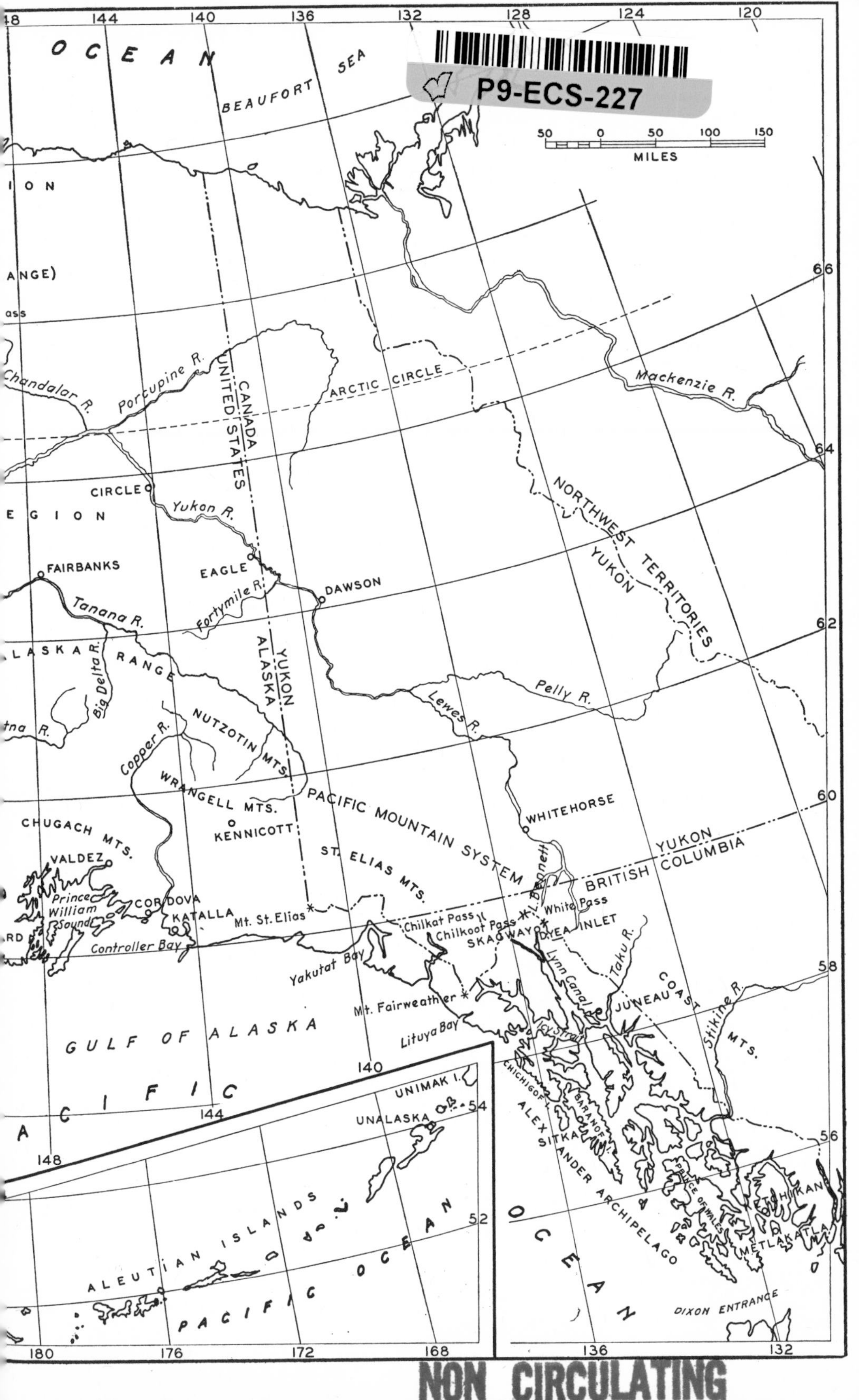

OCEAN
BEAUFORT SEA
MILES
ARCTIC CIRCLE
CANADA
UNITED STATES
Porcupine R.
Chandalar R.
Mackenzie R.
CIRCLE
Yukon R.
EAGLE
FAIRBANKS
DAWSON
Fortymile R.
Tanana R.
NORTHWEST TERRITORIES
YUKON
ALASKA RANGE
Big Delta R.
YUKON
ALASKA
Pelly R.
Lewes R.
NUTZOTIN MTS.
Copper R.
WRANGELL MTS.
PACIFIC MOUNTAIN SYSTEM
WHITEHORSE
KENNICOTT
CHUGACH MTS.
VALDEZ
ST. ELIAS MTS.
YUKON
BRITISH COLUMBIA
L. Bennett
Prince William Sound
CORDOVA
KATALLA
Mt. St. Elias
Chilkat Pass
Chilkoot Pass
White Pass
SKAGWAY
DYEA INLET
Controller Bay
Yakutat Bay
Taku R.
Lynn Canal
COAST MTS.
Stikine R.
JUNEAU
Mt. Fairweather
Lituya Bay
Icy Strait
GULF OF ALASKA
PACIFIC
CHICHIGOF I.
BARANOF I.
SITKA
ALEXANDER ARCHIPELAGO
PRINCE OF WALES I.
KETCHIKAN
METLAKATLA
OCEAN
DIXON ENTRANCE
UNIMAK I.
UNALASKA
ALEUTIAN ISLANDS
PACIFIC OCEAN

BLAZING ALASKA'S TRAILS

ALFRED HULSE BROOKS
(1871-1924)

Blazing Alaska's Trails

By

ALFRED HULSE BROOKS

Late head of the United States Geological Survey work in Alaska

ILLUSTRATED

Edited by Burton L. Fryxell, formerly professor of English, University of Alaska, with Foreword by John C. Reed, Arctic Institute of North America

SECOND EDITION
including

Memorial of A. H. Brooks
by Philip S. Smith

University of Alaska Press
Fairbanks, Alaska 99701

Library of Congress Catalog Card No. 73-88211
ISBN: 0-912006-01-3

Printed in the United States of America

cover design by Dennis Tani

Preface to Second Edition

The University of Alaska's happy association with the memory of Alfred H. Brooks has continued over the years, ever since the day in July 1952 when its then new School of Mines building was named for him, and the decision made to publish BLAZING ALASKA'S TRAILS as a literary summation of Brooks' life work. By the mid-nineteen sixties all copies of the original printing of twenty five hundred had been distributed. The continuing requests from University alumni, and others interested in Alaska and its history, as it appeared half a century ago to the most distinguished Alaskan scientist of his day, have caused us to publish this new edition.

The reader is offered what is essentially a reprint verbatim of the first edition, but with additions at the end which convert this volume into a true new edition. And to the extent that it is a new edition the editors may be considered to be Ernest N. Wolff of the Mineral Industry Research Laboratory, Charles J. Keim, Professor of Journalism and English, Earl H. Beistline, Dean of the College of Earth Sciences and Mineral Industry, Executive Officer and Provost, and the undersigned.

The sympathetic biography of Brooks, by his colleague Philip S. Smith, which appeared in a 1925 bulletin of the Geological Society of America, has been reproduced in full at the end of this new edition, including the full life-time bibliography of over 100 titles of all Brooks' publications.

The historic controversy regarding the claim of Dr. Frederick A. Cook to have made the first ascent of Mt. McKinley in 1906 had for a while involved Alfred Brooks and embarrassed him. Evidently stung by this, Brooks in 1914 became the first historian (with his MOUNTAIN EXPLORATION IN ALASKA) to set forth the modern account of the true first ascent some years later. In this second edition, we quote Brooks' own publication about this event, where in the first an editorial reconstruction was presented. The minor errors and misprints which inevitably emerge during the years following a first edition have been collected and corrected in an addendum at the end of this second edition.

Alfred Brooks would undoubtedly be thrilled to learn of the immensity of today's North Slope oil discoveries for he was widely quoted in the press in June, 1922, when he told a group in Seattle: "I have every confidence that oil will be found in Alaska, and that the areas in the Territory are extensive." It was his optimistic 1922 assessment of the oil potential which was instrumental in bringing about a topographic and geologic survey of the area and the establishment of Naval Petroleum Reserve No. 4 on the North Slope.

Terris Moore

Note: This new edition has been made possible through the generosity of Terris Moore, Second President of the University of Alaska. In addition to this, Dr. Moore has contributed, by far, most of the research that has gone into it.

E.N.W., C.J.K., E.H.B.

Preface

THIS BOOK is the final literary work of Dr. Alfred Hulse Brooks, one of the great men in the history of Alaska, a man to whom the Territory owes enormous gratitude.

In preparing the book for publication, I have attempted to follow one basic principle: to make as few changes as possible in Dr. Brooks' original manuscript. It has not, however, been possible to adhere unswervingly to this principle and thus simply to print the manuscript in the form in which it came to me. While no effort has been made to bring the material up to date, to alter statements of fact, to improve the accuracy of hypotheses presented, or to increase the effectiveness of the basic style, some changes, nevertheless, have been deemed necessary.

As nearly as one can tell on the basis of internal evidence, the 27 chapters that constitute the book were written between the years 1914 and 1922, as separate and individual essays only loosely connected with each other, and not arranged into a final order to be used in book form. Dr. Brooks, in thus composing the essays over a period of years and interrupted by his service in World War I, frequently repeated himself and told the same story or used the same illustrative incident in several essays; and since he did not live to edit the material, to finish all that he contemplated doing, and to put everything together into book form, he did not delete these repetitions. Too, he left a number of blank spaces, evidently not having immediately available the specific figures or statistical data needed at the moment and planning to add the necessary material later.

Editorially, then, while trying to follow the basic principle already stated, I have attempted to complete the things that were left unfinished; and doing so has necessitated a few additional changes. I have organized the 27 essays into chapters in what seemed to me the most satisfactory and logical arrangement on the basis of subject matter dealt with and the chronology of events presented. I have deleted a number of repetitions with the thought that one version of the same story or illustrative incident was sufficient; but since the individual essays, now the chapters of the book, are organized according to topics, strict chronology has not been possible and a certain amount of repetition, consequently, still exists, especially in those chapters dealing with historical material. I have also deleted the loose threads or have made minor alterations in the script to weave them into the texture of the whole. Throughout, I have attempted to link the chapters together into a consistent and unified whole by providing appropriate transitions and cross references from one chapter to another. I have also attempted to make the spelling of names consistent, especially those of Russian, Indian, and Eskimo origin; this has been done by referring to Dr. Brooks' usage in his book, *The Geography and Geology of Alaska,* by consulting standard maps and other authoritative writers on Alaska, and by adopting a consistent method of transliterating from the Russian. I have corrected a few obvious slips in factual statements and, after consultation with recognized authorities, have provided the missing data to fill in the omissions in the manuscript, a task that often required a considerable amount of research. Finally, I have tried to check the accuracy of and to standardize the form of Dr. Brooks' footnotes.

But, in spite of these necessary alterations, the basic principle has been adhered to; any large changes are indicated in "editor's notes." I can only hope that Dr. Brooks would have approved of such editing as I have done. The text remains his work, and whatever merits the book has are due to him. The index, of course, is solely my addition; any errors of either omission or commission there are mine.

The illustrations are from two sources: official photographs selected from the files of the United States Geological Survey, as often as possible from the work of Dr. Brooks himself or that of his immediate associates; and maps prepared under the supervision of Ernest Wolff, research associate, School of Mines, University of Alaska, and by Dan C. Wilder, draftsman, Geophysical Institute, University of Alaska. The kind cooperation of both in making possible this essential feature of the book is greatly appreciated.

It is my sincere hope that the book will stand as a worthy monument to Dr. Brooks. Publication was arranged through a publication committee consisting of Dr. Charles E. Bunnell, president emeritus of the University of Alaska;

Dr. John C. Reed, a governor of the Arctic Institute of North America; Earl H. Beistline, dean of the School of Mines of the University of Alaska; and myself. Publication was made possible through the approval by the Board of Regents of the University of Alaska of the use of a portion of a special research fund for that purpose.

BURTON L. FRYXELL,
Editor

College, Alaska
1952

Contents

Illustrations

Foreword

ALASKA has been much in the public eye since shortly before World War II; and, judging from the pace of development there and the continued and expanding economic and strategic interest in the Territory, it apparently is destined to remain so for a long time to come. Seldom does the modern Alaskan, or non-Alaskan, pause to think that, deficient as our detailed knowledge is about Alaska—its resources, environments, and potentialities—much that has gone on there since the late '30's was based on a general fund of information gathered in earlier years by explorers and scientific pioneers or accumulated from the experience of the hardy souls who pursued and captured the hordes of silvery salmon, trudged lonely trap lines, or wrested a golden harvest from isolated creeks.

One of the greatest, perhaps the greatest of all Alaskan explorer-scientists, was Alfred Hulse Brooks. He is revered in memory by many old-time Alaskans as a scientist, as a man, and as one of the greatest exponents of the Territory. His name is honorably perpetuated on several Alaska geographic features, the most conspicuous being the great Brooks Range that describes a majestic arc from east to west across Alaska north of the Arctic Circle. In the summer of 1952 his memory was again honored by the naming for him of the new School of Mines building at the University of Alaska—the Brooks Memorial Mines Building. In the words of his biographer, Dr. Philip S. Smith, another outstanding figure in Alaskan geology and Brooks' successor as head of the Alaskan work of the United States Geological Survey, Brooks ". . . established a reputation not only in his chosen profession, but as an empire-builder, that made him more revered and better known than any other man connected with the development of this great Territory."

Brooks was a prolific writer, and his professional bibliography is long and notable. From his writings, from his famed and sparkling conversations, and from the many and various responsibilities that he undertook outside his special scientific field, it was evident that his interests and his contributions were exceedingly broad and betokened the best in a well-informed and thoughtful public-minded citizen.

Now it has come to light that this great Alaskan has left a written record of a breadth and scope hitherto unsuspected except by his family and perhaps a few close friends. That record appears in the following pages. It takes the form of a series of essays on subjects so diverse that they are revealing indeed of the broad horizons of the man's mind. It includes 27 chapters—six on the geography, geology, climate, flora, fauna, and early inhabitants of Alaska; ten on Alaskan history; six on mining and the mining industry; and one each on early transportation, fisheries, agriculture, education, and government. Collectively, this work constitutes a remarkably well-proportioned, authoritative, and readable picture of Alaska as of about 1920. To be sure, this is Alaska of a generation and a half ago; but it is the Alaska on which present-day Alaska is founded and as such even now it is timely, so timely in fact that thoughtful consideration of its contents is invaluable to those in whose hands today is entrusted the destiny of Uncle Sam's northernmost territory.

During all the period of the service of Dr. Brooks, his estimable wife was especially active in assisting him in collecting information from current publications both in the States and in Alaska. She arranged his files and typed his essays. Her interest in his work is evidenced by the fact that after his death she gave to the University of Alaska his library consisting of more than 2,000 bound volumes and several thousand pamphlets.

In 1950 Mrs. Brooks was planning to leave the Brooks' residence on Newark Street in Cleveland Park, Washington, and move to more suitable quarters. In her preparations it became necessary to go over many of the items left by Dr. Brooks—books, separate papers, notes, manuscripts, and the like. Much of this material, of course, had to do with Alaska; this was entrusted to Dr. Charles E. Bunnell, president emeritus of the University and long-time friend of the Brooks family, for sorting and organizing and eventually for preservation in accessible form at the University.

Among the valuable relics was the manuscript of this book—approximately 700 pages, yellowing with age and typed by Mrs. Brooks' own hands. Mrs. Brooks had long intended to make some appropriate disposition of this unofficial record of her husband's keen appraisal of the Alaskan scene. She was aware that his death had prevented the completion of several more chapters; but, even so, she visualized the publication of the almost-completed book. Apparently, some of Brooks' associates were aware of his effort and possibly had seen parts or all of it. Nevertheless, no steps were taken and, so far as is known, no knowledge even of the existence of the manuscript remained among those in the Geological Survey active in Alaskan work in 1950.

Finally, with the imminence of her change of residence, Mrs. Brooks called the attention of some of her husband's followers in the Alaskan work of the Survey to the manuscript and requested that attention be given to ways and means for its publication if it appeared to merit publication on careful and sympathetic consideration after nearly 30 years. Subsequently, the manuscript was referred to the Board of Governors of the Arctic Institute of North America, a joint Canadian-American association of those interested in research in the Arctic. Various chapters were reviewed by Institute authorities in appropriate fields, both Canadian and American, and the whole was reviewed by the Institute's editor. The comments were uniformly laudatory, and the Institute, with Mrs. Brooks' prior approval, decided to take up the matter of possible publication with officials of the University of Alaska.

This was done. The University representatives were President Emeritus Bunnell; Earl Beistline, dean of the School of Mines; and Dr. Burton L. Fryxell, professor of English. Meeting with the writer of these lines, this group on consideration felt, with the full concurrence of the Arctic Institute, that the manuscript should by all means be published; that it should appear under the joint sponsorship of the University of Alaska and the Arctic Institute of North America; that it would be fitting for the University to take the lead in providing the funds necessary for publication; and that any proceeds from sales, after all costs were met, would accrue to a special fund earmarked for research and equipment for the School of Mines of the University of Alaska. All felt that this procedure would be according to the wishes of Dr. Brooks, and the plan has had the approval of Mrs. Brooks.

The plan, sanctioned by the Board of Regents of the University of Alaska, was accordingly put into execution, with the task of handling the financial details entrusted to Dean Beistline. A publisher was found and a contract made —the result follows. Herein one can not only read Brooks' own words, appraise his keen analysis of the Alaska of his day, marvel at his appreciation of the historical roots from which his Alaska evolved, but also view selected photographs from Brooks' official Geological Survey collection, photographs taken in many instances at the very time Brooks was absorbing his Alaskan impressions.

By curious coincidence the plan for the book began to take form and substance at the precise time that Alaska, specifically through Igloo No. 4 of the Pioneers of Alaska and the University of Alaska, was preparing to commemorate the 50th anniversary of the discovery of gold in the Fairbanks district in July, 1902. Also at that time the new building to house the School of Mines at the University was nearing completion. The Board of Regents of the University appropriately decided that the new building should be named the Brooks Memorial Mines Building and that it should be dedicated at the anniversary celebration. Thus was provided a most opportune moment for the University, through Dean Beistline, to lay before a gathering of the most appropriate Alaskans that could be assembled the existence of the manuscript for this book and the plans for its publication.

The University of Alaska is proud to be a sponsor of this story of Alaska from its beginnings to 1920 by one of Alaska's greatest sons. The Arctic Institute of North America shares that pride and believes that its co-sponsorship of the volume is along the lines of its objective of sponsoring and coordinating North American arctic research. Both sponsors share the conviction that the book is an interpretation of major importance and lasting value of the Alaska of 1920 and that that interpretation is a prerequisite to an understanding of the Alaska of today and in anticipation of the Alaska of tomorrow.

JOHN C. REED
Arctic Institute of North
America

Washington, D.C.
1952

Alfred Hulse Brooks

(The Brooks Memorial Mines Building of the University of Alaska was dedicated July 22, 1952. Upon this occasion Dr. Charles E. Bunnell read from the pen of Mrs. Brooks the following biographical sketch of Dr. Brooks.)

THE LIFE of Alfred H. Brooks was devoted to a vision of developing Alaska. A scientist by inheritance and training, he chose geology as his profession, and his ideal of geology was as a foundation for progress and development.

On his graduation from Harvard in 1894 he was at once assigned to field work with Dr. C. W. Hayes, who had made an exploration in Alaska in 1891, and it was accounts of this trip which inspired him with the vision of Alaska as a field for development on scientific principles. He asked to be assigned to work in Alaska; but it was not until 1898, while he was studying at the Sorbonne in Paris, that he received a telegram offering him the opportunity. Within twelve hours he was on board the boat for Washington. This was indicative of the zeal which henceforth marked his devotion to Alaska. The long list of his reports, articles, and lectures denotes almost super-human industry.

Twenty-four times he made the trip to Alaska. In these days of the airplane it is hard to realize the time and effort such a trip involved; or the hardships of those early explorations with pack trains, chopping trails, fording streams, occasionally building a raft to cross a river, while at the same time gathering geological data. Brooks had personally explored many thousands of square miles when in 1903 he was put in charge of all United States Geological Survey work in Alaska. Thereafter he spent as much time as possible visiting parties in the field. He had personal knowledge of the whole country south of the Yukon, and his friends were scattered from Ketchikan to Nome, and from Fairbanks to Attu.

For Brooks had a rare gift of making friends. Men were drawn by his geniality, his keen sense of humor, and his sympathetic interest, but most of all by his fearless intellectual honesty that enabled him to see the truth and to interpret it, so that one came to rely on his wise counsel and frank criticism.

His service to Alaska was without stint and at the sacrifice of health. His interest extended to every aspect of the country's history and development, and his researches embraced all contiguous or similar countries, so that he became unquestionably the foremost authority on the subject of Alaska. Thus it happened that he was invariably selected to accompany high officials of the administration on trips of investigation into the Territory. And in 1912 he was appointed by President Taft vice-president of the Alaska Railroad Commission.

In the year 1913 he received two medals in recognition of his work: the Peter Daly Gold Medal of the American Geographical Society, and the Malta-Brun Gold Medal of the Geographical Society of Paris, France. Later he served as president of various scientific societies and was tendered high office in practically every organization of which he was an active member.

Several times he was offered positions of advantage, but he would never entertain the idea of giving up his chosen work.

A brief hiatus came in his Alaskan work when he served as chief geologist of the American Expeditionary Force in World War I from September, 1917, to February, 1919; and subsequently as chief of the Mining and Metallurgy Section of the American Peace Conference at Paris.

In 1920 the Secretary of the Interior appointed him chairman of a committee to advise on the development of Alaskan industries and resources. In the same year he received the degree of doctor of science from Colgate University.

But at last his indefatigable energy took toll of his health. In 1922 while accompanying Assistant Secretary Houston of the Department of Commerce on an industrial and economic survey around the world, he suffered an apoplectic stroke in Japan and was forced to return home. But, exclaiming that "there are some things that must be said about Alaska," he would not give up his work.

One more notable experience he had, when he went in 1923 to the second Pan-Pacific Congress in Australia, called for the purpose of discussing the problems of all nations bordering on the Pacific. Returning, he threw himself with renewed vigor into his task of interpreting Alaska, but his strength was unequal to the strain he put upon it. His final stroke came at his desk, just as he completed an important lecture on "The Future of Alaska."

His faith in that future was the guiding star of his life—a life not long, but how rich in accomplishment! It is given to few men to labor so happily in a chosen field, and to almost no one to see the country he served develop as did Alaska during his years of service. The bestowal of his name upon the Mines Building is a recognition of this service and a fitting crown upon his efforts to increase knowledge and development of Alaska's mineral deposits.

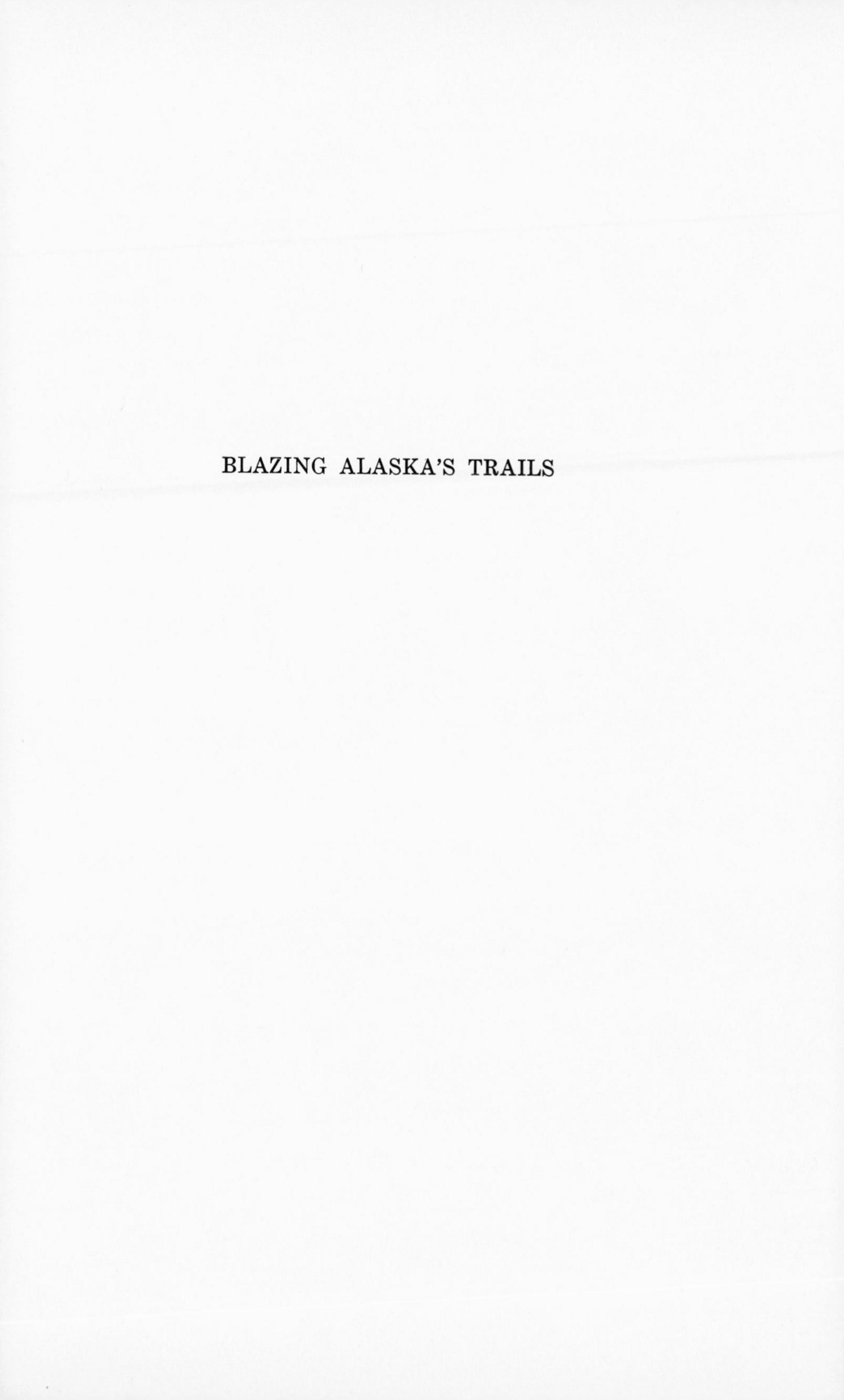

BLAZING ALASKA'S TRAILS

CHAPTER I

Relief and Drainage

ALASKA'S Pacific shore line is bounded throughout much of its length by rugged mountains in which lie great snow fields giving rise to many glaciers. This coastal barrier is especially prominent from Portland Canal on the southeast to Kenai Peninsula on the southwest. West of Cook Inlet there is another range which, with its southwestern extension in the Alaska Peninsula, also forms a coastal barrier. Inland of these mountains and adjacent to them are other parallel ranges of high altitude. The whole constitutes a rugged system forming, indeed, one of the larger features of relief in North America. These high ranges include some of the loftiest peaks on the continent; and as many of them rise close to sea level, they present scenes of grandeur elsewhere unsurpassed. The steep slopes covered with snow and ice present a forbidding landscape; and where the dense coniferous forests clothe the lower reaches, they add to the sombreness of the scene.

It is this aspect of Alaska's relief which has been most strongly emphasized in descriptive writing, and the fact that beyond these ranges there is a region of broad fertile valleys and rolling uplands draining to Bering Sea through the Yukon and Kuskokwim rivers is often lost sight of. This great inland region is in strong contrast, both as to topography and climate, as well as vegetation and soil, with the coastal barrier. It is, in turn, separated from the Arctic by another mountain system which stretches across northern Alaska, and falls off on the north to the barren grounds that skirt the polar sea.

Alaska thus falls into four large physiographic provinces —two mountain systems, one bordering the Pacific and one paralleling the Arctic, an intermontane region of lesser relief, and a lowland area separating the northern system from the Arctic Ocean. Of these, the two mountain systems, together with the intermontane region, are a northwesterly extension of the Cordillera of North America that forms the grand feature of relief in western United States and Canada. The fourth province of Alaska corresponds in a general way to the Great Plains region, which stretches eastward from the base of the Rocky Mountains both in Canada and the United States.

These four provinces have been named, from south to north, the Pacific Mountain System, the Central Plateau Region, the Arctic Mountain System, and the Arctic Slope Region. Each has a certain topographic unity that distinguishes it from the adjacent province; each is also divisible into a number of lesser provinces differing from each other. Thus, the mountain systems are made up of numerous distinct ranges, and the Central Plateau Region includes uplands, broad lowlands, and some minor ranges.

These larger features of Alaska's topography have in large measure controlled the climate, the soil, and the distribution of vegetation and animal life and, because of this and of the barriers to communication, have had an important effect on man's occupation of the land. Therefore, Alaska's natural and political history can only be understood by a clear grasp of its physiographic features. These will therefore be described in some detail.

The rivers and streams have been a dominating influence in determining man's occupation of Alaska. These were important to the natives because they furnished a large part of the food supply and because the rivers marked the main routes of travel both in winter and in summer. The approach of the white man was also largely dominated by the watercourses. On the Pacific seaboard he was long held in check by the turbulent glacier-fed watercourses which drain this part of the Territory. On the other hand, easy access was had to the vast interior beyond the coastal barrier by the rivers emptying into Bering Sea. Along the rivers the pioneer could transport necessary supplies in crude rafts or boats built of the timber which grows on the banks; subsequently the steamboat succeeded craft propelled by hand. Later overland routes were determined by the river valleys, first followed by trails, then by wagon roads and railroads.

Not only has the drainage system determined the avenues of approach, but the valleys have yielded most of the placer gold and have provided the water power needed for industrial developments. Moreover, the best timber and most of the arable land are found on the river banks and along the valley floors and slopes. In short, the watercourses are and have been the most important physical features of inland Alaska. Therefore, the larger drainage features of the Territory first merit a brief description. A more detailed account of the principal rivers will be included in the description of the different physiographic provinces.

Alaska's drainage is tributary to three oceans—southward to the Pacific, westward to Bering Sea, and northward and northwestward to the Arctic. The waters of about one-fifth of its area, including the major part of the Pacific Mountain System, are carried to the Pacific. Nearly one-half, including the great interior region, finds its way to Bering Sea, chiefly through the Yukon and Kuskokwim rivers; and the rest goes into the Arctic, whose watershed includes the northern part of the Territory.

In general it is true that the rivers emptying into the Pacific are turbulent and silt-laden, difficult to navigate in small boats, and impossible for steamers except in their lower courses. They drain a region of strong relief, and many spring directly from glaciers. In contrast to these, most of the rivers emptying into Bering Sea and the Arctic Ocean have sluggish currents for a long distance up from their mouths, making them navigable not only for small boats and canoes but also for steamers. These streams flow through regions of comparatively low relief, though some of their headwaters are in mountains and a few have their sources in glaciers. The Arctic drainage is in part of the turbulent type, in part rivers having sluggish meandering courses. A few small glaciers drain into the Arctic Ocean.

In looking at a map of Alaska one notices the great crescentic sweep of the southern coast line which partly envelops the Gulf of Alaska. This great bend of the shore is paralleled by all the larger features of the relief. The Pacific Mountain System trends northwesterly to about the meridian of Mount St. Elias, then bends westerly, and finally, in the longitude of Mount McKinley, trends to the southwest to be continued by the Alaska Peninsula and the Aleutian Islands. The Central Plateau Region makes a similar crescentic sweep, while the Arctic Mountain System, that trends east and west across Alaska, is continued to the southeast by a range that knits it to the northwesterly trend of the Canadian Rockies.

This crescentic surface plan of Alaska's relief is, then, the dominating feature of its topography and differentiates it from the rest of the North American cordillera, which preserves its northwesterly trend throughout the States and

Western Canada. Just as the great peninsula of Alaska stretches out to the west and southwest to meet the northeastern extension of Asia, so its mountain ranges change their northwesterly trend to the west and south toward the northeasterly trend of the mountains of Siberia. Alaska is, therefore, the meeting place between the mountain trends of the Old World and the New. This great hinge line of the mountain systems of the two continents is a deep-seated structural feature of the rock terranes which make up the mountains.

What has been described is the surface expression of the larger structures that dominate the bedrock formations. This change of trend line is especially striking in the Pacific Mountain System, which will first be considered.

Pacific Mountain System

The Pacific Mountain System is made up of a number of distinct ranges forming a mountainous belt paralleling the seaboard, together with some areas of lesser relief. In Southeastern Alaska it averages about 50 miles in width but broadens to the northwest so that at Prince William Sound it measures 200 miles across; it then narrows down again in the Alaska Peninsula. Its mean altitude varies from 5,000 to 10,000 feet, with many lofty peaks whose summits are from 10,000 to over 15,000 feet high and one, Mount McKinley, towering more than 20,000 feet above sea level. Some broad valleys, lowlands, and plateaus are included in the system, and the coastal barrier is traversed by a number of large rivers whose valleys lie athwart its course. It is these valleys and several passes which give access to the interior through the coastal barrier. The principal ranges of the system are the Coast, the St. Elias, the Chugach, and the Aleutian ranges, which lie close to the sea, and the Alaska Range, that forms the inland member of the system.

The mountains designated as the Coast Range stretch north from the boundary at Portland Canal for some 300 miles across the head of Lynn Canal and, again crossing the boundary, pass inland behind the St. Elias Range. They have no culminating crest line, but are made up of an irregular aggregate of peaks with connecting ridges, forming an elevated tract from 40 to 80 miles in width. Their general summit altitude has a marked uniformity, for only here and there a peak rises above the general level. At Portland Canal the relief is between 5,000 and 6,000 feet, but the altitude increases to the north, heights of 8,000 and 9,000 feet being reached at the head of Lynn Canal. Within the higher parts of the range there are some large ice and snow fields, and these give rise to numerous glaciers that discharge on both sides of the range, but the largest are on the seaward side. The boundaries of the Coast Range are ill-defined: on the south it is continued as the Coast Range of British Columbia; on the north and east it merges with the higher parts of the British Columbia plateau; on the west no sharp line can be drawn between it and the mountains of the Alexander Archipelago. Numerous fiords (see picture, page 61) break the western face of the range, some of which penetrate far inland. Indeed, Portland Canal on the south cuts through almost the entire range.

Viewed from the sea these mountains present for the most part steep scarps rising from the water's edge or from narrow rocky beaches. The lower slopes are clothed in a dense growth of evergreens, giving the scene a sombre tone. Here and there a cataract leaps from a high basin to the sea, and most of the watercourses draining the west front of the range occupy narrow and steep valleys.

The boundary between Alaska and British Columbia lies within the Coast Range, so that only a small part of this mountain mass lies within Alaska. The boundary is an irregular line connecting some of the more prominent peaks that lie not far from the sea front of the range. Only at White and Chilkoot passes does the boundary follow the watersheds.

In the higher parts of the Coast Range most of the precipitation is in the form of snow, and much of the drainage is that of glaciers. On the lower slopes mountain torrents carry the heavy precipitation to the sea. Here and there a larger stream emerges from the mountains through a steep-walled valley, but in general the drainage is through many smaller watercourses.

Several large rivers find their sources far beyond the Coast Range and reach the sea through valleys that traverse this barrier. The largest of these is the Stikine River, which drains a large area in northern British Columbia. It traverses the Coast Range through a steep-walled valley and here receives the discharge of several glaciers. The Stikine River has long been one of the routes into the in-

ALASKAN GLACIERS

Upper: Tanana Glacier, photo by A. H. Brooks; center: Taku Glacier, photographer unknown; lower: close-up of Taku Glacier, photo by F. E. Wright.

of the Wrangell Mountains and thence by a great crescentic sweep encircles the western flank of the mountains, while its principal tributary, the Chitina River, drains the southern flank. Its basin is a broad area of relatively low relief separated from the Yukon basin on the north by the Alaska Range and on the south bounded by the Chugach Mountains through which it finds its way to the sea by the usual steep-walled valley. Much of this basin has been deeply buried in glacial silts and clays into which the Copper and its tributaries have entrenched their steep-walled valleys. The silt-filled part of its basin stands at 1,000 to 1,500 feet above sea level and has been called the Copper River plateau. Much of its surface is an ill-drained swampy area dotted with lakes and supporting only a scant vegetation of stunted spruce and moss. The valley bottom and slopes, however, have a more luxuriant growth of spruce and herbaceous plants.

The Copper River plateau stretches to the westward, where its margin is drained by streams flowing into the Susitna River. There is thus no well-defined watershed between the Copper drainage on the east and the Susitna on the west. Here the streams of the two watersheds interlock irregularly.

Beyond Prince William Sound the Chugach Mountains swing to the south and are continued by the Kenai Mountains, which form the backbone of the peninsula of the same name. This range rises steeply from the fiorded eastern shore of the Kenai Peninsula to altitudes of from 4,000 to 6,800 feet and is continued to its southernmost extremity. This mountain mass is from 30 to 60 miles in width with numerous sharp crest lines, in part broken by broad valleys. One of these furnishes the route of the government railroad extending inland from the town of Seward. Its higher southern portion is marked by a great ice cap above which only the higher peaks are exposed. On the west the Kenai Mountains fall off to a relatively flat upland that slopes down to the shores of Cook Inlet. Near the western margin of these mountains there are a number of large picturesque mountain lakes, the largest of which is called Kenai Lake. The shore of this lake is skirted by the government railroad.

The valley of the Matanuska River marks a broad depression separating the Chugach Mountains on the south from the Talkeetna Mountains on the north. This range comprises a roughly circular area in which peaks from

6,000 to 8,000 feet in altitude, with connecting sharp ridges, are rather irregularly distributed. The mass is broken by the valleys of several large rivers that flow westward to join the Susitna. To the north the range is connected by some irregular highlands with the Alaska Range; on the east they fall off through a series of foothills to the Copper River plateau.

The great depressed area, of which the lower part lies under the sea and forms Cook Inlet, stretches northward from tidewater for upwards of 100 miles. It here forms the Susitna lowland, traversed by the Susitna River and bounded on the east by the Talkeetna Mountains and on the west by the foothills of the Alaska Range. At the mouth of the Talkeetna River, the largest eastern tributary of the Susitna, the valley walls are contracted, and above this point the Susitna lowland is represented by only the flood plain of the river.

The Susitna River, which receives the drainage from much of the Talkeetna Mountains, springs from a glacier at the southern margin of the eastern part of the Alaska Range. It traverses a belt of foothills through a broad gravel-filled valley, then, bending westward for some 20 miles, cuts through its steep-walled rockbound canyon. Emerging from this canyon, it takes a southerly course through an open valley whose walls gradually recede to encompass the broad lowland of the lower Susitna.

West of the Susitna lowland is a series of foothills and beyond the snow-covered crest of the great Alaska Range. This is a rugged mountain mass which sweeps as a great crescent around the Susitna and Copper basins, constituting for the most part the watershed between the Pacific Ocean and Bering Sea. Trending northeastward from an unexplored region near Lake Clark, the range continues to the east as far as the Delta River. Here the axis takes a southeasterly direction and is continued, in the so-called Nutzotin Mountains, eastward to the international boundary on the White River.

The axis of this range, which has a parabolic form, is between 500 and 600 miles in length, and the range is from 50 to 80 miles wide. In the southern part of the range the peaks are from 5,000 to 8,000 feet in altitude. When traced northward and eastward, the crest line is found to maintain an altitude of 7,000 to 10,000 feet to the vicinity of Mentasta Pass, beyond which it is continued by the Nutzotin Mountains at a lower altitude. Its longitudinal extent, breadth, and mass make the Alaska Range one of the most prominent mountain chains of the continent. It is both higher and broader than the Sierra Nevada and of greater relief and extent than the Alps of Europe.

The region lying between Cook Inlet and Lake Clark, about 80 miles wide, has been little explored but is known to be of high relief. These mountains stretch northward for 100 miles and probably include a number of high ridges trending north and south, separated by rather broad valleys, and with peaks 8,000 to 9,000 feet high. From the Susitna lowland the eastern face of these mountains can be seen as a rather abrupt scarp which rises to a summit level covered with snow and is broken by a number of glaciers discharging into streams flowing into the Susitna River. In the head-water region of the Yentna there is a break in the Alaska Range, and several gaps from 2,900 to 3,000 feet high afford easy routes of travel between Cook Inlet and the Kuskokwim.

The Alaska Range maintains the same general character 100 miles northeast of the Skwentna basin. Here the inland slope rises abruptly from the gravel-floored plateau to the

THE ALASKA RANGE

A portion of this majestic range, east of Mount McKinley, is shown here; for views of Mount McKinley, see page 293. Photo by F. H. Moffit.

crest of the range, not more than five to ten miles distant from the mountain front. The crest line, a high serrated ridge 7,000 to 10,000 feet high, joins a series of dominating peaks, including Mount Dall (9,000 ft.), Mount Russell (11,350 ft.), and the two giant peaks, Mount Foraker

(17,000 ft.) and Mount McKinley (20,300 ft.). East of the crest line are other high peaks which probably attain altitudes of 10,000 to 15,000 feet. Here valleys of the southeastward-flowing streams reach far back into the mountains and are, as a rule, filled with glacial ice well out toward the Susitna lowland. These glaciers form the most extensive ice sheets of inland Alaska. The valleys of the westward-flowing streams are short and are only in part filled with glacial ice.

That part of the range which lies between the head of the Chulitna, west fork of the Susitna, and the Tanana valley includes a mountainous area in which at least three subordinate ranges can be recognized, with an aggregate width of nearly 100 miles. The broad valley of the Nenana, traversing two of these ranges, is connected by a broad, low gap called Broad Pass (2,400 ft.) with the valley of the Chulitna, a stream that flows south.

The range is continued in a southeasterly direction by a broad mountain mass. Here the peaks are from 8,000 to 10,000 feet high, but the snow-capped summit of Mount Hayes stands over 13,000 feet above sea level. From the Delta River, which traverses the entire range, to Mentasta Pass the mountains are unbroken, the snow-covered crest line averaging probably 7,000 to 9,000 feet in altitude. Mentasta Pass is a broad, flat depression, 3,000 feet high. From Mentasta Pass the range finds its continuation to the southeast as far as White River in the Nutzotin Mountains, which embrace a rugged area 100 miles in length and 40 miles in width. These mountains stand at elevations between 7,000 and 8,000 feet, but above this level rise several peaks that are 9,000 to 10,000 feet high.

The southwestern part of the Alaska Range is separated from Cook Inlet by the Chigmit Mountains whose axis parallels Cook Inlet. Mount Spurr (10,500 ft.) and a number of peaks form the northeastern end of this range, which stretches to the southwest with decreasing altitude and at Iliamna Bay constitutes only a low, narrow ridge broken by numerous passes. Within the Chigmit Mountains are the two active volcanoes, Mount Iliamna (12,066 ft.) and Mount Redoubt (11,270 ft.).

Close to Cape Douglas, marking the entrance to Cook Inlet on the south, is a group of high snow-clad peaks which constitute the northeastern end of the Aleutian Range. This range parallels the southern coast of the Alaska

Peninsula. Near Cape Douglas the peaks reach altitudes of 5,000 feet and more, and here several glaciers of considerable size originate in the mountain mass whose crest line is here well defined. To the southwest the range decreases in altitude, though its crest is marked by many peaks, the highest of which are active or extinct volcanoes. If the range be traced to the southwest, its average summit level will be found to decrease in altitude, at Herendeen Bay the highest peaks being only about 4,000 feet in height. Here many broad, flat gaps break the continuity of the range. A further southwest extension is found in the mountainous Aleutian Islands, which carry the axis of the range for some 800 miles to the westward. Here the peaks reach altitudes of 4,000 to 8,000 feet. The peaks are all of volcanic origin, and the highest are found on Unimak Island where are the active volcanoes of Shishaldin (9,387 ft.), Pogromni (6,500 ft.), and Isanotski peaks (8,032 and 8,088 ft.).

The axes of the southern end of the Alaska Range and of the Aleutian Range are parallel. These highlands form the southwestern extension of the Pacific Mountain System. West of Cook Inlet the system has a width of some 40 or 50 miles, which gradually decreases to five to ten miles in the southwestern part of the Alaska Peninsula. North of Bristol Bay is a minor northeasterly-trending range called the Ahklun Mountains. Its relation to larger physiographic provinces has not been determined, for it lies in an unmapped region.

Central Plateau Region

Beyond the inland front of the Pacific Mountain System the aspect of the country changes abruptly. Rugged snow-clad ranges and narrow steep-walled valleys give way to a broad, rolling upland, diversified by extensive plains and broad, flat valleys. There are no glaciers in this part of Alaska, and the grasslands and timber, with the gentle slopes, give a pleasing aspect to the landscape. Here the interstream areas are in many instances flat-topped with a mesa-like form. Hence the name for this province, Central Plateau Region. A few minor ranges and many rounded domes rise above the general summit level. This region, a northwesterly extension of the central plateau of British Columbia, crosses the international boundary with a summit level of 3,000 to 4,000 feet and then sweeps westward with decreased altitude as it approaches Bering Sea. It has its minimum width near the meridian of Mount McKinley, where it measures some 150 miles between the front ranges of the Pacific Mountain System on the south and the Rocky Mountains on the north. To the westward it broadens out as the southerly system of ranges recedes.

This central province drains to Bering Sea, chiefly through the great Yukon and Kuskokwim rivers. While its general outline is fairly well defined, there are many places where it is not possible to make a sharp distinction between the Central Plateau Region and the bounding mountain system. It has a fairly definite southern boundary westward from the 141st meridian beyond Mount McKinley. Here the plateau province abuts abruptly against the inland front of the southern ranges, and here the flat, moss-covered interstream area abuts directly against the scarp marking the abrupt inland slope of the high ranges. Southwest of McKinley, so far as the region has been explored, there appears to be less of a contrast between the two provinces.

The northern boundary of this central province has only in part been explored, but it appears that here too the differentiation between plateau and mountains is not everywhere well defined. In places, however, as in the upper Koyukuk basin, the northern ranges fall off rather abruptly to the plateau level.

There is another element which complicates the topography of this region. Between the Yukon and Porcupine rivers the northwestern extension of the Rocky Mountain system penetrates the plateau province. In British Columbia and in the southern part of the Yukon Territory the eastern boundary of the plateau is fairly well defined by the front ranges of the Rocky Mountain system of Canada. The axis of these mountains on approaching Alaska swings gradually to the west, crossing the international boundary north of the Yukon, and is traversed by the valley of that river south of the town of Circle. Here the mountains are not well defined as a distinct topographic unit, but the extension of this uplift is found in the Crazy and White mountains west of Circle. These two minor ranges stand conspicuously above the general plateau level. It seems probable also that the same axis is to be recognized in the mountains which form the divide between the Yukon and Kuskokwim rivers in the Innoko-Iditarod region and to the southwest. West of the Yukon the Rocky Mountain element of the topography is by no means well marked, for the ranges described above do not form very conspicuous features of the relief as compared with the plateau features. This account of the northwesterly extension of the Rockies must be regarded as provisional until the region lying east of the upper Yukon and north of the lower Porcupine has been better explored.

The plateau region is also diversified by other minor ranges, such as the Glacier Mountains in the Fortymile basin, the Ahklun Mountains north of Bristol Bay, and Kigluaik and Darby mountains of Seward Peninsula. A much more striking feature of the Central Plateau Region is the lowland areas. These include the broad coastal plain which marks the deltas of the Yukon and Kuskokwim rivers and extends northward to include much of the eastern shore of Norton Sound. They also include the broad basin lowlands which form a part of the valley system of the Yukon and Kuskokwim rivers and their tributaries. The best known of these is the Yukon Flats, lying adjacent to the Arctic Circle, but almost equally extensive are the basin lowlands of the lower Tanana, the upper Kuskokwim, and the middle Koyukuk rivers. These are of the same general type—flat areas across which the watercourses take meandering courses, bounded by the scarps of the upland. The main watercourses, traversing these lowlands in broad meanders, often enter and leave the basins through narrow steep-walled valleys.

Viewed in detail, the topography has certain striking characteristics. All except the smallest watercourses have rather broad flood plains; steep-walled valleys are the exception rather than the rule. Rounded forms and smooth slopes are the rule; scarps of bedrock and finely dissected slopes, the exception. The flood plains merge with the valley slopes at least on one side of the valley, and these slopes are continued to summit levels at low angles. The flat-topped interstream areas are broken here and there by rocky knobs which end abruptly on the smooth or moss-covered slopes.

Bering Sea receives the drainage of nearly all the vast Central Plateau Region and much of the inland slopes of its bordering ranges—an area comprising not only over half of Alaska but also a considerable part of Yukon Territory and northern British Columbia. Most of this large drainage finds its way to the sea through the Yukon and Kuskokwim rivers.

The Yukon is the largest stream of Alaska, the main

artery of an extensive drainage system which gives easy access to much of the vast intermontane region. To the natives the river is and has been all important, for through countless generations its waters have furnished them fish for food and easy routes of travel by canoe and raft in summer, by sled and dog team in winter. The white men, too, found access to the interior by this river. The Russians, coming from the west in search of furs, dragged their clumsy boats for a thousand miles against its current; while the English traders, who reached its headwaters from the east, descended in their bark canoes for hundreds of miles. One of the headwater tributaries, rising in the Chilkoot Pass not two score miles from tidewater on the Pacific furnished an inland route to the coast natives and later to the prospectors who discovered the Yukon gold fields. Now the railway through the Coast Range makes the upper Yukon basin still more accessible. Scores of steamers navigate the Yukon during the summer months, and its frozen surface affords a highway for winter travel. In short, the settlement by natives and whites and the development of all the mining interest of the great interior region of Alaska and Northwest Canada were only made possible by the Yukon waterways.

The Yukon, with its longest tributary, the Lewes-Teslin, has a length of about 2,300 miles, of which about 2,000 miles are navigable, and a catchment area of about 330,000 square miles, over half of which is in Canada. The following table shows it to be fifth in rank among the rivers of North America:

Length and Drainage Area of Five Chief Rivers of North America

Rivers	Approximate Length (Miles)	Approximate area of drainage (Square Miles)
Mississippi, with Missouri	6,000	1,244,000
Winnipeg and Nelson	3,840	486,500
Mackenzie	2,868	677,400
St. Lawrence	2,600	565,000
Yukon, with Lewes and Teslin	2,300	330,000

The volume of the Yukon River, draining as it does a semiarid region, is far inferior to that of other streams draining equal areas. The measurements made by Porter and Davenport[1] at Eagle, near the international boundary

[1] Porter, E. A. and Davenport, R. W., "The Discharge of the Yukon at Eagle, Alaska," *United States Geological Survey, Water Supply Paper, No. 345*, Washington, D.C., 1914.

showed the Yukon to have a volume of 100,100 cubic feet per second at a low-water stage in April and a volume of 249,000 cubic feet per second at a high-water stage in May. In 1900, G. R. Putnam computed the volume of the Yukon at the head of its delta (73 miles from the mouth), some 1,200 miles below the boundary, as 436,000 cubic feet per second in September, probably a medium low-water stage. Making allowance for high-water stage, it is estimated that the average discharge of the Yukon at its mouth is about 500,000 cubic feet per second. This may be compared with a discharge of 6,750,000 cubic feet per second for the Mississippi or even the 900,000 cubic feet per second of the St. Lawrence. The drainage basin of the latter is about two-fifths larger than that of the Yukon, and it also receives an average precipitation of about 35 inches, compared with about 12 inches for the Yukon.

The sources of the Yukon lie in British Columbia. All of its upper drainage channels trend north and northwest until it reaches the Arctic Circle, where it makes a right-angled bend to the southwest, and continues in this general course until it empties into Bering Sea. From latitude 60° to about latitude 65°, where it enters Alaska, it flows through the Yukon Territory, and less than half of its basin lies in Alaska.

The Yukon basin, comprising an irregular area in Alaska and adjacent portions of Yukon Territory and British Columbia, is roughly outlined on the north, east, and northeast by the Rocky Mountain system, and on the south by the Pacific Mountain system. There are no considerable highlands on the southeast, for there the tributaries of the Yukon, Liard, and Stikine interlock irregularly within the plateau region. The main tributaries of the Yukon are the Koyukuk, Tanana, Porcupine, White, Pelly, and Lewes, the main stream beginning with the junction of the Pelly and Lewes, which are entirely within Canadian territory.

The Yukon proper—that is, that part of the river below the junction of the Pelly and Lewes—has a length of about 1,500 miles. Its course is northwesterly, and for some 500 miles it flows through a steep-walled valley with only a narrow flood-plain as far as the town of Circle. The Yukon below Circle enters the great lowland called the Yukon Flats through which it takes a meandering course for some 200 miles. Within the flats and at the Arctic Circle the river makes its great bend from northwest to southwest.

THE YUKON RIVER

Showing some of the different country through which it flows. Upper: Looking up the Yukon from the White River, photo by A. H. Brooks; center: Yukon valley at Eagle, photo by J. B. Mertie; lower: Riverboat pushing barges on lower Yukon, photo by J. B. Mertie.

The Yukon Flats comprise a great lowland, swampy area bounded by a rim of highlands with a length of some 200 miles and a width of 40 to 100 miles. No surveys have been made of this part of the river, but in places the various channels probably include a width of 10 to 20 miles. It is here made up of an intricate network of shallow channels and sloughs. Many oxbow lakes have been formed by the shifting channels. From the steamer deck the Yukon Flats present a monotonous expanse of sand bars and low, densely forested spruce islands through which the boat follows a tortuous channel among a bewildering maze of tributary and distributary watercourses, with an occasional glimpse of the distant rim of the plateau which surrounds the lowland. The presence of man in this dreary tract is made manifest only in the clearings, from which the timber has been cut for fuel, or the occasional small trading post or Indian settlement. At low water 10 or 15 feet of silt are exposed in the banks, but during floods the river is almost even with the surface of the islands. The ever-shifting channels make navigation a constantly changing problem to pilots.

Within the flats the Yukon receives one of its largest tributaries, the Porcupine, whose mouth lies at the great bend of the main river and just within the Arctic Circle. The source of the Porcupine is within 60 miles of the Yukon, in latitude 65° 30′, whence it flows northwesterly and, impinging on the mountain barrier which separates the Yukon and Mackenzie basins, bends sharply to the north and thence southwest, forming a great loop.

Within the flats the Yukon receives only two important tributaries, the Porcupine and Chandalar. Near the 66th parallel of latitude the flats end abruptly at a scarp which forms the northern boundary of a part of the plateau. This stands between 1,800 and 2,000 feet above sea level, and is often called the Lower Ramparts of the Yukon. The Yukon traverses this upland by a narrow, somewhat winding valley, whose walls often rise rampart-like, either directly from the water or from a narrow terrace. The stretch of the valley, about 120 miles long (measuring around the bends) and one-half to three miles wide, continues unbroken from the Yukon Flats to the mouth of the Tanana.

The Rampart region with the broad, sweeping curves of the river and the steep valley walls, clothed with spruce, cottonwood, and birch, varied by bare cliffs, is the most picturesque part of the Yukon. The Russian explorer, Lieut. L. A. Zagoskin, in 1843, reported the Yukon as unnavigable above the lower end of the ramparts, though its ascent and descent by steamer are attended by much less difficulty than in any other part of the river, for the current probably does not exceed five or six miles per hour, and there are few shifting sand bars to contend with.

The Ramparts end at the mouth of the Tanana, where there is an abrupt change in the contour of the valley. The gorge suddenly opens to a broad lowland, which along the Yukon is 15 to 20 miles in width, but which stretches up the tributary Tanana valley for a distance of 200 miles with a width of 20 to 100 miles. The northwestern boundary of the valley is a series of low mountains whose base the Yukon hugs. The southern wall is 15 to 20 miles distant near the Tanana, but gradually approaches, thus reducing the width of the valley. Then for some ten miles the valley is well defined by both walls; but, ten miles below, the eastern wall recedes and is seldom visible from the river. Throughout its course to the head of the delta the Yukon continues to skirt the north bank, and the river itself flows through many channels and is broken by numerous islands and sand bars.

The delta begins near the 63rd parallel of latitude where the river divides into a number of divergent channels which find their way to the sea with generally northerly and northwesterly courses. Apoon Pass, the northernmost, and Kwikluak Pass, the most southerly of these waterways, reach the open sea at points about 75 miles apart in an air line and 40 or 50 miles from the head of the delta. An intricate maze of waterways lies between the two channels, some of which flow chiefly to the Bering Sea; others connect with such channels, but many are blind sloughs affected only by the ebb and flow of the tide. The interstream areas, not more than ten feet above low tide, are swampy and dotted with innumerable small lakes. Here, as in the flats, the Yukon is constantly shifting its channel. The changes are brought about largely by the current and tides, but aid is given by the scouring of the ice which accumulates in the delta after the break-up in the spring and forms dams that cause new channels to be cut and old ones to be silted up.

Though the Yukon delta properly includes only that part

of the coastal plain included between the distributaries of the river, the broad lowland which embraces the deltas of the Yukon and the Kuskokwim has an extreme breadth of upward of 200 miles and might well be grouped with the delta flats. There can be no doubt that at some time a part of the Yukon water found its way across these lowlands and deposited the sediments by which they were made to encroach upon the sea. This region embraces a flat which is but a few feet above tidewater and is drained by sluggish, meandering rivers and dotted by many lakes. Its smooth surface is interrupted here and there by low, isolated hills, and the shore line is broken by inlets and tidal lagoons. At low tide this low coastal plain is extended a long distance seaward by mud flats.

The scenery of the lower Yukon offers but little of interest to the traveler. The mighty river, with its dark-yellow waters, is not without its grandeur, and the rounded valley slopes, dotted with spruce and deciduous trees, are not without picturesqueness; but for hundreds of miles there is almost no change in the aspect of the landscape. The upper reaches of the lower Yukon are heavily forested, but as the sea is approached the trees become more scattered and finally, a few miles above the delta, give way entirely to the tundra with its dreary, monotonous view. Inland the moss- and grass-covered lowlands stretch almost unbroken to the horizon except for distant, rounded highland masses, while seaward there is no break in the lowland, and its smooth surface merges with the plain of the sea. The delta supports a large, though migratory, Eskimo population which finds its way among the intricate waterways in large skin boats (umiaks) and kayaks, and is almost entirely dependent on the sea for food.

The Tanana River, the longest tributary of the Yukon whose basin lies entirely in Alaska, empties into the latter just where it emerges from the Ramparts and is about 400 miles long. The valley trends northwesterly, parallel to the main stream above the big bend, and drains an area of probably 25,000 square miles. The Alaska Range bounds the basin on the south and is the breeding ground of the glaciers from which most of the southern tributaries of the Tanana spring. The headwaters of the many tributaries from the north interlock with streams which flow directly into the Yukon above the Ramparts.

The Koyukuk joins the Yukon from the northwest about

450 miles from Bering Sea. Its drainage basin has an area of approximately 25,000 square miles and includes the southern ranges of the Arctic Mountain System which here form the Yukon-Arctic watershed. The valley of the Koyukuk, including that of its longest fork, is upward of 300 miles in length, while the river measured around the bends must be 600 or 700 miles long.

The area roughly blocked out by the Alaska and Aleutian ranges, the Tanana and Yukon rivers, and Bering Sea has been explored only in part. Its topography, as far as is known, consists of rounded hills and low mountains, seldom exceeding 2,000 feet in altitude, interpenetrated by broad river valleys and many lowlands; and the greater part of the drainage is carried to Bering Sea by the Kuskokwim River, the second in size in Alaska, possessing a catchment basin of probably more than 50,000 square miles.

Many headwater streams of the Kuskokwim rise in glaciers on the inland slope of the Alaska Range and flow northwesterly, their channels gradually uniting into four or five rivers which are tributary to the two trunk streams, whose junction in latitude 63° can be regarded as the beginning of the Kuskokwim proper. Geographic usage has applied the name Kuskokwim to the southern fork, while the other, whose valley trends northeast and southwest, is called the North Fork of the Kuskokwim. The Kuskokwim River proper rises in the unexplored mountain mass at the southern extension of the Alaska Range, and its headwaters probably interlock with streams tributary to Lake Clark.

The valley of the Kuskokwim below the forks is broad, and on the south the river is in most places bounded by wide lowlands that have been but little explored. One hundred miles above its delta the valley walls disappear, the uplands being represented only by occasional rounded hills or low ridges. The delta of the Kuskokwim on the north coalesces with that of the Yukon and is of the same general type. Unlike the Yukon delta, a relatively deep channel winds through the Kuskokwim delta, making it possible to bring small ocean vessels into the mouth of the river. Above, the river is navigable for river steamers for some 800 miles.

The Seward Peninsula, though it belongs to the Central Plateau Region, is isolated from the rest of the province. It is essentially a region of flat-topped uplands bounded near the sea by coastal plains. In places these give way to abrupt bluffs whose bases are washed by the waves of the ocean. This upland is diversified by some minor ranges, of which the Kigluaik, with peaks up to 4,000 and 5,000 feet in altitude, is the highest. The upland is broken by broad, flat valleys having gentle slopes. The drainage of the peninsula is both to the Arctic Ocean and Bering Sea.

Arctic Mountain System

The Central Plateau Region is bounded on the north by the Arctic Mountain System which stretches across northern Alaska as a broad highland belt forming the watershed between the Arctic Ocean and the Yukon basin.

The Arctic Mountain System enters Alaska as a broad belt north of the Porcupine River, here trending nearly east and west. It then bends somewhat to the southwest, terminating near Kotzebue Sound. These mountains are but imperfectly known.[2] At the boundary the system is made up of several parallel but ill-defined ranges, varying from 4,000 to 8,000 feet in altitude. Along the valley of the Colville River, whose course is at right angles to the system, two mountain axes are distinguishable, the southernmost of which has been termed the Endicott Mountains. As it approaches the Arctic Ocean to the west, it loses its definiteness and is split up into several minor ranges by the valleys of the Selawik, Kobuk, and Noatak rivers, whose courses lie parallel to the general trend of the system. The northernmost of this group of ranges lying north of the Noatak valley has been called the DeLong Mountains. The Baird Mountains lie between the Kobuk and the Noatak; they are from 4,000 to 6,000 feet in height. The southern face of the Arctic Mountain System is not everywhere sharply differentiated from the plateau region, for the two provinces merge through a series of foothills. The north face, on the other hand, falls off abruptly to a piedmont plateau to be described below.

The Arctic Mountain System is drained in three directions —southerly to Bering Sea and chiefly through the Yukon; westerly to the Arctic Ocean at Kotzebue Sound through the three large rivers, the Selawik, the Kobuk, and the Noatak; and northerly to the polar sea through many watercourses of which the Colville is the largest. This river rises in Chandler Lake, flows westerly, then, making a

[2] They are, of course, much better known now than they were when this manuscript was written. They are now called the Brooks Range in honor of the author of this book.—*Editor's note.*

great bend, takes a northerly course to the sea. The aspect of the Arctic Mountain System is one of a rugged topography but broken by many broad gaps. Timber is found in only sheltered valleys, and much of the mountain mass is barren of vegetation except for moss. Few of the peaks rise to the line of perpetual snow, and there are only a few small glaciers in the entire mountain mass.

The Arctic Mountain System east of the boundary is knit to the northwestern extension of the Rocky Mountains by a minor range which forms the watershed between the Mackenzie and the Porcupine rivers. In Canada the plateau province is bounded on the east by the Rocky Mountain system whose ranges, as has been shown, bend to the westward and, after crossing the boundary, are lost in the uplands of the plateau region.

Arctic Slope Region

At the international boundary the northern face of the Arctic Mountains rises almost directly from the sea, with only a few miles of low coastal plain between it and the Arctic Ocean. To the west the coast line bends northward and the mountain front retreats southward, thus widening out the coastal belt to more than 150 miles near the 156th meridian. This province, which embraces both a plateau and a coastal plain, is called the Arctic Slope Region.

Along the valley of the Colville River, the Anaktuvuk Plateau and the coastal plain go to make up the Arctic Slope Region. The former lies immediately adjacent to the mountain front, where it has a height of about 2,500 feet; thence it stretches northward, retaining its character as a rolling upland and sloping gently toward the Arctic for about 80 miles from the mountains, where the coastal plain begins. It is inferred that there is a gradual transition between the two topographic forms, their differences lying in the fact that the plateau has a gently rolling surface, while the plain is absolutely flat. In genesis, however, the two types differ, for the plateau is an uplifted, eroded surface, and the coastal plain is a constructional form, largely built up of horizontal stratified sediments.

It seems likely that the whole region lying north of the Arctic Mountains has essentially this type of topography, but it is almost unexplored. At Cape Lisburne there are remnants of a former plateau surface at an altitude of about

1,500 to 2,000 feet, which is probably a westward extension of the Anaktuvuk Plateau.

A number of rivers and streams traverse the Arctic slopes through broad valleys. These rise in the mountains, where they have steep gradients and swift currents. Emerging from the highlands, they take tortuous courses to the sea. The Colville, the largest of these watercourses and the only one surveyed, has already been described. The Arctic Slope Region is devoid of all timber except for a thin fringe of willow which hugs the watercourses. Grass, too, is scant, and most of the land is covered with moss and some herbaceous plants.[3]

[3] A great deal of exploring and of more accurate mapping and surveying than is indicated in this chapter has been done in recent years. Of all this, Dr. Brooks, of course, could have no knowledge when he wrote his manuscript. Consequently, a few of his references to nomenclature and some of his figures on mountain heights are subject to correction. For example, the Yukon River by official decree of the Canadian government is no longer considered to begin at the junction of the Pelly and Lewes, but now includes as part of its over-all length what was formerly known as the Lewes. Or again, the altitude of various mountains as given by Dr. Brooks is occasionally at variance with later, more precise measurements; nevertheless the figures quoted in his manuscript are the ones that have been used. In a number of instances, however, he had left blank spaces, apparently to be filled in later, for the heights of different peaks; these have been supplied by reference to *A Dictionary of Altitudes in the United States*, fourth edition, published by the United States Geological Survey as Bulletin No. 274, 1906.—*Editor's Note.*

CHAPTER II

Climate

PROBABLY none of the physical features of Alaska is generally less well understood than is the climate, regarding which there is much confusion of thought. The average man finds it hard to reconcile the long-familiar tales of ice and snow and perils of winter travel with the more recent propaganda about vast tracts of fertile land and equitable climate; and as a rule he stands by his earlier and more deep-rooted conceptions. The reason is that the world at large gained its first permanent impression of Alaska during the Klondike days, when thousands of amateur gold seekers told their stories of perils and privations. The wintry blast and the great white solitude have been pictured by the romancer, the poet, and the dramatist, almost to the exclusion of all other Alaskan themes. Such features lend themselves better to a heroic literature than do the long, mild summer days, the broad meadows, and the profusion of wild flowers that are equally indicative of Alaska's climate.

The camera, too, with its endless record of glaciers and dog teams, has played false to a true conception of Alaska's climate. It is such data, presenting only one phase of the subject, that have given the world at large a false conception of the climate of this northern land. Nor is this strange, for in like manner the early literature dealing with Eastern Canada and New England conveys the impression of a land almost uninhabitable because of the rigorousness of its climate. The survivors of the first winter at Plymouth undoubtedly regarded the climate as a serious menace to the settlement of New England. If our only knowledge of the Atlantic seaboard had been gained from many of the early narratives, we might decide adversely as to its suitability as a permanent home for the white race. This fertile eastern border of the continent, on the basis of such information, might be pictured as falling into two zones, one with a winter climate so rigorous as to be almost unfit for human habitation, and another a tropical and fever-ridden zone.

For these reasons, many will probably have to divest themselves of all previous conceptions to understand Alaska's climate. Yet such an understanding is necessary to a comprehension of the distribution of animal and vegetable life, to an understanding of man's advances in the Territory, and above all to an evaluation of this northern province as a permanent abode for the white race.

First, it must be understood that there is no such thing as an Alaskan climate. The climates of different parts of the Territory are too diversified to permit of such a generalization. There are within this northern province even greater contrasts of climate than exist between Florida and Maine, or between Puget Sound and Montana. These great diversities are due to a contrast of physical conditions, caused by geographic position and extent relative to oceanic bodies of water, and, above all, to the presence of the great mountain barriers already described.

Alaska's great latitudinal and longitudinal dimensions, already suggested in the previous chapter, are in themselves sufficient to account for great diversities of climate. Its westernmost point is thrust far out into the warm waters of the Pacific, whose waves also beat on a tremendous stretch of its southern coast line. On the other hand, its western boundary is marked by the cold waters of Bering Sea, and the still colder waters of the Arctic Ocean border the Territory on the north.

The major movements of the Pacific waters are circulatory, from west to east, and this great ocean current impinges on the land near the southernmost point of Alaska, causing this part of the Territory and the adjacent parts of British Columbia to have an equitable climate. North of this major oceanic movement and within the Gulf of Alaska, there is a subordinate circular current which carries the warm waters of the Pacific along the Alaskan seaboard and much ameliorates the climate of the adjacent littoral. The great circulatory movement of the Pacific passes close to the Aleutian Islands; in fact, part of its warm waters are sent northward into Bering Sea between the western end of the Aleutian chain and the Commander Islands of the Asiatic coast. These conditions have had a marked influence on the climate of the Aleutian Islands, noteworthy in their fogs and excessive precipitation.

The Bering Sea is for the most part a cold body of water, for upwards of one-third of it is covered with ice during the winter months. While it receives warm waters from the

Pacific, these waters circulate only in its southern and deeper parts. The northeastern half of this sea is shoal, and its temperature is determined largely by the access of cold water received from the Arctic Ocean through Bering Straits. Its shores, therefore, bathed chiefly by cold waters, have a much more rigorous climate than has the Pacific littoral. The Arctic Ocean, with its polar ice cap completely frozen for about ten months, gives the adjacent land that rigorousness so often associated in the popular mind with the climate of all Alaska.

In strong contrast to these maritime climatic provinces is the great inland region, which is essentially continental in its character. The great drainage basins of the Yukon and Kuskokwim rivers are shut off by high ranges from the ameliorating influences of the Pacific Ocean on the south, and by other ranges from the rigors of the Arctic Ocean littoral on the north. This province, however, opens out to Bering Sea, and its climate gradually merges with that of the Bering Sea littoral. Inland Alaska is essentially arid, with short, comparatively hot summers and long, cold winters.

The climatic effects of the conditions described above are especially marked in their influence on the distribution of precipitation. The moisture-laden winds of the Pacific, sweeping the high coastal ranges, precipitate their contents and give to this littoral the wettest climate on the continent. On the other hand, the air currents over the cold waters of Bering Sea are relatively dry, and there is, moreover, no coastal mountain barrier to induce precipitation. These winds, sweeping up the Yukon and Kuskokwim valleys, only gradually lose their moisture, and there is therefore no marked coastal rainy belt.

Still smaller precipitation occurs in the Arctic coast province. Here the very low temperature of the ocean leads to but very little evaporation, and the winds are relatively dry. Therefore the whole Arctic littoral is a region of small precipitation. These facts are graphically illustrated by the accompanying map showing the distribution of precipitation. A heavy precipitation is indicated along the Pacific seaboard, a much lighter one along the shores of Bering Sea, and an almost insignificant one on the Arctic coast, while the entire inland region is semiarid.

Strong contrasts are exhibited in the mean annual temperature of Alaska. The distribution of the annual isotherms

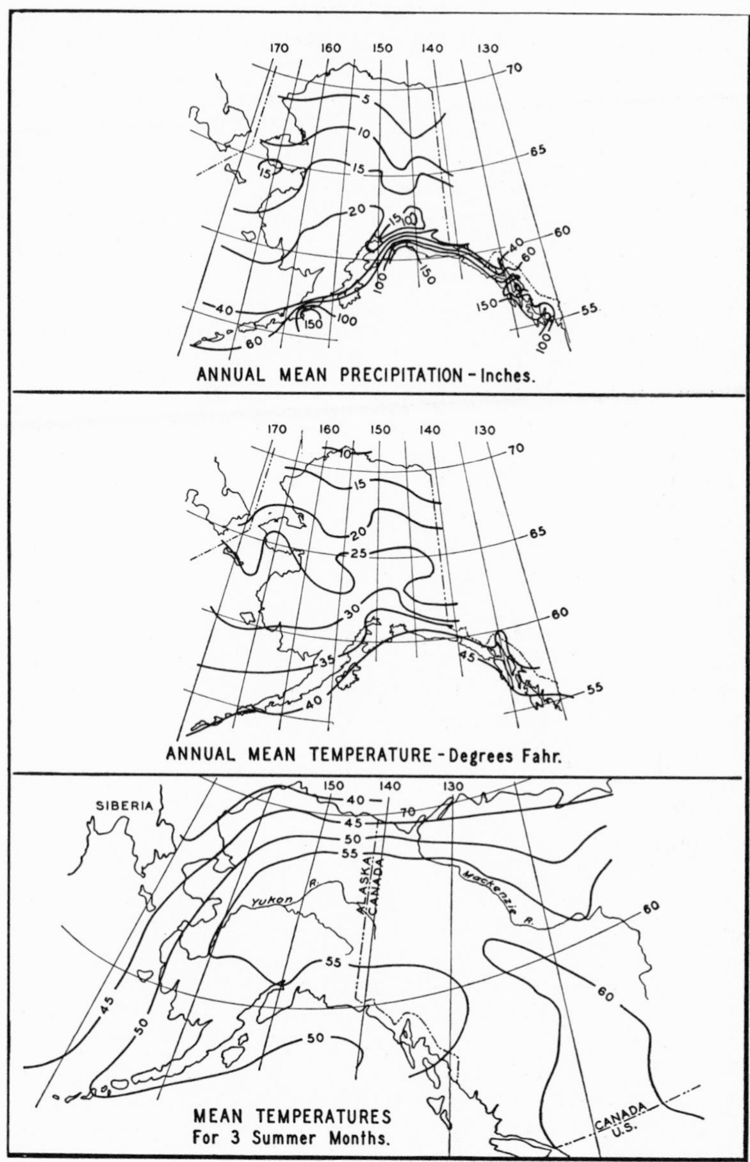

CLIMATIC FEATURES IN ALASKA

is largely dominated by latitude and by the physical features, and hence, as the map shows, they parallel the southern seaboard. The 45° F. isotherm is the highest and traverses the southern part of Southeastern Alaska. Most of the Pacific seaboard region, however, has a mean annual temperature of 30° to 40° F. Beyond the mountains the 25° and 30° F. isotherms course through the Yukon basin, paralleling the southern seaboard. Going northward, the mean annual temperature falls, till finally at Point Barrow it is less than 10° F.

The isotherms of the three summer months exhibit great irregularity, and as these mark the growing season their position is of more importance to Alaska's future as an abode for man. The map shows that the summer isotherms of Western Canada make a great northwesterly sweep as they approach the Pacific seaboard. While the mean annual temperature of the Pacific coast region is about 50° F., that of the inland region is 55° F. The isotherm marking 60° reaches almost into the Yukon basin, though it does not touch Alaska.

A general understanding of Alaskan climate can best be obtained by considering it as divided into three general provinces: (1) the Pacific seaboard, with heavy precipitation, cool summers, moderate winters, and no extremes of temperatures; (2) the inland region, with low precipitation, hot summers, and extremes of summer and winter temperatures; and (3) the northern Bering Sea and Arctic coast region, with low precipitation, short cool summers, and long cold winters. The general features of these larger provinces will first be presented, but the more exhaustive analysis to follow will show that each admits of subdivisions into a number of subordinate climatic provinces.

The maritime province, lying adjacent to the Pacific Ocean, has a heavy precipitation (50 to 190 inches), comparatively high mean annual temperature (40° to 48° F.), cool summers (mean temperatures of 50° to 55° F.), and mild winters (mean temperatures of 20° to 35° F.). It has small variations of annual temperature compared with the interior, the records showing from –12° to 84° F. The second is the inland province, lying beyond the coastal mountains, with a continental climate characterized by semiaridity (precipitation nine to 15 inches), comparatively warm summers (mean temperatures of 50° to 58° F.), and cold winters (mean temperatures of 0° to –15° F.). Its most striking feature is the extreme annual variation in temperatures, which are from –76° to 90° F. The mean annual temperature varies from 15° to 27° F. The third province includes the region tributary to the Arctic Ocean, which, according to a few records, has a precipitation of only about six to eight inches, an average summer temperature of from 40° to 45° F., a winter temperature of about –10° to –16° F., and an extreme variation, according to a few records, of –54° to 60° F. With this is here grouped the region tributary to northern Bering Sea, though here the precipitation is from 10 to 20 inches and the summer temperatures higher.

The climate of the coastal province is comparable with that of Scotland and the Scandinavian peninsula in Europe, but is somewhat warmer. That of the inland region is not unlike the climate of Alberta, Saskatchewan, and Manitoba in Canada. The northerly province bordering the polar sea is the only one in which Arctic conditions prevail. Of the Pacific seaboard province, the Alexander Archipelago and adjacent portions of the mainland, called Southeastern Alaska, have the most temperate climate of the Territory. But even in this subordinate province there are great local variations of climate.

The precipitation in Southeastern Alaska varies from about 147 inches at Ketchikan to less than 30 inches at Skagway. While there is but little snow at sea level, there is a very heavy fall in the mountains. At White Pass the winter snowfall is probably 25 to 30 feet, but it is probably less than four feet on the Chilkat summit. Records show that the mean annual number of days on which precipitation occurs in Southeastern Alaska varies from 85 at Skagway to 235 at Ketchikan. The mean temperatures of the three summer months in this province vary from 50° to 55° F., of the three winter months from 20° to 30° F.; the mean annual temperature is between 40° and 48° F. The highest recorded summer temperature in Southeastern Alaska is 92° F., the lowest winter temperature –40° F. The temperature extremes at Sitka show for August, the hottest month, an extreme range of from 35° to 87° F., and for the coldest month, February, a range from 3° to 54° F. The mean temperature for January is 33° F. and for August 50° F. Sitka, located on the outer islands, is subjected to all the ameliorating influences of the warm waters of the Pacific. Juneau, on the mainland, is less subject to these oceanic influences. The extreme of winter temperatures recorded was in February and showed a range of from –4° to 50° F.; the extremes in summer (July) are from 38° to 80° F. The growing season on the outer islands is about 200 days in length, that of the mainland about 175 days.

In general, the climate of Southeastern Alaska is one of great humidity. About three-quarters of the precipitation falls in the winter months from November to March, and is characterized by long, incessant rains and drizzles. On the seacoast there is little snowfall, but in the high ranges there is a very heavy snowfall. The summers are cool and pleasant, though bright clear days are the exception, there being on the average less than 100 days in the year when the skies are not overcast. The winters are mild and not unpleasant, save for the heavy precipitation.

The coastal strip lying west of Southeastern Alaska and stretching through to the entrance of Cook Inlet has a somewhat lower temperature and higher precipitation than the region described above. Here the average temperature for the three summer months is about 51° F., of the three winter months from 20° to 30° F. The lowest temperatures recorded in this region are –14° F., the highest 82° F. Incomplete records show an average annual precipitation of from 51 to 135 inches, varying according to locality. The precipitation is about 127 inches at Katalla, 132 inches at Cordova, 135 inches at Childs Glacier, Copper River, 74 inches at Valdez, and 54 inches at Seward. The records indicate an average at different localities of from 90 to 240 days on which some precipitation occurs. The total snowfall is about five to eight feet at Seward, 12 feet at Valdez, six feet on the Trail Creek summit along the Alaska Northern Railroad, 30 feet at Childs Glacier on the Copper River Railroad, and about 15 feet at Thompson Pass, crossed by the military road from Valdez. Here, as in Southeastern Alaska, the inland fiords are decidedly colder with less precipitation than the outer shore line. Thus, both summers and winters are colder at Valdez than at Cordova or Katalla. The precipitation at Valdez is not more than half as much as that on the outer coast.

In a general way, it may be said that the severest storms along the central part of the Pacific seaboard of Alaska are from the south and southeast, and that they are more frequent from October to March than during the balance of the year. Of importance to commerce and habitation too are the violent winds which blow in and out of the valleys that traverse the coast ranges and their connecting fiords. These generally blow toward the land in summer and toward the sea in winter. The severest are the outward winds, which are most common from January to March when velocities of 60 to 70 miles an hour are said to be not infrequent. These winds are known as glacial winds, as they are especially prevalent where the break in the range through which they blow is partly filled with ice. Examples of such winds are found at Taku Inlet, Lynn Canal, Bering River, Copper River, Lowe River, Valdez Glacier, Resurrection Bay, Turnagain Arm, and Iliamna Bay.

Cook Inlet has quite a different climate from that of the outer coast line. Here the precipitation is only 25 to 40 inches, with a snowfall of four to five feet. Some precipitation occurs on about 100 days in the year. The mean annual temperature varies greatly in different parts of this region, being from 33° to 42° F., while the average temperature of the three summer months is about 53° F., of the three winter months about 10° to 25° F. The highest recorded summer temperature is 87° F., the lowest winter temperature –46° F. The growing season is probably about 100 days in length.

The climate of the lower Susitna and of the Matanuska valleys differs, again, from both that of Cook Inlet and that of the outer coast line. Here there are very few records, but the summers are known to be warmer than on Cook Inlet, and the winters are probably milder. The precipitation is small, one year's record on the Chickaloon in the Matanuska valley indicating a total of only ten inches, but this was probably an unusually dry year. The lowest temperature recorded at this locality during the same period was –12° F., the highest 84° F. There are no records of the growing season, which is probably about 125 days in length.

The lower Copper River valley has much the same climate as that of the coast, but as one ascends the river above Tiekel a gradual transition to inland conditions is noted. There are no records at Chitina, but the precipitation is known to be small, the summers warm, and the winters cold. At Kennicott, the inland terminal of the Copper River Railway, the snowfall is about four feet, and the extremes of temperature recorded are –31° and 76° F. This station is 2,000 feet above sea level and close to a glacier. At Copper Center the total precipitation is about ten inches, and the snowfall about three feet. Extremes of temperature of –50° and 85° F. have been recorded. The average temperature of the three summer months is about 55° and of the three winter months about 10° F. It is estimated that the snowfall at Paxson, a few miles south of Isabella Pass, is between three and four feet, and the total precipitation somewhat greater than at Copper Center.

The Alaska Peninsula and adjacent islands constitute a subordinate province with essentially oceanic conditions. On the Bering Sea, or northern side of the peninsula, the rainfall is between 25 and 30 inches; on the southern, or Pacific coast, side, it is from 45 to 60 inches. At Kodiak a rainfall of 57 inches has been recorded, at Unga one of 45 inches. Precipitation is pretty well distributed throughout the year, but the driest season is from January to August. Mean summer temperature varies from 50° F. on the north side of the peninsula to 55° F. on the south side. Mean temperatures of the three winter months average about 30° F. at Kodiak.

The Aleutian Islands and Alaska Peninsula have a climate characterized by moderate temperatures, limited range of temperatures, and less humidity than that of the Pacific coast littoral to the east. The total precipitation is about 80 inches, which falls mostly as rain. A mean summer temperature of 50° to 55° F. and a mean annual temperature of about 40° F. are indicated by the meagre data at hand. The extremes of temperature recorded at Unalaska, the only station where any records have been kept, are 78° F. in July and 5° F. in January. The summer of the Aleutian Islands is characterized by fogs. alternating with severe southwesterly gales accompanied by rain. June, July, and August are the months of least precipitation. The climate of the Aleutian Islands is not unlike that of Scotland, though it lies in a somewhat lower degree of latitude.

The climate of the shores of Bering Sea is characterized by a summer temperature of from 45° to 55° F. and a mean annual temperature of 25° to 40° F. The extremes of temperature recorded at Nome are a maximum of 84° F. in July and a minimum of –47° F. in January. The precipitation, which is about 30 to 40 inches in the northern half of Bering Sea, decreases at its northern shores to 15 and 17 inches. At St. Paul Island the precipitation is 40

THE ARCTIC REGION

Upper: Coastal plain near Point Barrow, photo by E. D. Leffingwell; center: Difficult sledding on the Beaufort Sea, photo by E. D. Leffingwell; lower: Iceberg about 30 feet high, photo by D. F. Higgins.

inches, at St. Michael 17 inches, at Nome 15 inches. At Nome the winter snowfall is from six to eight feet. The climate of the northern half of the Bering Sea littoral is comparable to that of the province of Archangel in northern Russia, a region which supports some agricultural population.

The Arctic province, which includes the littoral of the polar sea and the region lying north of the Arctic Mountains, is similar to that of the northern part of Bering Sea, but colder. At Point Barrow, the northernmost cape of Alaska, the mean annual temperature is less than 8° F. and the mean annual precipitation less than eight inches. The highest temperatures recorded at Point Barrow do not exceed 65° F., the lowest –55° F.

The precipitation, according to records available, is between six and eight inches. In the winter it falls in the form of fine snow and, on account of severe winds, drifts very much. The greatest rainfall is between July and October. Frosts are liable to come during any of the summer months, but according to the meagre records, they are rare in June and July. The climate of the northern field is distinctly arctic in its character. It is similar to the rest of the circumpolar region.

Inland Alaska, including the great valleys of the Yukon and the Kuskokwim, as well as of the Susitna and Copper rivers, is continental in its character. Bright, clear days with scant rainfall typify the summers, and the winters are severe; but on account of the aridity of the climate, they are not a great strain on mankind.

The total annual precipitation in the upper Yukon basin varies locally from 10 to 16 inches. At Fairbanks it is about 11.5 inches, at Eagle 12 inches, at Dawson 13 inches, at Fort Gibbon (now Tanana) at the mouth of the Tanana about 14 inches. The snowfall in this district is from three to five feet. It is reported that the snowfall in the upper White River basin is only two feet. Some precipitation occurs for about 80 days in the year. The mean temperature for the three summer months at Fairbanks is about 56° F., the mean temperature for the three winter months about –12° F., and the mean annual temperature about 25° F. A minimum temperature of –70° F. has been recorded, and a maximum of 90° F. The precipitation in the lower Yukon and Kuskokwim is about 17 to 20 inches. The average summer temperatures are a little lower than at Fairbanks, and the winter temperature about the same. The growing season in the inland province is from 90 to 120 days in length, depending on local features of relief.

The experience of those long resident in Alaska has shown the climate to be very healthful. No extremes of heat or cold occur along the Pacific seaboard. The excessive rains characteristic of many parts of this district are, to be sure, disagreeable, but experience demonstrates the fact that they have no adverse influence on health. It must be remembered too that the excessive precipitation is by no means universal in this maritime belt. It has been shown that at Skagway, for example, the total precipitation is less than 30 inches, and at Seward about 55 inches. Probably the most trying feature of the coastal climate is the strong winds which blow in the winter from the valleys traversing the coastal barrier.

The Cook Inlet and Susitna regions have a climate similar to that of the interior, and warmer summers than those on the coast, with less precipitation. The same holds true of the Copper River basin. Of the Yukon it may be said that the summers are cool and that bright, clear weather prevails most of the time. The aridity of the climate makes the extreme temperatures of the winter easy to resist. All who have lived in this inland region are agreed that the winter climate is far more healthful than that of many parts of the States where the temperature is higher but with an excess of humidity. Residents of the interior have no fear of the extreme cold that often prevails during the winter months. The winter journey between Valdez and Fairbanks is made by men, women, and children and offers no serious handicaps except when storms are encountered.[1]

[1] As at the end of Chapter I, it is again necessary to note that much more complete data are now available than were when Dr. Brooks wrote his manuscript. Hence, some of the figures used in this chapter are subject to correction, especially those recording maxima and minima temperatures. Still, it has seemed advisable to adhere to the policy of altering his manuscript as little as possible and, consequently, to use the figures he gives. A few blank spaces in his manuscript have been filled after consulting the readings given in *Climatological Data*, the annual reports on Alaska prepared by the United States Weather Bureau.—*Editor's Note.*

CHAPTER III

Sketch of Geology of Alaska

IT HAS ALREADY been pointed out that the mountain systems of Alaska are parallel, that they trend first northwest from Canada into the Territory, then bend southwest toward Asia. These larger features of the relief are, therefore continental in their magnitude, and their genesis must be sought in the attitude of the rock formations of which they are built up. An understanding of the geography of Alaska must take into account its geology. Moreover, the geologic constitution of Alaska has determined the occurrence of its mineral resources. Also, the soils which determine the distribution of the vegetation and arable lands are primarily the result of geologic agencies. Without following this argument any further, it will be evident that an understanding of the geology of the Territory is essential to a comprehension of its history and resources as well as its future.

As this writing is intended for the non-technical reader, it will be desirable to present briefly the geologic principles to which reference will be made in the discussion to follow and to define certain technical terms whose use can hardly be avoided. Thus it is hoped that this analysis may be comprehensible to the layman not versed in geologic lore without his having to consult any of the excellent text books of the science.

That part of the earth's crust accessible to man—the only part on which direct observations can be made—is, as is well known, built up of a great sequence of rock strata, now in part tilted up but all originally laid down as horizontal strata. These sediments, laid down as beds in the oceans of the past, have been diversified by igneous masses of more or less irregular outline. It will be evident that the determination of the sequence of rock strata is fundamental to the understanding of the geology.

All sedimentary rocks have been derived, by more or less alteration, from material originally laid down in horizontal beds on the floor of an ocean or other body of water. Such deposits are of two general types: (1) deep-sea sediments, in which calcareous matter derived from organisms dominates; (2) shallow-water sediments which comprise clays, sands, and gravels derived from the erosion of near-by land masses. The accumulation of sediments, though a relatively slow process, measured in geological time goes on very rapidly. Thus, during one of the minor geologic subdivisions of the past thousands of feet of strata may accumulate, and the deposits of a larger subdivision, such as the Paleozoic, may attain a thickness to be measured in miles.

If the sediments remain undisturbed, the more deeply buried beds become altered to hard rock by the physical changes wrought through the blanketing effect of the superimposed strata. This change to hard rock is often accelerated by crustal movements which disturb the strata. Such movements are also often accompanied, as will be shown, by the upward injection into the sediments of molten rock masses from the abyssal regions. Both the crustal disturbances and the injection of igneous rocks produce more or less chemical and physical changes in the sediments, and this change is termed "metamorphism." Igneous intrusives when consolidated at depth may form an integral part of a geologic succession. The same is also true of volcanic rocks comprising those of igneous origin consolidated at the surface. This process, known as "vulcanism," will be discussed below.

Certain kinds of mineral deposits are of sedimentary origin; that is, they were laid down with the bedded rocks with which they are now found associated. The most important of these is coal. This is derived by alteration from vegetable material, either peat or wood fragments; subsequent burial and alteration caused by folding have changed this vegetable matter to coal. If only partly altered, it becomes lignite; if profoundly altered, bituminous coal or anthracite. All these grades and transitions between these are found in Alaska. Petroleum too is found only in sedimentary rocks and is probably derived from organic matter deposited in the rock strata. It differs in occurrence from coal, inasmuch as, being liquid, it can migrate from one horizon to another. Thus, some of the Alaska petroleum occurs in rocks of Tertiary age, but it probably had its origin in much older strata. Certain kinds of iron ore are also found in bedded rocks, but such have not been found in Alaska. Alaska's gypsum deposits furnish another example of a valuable mineral found in sedimentary rocks, as do also her beds of marble.

Many of Alaska's gravel beds carry more or less fine particles of native gold. When the gold is present in sufficient quantities to permit its profitable extraction, such auriferous gravels become placers. Therefore what is today simply a deposit of auriferous gravel without value may in the future, when costs of operation are reduced by railway or road construction and by use of improved machinery for recovery, become a valuable placer. As gravel deposits are, properly, bedded rocks, even though unconsolidated, the gold placers must be classed with the ore deposits of sedimentary origin. In addition to the gold, native copper and the mineral cassiterite, known as stream tin, have also been found as placer deposits in Alaska; and a few minute particles of platinum have been found in some of the Alaskan gold placers.

In general, it may be said of the mineral deposits found in bedded form that they have far more regularity of occurrence than those found in veins, to be described below. Thus, given a tract of coal land, it is possible, from the natural exposures supplemented by excavations and borings, to estimate within a few degrees of accuracy the amount of coal available. The same is true of a placer, though here the gold is usually all under a cover of sand and gravel, and recourse must be had to excavation to find the amount and distribution of gold. By the proper testing of ground under the management of qualified engineers, the element of chance can be almost entirely eliminated in a coal or placer mining venture. Unfortunately, the public has not been convinced of this fact, and in Alaska alone hundreds of thousands of dollars have been squandered in mining ventures which would have been saved by proper preliminary testing of the deposit.

The component rocks of Alaska are the products of these processes of sedimentation, intrusion, vulcanism, and alteration which have been operating through a long period of time, extending back to the Archaean, the earliest of the geologic subdivisions. Some of these agencies have continued to be active to the present, but the youngest strata (sediments that have become indurated) belong to the early Tertiary.

It is not to be supposed, however, that the rocks form an unbroken succession of strata deposited in the same ocean.

As a matter of fact, there were recurrent periods of movement which altered and deformed the strata deposited in any one epoch, many of which brought the rock above sea level as land masses and thus inaugurated periods of erosion. These periods of erosion, which furnished the sediments for the sedimentary rocks of other areas, were in turn followed by submergence and the recurrence of sedimentation. Epochs of erosion, which afford an important clue to the geologic history of a province, are made evident in the rocks now exposed by the discordance of the beds of different formations; these are termed "unconformities."

The general stratigraphic sequence is shown in the accompanying table, which undoubtedly will be modified when more detailed studies have been made.[1]

Rock strata which have been disturbed from the original horizontal position by movements within the earth's crust stand at various angles. The attitude in space of such disturbed beds is termed "structure." It is due to such disturbances and subsequent removal by the agencies of erosion of a part of the rock sequence that the older formations become exposed on the earth's surface.

The "strike" or "strike line" of a formation is the intersection of the bedding planes of the terrane with a horizontal plane. In a region of complex folding, the strike often varies from place to place; but the dominant structures usually follow a well-defined system, and generally where there is strong relief these are parallel to the major topographic features.

The "dip" of the strata is the inclination of their bedding planes with the horizontal. While in this discussion the absolute angle of dip is of small importance, its direction is essential to a comprehension of the structure of the strata —for the direction of dip along a line at right angles to strike indicates whether the fold is an arch or trough, the first being called an "anticline" and the second a "syncline." The great Alaska Range, for example, is built up of strata having a general synclinal structure—that is, they form a trough, the strata dipping toward the center of this trough from both margins.

The movements in the earth's crust produce not only folds, but also breaks in the strata. That is, a bed or a series of

[1] Dr. Brooks' manuscript did not include this table. I have, accordingly, inserted the stratigraphic correlation that he prepared for his earlier book, *The Geography and Geology of Alaska*, which is, consequently, here reprinted.—*Editor's Note.*

beds is broken through and the two sides of the break have moved in opposite directions. These are termed "faults," and are of varying degree of magnitude. For example, a few square inches of laminated slate may show hundreds of minute dislocations, each of which is a fault. On the other hand, a fault may mark a dislocation measured by thousands of feet, if not by miles. Thus, rocks of very different positions in the stratigraphic column may be brought into juxtaposition. For example, in the upper Copper River region there is a fault marking a dislocation of over seven thousand feet.

The plane of movement in such dislocations is called the "fault plane," and this may slope at any angle. In some instances, where the slope of the fault plane is gentle, the lower strata are thrust up over the higher beds, and this is called a "thrust fault." There are many examples of thrust faults along the inland base of the Alaska Range.

In the presentation of an analysis of bed rock structure of Alaska, it must be noted that during the past geological ages there have been a number of periods of folding and that, therefore, the present attitude of the terranes is the final result of several crustal movements. Lack of detailed studies makes it impossible to differentiate to any considerable extent the structures of the various periods of stress, but in the sketch of the sequence of geologic events given below these will be briefly touched upon. It is proposed, however, to consider here chiefly the present attitude of the bed rock strata irrespective of the period of deformation to which they may be assigned.

Igneous rocks have already been referred to as contributing an important element of the earth's crust, especially in Alaska. The intrusive igneous rocks—namely, those that have been injected from below along fissures or lines of weakness but that hardened and crystallized before reaching the surface—are particularly abundant in Alaska. Among these are rocks that may be grouped together as granites. These are the dominating types, though they vary somewhat in composition. These occur in large areas, as in the Coast Range of Southeastern Alaska. Here they have been intruded in great volumes, called "batholiths," to be measured in thousands of cubic miles. Such injections have disturbed and altered the adjacent strata. They are also found in more restricted areas and are then called "stocks." An example of a granite stock forms part of Mount

McKinley. A third occurrence is that of the filling up of fissures; this type is called "dikes." All of these intrusions occurred under a blanket of thousands of feet of strata, and it is only the removal of the superimposed strata by erosion that makes them visible.

GEOLOGICAL PICTURES

Upper left: Quartz veinlets in graywacke boulder, photo by S. R. Capps; upper right: Silurian fossils in limestone, photo by J. B. Mertie; center left: Folds in slate and graywacke, photo by Sidney Paige; center right: Dike in leaf-bearing beds, photo by F. H. Moffit; lower left: Faulted graywacke, shale, and sandstone, photo by F. C. Schrader; lower right: Thrust fault, photo by A. J. Collier.

Closely connected with these igneous intrusions are the ore bodies. These, like the igneous rocks, have been forced up from the abysmal regions of the earth and have thus invaded the higher strata. The most common are the auriferous quartz veins. A vein of quartz is a rock fissure which has been filled by quartz. Often such veins carry other minerals. Quartz veins are usually abundant in regions which have been intruded by igneous rocks, and in their origin have much in common with dikes of igneous rocks. Under certain conditions of origin, only in part understood, quartz veins carry metallic minerals, such as gold and other metals and their compounds. When the metallic contents of the veins are large enough and the veins of a sufficient size to permit of economic mining, such metalliferous quartz veins constitute ore bodies. The genesis of such ore bodies is only partly understood, but it is fairly well established that it is closely connected with igneous intrusion. Examples of auriferous quartz veins closely connected with igneous intrusion are those found at Juneau and at Fairbanks.

Most of the ores, including silver, copper, tin, lead, and others, have a genesis in a general way comparable with that of the auriferous quartz veins described above. For reasons also not well understood the ores in metalliferous minerals are usually unevenly distributed in the veins. Thus, one part of the vein may be rich enough to be profitably worked and another part practically barren. These localized masses of ore in the vein are termed "mineral shoots." The irregularity in the occurrence of the metals in the vein and the irregularity of the vein itself, now narrowing, now widening, give the lode mining industry that element of speculation which has been both a blessing and a curse—a blessing because it has attracted adventurous spirits, a curse because it has frequently led the industry into a field of mere speculation.

It will be evident that the question of costs of mining and, therefore, of transportation will be the determining factor in the valuing of an ore body. Had the ore body of the great Treadwell group of mines, which have produced gold to the value of over fifty millions of dollars, been located far from tidewater, the cost of mining would have been so great as to make this very low-grade deposit worthless.

The intrusive rocks, as already pointed out, have been

formed of magmas forced up from abyssal depths to the upper crust of the earth, but cooled and crystallized long before they reached the surface. Such rocks have a coarse texture like granite. Some of these invading magmas have continued their course until they break through to the surface and then cool relatively rapidly under the atmosphere, giving them a much finer grain than the intrusive rocks like granite. These surface-cooling rocks are the lavas, familiar in volcanic regions. Their most common form of emergence is through vents of volcanoes, which are themselves built up of igneous ejecta. Volcanic eruptions of the explosive type furnish the ash or tuff deposits or, when this material is mixed with water, the volcanic mud, such as overwhelmed the town of Herculaneum during the famous eruption of Vesuvius in the year 69. Periods of volcanic activity have occurred at many different times during the geologic past. The most evident results of vulcanism are the volcanoes of the present or immediately preceding geologic period, whose material still forms protuberances, including great mountain ranges, on the earth's surface. Vulcanism is an important feature in Alaska's geology. The great Wrangell Mountains, including some of the highest peaks of the Territory, are built up of volcanic material. The Aleutian chain of islands and many of the mountains of the Alaska Peninsula are largely made up of volcanic material. Lesser evidences of recent volcanic activity are found almost throughout the province. At many places in Alaska and Northwest Canada there has been local welling out of lavas, leaving no well-defined vent. Thus, at Miles Canyon and at White Horse Rapids just below, the Lewes River was dammed by such a lava flow. At the canyon the walls of lava still remain, representing a part of a flow through which the river has incised a channel.

The only mineral deposit connected with any of the Alaskan volcanoes is the sulphur found around some of the vents. The ejecta of Mount Edgecumbe, the beautiful volcanic cone near Sitka, have helped to enrich the lands of the vicinity.

The processes that have built up the earth's crust have been outlined in the preceding pages. It has been shown that crustal movements fold up the strata, and it should be added that both local and regional elevations and depressions take place in which the land is moved in great blocks with little or no folding. Thus the presence of sea shells on the slopes of Mount St. Elias 5,000 feet above tidewater, not unlike those in the adjacent waters, shows that this mountain mass has been recently elevated. On the other hand, the fiorded coast line of Southeastern Alaska indicates a general depression. Here the land has been lowered relative to the sea, and tidewater has invaded what were formerly valleys and thus formed the fiords and passages along the familiar tourist route.

Most of these movements of the earth's crust are so slow that the space of man's chronology gives little direct evidence of it. Yet, some more direct evidence is available. Thus, it is known that during Alaska's great earthquake of 1899 the beach on part of Yakutat Bay, on the Pacific seaboard, was elevated along a break for 14 feet by one such earth movement.

It will be evident that the constructive processes described constitute only a part of geologic history. All the land is constantly exposed to the wearing away processes called erosion. The material of the slopes is carried to the streams and rivers which, in turn, transport it to the sea, where it finds rest. Thus, the muddy Yukon builds out its delta into Bering Sea from material derived from the region which it drains. Therefore, the processes of erosion and of deposition are the complements of each other.

Erosion is constantly tending to reduce the surface of the earth to a level plain. Therefore, were there no crustal disturbances to counteract erosion, all mountain ranges would disappear. The relief as we see it now is, then, the result of the interaction between the forces of construction, which build up the outer crust of the earth by folding and elevation or by intrusion and volcanic ejecta, and the destructive force of erosion, which tends to reduce all elevated land masses to sea level. In general, it is true that mountain ranges or other areas of high relief are the scenes of recent geologic elevation or igneous extravasation. The St. Elias Range is an example of the first, the Wrangell Mountains of the second. On the other hand, the areas of lesser relief, like the central Yukon basin, are evidences of long continued denudation by processes of erosion. It must be noted, however, that the rocks forming the crust of the earth are of varying degrees of resistance to the forces of erosion. It thus frequently happens that a mountain peak is left towering above the adjacent region because it is made of rocks more resistant to erosion than are the surrounding areas. Thus, Mount McKinley is a granite boss surrounded by more easily eroded slates. The geology of Mount St. Elias too is of a similar character. Both these mountains are in the loci of the highest part of the uplift of the ranges of which they constitute a part, yet their present relief is in a large measure due to the resistance to erosion of the rock of which they are composed.

The reader's attention is here directed to the main features of relief of the trans-Mississippian region of the United States and of Western Canada and to the fact that they find their counterpart in Alaska. The northwest trend of the two great mountain systems of the western part of North America makes in Alaska a sharp southwesterly bend and continues the course of the mountains in this direction to meet the continent of Asia. These trends of the mountain masses are but a surface reflection of the attitude of the strata which constitute the ranges. In other words, the strike line of the dominant structural features of Alaska is first northwesterly, then southwesterly, forming a great concentric sweep around and parallel to the southern shore line. This structural trend is the most important primary conception necessary to an understanding of Alaska's geology. It is seen not only in the attitude of the component strata of the mountain ranges, but also in the rocks which occur in the areas of lesser relief lying between the mountain systems.

Geologically as geographically Alaska is the meeting point of the Old World and the New. The northwesterly trend of the axis of folding is North American, the southwesterly trend is Asiatic.

The marked parallelism of the larger bed rock structures throughout Alaska has had a wide influence on the distribution of the various formations found in Alaska. As a result of these lines of folding, or tectonic lines as they are called, many of the geologic subdivisions occur in belts which parallel the Pacific seaboard. This being the case, it is to be expected that the larger features of the geology of western United States and Canada should find expression in the Territory, and such is the case.

To consider these from the southern coast northward:

The ranges of the Pacific Mountain System have the same geology as their southern extension in Canada and the United States. They are constituted of close-folded and dislocated sedimentary strata, vast intrusions of igneous rocks, and extravasations of volcanic material. Their present high relief is due to geologically recent elevation, so that the forces of erosion, ever active on all elevated tracts, have not yet had time to reduce them. Far different is it in the Central Plateau Region. Here too the component strata are closely folded, because of mountain building forces, but this disturbance was in the past, and since then erosion has reduced the region to one of relatively low relief. Here the strata are a great sequence of sediments with igneous intrusives, the counterpart of the formations making up the intermountain region of British Columbia. To the north of this intermountain province is that extension of the Rocky Mountains, the Arctic Mountain System, a region again of comparatively recent elevation where the reducing agents have not yet had time to work. The component strata of these mountains are Paleozoic and Mesozoic, which have been thrown up into large folds with some extensive dislocations. Here too there is a close parallelism with the geology of Western Canada. The Arctic Slope Region, that plateau descending toward the polar sea from the north base of the Arctic Mountains, is built up of a succession of little-disturbed Mesozoic and Tertiary sediments. These strata have a northerly dip and are also gently folded. The geology of this province is analogous in every way to that of the Great Plains region of the western United States and Canada.

It will, next, be in order to consider briefly the sequence of events by which the geologic terranes of Alaska have been formed, including the processes of deposition, mountain building, and volcanic activity as well as the periods of erosion that have operated in the past. Such a discussion of geologic history can even in well-known regions be given only in general outline. Still greater difficulties are met with in deciphering the geology of a province like Alaska, much of which still remains almost unknown.

The earliest epoch of Alaska's geologic history is one of sedimentation. In a sea which probably covered most of the Territory, as well as much of adjacent Canada, vast deposits of sediment were laid down. These were in large measure detrital deposits; that is, deposits formed of debris derived from the erosion of the land. The location of this land is not known, and it is probably now buried under some of the younger strata. With the detrital material some calcareous matter was laid down, indicative of deep-sea conditions. It is quite possible that sedimentation was interrupted by folding and elevation of the sea floor, and a land surface exposed to the agencies of erosion, but of this no evidence has yet been found. All that is known is that many thousands of feet of sands, clays, and some limestones were laid down in this ancient sea. During a later but still very ancient period, these sediments were folded and altered, and at the same time intrusions of granites and other igneous rocks took place. As a result of these earth stresses a land mass arose from the sea, probably one of high relief. This was attacked by the agencies of erosion, stream and river systems were developed, and thus the mountains were gradually reduced in elevation.

The period of earth stresses which belongs to the earliest epoch of the manifestation of mountain building forces of which there are any records in Alaska not only hardened the sediments, but so altered them as to recrystallize the materials of which they were composed. Thus, the limestones were marmorized, the sandstones became quartzite, the shales became mica schists, and even the granite and other intrusives were rendered more or less schistose.

All this action is believed to have taken place in pre-Cambrian times and can be conveniently referred to the so-called Archaean epoch. The rocks resulting from this epoch form a broad belt in the upper Yukon, notably in the region blocked out by the Yukon and Tanana rivers. Here they include the so-called Birch Creek schists which form the bedrock in much of the placer-bearing region of the upper Yukon. They are found in the Koyukuk basin and stretch westward into the drainage basin of the Kobuk River. Similar rocks which are possibly of the same age occur in the Seward Peninsula, where they are known as the Kigluaik Mountains. Series of ancient crystalline rocks are also found in the intermontane region of British Columbia. The resulting rocks in all these areas, whatever their relative ages may be, are to be regarded as the floor on which the northwestern part of the American continent has been built up.

All that is definitely known about this ancient complex of sediments is that sometime in the early part of the Paleozoic they emerged from the sea in very much their present condition. It is probable that this, the oldest land mass forming the nucleus of what is now Alaska, had an attenuated outline stretching through the upper Yukon basin and possibly connected with another land mass in the Seward Peninsula. Just when this emergence took place is not known.

There is no clue as yet to the conditions which prevailed during early Cambrian times, and conditions of sedimentation or erosion may have prevailed. It is certain that during late Cambrian times most of Alaska was submerged, and limestone deposits were formed. Marine conditions probably prevailed without interruption through Ordovician and Silurian times, for the deposits found belonging to this period are all chiefly of deep-sea origin. It is of significance to note that, while the organic remains found in the Cambrian rocks are closely similar to those of other parts of North America, the fossils of the Ordovician horizon and in part of the Silurian epoch indicate the invasion of marine organisms from Asia and Europe.

Conditions of deposition and erosion were not the same throughout Alaska during early Paleozoic times. In the Canadian Yukon, Cambrian sediments are found which appear to be absent on the Alaskan side of the boundary. In the Yukon-Tanana region, the Cambrian appears to be wanting and the Ordovician (?) lies directly on the Archaean schist. This supposed Ordovician is made up of fragmental rocks derived from the Archaean rocks, indicating that there was a land mass in this region. On the other hand, in the Seward Peninsula Cambrian limestones have been found, as well as what are believed to be older schistose rocks. In Southeastern Alaska, the oldest horizons known are Ordovician limestones. Elsewhere in the Territory, the older rocks are all buried under younger sediments, and there is therefore no clue to the physical conditions in early Paleozoic times. This fragmentary evidence can probably be interpreted best by believing that during Cambrian times there were some isolated land masses which stood above the sea, that orographic movements took place after deposition of Cambrian rocks, and that during the Ordovician there were also islands in the sea, though these were probably in part different from those of the previous epoch.

Following the Ordovician, deep-sea conditions probably prevailed over much of Alaska, throughout Silurian times and extending into the Devonian, for the known rocks of this epoch are mostly limestones. There are indeed some fragmentary beds in the Alaska Range which may belong to this period, but there is no evidence of the location of the land mass from which they were derived. So far as the direct evidence goes, it indicates that deposition continued without break from Silurian into Devonian times. Indeed, in many quarters of the province there appears to have been no interruption in deep-sea conditions from the Cambrian to the Devonian.

In Middle Devonian time a wide-spread epoch of vulcanism occurred. Throughout Alaska south of the Arctic Circle volcanic rocks are found with the Devonian limestones. The evidence at hand indicates that there were certain centers of vulcanism where the outflows of lavas and ashes were more intense than elsewhere, but the outbursts of volcanoes were widespread. These volcanoes poured out lavas and threw out tuffs which became intermingled with the limestones being deposited at the same time. So close is this intermingling that it seems probable that much of the material was directly deposited in the sea. A picture of a broad ocean dotted with innumerable islands made up of volcanoes which poured out great lava streams and threw into the atmosphere great volumes of ash will probably meet the condition of facts now known. Many submarine volcanoes were also present whose ejecta never reached the atmosphere. It must not be supposed that this epoch of vulcanism was any more intense than some that have followed. For example, the volcanic epoch which had its maximum intensity in late Tertiary times and is continued today in the present active volcanoes of Alaska was as widespread and extensive as that of Devonian times. To believe this, one has only to picture the volcanoes of the Wrangell Mountains and of the Alaska Peninsula and the Aleutian Islands, as well as the lesser outbursts along the shores of Bering Sea and of the Yukon basin.

Devonian vulcanism was followed by a period of mountain-building movements when the volcanic rocks and associated sediments were folded and faulted. At its close, a part of Alaska stood above the sea and was subject to erosion. This was followed by a depression when probably the whole of Alaska was sunk beneath the sea. The late Devonian epoch was one of widespread limestone deposition, and this condition continued until Carboniferous times. While conditions of deposition did not change, new forms of organic life made their appearance in the Carboniferous sea of Alaska, and these are European and Asiatic in their character rather than North American. Limestone deposition went on until probably several thousand feet of strata were accumulated.

In parts of Alaska deep-sea conditions probably prevailed throughout Carboniferous times. There is evidence that in the upper Yukon basin limestone deposition was interrupted by a period of uplift and erosion followed by the deposition of gravels, sands, and silts. This gravel and silt deposit was undoubtedly laid down by rivers, indicating a considerable land area—a condition not unlike those now existing. There is some evidence that this epoch of subaerial deposition included a large part of what is now Alaska. On the Yukon a few small beds of coal are found with the fluviatile deposits, but these are without commercial value. Some coals, of value, are also found in the Carboniferous near Cape Lisburne on the Arctic Ocean. Taken as a whole, however, the Carboniferous epoch, which included the great coal-bearing horizons of the world, was not the time of coal deposition in Alaska, whose coals are for the most part much younger. The reason is that the Alaskan Carboniferous rocks were for the most part laid down in the deep sea, while the accumulation of vegetable matter sufficient for coal formation is possible only in fresh water or in beds formed close to the shore.

After the interruption by the epoch of gravel and sand deposition in Middle Carboniferous times, the land was again lowered beneath the sea, and limestone formations continued up to the close of the Paleozoic and in the Yukon during the Mesozoic. On the Yukon, the Triassic or oldest epoch of the Mesozoic period is limestone, and there is no break in the deposition of this and the Carboniferous limestones. Elsewhere in Alaska an erosion interval may have intervened between the two epochs, but this is uncertain. In most of Alaska the Triassic is represented by limestone deposits, but these were in part accompanied by fine sand sediments now represented by slates. Locally, at least, there was another outburst of vulcanism in late Carboniferous or early Triassic times. This is represented in the Copper River region by several thousand feet of lavas known as the Nikolai greenstone which is important because it is the locus of valuable copper deposits. Greenstones which are probably of the same age also occur in other parts of Alaska which have been assigned to this period. In

Southeastern Alaska slates are associated with the ancient lava flows belonging to the Carboniferous.

The Triassic beds were succeeded by the deposition of a great series of sediments, chiefly of a detrital nature. These are now represented by shales, slates, sandstones, and conglomerates, aggregating many thousands of feet in thickness and belonging to the various subdivisions of the Carboniferous. The lowest of these beds appears to have been laid down on an eroded land surface. It is, therefore, probable that after the deposition of the Triassic limestones there was an elevation which brought up land surface.

The extent of this Triassic or early Jurassic land is not well known. A unique formation of Jurassic time was the great coal-bearing series of northwestern Alaska, found near Cape Lisburne and probably to the east. This has not been recognized elsewhere in Alaska, but it probably occurs in northern Siberia.

During Jurassic times there were local recurrent epochs of vulcanism, especially well developed in the Alaska Peninsula region. This was also the beginning of the great epoch of intrusion which was to continue for several geologic epochs but probably reached its maximum in late Jurassic times. It was during this epoch that the great intrusions of granite and diorite occurred. This intrusion was continental, even intercontinental, in extent. It produced the great masses of igneous rocks of the Andes, of the Sierra Nevada, of the Coast Range of Southeastern Alaska and British Columbia, and possibly those of eastern Siberia. During this period also the extensive granite and diorite of the Yukon were injected. It was indeed one of the most profound and far-reaching revolutions of all geologic history. It began in the Triassic, continued with increased vehemence in the Jurassic, and began to die down in the Cretaceous. The Tertiary granites and other intrusives of Alaska and of Japan may be considered the last evidence of this profound disturbance.

All these rocks were intruded under a heavy blanket of sediments, probably to be measured in thousands of feet. Their intrusion in such masses as are found in the Coast Range caused profound disturbances, owing to their bulk alone. The intrusives, though wide-spread, followed certain well-defined axes, the most pronounced of which is that following the western border of the Pacific from South America as far as Lynn Canal, where it passes inland of the St. Elias Range and to the northwest merges with the axis of the Alaska Range.

This epoch of intrusion was accompanied and followed by folding, and it is the lines of movement thus caused that determined the present relief of Alaska. While none of the present relief is caused by this period of earth movements, yet these stresses followed lines of weakness which have determined the position of all the subsequent major folding.

One can picture, at the close of this movement, Alaska as a land not unlike that of today in its larger features. The Pacific Mountain System was then, as it is now, marked by high ranges, while to the north was another series of ranges not unlike the present Arctic Mountain System. The area between, comprising the Central Plateau Region, was probably of lesser altitude and may in part have been occupied by an arm of the sea. The Aleutian Islands were probably non-existent, but to the north it is not improbable that the continents of Asia and America were connected.

On this land mass erosion was active and probably continued for a long period of time, possibly long enough to remove most of the relief. General depression followed, and the sea swept over most of the Territory. In Lower Cretaceous times marine sedimentation took place over a large part of Alaska. These sediments include much terrestrial material, suggesting the presence of islands from which they could have been derived. Evidence of the presence of a Lower Cretaceous sea has been found in nearly all parts of Alaska, but in no considerable areas, so that it may have been a sea within a large archipelago.

This sedimentation was interrupted by another profound disturbance in which folding took place along the same axes of movement as those of the previous epoch. The injection of granitic magmas at depth also took place, but with less vehemence than that which had gone before. With the dying out of the igneous activity came another all-important event—the injection of the gold-bearing quartz veins. These, as already shown, are closely connected with the granodiorite intrusives. They are found widely distributed and, everywhere except on Seward Peninsula, occur in and near the igneous intrusives. Some of the copper deposits also belong to this epoch, while the tin of the York region, near Cape Prince of Wales, is contained in granitic rocks. It is not improbable that the injection of metalliferous veins locally continued into Tertiary times. There is some evidence of this in Alaska, and it is certainly the fact in the Japanese islands.

This epoch of deformation was the last one which was profound enough greatly to alter the rocks which were included in it. The Tertiary folding which followed, while it profoundly disturbed the strata, did not metamorphose the rocks. A depression followed, and the Upper Cretaceous sea invaded the land at least as far as the Ramparts of the Yukon. The greater part of the Alaska Peninsula was then submerged, and erosion continued in most of the Territory. Then an elevation took place, and Alaska arose from the sea with most of its present outline and probably a strong similarity in relief. A long period of land erosion followed during which a great river system was developed. The land carried a flora not unlike that of part of the States. Maples, sequoias, poplars, and birches give evidence of the climatic conditions, for their remains are found in the river beds deposited at this time. Nor were these warm climatic conditions confined to Alaska alone. A similar flora has been found in beds which are in the lands encircling the pole, such as Siberia, Greenland, and Spitzbergen. This period, assigned to Eocene Age by American geologists and to Arctic Miocene by European geologists, affords striking evidence of one of the many changes in climate recorded in geologic history.

An important event to Alaska of this epoch was the formation of great coal deposits. These were laid down as vegetable matter in the rivers and lakes and along the seaboard. Subsequent movements of the rocks in which they are contained altered them in part to lignite, in part to bituminous and anthracite coal. The Eocene is the great coal-making period of Alaska's history, as was the Carboniferous the coal-making period of the Appalachians.

Deposition of Eocene times was terminated by a profound revolution, the last of continental extent in the history of Alaska. By a thrust which came from the Pacific, profound disturbances were caused which, however, followed the lines of previous movements. It was then that the mountain-building forces folded and faulted the component strata of the Alaska Range and of probably most of the other ranges of the Pacific Mountain system. Folding also took place along the northern front of the Rocky Mountain system and possibly disturbed the formations of other parts of this system. The areas lying between these axes of disturbance were, however, little affected, for the Eocene beds are found in the Susitna and Yukon basins, as well as elsewhere, lying almost horizontal.

It was about the close of this epoch of disturbance that the second great period of vulcanism broke forth. The volcanoes of this period include those of the Wrangell Mountains and of the Alaska Peninsula and Aleutian Islands, besides smaller outbursts elsewhere. The continuation of this period of vulcanism is found in the present, but with decreasing violence.

At the close of this period of disturbance erosion took place, and in the inland region lasted long enough to reduce much of the land to a plain of little relief, but with here and there a rounded mountain mass or dome rising above it. The conditions along the Pacific seaboard are less well understood, but it is probable that deposition was taking place near what is now the present coast line, as it is known to have along the northern border of the Territory.

With the close of this cycle, Alaska's land and drainage features were much as they have already been described. Climatically, there had been great changes from the time when the southern flora had invaded this northern land, for the period of glacial invasion was now inaugurated. A great ice sheet, known as the Cordilleran Glacier and formed in the intermountain region of British Columbia, moved northward into the borders of Alaska. Besides this, all the high ranges were centers of ice accumulation. Thus, ice moved out in both directions, from the Alaskan Coast Range and from the Wrangell Mountains. The Rocky Mountain ranges too were sources of glaciers which, on one hand, moved south into the Yukon basin and, on the other, moved north toward the Arctic Ocean. There were also innumerable minor ranges within the Yukon basin where glacial ice accumulated. With it all, Alaska's glaciation was local rather than continental. There was no such overriding of the entire land surface as occurred during the glacial epoch of the Eastern States. With the retreat of the ice came floods of silt-laden water which deposited vast quantities of material, later dissected by streams and now left as benches along the watercourses.

The recent land movements of Alaska are complex and but imperfectly understood. The fiorded coast line of Southeastern Alaska and Prince William Sound is in part due to glacial erosion, but is in part due also to an invasion of the land by the sea caused by a general depression. Thus, the former valleys form fiords and channels. On the other hand, elevated benches are found in this part of the seaboard which carry marine fossils. Such have been found on the slopes of Mount St. Elias, 5,000 feet above the sea. On the Seward Peninsula too there are evidences of elevation and depression. All these facts indicate an instability of the strand and make generalization impossible.

The post-glacial deposits include the sands and gravels of the present watercourses, as well as those which are being formed along the strand line. It is in these post-glacial gravels that most of the placer gold occurs that has been thus far mined. It is possible that some of the gold deposits of Fairbanks and other camps are older than the post-glacial deposits, but this has not been determined definitely. At Nome gold is found not only in the existing beach but also in the elevated beaches, which are much older.

The outline of Alaska's geologic history shows that both the present condition of the strata and the land forms are the result of many different events. An almost infinite sequence of deposition, elevation, folding, and erosion has taken place. While many of the events of the early geologic history are as yet but little understood, there is no reason to believe that they differ either in magnitude or in process from those of recent history.

CHAPTER IV

Vegetation

THE TRAVELER approaching Alaska by way of the southeastern panhandle will see a land densely clothed with vegetation. Great coniferous trees, five and six feet in diameter, are scattered in the flat regions; and these, with the smaller timber, shade the ground, mantled with a thick coating of moss. He who approaches it from Asia across the Bering Straits gains a totally different impression of its vegetation. Here forests are entirely absent and the land is clothed in moss and low stunted shrubbery, with only patches of willows along the watercourses. Southeastern Alaska is tropical in the luxuriance of its vegetation, but northern Alaska has a strictly arctic flora. The inland region is still different with its broad meadows of grass, extensive swamps, and open growth of spruce and other trees, all more or less stunted compared with the trees of the coastal region. The grassland province of the southwest, including the Alaska Peninsula and the Aleutian Islands, is a fourth vegetation type, characterized by absence of trees and abundance of grass. To these four main subdivisions must be added the Alpine region with its stunted plants and absence of timber, merging upward in the high ranges to rocky slopes carrying lichens alone. These vegetation provinces in their typical development are entirely distinct, yet merge into each other at their boundaries. Those who would understand Alaska's flora must keep these types in mind.

Southeastern Alaska possesses most of the true forests of the Territory. There are, indeed, small areas of good timber in the tidewater region west and north as far as Cook Inlet, but their aggregate area is small. The general aspect of Southeastern Alaska is sombre. The dark green of the dominating coniferous trees is broken only by the occasional lighter green of smaller deciduous trees. Western hemlock, with trees up to five and six feet in diameter occurring at favored localities, forms probably 70 per cent of the stand of timber, and the Sitka or tide-land spruce, probably 20 per cent. Among other trees may be mentioned

SCENIC SOUTHEASTERN ALASKA

Upper left: Fairweather Mountains rising almost directly from the sea, photo by F. H. Moffit; upper right: Mount Edgecumbe, photo by C. W. Wright; lower left: An Alaskan fiord, photo by J. C. Reed; lower right: Small cove on Prince of Wales Island showing heavy forests of this region, photo by A. H. Brooks.

the red and yellow cedar. The last named is in sufficient quantities to have timber value, but the best stand is confined to the southern part of the panhandle. There are also more stunted shore pines and, at higher altitudes, mountain hemlock. The deciduous cottonwood trees are chiefly alders and willows and birches, though the botanists report that the northern limit of the broad-leafed maple and western yew extends into the extreme southeastern limit of Alaska. Data in regard to the coniferous trees indicate a growth of one inch in diameter in from five to ten years.

This coastal region is so wet that forest fires seldom maintain themselves sufficiently long to be destructive. In the last 15 years there have, however, been at least two summers dry enough to permit of fires sweeping over several square miles. In the absence of fire and with very small destruction by man, primeval forest conditions prevail. There is much fallen timber and, viewed from a distance, many dead trees are seen among the evergreens. In the language of the forester, the forests are over-ripe and the utilization of the mature trees should be encouraged in every way possible. The possibility of developing a pulp industry in this coastal region is evident, for much use is being made of similar forests in the adjacent portions of British Columbia.

The timber-covered flats of Southeastern Alaska, which are not abundant, consist chiefly of larger timber, with a soil densely covered with moss. Shrubbery, grass, and flowering plants are scant in this forest type. There are, however, occasional meadows where grass is found, usually on newly made ground along valley bottoms where the timber has not yet had time to establish itself. On the better drained hill slopes, shrubbery and flowering plants are more abundant. Notable among the shrubs is the broad-leafed devil's club whose spines perforce attract the attention of the most unobservant wayfarer. Among other shrubbery are the salmonberry, the elderberry, the high bush cranberry, and the huckleberry. One of the striking features of the hill slopes is the thin coating of soil among the rocks which suffices to support even large trees. Higher up, the trees decrease in size, and grass and flowering plants become more abundant, reaching their maximum near the upper limit of shrubbery and timber, which varies locally from 1,500 to 3,000 feet. This vegetation phase merges into the Alpine vegetation above until finally only lichens are found.

One of the striking features of the vegetation, locally, is its luxuriance almost at the margin of the glaciers which discharge into the sea. Even the land which is uncovered by the retreat of the ice soon has a plant covering. This is brought about by a sequence of growth, the first plant to make headway over the bared surface being the creeping willow, followed by larger willows and other shrubs; alders and herbaceous plants and grasses next appear, and finally the spruce forest obtains a foothold.

The moist climate of Southeastern Alaska is favorable to the growth of ferns which are locally in great profusion at altitudes below 1,500 feet. Wild flowers, while also present, are not so abundant as in other parts of the Territory. Later in this chapter the presence of an inland flora at Skagway, near the head of Lynn Canal, will be discussed.

There are few data to estimate the average stand of timber in Southeastern Alaska. The best of the forest will probably run 30,000 to 80,000 feet (board measure) per square mile, while the average may be 5,000 feet or more. It is probably safe to say that the well-forested areas, including large trees, constitute between 40,000 and 60,000 square miles and that in addition an area about half as large includes timber of lesser size.

In the Pacific coast littoral west of Southeastern Alaska as far as Cook Inlet, the same general floral aspect is maintained, though the forested areas are smaller and the trees usually smaller. There are, however, some good stands of hemlock near Yakutat Bay, on the east side of Prince William Sound, near Seward on Resurrection Bay, and on the streams tributary to Turnagain Arm. The Sitka spruce occurs at many localities throughout this belt, but in no considerable stands. Timber line also becomes lower as one goes westward. Large trees are practically limited to valley floors, and the upper limit of tree growth is from 500 to 1,500 feet above the sea. With the sparser growth of trees, herbaceous plants and grasses increase. The shrubbery of Southeastern Alaska is also found in many of its species to the westward, but more stunted in growth. The devil's club, which attains heights of ten feet or more in the Ketchikan region, is only two feet high on Cook Inlet. On the Copper River, on Lowe River near Valdez, and on Cook Inlet are found examples of the transgression of the inland flora on the coast province.

The Kenai Peninsula vegetation is of intermediate type, having features in common with the forested coastal region, with the woodlands of the interior, and with the grasslands to the southwest. In the flat stretching northward from the head of Resurrection Bay, there is a heavy stand of hemlock and spruce, with many large trees. Elsewhere on the peninsula the timbered areas are of the woodland type to be described below—so typical of the interior of Alaska. In the lowland on the west side adjacent to Cook Inlet are some grassy meadows suggestive of the grasslands of Kodiak Island with the same species of plants.

This central coastal region of Alaska is, indeed, a whole transitional zone between the forest formation and grassland formation of southwestern Alaska. The northeastern part of Kodiak Island is timbered, but beyond to the westward are only grasslands. The base of the Alaska Peninsula also carries a few trees, but its main mass lies in the grassland province. The timber line is fairly sharply drawn, a fact which has led to much speculation as to the cause of the unforested areas. Summer temperatures and moisture are favorable to growth of trees, and their absence is probably due to the cold winds which blow during the winter. This agency is hostile to the growth of any except perennial plants. Sitka spruce trees, planted by the Russians at Dutch Harbor in the eastern end of the Aleutian Islands in 1804, have maintained themselves. But they are in a sheltered nook, and there is no evidence that they have propagated. After more than a century of growth the largest is barely 24 inches in diameter. Probably similar stands could be obtained in sheltered places, but it is unlikely that the tree growth could extend itself over the divide where the trees would be exposed to the winter winds. While timber is absent, dense willow thickets mark the position of many of the watercourses in this grassland region. There is also some other low shrubbery, with alder growing often in dense patches.

The vegetation of Kodiak Island, except in the northern part, and most of the Alaska Peninsula is characterized by an abundant growth of grass up to altitudes varying from 1,000 to 2,000 feet. Blue top is the dominating grass and affords excellent pasturage. Blue grass, beach rye, and wild barley are also found. Cattle raising has been carried on in a small way for upwards of 100 years on Kodiak Island and at other places in southwestern Alaska. This is evidence of the nutritive value of the grasses. With these grasses is a profusion of flowers. Ferns are also common. The higher slopes of this region gradually merge into the typical tundra with its moss and tufts of grass. So far as is known, the lower limit of the tundra type of vegetation gradually descends toward the southwest. On Unalaska Island, the grasslands are chiefly confined to the valley floors and the lower 200 feet of the hill slopes. The tundra type of vegetation in turn passes at higher altitudes into the Alpine type.

On the flats on the north side of the Alaska Peninsula grass is also found, but here it is more scattered and interspersed with moss. This is, indeed, the zone of transition to the tundra type, though the real tundra does not reach its typical development until the northern part of the Bering Sea littoral is reached. This much abused term, tundra, can be defined as a treeless region having an arctic vegetation, chiefly moss and lichens, with some grass, in scattered patches, a few varieties of low shrubbery, and an abundance of flowering plants. There is considerable local variation in flora, so we may have an upland tundra where mosses and lichens predominate and a lowland tundra where the mosses and lichens are broken by patches of grass and thickets of small woody plants.

The tundra has a peculiar type of coloring caused by the merging of the pale green of the lichens and the darker green of the mosses, grasses, and other vegetation. The

CONTRASTS IN VEGETATION

Upper left: Tundra, photo by A. J. Collier; upper right: Close-up of niggerheads, photo by S. R. Capps; lower left: Grasslands, photo by A. H. Brooks; lower right: Forest fire in Chitina district, photo by F. H. Moffit.

undrained depressions are usually moss covered, while in the higher lands and drier areas the lichens predominate. In the valley bottoms along the lower slopes patches of grassland, and in places considerable meadows, are not uncommon, and these afford forage for stock during the short summer. Among these are found bunch, rye, and blue grasses. There is also a variety of sedge known as tundra or cotton grass. This grows in thick tufts which project above the intervening moss carpet and forms the so-called "nigger head" which is so difficult to traverse. This sedge is an inferior forage plant.

In places the slopes are covered with dense growths of a dwarfed variety of birch, growing to heights of not more than two or three feet. These, with the patches of stunted willow which mark the watercourses, are practically the only woody plants found in the tundra. The willows, while they may reach lengths of eight or ten feet, are usually gnarled and recumbent. They furnish a valuable supply of wood to the traveler in the absence of all other sources of fuel. While the tundra yields but little in the way of food plants, several varieties of berries long used by the Eskimos are found. Among these are blueberries, raspberries, cranberries, and above all the salmonberry.

The climatic conditions which determine the tundra vegetation are the low temperatures of the soil, much of which remains perpetually frozen a foot or two below the surface; the cool summers with, nevertheless, a relatively large amount of heat from the direct rays of the sun during the long summer day; and the shortness of the growing season. The rainfall is relatively low, but it is fairly evenly distributed during the growing season. The winter winds prevent growth of trees.

The description given above applies more especially to the tundra of Nome and the Seward Peninsula. To the north the grassy tundras become less prominent, and to the south along the shore of Bering Sea the tundra vegetation gradually merges into the grasslands. The mountains within the tundra region have the Alpine type of flora, modified by local conditions of climate. Inland, the tundra merges with the woodland formation by the appearance of cottonwoods and spruces and an increase in the percentage of grasslands.

Probably over a third of Alaska is characterized by the woodland type of vegetation. This includes the basins of the

Yukon, Kuskokwim, Copper, and Susitna rivers. It is broken by upland areas whose vegetation approaches the tundra formation and by high mountains with the Alpine type of vegetation. It is typified by open growth of spruce, broken by meadows of grass, and merging at higher altitudes into dominant grasslands and thus into moss- and lichen-covered uplands. The drier lands, including the lower slopes and gravel river bottoms, include groves of cottonwood (quaking aspen and balm of Gilead) and white or canoe birch. In the valley floors are open moss-covered swamps, with scant growth of spruce, and grassy swamps surrounding small lakes and ponds. These lowland swampy areas, though often miscalled tundras, are properly designated as muskegs, a name borrowed from the Ojibways and in common use in Eastern Canada. Dense growths of spruce of better quality than elsewhere line the banks of many of the rivers, and the presence of these has led to the frequent misconception of the quantity of timber on the part of the casual traveler. Thickets of willow and alder are also found, but the growth is not so dense as in the regions nearer the coast.

To consider the timber in greater detail: The most valuable tree is the white spruce found along the river banks and lower slopes of the valleys. This tree reaches its best development on unfrozen ground, a condition relatively rare. In favorable places individual trees reach diameters of two and a half feet or even more. Timber of this size has been found along the Copper near Chitina, at various places on the Yukon, but more especially along the Tanana. As it grows in ground usually well watered, it has been less damaged by forest fires than have the other varieties of timber. The black spruce is the most widely distributed of the trees. It occurs in sheltered valleys on the Arctic slope near the international boundary, in the eastern part of the Seward Peninsula, throughout the Yukon basin, and in the Susitna and Copper valleys. In the absence of better timber, it has been invaluable to the pioneer both for lumber and for fuel.

The trees popularly grouped together as cottonwoods are almost as widely distributed as the spruce. They usually grow in drier soil than the spruce. They are especially well developed in the gravel flats of parts of the Copper and Susitna basins. They occur near Skagway where the inland flora reaches the coast and are also found in a few scattered groves beyond the western limit of spruces on the Seward Peninsula. In the Susitna bottom lands the aspen grows to large size, trees two to three feet in diameter at the base being found. In the Yukon basin the aspen and poplar seldom exceed 18 inches in diameter. The white birch is almost as widely distributed as the spruce, but does not reach such high altitudes and is numerically far less abundant than the coniferous trees. It occurs in groves composed almost entirely of birch and also in mixed forests of birch and aspens, as well as in the spruce forests. These groves have furnished a valuable source of fuel in the Yukon camps. The birch forests are indicative of better soil than are the other trees; and as the land is easily cleared, they mark the loci of potential agricultural lands.

On the river banks some large varieties of willows are found, mixed with the spruce forests. Smaller species of willows are found along the lesser watercourses. Willow thickets are also the only forest growth on the great delta of the Yukon where the transition between the interior woodland formation and the tundra vegetation takes place. The Alaska larch or tamarack has a limited distribution in the central Yukon basin. It is found distributed along the Yukon valley from near the international boundary for about 800 miles downstream, and reaches up the Tanana above Fairbanks and westward across the divide to the Kuskokwim. The interior woodlands have but little underbrush. Huckleberries are abundant above timber line, and raspberries and currants are found at lower altitudes. The grasslands of this province are of two occurrences. Grass grows abundantly in most places at or near timber line, and also as a second growth in the burnt-over areas at lower altitudes. In the lowlands marsh grasses are found surrounding the lakes and ponds. A species of wild pea grows abundantly in the gravel bottoms of some of the tributaries of the upper Yukon; it seems to thrive under semiarid conditions and is not found in the region of greater rainfall of the lower Yukon.

The bunch, the blue, and the rye grasses, as well as the wild pea mentioned above, furnish excellent forage. There is hardly any part of the Yukon basin where good summer grazing can not be found. In the upper basin, with its low precipitation, some of the forage plants cure on the stalk and with the small amount of snowfall, furnish winter pasturage.

A typical section of the Yukon region will show white spruce along the river banks, then groves of aspen, birch, and black spruce, grading upward into a region in which the black spruce predominates. Here extensive grasslands are found, still higher are found the huckleberries, and finally the uplands are covered with moss and lichens and other plants of the tundra type. The variety and abundance of wild flowers are striking features. The old burnings are in part covered with grass and often with a brilliant red covering of fireweed. In these old burnings are also found tangles of berry bushes. The forest fires are, therefore, not an unmixed evil, for the burnings are often soon covered by a luxuriant growth of grass.

In general, the black spruce forests are open; and in fact, except along the watercourses, all the trees in the inland region are widely spaced, so that a rider can traverse the country at will. The only serious obstacles are the dense willow and alder thickets found along the watercourses. The heavy timber of white spruce is practically limited to the valley bottoms and the upper half of the Yukon basin. Black spruce is found in altitudes varying from about 3,500 feet at the boundary to 100 or 200 feet near the western limit of timber as one approaches Bering Sea. In general, the timber line varies between 2,800 and 3,400 feet, but there are very great local variations. The upper Kuskokwim flats are heavily timbered, but the timber decreases rapidly as one goes downstream.

The vegetative coloring is chiefly dark green, showing the predominance of the coniferous trees. This is varied by the light foliage of the birches, aspens, and poplars. The higher altitude gives a bluish aspect to the landscape because of the mosses and lichens. As one views the landscape in greater detail, the varied coloring of the wild flowers becomes evident, as well as the meadows of the grassland. The finest color effects are obtained in the fall, when the frosts have turned the birch and other deciduous foliage into delicate shades of yellow which contrast strikingly with the sterner dark greens of the spruces.

The vegetation of the Yukon and Kuskokwim basins is of a semiarctic character. As much of the subsoil is permanently frozen, the roots can not strike deep and the tree roots spread out in a great circular mass of no great depth. The comparatively hot summer, with its long days, is favorable to rapid plant growth, but more particularly to perennial plants. On the other hand, the small precipitation limits the plant species to such forms as are adapted to semiarid conditions. Many of the lowland depressions are underlain by heavy layers of peat and humus whose acid soil is another factor in the determination of the vegetation.

Different conditions are found on the river banks and terraces where the ground is thawed and vegetation can grow more luxuriantly. It is in such localities that the largest trees of white spruce, birch, aspen, and poplar are found.

At best, the timber growth is very slow and hence the trees are small. In only favored localities do the birch-aspen groves yield more than 20 cords of wood to the acre. The individual trees in such groves average about eight inches in diameter with a maximum of 18 to 24 inches. The black spruce rarely exceeds six inches in diameter, the tamarack is even smaller, and the willow does not grow large enough to furnish any cordwood. White spruces attain diameters of two to two and a half feet and a height of about 75 feet. The growth of the white spruce probably averages about one inch in eight or nine years, and that of the black spruce is probably less than one tenth as rapid. It is estimated that the white birch grows one inch in about 12 years. The growth of larch probably corresponds with that of the black spruce.

Forest fires have destroyed much woodland in the Yukon basin since the advent of the white man. These have been mostly the result of accident or carelessness. Some woodlands have been deliberately burned over to obtain dried timber or better grass, or to get rid of the mosquito pest. Forest fires also occurred, as shown by old burnings, before the advent of the white man. I have traced one forest fire to a native camp, and probably the older fires were due to the carelessness of the natives. In the almost entire absence of thunderstorms, it must be presumed that the old burnings are to be credited to the natives, and there are some which must date back at least 50 years and possibly a century. In the dry inland region, protection of forests against fires is of vast importance. The destruction of trees for fuel and timber is but infinitesimal compared with that which has been burnt up. Public opinion is gradually changing in its attitude toward this question since many of the camps are experiencing a shortage of cordwood. Fire patrols should be established for the months of July, August, and September, and rigid laws passed to prevent careless and willful burning. The preservation of the inland forests is far more important than that of the coast forests where fires are almost unknown and tree growth is much more rapid. There is reason to believe that some of the burnt-over areas where the ground has been thawed could be reforested by better and more rapidly growing timber. Certainly an experiment in this matter is worth trying.

The Susitna basin has a flora similar to that of the interior, modified somewhat near the coast by changes of climatic conditions. At Turnagain and Knik arms, the coastal forest type and the inland woodland type are close together. The inland type, however, maintains its general characteristics; and the two varieties of spruce, the cottonwoods, and the white birches are the dominating trees. A section on either side of the lower Susitna valley will show a bottom land of large cottonwoods and spruce; above on the benches is a growth of birches, aspens, and poplars. As one climbs higher, the forests become more open, with large patches of luxuriant grass. This merges into a beautiful park-like region where grasslands are broken by groves of spruce and deciduous trees. This is perhaps the most beautiful fertile region of Alaska. At higher altitudes the trees become less plentiful and grasslands predominate. Finally the grassland gives way to the moss- and lichen-covered slopes characteristic of the formation intermediate between the woodland and Alpine vegetation formations.

On the west side of the upper part of Cook Inlet the Sitka spruce, devil's club, and other species of coastal type of flora are found intermingled with the birches, spruces, and other vegetation belonging to the inland formation.

The Iliamna region to the southwest is again of the inland type. Here, however, the grasslands are relatively scant, and there is a rapid transition to the tundra type of flora on the one hand and the Alpine type on the other.

The Copper River basin belongs entirely to the inland vegetation formation. There is no timber on the Copper below the mouth of the Bremner, except for some cottonwood along the gravel bottoms and a few scattered spruces. Near the canyon some fairly good spruce is found. Large spruce also occurs along the banks of the Copper and some of its tributaries. These are most abundant near Chitina and at the mouths of some of the larger streams. The white spruce, which furnishes the heavy timber, usually does not occur more than 100 or 200 feet above the river bottoms. The park-like type, such as has been described on the Susitna, is but little represented, and the grasslands are far less abundant than in other parts of the inland region. Good grass is, however, found on lower slopes where timber has been burned and also in the upper reaches of the Copper.

The gravel- and silt-floored upland which stretches westward from the Copper to the Susitna basin is essentially a region of stunted vegetation. It is sparsely timbered with black spruce and some deciduous trees. These grow out of a mat of moss, and grass is relatively rare. This formation is difficult to explain, for the climate, so far as is known, is no more hostile to vegetation than are other inland regions which are better timbered. It is probable, however, that the humus and peat soil is too acid and that the undrained character of the land is the most important factor determining the vegetation. Burning the moss and giving the sun's rays access to the frozen subsoil together with drainage might improve the condition of present growth. I have noted that in some places the second growth of trees after a fire seems to be much more rapid than that of the primeval forest. To the north, this upland region merges with the foothills of the Alaska Range, and here good timber of the inland type is again found.

The Alsek valley, which reaches into the inland region, is practically without timber on the Alaskan side of the boundary. Except for some cottonwood and some willow and alder thickets, there is no timber on the lower Alsek.

At Skagway on Lynn Canal the inland flora reaches tidewater, though here mixed with species belonging to the coast forests. The flats of Skagway River were originally covered with a dense growth of timber, including poplars and Sitka spruces. On the lower slopes the coniferous trees dominate, and still higher is found a dwarfed birch together with huckleberries and other shrubs. This zone passes up into one in which mosses and lichens dominate and in which there is in general an Alpine flora. The Stikine valley which traverses the Coast Range presents another transition between coastal and inland floral conditions. That part of the valley lying below the boundary is almost without forests, and the slopes are too rugged to support anything but a scant vegetation.

Several attempts have been made to estimate the timber resources of the inland wooded region, but at best these can be regarded as little more than intelligent guesses. No forest surveys have been made, and there are estimates of stands at only a few localities. It is probable that the original stand of heavy large timber did not cover more than 5,000 square miles and that the stunted growth, of no value for lumber but affording fuel, covers probably 60,000 to 70,000 square miles.

The Alpine vegetation zone has no such marked characteristics as the others described have shown, which are striking even to the layman. Nearly everywhere in Alaska the upper zone of timber passes into a region of low shrubbery with some grass and many wild flowers. The shrubbery and grasses give way at higher altitudes to the moss and lichens, with the hardier wild flowers and other plants. Among these are Alpine junipers together with heather and various heather-like plants. The plants in general have short leaves and axes. At the highest altitudes only the lichens are found. The chief climatic conditions under which this vegetation maintains itself are a short growing season and rarefied air, which acts directly on the plant and also affects heat, light, and precipitation. Precipitation is much greater in the Alpine zone than at other altitudes; snow is deeper and lies much longer in the summer. The flowers are usually bright colored and are often found blooming close to snow banks. Another element is the soil which, at best, is thin and finally, among the rocky summits, is almost entirely absent. It should be noted that the climatic conditions in the tundra and Alpine regions are in many respects very dissimilar, and have resulted in differences of vegetation between the two formations, though the presence of mosses and lichens in both gives them a similar general aspect.

The vegetation of the Alpine zones of Alaska has been but little studied, but it is believed to have the same general character in the different ranges. To describe the distribution of the Alpine flora would be to duplicate the account of the mountain ranges already presented. In general, it may be said that the Alpine zone is reached at an altitude of about 3,000 feet in the coastal region and at a somewhat lower altitude on the inland slopes. Its lower zone descends again in northern Alaska. In the tundra region there is an Alpine zone among the higher ranges, but here the contrast is less striking than in the timbered region, and to determine its lower limit will require closer study than has yet been given the subject.

CHAPTER V

Animal Life

IT WAS the fur-bearing animals that first attracted the white man to Alaska and for more than a century were the only justification for its permanent settlement. Even today, after a century and a half of the ravages of the fur hunter, Alaska's furs still yield a considerable revenue. Though the sea otter has almost disappeared and the revenues from seal herds are comparatively small, a large number of natives and quite a few whites are largely supported by trapping fur-bearing animals. The game of Alaska has been second only to fish and sea animals in supporting the native tribes. It has been and now is an important source of food supply to the prospectors and other pioneers, though diminishing in the more settled regions.

The disappearance of the fur-bearing and larger game animals from certain regions with the advent of the settler is inevitable. Nor is this to be deplored, provided it is not due to ruthless and useless slaughter. If the farmer, sheepherder, and cattleman make progress at the cost of driving out the moose, the caribou, the big bear, and the wolf, it is but an evidence of the progress of civilization. A fundamental principle of advancement of civilization is that the land must be put to its best possible use for the welfare of mankind. Our people have never taken kindly to the European system of game preserves which benefit the few at the expense of the many. All this does not mean that we shall not make every effort to preserve wild life so long as it does not conflict with the legitimate demands of the settlers.

There have been some wise restrictions put on the killing of game and fur-bearing animals, but some actions taken have been regarded by Alaskans as of more benefit to the non-resident hunter and the occasional visiting naturalist than to the residents of the Territory. For example, some of the game laws indicate a desire to preserve for use of the large brown bear areas which might be used for cattle or sheep. So far, these laws have worked few hardships, as the region is but little settled. As soon as the settlers demand it, such laws will inevitably disappear before advancing civilization, and the bear will be relegated to haunts not available for better purposes. Lovers of wild animals and sportsmen who look askance at the occasional killing of game birds out of season by those in want of fresh meat may comfort themselves with the thought that there are extensive tracts, like the Yukon delta and other inaccessible regions, where wild life will remain unmolested for generations to come.

While one can look with equanimity on the reduction of the area populated by the big brown bear, this attitude does not countenance the destruction of such animals as the fur seal, the sea otter, and the beaver. These animals live under conditions by which their presence in no way interferes with the advancement of settlement. Their realm is one that can not be used for other purposes, except that at some time the beaver meadows may be put to better use. The destruction of the otter, seal, and beaver has been purely for their pelts, and the disappearance of those valuable fur-bearing animals has been solely due to greed. The disappearance of the caribou and moose from certain regions is unfortunate but unavoidable. The moose especially is a timid animal and can not be expected to survive near settlements. On the other hand, the caribou ranges will eventually be utilized for reindeer, which will furnish a better meat supply than the wild animal does.

While the destruction of the fur-bearing animals is chargeable to the greed of the white man, the disappearance of moose and caribou is largely due to their indiscriminate slaughter by the natives. The Alaskan native, who for one or two generations has been taught the use of modern firearms, has still to be taught some providence for the future. At present he is inclined to shoot as long as ammunition holds out and with no thought of the future. This is in strong contrast with the white man who as a pioneer seldom needs the restrictive influence of game laws, for he will as a rule hunt only when he needs meat. In some respects he is the superior of the so-called true sportsman, who will kill animals he can not use. It is to be noted that the killing of wolves, on which there should be a bounty, has done much to promote the increase of both caribou and moose.

As recently as within the last century musk ox roamed over northern Alaska, at least as far west as Point Barrow. The Eskimos of Alaska still have traditions of the killing of musk ox by their forefathers, and several skulls have been picked up on the tundra. The evidence in hand indicates that the musk ox disappeared from Alaska late in the 18th or early in the 19th century, before the coming of the white man and before the natives had firearms.

SOME ALASKAN ANIMALS

Upper left: Moose, photographer unknown; upper right: Mountain goats, photo by D. J. Miller; center left: Bear and cubs, photographer unknown; center right: Fox, photo by J. C. Reed; lower left: musk ox, experiment in domestication, photo by J. B. Mertie; lower right: Caribou, photo by S. R. Capps.

In this discussion of the distribution of animals emphasis will be laid on the original condition existing before the whites brought in the destructive rifle. The game and fur-bearing animals are not distributed in such definite zones as are the plants. While the naturalist will find distinctions between varieties of the same species occurring in different vegetative zones, these are in many cases not striking enough to impress the layman. Animals like the bear, the wolf, and the caribou are found in several of the different vegetative formations. The black bear, for example, occurs both in the coastal forests and in the inland woodlands, and at certain seasons of the year far above timber in the Alpine zone. Again, the several varieties of caribou occur in the southwestern grassland, in the woodland, and in the tundra regions. Here, of course, the zoologist makes a distinction and differentiates the woodland and the barren ground and grassland caribou. It will be well, therefore, in the case of animal life to leave to the specialists the distinction of life zones and to point out here only the distribution of some of the better known animals.

The deer is known only in Southeastern Alaska and, in fact, is for the most part confined to the larger islands of the Alexander Archipelago. This animal is the so-called Sitka deer, closely related to the black deer. It is abundant on Prince of Wales, Admiralty, Chichagof, Baranof, and some of the smaller islands. So far as is known, it does not occur in any abundance on the mainland strip where the strong relief is unfavorable to its habits. Had not wise legislation stopped the slaughter of deer for its pelt, this animal would soon have been exterminated. Previous to the enactment of protective laws, over 40,000 deer skins were shipped from one small settlement. The carcasses of these slaughtered animals were, of course, left rotting in the forest, benefiting no one. This is an illustration of the fact, already set forth, that it is the fur trader and not the pioneer who needs restriction.

The caribou is the most widely distributed of the large Alaskan mammals, a fact which is in accord with its range in other parts of North America. This animal originally ranged through all the northern part of the continent from Maine westward to northern British Columbia and Alaska and northward to Labrador, Greenland, and the Arctic archipelago. Its vertical distribution is equally varied, for it is found in the barren grounds at sea level and at certain seasons of the year far up among the glaciers of the high ranges. It appears to be an exceedingly plastic animal, varying locally in color, in size, and in other features.

The naturalists have recognized several species or varieties of Alaskan caribou among which the size is the most striking feature to the layman. The so-called barren ground caribou is the smallest, the carcass dressing about 100 pounds. Next in size is the Stone caribou, sometimes called the woodland caribou, and the largest is the mountain or Osborn caribou. Gradations between these varieties are found which are difficult to classify. It will suffice here to recognize only two varieties: the larger, which will be called the woodland caribou, and the smaller, the barren ground caribou.

Woodland caribou are found in the highlands of the intermountains of the Yukon down to the limits of timber near Bering Sea and in the upper Susitna and Copper basins. They were formerly abundant on the Kenai Peninsula, the only place they reached near tidewater, but now only a few are left; fortunately, these are protected by law.

While the woodland caribou have decreased since the white man first came to Alaska, yet they are still abundant in certain regions. Among these are the highlands of the Yukon-Tanana region and the inland front of the Alaska Range. They are not found in the larger valleys, except when migrating, but belong essentially to the region at and above timber where they find the lichens, their favorite food. In the summer they are found in bands of from two to 12, with an occasional isolated buck. In the fall of the year they congregate in great herds numbering up to the thousands. Their routes of migration in the fall seem to be not well-defined, naturalists reporting that they generally travel against the prevailing wind. However, in the fall of the year they usually traverse the high divides which lie between the towns of Fairbanks and Circle and are here often shot in great numbers to supply a store of winter meat to the neighboring mining camps. This killing is usually after the meat will remain frozen, and in this condition it can be stored throughout the cold season. This slaughter is to be deplored, yet it must be remembered that the carcass is put to good use. There is no definite evidence that there has been any marked diminution in the size of these migratory herds, though the absence of caribou in certain districts where they were formerly abundant has been noted. This decrease was noted before the large mining camps were established and is chargeable, in part at least, to the use of the modern rifle by the native.

The natives formerly killed the caribou by driving them through openings in long fences built of fallen trees. Here they were snared, speared, or killed with bows and arrows. Such caribou fences sometimes extended for miles. I have seen such a fence in the upper Fortymile region. It was built of uprooted small spruces in the form of an entanglement rather than a fence. While such a barrier could easily be traversed by a caribou, his instinct seems to be to follow the path of least resistance and thus to follow the fence to the opening where the snare or the hunter awaited him.

My experience indicates that the caribou is not a timid animal and that it depends on scent rather than on sight or hearing to avoid danger. Its curiosity seems unbounded, and small bands will follow a pack train for hours, paying no heed to the jangle of the bell of the lead horse. They will frequently gallop in large semicircles, stopping every now and then to gaze at the unfamiliar sights. Occasionally they will approach within pistol shot.

The tundra is the home of the barren ground caribou, though in the fall he makes incursions into the margin of the inland woodland. Formerly abundant on all the tundras of the Bering Sea and Arctic Ocean littoral, he is now limited to the less-visited part of this province. As the coastal natives were the first to receive firearms, the barren ground caribou has decreased far more than has the allied species of the interior. This is also due to the fact that the Eskimos of the coast are far more abundant than are the Indians of the interior.

The caribou has almost disappeared from the tundras of the Yukon delta, Norton Bay, and Seward Peninsula. To find this animal in abundance, one must seek it in the north Arctic slope, a region little traversed even by natives. In its general habits, the barren ground caribou is similar to those of the inland region. Scattered in small bands in summer, it congregates in large herds in the fall to move southward to the foothills of the high ranges and then moves northward again in the spring. Its food is principally the reindeer lichen, found in the drier parts of the tundra.

Before they had the use of firearms, the Eskimos used to drive caribou into small lakes, favorably situated at the mouths of valleys, barricaded more or less at the sides by stone mounds behind which the bowmen took stand. Most of the killing was done by lances after the animals were in the water. The lancemen were stationed in kayaks along the margins of the lakes.

A somewhat larger variety of caribou than the true barren ground animal is found in the Alaska Peninsula grassland region. These are said to be abundant on Unimak Island, which is separated from the mainland by only a narrow gut of water. The caribou does not occur on the Aleutian or other islands of the Bering Sea except on Unimak, as noted above, and on Nunivak Island. This latter is separated by only a narrow strait from the mainland which is often blocked with ice in the winter.

The Alaskan moose, the largest species of the deer family, inhabits the woodland area of inland Alaska and is very widely distributed. It ranges from the upper Yukon nearly to the mouth of the river, reaching as far as Anvik. Occasional stragglers are found in the delta of the river beyond the limits of timber, but this occurrence is rare. It has been found to the north on the Arctic side of the divide near the international boundary. It occurs in the Kobuk valley and is abundant in parts of the Kuskokwim basin. It is found to a limited extent in the Iliamna Lake region, which lies near the limits of timber. The moose occurs in the Susitna and Copper basins, but is entirely absent on the Pacific slope of the coastal ranges except in the Kenai Peninsula. This latter province appears to be particularly favorable for the moose and today affords the best accessible hunting ground in Alaska. While typical of the lowlands and forested areas, moose is occasionally found above timber line. I have seen it in the Alaska Range a thousand feet above timber.

The habits of the moose are such as to make it less susceptible to wholesale slaughter than the caribou. It is a more wary animal and, as a rule, quickly deserts the vicinity of settlements. In summer it is found in bands of from two to eight but more often scattered—the does with the fawns and the bucks apart. The moose browses on the small shrubbery of willow, birch, and cottonwood, which constitute a large part of its food, though it also eats grass and other vegetation. In winter it finds nourishment in the tender twigs of the deciduous trees. It then joins others in bands which, after the snow has fallen, tramp down the snow in the so-called "yards." With the heavy fall of snow, especially after a crust is formed, a moose is often quite helpless and can be easily run down by a hunter on snowshoes. This used to be the chief method of capture by the natives before the firearm was introduced. Once run down, the moose could be killed with arrows and lances. Moose were also captured by snares hung from trees along their regular runway. As a moose will often dress 1,000 pounds, this was an important source of food; hides, too, were valuable for moccasins and clothing. The size of the moose makes it almost wrong to kill them for sport, because it is only in rare instances that a carcass is fully utilized.

While the moose is likely to leave the vicinity of settlements, yet it is by no means certain that the animal is now decreasing at a rapid rate. One of the best hunting grounds, as already stated, is on the west side of the Kenai Peninsula, which has been settled since the Russian days. For upwards of a century this has been a hunting ground, yet it is not likely that the animal is decreasing. The killing of wolves has no doubt had a beneficial effect on the moose, for the wolf is its greatest enemy. While not attacking the adult animal unless it is disabled, and then only in packs, the wolf is very destructive to the fawns. Wolves are constantly following the does and fawns awaiting an opportunity to attack the young. In 1898, when the lower White River was a good moose region, I noted that in nearly every instance moose doe and fawn tracks were followed by the track of a wolf.

It must not be supposed that the evidence of the Kenai Peninsula of the moose holding their own is universally true. On the Yukon, for example, the moose is now seldom seen, though formerly abundant. On the lower Tanana, where moose were fairly abundant 16 years ago, they are now rare. On the other hand, there is good moose hunting on tributaries of both the Tanana and the Yukon. The evidence in hand indicates that, taking Alaska as a whole, there has not been any great decline in the total number of moose during the last generation of natives, which is the one supplied with modern rifles. There is no question, however, that the moose has been driven from certain districts.

The Alaskan mountain goat, which is a variety of, or closely allied species to, the Rocky Mountain goat, is found only in the coastal ranges, a region of heavy precipitation. As this habitat may be considered strange, in view of the fact that the Asiatic goat is essentially at home in an arid region, it should be noted that the Alaskan goat belongs to a different genus, which naturalists believe to bear a resemblance to the antelope. There have been many reports of ibex in Alaska, but these animals appear all to belong to the mountain goat family and are probably only individuals with unusually large horns. As the goat is not a migratory animal, it is to be expected that variations, indigenous to particular localities, will occur. So far, however, no subdivisions of the goats have been made. The mountain goat is found on both slopes of the Coast Range of Southeastern Alaska, but is more common on the seaward side of the mountains. It is not known on any of the adjacent islands. It is also found on both slopes of the St. Elias and Chugach ranges and is known to occur as far west as the mountains north of Turnagain Arm, in the Cook Inlet region. It is not found in any other part of Alaska. Goats are found in the region of Kennicott Glacier, on the south slope of the Wrangell Mountains. They are here intruders in a province belonging to the mountain sheep, and this occurrence is one of the few localities where the two species are found together.

The mountain goat is essentially an animal of the high ranges, but in winter is driven to lower altitudes where it feeds on willow and other shrubbery which stands above the snow. It preserves its white color throughout the year, though often in a yellowish shade. Though it has been described as a timid animal, this statement is not borne out by my own observations. Near Port Valdez I saw goats which frequented the vicinity of a prospector's camp all summer, paying no heed to the daily blasting. Its persistence in remaining in one drainage basin is likely to lead to its destruction for food, as it is often the only source of fresh meat to the outlying prospecting camps. On the other hand, the meat is not very palatable, which is something of a protection to the animal, as is also the fact that its native range is difficult of access.

The white mountain sheep is widely distributed in Alaska, but is limited to the high ranges. It is found in both the Pacific Mountain and Rocky Mountain systems of Alaska and also in the minor ranges which break the upland lying in between. A map indicating distribution of sheep would show a rather narrow belt of sheep country lying north and south of the Yukon and Kuskokwim valleys, with some smaller patches in which sheep occur lying in scattered areas and marking the minor ranges of the plateau region. The isolation of many of these smaller areas of sheep country would lead one to expect many variations from type. Mr. Charles Sheldon, who has given close study to the Alaskan sheep, assigns them all to one species, *Ovis dalli*. He does show, however, that in northern British Columbia there is a transition from the Alaskan white sheep to the darker colored *Ovis stonei,* closely akin to the Rocky Mountain big horn.

The above general description of the distribution of the sheep is subject to many minor variations, some of which are worthy of consideration. There are, for instance, no sheep on the seaward slope of the Coast Range. Therefore, so far as Alaska is concerned, no sheep are found in the southeast panhandle, nor westward until the basin of Copper River is reached. Here they are locally abundant, being found on both slopes of the Wrangell Mountains and to the north in the Alaska Range.

In the Chugach Mountains sheep are found only on the inland slope. In other words, in their distribution the sheep and goats are more or less complementary to each other, the sheep being chiefly confined to the dry inland slope, the goats to the wet coastal slope. Sheep are abundant in parts of the Kenai Peninsula, where the goats seem to be entirely absent. Sheep are abundant also in the Talkeetna Mountains, north of the Matanuska, and on the inland slope of the Alaska Range. They are not found on the seaward slope of the Alaska Range west of Broad Pass. They are especially abundant in the Alaska Range along the foothills near Mount McKinley. The sheep country stretches as far south as Lake Clark and includes the mountains lying west of Cook Inlet. Among the isolated occurrences of sheep may be mentioned the Glacier Mountains, in the Fortymile region of the Yukon, and the White Mountains, lying southwest of Circle on the Yukon. Sheep are also found in the highlands between the Yukon and the Koyukuk. The ranges grouped together as the Rocky Mountain system are inhabited by the white sheep. They have been seen along the international boundary east and north of the Yukon; in the Koyukuk and Chandalar basins; and westward in the mountains limiting the Kobuk and Noatak mountains. They have been found near Cape Beaufort, on the Arctic Ocean, the only place, so far as is known, where their habitat approaches sea level. They thus are found on both the Arctic and Yukon slopes of the Rocky Mountain ranges.

In summer the sheep frequent the high ranges on slopes difficult for man to ascend. I have seen their trails cross to places where it was difficult to believe that anything but the well-equipped mountaineer could traverse. In the winter they are driven to the lower slopes to find their food in the willow thickets and are then hunted by the natives. They have, however, never constituted any important food supply to the native, chiefly probably because of the difficulty of their capture. To the experienced hunter with the modern rifle, the killing of sheep offers no difficulties except in some localities where much climbing is necessary. I have seen sheep in flocks of 20 to 40 in the foothill region near Mount McKinley where they could be approached without any difficult climbing. In general, the sheep hunter has to do less climbing than the goat hunter. The white color of the sheep in the treeless region which they inhabit makes them very conspicuous objects on the landscape. This coloring seems to be at variance with the usual provision of nature for making the wild life inconspicuous in its natural habitat.

The haunts of the sheep in the high ranges have been for the most part distant from the settlements and the camps. As a consequence there has been little inducement to the extensive killing of sheep. Where the home of the sheep has been invaded by mining camps, the animal has become more timid, giving him more natural protection than in his entirely primitive state. These conditions augur well for the continuation of the sheep in the higher ranges under reasonable protective laws.

To the layman, Alaska's bears are roughly divisible into three general groups: the black, the polar, and the brown bear. Of these, the first two are definite species, recognized by the naturalists, but the so-called brown bear includes not only a number of different species but probably many subspecies or varieties as well. It should also be noted that some of the animals classed as brown bears are grizzlies, differing very materially from the true Alaskan brown bear.

The black bear—one of the most widely distributed animals in North America—ranges over the entire timbered region of Alaska. He is found in the coastal forest zone and throughout the woodlands of the interior. He is observed at certain seasons catching salmon along the rivers and at other seasons finding his sustenance in the berries growing far above timber line. He occurs in the islands and coastal strip of Southeastern Alaska and along the Pacific seaboard north and west to Kenai Peninsula and Cook Inlet. He roams over the entire woodland region of the interior, but does not occur in the barren grounds. Essentially a shy animal, he is not frequently seen and never shows fight except as a last desperate effort at self preservation. Black bear skins play no inconsiderable part in the fur trade, but are valuable only in their prime.

The so-called glacier or blue bear is believed by naturalists to be a closely allied species, or possibly a local variety of the black bear. This bear, so far as is known, has never been seen by white men, though several skins have been secured by natives. I have seen only three pelts of the glacier bear. The color of the pelt is silvery gray mixed with black or bluish gray; hence the name blue bear. The hair is long. Of the three blue bear skins I have seen, two were from the coastal region between Yakutat and Controller bays, and the third was sold at Nome, its source being unknown. It is generally believed that the home of the blue bear is in the St. Elias region, but little is known of it.

Naturalists report the range of the grizzly as extending along the coast westward as far as Kenai Peninsula, in the Copper basin, and in the upper Yukon region. The coastal and inland grizzly are said to belong to different species.

The Alaskan brown bear is the typical big game animal of the Territory and one of the largest of the bear family known in the world, being much larger than the grizzly. There are a number of different species, some of which have been described. It is especially abundant on the Kenai Peninsula, in the Susitna valley, in the southern part of the Alaska Range, on the Alaska Peninsula, and on Kodiak Island, as well as on islands of Prince William Sound. While naturalists report the Kodiak brown bear as the largest of the species, the largest skin I have seen came from the Alaska Peninsula. The brown bear is also found in the Yukon basin, but this seems to be a somewhat smaller variety than that of the coast and there is some question whether these inland brown bears are not all grizzlies.

The brown bear is a huge animal. I have seen skins which were 11 feet long. An adult will frequently weight 1,200 pounds. The skulls are much larger than those of the true grizzly. The brown bear varies greatly in color, ranging from dark brown to a very light brown, sometimes almost yellow. The light-colored variety has led to occasional reports of polar bear in the inland region.

Testimony as to the ferocity of the brown bear is very conflicting. While it is generally believed that they are less aggressive than the true grizzly, several cases are reported of their attacking men, apparently without provocation. It is also a significant fact that the Alaskan natives have a fear of them. As they are not sought by the Indian for food or for their pelt, there seems no reason why the native should come in conflict with the bear unless the latter were the aggressor. On the other hand, my own personal experience with she bears and cubs leads me to believe that they will attack man only as a last resort in protecting their young, much preferring to seek safety in flight. On the other side of the argument again is the evidence of men who have been mutilated, crippled, or even killed by bear under conditions when the animal is said to have been the aggressor. It seems possible that this conflicting evidence indicates that at certain times in the year the brown bear is in a more nervous and aggressive state than at others and that at such times he will occasionally attack man.

In general, it is true that the brown bear has decreased but little since the coming of the white man. The modern rifle of the native is seldom turned on this huge monster; he still inspires awe in the primitive man who but a generation or two ago was armed only with the bow, lance, and knife. On the other hand, it is certain that so huge an animal can not maintain itself in a settled region. Whatever legislation there may be, the settler will regard the bear as a menace to his sheep, young cattle, or even children and will seek his extermination. The bear is an omnivorous animal, but as a rule depends on fish, roots, berries, and small mammals for food. He will, however, attack the young of the larger animals when hungry. The sheepfold is hardly possible in the presence of such an animal. These conditions will make it impossible to preserve the great brown bear in the regions available for settlement and agriculture, and already he has been driven from the haunts of man. On the other hand, there are many regions where he will be unmolested for generations to come. When, however, the final choice has to be made between the settler and civilization on the one hand and the big bear and unsubdued wilderness on the other, there can be no question what the result may be, however we may regret the loss of this unique animal.

In the barren ground is found another variety of brown bear, similar in general appearance to the lighter colored varieties of the true brown bear. This barren ground bear is, however, much smaller than the bear of the Pacific littoral. The barren ground bear ranges throughout the tundra region and is still found on Seward Peninsula in spite of the relatively large mining population.

The polar bear of Alaska differs in no way from the species found in the circumpolar region. His habitat is the Arctic coast littoral, and he seldom leaves salt water, whose organisms furnish him with food. Nearly every year a few polar bear find their way to Bering Sea, and on the retreat of the ice in summer some of these may become stranded on St. Lawrence Island or even on the mainland. The polar bear is much sought for his pelt by the natives, and it finds a ready market. It does not seem likely that these inroads have as yet seriously depleted the number of polar bear, and the law regulating the exportation of the skins will probably assure the preservation of this animal, which inhabits a region of little use to man.

The seal and the sea otter were in the past the most important of the fur-bearing animals of Alaska but are now of relatively small importance in the fur trade; they will be referred to in later chapters. The beaver, too, of late years has become so scarce as to furnish but few skins, and now its trapping has by wise legislation been entirely interdicted until 1915. This leaves the muskrat, mink, marten, fox, and ermine as the most important fur-bearing animals at present. To this list must be added the wolverine, wolf, and black and polar bear.

In 1912, 123,925 muskrat, valued at $49,570, were shipped from Alaska. The typical habitat of the muskrat is the swampy land in the borderland between the interior woodland and the coastal tundra, more especially in the lower Yukon and Kuskokwim basins. Muskrats are also found in the small lakes and sluggish streams of the open swamps in other parts of Alaska.

Mink are found along the clear-water streams of the inland region throughout Alaska and also, in lesser numbers, in parts of the tundra region. The mink from the woodland are chocolate brown; those of the tundra reddish brown in color. In 1912, 31,363 mink, valued at $141,133, were shipped from Alaska, the value of the shipments being almost exactly equal to that of the fur seal for the same year.

The marten inhabits the forested region and differs locally in color and hence in value of the pelt. Some 12,999 marten skins were shipped from Alaska in 1912, having a value of $162,487. This is the highest value of any one species of fur shipped during the year. Alaska ermine is the name given to the white winter coat of the weasel. This animal is found throughout the inland wooded region. The shipments of ermine in 1913 totaled 7,957, valued at $10,821. Considering its small size, the ermine is one of the most expensive of Alaskan furs.

The land otter is one of the most widely distributed of the Alaskan fur-bearing animals, being found in the wooded regions and also in parts of the tundra. In 1912, 1,480 land otter were shipped from Alaska, valued at $20,720.

The wolverine is a relatively unimportant animal in the fur trade. In 1912, only 189 skins were shipped, valued at $1,890. The wolverine has a wide distribution in the inland region, and its thieving habit makes it a pest to both whites and natives. Its skin has value for trimming the hood of the parka, as the coarse hair does not hold the moisture of the breath and cause icicles to form about the face, as do other furs.

The wolf is found almost throughout Alaska and is the enemy of nearly all other mammals. It ravages the small mammals and the young of the larger ones. Wolf-skin robes are largely used in the Territory, but the export of wolf skins is small, that of 1912 being only 103, valued at $927.

The lynx, only member of the cat tribe, is found almost throughout Alaska, but is so wary an animal that it is seldom seen. Its chief food is the rabbit or hare, and its abundance varies directly with that of these little animals. In 1912, 2,720 lynx skins were shipped from Alaska and were valued at $58,480.

The red squirrel is common in the coniferous forests, and its fur is utilized for clothing by the natives. The snowshoe rabbit or varying hare is abundant in the woodland region of the interior. Its numbers are subject to periodic decline and increase. It appears that at intervals of about seven years the hare reaches its maximum, then rapidly declines, almost to the point of apparent disappearance, then increases again. In its greatest abundance the hare can be counted by the hundreds along a route of travel through favorable districts. In the years of maximum abundance the hare sometimes plays havoc with the winter pastures. On the other hand, during the lowest ebb in numbers the natives often suffer for lack of food, for the hare has long furnished an important source thereof. It is relatively easily snared, and many an Alaskan pioneer has eked out a shortage of food by use of this little animal. The Arctic hare is the complement of the varying hare, occupying as it does the tundra region which the former does not invade.

Among the smaller mammals are woodrats and mice and porcupine, which are found in the timbered region. The porcupine is especially abundant along parts of the Pacific seaboard, notably in the Kenai Peninsula. The whistler or hoary marmot inhabits the Alpine zone far above timber. Its upward range is far above that of any other mammal.

The fox is the most widely distributed of Alaskan mammals, its various species being found throughout the Territory. Of the several varieties, the red fox is the most abundant, occurring as it does from the forested region of the Pacific seaboard to the margin of the northern Arctic tundra. The red fox also occurs to the southwest in the Alaska Peninsula and in the Aleutian Islands. This animal even invades the domain of the white fox in the tundras of Bering Sea and the Arctic Ocean. The much rarer black, silver, and cross foxes have the same habitat as the red fox.

The home of the blue fox is in the Alaska Peninsula and the Aleutian Islands. Man has, however, extended the distribution of this species, which now occurs on the Pribilof Islands and in a semidomesticated state on a number of small islands along the Pacific seaboard. There is some reason to believe that the distribution of the blue foxes in the Aleutian Islands was accomplished by the Russians and that the animal is only indigenous to the Alaska Peninsula.

The white fox is an animal of the tundra. As the blue fox occupies the grassland province of southwestern Alaska, so the white fox occupies the tundra stretching along the eastern shore of Bering Sea and northward across the Seward Peninsula to the Arctic Ocean and thence along its littoral northward and eastward along the boundary.

The fox skin has always been an important element in Alaska's fur trade. In 1912, the value of the fox skins was greater than that of any other pelts. In that year some 8,018 red foxes valued at $68,153; 3,037 white foxes valued at $39,351; 884 blue foxes valued at $44,298; 603 cross foxes valued at $10,251; 142 silver-gray foxes valued at

$35,500, and three black foxes valued at $1,800 were shipped from Alaska.

The bird life of Alaska is varied chiefly by the presence of the large number of migratory birds which winter in southern latitudes. Of the permanent dwellers, the ptarmigan is perhaps most typical of the Northland and is found in a large number of varieties. Its habitat is chiefly in the lower Alpine zone of the interior and in the southwestern grasslands. In the latter province it is found close to sea level. Its beautiful variations in color from snow white in winter to the darker summer hues make it a constant source of interest to the traveler. The best known and probably most abundant and widely distributed varieties of ptarmigan are the large willow ptarmigan associated with the upper growths of willows and the smaller rock ptarmigan of the higher zone. In the Aleutian Islands there are several varieties of ptarmigan indigenous to that part of the Territory. When in the fall of the year the ptarmigan assume their white plumage and gather in great flocks, they simulate a cloud of snow.

In the wooded regions several varieties of grouse are common, including the Canadian and ruffed grouse. The Alaskan jay, better known as the camp robber, is the most friendly of Alaska's birds, as he haunts the abode of man.

The great bald eagle is a familiar sight along the Pacific seaboard of Alaska. Here also are found the raven and large crow which feed on the mussels exposed on the beaches at low tide. Naturalists report the presence of hummingbirds as far north as Sitka, and the sight of these delicate little organisms reminds the wayfarer that the rigorousness of the Alaskan climate has been much exaggerated.

Among the birds familiar to more southern climates which are found along the Pacific seaboard are the barn and Townsend sparrow, song sparrow, golden-crowned sparrow, warbler, red poll, magpie, dwarf thrush, hermit thrush, a variety of finch, and kingfisher. One of the typical and common birds of the interior is the loon. Along the Yukon and its tributaries are found a number of varieties of both hawks and owls, the kingfisher, and several species of woodpecker. The raven is also found along the Yukon as are warblers, waxwings, and swallows. In most of the interior robins are among the summer visitors.

The waterfowl are the most abundant of the migratory birds. Myriads of ducks, geese, and brant nest in favorable localities along the Yukon and its tributaries, but more especially in the low-lying Yukon delta. Sandhill cranes, swans, sandpipers, and many other water birds are found in the same province.

In general, the inland region is not conspicuous for its bird life. The forests are silent, and even such bird life as exists has a sombre coloring. Far different is it in southwestern Alaska, notably on Kodiak Island, where birds are common and in great variety.

Insect life is not abundant in its variety or in numbers save solely for the mosquito, black flies, and horseflies. Butterflies are found in both wooded and tundra regions, but are not abundant enough to be conspicuous.

The mosquito is omnipresent. Making his first appearance as soon as the winter's snow disappears under the sun of the long spring day, he remains until the killing

THE MOSQUITO PEST
The mosquito plagues man and beast indiscriminately and makes some sort of protection necessary. Photos by J. B. Mertie (left) and P. S. Smith (right).

frost in the fall. June and July are, however, the only months when the mosquito pest is serious, but at that time the traveler seldom escapes them. They are active 24 hours in the day, but not quite so vicious during the short summer night as in the sunshine. They are found along the watercourses, around the lakes, in the swamps, and far above timber where they breed in the wet moss. They follow man and beast in swarms like a cloud, never relaxing their attack. The only relief besides a covering is a strong wind which they are not able to withstand. The quantity of mosquitoes varies greatly. A wet spring followed by clear bright sunshine is favorable for their breeding. A very dry or very wet summer is unfavorable. Their larvae are hatched out in the stagnant pools and in the saturated moss under the influence of the summer sun. All the mammals, both wild and domestic, suffer under their attack. Moose, caribou, and deer during the mosquito season seek the river bars or the areas above timber where a wind is likely to be found. On the other hand, there are but few mosquitoes in the settlements where the destruction of the moss has left them no breeding ground. Forest fires also destroy the mosquito pest.

The small gnats are almost equally annoying, but these last only two or three weeks in late July or early August. Horses as well as some of the wild animals also suffer under the attacks of the large horseflies, whose season is the month of June. These are found only in the lowlands and can be avoided if a trail above timber can be chosen. While they last, they are a serious menace to the stock, for, with the mosquitoes, they harass the poor animals day and night, giving them no chance to rest or feed.

Take it all in all, the insect pest is the only serious hardship to summer travel in Alaska. No experienced traveler will neglect his mosquito-proof headdress or his gauntlet gloves. The mosquito-proof tent with floor sewed to sides and door closed by drawstring is not a luxury but an absolute necessity to the explorer in Alaska. During the day the exigencies of the work may necessitate the removal of headdress and gloves. Sighting a rifle, using an instrument, or handling an axe often make it essential to remove the mosquito bar; in running rapids, too, he must have eyes and hands free. Then the mosquito has his opportunity. After camp is made, the explorer can retire to his mosquito-proof tent and secure the rest necessary to prepare him for another day's toil. Without this relief from the insect pests, life would be almost unbearable.

CHAPTER VI

Native Tribes

THE NATIVE tribes of Alaska offered but little resistance to Russian subjugation. These Russian aggressors found a people armed with only primitive weapons and with but little tribal organization. On occasions the natives of communities united to repel the invaders, but usually the communities acted independently and could offer but little resistance to the Russian freebooters provided with firearms. Moreover, the Russian aggressors came of the same warlike stock which for two centuries had fought its way across the continent of Asia and had at least the tradition of military organization. To prove the dominance of the Russians, it is only necessary to note that less than 500 held in subjugation a native population of nearly 20,000.[1]

When the Russians overran Alaska between the years 1765 and 1842, they first clashed with the natives of the Aleutian Islands and adjacent mainland, the Aleuts, an inoffensive people whose lack of organization made them easy to cope with. Following the coast eastward and southward, they encountered the warlike Tlingits, who offered considerable resistance, chiefly because of better organization. Later the conquest was gradually extended northward to Bering Sea, and here the Eskimo tribes offered some resistance. Finally the conquerors pushed their way inland by the Yukon and Kuskokwim valleys and here met with tribes of true North American Indian stock. The Russian posts in the interior were but few, and the Indian tribes were never subjugated.

Ethnologists have recognized four linguistic stocks among the natives found by the Russians in Alaska. These are the Haidas of Prince of Wales Island; the Tlingits of the rest of Southeastern Alaska and extending along the coast as far west as the Copper River delta; the Eskimo, including the Aleuts and occupying all the rest of the Alaskan seaboard; and the Athabascans, whose domain included the entire

[1] This figure includes only the natives of that part of Alaska actually occupied by the Russians. In addition to these, there were probably 5,000 of upper Yukon Indians and Arctic coast Eskimo with whom the Russians had little intercourse.

inland region and some of whose tribes touched the coast at Copper River and Cook Inlet. The general question of permanency of language and its coordination with physical type and cultural stage need not here be discussed, though in Alaska there is a rather close correspondence between language, physical type, and cultural stage. The Tlingits and Haidas had, indeed, about the same cultural development at the coming of the white man and exhibited no marked anthropological differences, though their languages are of distinct stocks. Dr. John Swanton[2] has, however, pointed out that there are certain similarities between the Haida and Tlingit languages; but he has also recognized certain morphological similarities between these and the language of the Athabascans of the interior. The Haidas and Tlingits are so closely allied in habits of life and social organization, and in these matters differ so greatly from the other Alaskan natives, that for the purpose of the present description they can be regarded as a unit. The native Eskimoan linguistic stock is also for the most part of a distinct physical type and cultural stage. Their true environment is in the treeless coastal tundra where their habits of life are fixed by that environment. Tribes of Eskimoan stock are also found along the wooded shores of Prince William Sound and on Kodiak Island, but here their habits of life are different from the mass of these people. The inland Athabascans form a linguistic physical and cultural unity.

In its simplified form, then, the classification of Alaskan natives falls into three groups: (1) the Haida-Tlingit, (2) the Eskimoan, and (3) the Athabascan. Where these groups come into contact, transitions in language, anthropology, and culture exist. These are in part the result of mixture of blood, in part the result of bringing a stock out of its true physical environment and consequent change in modes of life. Each of the linguistic stocks is divisible into many tribes, differing chiefly in language.

To review the geographic distribution: the great inland region, cut off from the coast by mountain barriers, is occupied by true North American Indians of Athabascan stock whose domain reaches tidewater only at the head of Cook Inlet and at the mouth of the Copper River; the whole Bering Sea and Arctic coast line is occupied by people

---

[2] Swanton, John R., "Tlingit," *Bulletin of the Bureau of American Ethnology, No. 40, Part I*, Washington, D.C., 1911, p. 164.

SOME ALASKAN NATIVES
Upper: Eskimo family on Flaxman Island, photo by E. D. Leffingwell; center: Indian family from Copper River, photo by F. C. Schrader; lower: Natives in winter dress, photographer unknown.

of Eskimo stock, and closely allied to these are the Aleuts of the Aleutian Islands and scattered tribes occupying the Pacific seaboard as far as the Copper River delta; Southeastern Alaska is occupied by the third group, chiefly the Tlingit tribes but with some Haidas whose stronghold is farther south in British Columbia.

Such was the distribution at the coming of the white man. The Russians, however, finding the Aleuts good boatmen and hunters, practically enslaved the people and scattered them over much of the Pacific seaboard as far south as Sitka. In 1886 another element was introduced by the migration of the Metlakatla Indians of Tsimshian stock who belong in British Columbia. Changes of language were also brought about by the Russian conquest. The Aleuts now talk a mixture of their own language and that of their conquerors. Even the Yukon Indians as far north as the Tanana River have a large admixture of Russian words in their vocabulary. It was natural to use the Russian word for the new articles supplied by civilization.

The Haida-Tlingit Group of Southeastern Alaska

The Tlingits form the dominating stock of native tribes in Southeastern Alaska and the coast as far west as Controller Bay. In Southeastern Alaska, Prince of Wales and some of the adjacent islands are occupied by Haidas, racially closely akin to the Tlingits, and Metlakatla Island is occupied by newcomers from British Columbia; but the natives of all the rest of Southeastern Alaska are Tlingits. According to the census of 1909 the Tlingits numbered 4,458, compared with 6,400 in 1880.

The Tlingits and Haidas are of medium stature, dark skin, and erect bearing. Their large black eyes are their handsomest features. The women have small hands and feet, and the young girls are usually comely and often handsome. The hair is coarse, stiff, coal black; their eyebrows are dark; and their cheeks bones protrude. They are intelligent and kindly, and show marked manual facility; under proper training they are industrious and not so improvident as most of Alaska's natives.

The Tlingits are a coastal people. They usually travel by water, much of their food is derived from the sea, and all their permanent habitations are at or near tidewater. The temperate climate, abundance of food, and ready means of communication by the inland waterways led to their being much more highly civilized than any other Alaskan natives at the first coming of the white man. At the time of their first contact with Caucasians they already cultivated a species of tobacco.

The social organization of these people is based on their large subdivision into two brotherhoods, or phratries, called the raven and the wolf or eagle. According to the native myth, each phratry is descended from an ancient hero or god, who procured for their respective peoples the advantages they now enjoy. The legend of each is interwoven with the animal that now forms the totem of the phratry. As the social law provides that marriage may only be between individuals of different phratries, it is evident that both are represented in each household. The children belong to the phratry of the mother. The phratry must not be confused with the tribal or clan subdivisions and is in no sense a geographic subdivision.

The phratries are each again divided into a large number of clans, 20 to 30 of which have been recognized. Each of these clans has special right to a certain emblem or totem, usually an animal such as the bear, shark, frog, or salmon. As in the case of the phratries, intermarriage between members of the same clan is prohibited by custom, and the clan descent is through the mother. An individual may, however, be adopted from one clan into another and then has the same status as if joined by ties of blood. The clans are smaller groups than the phratries and have some geographic significance, but here again two clans are represented in each household. However, a clan is not a fixed subdivision, as a chief may rise to power and, upon his choosing a totem, his village may adopt it and thus form a new unit. In this way the clan becomes a political organization.

Every community forms a political unit dominated by some chief who, with his immediate family, forms an upper caste. As in more civilized communities, wealth has much to do with the selection of a chief, but the choice is also based on ability. Strictly speaking, a chieftain's son inherits neither the wealth nor the totem of his father, these passing to the sister's children. There is, therefore, a constant shifting of totems, authority, and wealth in different generations. There are, however, means of evading this custom, and a chief may transfer his totem right and his wealth to his own son.

It is evident that in such a shifting social and political organization there could be little unity and not much hope of concerted effort in warfare. It happened, though, that some strong man would for a time dominate several communities and by such means could muster and command a considerable fighting force. It was such a condition that enabled the natives to attack the Russians several times with considerable force.

The village, made up, as has been shown, of members of different phratries and totems, is the social and political unit of the Tlingits. Each is dominated by some chief whose power is ill-defined and whose influence depends on his wealth and ability. There are also petty chiefs who dominate the households and families. These together used to form a superior class which included the shaman or medicine man. A second class was made up of the common people, including all the freemen of the community.

The slaves constituted the third class of the social organization. These comprised (1) the prisoners of war, (2) the slaves secured by barter with the southern tribes, and (3) all descendants of slaves. It is estimated that in 1841 one-third of the entire population were slaves. The slaves performed the manual labor and served their masters in time of war. They were not permitted to set up their own households or to own property, and their masters had absolute power of life and death over them. Slaves were sometimes freed and then adopted into one of the totems. At the deaths of chiefs and in certain other ceremonies, slaves were killed. Slavery has now, of course, been entirely abolished, and the caste distinction between freemen and chiefs is disappearing.

There was no well-defined civil government, but when occasion arose councils of head men were called to determine matters of tribal policy. In these the women expressed themselves as freely as the men. Interhousehold disputes were usually settled by the petty chiefs.

Slaves were the chief property, a man's wealth being counted by the number of his slaves. After the coming of the white man, wealth was measured by the number of blankets. A man owned his own house, but the fishing grounds were the possession of the community, though usually dominated by some chief. Among the Haidas, property rights of individuals in fishing rights at certain localities were recognized, this being the only example among the aborigines of the northwestern part of the continent of ownership of land.

The men were the hunters and warriors of the communities, and the more domestic duties fell to the share of the women. In the special season of fishing, the work was shared alike by both sexes, though the chiefs were usually exempt from manual labor and the drudgery was largely performed by slaves. There was more or less specialization in the industrial arts. Thus, a house builder would work for others and in turn be served by canoe makers, blanket weavers, or basket makers. These artisans were divided among both sexes, the woman doing the weaving and basket making, the man the carpenter work.

The native villages of Southeastern Alaska are invariably located near the shore and with a convenient gravel beach at hand for canoe landing. The proximity of fishing grounds has always been a controlling factor, and in former times susceptibility of defense was an important element in the choice of village sites. At the coming of the white man many of the settlements were provided with fortifications to which retreat could be made in time of war.

The houses of permanent habitation are of substantial construction. A framework is made of hewn plank, morticed together, and the roof is a low gable supported by posts at either end. The roof is covered by split logs or hewn boards, and the sides by vertical planks closely joined. The interior consists usually of three levels. The lowest has a dirt floor, and here is the fireplace, the smoke escaping through a hole in the roof. Above this is a plank floor about three feet above the hearth level, and surrounding this a platform three feet higher where the inmates sleep with feet toward the fire. In some instances, some privacy is secured by partitions dividing off the sleeping platform. Totemic emblems are used for exterior decorations, and the front central post is often carved into a totem.

The above description of the dwellings indicates a high type of development in mechanical skill. It is especially striking in view of the fact that these buildings were formed and erected without the use of any metal tools. The Haidas' dwellings are, indeed, the highest type of wooden architecture developed by any of the North American races.

Temporary dwellings consisted of cedar bark tents that

could be transported in canoes. Summer habitations at salmon streams were made of a light framework with bark covering. Fur sleeping robes or blankets, with cooking utensils and wooden boxes, constituted the only interior furnishings. All this has, of course, been modified by contact with the whites. Stoves are now in general use, and houses are built after civilized pattern.

The Tlingits and Haidas are essentially a seafaring people, for their routes of travel were by the sea and marine life their principal food. Under these conditions they became the most expert boat builders on the continent. The canoes varied, according to their purpose, from 12 or 15 feet to 65 or 70 feet in length. The smaller size are used for fishing and hunting in the protected waterways and bays, the largest for voyaging and war purposes. A large canoe might have a beam of six to eight feet and be capable of holding 40 to 50 men. The canoes have long, overhanging, tapering bows and sterns and have good lines. They are equipped with sails and paddles, the latter having sharp points. Though the natives had no knowledge of the oar, they were quick to adopt it from the white man. In their larger boats the natives made long voyages and had no hesitancy during their seal hunts in putting out some distance into the open ocean. Their navigation was, however, essentially coastal, and, so far as is known, they depended on landmarks and not on the constellations as guides.

The building of these crafts would do credit to a people who had all the modern implements. Stone axes were used in felling the trees for canoe manufacture, and the rough shaping was done with wedges and axes. All the fine work was accomplished with adzes formerly made of stone. After it had been wrought out, the shape was modified by steaming accomplished by the use of water and hot rocks. The smoothing was done with rough stones and shark skins. White men's tools were quickly adopted in canoe manufacture. The yellow cedar was utilized for all the large canoes, but smaller ones were manufactured of Sitka spruce.

The primitive dresses of the natives were made of furs, including seal and sea otter, roughly sewn together, and of tanned skins, chiefly deer. The southern Indians also used a cloth made of fibre of cedar bark. Blankets made of twisted bark thread and the wool of mountain goats were highly ornamental and used only on ceremonial occasions.

The Chilkat blankets were especially famous and have now become rare curios. Both sexes went barefoot for most of the year, but moccasins were worn in winter. Hats were woven of grass, but the natives mostly went without head covering. Needless to state, all this is a thing of the past. The natives now have civilized garb, the primitive dress being confined to ceremonial occasions.

Salmon and halibut were the chief native foods, supplemented by herring, cod, and candle fish. Seals and porpoises were one source of the large amount of oil used by the native cooks. Geese, ducks, and other wild fowl captured when young were much esteemed as articles of food. At certain times of the year birds' eggs were collected in large quantities. These natives were not essentially big game hunters, but deer, bear, and goats supplied a part of the food. The sea also furnished them with clams, crabs, cuttlefish, and mussels; and a variety of marine algae also added to the larder. Seaweed was dried for winter use.

Among the land plants the berries were most important in the food supply. These included raspberries, salmonberries, strawberries, currants, huckleberries, and cranberries. Certain roots, including wild parsnips and a wild lily, were also eaten. The scraping of the inner bark of the hemlock also furnished a vegetable food. Potatoes were early introduced by the Russians and have been grown by the natives for many years. In primitive times the only cultivated plant was a variety of tobacco about which little is known.

The natives of Southeastern Alaska have for several generations been provided with firearms, so that the art of making their primitive weapons has almost been lost. They still fashion knives and daggers very much as they did in the ancient days. These were formerly made of stone, sometimes of copper, the handle being wound with buckskin. Sometimes the knife was carried by a thong, sometimes in a buckskin sheath. The copper was secured from the northwest by intertribal trade. Even at the first coming of white men some iron knives were found among the natives. The material from which they were fashioned may have had a Spanish source far to the southeast, may have been passed across the continent from the Hudson Bay posts, or may have come from Siberia. A spear or lance was another native weapon. The heads of these, like the knives, were fashioned of various materials. The bow and arrow was also in use in this coastal region, but the club was the favorite weapon of war. Armor of wooden shafts woven together, with leather and copper shields or skin-covered bucklers, and wooden helmets and visors were the weapons of defense.

More important than the above as food producers were the fish nets, hooks, weirs, and spears. These, together with the basketry and carving, required much manual skill in their fashioning. The basketry of these natives ranks among the best in Alaska. Now, the use of colored yarn in their manufacture, aniline dyes in coloring, and, above all, the departure from shapes made for utility and an attempt at copying the white man's utensils have detracted much from the value of the baskets. Mats woven from grasses are another native industry, though they are now only made as curios.

Copper was the only metal possessed by the Alaskan natives before the coming of the white man. This was obtained by the Tlingits and Haidas by barter with both the Copper River natives and the interior Indians. The metal was highly prized and was fashioned into weapons and ornaments. Their experience in fashioning this copper made it easy for them to take up the vocation of silver-smithing. Many silver ornaments are now made for the tourist trade, and while this work is not one of their primitive industries, it shows their natural handicraft.

Bone and shell ornaments were also fabricated by these tribes but are now seldom seen. The primitive adornments included lip, nose, and ear rings, necklaces, and bracelets. Among the Haidas, tattooing of the body was commonly practiced, the emblems being the totems. On ceremonial occasions and at war time, the natives painted themselves, the colors being black, red, green, and white. The pigments used were ochre, cinnabar, and some of organic origin; these were mixed with oil.

Like all primitive peoples these natives had many myths and superstitions that played an important part in their lives. The earth is conceived as flat, supported on a post that is in charge of an old woman. Under certain conditions the earth moves on this support, giving the quakes that are not unfamiliar phenomena in this region. The Tlingits believed in the immortality of the soul and in a happier existence after death. Certain of their myths include the resurrection of the dead. A raven with some human attributes is the creator of all things and the benefactor of mankind. He is also the ancestor of all the Indians and has his abode in the headwater region of the Ness River in northern British Columbia. The entire universe is peopled by innumerable minor spirits who must be propitiated in various ways. Thus, an old woman lives at the head of each salmon stream. Offerings of food, tobacco, and ornaments were made to these spirits and special heed was given not to speak of them lightly, as otherwise troubles would follow. Many of the myths are connected with some particular animal, the grizzly bear, mountain goat, and otter being held in special reverence.

The shaman or medicine man played an important part in the social fabric. He led the ceremonials and treated the ill. There was an elaborate equipment of wooden masks, headdresses, blankets, and rattles provided for ceremonial occasions. The pharmacopoeia of the shaman included numerous concoctions and charms, used as cures for various ailments and as bringers of good luck.

Among the numerous ceremonial festivals, the potlatches or "givings" are the most familiar. The potlatch is essentially a great feast at which the host makes valuable presents to his guests. It was usually given by some chief or wealthy man who aspired to a chieftainship. The host sometimes stripped himself of all his possessions at these gatherings and thus achieved popularity in his settlement. He, again, benefited by the potlatches of others.

The ceremonial meetings were attended by dancing and singing. A fondness for vocal music is one of the characteristics of the natives of Southeastern Alaska. The songs include those used at meetings for barter, the war songs, and other types. The melodies are simple and not inharmonious. Drums, rattles, and wooden trumpets and whistles constitute the musical instruments.

The mortuary customs differed in various localities. Cremation was the general rule among the Tlingits, but it was by no means universal. The ashes were deposited in a box which was placed on a wooden post, frequently carved with totemic emblems. Where inhumation was practiced, the remains were placed in a coffin and covered with a small wooden structure. For the chiefs a totem pole was erected. The shamans' bodies were always disposed of in this way. The place of burial was always in some sightly place, like

NATIVE BURIAL PLACES

Alaskan natives disposed of their dead in a variety of ways, two of which are shown here: a simple raised Eskimo grave (left, photo by F. C. Schrader) and a more elaborate Tlingit Indian burial place near Ketchikan (right, photo by A. H. Brooks).

an island or promontory, and at some distance from the settlements.

While the preceding account pertains particularly to the Tlingits, it applies in many ways also to the Haidas, who are of kindred stock. Some differences in canoes, carvings, and basketry are to be noted between the two tribes. The social organization was essentially the same, the two phratries and the many totems being represented in both. The Haidas excelled somewhat in carving, being particularly noted for their work in slate. This slate, like the pipestone of the western states, has the peculiar property of being soft when quarried and hardening on exposure to the air.

There were 530 Haidas in Alaska in 1909; in 1880 they numbered about 800. They are, if anything, more intelligent and industrious than the Tlingits.

The ready means of communication along the inland waterways made the natives of Southeastern Alaska travelers and traders. Their intercourse extended far south in British Columbia where they procured slaves by barter from tribes who obtained them by war with the Flathead Indians. The Copper River natives supplied them with copper. They were the superior of the inland natives, who were not permitted to visit the coast. The Tlingits, however, made trading journeys far into the interior and even impressed their own language on the Tagish natives whose home lay on the inland side of the Coast Range. The Chilkat tribe of Lynn Canal were especially well-known as traders. They controlled the passes leading into the interior, notably the Chilkoot. This pass was an avenue of trade for a long time. Even after the Russian occupation, all trade with the interior natives was through the Chilkats, who jealously guarded their long-established and lucrative rights of middlemen. When Hudson Bay Company traders reached the Yukon, in the middle of the 19th century, this monopoly was broken. The Chilkats did not, however, give up without a struggle, for in 1848 they sent a marauding expedition across the Chilkoot and 300 miles beyond to destroy the Selkirk post, hoping thus to re-establish their monopoly.

The Tlingits had some jade, which must have come from northern Alaska or from Asia. This suggests barter with the tribes still farther west, though the jade may have passed from tribe to tribe before it came into possession of the Tlingits.

It is generally believed that the Tlingits came from the south and that their invasion of Southeastern Alaska took place not many centuries before the coming of the white man. They are believed to have been actively pushing their aggression to the west when the white invasion put a stop to their tribal movements. When Bering made his voyage to the Alaskan coast in 1741, they had already reached the eastern part of the Copper River, here being in contact with a people of Eskimo derivation. Had this invasion not been terminated, they would probably soon have occupied the whole coast of Alaska at least as far as the limits of timber on Cook Inlet.

The Haidas are regarded as still later comers to Alaska. Their invasion, which was also from the south, probably took place in the early part of the 17th century, and they presumably displaced the Tlingits of the region they overran.

No evidence has been found of any earlier inhabitants of Southeastern Alaska, and it is quite probable that the Tlingits were the first. Not many centuries before, this entire coast region had been occupied by glacial ice which filled the valleys, fiords, and channels. Under such conditions there would be little to support man, and it is quite possible that this part of Alaska has only recently been occupied by mankind. Even after the retreat of the ice, the region for a time would still be barren and inhospitable until vegetation had acquired a foothold and animal life had come in. Among the Tlingits' traditions are some indicating that the valleys of the Coast Range were still blocked with ice at the time of their invasion. Special reference is made in some of their myths[3] to ice blocking the Stikine and Alsek rivers.

Speculations concerning the Mongolian origin of these coastal tribes have not been uncommon. Their facility at handicrafts, especially at carving, and the physiognomy of some individuals are suggestive of Mongolian ancestors. The anthropologists and ethnologists have, however, found little evidence of an Asiatic origin of these people. The facts noted suggest the occasional infusion of Asiatic blood, caused perhaps by junks being blown across the Pacific. Such wrecks have been reported repeatedly during historical time, in many instances with part of their crew still living. Improvements in handicraft might well have been brought about by the influence of the occasional shipwrecked Chinese or Japanese mariner. When the crew of the English ship *Boston* in 1803 was massacred by the natives of Nootka Sound, they preserved the life of the armorer, John R. Jewitt, to forge and teach them how to forge weapons. They were evidently intelligent enough to take advantage of this opportunity to improve their arts; they may well have done so on other occasions of which there is no historical record.

The Aleut-Eskimo Group

The Eskimo peoples of Alaska fall into two large groups: the Innuit, usually known as Eskimo, that originally inhabited most of the coastal region west of Controller Bay; and the Aleuts that occupied the Aleutian Islands and adjacent parts of the Alaska Peninsula. At Controller Bay these peoples were in contact with the Tlingits, and on Cook Inlet, on the lower Copper, Yukon, and Kuskokwim rivers with the Athabascan or Indian tribes. Where this contact occurred, there was more or less admixture of blood, and tribes were developed that partook somewhat of the character of both stocks. With this racial blending there was also a merging of customs, implements, and industries.

The tribes of Eskimo origin on the Pacific had for the

[3] Swanton, John R., "Social Conditions, Beliefs, and Linguistic Relationships of the Tlingit Indians." *26th Annual Report of the Bureau of American Ethnology, 1904-1905.* Washington, D.C., 1906, p. 410. Cf. Swanton, "Tlingit Myths and Texts." *Bulletin of the Bureau of American Ethnology, No. 39,* 1909, p. 67.

most part a strong admixture of other stocks. Therefore these—that is, the natives of Prince William Sound, the southern coast of Kenai Peninsula, Kodiak Island, and the base of the Alaska Peninsula—show but few of the Eskimo traits. Their differentiation, though they belong to this linguistic stock, is the more difficult because they came into such intimate contact with the Russians. Now the natives of these supposedly Eskimo tribes include many creoles, as the Alaskan half-bloods are called. They have lost many of their primitive arts and have changed their modes of life so that the ethnologist finds it difficult to trace their affinities. They use in part the Tlingit dugout canoe, in part the skin-covered boats of the Eskimo.

These people are of moderate height, stocky, with broad faces and coarse black straight hair, and are somewhat redder in coloring than the western Eskimo. They were essentially a littoral people whose main food supply came from the sea, including fish and whale blubber. Shellfish, roots, and berries were also a part of their food. Their clothing was made of seal and sea otter. Those of Kodiak Island and the Alaska Peninsula used the skin boats, but in Prince William Sound the dugout had also been introduced because of the Tlingit influence. Their weapons were the bow and arrow, the harpoon and spear; their tools, axes and adzes. They lived in large single-roomed houses, in part made by excavation, in part of logs. They had little tribal organization, government being by households rather than by communities. In spite of this lack of political organization, these people maintained themselves against the Russians. Though they became the most Russianized of Alaskan natives, it was by adoption of Russian implements, customs, and religion rather than by enslavement, as was the case with the Aleuts.

The peoples described occupied the coastal region, except Cook Inlet, from the Copper River delta to about the Shumagin Islands, and also Kodiak Island. The rest of the Alaska Peninsula and adjacent islands, including the Aleutian chain, was the home of the Aleut. The physical appearance of the Aleuts is similar to that of the western Eskimo, except that their stature is somewhat greater. Their complexion is light yellowish-brown; the hair coarse, straight, and black; the cheek bones broad and high; the nose flat and fleshy; the lips thick; the eyes wide-set, small, and jet black; and the beards and eyebrows scanty. It must be said that the Aleuts, like the other Eskimo tribes, have a Mongolian rather than a North American Indian appearance.

Food supply largely determined the choice of locality for settlement. A good boat landing was also a prime requisite, as was an available supply of fresh water. Susceptibility of defense also influenced choice of settlement. Localities near salmon streams or mussel banks, with other conditions specified above, were generally chosen. Communal ownership in fishing grounds and village sites was absolute and was defended by arms, if invaded by others. The social organization of the communities was essentially patriarchal. While the head of a household dominated the family, there was also a chieftainship, possessing more or less authority in community matters. These chiefs constituted an aristocracy which was based largely on wealth and ability. Chieftainship was a matter of inheritance, but the oldest chief in the community was recognized as the leader. A chief might be deposed for cowardice or for other reasons. The freemen of the community constituted a second class, and the slaves a third. The slaves and their descendants were the prisoners of war. They were not so plentiful as among the Tlingits and had, on a whole, a better lot than those of the more southern tribes.

Punishment by death was inflicted only after communal council and vote, and only for murder and treason. Minor crimes were punished by public reprimand, tying and exhibition of the culprit, and in some instances by beating. Beating, however, was seldom inflicted on freemen. Freemen were killed by spears, slaves by clubs. Slaves were also punished by mutilation. Wars were carried on by individual communities under the leadership of chiefs. In some cases, several communities on one island united for purposes of war under the senior chief of the island.

The Aleuts' supernatural conceptions were those of pantheism. Although there was one creator of the universe, it was the minor gods who must be placated by various religious observances. Their beliefs included the immortality of the soul, and slaves were killed at the death of the master so he might be served in the next world. The Aleut myth of an original uninhabited world, the creation of two beings, and the subsequent dispersal of the descendants of these to people the world bears such a strong resemblance to the Hebraic legend that its authenticity might be questioned.

The food of primitive Aleuts came mostly from the sea and included salmon, cod, herring, candle fish, sea urchins, mussels, seal, whale, and sea lion. This diet was varied by different edible roots and plants, sea weed, and waterfowl. Largely through their improvidence the Aleuts often suffered from hunger, sometimes dying of starvation. Food was chiefly eaten raw.

In pre-Russian days the Aleut's dress was a parka made of fur, chiefly sea otter, and of bird skins, such as the puffin and the diver. Boots were made of hair seal skin. A waterproof over-garment was manufactured of the entrails of the sea lion. Hats, when worn at all, were of thin strips of wood, bent and woven together. Mats were woven of grass. The sea otter skins were largely used for bedding.

Their weapons were bows and arrows and darts and lances, the latter propelled with the aid of throwing sticks. They had at the coming of white men no metal except some copper, and weapons were pointed with bone or flint. Shields for defensive purposes were made of wood, but they seem to have had no body armor, as had the western Eskimo and the natives of Southeastern Alaska. There is no timber on the islands, and all wooden implements were made of driftwood. At the coming of the white man the Aleuts had only stone implements, and only knives, hatchets, and chisels. Fire was obtained with two flints rubbed with sulphur, igniting dried moss powdered with sulphur. The sulphur was obtained from some of the volcanic vents of the islands.

Their dwellings were large, and each held several, sometimes many, families. These were dug in the earth, lined and roofed with drift wood, and covered with turf. Entrance was by holes in the roof. They used no fire, the only source of heat being oil lamps.

Their travel was by sea in skin boats, now generally called by the Russian name *bidarkas*. These were of the familiar kayak form, often built with two hatches. Both double and single paddles were used for propelling the craft. The Aleuts are skilled boatmen and hunters, a fact which led to their employment by the Russians as hunters. They manufactured bone hooks and lines and nets of seal skin, whale sinew, or twisted moss.

The Aleuts are the most skillful basket makers in Alaska.

Basketry is their only highly developed art, though they are also skillful wood carvers. The baskets are woven from native grasses, the most delicate being woven under water. Most valuable of all are the Attu baskets which, now that the art has become almost lost, command fabulous prices. Their wood carvings were chiefly confined to masks used in ceremonial dances. Many small implements, such as needles, were carved out of bone.

The Russians found the Aleuts a kindly, hospitable, and inoffensive people. They were not warlike but by no means cowardly. Their general code of morality was high considering their low status of development. The first 50 years of Russian aggression saw the Aleuts robbed, murdered, and enslaved by the pitiless bands of marauding fur hunters. Although they fared better after Russian America became an organized colony, they never recovered from this treatment. Some settlements were wiped out, others were transplanted; customs and traditions were violated, and the valuable sea otter hunting grounds were ravaged. Large numbers of Aleuts were transplanted to other parts of the colony—for example, the inhabitants of the Pribilof, or Seal, Islands are the descendants of Aleut hunters taken there by the Russians. The number of Aleuts has declined greatly from an estimated 16,000 in 1740. In 1909, they numbered 1,491, which included 489 of mixed blood. In still later days these conditions have become more serious, as the sea otter, their chief source of furs, has been almost exterminated. There is nothing on the islands except foxes, and by the trapping of these, with the aid of the fisheries, the natives maintain a precarious existence. Their native customs, including dress and social organization, have, of course, long disappeared. They now live chiefly in wooden houses, furnished with stoves, and are dependent on white man's food. Their most important settlements center around the Russian missions at Unalaska and Attu. Attempts have been made to improve their condition by the introduction of reindeer on some of the islands.

It is now generally believed that the Aleutian Islands were first settled by a people coming from the mainland of Alaska. This belief is supported by the anthropological and linguistic affinity of the Aleuts to the true Eskimo and also by their own traditions. The presence of ancient shell heaps and village sites, in some of which at least two stages of development are recognized, indicates that the

Aleutian Islands have been inhabited for centuries, if not for a period exceeding a thousand years.

The natives occupying the eastern shores of Bering Sea and the entire coast line of the Arctic Ocean can be conveniently grouped together as Eskimo proper. They are tied together by anthropological characteristics, by linguistic affinities, and, in large measure, by modes of life and state of culture. As already shown, the same stock is represented by the inhabitants of Kodiak Island and along the Pacific seaboard eastward as far as the Copper River delta. These southern Eskimo have, however, been modified both by contact with other native stocks and by the different environment to the extent that they have lost many of their original characteristics. According to the census of 1909, there were in all Alaska 12,652 natives of Eskimo stock, of whom 787 were of mixed blood.

These Eskimos are essentially a littoral folk. They have, however, penetrated some distance inland along the larger waterways, and some tribes have permanent habitations on these rivers. Thus, they are found up the Kuskokwim as far as Kolmakof, some 600 miles from the sea, and on the Yukon nearly to Anvik, 400 miles from tidewater. The entire Seward Peninsula belongs to their domain, and they also dominate the drainage basins of all the rivers flowing into the Arctic Ocean. These have more or less modified the habits of life of the inland Eskimo because of the different environment. Where they come into contact with the interior Indians, there have been physical changes caused by the admixture of the different stocks. The Eskimo type must, therefore, be sought among the coast dwellers.

When the Russians established themselves on Bering Sea a century ago, the Eskimos of this province were still in the stone age of development. Since that time marked changes have been brought about by contact with the whites. There still remain, however, in northeastern Alaska some tribes that, except for the use of firearms, are almost as primitive as at the first coming of the white man. What follows will be an attempt to describe the Eskimos in their primitive condition, their more recent development being for the most part ignored.

Typical Eskimos are of medium stature but with broad shoulders and heavy build. When well fed they incline to corpulency. Their complexion is light brownish-yellow, often with ruddy cheeks. They have broad cheeks, high noses, and long heads with black straight hair. The eyes are dark and slightly oblique, giving them the Mongolian character so frequently noted.

The Eskimos are intelligent, with a strong sense of humor. They have a sturdy independence which is not always broken down, as is the case with so many primitive people, by contact with a superior race. They have remarkable physical endurance, and their industry is greater than that of most barbaric people.

Like those of other maritime people, the Eskimo settlements were determined by food supply, boat landings, and, in pre-Russian days, by means of defense. Fishing grounds were an important element. This means one type of location for those dependent on whales and walrus and another for those eating salmon and tomcod. For various reasons the mouths of the larger waterways were favorite locations for settlement. These were the scene of salmon fisheries and offered routes of summer travel by boat and winter travel by dog sled. Inlets and lagoons also afforded advantages for settlement above those of the open coast line. In the absence of all such advantageous natural features, Eskimo settlements were still maintained on rocky and exposed shore lines.

The Eskimo seems to have had even less social organization than other Alaskan natives. Each settlement was dominated by a head man, but he had little authority. Much influence was wielded by the shaman, or medicine man, who was called in council in case of danger or sickness. Punishment for murder was usually an individual matter for the relatives of the victim. Minor crimes were punished by public reprimand of the culprit. That the Eskimos have a sense of community responsibility is made evident by numerous records. For example, when the missionary Thornton was killed by three Eskimo boys at Cape Prince of Wales in 1894, two of the murderers were captured by the villagers the same night and executed before the horrified eyes of Mrs. Thornton the next morning. The third, who had conspired with the others, though he had done no actual shooting, was later also killed by the natives when Captain Hooper of the Revenue Cutter Service, on his annual visit the following summer, represented to the village elders that he was equally guilty with the others.

Community matters were settled by council of the village elders, in which the women also took part. Fishing rights and hunting grounds belonged to communities and in some cases, possibly, to individuals. These passed by inheritance through the male line. Houses, goods, and chattels were also the property of individuals.

The typical Eskimo dwelling is the igloo. This is an underground habitation consisting of two or three rooms. The walls are made of driftwood covered with turf and soil. Entrance is either through the smoke hole in the roof or through a narrow tunnel. Some have a covered passageway for summer use. Some of the Alaskan Eskimo used wood for fuel; others depended solely on the oil lamps.

Every settlement had a large igloo or community house, called by the traders of the Bering Sea "kashim," used for every kind of community assemblage including councils and dances and feasts. In large settlements there are often two kashims. Where timber or driftwood is available, a store house on four posts, generally known among the whites as a cache, is used for sheltering supplies. In the absence of suitable timber, underground store houses are used.

Modifications of dwellings are found among the tribes living in the timbered regions. Here crude log cabins take the place of the igloo. Other types of abode are used by those living away from the driftwood supply of the coast. Here dome-shaped houses are built of willow, moss, and turf. The summer houses at hunting and fishing camps were in primitive times lodges covered with skins or wooden mats. Now, of course, tents are in general use. On travels, the family boats, or umiaks, to be described below, were turned up and used as shelters from the wind.

The food of the Eskimo varied according to locality. The Bering Sea natives ate chiefly salmon, cod, and seal, with some caribou. Along the Arctic coast, whale, seal, and walrus formed important elements in the food of the natives. The inland Eskimo of the Arctic slope subsisted largely on the barren ground caribou. Marmots, rabbits, and ptarmigan were also snared, and sea fowl and their eggs furnished a further variety. Berries, notably the salmonberry, and certain roots were used by all. Famines resulting from various natural causes have not been uncommon in the past and have materially kept down the population.

The Eskimo is both a sea and land traveler. Boats are of two kinds: the large traveling and family umiak and the small hunting kayak. Umiaks are made from 15 to 40 feet long. The framework is of wedge-shaped pieces of driftwood, and the whole is covered with seal skins or walrus hides. The single-bladed paddles originally used have now been superseded by oars. Sails, formerly made of woven mats and deer skins, are now made of canvas. The umiak is very seaworthy and an excellent surf boat, when skillfully handled. When making landings in surf, the steersman waits until there is a wave just suitable for his purpose and then floats to shore on top of it. The crew seize the boat as soon as it touches the beach and carry it out of reach of the surf. Excellent care is taken of umiaks, they being carefully washed out after every voyage and turned up on edge to dry out. The kayak (see picture, page 414) is so familiar to all that it needs no special description. It differs somewhat in shape in various districts, but is essentially a small decked canoe, 12 to 18 feet long, made of a framework of wood covered with skins. The manhole is small, and the high gunwale prevents the waves from swamping the boat. Further protection is by a garment which covers the boatman and manhole and keeps out all water. The kayak is propelled by a single paddle which varies in shape according to locality. The under deck space is used for storage, articles being hauled by means of boat hooks. I have frequently seen children packed away in this small space, sometimes one at either end of a kayak.

In travel along stretches of sandy beach or river bars dogs are often utilized to haul the umiak. The work of the dogs is, however, more properly that of hauling sleds in winter. They are also used as pack animals on summer inland hunting trips. Winter equipment for travel includes dog sleds, hand sledges, snowshoes, ice staffs with sharp points, and ice creepers to prevent slipping. All the equipment, manufactured by the natives themselves, was, before the coming of the white man, made with no metal.

The clothing of the Eskimo consists of trousers, boots, and smock, or parka, as it is called. In primitive days men and women dressed much alike. Reindeer skin is the commonest material, being partly of wild caribou and partly of domesticated reindeer obtained by trade with the Siberian natives. Marmot and seal skins are also used in clothing. Waterproof garments are made of fish skins or walrus intestines. Similar material and seal skin are used for the waterproof high moccasin or mukluk, as they are called, universally worn except in winter when a reindeer fur boot is substituted. Head coverings consist usually of the hood of the parka or waterproof garment.

The offensive weapons of the Eskimo are the lance, the spear, used with throwing stick, bow and arrow. Armor made of ivory plates woven together with thongs was formerly in use. Lances, arrows, and the like were tipped with bone, sometimes with flint or jade. Fish nets and traps, hooks, and lines were an important element in securing food supplies.

One of the important characteristics of the Eskimo is their skill in carving. Walrus ivory and fossil mammoth ivory were the usual materials, but some wood carving was also done. Innumerable utensils for use of the household or of the chase were finely fabricated and often ornamented. These include such a variety of articles as structural parts of boats and sleds, fishhooks, net making implements, spoons, pipes, ornaments, and toys carved of ivory; and dippers, masks, and other articles carved of wood. Baskets and mats were also woven of grass and roots, and to this art belonged the bird and fish nets.

The ability of the Eskimo in the graphic arts is so well known that it needs no special description. Much of the ivory and wood work is pictorially ornamented. The natives are especially skillful in drawing maps and have a strongly marked sense of distance and direction. I recall seeing an Eskimo map of the lower 1,200 miles of the Yukon which, though based entirely on memory, contained many of the intricate details of tributary watercourses.

Tobacco seems to have been used among the western Eskimos before the coming of the Russians, perhaps secured through trade with Asiatic natives. It is at least an interesting speculation whether tobacco must not have reached Asia in pre-Columbian days rather than assuming that it encircled the globe, traveling eastward, and reached these distant aborigines not much over two centuries after it had been brought to Europe.

The western Eskimo were in close contact with Asia at Bering Straits. In fact, the western side of the straits was inhabited by people of their own stock. This narrow strait, whose bounding headlands are intervisible, was easily traversed in the great sea-going umiaks, and intertribal communication here took place between the two continents long before the Russian days. This intercourse has been

NATIVE DWELLINGS

Upper: Eskimo houses at St. Michael, photo by J. E. Spurr; center: Aleut barabara at Unalaska, photo by I. C. Russell; lower: Indian house and cache, photo by A. H. Brooks.

continued to the present time, and up to recently many of the Alaskan Eskimo were clothed in the skins of the domesticated reindeer secured from Siberia in barter. Fox skins, seal oil, and possibly jade were exchanged with the Asiatics. In return, the domesticated reindeer of the Tchuckchus, the natives of the inland regions of this part of Siberia, furnished the imports. In this trade the Cape Prince of Wales natives were the middlemen and found thus a lucrative monopoly. They were, in fact, the wealthiest and most independent natives on the American coast. There was also some barter with the interior Athabascans, but this seems to have been less well organized, probably because these inlanders had few, if any, articles not equally accessible to the coastal Eskimo.

The Athabascan Indians of the Interior

It remains to consider the inland natives, who, though they include many different tribes, each with its language or dialect, all belong to the Athabascan linguistic family. They are also all of the same general physical type and have essentially the same mode of life and cultural stage. Of these Athabascans there were, according to the census of 1909, 3,916 in Alaska. Since this was the first accurate census, there is no means of knowing how rapidly they have decreased. However, there is much evidence that they have decreased since they first came into contact with the whites only a century ago.

The Alaskan Athabascans, or Tinneh, constitute but a small part of that great family of North American natives which originally was represented as far south as Mexico and almost as far east as Hudson Bay. They are of the same general physical type as the North American Indians in general. They are taller than the Eskimo, not so stocky, and somewhat more swarthy in coloring. They have high cheek bones, piercing black eyes, and black hair. These inland natives were divided into numerous tribes that need not here be considered.

More significant was a certain geographical grouping that materially affected their mode of life. Much the greater number lived on the large rivers and their tributaries, visited annually by salmon which furnished an important part of the sustenance of these Indians. A small part lived in the headwater regions, notably on the upper Tanana beyond the migration of the salmon. These were essentially meat-eaters, their only fish diet being the Arctic trout, or grayling, and a small whitefish. These highlanders, as they might be called, were the last to come into contact with the whites and hence preserved many of their original customs up to recent times. In 1898 and 1899 I found such men living on the upper Tanana who, except for their firearms, exhibited but little evidence of intercourse with the whites. Most of the men and some of the women were dressed entirely in buckskin, and their bedding was made of furs. Here I saw an Indian hunting with bow and arrow. His arrows were tipped with copper from the gravels of near-by streams. On this same stream, the Kletsandek, a tributary of the upper White River, I found a party of natives searching for the native copper pebbles in the gravels, their digging implements being caribou horns.

The primitive dress of the native is buckskin parka, or shirts, pointed both in front and behind. Breeches were also of buckskin, and the moccasin completed the garb. There was little difference between the dress of women and men. To this was added rabbit skin undergarments. No headdress, except sometimes a small round ornamental cap, was worn in summer; but in winter a fur cap and sometimes outside fur garments were worn.

Their houses were, for the most part, crude affairs—a framework of poles thatched with bark and brush. In shape, these were much alike—a wall tent with low walls and a gradual slope to a peak. An opening at the peak was left for smoke to escape. Chinks were caulked with moss, and a double door gave greater protection against the severe cold of the winter. Summer habitations were of the same general style but of more flimsy construction.

A cache or store house, built usually as a platform in trees but sometimes on posts, guarded the supplies from predatory animals. Most of the inland natives made sweat houses. These were hay-cock frameworks made of willow and covered with skins. Hot rocks were placed inside, and a dash of water furnished the steam.

Some of the tribes built more substantial houses, notably those of the Cook Inlet region. These were of logs, built much like the cabins of white men. The logs were grooved on one edge so as to fit on to the adjacent ones, making the houses very tight. A hole in the roof, which was of bark, served as smoke vent. Inside, there was a platform like that of the Tlingit houses from which the idea may have been borrowed. On the lower Yukon, houses were also built of upright logs more or less flattened by hewing.

The social organization was of the simplest. Each group was dominated by some man who, by common consent, was recognized as chief, but had only such authority as the individuals were willing to grant him. Community affairs were settled by general council in which the chiefs and old men ruled by custom. There was no tribal organization outside the individaul communities, though alliances were sometimes made in time of war.

Intellectually, the inland natives were far below those on the coast. Their myths embraced a kind of demonology, but they had no conception of one supreme being or immortality.

Men and women shared alike in most of the hard work. Of course the men were the hunters and the women the clothing makers. The labor during fishing season was shared by all, men, women, and children.

Salmon furnished an important part of the food supply of many of the Athabascan tribes. These were speared, caught with scoop nets, and snared in fish traps. They were dried and stored away for winter use, for dogs as well as for men. The natives beyond the salmon area dried the smaller whitefish but lived more on the game. All the natives killed caribou and moose. The former, as has been previously described, were driven through openings in long fences built of brush where they were snared or speared. In the days of bows and arrows, the moose were little killed except in winter when, under favorable conditions, runners on snowshoes could overtake the wily animal. Like the caribou, they were also to a certain extent caught by snares hung from trees, and sometimes they were killed with bow and arrow. The moose, however, was much too wily an animal to be caught readily. The moose skin was highly prized because the toughness of its hide made it useful for accoutrement and some forms of clothing. Rabbits were snared in great numbers during the good seasons. This little animal is, however, as already pointed out, only abundant at certain periodic intervals, and during the lean rabbit years there was likely to be suffering, if not starvation, among the natives. Grown ptarmigan and young waterfowl were also a part of the Indian's diet, as were the eggs of many birds. These birds were snared, clubbed, and killed with bow and arrow.

Various fur-bearing animals were used in clothing, such as land otter, mink, marten, and fox. The wolverine was especially prized, for its fur has the property of not carrying icicles, and it was used in collars and capes that were likely to be moistened by the breath. The black bear was also killed by natives, but they apparently feared the large brown bear and grizzlies, which were seldom molested before they had firearms. They also seemed to fear the wolf. When they made camp in winter, a wisp of dried grass or birch bark was wrapped around a stick which was thrust into the ground near the fire. If a wolf approached after the fire burned low, a blaze could be quickly obtained by thrusting the stick and moss into the fire. With the aid of this fire wand, the animal was frightened away.

Berries and certain roots furnished the inland natives with their only vegetable food. In the spring the inner bark of the spruce was scraped and a brew concocted which they drank because it was good medicine. It can be regarded as antiscorbutic.

Primitive weapons included the bow and arrow, the spear, and the club. Knives were fabricated of copper or stone, as were spear and arrow heads. Axes, adzes, and knives were made of stone.

The inland natives have no marked manual dexterity. Their bark canoes (see picture, page 414) are probably the highest examples of manual skill. These are 10 to 12 feet long and consist of a light framework bound together and covered with birch bark. They are propelled with a single-bladed paddle and with great skill. They can not be used in swift water and are chiefly of use in fishing and hunting trips. Two short sticks form part of the equipment of each canoe. These are used for propelling the boat up shallow and sluggish streams. With a stick in either hand, the native can push the light craft at a remarkably rapid rate. The canoes are too small to transport supplies, so this was done on land by back-packing in summer and sleds in winter. When a river had to be crossed in summer, a raft was built. Fallen spruce was used before the days of axes and was fashioned into right lengths by burning if necessary. The logs were lashed together by roots, and the crude raft thus fashioned was guided, so far as it was possible, by poles.

Another form of craft occasionally resorted to was fashioned of raw moose hides. A hunting party having killed some moose would make a framework of light poles fastened together by roots or thongs. Over this, the moose skins would be stretched and the crude craft used to transport the meat back to camp. Sleds and snowshoes were also made of spruce lashed together by thongs. Some of the natives also made short skis of spruce wood; the end was turned up by steaming.

At the coming of the white men their cooking utensils were of the simplest pattern. The salmon and other fish were smoked, but not otherwise cooked. Meat was roasted in the fire. The only utensils were birch baskets, in which water was heated by the use of hot rocks, and wooden troughs or plates. The horns of the Alaskan mountain sheep were utilized in the manufacture of spoons with curved handles. Birch bark baskets were skillfully made of many sizes and patterns, and were the chief household utensil. Mats were also fashioned into hampers.

Clothing was ornamented with porcupine quills. The needlework of the women was very skillful. This art is noticeable in the moccasin, still made, the only original article of native dress still preserved.

The Athabascan tribes of the interior, though they annually made long hunting trips, were essentially a sedentary people. Each tribe had its permanent habitation and well-defined hunting ground. These were jealously guarded, as were also the fishing grounds. As a rule, the inland native knows little or nothing of the region lying beyond his own hunting grounds, which were determined by natural physiographic boundaries. Thus, the natives of the Susitna basin seldom ventured into the Kuskokwim valley, though low passes offered good means of communication. I had an example of this on a journey from Cook Inlet through the upper Kuskokwim to the Tanana. I found that most of the Tanana natives knew nothing of Cook Inlet from personal observation. One old man seemed familiar with the route and possibly had made the journey as an envoy. Ivan Petrof makes special mention[4] of the arrival of two Tanana Indians on Cook Inlet in 1866 and states that the oldest man among the coast natives remembered only two previous visits by Tanana Indians.

---

[4] *First Annual Report, Bureau of American Ethnology, 1879-80*, Washington, D.C., 1881, p. 482.

There is an intertribal law among these natives by which the tribe is responsible for the life of a visitor from other tribes. If such a visitor loses his life while on such a journey, the tribe whose domain he has entered is required to make indemnity to the visitor's tribe. Not many years ago, for example, a Tanana native was accidentally drowned while visiting the Fortymile region. Demand was at once made by the Tanana natives for indemnity from the Fortymile natives for the loss of life, though the latter could not have prevented the accident. It is a curious thing that this elementary principle of international law should have been developed among a people of such low cultural status. Evidently, therefore, the principle is based on a natural evolution and can not be considered the result of a highly organized society.

In this connection, it may be noted that a visitor from a neighboring tribe might not catch fur-bearing animals except as food. He was privileged to kill any animal for food, but the pelt must be delivered to the tribe owning the hunting ground.

It is difficult to determine just how much intertribal trade existed before the invasion of the whites, which quickly changed the habits of the natives. There is no doubt that certain of the Athabascan tribes furnished the coast natives with copper which they secured from the upper White and Chitina River basins long before the coming of the white man. They undoubtedly received in return articles of coast manufacture, but just what these articles were is not known. Copper was also distributed in the same way among the Athabascan tribes. Aside from this copper, no inland tribe had articles or materials not accessible to the others.

Conditions changed when the Russians reached the coast and, half a century later, the Hudson Bay traders reached the Yukon. Then the natives immediately adjacent to the trading posts obtained many articles which they bartered with the more distant tribes. In time these distant natives visited the posts themselves and thus avoided the profits paid to the middlemen. Thus, even the Tanana natives used to congregate annually at the mouth of that river and barter their furs with the white traders. Those of the upper Tanana reached the Yukon and Fort Selkirk for the same purpose by a more direct route.

Professor George Davidson[5] has described the route of the Chilkat chief to burn Fort Selkirk. His information came from Kohkluk, the chief himself, and the geographic data are in such detail as to make it certain that the region was familiar to the narrator. It also appears from this account that the Chilkat chief had also descended the Alsek to the sea. The Chilkats also appear to have been familiar with the copper deposits in the upper White River region. They called the White River the Irkhena, which means copper. The coast tribes also had a route of inland communication along the valley of the Taku and Stikine rivers. So far as is known, these do not seem to have been as much used as the more northern passes. The reason may have been that the Chilkat routes were available and established before the other two rivers were cleared of glacial ice.

Intertribal warfare was probably less common among the Athabascans than among the coastal tribes, probably because the natives were more widely distributed and the primitive means of transportation prevented any close contact. Moreover, the physical conditions of life were much the same throughout the entire province and, as has been shown, except for the copper deposits of certain tribes none of them had property likely to excite the cupidity of others. Also, in the absence of slavery one motive for foraging expeditions was lacking.

On the other hand, there was constant friction along the frontiers of the different races. The Tlingits and Haidas of the coast clashed more or less with the inland Athabascans, though their higher cultural development gave them every advantage in warfare. More important were the wars between the Athabascans and Eskimo tribes, especially along the lower courses of the Yukon and Kuskokwim rivers, where there was no physical obstacle to tribal intercourse. This is seen from the zone of mixed bloods found along the border of the two stocks. Here there are several tribes that have affinities, both physical and cultural, with both stocks.

In spite of this evidence of tribal intercourse, there was almost continuous conflict between the tribes of the two stocks, though more often intercommunity clashes than actual warfare. Of these wars, there is no record except

[5] Davidson, George, "Explanation of an Indian map of the Rivers, Lakes, Trails, and Mountains from the Chilkaht to the Yukon, drawn by the Chilkaht chief Kohkluk in 1869," *Mazama*, April, 1901.

tradition, but there is no evidence that they were ever waged on a large scale or in a systematic manner. They usually consisted of surprises and accompanying massacres from which neither age nor sex was exempt. Samuel Hearne has left a graphic picture of such a fight between the natives of Athabascan stock and the Eskimo which took place in 1763 on the Copper Mine River of Northern Canada. Of the intertribal wars of the Athabascans, there is even less record. In general, the hunting Indians, like those of the upper Koyukuk and Tanana, seem to have been held in dread by the fish-eaters of the larger rivers.

The origin of the natives of Alaska involves the far-reaching ethnologic problems relating to the origin of all the aborigines of North America. There is still much difference of opinion on this matter among the students of the subject. It is, however, probably safe to make two generalizations. The first is that Alaska was first settled by people coming from the south and east. In other words, the natives are of North American and not of Asiatic stock. This statement refers to the natives of Alaska as found by the white men a century and a half ago. Whether in a much earlier stage North America was peopled from Asia by way of Bering Straits or the Aleutian chain will not here be discussed, as that question has no bearing on the genesis of the present Alaskan natives. The second generalization is that Alaska was peopled in comparatively recent time. Both Haida and Tlingit traditions show that these people came from the south, as do also their physical and linguistic affinities to more southern stocks. This northward migration must have taken place since the retreat of the glaciers from the fiorded coast line. If one were to venture a guess as to the length of this period, it might not exceed 500 years. It could not have been longer than a sufficient time after the retreat of the glaciers for vegetation to establish itself enough to support animal life. It is fair to assume that the Tlingit invasion took place not over 500 years before the coming of the white man.

The Eskimo of Alaska are also newcomers. They followed the Arctic shore line from the east, eventually spreading down into Bering Sea and finally to the Pacific. They had probably reached the western end of the coastal ice barrier formed by Malaspina and Bering glaciers when the Tlingits approached it from the southeast. This glacial mass was one of the last to retreat, and within a few centuries ago it probably occupied the entire shore line from the Alsek to Controller Bay, a distance of over 200 miles. Such an ice front would have held in check the littoral tribes on either side of it, unless they were impelled by some strong motive such as search for food or escape from invaders. The abundance of sea food on both sides of the barrier shows that there was no reason for the first, and there is no evidence of the second. It was probably only about the time of the coming of the white man that the Tlingits had reached Controller Bay and here came into contact with the Eskimo. The gradual retreat of the Copper River glaciers opened a way to the coast for some of the inland natives, but this condition was probably a recent development when the whites came. On the other hand, the Susitna River route had long been free of ice, and here the coastal natives had not only reached tidewater but had occupied the shores of Cook Inlet. It is probable that they already occupied this field when the Eskimo arrived from the west. The date of the Eskimo incursion into Alaska by way of the mouth of the Mackenzie has been put as recent as 600 years ago. Certain evidence has been presented supporting this view, which relates to the distribution of the musk ox. Whether the westward movement of the Eskimo was held in check by glacial ice is not definitely known. There were glaciers on the north coast, but their retreat seems to have been much earlier than that of those on the south. Therefore, it may have been other factors which kept the Eskimo out of Alaska until comparatively recent times.

The Athabascan tribes of the interior are so closely related to the plains Indian of Western Canada and the United States that a common origin is without question. While there is no direct evidence of the direction of migration, it is probably safe to regard it as having been northwesterly. The cordilleran ice sheet that once occupied the intermountain parts of British Columbia disappeared long before the coastal glaciers of Southeastern Alaska. There is no measure of the time that has elapsed since the disappearance of this ice, but it was probably long before the occupation by the natives. It is quite possible that inland Alaska was peopled long before the border coastal zone.

The evidence toward a comparatively modern settlement by mankind of the Alaskan littoral is all in accord, except some facts presented by Dr. William H. Dall with reference to the Aleutian Islands. It has been shown that the Aleuts are of Eskimo stock and that they came from the east. It would be the natural inference to believe, in accordance with the other evidence, that the Aleutian Islands were only recently peopled. Dr. Dall has, however, obtained evidence from kitchen middens, cave dwellings, and other anthropological finds that the islands have been peopled for at least a thousand years.[6] In his excavations he finds evidence of three different cultural stages. The skulls found in the second stage are of the Eskimo type. In his opinion, the present inhabitants of the islands are the descendants of those represented by the earliest cultural stage. This evidence evidently contradicts the theory that the Eskimo invasion is of recent date. Unless the anthropological evidence be taken as conclusive, it might be asserted that the two earlier cultural stages represent inhabitants of the Aleutian chain antedating the Eskimo migration. It is not impossible that the Aleutian Islands might have been habitable while the rest of the shore line was still occupied by ice; that a primitive race occupied these islands before the invasion of the present stock; and that the Aleuts are in part of Eskimo descent, with possibly an infusion of the blood of an older stock which already occupied the islands at the time of the coming of the Eskimo. This explanation at least makes the whole scheme of primitive migration consistent.

---

[6] Dall, William H., "On Successive Shell Heaps of the Aleutian Islands." *Contributions to North American Ethnology*, I, (1877), 41-92.

CHAPTER VII

Discovery and Early Exploration

VITUS BERING, sent by Russia to find the American coast east of Asia, made landfall near Mount St. Elias on July 16, 1741, and thus discovered what is now known as Alaska. He and his subordinate, Alexis Chirikof, traced sufficient of the Pacific littoral along the Gulf of Alaska to determine that it was the mainland and thus fulfilled the mission with which they were charged.

It is certain that the presence of land beyond Bering Straits was known to the Russians previous to Bering's voyage in 1741. In fact, a Russian party had landed on Seward Peninsula in 1732. This was known to the Russians[1] as the "Large Country" and they had probably gained knowledge of it through the Tchuckchu natives who for many generations had traded with the Alaskan Eskimos. Gvosdef, who made the landing on the mainland, believed he had reached only a large island. Other voyagers may have had sight of the Alaskan coast or some of the Aleutian Islands, but these have left no definite records. It is more than likely, too, that Japanese or Chinese vessels had reached the American coast, but no direct evidence of such discoveries has yet been found.

In the 16th century there were many efforts by European cartographers to reconcile the conflicting data on the relation of Asia to North America. The voyages of Magellan and Drake had shown the wide expanse of the ocean separating the west coast of North America from the Cathay of Marco Polo. But the North Pacific and Bering Sea were entirely unknown and could be filled in only from the vague information about countries northeast of Cathay which Marco Polo had brought back to Europe in the 13th century. This did not prevent the cartographers from indicating in some detail the seas and lands in these unknown regions.[2] As the latitude of Marco Polo's journey was unknown, Cathay was represented far to the north of its actual

[1] Golder, Frank A., *Russian Expansion on the Pacific, 1641-1850*, Cleveland, 1914, p. 160.

[2] Cf. Sykes, Godfrey. "The Mythical Straits of Anian," *Bulletin of the American Geographical Society*, XLVII, 161-172.

position and a great bulge of the North American continent was indicated to meet it from the east. Their cartographic representation of the northwest part of America was near enough the truth to be prophetic of the discovery of Alaska. The best known map of this period is one by Zaltieri, a Venetian cartographer, published in 1566, and on this the "Anian Straits" appeared as separating America and Asia. A superficial examination of this map gives the impression of a geographic knowledge far ahead of the time. The American coast as represented is not unlike its actual contour. One jutting land mass is indicated that might represent the Alaska Peninsula, and another might be taken for Seward Peninsula. Closer study, however, reveals the fact that these peninsulas lie only a little east of the meridian of Japan, represented by an area located in the middle of the Pacific. It is likely, therefore, that they may represent the Kamchatka Peninsula, information about which had reached Europe about this time through Jesuit missionaries in Japan.[3] It seems necessary, therefore, to reject Zaltieri's map as evidence of any such complete knowledge of the North Pacific as its general features suggest. If the Alaskan coast was well known at this time, the knowledge was confined to China and Japan, and any records of voyages in these seas were not available to European cartographers.

It now seems certain that the Anian Straits constituted an attempt to indicate graphically Marco Polo's verbal account of the information he obtained about the region northeast of China. The Anian Straits may quite likely represent Chinese knowledge of the waters separating the southern end of the Peninsula of Kamchatka from the mainland or the Japanese Islands. Anian has been identified with the ancient people of Zezo, the northern Japanese Islands.[4]

Francis Drake in 1579 extended the Spanish exploration on the west coast of North America as far as Oregon, but this fruitful field of discovery was not followed up. By 1741, the west coast of Bering Sea was roughly outlined by Russian discoveries, and it was known that Asia and America were not connected. The Arctic Ocean was then believed to be separated from the Pacific, but the chain of

[3] Golder, *op. cit.*, p. 118.

[4] Cf. Ruge, S., *The Term Anian*, Dresden, 1872; Sandler, C., "Die Anian Strasse und Marco Polo," *Gesellschaft für Erdkunde zu Berlin*, XXIX, 1894, 401-408.

the Aleutian Islands that formed the barrier between the Pacific and Bering Sea was yet unknown. Somewhere beyond the eastern margin of Asia lay America, but how far no man knew. The great stretch of the continent between the Great Lakes and Bering Straits had not yet been seen by Europeans. Thus it fell to Bering, sailing out into unknown seas from Asia, to seek the continent to which Columbus' voyage had led the way. This time the route lay eastward and the starting point was that continent whose southern margin Columbus had sought and died believing he had found. This eastward voyage of discovery was the only important one made in this direction since Vasco da Gama had in 1499 found the water route to India by circling the Cape of Good Hope. To understand this reversal of exploratory routes, a brief review of the Russian conquest of Siberia must be given. And to understand the conditions that brought about the Russian conquest of Siberia and later of the northwest part of America requires a brief consideration of certain features of European history.

The golden period of ocean exploration which began with Columbus' voyage westward to America and Vasco da Gama's voyage eastward to India and which culminated in Magellan's rounding South America and encircling the globe was the geographic result of the Renaissance of Western Europe. At about the same epoch the little Muscovy kingdom, the precursor of Russia, was fighting a battle with oriental barbarism by maintaining itself against the Tatar hordes. In the same year that Columbus discovered America, Ivan III of Muscovy took the title of Tsar because of his alliance with a princess of the deposed Byzantine royal house and thus assumed that he had fallen heir to the old Eastern Empire, Constantinople being in the hands of the Turks. The struggle between Europe and the Orient was thus transferred from the shores of the Bosphorus to the banks of the Moskva. It was these conditions that prevented Russia's advance and for two centuries kept her far behind the culture of West European nations. Until Russia reached the shores of the Black Sea or the Baltic she had no contact with the Western World. The trade routes to the Orient lay outside of her possessions, and she was still further isolated by the new sea route to India. She was left rather as an Asiatic than as a European power. Her route to the west was blocked by the Polish Empire, the route to the Mediterranean and the Orient by the Turks. Her only possible zone of expansion was to the east. She indeed reached the polar sea at Archangel as early as 1583, but this afforded only an indifferent means of communication. Therefore, the only outlet for the new nation was eastward across the Urals into Asia. (See Map No. 4, page 166.)

The conquest of Siberia both because of geographic and because of political conditions was thus forced on a people that was beginning to feel its nationality. The instrument of this conquest was also at hand in the border people, known as Cossacks, who lived largely by pillage. Another element in the Russian people was also largely contributory to the conquest of Siberia. The stern rule of the Muscovite kingdom had during the reign of Ivan III through that of Ivan IV (1462-1584) developed order out of chaos and made it possible for commerce and industry to develop. The independent Hanseatic city of Novgorod had been swept into the Muscovite kingdom and with it the organized condition of commerce and industry that had been adopted from Western Europe. Relatively stable conditions were thus established and the merchant of Muscovy was ready to seek new paths of commerce.[5] The enterprise of the merchant furnished the motive and the Cossacks provided the means for an eastward movement of trade and with it of a nation. Meanwhile the conquest of Astrakhan and Kazan had opened the route to the Caspian and the Urals.

Yermak, the Cossack, is rightfully credited with starting this eastward movement, but in it Strogonof, the merchant, also played an equally important part.

Anika Strogonof had amassed a considerable fortune during the reign of Ivan the Terrible as a salt and fur merchant in the province of Archangel.[6] In this trade he came into contact with some of the Siberian natives. Ivan IV, recognizing the possibility of extending his dominions, made a land grant to Strogonof on the Kama River near the west slope of the Urals with the view of encouraging him in his trade with the Siberian natives. This trade had now developed into freebooting expeditions on the part of the Russian fur traders. Northwest Siberia had in the 11th and 12th centuries gradually been absorbed by the

[5] Some of the merchants of Novgorod had established trade relations in the reg'on beyond the Urals as early as the 11th century.

[6] Price, M. P., *Siberia*, New York and London, 1912, p. 175.

Hunni of Turkish stock, who came from central Asia and conquered the aboriginal Finnish tribes. Therefore, the peoples with whom the Russians came into contact were of mixed Turko-Finnish blood but dominated by the Turks. Some of the Finnish tribes were forced northward to the limit of habitable lands and there preserved more or less independence. The first traverse of Siberia was along the line of cleavage between the Turks and Mongols on the south and the Finnish tribes on the north. In the 14th century the Asiatic Empire of the Great Khan had already begun to crumble. Hence at the time of the Russian advent only the smaller units of this empire had to be contended with.

Strogonof was powerless to extend his trade into Siberia without military aid. At this time appeared Yermak, credited with the conquest of Siberia. Yermak's life and achievements are clouded in romance, and his history will probably never be authentically known. It is certain, however, that he was a Cossack chief from the Don who found his way to Strogonof's land grant in eastern Russia and here probably obtained the inspiration for a trans-Ural raid. His first expedition was a failure, but with a band of Cossacks probably armed and equipped by Strogonof in 1579 he invaded the possessions of the Tatar Khan Kuchum in Siberia, defeated that prince, and in less than two years triumphantly entered his capital, Sibir, located near the present site of Tobolsk.[7] The importance of this conquest was recognized by the Tsar when its success was reported to Moscow by Yermak's messenger, and reinforcements of Russian soldiers were dispatched. Yermak's death in 1584 led to a withdrawal of the Cossacks, but the rich fur country once discovered was soon again entered, and by the beginning of the 17th century the eastward march had well begun. The route followed the Ob, Yenisei, and Lena rivers. Yakutsk, at the great bend of the Lena, was founded in 1632. From here the Aldan River offered a route to the base of the Stanovoi Range, through which a pass was found that brought the conquerors to the waters of the Pacific at the Sea of Okhotsk in 1643. (See Map No. 4, page 166.) At about the same time the Lena and Kolyma rivers were descended to the polar sea. In 1646 a voyage was made eastward from the mouth of the latter stream.

[7] Coxe, William, *Account of the Russian Discoveries between Asia and America*, 2nd edition, London, 1781, pp. 180-184.

All this activity brought the Russians into contact with the Tchuckchus, a warlike race that occupied the northeastern extremity of Siberia. The rich booty of furs from the 1646 voyage led to further explorations, and in 1648 the Russians reached the valley of the Anadyr River. Before considering the explorations of the Tchuckchu Peninsula, which bears a close relation to the discovery of Alaska, it will be well first to consider briefly the organization of Russian Siberian possessions; and here I must rely almost entirely on Professor Golder's important researches, to which frequent references have already been made.

Siberia became an imperial colony as soon as conquered. It was open to the individual fur trader and never monopolized, as was Russian America soon after its first settlement. It was organized under the Office of Foreign Affairs of the Tsar, but after 1637 its administration was carried on under a separate unit of Russian government.[8] The sole policy of the administration was one of exploitation. Centuries were to elapse before the adoption of a farsighted policy of developing this rich land as homes for Russia's surplus populations and as a source of food and minerals. Reforms were introduced under Peter the Great, but these were more closely related to an improvement of the administrative machinery than to an improvement of the conditions of the Siberians.

For administrative purposes Siberia was divided into districts, each under the control of an official known as a *voyevode* whose authority was supreme. Only the collection of taxes was outside his province, this being in the hands of revenue officers known as *golovas*. The districts were subdivided, each with a subordinate official in charge. The headquarters for northeast Siberia were at Yakutsk, and in this part of Siberia fur hunting was the only industry. Natives were required to pay a tax in furs to the Government. This tax, while in itself not large, was greatly increased by the private levy of all classes of government officials for their own profit. The plundering of the natives was systematized, and the authorities in Russia were unable to prevent it any more than they could stop the grafting of government funds, supplies, and furs on the part of their own employees.

At first the officials were from an illiterate class, in large part of resident Russians; later they were in part drawn

[8] Golder, *op. cit.*, p. 191.

from among the exiles. The exile system was inaugurated before the time of Peter the Great, but it did not reach any great development until the reign of Catherine II. It included both political and criminal exiles, and it finally led to a large part of the civil and military officials being recruited from among the exiles. This, while it improved the intelligence of the official class, did not lead to any reform of administration, for these men were not likely to evince any great loyalty to the home government. The few honest and efficient officials only served to emphasize the corrupt character of most of them. It was probably this condition as much as anything else that led to a change of administration when Russian expansion led to the acquisition of Russian America, as Alaska was called.

Even before this time, monopolistic rights to the fur trade in certain provinces were in some instances granted. The general law, however, permitted any free Russian after paying for a license to engage in the fur trade. In addition to the license, a tax of one-tenth of the gross receipts of furs was levied on these free traders. The trader was, of course, at the mercy of the army of local officials to whom he, like the natives, was forced to pay unlawful tribute.

These were the conditions under which Russian expansion to the Pacific and eastward to Russian America took place. Aside from Bering's voyages, until the 19th century there were hardly any attempts at exploration, except those carried out by local officials whose sole aim was to find new fields for plunder. Under these conditions it is not a matter of surprise that the record of the early exploration is incomplete and the results of no great value or accuracy. It was not until naval officers were dispatched from St. Petersburg in the 18th and 19th centuries that any real progress was made in the scientific investigation of Russia's Pacific provinces.

The results of the first half of the 19th century in exploring the North Pacific and Arctic littoral were indeed worthy of Russian people. It was not until the sea route of the Pacific was utilized that properly organized and equipped expeditions could be dispatched to these distant lands. However, it must not be supposed that the authorities at St. Petersburg were entirely unmindful of the value of information about Siberia. Professor Golder[9] has shown that in the 17th century the local officials were charged

[9] *Ibid.*, p. 67.

with the duty of drawing maps of their districts and that some important results were thus achieved. Even the Chinese were not without geographic knowledge of Siberia with which they carried on a lucrative commerce. Thus in 1723 a Chinese official and historian who had visited Siberia wrote an account of the country and included a map of Siberia on which Lake Baikal, Lena River, and the mouth of the Amur were indicated.[10]

It should be borne in mind that, in spite of the lack of the proper kind of local officials to encourage explorations and survey, the incentive to seek new tribes that could be plundered led to many minor expeditions, both official and private. In this manner a local knowledge of Siberia was developed which, while not very exact, was sufficient for administrative purposes. Moreover, the strongly centralized government at Moscow, as well as the greed of the local officials, furthered this kind of exploration. As a result many Siberian maps reached at least manuscript form during the latter part of the 17th and early part of the 18th centuries.

The most glaring error in these maps was the discordance of orientation of different parts of the map. There appears to have been only a vague sense of the direction of flow of even the larger watercourses. Thus, a map of northeastern Siberia dated 1669 and reproduced by Professor Golder[11] shows the Lena and Amur as parallel rivers both flowing into an eastern ocean. A similar lack of understanding of direction is noted in other maps. One comes to the conclusion that such maps were drawn by those who made no use of the compass and who drew their maps after completion of journeys. They resemble the crude maps drawn by the Alaskan natives.

Of the 17th century explorations of Siberia one deserves special mention—the one usually referred to as the Deshnef expedition. As noted above, by 1646 the Russians had already reached the mouth of the Kolyma River and skirted the Arctic coast for some distance eastward. The rich booty of furs and walrus tusks resulting from this voyage soon led to further penetration into this field.

By many writers Deshnef has long been credited with rounding the East Cape of Siberia and reaching the Anadyr River through Bering Straits. If this is true, it was he

[10] Cahen, Gaston, *Les Cartes de la Siberia au XVIII siecle*, Paris, 1911, p. 136.

[11] Golder, *op. cit.*, p. 69.

and not Bering who proved that Asia and America were separated. After a re-examination and critical study of the original records, Dr. Golder[12] has entirely rejected this version of Deshnef's voyage, and from his account it seems clear that neither Deshnef nor his companions laid claim to the rounding of northeast Siberia. Dr. Golder's interpretation is briefly as follows:

Simeon Deshnef was a minor Cossack official who lived at Yakutsk. In 1647 he accompanied Fedot Alexief, agent for a Moscow merchant, in an attempt to reach the Tchuckchu country in four small vessels, by tracing the Arctic coast eastward from the mouth of the Kolyma. The voyage was unsuccessful because of ice. In the following year another attempt was made, this time with seven boats. Four appear to have been lost or to have turned back in the early part of the voyage. The others continued; and, in accordance with one interpretation placed on the scant records that have been left of this party, traced the north coast of the Tchuckchu Peninsula, passed through Bering Strait, and were wrecked somewhere south of the Anadyr River. Professor Golder has pointed out that there is little, if any, evidence in the records of such a voyage. His interpretation of the records is that the party was wrecked somewhere east of the Kolyma River and reached the Anadyr River by an overland journey.

Aside from the question of the interpretation of the scant records of this voyage, the inherent improbability of it because of the adverse physical conditions is great. As Professor Golder points out, the distance from the Kolyma to the Anadyr, following the windings of the coastline, is over 2,000 miles,[13] a journey almost impossible in the small boats used on the voyage without frequent landings for food. The Tchuckchu tribes were notoriously hostile for a century after Deshnef's time, and the strangers could expect nothing from them except armed opposition. Moreover, this voyage once accomplished would have opened a sea route to what became an important post on the Anadyr. It would certainly have been utilized by the Russians when opportunity offered, in lieu of the laborious overland route

[12] *Ibid.*, pp. 77-95.

[13] It is fair to assume that a journey in the small open boats would follow the shore line closely, especially since the purpose of the expedition was to find fur-bearing animals and natives.

from the Kolyma.[14] While the written records of Deshnef's voyage remained unknown for many years, yet he and his companions would, it seems, have communicated the facts about this route to others. The alleged journey was so remarkable that it appears that traditions of it would have remained at Anadyr and Yakutsk. If, on the other hand, they went by land from the Kolyma little attention would have been paid to their journey because it was duplicated by many others within a few years.

For the present writing the important fact of Deshnef's voyage was the discovery of the Anadyr River[15] and the establishment on its headwaters by 1650 of the permanent post of Anadyrsk. This, the first Russian settlement on Bering Sea, was within 400 miles of Cape Prince of Wales, the nearest point of Alaska. The Anadyr post was reached and supplied by a long overland route from the eastern tributaries of the Kolyma. Hence it was difficult of access.

Its garrison was much reduced after the establishment of posts in Kamchatka in the early part of the 18th century. From Anadyrsk the Russians gradually extended their conquest southward to Peninshin Gulf and finally to Kamchatka. They were here passing through the lands of the Koriaks, the most formidable tribes they had come into contact with, and the difficulties of keeping open a line of communication held them in check. By 1720 a new route to Kamchatka was established across the sea from Okhotsk which was reached from Yakutsk by way of the Aldan River and through a pass in the Stanovoi Mountains. This gave a more direct means of communication and avoided the warlike Koriaks. Anadyrsk now became only a secondary outpost, and Russian development on the Pacific became centered in the Kamchatka Peninsula. This threw the hub of Russia's commercial interests to the southern part of the Bering Sea and the adjacent Pacific, and it was for this reason that the Aleutian chain, rather than Tchuckchu and Seward peninsulas, marked the route leading to Alaska. Moreover, the explorations of the Kurile Islands led the Russians to Japan, and this together with the long-

---

[14] The ocean route from Bering Straits to the Kolyma River is now used by merchant vessels, though in some seasons seriously hampered by ice. Cf. A. Siberiakoff, "Uber den Seeweg zur Mündungen der Kolima und der Lena durch die Bering Strasse," *Deutsche Geographische Blätter*, Bremen. 1914, XXXVII, 19-22.

It needs to be rememberd that navigation by steamers may be possible when it would be impractical for sailing vessels. It is also possible that the Arctic ice pack may have retreated since Deshnef's voyage.

[15] Professor Golder even questions whether Deshnef was the first Russian to reach the Anadyr.

established commercial relations with China drew the Russian interests to the south. Kamchatka with its comparatively temperate climate, abundant timber, and agricultural possibilities, as well as the good harbors, was far more desirable than the bleak tundras of the north. But the most important effect of the occupation of Kamchatka on the trans-Pacific expansion of Russia was its development of a seafaring population. The voyage to Okhotsk demanded some knowledge of navigation and, once the Russians had become accustomed to the sea, the adjacent shore lines were explored.

It is not to be supposed that the Russians at Anadyrsk entirely neglected the search for new fur fields in the adjacent region. The post was, however, beset by the warlike Tchuckchus to the northeast and the Koriaks to the southwest, and exploration was both difficult and dangerous. As already shown, efforts were chiefly directed toward establishing a route of communication with the Sea of Okhotsk and the Kamchatka Peninsula. There were probably some inroads to the northeast, and an account of one of these has been printed. About 1711 a Cossack, Peter Popof, penetrated the Tchuckchu Peninsula northeast of Anadyr with the purpose of making the natives pay tribute.[16] In this he was unsuccessful, but he appears to have brought back some account of Bering Straits, the Diomede Islands, and the "Great Country" which lay beyond.[17]

Thus at the close of the reign of Peter the Great, the Russian exploitation of northeastern Siberia had resulted in the occupation of the Lena, the Kolyma, and the Anadyr valleys, the Kamchatka Peninsula, and the shores of the Sea of Okhotsk, and in the establishment of a route through the Stanovoi Range and Aldan River to Yakutsk. It also appears through native reports that there was some vague idea of the Tchuckchu Peninsula and of the "Great Land" that lay beyond. No evidence has been found that any knowledge of the proximity of North America was current among the Russians of northeastern Siberia.

Be it remembered that at this time the trans-Mississippian region of North America was unknown except for the incursion of the Spaniards into what is now California and Arizona and that the west coast had been traced only as far north as the present southern boundary of Oregon.

[16] Bogdanovich, K. I., *Sketch of Tchuckchu Peninsula*, St. Petersburg, 1901, p. 82.
[17] Bancroft, H. H., *The History of Alaska*, San Francisco, 1886, p. 27.

Though the eastern and southern shores of Hudson Bay had by this time been occupied by the fur traders, the western shore was known only to the mouth of Churchill River. Three thousand miles of unknown land and seas separated the westernmost Hudson Bay post at Churchill River from Anadyrsk, the easternmost Russian settlement. European scholars still dreamed of a northwest passage to the Pacific and hence a route to China by way of Hudson Bay.

Such were the conditions when Peter the Great turned his attention to Siberia. One of the principal objects of his life had been to make Russia a maritime power, and the navigation and exploration of the Pacific naturally appealed to him. He probably had a fairly good grasp of what was known of Siberia, for even the minor local officials were frequently called to St. Petersburg for conference and report. Peter was well aware of the value of the fur trade and when in London showed special interest in the Hudson Bay Company.[18] It is not to be wondered at then, in view of these facts, that he desired to extend Russian influence beyond the Pacific.

The first matter to be settled was the question of whether Asia and North America were connected. Aside from the geographic importance of this problem, which no doubt appealed to the great monarch, it might have a far-reaching political importance. If the Russian Cossacks at Anadyrsk and the English traders at Hudson Bay were on the same land, many important questions of jurisdiction might arise since, of course, it was not then known that these two countries were thousands of miles apart. Peter recognized as the first task the determination of the relations of the two continents. His navy, the first built by Russia, was officered to a large extent by men recruited from the maritime countries of Europe. It was, therefore, natural that the Pacific exploration he had in view should be entrusted to a man of foreign birth, namely Vitus Bering, a native of Denmark.[19] Bering's instructions provided that he should determine whether Asia and America were united, visit some settlement under European jurisdiction, chart the coast, and return and report.[20] These instructions were

[18] Willson, Beckles, *The Great Company*, London, 1900, I, 308.

[19] Peter had sent two Russians, Feodor Luzhin and Ivan Yevreinof, to Kamchatka in 1720 with orders to "determine whether Asia and America are united," but the expedition was unsuccessful. See Golder, *op. cit.*, pp. 114-115.

[20] *Ibid.*, p. 134.

signed in 1724, only a month before the great Tsar's death.

Bering's selection for the leadership of this important expedition was based on the recommendation of the Russian Admiralty. His service for 20 years in the Russian navy had proved him to be a skillful navigator and a brave soldier. While he appears to have lacked the spirit of scientific inquiry that was possessed by English navigators and that made the voyages of such men as Cook and Vancouver so fruitful of scientific results, yet he had many qualities that fitted him for the task. It must be remembered that Russia had in Bering's day but recently entered the field of science and that there was no background of scientific research such as permeated the England of the days of Captain Cook. Like the navigators, the scientists of Russia were mostly foreigners, and the administrative circles of St. Petersburg that organized the expedition had little interest in science. We must, therefore, look upon Bering as a soldier who was willing and anxious to perform the task assigned to him but who looked little beyond the orders received from his superiors. Then, too, he had to contend with that strong undercurrent of opposition to the new order of things that vexed Peter throughout his reign and that at times threatened to nullify the work of the great Tsar.

When Cook embarked on his famous voyage in 1776, five months had elapsed since he had received orders to explore the Pacific. Vessels were secured from the British navy and every facility provided for a successful execution of his task. When Bering received his orders, his ships were unbuilt and 4,000 miles of land separated him from the forests of Kamchatka where the timber was to be felled to construct the first Russian naval vessels on the Pacific. Before him lay the Herculean task of transporting supplies and equipment to the distant Kamchatka. His successful march across Asia, which took three years, and his overcoming the opposition of the local Siberian officials alone are sufficient to attest to his ability as a leader as well as to his determination to make the project a success. His ship's company included Martin Spanberg, a Dane, afterwards to distinguish himself by his exploration of the Kurile Islands, and Alexis Chirikof, a Russian, who was to share with Bering the honor of the discovery of the mainland of Alaska. Three years after leaving Moscow, the entire party had assembled at the Kamchatka River and had built two vessels, the *Fortuna* and the *Gabriel,* in which they sailed northward on July 26, 1728.

The course was laid to the north parallel to the coast, and several headlands and bays on the Siberian coast were sighted and named. On August 21 St. Lawrence Island was discovered and named, the first part of Alaska to be seen by a European. What was afterwards called Bering Straits was traversed in foggy weather while in view of the Siberian coast, but without report of the Diomede Islands or the Alaskan mainland beyond. The voyage was continued to latitude 67° 18′, which carried the expedition well into the Arctic. Returning, the vessels reached their starting point on September 2, having been gone a little more than a month. The following June (1729) Bering again put out to sea, this time taking an easterly course, to reach the reported land lying east of Kamchatka. Heavy winds blew him to the south, and he must have come close to the Commander Islands. This voyage closed after three weeks, having determined that no land lay within 150 miles of Kamchatka. Bering now set out for St. Petersburg where he arrived in March, 1730.

His report of results met with much criticism. To the simple-minded sailor, it appeared that his orders had been obeyed to the letter. He had proved to his own satisfaction that Asia and America were not connected. It was a fair inference from his explorations, as he states that by sailing westward he would have reached the Kolyma River and he so indicated on his chart.[21] He had not been ordered to go to the Kolyma and probably had some doubts as to whether the polar ice cap, already known to the Russians, would permit such a voyage. On his second voyage, he had sought land east of Kamchatka and failed to find it. Bering, having failed to see the Alaskan shore at Bering Straits, drew the fair inference that the American continent was far distant and that his orders did not contemplate an extensive eastern voyage. He had obeyed his orders as he understood them and now returned, anxious to obtain authorization for further explorations. The fact that he desired to extend his explorations proves both that he was no coward, as has been charged, and that his imagination had been excited by the voyages into unknown seas. While

[21] Dall, William H., "Early Expeditions to Bering Sea and Straits," Appendix 19, *Report for 1890, United States Coast and Geodetic Survey,* Washington, D.C., 1891.

Bering was preparing for his second expedition, others were extending the exploration towards Alaska.

The next expedition was a military one that had for its purpose the conquest of the turbulent Koriaks and Tchuckchus who had so long vexed the Russians of the Anadyr. Evidently "new lands" were to be looked for. Of the military aspects of this expedition, nothing need be said here except that they were unsuccessful. Important geographical results were obtained by one unit of these expeditions. This comprised a party under the leadership of Fedorof, but in which the surveyor Gvosdef was the leading spirit. Using one of Bering's vessels, the *Gabriel,* the party encircled the Peninsula of Kamchatka[22] and then traced the coast line northward to Bering Straits. Here the Diomede Islands were discovered and the adjacent parts of the mainland of North America. The mainland was termed the "Great Country," and its discovery confirmed the traditions that had long existed among the Russians of northeastern Siberia. Fedorof and Gvosdef are most likely the first Europeans to have seen any part of the mainland of Alaska. They, however, did not realize that this was the mainland and not an island, or that the coast of America had been found. Worthy of note is the fact that a mineralogist or "ore finder" by the name of Herdebal[23] accompanied the party. There is no record that this man made any report or investigation, but he was the first man to go to Alaska to find mineral wealth.

Meanwhile, Bering had laid before the authorities a plan to search for a continent beyond the seas. The Tsarina Anna appears to have had little interest in the project, but Bering had influential friends and through their efforts the plan was approved in spite of the opposition of the conservative element which was inimical to the foreigners in the Russian service.

In 1731, orders were issued to inaugurate the plan, but it was not until nine years later that the trans-Pacific voyage was actually begun. Bering's expedition is generally known as one which sought lands beyond the Pacific. It was, in fact, far more comprehensive than this. The orders of the navigator involved not only a search for the west coast of America but also an exploration to the south to Japan and one to the north to traverse the Arctic coast of

[22] Golder, *op. cit.,* pp. 160-162.

[23] Bancroft, *op. cit.,* p. 37.

Siberia. His little army included not only navigators and naval officers but also many scientists or alleged scientists, architects, engineers, and mechanics of all kinds. The plan was, indeed, a scientific exploration of Siberia and adjacent lands. If one were to venture on a guess based on the scanty records that have been published, it is that behind all this was the plan of some master mind which went far beyond the imagination of the simple Danish sailor whose principal desire seems to have been to traverse the ocean whose shores he had become familiar with. Whoever may have been responsible for the project, it is certain that this was the first comprehensive plan of scientific exploration in the history of the world. Indeed, it is only in very modern times that any government has attempted such a far-reaching survey of its possessions. Concerning the results of Bering's expedition other than those pertaining to Alaska, it is not proposed here to speak; but in estimating Bering's service to mankind, one should remember that these other fields of exploration were far more fruitful of results.

After years of toil and vexatious delay, Bering reached Okhotsk in 1737; there the two vessels, *St. Peter* and *St. Paul,* destined for the trans-Pacific exploration, were launched in 1740.[24] In the same year the two vessels sailed to Avacha Bay on the Kamchatka coast where the present town of Petropavlovsk was founded. Here the voyage was begun on June 4, 1741. The two vessels built for this voyage, which were brigs, were by far the largest that the Russians had then built on the Pacific; each was 80 feet long with about 108 tons burden. It is a significant fact that the smaller of the two vessels used by Captain Cook to explore the same seas some 30 years later was nearly three times the size of Bering's.

When Bering set forth on his momentous voyage, ten years had passed since the first order for the expedition had been given. During most of this time Bering had labored incessantly. He had organized expeditions for the exploration of the Arctic seaboard and of the Kurile Islands and Japan. He had established iron works, built ships, towns, and forts. He had worked under the constant strain

[24] The most complete accounts of this voyage are contained in the frequently referred to work by Frank A. Golder, *Russian Expansion on the Pacific,* and in George Davidson, "The Tracks and Landfalls of Bering and Chirikof on the Northwest Coast of America," a paper read before the Geographical Society of the Pacific on June 29, 1892, and since published in San Francisco in 1901.

caused by friction within this heterogeneous company brought from Moscow and with the local Siberian officials. Thousands of tons of supplies had been transported across Siberia, yet through no fault of his own, his own two vessels were but ill-equipped. Instead of a year and a half's supplies, he was provisioned for barely five months. Under this stress he had lost the elasticity of youth, and the great plan he had conceived of finding lands beyond the unknown seas now seems to have been reduced to the carrying out of his instructions. He was too well-trained a soldier not to obey his orders, but the quest for the unknown no longer seems to have inspired him. A man of 60, whose physical strength had been broken by long years of work and exposure in Siberia, could not be expected to evince the same enthusiasm for exploration as had been his when the plan was made. These conditions do not seem to have been taken into account by the many who have so severely criticized Bering.

Bering commanded the *St. Peter* and with him was the German naturalist, G. W. Steller, who was surgeon to the expedition. Lieutenant Alexis Chirikof, an able and experienced naval officer of Russian birth, commanded the *St. Paul.* Louis Delisle [de la Croyere], a man of adventurous disposition and half brother of Joseph Nicholas Delisle, the famous French astronomer, in the Russian service, accompanied Chirikof. Officers and crew numbered a total of 76 on each vessel, which necessitated close crowding and hence was one of the contributing causes that led to sickness among Bering's crew.

The charts of the day, notably the one furnished the expedition by the Admiralty, and drawn by Delisle the astronomer, showed a land mass southeast of Kamchatka known as Gama Land. In accordance with the Russian naval regulations, the council of officers, and not the commander, determined the route of the expedition. This council, made up of officers of both vessels, decided in opposition to Bering that a search for Gama Land should be made. There has been much criticism of this decision and the chart on which it was based. The chart was an attempt to reconcile the conflicting data at hand. Bering's voyage of 1729 had shown that there was no land for 150 miles east of Kamchatka, and it was logical, therefore, to seek it to the southeast where land had been reported. It was the duty of this expedition to lay its course for the nearest reported land mass and then, if this were not found, to sail into the unknown seas beyond. Therefore, the council should not be taken to task in first searching for the nearest reported land.

A southeast course was laid and both vessels set sail on June 4, 1741, keeping this direction in company for a distance of 600 miles, which carried them through the supposed Gama Land. This part of the purpose of the voyage being accomplished, a north-northeasterly course was set on June 12, and eight days later the vessels became separated in a storm. After some search for each other, both vessels took a general northeasterly course, and for the rest of the voyage they had quite different experiences.

Chirikof, in the *St. Paul,* was the first to make landfall, which he did on July 15. According to Davidson, this was about in latitude 55° 21′, or about the entrance to Chatham Straits. He then turned northward and probably near the latitude of Sitka came to anchor and sent a boat and ten men ashore for water. These not returning, the second boat was dispatched two days later. The next day two boats approached and were found to be full of natives. Chirikof decided his men had been captured or killed, and, as he had no other boats and a strong west wind was blowing, he was forced to weigh anchor and beat off the coast. He stood in and off for several days, but learned no more of the fate of his men. A council of the officers then decided that no further explorations were feasible. About one quarter of the crew and both ship's boats were lost. Davidson, whose long experience on the Alaskan coast well fitted him for interpretation of the records of this voyage, held that Chirikof's loss of boats was at Sitka Sound.[25]

Abandoning all hope of learning the fate of his men, Chirikof sailed northwestward to the mouth of Cook Inlet, thence southwestward along the shores of Kodiak Island. Without boats he could make no further landings, and the possibility of building a ship's boat does not seem to have occurred to him. He anchored in a bay of one of the westernmost of the Aleutian Islands, where he saw natives. Shortage of water, poor food, and the strain of the long voyage told on the health of his crew and many died,

[25] Professor Golder has suggested (p. 187) that the place of anchorage might have been Lituya Bay and that the boats were lost in the well-known rip tide of the very dangerous entrance. This interpretation does not fit with Davidson's computation of position, nor does Chirikof's description of the environment seem to correspond to the topography of Lituya Bay.

BERING'S LANDFALL

The sight of the snow-covered peak of Mount St. Elias in the distance (upper photo) led Bering to his first landfall in Alaska on July 16, 1741. He sent a boat ashore on July 19 in the vicinity of Kayak, Wingham, and Kanak islnads (lower photo). Photos by D. J. Miller.

including his two lieutenants. He reached Avacha on October 8,[26] he himself broken in health, and Delisle dying before he could be taken ashore. The following May he again sailed eastward to search for the American coast and his commander. He reached Attu and Atka, but because of storms soon returned.

Meanwhile, Bering in the *St. Peter* had made his first landfall by viewing the distant snow-covered summit of Mount St. Elias on July 16. The course steered was now westerly and northwesterly and on July 19 the now well-known navigator's guide, Cape St. Elias, a rocky headland with a detached pinnacle, was passed and named. The next

[26] Golder, *op. cit.*, p. 189.

day anchor was dropped near the southern end of Wingham Island and not far from the entrance to Controller Bay.

One boat was sent to explore the coast and probably visited Wingham Island and possibly Kayak Island, the latter lying north of the entrance to Controller Bay. The second boat was used to fill the fresh water casks and in this Steller, the naturalist, was allowed to go ashore. Bering seems to have had little interest in the work of this naturalist who had succeeded in antagonizing the entire ship's company. Poor Steller, who had had high hopes of scientific explorations, now found that his scientific work was to be limited to a few hours with but an ignorant Cossack assistant. He bewailed the fact that ten years had been spent in preparation for an expedition whose sole purpose seemed to be to fill the water casks. He soundly berates the commander and officers of the expedition for this, and not without justification. These simple seamen seem, on the other hand, to have regarded him as a rather disagreeable passenger who, while employed as surgeon, was constantly injecting himself into matters that did not concern him. Steller made the best of his meagre opportunities for his cherished scientific work. During the few hours spent on shore, he feverishly collected everything he could lay his hands on, and his notes on the brief excursion bear proof of his wide scientific interests. He was finally peremptorily called aboard and only obeyed orders when he was assured that the commander would sail without him. It is noteworthy that, as appears from records, this famous exploratory expedition made no actual landing on the mainland.

On the morning of July 21 Bering weighed anchor and laid a westerly course roughly parallel to the mainland. This precipitous departure from the goal he had so long sought has led to much adverse criticism of the great explorer. Anyone who has lain at anchor in the lee of Kayak Island when the ship rolled gently in the swell will wonder why Bering should have been in such haste to depart. Far different, however, is the aspect of the traveler should he lie at the same anchorage when the seas roll in under the influence of a southerly or southwesterly gale. Bering was on an uncharted coast line, on the lee shore. So far as he knew, he might have to beat out to sea to avoid shipwreck. A third of his crew were ill with scurvy. He had only provisions to take him back to his home port.

He could not winter on this strange coast; and if he was to avoid risk of starvation, he must turn westward at once. Moreover, he had obeyed his orders, the American coast had been found, and it was for him to return and report the results. There can be no doubt, too, that Bering's own loss of strength, for he was already an ill man, was an important factor in the decision. As a matter of fact, even had Bering lingered on the American coast, which at best could not have been more than a few weeks, it is unlikely that anything of great importance would have been discovered. A few bays would have been charted, a few more mountains sighted, and Steller would have increased his small collection.

The great object of the expedition, to find the American coast east of Siberia, was accomplished and the supplementing of this great accomplishment could well be left to future voyages. Moreover, the course that Bering laid on his return voyage, even if only by chance, was well calculated to secure further geographic information. Wind and fog, indeed, prevented his taking full toll of this opportunity, but as a matter of fact he traced the salient features of coast line from Kayak Island through to the Aleutian chain.

Bering's return voyage will not here be considered in detail. He saw Kodiak Island which he believed part of the mainland, sighted several of the higher peaks on the Alaska Peninsula, buried one of his crew, Shumagin, on one of the group of islands which still bears his name. The course lay to the southwest, paralleling the axis of the Alaska Peninsula and the Aleutian chain, and many elevated points were seen. There was now no thought of landing or exploration, for the scurvy was rapidly depleting the crew. The sole purpose of the ill commander was to save as many of his men as possible, though no doubt the duty of returning and reporting the results of the voyage was also an impelling motive in Bering's actions.

By October the crew was so depleted by death and sickness that they could no longer man the vessel. A landing was imperative, and when what is now the Commander Islands were sighted attempt was made to find anchorage. Two anchors were lost and the heavy seas carried the small craft over a reef into quiet waters. Landing was made on November 7, and finally the entire ship's company including the sick were sheltered in crude cabins, in part dugouts,

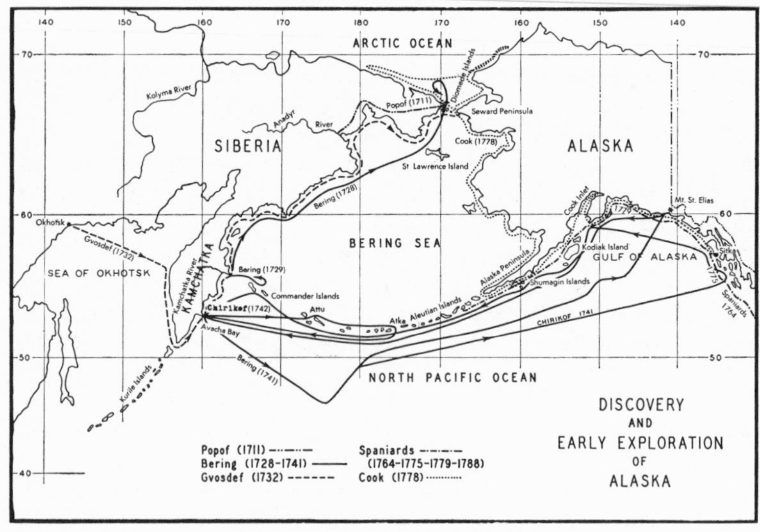

ROUTES OF EARLY EXPLORERS

in part built of driftwood. The vessel was cast ashore, and death rapidly carried off many of the survivors. Bering died on December 8.

Food was chiefly the meat of the sea otter, which were abundant on this uninhabited island, supplemented by some flour and rye meal saved from the wreck. By January the scurvy had disappeared, and the rest of the winter was passed without lack of food. In the following July, a 32-foot boat was built of the wreckage, and in this the 46 survivors sailed westward on August 14, reaching Avacha Bay on August 27. Among the survivors were Steller, the naturalist, whose journal offers a vivid picture of the voyage, and Waxel, the sailing master, who made the official report which as yet has not been published in complete form.

Bering's two vessels had established the larger contour of the Pacific seaboard of Alaska. Something had been learned of the Aleutian chain which, with the Commander Islands, links North America and Asia. Details of this coast line were lacking, and the concepts of the larger features were vague, but the long voyage that ended so tragically had fulfilled its chief purpose.

CHAPTER VIII

Explorations of Northwest Coast By Rival Nationalities

DRAKE'S voyage to the Pacific in 1579 with its raid on Spanish commerce was the first challenge to the Spanish domination of the Pacific seaboard of the continent. Though Drake's incursion was prophetic of the waning of Spanish rule in the Americas, it was for the time being simply an interruption and not a curtailment of Spanish ascendency. While Spain was to maintain her American colonies for upwards of two centuries yet, her oversea possessions won by Balboa, Cortez, and Pizarro were but little extended, and after the 16th century Spain contributed not greatly to geographic exploration.

The Russian activities on the North Pacific seaboard brought about for a time a renaissance of the old Spanish spirit of exploration and conquest.[1] As a consequence, the Viceroy of Mexico was ordered to extend Spanish settlement northward from Mexico and into the present state of California. San Diego and Monterey were founded in 1764, the latter becoming the seat of government of upper California, though under the Viceroy of New Spain as Mexico was then called.

Spain at this time had a large fleet on the Pacific, and her west coast ports gave her convenient points of departure for the exploration of the North Pacific, an advantage possessed by no other European nation. It is no wonder, then, that Spain too should have also played a part in Alaskan exploration; but it is indeed remarkable that, with every advantage of geographic position, she accomplished so little in this field. It should be noted that the extensive commerce between New Spain and the Philippines was carried on by voyages that did not reach into the higher latitudes. The westward voyage was made by way of Guam and the return by a more northerly route, both laid

[1] This revival was also caused by Spain's being driven out of Florida by the English in 1763. Spain, fearing a loss of the Atlantic seaboard, sought to recoup herself on the Pacific.

so as to take advantage of prevailing winds and ocean currents. One consequence was that, though Spanish navigators had encircled the Hawaiian Islands for centuries, it remained for the Englishman Cook to discover this archipelago.

Spanish occupation of California did not, however, end her attempt to invade the seas about which the Russians were bringing back information. Voyages of discovery, with plans of annexation, formed a part of this policy. The first expedition was under command of Juan Perez[2] who in 1774 was dispatched by Revillagigedo northward with instructions to reach the lands discovered by the Russians. He appears to have reached Dixon Entrance which marks the present southeast boundary of Alaska.[3] In 1775, Bruno Heceta was sent north with two vessels. The smaller, only 36 feet long, commanded by Lieutenant Juan Francisco Bodega y Quadra, alone reached Alaska.

The first landfall in Alaska appears to have been made near Sitka and, according to Bancroft, formal possession was taken at the first landing which was on either the Kruzof or Chichagof islands. A second landing was made on the west coast of Prince of Wales Island, and the ceremony of taking possession in the name of Spain was not omitted.

In 1779, a third expedition was sent out, commanded by Lieutenant Ignacio Arteaga in the *Princesa,* with a second vessel, the *Favorita,* commanded by Bodega y Quadra. They sailed to Bucareli Sound where landing had previously been made. After spending some time in charting the west coast of Prince of Wales Island, they continued their voyage to the northwest, passed St. Elias, entered Prince William Sound, and continued to the entrance to Cook Inlet.

This voyage seems to have satisfied the Spaniards that they had no rivals on the west coast as they had seen no settlements of Europeans, and it was not until after they had learned of the voyages of Cook and others and of the Russian settlements that they again became alarmed. By 1788, they had again taken up the work of extending their domain. Jose Martinez and Lopez de Haro were sent in two ships to learn of the aggressions of other nationalities.

---

[2] The data on Spanish exploration are largely from H. H. Bancroft, *The History of Alaska,* San Francisco, 1886.

[3] Bancroft, *op. cit.,* pp. 195-196.

These navigators entered Prince William Sound, explored Shelikof Straits, visited the Russian settlement at Three Saints Bay, and extended their voyage to Unalaska. They appear to have been thoroughly impressed with the fact that the Russians had occupied Northwest America and could not be ejected except by an armed force. A subsequent exploration of Prince William Sound practically ended Spanish contributions to the Alaskan coastal explorations, though something was later accomplished by the Italian Malaspina who sailed under the Spanish flag.

Names like Valdez, Cordova, and Revillagigedo commemorate the attempt of the dying Spanish Empire to add to its domain in these northern latitudes. The Spanish field of colonization had not been in northern latitudes, and the fur trade had never attracted this nation whose activities at development in the New World had been largely stimulated by the search for gold and silver.

While these feeble efforts at Spanish dominion of Alaska were being made, England turned her attention to the same field. As a result of the war with France, England controlled the entire Atlantic seaboard of North America. The enterprises of her fur traders had already given her the lands tributary to Hudson Bay. India and other distant possessions laid the foundations for the British Empire. The genius of William Pitt had inaugurated the epoch of modern England, though it was still to receive a serious check during the reactionary reign of George III.

The renaissance of exploration by Englishmen during the last half of the 18th century had resulted in many voyages, notably to the South Seas and Australia and to some fruitless searches for a westward passage from Hudson Bay. Among the many navigators none compared with Captain James Cook. Of humble origin, he had raised himself to become an officer of the British navy. Two important voyages by him had been made before he entered on the last which was to make him the greatest navigator of his time. When he was dispatched to the North Pacific by the British Admiralty, the possible political results were an important motive. It was well for England to become acquainted with these lands which were being occupied by the Russians and explored by the Spaniards. The principal motive was, however, the hope of a passage to the Pacific which would avoid the long voyage around the southern capes of Africa or America. Hudson Bay was known to possess no connection with the Pacific, but it was thought possible that a navigable route might be found northwest of Hudson Bay. Samuel Hearne of the Hudson Bay Company had, indeed, reached the Arctic Ocean at the mouth of Copper Mine River in 1771, and his report of ice fields would not, it seems, have encouraged further search for a northwest passage. Nevertheless, it remained to be proved that such a passage did not exist.

Cook's voyage was the first to be organized and carried out under a scientific banner. Himself a learned astronomer, he inspired his entire staff with the spirit of accuracy and research. This is in strong contrast to Bering's attitude, for he was but a simple sailor and soldier who had no grasp of scientific accuracy except so far as it related to his navigation. Bering had no comprehension of scientific research and tolerated rather than supported attempts at scientific observation.

Cook's orders were not to touch on any Spanish possessions unless driven by necessity and not to interfere with the subjects of any European state. His vessels were the *Discovery* (300 tons), commanded by himself, and the *Resolution* (462 tons), commanded by Captain Clerke, to whom fell the leadership of the expedition after Cook's death in the Hawaiian Islands. Among the other officers were the lieutenants James King, John Gore, and James Burney. The midshipmen were George Vancouver, George Dixon, and Nathaniel Portlock, who in later years were to extend Cook's Alaskan explorations. Worthy of mention also are Joseph Billings, an astronomical assistant who later led a Russian expedition into Alaskan waters, and John Ledyard, corporal of marines, a Connecticut Yankee whose more or less visionary schemes led Thomas Jefferson to organize the Lewis and Clark expedition. There is probably no greater measure of Cook's genius as a leader than the large number of his companions who were inspired to continue his explorations.

Cook sailed on July 12, 1776, hence eight days after the signing of the Declaration of Independence. As he lay at anchor in Portsmouth, three transports sailed loaded with English and Hessian troops to suppress the American rebels. Later, by special convention Cook's vessels were made exempt from capture. This was a recognition even before the voyage was completed of the international benefits expected from the expedition.

Cook reached the Pacific by way of Cape Horn and made important explorations in the South Seas. He then, according to his instructions, turned northward, sighted Cape Flattery, and visited Nootka Sound on Vancouver Island. He first fell in with the Alaskan coast in May, 1778, near the present site of Sitka, probably not far from the place where Chirikof had made his disastrous landing and where also the Spaniard, Bodega y Quadra, had made his first landfall three years before Cook sighted and named Mount Edgecumbe. Skirting the coast of Chichagof Island, he entered Cove Sound; thence he proceeded westward and named Mount Fairweather. He seems to have mistaken the mouth of the Alsek for an embayment and erroneously[4] recognized it as the scene of Bering's landing;[5] hence he called it "Bering Bay." He landed on the south side of Kayak[6] Island and here, to quote from his record, "at the foot of a tree on a little eminence not far from the shore I left a bottle with a paper in it on which were inscribed the names of our ships and the date of our discovery." Thus he took possession in the name of George III of the south side of an island, the north side of which had been visited by Bering a generation before. Wingham Island is also described, and Controller Bay was named though it was not explored. Prince William Sound was now entered and explored to about the entrance to Port Valdez which Cook decided would not afford any hope of a northeast passage.

His course now lay to the southwest, tracing the shore of Kenai Peninsula. Cook Inlet was entered and the volcanoes, St. Augustine and Mount Redoubt, recognized. Slowly beating his way up Cook Inlet, he finally dropped anchor in a cove at the south side of the entrance to Turnagain Arm. Here at Point Possession the ceremony of planting a bottle with records was not omitted. A ship's boat was sent to the head of Turnagain Arm, and the hope of finding a northeast passage was thus again blighted. Cook did not see the Susitna but supposed that the inlet which now bears his name was the mouth of a great river and that Turnagain Arm was also a river.[7]

A course was now set to the southwest paralleling the Alaska Peninsula and the adjacent islands. At the Shuma-

[4] There is a lagoon here called Dry Bay.

[5] Cook himself had questioned this identification.

[6] Named by Cook Kaye Island, but subsequently corrupted to Kayak.

[7] On the chart of his voyage the inlet is named Cook River, and Turnagain Arm is called Turnagain River.

gin Islands a native brought on board a letter written in Russian which Cook could not read; but it contained the dates 1776 and 1778, which he could make out, and thus he was apprised that he was entering the domain of the Russian fur trader.

The voyage was extended by rounding the Alaska Peninsula and exploring Bristol Bay, Norton Bay, and the southern shore of Seward Peninsula. The Bering Straits were then traversed, and then the Siberian coast as far as Cape North and the Alaskan coast as far as Icy Cape. Plans were made for a further exploration of these seas in the following season. This work was faithfully carried out by Clerke after Cook's death, but he too died on the voyage and the vessels returned to England under command of Gore, the senior lieutenant.

The most significant incident of Cook's voyage was his meeting with the Russians on Unalaska Island. Curiously enough, the first of Cook's command to meet with the Russians was John Ledyard, the American, who made an overland trip for this purpose. Cook was visited by the chief Russian trader, Gerasim Grigorovich Ismailof. From him he gained the impression that the Russians had but vague conceptions of the lands lying to the east. Either because of the lack of an interpreter or intentionally, the Russians gave Cook to understand that they had voyaged but little east of Unalaska. They knew of the mainland which they called "Alaschka."

Cook's contribution to geographic knowledge of Alaska comprises the actual tracing of the main features of the coast from the latitude of Sitka in the Pacific to Icy Cape in the Arctic Ocean. After the completion of his exploration, Alaska was practically outlined as it is today. He also brought confirmation of Bering's conclusion of there being no land connection between Asia and America. His results conclusively showed that there could be no waterway through the American continent, though this conclusion was not fully accepted until many years later.

Great as was Cook's contribution to the geography of the Alaskan coast, perhaps of still more lasting importance was his inauguration of a new era in the exploration of these northern waters. The vague and haphazard reports of the previous explorers were replaced by concise charts and accurate observations, many of which have stood the test of more detailed investigation.

Cook's officers and crew had secured by barter a number of sea otter skins on the Alaskan coast. They had little idea of their value until they offered them for sale at Macao, on the Chinese coast, where they touched on their return voyage. To the surprise of these seamen, who knew nothing of the fur trade, these sea otter sold at what seemed to be fabulous sums, considering that their cost was only that of a few trinkets and some pieces of iron.

Both officers and crew now had visions of fabulous profits to be made out of this fur trade, and in spite of the rigid discipline there was almost a mutiny among the seamen who desired to return and engage in this lucrative traffic. Upon their return to England in 1780, the news of the value of the sea otter pelts was soon noised abroad and was for a time to have much influence on the exploration of the Alaskan coast. It is a significant fact that it was the sea otter skins brought back by Bering's crew that led the Russians to Alaska and the sea otter skins secured by Cook's crew which brought the English to the coast of Alaska.

Up to this time the Russians, probably for lack of skillful seamen, had not taken advantage of the direct sea route to China from the Alaskan fur fields. This new trade route was, therefore, still open when Cook's voyage showed its commercial importance. The first of the merchant marine to make this voyage appears to have been Captain James Hanna, an Englishman, who under the Portuguese flag sailed from China to King George Sound on the British Columbia coast in 1785 and returned with a rich cargo of furs. Others followed his example, and the English fur trader soon became a familiar figure on the northwest coast of the continent.

In the same year as Hanna's voyage, two of Cook's officers, George Dixon and Nathaniel Portlock, set sail from England under a charter from the South Sea Company on a trading voyage to the northwest coast. They reached Cook Inlet the following year and here encountered Russian traders. They wintered in the Hawaiian Islands, and the following year returned to the northwest coast. Their cargo of furs was disposed of in China, and the vessels returned to England. While the aim of this voyage was commercial, yet the training of Dixon and Portlock under Cook led them to make many scientific observations.

The fame of the new fur country reported by Cook was

to extend to New England where nine ship owners began to think of the Pacific as a new field for ventures. Probably John Ledyard's return to his Connecticut home after his desertion from the British navy had some influence. Ledyard made an attempt to interest American ship owners in a trading voyage to the Pacific, for he was possessed with the idea of returning to the scenes of his adventures with Cook. He then made a similar attempt in London. In both he was unsuccessful, so he later went to Paris to obtain support. There his venturous mind conceived a new plan, that of reaching the Pacific by a land journey across Siberia. This he talked over with Thomas Jefferson, then American Minister to France. With only scant funds he finally started on this wild project, but was later turned back by Russian authorities.

Though Ledyard died without seeing his hopes realized, yet the project which he proposed and which was scoffed at by the ship owners of that time was actually entered upon by Boston merchants not ten years later. In 1787, the *Lady Washington,* commanded by Robert Gray, and the *Columbia,* commanded by Robert Kendrick, set sail from Boston for the northwest coast. Kendrick was the senior commander, but Gray was the more enterprising of the two. They reached Nootka in the same year. Gray subsequently explored waters lying on the west side of Queen Charlotte Island and visited the southern part of what is now Southeastern Alaska. Gray returned to Boston by way of China, being the first to carry the American flag around the world. In a later voyage in 1790 he appears to have again visited the southeastern part of Alaska, but his important contribution to geography was the discovery of the Columbia River.

The voyages of Gray, Dixon, and Portlock were but conspicuous examples of the many made to the northwest coast for furs. This trade was regarded with apprehension by the Russians and Spaniards. Of the vast coast line stretching from California to the Aleutian Islands, the Spaniards were in possession of the southeastern and the Russians of the northwestern part. In between, lay thousands of miles of no man's land, claimed, however, by Russia on the basis of Bering's discovery; by England because of Cook's voyage and subsequent visits of English ships; and by Spain by virtue of both her ancient right to the Pacific seaboard and the acts of acquisition made by the Spanish navigators as already recorded. The dispute between England and Spain, a waning power, was to be settled soon, that between England and Russia a quarter of a century later. A relic of the latter dispute was inherited by the United States, in the Alaskan boundary dispute that was not settled until nearly a century after the first questions of jurisdiction arose.

Spain was not, however, to relinquish her ancient claim to the west coast of North America without a protest. The explorers dispatched by the Viceroy of Mexico in the last quarter of the 18th century had found a vast stretch of the coast line as far north and west as Kodiak still unoccupied by the Russians or any other Europeans. To this Spain laid claim, both on the basis of ancient rights and by virtue of the discoveries chronicled above.

The report of Haro's voyage of 1788 had alarmed the Spanish government as to Russian aggression, and hence in 1789 the shadowy Spanish title to the northern coast line was asserted in more definite form by the formal act of taking possession of Nootka Sound on the west coast of Vancouver Island. This excellent harbor was at that time already a favorite rendezvous of English traders. To substantiate their claim to this coast, the Spaniards seized two English trading vessels at Nootka and thus came into direct conflict with British interests. The matter was settled by the Nootka Convention, signed by Spain and England in 1790. By the terms of this treaty British subjects had an equal right with Spain to settle and trade on this northwest coast, so long as the lands were not already held by Spain. The treaty was mutual and reciprocal, but as England had no possessions on the west coast, the advantage lay all with her. Moreover, trading rights were of no use to Spain, as she had no interest in furs. Spain was forced to this humiliating position, for with the French Revolution she was isolated and her power was on the wane, though her government had successfully resisted the political reconnaissance inaugurated by the great French upheaval. The treaty was of particular benefit to Americans as it in effect left the trade open to all comers and in this respect legalized Gray's incursion into what was nominally a Spanish possession.

One of the important results of this convention was the dispatching of George Vancouver to the northwest coast. His mission was twofold: he was to take over Nootka Sound from the Spaniards and he was to survey the coast from the 35th to the 60th parallels—that is, from what is now central California to Cook Inlet, a distance of 2,500 miles. In other words, he was to bring back information about the little-known coast line which tied together the Spanish possessions on the south and the lands on the north which were already in the possession of the Russian fur trader.

The English fur traders had already invaded this zone and the Spaniards been virtually ejected by the convention of 1790, which provided that trading privileges were to be free to all nations and which, in practical effect, advanced the British interests. It remained, however, not only to learn more of this no man's land but also by an official survey to strengthen England's claims at some time in the future. England had lost her American colonies except for Canada. The Canadian fur hunters had already established posts within 500 miles of the Pacific, and indeed, though it was unknown in England, Alexander Mackenzie had already started on his canoe voyage across the continent.

Therefore, Vancouver's expedition was based on a far-sighted piece of statesmanship. Chiefly as a result of it, England was later able to lay claim to what is now the British Columbia coast and thus make Canada a continental power and not an Atlantic province. Were it not for Gray's discovery of the Columbia River at this time, there is strong reason to believe that England might have made good her claim to what is now Oregon and Washington. The charting of the coast line, now frequented by English ships, and an alleged search for the mythical northeast passage afforded a good excuse for Vancouver's voyage, so that the large reasons of statecraft could be kept entirely in the background. It is quite likely that even Vancouver himself had no more than a vague conception of the real purpose of this voyage. Be that as it may, the expedition was manned and equipped with a view of maintaining the same high scientific ideals established by Cook under whom Vancouver had obtained his training.

Vancouver's own vessel was the *Discovery,* a sloop of war with 20 guns, manned by 100 men. With him went the tender *Chatham,* armed with ten guns and with a crew of men under the command of W. R. Broughton. Archibald Menzies accompanied the expedition as surgeon and botanist. The voyage was started on April 1, 1791, and a course laid to the Pacific around Cape of Good Hope. A year later Vancouver fell in with the American coast near Cape Mendocino. Sailing northward, he next encountered Captain Gray who reported the discovery of the Columbia River. Exploring Puget Sound and then encircling Vancouver Island on the east, he reached Nootka in August. Here the Spanish commander, Bodega y Quadra, politely but firmly refused to vacate the sound, and the first part of the plan—namely, the ejecting of the Spaniards—went temporarily amiss, though they later did withdraw to their California colony.

Of Vancouver's explorations and surveys to the north which occupied him about a year, it is not necessary here to speak. He sailed north again in the summer of 1793, and in July obtained his first view of what is now Alaska, at the entrance of what he named Portland Canal. The winding passage of the fiord he traced to its head, and his charts and descriptions were destined more than a century later to play an important part in the boundary controversy between Canada and the United States.

Vancouver's voyage of this year took him as far north as the mouth of the Stikine River, which, however, he did not recognize as a river. It is rather remarkable that, with all the painstaking accuracy of Vancouver's survey, he failed to discover the mouths of the several large rivers which he passed. This is true not only of the Stikine, but also of the Columbia, Fraser, Copper, and Susitna. After another voyage to the south for the winter, Vancouver again turned north, and April 1794 finds him entering Cook Inlet. At the upper end of this inlet he found the Russians already in possession, and they informed him that they had been there four years and also that there were Russian posts at Kayak Island and on Prince William Sound. Vancouver charted Turnagain Arm and Knik Arm, though the latter he called a river. Later he made surveys in Prince William Sound, visiting Port Etches where he was well received by the chief of the Russian post. He learned of the Russian post at Kodiak and also of the shipyard on Resurrection Bay, near the present site of Seward. The coast was now traced southeastward and Yakutat Bay visited, referred to by Vancouver as Port Mulgrave. There were no Russian posts here, but there was a large fleet of native boats under charge of Russians searching for sea otter. He later entered Cross Sound, passed through Icy

Strait, surveyed Lynn Canal, and carried his mapping southward to connect with that of previous years, completing the work in August, 1794.

Vancouver evidently regarded that part of Alaska lying west of Ann Sound as already belonging to Russia, but from Cross Sound southward he considered a new land. He called it New Norfolk as far as Prince of Wales Island. Southward, thence, along the present coast of Alaska and British Columbia he called New Cornwall; and south of this lay New Georgia and New Hanover. He clearly shows by these names the main purpose of his expedition, which was to lay claim in the name of King George of England to all the coastal strip from Spanish California to Russian America.

These hopes of annexation were only in part to be fulfilled, but Vancouver's remarkable voyage and the resulting charting will stand as one of the most notable achievements of mensuration. In three summers he and his associates had charted literally thousands of miles of unknown coast line, and his work stood the test of later navigators for over a century. It has been only the recent refinements of coastal surveys that have made it possible to supersede Vancouver's charts. His would have been a difficult task even in the age of steam, but to thread the intricate waterways of this region with their dangerous rip tides in sailing vessels, penetrating every irregularity of the broken coast line, was little short of marvelous.

The service rendered by Cook and Vancouver in exploring the Alaskan coast is permanently recorded in many of the geographic names now seen on the charts. Among them are Portland Canal, Prince of Wales Island, Frederick Sound, Lynn Canal, Admiralty Island, Cross Sound, Prince William Sound, Cook Inlet, Norton Sound, Cape Lisburne, and a host of others.

Vancouver's detailed examination of almost the entire coast line connecting the Spanish colonies on the south and the Russian possessions on the north left little for others to do except to fill in the detail. Much of this work, so far as the Alaskan shore line is concerned, was done by the Russians before the transfer of the Territory. Other nationalities, however, also took part, even before Vancouver's voyage.

The French made an effort to establish some claim to the lands made known through Cook's voyage. In 1785 Jean

Francois de Galoup la Perouse, in command of an elaborate scientific expedition including two vessels, was sent to explore the Pacific. He reached the Alaskan coast near Mount St. Elias and went to Lituya Bay where he lost two of his ship's boats in an attempt to explore this dangerous inlet. This was his only contribution to Alaskan exploration, and later both ships and all hands were lost under circumstances that have never been revealed. Fortunately, the record of the early part of this voyage had been transmitted to Paris, and it preserves the record of a careful, scientific investigator. Soon after Louis XVI had dispatched La Perouse, the Revolution broke out, so even had he returned, France would have been in no position to follow his recommendation of invading this new field of fur trade. This voyage was one of the last acts of the old regime, and it is fortunate that during the turmoil of the Revolution La Perouse's valuable report was not lost and was given to the world by Napoleon.

The last attempt at Spanish exploration in these waters was that of Alessandro Malaspina, who traced the shore line with two vessels from Sitka to Prince William Sound in 1791. This one voyage is especially associated with Mount St. Elias, for Malaspina was the first to measure its altitude and, although his measurement was more than 2,000 feet in error, it was more nearly correct than any made later until an accurate triangulation was accomplished in 1892. Malaspina was an Italian, the only one of that nationality to contribute to the knowledge of Alaskan geography until a century later when Prince Luigi made the first ascent of the peak which his countryman had been the first to measure. Malaspina's name is now attached to one of the great piedmont glaciers which has its source in the St. Elias Range.

While the rival nationalities were striving for rights along the northwest coast line, the French, and later the English, fur traders were heading for the same goal by an overland route from the east. The Hudson Bay Company, during the last half of the 18th century, gradually extended its domain to the westward and dispatched several expeditions to seek a waterway to the Pacific. Long before this, the French fur hunters had penetrated the region beyond the Great Lakes. About the time of Bering's discovery of Alaska, Verandrye had reached the foothills of the Rockies from the upper Missouri basin. Ten years later another pioneer trader established a post at the present site of Calgary, Alberta, at the very base of the Rocky Mountains and only 500 miles from Pacific waters. This, with all the other western posts, was abandoned when Canada in 1763 passed into the hands of the English.

Henceforth, the English fur trade gradually expanded into the region which had been pioneered by the French. The Rocky Mountain barrier for a long time marked the limits of this westerly fur trade. It remained for Alexander Mackenzie to surmount this barrier and to introduce a new factor into the development of Alaska. Mackenzie, who was a member of the Northwestern Fur Company, the great rival of the Hudson Bay Company, ascended the Peace River from Lake Athabasca, crossed the Rockies, then traversed the headwaters of the Fraser, and, after crossing the Coast Range, reached Pacific waters in the latitude of Queen Charlotte Sound. This journey, which was the first made across the continent north of Mexico, was accomplished in 1793, at the same time that Vancouver was surveying adjacent waters. It was the forerunner of the fierce rivalry which was to spring up between the two great competitors in the fur trade, the Russian American and the Hudson Bay companies.

Meanwhile, a new era for Russia had dawned under the reign of that remarkable sovereign, Catherine II. Her attention, it is said, was directed to her American possessions by the account of the Russian discoveries in America published by the Englishman, William Coxe, which, it is said, she had translated into Russian for her own perusal. Be this as it may, Catherine had the breadth of view to realize the importance of a Russian expedition to this field, a plan suggested and supported by Pallas, the astronomer. The matter was brought to a focus by the report of La Perouse's expedition having sailed on a similar mission.

Joseph Billings was chosen as commander of this expedition more because he had been with Cook, holding the position of assistant astronomer, than because of any particular ability. The party made its way across Siberia by the usual route, to be described in the following chapter. At Yakutsk they encountered the American, Ledyard, who was bound on a somewhat similar mission but on his own initiative. Ledyard, who had received a safe-conduct from Catherine, was arrested while with Billings at Yakutsk and forced to return to Europe. No reason for this action is given, but it is probable that Catherine, after his departure from St. Petersburg, saw in his journey a possible rival to Billings' and took this summary way of getting rid of him.

Billings sailed from Kamchatka in 1789 and, passing through Bering Straits, penetrated the Arctic Ocean to about latitude 69° and then returned to Kamchatka. In 1790 he made a second start, and the two vessels of the expedition, after stops at Unalaska and Kodiak, reached Prince William Sound and then again returned to the point of debarkation. In the following year, a third start was made, and Billings once more reached Unalaska, whence he sailed northward, touching at the Pribilof Islands, Seward Peninsula, and St. Lawrence Island. Billings himself was afterwards landed on the Tchuckchu Peninsula in Siberia where he made a hazardous, but apparently bootless, journey inland. The two vessels wintered at Illiutluk, Unalaska Island, and the following year returned to Kamchatka. Elaborate orders had been issued for the conduct of the expedition, which in its preparation and execution had cost seven years of time and large sums of money, yet it accomplished relatively little. Probably its most important result was the directing of the attention of St. Petersburg authorities to the abuse of the natives by the Russian fur hunters. Billings laid special emphasis on these cruelties in his official report, an extract from which reads:

> The hunters were accustomed to act as follows: Upon the arrival of any vessel at an inhabited island the Peredovchik [chief of hunters] sent an armed boat to the habitations to take from the natives all furs and valuable articles they possessed and if the least opposition was made they were silenced by the muskets of the hunters. Wives were taken from their husbands and daughters from their mothers; indeed the barbarities of these subduers to the crown of Russia is not to be described. They used, not infrequently, to place men close together and try through how many the ball of their rifle-barreled musket would pass. Nor were the hunters more kind to their own brethren, for if two parties in different interests met, they fought together for the possession of the natives or formed themselves in one company.

No doubt, attempting to stop this abuse was an important influence in the granting of monopolistic control of Russian America to a single corporation. It is the development of this company and its rule of Alaska that must next be considered; but first a discussion, in the two following chapters, of the conditions and the people that prepared the way for the Russian American Company and governed much of its activity is necessary.

CHAPTER IX

Routes of Commerce In Russian America

MAN'S advances in a new land are primarily controlled by geographic features. The extent of this control is in more or less direct proportion to the degree of his civilization. An ocean or turbulent glacial river or mountain barrier which might entirely check the wanderings of savage tribes can be overcome by means available to civilized man. Each stage of advancement in civilization gives man greater power in surmounting physical obstacles. The sailing ship can traverse oceans unnavigable for the primitive dugout; the steamer makes accessible to commerce regions almost impossible to wind-driven vessels. The upper part of Cook Inlet, now an established route of commerce, was almost inaccessible to the cumbersome sailing vessels of the Russians. The Russian settlements in Alaska—for example, Sitka, Kodiak, Nuchek, Unalaska—were all near the open sea because such ports could be entered readily by sailing ships. Now that steamers are used, many of the most important Alaskan ports—for example, Ketchikan, Juneau, Cordova, Valdez, Anchorage—can only be reached through constricted channels, many with strong tides and ill-situated for wind-borne commerce.

Before a presentation of the early development of transportation routes in Alaska, it will be desirable to review briefly some of the geographic factors which have controlled them. These include (1) position relative to other land masses, (2) extent and character of coast line, (3) mountain barriers, and (4) watercourses. Climate affects all these factors; for example, in determining the prevailing winds and ice-free ports, in ocean navigation, in snow and ice on mountain barriers and watercourses.

The proximity of Alaska to Siberia has already been shown to be the reason that Alaska was explored and first settled from the west. That this first invasion came by the Aleutian chain and not by Bering Straits is due to the short open season for open navigation in the north part of Bering Sea.

Alaska, as we have seen, thrusts out as a peninsula into the Pacific. Bering Sea and the Arctic Ocean give her an enormous shore line which greatly accelerated the exploration of her littoral. As was indicated in the previous chapter, within a century after Bering's discovery, the larger features of Alaska's shore line had been traced; but the full exploration of her watercourses promises to take nearly another century. The broken shore line of the Pacific seaboard of the Territory, with its fringes of islands, many harbors, and deep water close to land, favored settlement and made large areas accessible from tidewater. Furthermore, these coastal waterways, except for parts of Cook Inlet, are ice-free throughout the year. On the other hand, the strong tides and currents caused by the irregular coast afforded serious difficulties to the early navigation by sailing ships. In strong contrast to the southern coast line are the smooth shores with but few harbors and with shoal waters far from the land that mark the prevailing littoral of northern Bering Sea and the Arctic Ocean. Then, too, these northern waters are locked in ice for a large part of each year. Where these conditions prevailed, the Russians had only one settlement, St. Michael, and that only because it was absolutely essential for the fur trade of the Yukon.

The great mountain barrier of southern Alaska, stretching from Dixon Entrance to the head of Cook Inlet, effectually shut the Russians out of any direct route into the interior. It was broken by the valleys of a number of turbulent rivers such as the Stikine, Chilkat, Alsek, and Copper, and by numerous passes such as the Chilkoot, White, and Thompson, all of which have been used as routes of approach to the interior by the white man since the Russians ceded their territory. The snow and glaciers of the mountain barrier have been and still are a serious obstacle to routes of transportation. The Russians, however, explored and exploited areas in the lower Yukon and Kuskokwim valleys, which open up invitingly on the eastern shore of Bering Sea. Those great arteries of travel and commerce which until recently have been the sole means of reaching the great inland region beyond the mountains were never fully utilized by the Russians, for they had neither the enterprise nor the means of using this great system of navigable waters. For their crude boats, the upper Yukon and Kuskokwim rivers were entirely unnavigable.

Russian America remained throughout its history an isolated possession difficult of access and without organized means of internal communication. Sitka, its capital, lay across 2,300 miles of the stormy waters of the Pacific from

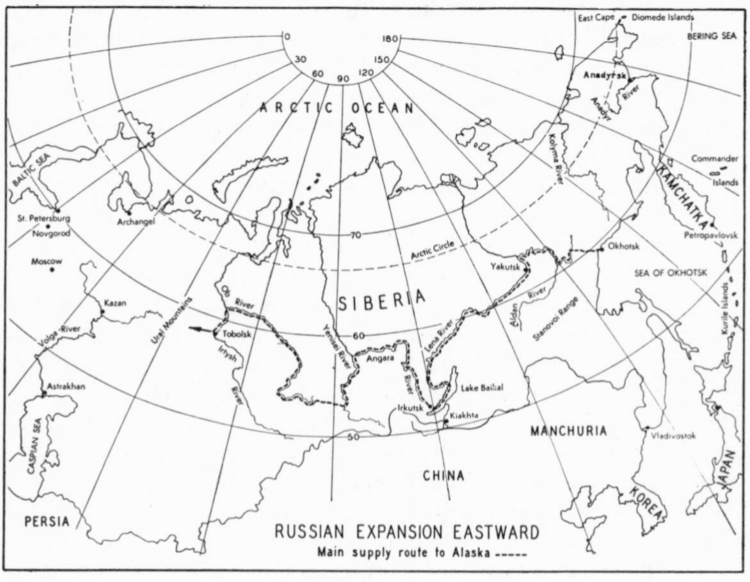

RUSSIAN ROUTES IN SIBERIA

Petropavlovsk on the east shore of Kamchatka, the nearest Siberian port. This port in turn was chiefly supplied from Irkutsk in central Siberia. The route of communication between these two places was by sea to Okhotsk, a port open to navigation only for a part of the year, and thence by a nearly 3,000 mile overland and river journey to Irkutsk. After 1803, direct ocean communication from the Baltic to the Pacific ports was indeed established. But this involved a voyage of nearly 20,000 miles, encircling Africa and, indeed, half the globe. Up to the close of the Russian occupation of America, the direct ocean route was used only to supplement transportation by the land route. This was in part because the Russian expansion has always been by land and not by sea, and in part because one of the principal markets for Alaskan furs was in Asia and not in Europe. Because of these conditions, commerce with Russian America was beset with such great difficulties as to check the industrial development of the colony, and this fact in turn led to its ultimate transfer to the United States.

Both the relief and the watercourses of Asia favored the trade route across Siberia. The great cordillera of Central Asia reaches only into southern and eastern Siberia, while north and west of the mountains is a province of plains and low uplands traversed by many large northerly-flowing rivers. To consider the geographic features of the trans-Siberian trade route in greater detail:

The low Ural Mountains are no serious barrier to advance from Europe into Asia, for their many broad passes offer easy routes of communication. From the base of the Urals a broad area of low relief sweeps eastward three-quarters of the distance to the Pacific and southward to the foothills of the great *massif* of Central Asia. This province, generally known as the "Great Siberian Plains," though it includes enormous lowlands, is not strictly a plain. East of the Ob River it includes many rolling upland areas, broken however by many broad river valleys, and entirely devoid of any high crest lines that might prove an obstacle to man's advance.

It is the great river systems of northern Siberia which especially favored routes of communication. These great northerly-flowing rivers with their interlocking tributaries separated by only low passes have given the physical conditions favoring the trade routes across northern Siberia. The three largest river basins whose waters determine these routes are the Ob, the Yenisei, and the Lena. From eastern tributaries of the Ob, it is only a short portage across to the Yenisei, which in turn has one of its sources in Lake Baikal. One of the tributaries of the Lena rises not far from Lake Baikal. Therefore, only two short portages separate the Ob waters from those of the Lena, whose most easterly point near Yakutsk lies by air line over 2,000 miles from the Urals. In summer all these rivers were navigable for the crude boats of the Cossacks, and their smooth surface afforded a favorable winter route of travel.

East of the Lena River, the physical conditions were quite different. Here the rugged Stanovoi Range forms a barrier between the navigable waters of the Lena and the Pacific at the Sea of Okhotsk. These mountains are an offshoot from the great *massif* and stretch northeasterly as a Pacific coastal barrier into the little-known regions of northeastern Siberia. To the northeast they appear to lose their identity, merging into an upland region of no great altitude. As has been previously pointed out, the first traversing of these mountains by the Cossacks was in the headwaters region of the Kolyma, whose waters are separated by only low passes from streams tributary to the Anadyr River flowing into Bering Sea; and later they found a route through the Stanovoi Mountains from the Aldan, a tributary of the Lena, to the Sea of Okhotsk. This became the main trade route to the Pacific and hence a part of the line of communication with Russian America.

One other feature affecting trade routes across Siberia deserves notice; that is, that the Amur River, whose headwaters interlock with southern tributaries of Lake Baikal, traverses the mountain systems of eastern Asia and affords a ready egress to the Pacific. For more than a century Russia struggled to obtain control of this natural highway, but it was not until the treaty of 1859 with China that control of its navigation was secured. This resulted at once in the shifting of the trans-Siberian trade route from the Lena southward to the Amur. This change came, however, too late to affect the communication with Russian America.

There is a rather striking parallel in the trans-Siberian trade route with that across Canada in the early days of expansion toward the Pacific. In both instances the interlocking arms of great river systems furnished feasible routes for the fur hunter and trader. In Siberia, the waterways on the east reached a coastal barrier; in Canada, the cordillera on the west long held in check the extension of the fur trade to the Pacific. The Canadian voyageur, however, found routes to the Yukon basin through this barrier which required no long portages, while until the Amur River route was opened the Russian was forced to cross the high Stanovoi Range. On reaching the Pacific, the Russian, with his lack of seafaring traditions, used open transport only as he had to, while the Englishman on the other hand, with more than a thousand years of seafaring history, at once took advantage of the ocean-borne commerce. Thus, while Russian America was supplied by means of the long overland Siberian route, commerce with the Hudson Bay factors on the Pacific was by means of vessels encircling Cape Horn. Under such a decided handicap, it is not to be wondered at that the Pacific coast fur trade, even including Southeastern Alaska, fell to the Hudson Bay rather than to the Russian American Company.

It will be well to recall here the physical features of Russian America so far as they affect commerce. The Pacific seaboard, where the principal Russian settlements were located, is separated from the interior by a rugged mountain barrier, broken only by a few rivers like the Stikine and Copper which could be ascended only with great difficulty by the clumsy Russian boats. The Susitna River, indeed, afforded more favorable conditions; but because of the difficulty of navigating the upper Cook Inlet, this was not adopted by the Russians as an inland route. The mouths of the great Kuskokwim and Yukon rivers were blocked by ice for eight months in the year, and this fact will perhaps account for the small use made of these great highways into the interior.

The broken shore line of the Pacific littoral afforded an infinite number of harbors, ice-free throughout the year. Only the upper part of Cook Inlet was ice-bound during the winter months. Furthermore, the strong tides and heavy winds, with a consequent choppy sea, made the head of Cook Inlet relatively inaccessible to the sailing vessels of the Russians. The difficulties of navigating these waters are indicated by the following extract from the official Russian sailing manual:[1]

> It is difficult to convey an idea of the choppy sea [in Cook Inlet]. The roaring sea boils with short steep waves rising in all directions. The crests of the billows, often even the billows themselves, tumble down upon the ships, pitching violently among them. Even with a strong favorable wind the lower sails often lie against the mast while the upper ones are filled. The ship obeys the helm with difficulty, or not at all. All the hatches have to be closed, everything has to be made fast, and nothing can be done but try to keep the course. In the autumn the chopping seas are fierce and more dangerous.

This description serves to account for the fact that the Russians never fully occupied the head of Cook Inlet or harvested the rich fur fields of the Susitna River basin. Indeed, their principal approach to this province was across the Portage Glacier from Prince William Sound, thus avoiding the navigation of Cook Inlet.

The fogs and innumerable rocks and reefs, together with the strong currents of the broken Pacific littoral, presented

[1] Tebenkof, M. D., *Hydrographic Notes to the Northwest Shores of America*, St. Petersburg, 1852.

many dangers to Russian navigation. Their principal settlements, such as Dutch Harbor, Nuchek, Kodiak, Yakutat, and Sitka, lay near the open sea and were more readily accessible to sailing ships than are the modern towns of Ketchikan, Juneau, Skagway, Cordova, and Valdez, which are only conveniently reached by steam-driven vessels. These geographic conditions, though imposing serious difficulties, would not have greatly retarded the commerce of seafaring peoples like the Americans, the British, and the Dutch. The Russians, however, had always been a land folk. Their development of a naval and merchant marine during the 18th and 19th centuries was not a natural evolution, but was largely superimposed by an autocratic government upon a people which had no seafaring traditions. Russia had no great littoral population to draw upon, as had the nations of the West. Her northern ports, first on the White Sea and later on the Baltic, were locked in ice for a good part of the year. Even after she gained a foothold on the Black Sea, the free outlet to Europe was blocked by the Turk at the Dardanelles. Russia had, therefore, no fishing folk from whom to draw seamen, and for generations many even of her naval officers came from other countries.

The Cossack freebooters who overran Siberia during the 17th century when they started at the Urals were essentially landsmen, but during their century of advance they perforce acquired knowledge of river navigation, since the easiest routes of advance were along the great northern river system of Siberia. Therefore, when they reached the Pacific, they had become skilled in the construction and use of the small river crafts which they had used for the transportation of supplies and pelts.

Incidental to the conquest of Siberia and the harvesting of its rich fur resources, another and more daring type of boatman was developed. This was the north-coastal navigator who in his search for furs found means to overcome the difficulties of traversing the shallow polar sea with its constant menace of drift ice. Even before Yermak began the conquest of Siberia in 1579, the Russian fur hunters had traced the shore line eastward from Archangel as far as the mouth of the Ob River, and during the following century their successors extended their voyages nearly to Bering Straits. These daring voyages were made in vessels constructed without the use of nails. The smaller boats were made by hollowing out logs, the sides being built up with crude planks lashed together by woody fibres, chiefly willow, or by leather thongs. Larger boats appear to have been clinker built on a framework, but all were fastened together by lashing. Moss was used for caulking, made waterproof by gum from coniferous trees. The boats were provided with lugger sails of reindeer hides, which also furnished the material for rigging. The larger boats were decked and were 30 to 40 feet in length with a 12- or 15-foot beam. Anchors were fashioned of roots weighted with stones lashed to them. It was in such primitive craft, guided by men who knew nothing of the use of the compass, that the ice-bound shore of northern Siberia was traced. These ignorant men added but little to geographic knowledge, for their concept of charts was very crude. Yet their successors were to aid Russian expansion across the Pacific. Primitive as was their knowledge of the sea, they were the only sailors that Russia had to draw upon on her distant eastern seaboard.

During the century of the conquest of Siberia which developed the Cossack boatman and the coastal navigator, relatively little advance was made in European Russia in the matter of ocean transport. Since the days of Peter the Great Russia's driving force has been to seek an outlet to the sea, and most of her wars have been to this end. Locked in the ice on the north, blocked by the Turkish forts on the Dardanelles, clashing with Japan at Port Arthur, and prevented by Great Britain from seeking an outlet through Persia, she has vainly sought to become a maritime power. One result is that Russia's foreign commerce has been chiefly by land, and her commercial like her political expansion has been eastward into Asia rather than by sea routes. Russia's merchant adventurers up to the 19th century sought their profits along the caravan routes of Asia rather than in distant seas.

It was the fur trade of America that first drew Russian commerce overseas, and the Russian American Company was the first corporation to venture beyond the continental limits. Russia's first real maritime commerce developed on the Pacific in the 19th century. Methods and means for this commerce, known for many centuries to the people of western Europe, had to be gradually developed. There is good reason, therefore, for Russia's apparent lack of developing efficient direct-ocean transport to the American colony and giving preference to the long and difficult land route to the Pacific.

Such were the general features of the overland Siberian trade route and the conditions under which it was developed. Now it will be well to trace it in somewhat greater detail. It will not be necessary to consider the Amur River route since it was not used until after the middle of the 19th century and hence played no important part in the Russian American commerce. It was, however, somewhat used by the Russian American Company as early as 1854, though not officially recognized until 1857, when it was seized by order of the Tsar. In 1860 China was forced to recognize this annexation by treaty, which also released to Russia the Manchurian territory north of Korea. This gave Russia Vladivostok, later to become the Pacific terminal of the Trans-Siberian Railroad. This port, being ice-bound for a part of the year, did not meet the Russian needs completely, a fact which led to further advances southward and the seizure of Port Arthur—from which Russia was ejected by Japan half a century later.

Irkutsk, the capital of eastern Siberia, was also the trade and industrial center of Siberia. From here radiated the trade routes westward to Europe, southward to China, and eastward to the Pacific. Irkutsk is centrally located, lying about half way between the Pacific and the Ural Mountains and but 100 miles from the Chinese border. Before the middle of the 19th century Irkutsk had become an important manufacturing center. Its factories and workshops supplied cloth, glass, paper, and manufactured iron products. Irkutsk lies at the eastern margin of the black soil belt of southwestern Siberia. This zone of rich soils widens out to the westward, and by the early part of the 19th century farming and cattle raising had already become an important industry in the region tributary to Irkutsk. In 1839 the province of Irkutsk produced nearly 2,000 tons of grain and was not only self-supporting but also able to supply eastern Siberia with food, manufactured goods, grain, and cattle. Irkutsk was, furthermore, the fur trade center of Asia. Most of the furs from Siberia and Russian America passed through Irkutsk on their way to the Chinese and European markets.

The trade route from Irkutsk to Siberia led down the Angara River, the outlet of Lake Baikal, to the Yenisei, thence by short portage to the waters of the Ob. This was descended to the mouth of the Irtysh and up that stream to Tobolsk, where there are overland routes to European Russia. A more direct route to Tobolsk from Irkutsk was overland, but this was used principally in winter. It was mainly by this route that the Alaskan furs, and the tea and other Chinese products obtained by barter with Alaskan furs, found their way into Europe. Irkutsk was the principal source of supplies for the American colony, though, as will be shown, some came direct by ocean vessels from the Baltic.

The Chinese trade route from Irkutsk was across Lake Baikal and up the Selenga River to the frontier at Kiakhta, which was the trade mart of the Siberian and Chinese merchants. After the seizure of the Amur River, this route was utilized as a more direct route to the Pacific.

The Lena River finds its source in the mountains which skirt the northern margin of Lake Baikal. A pass through this range afforded means of reaching navigable waters in the Lena River, and the trade route went down that stream for over 1,500 miles to Yakutsk. Near Yakutsk on the Aldan River, a southeasterly tributary of the Lena, was the nearest approach to the Pacific which could be reached by navigable river waters. Thence the traffic was by difficult trail over the Stanovoi Mountains to the sea at Okhotsk.

The river routes described above are available to water transportation from May until October, but their frozen surfaces in winter also afforded favorable routes of travel. Transportation by these river systems was among the earliest industrial developments of Siberia. Previous to the introduction of steamboats, river commerce was carried downstream by the current and upstream by vessels towed by horses or oxen. In 1839, the water-borne commerce of Siberia was carried by 180 river and lake craft, large and small. This commerce was very greatly increased by the introduction of steamers, first used on the Ob River in 1845 and during the next 20 years on the Amur, Lena, and other Siberian rivers.

The crossing of the Stanovoi Range from the Aldan to the Sea of Okhotsk was the most difficult and expensive part of the old trans-Siberian trade route. A worn trail 800 miles in length led from Yakutsk to Okhotsk, traversing a pass over 3,000 feet in altitude. During high water stages the distance of land transportation could be shortened somewhat by river transport on the two sides of the range.

By this laborious and expensive transport, the Russian American Company carried a large part of its supplies. At times the company used as many as 4,000 pack horses. Until the ocean route to the Baltic was inaugurated, even the heaviest material, including all metal and cordage used for vessel construction, reached the Pacific by this laborious route.

To summarize: The trans-Siberian trade route led for some 175 miles across the stormy sea of Baikal, thence by a short portage to navigable waters on the Lena River. The Lena River route to Yakutsk was over 1,500 miles in length, and the mountain trail to Okhotsk added 800 miles more. This made the total distance from Irkutsk to Okhotsk over 2,500 miles. Further difficulties were presented by the indifferent harbor of Okhotsk, locked in the ice for the greater part of the year. Supplies were sent by sea to Petropavlovsk on the east shore of Kamchatka, which was the supply point for the American colony. There still remained over 2,000 miles of the stormy Pacific to cross to reach Kodiak and Sitka. But even this was not all, for the supplies had to be further transported to the local trading posts along the Pacific coast and the Yukon and Kuskokwim rivers. As a consequence, rye meal purchased at one-half ruble a poud (36 pounds) at Irkutsk cost the Russian American nine rubles, or 18 times as much delivered at Sitka. It was only the enormous value of the furs, especially the otter and seal skins, shipped for the most part by the same laborious route, which could compensate for the enormous expense of supplying the American colony. Though accurate figures on profits are not available, it is probable that furs were sold in China and Europe at more than 20 times their cost in America. According to C. L. Andrews, the cost of freight from Irkutsk to Sitka was from 540 to 630 silver rubles ($270 to $330) by direct sea route, and from Kronstadt to Sitka 193 to 254 rubles ($96 to $227) a ton.[2] With such costs, the company made every effort to supply the American colony with cheaper provisions, brought by American ships and secured by trade with California and Hawaii.

The difficulties of communication made it impossible for the directors of the Russian American colony to exercise more than a very general supervision over the American

[2] Andrews, C. L., "Alaska under the Russians," *Washington Historical Quarterly*, Seattle, 1916, VII, 229.

affairs of the corporation. Mail facilities were no better than supply transport. The post arrived at Sitka only once a year, and an exchange of letters usually required two years. Even an Imperial dispatch bearer, given every facility for rapid travel, occupied two months in the journey from Moscow to Okhotsk.

The Russians made no attempt to develop any definite system of interior transportation in their American colony. No roads, except for short stretches at Sitka and Kodiak, were constructed, and indeed hardly a trail was built, though some long-established Indian portage routes were used by the Russians. Though the Russian American Company used thousands of pack horses on the route from the Lena River to the Sea of Okhotsk, none was brought to the American colony, and though they made much use of reindeer in the transport service of northeast Siberia, it never seems to have occurred to them that the animal might be of use in America.

The Russians had no craft the equal for river navigation of the Ojibway bark canoe or of the narrow poling boats used by the Hudson Bay Company on the Yukon. Their clumsy skin-covered boats could be towed upstream only with the greatest difficulty, even where no rapids were encountered. It is said that the annual voyage up the Yukon to Nulato made by man's towing went so slowly that at night a man walked back to the previous bivouac to bring up a brand to light the evening campfire. Indeed, the Russian ascent of the Yukon was so laborious that their supplies were freighted by dog teams from Andreafsky over the portage rather than by making the upstream trip from the mouth of the river. It was the lack of proper river craft that led the Russians to report that the Yukon was unnavigable above the mouth of the Tanana, although the Hudson Bay voyageurs frequently made journeys from Fort Yukon down to this place and back in their bark canoes.

The Russians were better provided for their coastal journeys, for they adopted the boats of navigators developed by long evolution to this purpose. These included the large skin boats, or umiaks, of the Eskimos and Aleuts and also their small decked-boats, or kayaks. The latter were enlarged and modified by the Russians. As used by the natives, the kayak was a one-man craft with but a single cockpit. The Russians built it larger and provided it with two or three cockpits for a crew of two or three. These boats were termed *bidarkas* (small boats) by the Russians. Being very seaworthy, they were admirably adapted to coasting voyages and for seal and otter hunting. The Russians also made use of the larger cedar dugout canoes of the Tlingits and Haidas of Southeastern Alaska.

The dog team was the only Russian means of land transportation. Their sleds were well-fashioned, being the result of their own long experience in this form of Siberian transport, modified by the new conditions encountered and by the experience of the natives with whom they came into contact. In the same way they became familiar with and adept in the use of snowshoes. But along the Pacific seaboard, where the principal Russian ports were located, the climatic conditions prevented any great use of this form of transport. Here, land transport, so far as it existed at all, was on the backs of men.

Russian trade routes in Alaska were almost entirely confined to the Pacific and Bering Sea littoral, to the lower Yukon and Kuskokwim rivers, and to some smaller rivers tributary to Bristol Bay. They knew something of the lower valleys of the Susitna and Copper rivers, but these were not much used by them. The only portages extensively employed by the Russians were as follows: The route from Portage Bay on Prince William Sound to the head of Turnagain Arm was used, evidently to avoid the long sea trip around Kenai Peninsula and up Cook Inlet. Several Indian trails from Pacific waters to those of Bering Sea also were used. The shortest of these led from Iliamna Bay on the west shore of Cook Inlet to Iliamna Lake, where the Russians maintained a post. Another led from Katmai Bay on Shelikof Strait by way of Nushagak Lake to the mouth of the Nushagak River. A third led from one of the bays south of Cold Bay across Ugashik Lake and down the river of the same name to Bering Sea, where there was a Russian post. The Russians reached the Kuskokwim from Bristol Bay up the Nushagak and down the Chulitna. The more usual route of approach was from the Yukon across the water and land portage. The most important of the Russian portages extended from Unalakleet on Norton Bay to Kaltag on the Yukon. Much of their trade with the Yukon was carried on by this route, about 70 miles in length, over which dog sleds were used. It will be seen from this brief review that land transport played but a relatively small part in the Russian American fur trade. Of the water transport, more will be said.

The first impetus to Russian navigation of the Pacific came, as we have seen, from Peter the Great. In 1714, by his orders a ship's carpenter was dispatched to Okhotsk, and here in the course of two years he built a vessel 52 feet long with an 18-foot beam, the largest Russian vessel yet to be built on the Pacific coast. It was intended to establish ocean communication with Kamchatka, until then only reached by the land route. Bering's first exploration, which carried him through Bering Straits in 1725, was made with two vessels about 60 feet long. In his second voyage to the coast of Alaska 15 years later he had vessels some 80 feet long. These figures indicate fairly rapid progress in the art of ship-building on the Pacific, though the building was done entirely by the Imperial Government. There was as yet not sufficient incentive for an individual to undertake the building of vessels because of the prohibitive cost of all material except lumber which had to be brought across Siberia.

The first voyages to the scene of Bering's discoveries were in search of sea otters and were made in the crude *shitiks*, of which the planks were lashed together and in which no iron was used. About 1750 the use of better constructed vessels was begun.

By the time that the first Russian colonies were established in America in 1784, larger vessels of from 80 to 100 tons had come to be used in the trade. Indeed, it was only by the use of such vessels that a colony could be at all maintained in the distant possession. These were commanded by masters who had at least a rudimentary knowledge of the art of navigation. There was, however, always a dearth of skilled navigators for the Russian American colony; and the lack was only in part supplied by naval officers taken into the service of the company and by the training of creoles, as the Russians called the half-bloods, in the elements of navigation at the Sitka school and at St. Petersburg. Many of the important inland and coastal explorations, as we shall see, were made by creoles educated at Sitka.

Properly trained shipwrights were also lacking in the Russian Pacific settlements. The first vessel built in Russian America was under the direction of an Englishman named Shields. She was launched in 1794 near the present site of Seward on Resurrection Bay. Since no large saws were available, the timbers were laboriously hewn out of solid logs. All other material, including nails, oakum, and rigging, had been laboriously brought across Siberia by the long land and river route. Later, four small vessels were built at Kodiak and two at Yakutat. The principal shipyard was, however, at Sitka, where in 1835 a water-driven sawmill was erected, the second on the Pacific coast of America.[3] Sitka was also provided with machine shops, a small foundry, and eventually a shop for making nautical instruments. This equipment and a considerable number of well-trained mechanics made possible the construction of good vessels. In 1841, the steamer *Nicholas the First* was launched at Sitka, the first built on the Pacific seaboard.[4] Its 60 horse power engine was imported from the States. A little later, a sea-going tug was built, its engine being entirely constructed in the Sitka machine shop. The largest vessel to be built at Sitka was a brig of 400 tons, but several were constructed of 150 to 300 tons. In all, about a score of vessels were constructed at Sitka, but during the last two decades of the Russian regime only small boats were built. It was found that better and cheaper vessels could be secured by purchase from the Americans, who brought them around the Horn from New England shipyards. Though there was fairly good ship timber at Sitka, the Russians did not realize the necessity of allowing it to season. Hence, their vessels were usually short-lived, in spite of the fact that the larger ones were copper-sheathed.

American vessels, indeed, were an important element in the commerce of the Russian American colony. This was in the days when American ships carried much of the ocean commerce of the world. Captain Gray, the discoverer of the Columbia River in 1792, was the first of the American skippers to visit the northwest coast, but he was followed by many others. The total Atlantic-Pacific ocean traffic was, indeed, small until after the discovery of gold in California,[5] but previous to that time the destination of a large percentage of the vessels rounding Cape Horn was the fur fields of the northwest coast. At first the Russians

[3] The first was built on the Columbia River by the Hudson Bay Company.

[4] The *Beaver*, owned by the Hudson Bay Company, the first steam vessel on the Pacific came around Cape Horn in 1835.

[5] In 1849, 698 vessels cleared for California from Atlantic ports.

were inclined to resent this invasion of their domain, but they soon found that it was to their financial advantage to trade with the American skippers. The first to arrive was Captain James Scott, who visited Kodiak, and his cargo of provisions was most welcome to Baranof, the manager of the company, for his half-starved colony. Later, American vessels not only brought supplies but were also employed by contract in the sea otter hunt. The War of 1812 drove American ships into Russian harbors to avoid British cruisers against which they had no defense except their own small batteries and ill-trained crews. This enabled the shrewd Baranof to drive some hard bargains for vessels which he could buy at his own price.

The St. Petersburg authorities became alarmed at the inroads of American and British vessels along the coast of Russian America, and consequently a ukase was issued by the Tsar in 1821 declaring all the west coast of America north of the 51st parallel to be Russian territory and forbidding foreign ships to approach within 100 miles of the shore unless in distress. This was done under the plea that, as the Russians controlled both shores of the sea, they also maintained the dominion of the intervening ocean. Both the American and British governments promptly challenged this absurd claim, and the incident was one of the causes of the enunciation of the Monroe Doctrine. Hence, treaties were made by Russia with the United States in 1824 and with Great Britain in 1825 which recognized the southern boundary of Russian America to be 54° 40′, the present boundary of Alaska. Russia furthermore conferred rights of fishing and trade on both American and British subjects in Russian American waters, that is within the marine league limit, but she did reserve the right to abrogate this permission after ten years. The treaties also forbade the barter of arms or intoxicants with the natives.

These two treaties were destined to play an important part in later diplomatic negotiations of the United States. On the one hand, they were the principal cause for the rejection of claims to the shutting out of all foreign vessels from pelagic sealing in Bering Sea; on the other hand, it was these treaties which gave the principal support to our contention for the inland position of the territorial boundary of Southeastern Alaska, settled in our favor in 1903.

Russia could not have denied the privileges granted in these treaties, for she was not a maritime power and was dealing with the two strongest maritime powers in the world. Moreover, her American colony would have been industrially throttled without the commerce brought by American and British vessels. At this time American and some British ships would bring supplies to the Russian ports, barter them for furs, sail to China, exchange the furs for tea and other Oriental products, and return to their home ports. The Russians, having no merchant marine, could not gain an entrance into this triangular trade. The Russian American furs were chiefly sent to Okhotsk, and thence overland to Irkutsk. From here they were sent to the Chinese border, where they were bartered for tea and other Chinese products, which were sent to Europe by way of the Ural passes.

The set of oceanic currents in the North Pacific is eastward, favoring voyages from Asia to America. Vessels from trans-Pacific ports usually arrived at Sitka and Kodiak in August and September, thus taking advantage of the prevailing westwardly winds. The westerly voyage from Sitka was made preferably in April, when some easterly winds were to be expected. As a rule, however, much of the westerly voyage had to be made by beating to windward, even during the spring months.

The contrast between Russian and American seamanship is referred to by Dana in his *Two Years before the Mast.* In 1835, he fell in with a vessel from Sitka at San Francisco. After paying his compliments to the over-manned little brig, which mustered six officers and a crew of 20 to 30, he says:

> The vessel was no better than the crew. Everything was in the oldest and most inconvenient fashion possible: running trusses and lifts on yards, and large hawser cables, coiled all over the decks, and served and parcelled in all directions. The topmasts, top-gallant-masts, and studding-sail booms were nearly black for want of scraping, and the decks would have turned the stomach of a man-of-war's man.

Cochrane, the eccentric British naval officer who crossed Siberia on foot in 1823, evidently had a somewhat similar opinion of Russian seamanship, based on his observation of Okhotsk and other Pacific ports.[6] Out of respect to his hosts, however, he speaks in more guarded terms than did the young American sailor, Dana. The testimony of these two seamen gives evidence how primitive Russian seamanship was compared with American and British.

[6] Cochrane, James D., *Narrative of a Pedestrian Journey through Russia and Siberian Tartary, 1820-1823.* New York, 1824.

The credit for both the plan and execution of the first direct ocean voyage from European Russia to the American colony belongs to A. J. von Krusenstern, an officer of the Russian navy. He was a well-trained seaman, having served in the British fleet during the American war and later made a voyage to Canton in a British merchantman. He appears to have been the first to recognize the advantages of ocean communication with America and the possibility of a direct fur trade with China. It was during this Canton voyage that Krusenstern drew up his memorial asking that a direct voyage be made to the Pacific. Authority for this was granted in 1802. It is significant of the status of Russian ship-building of the period that both ships used on the voyage were purchased in England. The one named *Nadeshda* was commanded by Krusenstern in person; the other, the *Neva,* by Lisianski, also an experienced naval officer. The original plan was expanded so as to include a diplomatic mission to Japan. Nikolai Petrovich Rezanof, of whom more will be said later, accompanied the vessels in the dual capacity of Ambassador to Japan and new governor of Russian America. As the Russian America Company was to benefit directly from the voyage, half of the cost was charged to it. The embassy to Japan signally failed, and Rezanof's governorship of the colony was short-lived. The vessels sailed from Kronstadt in August, 1803. They reached the Pacific in the following year by way of Cape of Good Hope and, after various adventures, reached Kronstadt again in 1806, the first vessels to carry the Russian flag around the world.

Though the mission failed to establish diplomatic relations with Japan, or even to obtain commercial rights in Chinese ports, it inaugurated a direct sea service with Russian America. Before 1841, 41 vessels cleared from Kronstadt for America. Of these six were lost on the outward voyage and three on the return, and 23 sailed around the earth. This was an average of only one successful voyage a year, an average which was not increased during the Russian occupation of Alaska. There was practically no direct trade developed between Russian America and Chinese ports, and American furs went westward chiefly by the overland route. Exception to this is found in the American furs carried by American ships from Russian America to Chinese ports.

The commercial failure of the American colony was directly due to the lack of a Russian merchant marine. Never in their entire history have the Russians developed any facility in navigation or seafaring. The attempt to develop a seafaring people begun by Peter the Great may be said to have ended with the naval battles of the Russo-Japanese war three centuries later. In Alaska the lack of knowledge of the sea prevented adequate communication with the outside world, made the attempts at whale-fishing a failure, and left to American fishermen the development of the enormous resources in cod along her shores.

CHAPTER X

The Fur Hunter In Alaska

THE SURVIVORS OF Bering's expedition returned to Russia at a time when there was small hope that their great achievements would either be recognized or taken advantage of by the Russian Government. In the nearly two decades that had elapsed since Peter the Great conceived the great project and dispatched Bering on his first voyage, Russia had had four sovereigns, three of whom had reached the throne by revolutions, accompanied by executions and assassinations. Repeated wars had been waged with European powers, and at times it seemed as if the foundations of a great empire laid by the great Tsar must crumble and fall. Twenty years were still to elapse before the constructive statemanship of Peter was to be again taken up and extended by the genius of Catherine II. Therefore, Bering's discoveries of lands beyond the Pacific and the exploration of Siberia and Japan carried on under his direction excited small interest in the court circle of St. Petersburg. Men of science like Joseph Delisle attempted to coordinate the results, but as these were not available except in fragmentary form their importance was not accorded full recognition. A generation was to pass before Bering's discoveries were to be extended by other official explorations.

The log books and charts of Bering's voyage proved for the immediate work of exploring Alaska far less important than the sea otter skins and the accounts of the fur-bearing animals brought back by the survivors. A new and rich fur country had been found, and this fact was the motive for the explorations by Bering's immediate successors. As indicated in the previous chapter, the coastal navigation of Siberia had developed some knowledge of seafaring. There was, therefore, at hand a class of adventurers who were ready to seek this new land, the Siberian fur hunters or *promishleniki,* as they were called, who had some familiarity with coastal voyages. Their very ignorance of offshore navigation fitted them in a manner for the task they had undertaken, for experienced seamen would hardly have taken part in such utterly hazardous and foolhardy enterprises. As there was little or no iron available in Kamchatka, for it had to be brought overland, a species of vessel, as has already been described, was devised, constructed without iron, the planks being sewed together with thongs of raw hide in lieu of nailing. These rovers depended largely on the sea for food. In such crude vessels, manned largely by crews that knew little of seamanship and but ill-equipped and provisioned, these intrepid fur seekers boldly pushed out into unknown and stormy seas. Many lives were lost by wrecks, starvation, and scurvy, and many of the adventurers met deserved death at the hands of the outraged natives. The risks were great, but when successful the expeditions were enormously profitable and the necessary capital was easily secured from among the Siberian merchants.

Good sea otter skins were worth from 80 to 140 rubles in the Chinese market, and a single voyage sometimes resulted in several thousands of these skins being procured besides the seal skins, foxes, and other furs of less value. These fur hunting expeditions were financed by Siberian merchants and fur traders who often took part in them personally. They employed so-called navigators to command their ships at sea, but these were for the most part simply sailors who had made a few voyages and knew nothing of scientific navigation. The organizers and often the expeditions too were financed by a group of men who retained supreme command in everything except the actual navigation. The crews were engaged in Kamchatka or at Okhotsk and consisted of Russians, exiles, and native Kamchatkans and Koriaks. Usually the Government was represented on each vessel by one or more Cossacks whose duty it was to collect the tribute.

These adventurous fur hunters knew no law except that of their own making, and as a consequence the Aleuts suffered every form of abuse their conquerors willed. If the tribute was collected, the authorities in Siberia usually paid little heed to the actions of the hunters, though in rare instances their crimes were investigated and punishment was meted out to hunters on their return to Siberia. The records of the early voyages to the Commander and Aleutian islands have been only partly examined. Therefore, on account of the lack of precise data, it will not be worth while here to attempt more than a brief summary of results with occasional references to some of the principal actors in the drama.[1] It is generally believed that Emilian Basof was the first to visit the Commander Islands after the return of the Bering survivors. Basof, a sergeant of a Cossack troop in Kamchatka, made his first voyage in 1743. In the following year, a second voyage was made and the winter spent in the Commander Islands, and he is credited also with having visited Attu, the westernmost of the Aleutian chain of islands.

More important was a voyage organized by a group of fur traders in 1745. Their vessel was the *Eudokia* and the partners, not being seamen, entrusted the command to Michael Nevodchikof, said to have been one of Bering's crew. They sailed eastward from the Kamchatka River in September, passed Attu Island without landing, and continued the voyage to Agattu Island, the second one of the Aleutian chain. Here a landing was made and the first fight with natives of Alaskan soil took place. Though the Aleuts, with their bone-headed weapons, could offer little resistance to the Russian firearms, yet the fur hunters deemed it wise to retire and wintered on Attu Island where more slaughter of natives took place. After various other adventures, the survivors of the murderous crew finally reached Kamchatka with about 300 sea otter skins. The result of the voyage again roused the St. Petersburg authorities to some appreciation of possible valuable possessions beyond the seas. Bering's log and charts were sent to Siberia, and the newly discovered lands were put under control of an official stationed at Okhotsk. Tribute was to be collected from the natives through Cossacks assigned to that duty.

Other voyages soon followed, and in 1747 a small vessel built on the Anadyr River by hunters named Bakof and Novikof reached Bering Island, where the expedition was wrecked and the party, like the Bering survivors, were forced to make the return voyage in a boat built of wreckage. It is significant of the Russian bureaucratic methods that all landings were prohibited on Bering Island because government property, represented by the wreckage left by the Bering crew, was still on the island. Hence the boat of Bakof and Novikof and the few furs they brought back

[1] These notes are for the most part abstracted from William Coxe, *Account of the Russian Discoveries between Asia and America*, London, 1781 and from H. H. Bancroft, *The History of Alaska*, San Francisco, 1886. No attempt has been made to examine anything but these secondary authorities.

were confiscated by the authorities and sold at auction. This was the first government reservation in this northern region, and the reasons for its establishment were possibly as good as those for establishing certain government reserves in Alaska's recent history. It should be added that the freebooting fur hunters paid small heed to this order and continued to hunt on Bering Island. Meanwhile, the finding of native copper ore on these islands led to a second edict forbidding their being visited by the hunters. In 1755, Peter Yakovlef, a mining engineer, was sent by the Government to investigate the copper deposits. No attempt was made at copper mining, nor have the deposits since proved of value.

Government interference with the fur traders continued in other forms. In 1748, an Okhotsk merchant named Emilian Yugof obtained from the Russian senate the sole permission to hunt sea otter in the "Sea of Kamchatka" with the proviso that the Government should receive a third of the furs collected. Only one of the four vessels built reached its destination and returned, in 1754, with a rich cargo. Meanwhile, other vessels received charters for expeditions to islands not yet made tributary.

By 1756 the sea otter had practically been exterminated on the Commander Islands, and the fur hunters were forced to extend their voyages to the Aleutian chain. In 1758, Stepan Glottof reached Unalaska and Unimak where three years were spent in fur hunting and in friendly trade with the natives. This appears to be the first recorded voyage to the eastern end of the Aleutian chain. It is a significant fact that many of these early fur hunters still believed that there was a land mass south of the Aleutians to which the sea otter and fur seal migrated each year. Therefore, many fruitless voyages into the Pacific were made in search of this land. It is quite possible that with their utter ignorance of geodetic positions they may have believed that the continent found by Bering and Chirikof lay to the south of the Aleutian chain, or the belief may have been a survival of the mythical Gama Land of the early charts.

Glottof's peaceful intercourse with the Unalaska natives was soon interrupted by the arrival of less scrupulous hunters, and their abuse of the natives led to the slaughter of many Russians. The natives of the eastern Aleutians proved more formidable than did those to the west, and there was much killing before they were brought to subjugation. In 1763, Glottof extended his voyage to Kodiak Island and here obtained information about the mainland of Alaska. At Kodiak, much greater opposition was met with than among the Aleuts. This landing appears to have been made at Alitak Bay at the southern end of Kodiak.

No attempt has been made in the above to chronicle all the voyages of which there is record. It will suffice to state that by the time the first Russian reached Kodiak in 1763 most of the larger of the Aleutian Islands had been visited and the natives subjugated. This was accomplished by a ruthless slaughter of the natives, for the typical trader of this horde of adventurers had no compassion on the Aleut. It was through this murderous crew of traders that the world was first to learn of the long chain of islands that link Alaska and Siberia. While the principal landmarks along this route gradually became known, the crude navigators had no skill in making charts and but a poorly developed sense of direction. Therefore, their contribution to geographic knowledge was principally to show that the landfalls made by Bering and Chirikof on their return voyages marked for the most part islands and not part of the main continent.

After 20 years of this freebooting, the authorities at St. Petersburg again turned their attention to their oversea possessions, and orders were given to dispatch naval officers to explore these new lands. The first of these was Lieutenant Synd who sailed from Okhotsk in 1764 but did not leave the Kamchatkan coast until two years later. He sailed eastward and discovered St. Matthew Island. He then laid a course northward and appears to have sighted various points on St. Lawrence Island, which he mistook for a group of islands. He also appears to have made a landing on the southwest coast of Seward Peninsula, but his exact course has, so far as I know, not yet been established. In any event he brought back little information about this sea that was not already known either through Bering's or through Gvosdef's voyages.

Synd's results were chiefly important in exciting further interest in maritime explorations. Consequently, Captain-Lieutenant Peter Krenitzin was dispatched from St. Petersburg in 1764. For some reason secrecy was maintained about the object of the expedition. Two years later it sailed from Okhotsk in the *St. Catherine,* commanded by Krenitzin, and in the *St. Paul,* commanded by Lieutenant Michael Levashef, with smaller vessels as tenders. Three of these were lost before the voyage was actually entered upon, which was in 1768, when Krenitzin in the *St. Catherine* and Levashef in the *St. Paul* laid a course to the Commander Islands and thence eastward. They became separated. Krenitzin reached Unalaska Strait from the northwest and was later joined by Levashef. They again became separated, and Krenitzin wintered at Unimak and Levashef at Captain's Harbor. The natives had learned to mistrust the white men and some encounters took place. In June, both vessels returned to Kamchatka where Krenitzin was drowned. The most important result of the expedition was to show that no land lay north of the Aleutian chain. Something was also learned of the geodetic position of the Aleutian Islands and some charting was done. Considering the great preparations made and the time spent, the results were exceedingly meagre. It is certain that many of the freebooting traders managed their voyages better than did these naval officers. The voyage had, however, very important results of a different kind: the reported abuse of the natives by the fur hunters led to a royal ukase prohibiting the collection of tribute by the *promishleniki* and Cossacks.

Meanwhile, the fur hunters continued their voyages. Notable among these was that of Dmitri Polutof who commanded the vessel *Archangel St. Michael,* owned by the trader Kholodilof, who reached Kodiak Island in 1776. Perhaps the most remarkable was the voyage of Potop Zaikof who sailed in 1772 and, gradually making his way eastward to Unimak, did not return until 1779. He was an exception among his class because he made as careful surveys of the islands he visited as means would permit, and probably actually contributed more to the knowledge of the geography than did the elaborate naval expedition described above.

About this time occurred a dramatic revolt in Kamchatka, led by the adventurer Count Mauritius Benyowski. Benyowski was a Polish exile who, after the defeat of his countrymen, was sent to Kamchatka. He organized a revolt at Bolsheretsk in 1771, overpowered the garrison, and finally sailed away with 96 companions in two ships. His own memoirs of this voyage have been proved to a large extent to be false and there seems to be definite evidence that he did not visit Bering Straits, the Commander and Aleutian islands, or Kodiak, as he claimed.[2]

To this epoch properly belongs also the raid of a group of Russian hunters into Prince William Sound, though it took place at a much later date. In 1783, three independent hunting vessels voluntarily put themselves under the leadership of Potop Zaikof, the discoverer of Kodiak. They sought the gulf about which they had learned from Cook, namely Prince William Sound. Zaikof led them first to Kayak Island where they probably anchored in Controller Bay and thence made excursions to seek natives and furs. One of the three boat parties, under Nagaief, discovered the Copper River.

It was here at Kayak Island that the Russian traders first came into contact with the Tlingit stock of natives who were later to give them much trouble. Thence they made their way to Prince William Sound, called by the Russians "Chugach Gulf," and here they scattered out on their customary freebooting expeditions. But, unlike the Aleuts, the Chugach were warlike and refused to submit tamely to abuse as did the Aleuts for the most part. Many of the Russians were killed, meeting well-deserved deaths. This was the first incursion of the Russian fur hunters northeast of Kodiak, but it was quickly followed by others.

During the 40 years following the first raid on the sea otter of the Commander Islands, the ravages of the fur hunters had so greatly reduced these animals that the voyages had to be made longer and gradually extended to the eastward. As has been stated, Kodiak was visited as early as 1763, and Cook Inlet was reached by 1778. These longer voyages required better ships and navigators and hence more capital. Fur hunting had gradually taken on more the form of an established industry than merely the raids of individual adventurers.

Therefore, it had gradually fallen into the hands of better equipped men. Companies were organized, sending out groups of vessels with more experienced navigators and better equipment. This evolution eventually led to the monopolization of the fur trade in Russia's American possessions into one great company. It was the visiting of the fur trading interests of the American coast which led to the permanent settlement of Alaska by the Russians,

[2] *Memoirs and Travels of Mauritius Augustus Count de Benyowski*, London, 1904.

and the foundations of this project were due to the genius of Grigor Ivanovich Shelikof. Shelikof, who had been in the Chinese trade, dispatched his first vessel to the Aleutians in 1776. His activities in the fur trade, which belong properly to the epoch of Russian settlement, will be treated in the following chapter.

CHAPTER XI

Early Russian Settlement

THE EVOLUTION of the Russian American fur trade from the raids of irresponsible hunting parties to the organization of a powerful monopoly was a slow one. The gradual depletion of the sea otter first on the Commander Islands and later on the western Aleutian Islands forced the hunter to extend his voyages farther to the east, a condition that demanded larger vessels and better seamanship. By the time the hunt was carried to Kodiak Island in 1763, the days when the crude boats of the *promishleniki,* whose planks were sewn together with thongs in lieu of nails, was rapidly passing. Then, too, the Siberian merchants had become acquainted with the possibilities of rich returns from this field of venture. As a consequence, many partnerships and many small, loosely organized stock companies were formed to engage in this trade.

Among the many who took part in Russian American trade at this period, two stand out prominently, namely Grigor Ivanovich Shelikof and Ivan Larionovich Golikof. Shelikof had come to Okhotsk from the Chinese frontier where he had gained some experience and some capital in trade. Golikof was a merchant from the province of Irkutsk. It was the Kurile Island trade that led to Shelikof's first venture into the western seas, this in 1776. He then embarked in the Aleutian Island trade, and soon a joint venture with Golikof in this field was undertaken. Without attempting to chronicle their enterprises, it may be said that these two men, either in partnership or in association with others, dispatched a number of vessels to the American coast which, though not all successful, yielded as a whole bountiful returns. Their success was in a large measure due to the type of commanders they chose. One of these was Gerasim Grigorovich Ismailof, who made some important explorations on the Alaskan coast; another was Gerasim Pribilof, later the discoverer of the Seal Islands.

Shelikof was the first to realize that success in the American fur trade necessitated the passing away of the old order of things so that trade could be better organized, permanent settlements could be established, and, above all, the warlike natives of Kodiak and Chugach Gulf, as Prince William Sound was then called by the Russians, could be dealt with in some method other than the slaughter and enforced servitude that had been successful with the peaceful Aleuts. About 1782, Shelikof and Golikof organized a new company with paid up capital of 70,000 rubles divided into 120 shares. The purpose of the company was "to sail for 'Aliaska land called America' and for known and unknown islands, to carry on the fur trade and explorations, and to establish friendly intercourse with the natives." Three ships of the new company sailed from Okhotsk in August, 1783[1] Shelikof led the expedition in person and was accompanied by his wife, Natalia, who was destined to play an important part in the affairs of the company after the death of her husband.

The expedition included nearly 200 men, by far the largest single force of fur hunters that had set sail for Alaska. Its three ships became separated on the Pacific, but two reached Unalaska in June, 1784. Here repairs were made, fresh water secured, and a dozen Aleuts added to the crew; sail was then set for Kodiak. In August the two ships, including Shelikof's, anchored in an indentation on the southeast coast of Kodiak named after one of the vessels, Three Saints Bay. Shelikof's attempt at friendly intercourse with the natives proved unavailing, and these assembled in large numbers on a rocky islet near at hand which was one of their strongholds. This was finally attacked, many natives were killed, and about 400 were taken prisoners and held as hostages.

Dwellings and fortifications were erected on the bay, and thus the permanent habitation of Alaska was entered upon. During the next two years, several parties were sent out to explore and secure furs. Kodiak was circumnavigated; Controller, Yakutat, and Lituya bays and the mouth of the Alsek River were visited. Posts were established on Afognak Island and on Kenai Peninsula, and some small boats were built. Shelikof himself, according to his own account, labored assiduously to educate the natives and to convert them to Christianity. Undoubtedly Shelikof's story lost nothing in the telling, for he was anxious to impress

[1] Shelikof, Grigor, *Erste und Zweite Reise von Ochotsk in Sibirien durch den östlichen Ozean nach den Küsten von Amerika in den Jahren 1783 bis 1789*, St. Petersburg, 1893.

OLD RUSSIAN BLOCKHOUSE
During their occupation of Alaska, the Russians built a number of these as a means of protection against the natives. Photo by J. B. Mertie.

the Siberian authorities by his achievements and to show by contrast the superiority of his own methods of dealing with the natives compared with those of his rivals. Nevertheless, it must be noted that his observations on the geography, the natural history, and the customs of the natives are known to have been reliable; and there can be no question that he was a keen observer as well as a shrewd trader. Shelikof planted a garden at his settlement, the first within the present confines of Alaska. He noted the abundance of wild grass and later sent over some cattle. Before Shelikof's departure it appears that posts were established at several places on Kodiak, including Karluk on the adjacent Afognak Island, and at Kamishak Bay on the mainland. He also left orders that, when reinforcements arrived, posts should be built on Cook Inlet and Prince William Sound. Shelikof's broad interests are shown by his instructions that, in the course of the explorations for new hunting grounds, minerals, ores, and shells were to be collected for transmission to St. Peterburg. By this order the Siberian merchant inaugurated the scientific investigation of Alaska.

While Shelikof's colony was the only permanent settlement in Russian America, he realized full well that there were others who would be quick to take advantage of the results achieved through his pioneer work. He forestalled a part of this competition by obtaining large interests in the Lebedef-Lastochkin Company, probably the most important rival. He did not, however, have the force, let alone the authority, to drive out the independent fur hunters who were roaming along the coast line adjacent to his colony. Therefore, he aimed at nothing less than to secure a monopoly of the fur trade in the new province from the Russian crown. It was possibly this thought that led him to his philanthropic work among the natives with the idea that it would influence the Tsarina to eliminate the freebooting fur traders. Whatever his motives, he certainly was the first to pay any heed to the rights of the natives, and his native school and museum at Three Saints Bay was the pioneer effort to look after the educational needs of this people who previously had met with nothing but barbarity at the hands of the newcomers.

In May, 1786, he took his departure for Siberia taking with him about 30 natives, in part children to be educated in Russia, in part adults who by personal observation were to be impressed with the Russian power. It was apparently believed that upon their return they would influence their brethren to desist from warfare on the Russians by pointing out the hopelessness of such action. Shelikof went direct to Irkutsk and submitted a report to Ivan Jacobi, the governor, of this exploration and colonization. The story of his achievements, as already indicated, probably lost nothing in the telling, for he desired to impress Russian officialdom with the importance of the new realm. This report was dispatched to Catherine II, who had been already prepared for the importance of the activities of the new company through an audience which she had granted to Golikof, Shelikof's partner. Later, the two partners had a personal audience with the Tsarina. Meanwhile, an investigation of Shelikof's claims was made by the Russian Department of Commerce, which urged a grant of 200,000 rubles be made to the company for use as capital, to be loaned without interest. The Tsarina found a less expensive method of giving recognition by granting a sword and gold medal to each of the two partners.

The question of monopolistic rights was held in abeyance, but the governor of eastern Siberia was instructed to find means of establishing Russian sovereignty in the new possessions. Jacobi found a simple and inexpensive method by furnishing Shelikof with copper plates and wooden crosses suitably inscribed which were to be erected as evidence of Russian possession. Finally, on September 28, 1788, the Shelikof Company was granted exclusive privileges of the lands actually in its control. This was a substantial advance toward Shelikof's goal, though it was by no means all that he had sought. One of the first moves was to supplant Eustrate Delarof, a partner and manager of the company. Delarof, who was a Greek by birth, had an enviable record of justice and kindness in his administration of Kodiak.

Delarof's successor was Alexander Andreyevich Baranof, a Russian merchant some 43 years old, who had been engaged in trade with the natives of Kamchatka. He was given ten shares of stock, about one-sixth of actual issue, and became manager of the company in August, 1790. While it was Shelikof's broad vision that led to the Russian America fur monopoly, it was Baranof who put the plan into execution. Baranof's introduction to his new realm where he was to rule with despotic sway for over a quarter of a century was no easy one. His vessel bound for Kodiak was wrecked on Unalaska, and here the survivors passed a miserable winter, eking out their stock of provisions by shooting seals and sea lions and digging roots. In April, 1791, three boats were built, and in one of these Baranof, ill with fever, reached Three Saints Bay in June, 1791. He took over the management of affairs from Delarof who, in spite of his mild rule, had succeeded in holding Kodiak and adjacent islands from the rival traders and had established a station at Fort Alexander[2] on the eastern shore of Cook Inlet.

The establishment over which Delarof presided included about 50 Russians in addition to about 300 natives, chiefly women. These latter were held as hostages for the good behavior of several thousand natives living in the vicinity. A further control of the natives was maintained by the seizure of all the large boats. These, with native crews, were employed in sea otter hunting, the expeditions being sent out under the Russians. The settlement at Three Saints Bay[3] was made up of five buildings, the barracks, the offices, the storehouses, a carpenter and blacksmith shop, and a cooperage and a rope walk. Several of the Russians had their wives with them, others were married to native women. Cabbages and potatoes were raised in small gardens. A few cows and goats constituted the entire livestock. The Russian employees nominally received good wages, but as their purchases of luxuries as well as necessities were from the company at exorbitant prices, they were all deeply in debt. Such was the first permanent white settlement in Alaska.

The other posts in Alaska were of the most primitive type, consisting of rude shelters for a few Russian traders. In 1790 when Sweden and Russia were at war, the Swedish cruiser *Mercury* under command of Captain Coxe was dispatched to the Aleutian Islands to destroy the Russian settlements and to prey on the fur trade. Coxe found only a few half-starved Russians who could make no defense. His pity was excited, for they had nothing worth taking. Therefore, ignoring his orders, he supplied some of these poor exiles with provisions and sailed away without molesting them.

Baranof's chief rival in the fur trade was the Lebedef-Lastochkin Company which occupied the upper part of Cook Inlet and also the valuable seal rookeries of the Pribilof Islands. Other independent traders were to be found in the Aleutian Islands and on Prince William Sound. Moreover, the English and American fur traders were approaching the company's domain from the south and had already invaded Southeastern Alaska. Therefore, if the company

[2] This station was on Port Graham, near the present site of Seldovia.

[3] Sauer, Martin, *An Account of a Geographical and Astronomical Expedition to the Northern Parts of Russia Performed by Commander Joseph Billings*, London, 1802, pp. 172-174.

was to outstrip its rivals, an aggressive policy had to be adopted and for this purpose no better man could be found than the new director. Intelligent and farsighted, he was quick to grasp the situation and, moreover, had no scruples about the methods he should employ to further the interests of the company.

One of Baranof's first moves was to find a better location for the headquarters of the company. The absence of all timber and its distance from Cook Inlet and Prince William Sound made Three Saints Bay undesirable. He also sent to Okhotsk for shipbuilding material, deeming it an advantage not to be dependent on Siberia for the vessels needed.

The site for a post was picked on what the Russians termed Paulovski Harbor, now called St. Paul Harbor, near the northeast end of Kodiak Island. Here where the grasslands of southwestern Alaska meet the forests of eastern Alaska, Baranof in 1792[4] built the post which for a decade was to be the Russian trading center of Alaska, only to be superseded by Sitka when he found it advantageous to lay claim to what is now Southeastern Alaska. Baranof called his new settlement St. Paul, but it is now generally known as Kodiak.

In 1792 Baranof also sought to establish friendly relations with the Chugach natives of Prince William Sound. He was far from successful in this attempt, for his men on Nuchek Bay were attacked by the natives and a pitched battle was fought. He only succeeded in beating them off by the use of a small cannon. More success was attained on Cook Inlet where he now proceeded and strengthened his stations without interference on the part of the natives.

Returning to his headquarters at St. Paul, Baranof found a supply vessel from Okhotsk under command of Captain Shields, an Englishman in Russian employ. Shields had been a shipwright, and this occupation seems to have been the reason for his having been chosen to command the supply ship. The cargo included supplies for ship construction, except the iron which seems to have been left behind by mistake.

Baranof had recognized that the best timber near at

[4] The date of the transfer to this post from Three Saints Bay has not been definitely learned, but it was probably in 1792, though the Russians had previously had a minor post at the same place.

hand was that at the head of Resurrection Bay.[5] Here he took Shields and his crew, which also included four other Englishmen. Great spruce and hemlocks covered the flats at the head of the bay, including the present site of the town of Seward. With crude tools the workmen felled the trees and, in the absence of whipsaws, hewed out the planks for the vessel. The iron[6] was obtained from the rusty scraps picked up at the various posts, and a mixture of spruce gum, ochre, and whale oil was used in lieu of pitch. The vessel constructed was of large size for that day, being a two-decked craft 73 feet long with a 23-foot beam and of 180 tons burden. She was named the *Phoenix* and glided into the water in August, 1794, the first to be built in Alaska. Two smaller vessels, the *Dolphin* and the *Olga*, were launched the following year at the same place.

Meanwhile Baranof was beset with difficulties because of the rival fur trading interests. These not only attacked Baranof's men but also fought among themselves. Cook Inlet was the principal scene of the strife. Here the Lebedef-Lastochkin Company in 1786 had built their post of St. George at the mouth of the Kasilof River. Five years later another agent of the same company had built a second post and erected the stockade of St. Nicholas at the mouth of the Katmai River. The two representatives of the same company quarreled and fought among themselves and only joined to oppose the Shelikof men.

The same company also established itself on Prince William Sound and attempted to keep out Baranof's hunters. Baranof seems to have been loath to interfere, but finally when they threatened his shipyard on Resurrection Bay, he assumed an authority he did not possess. Konovalof, the chief trouble-maker, was seized, put in chains, and finally with eight of his companions shipped back to Okhotsk.

In 1794 matters were sufficiently quiet on Cook Inlet and Prince William Sound to enable Baranof to send a large party of hunters to Yakutat and Icy bays. At Yakutat trouble threatened with natives, but the arrival of Lieutenant Puget with one of Vancouver's vessels overawed the natives. Purtof, leader of the Russian party, also utilized the chance visit of the English trader Captain Brown in

---

[5] Known to the Russians as Voskressenski Harbor. The outer entrance was called Blying Sound by Vancouver and the inner bay Port Andrews by Portlock.

[6] It is stated by Bancroft that Baranof even attempted to smelt some iron ores found near by in an improvised furnace. Some of the copper ores of the region contain a large percentage of magnetite, and it is possible that this was the ore used.

the *Jackall* to further awe the natives. His raid was successful, and it gave the Shelikof Company further prestige by having extended its operations to the east.

While Baranof was furthering the interests of the company in Russian America, Shelikof had been equally zealous in pressing for larger grants to his company at St. Petersburg and for monopolizing the fur trade of both northeastern Asia and northwestern America. He died in 1795 without achieving his long-cherished plan, but his widow and his partner Golikof brought the matter to a conclusion. In 1797 a consolidation was effected of the companies that were trading in Kamchatka, northeast Siberia, and Alaska. It remained to obtain monopolistic rights, and they were obtained largely through the personal influence of Count Nikolai Petrovich Rezanof, chamberlain to the Tsar. Rezanof, who had become financially interested with Shelikof and had also married his daughter Anna, was a man of broad vision, and his interest in the fur trading enterprise was by no means limited to financial gain. His attempts to improve the conditions of both Russians and natives in the American colony and his plan for extending the Tsar's sovereignty in this region will be referred to again.

The charter was granted in 1799 by the Tsar Paul. It conferred monopolistic rights to the fur trade in Kamchatka, in the Kurile Islands, and in the Okhotsk district. The details of the privileges granted will receive consideration in the next chapter, but it is important here to note that in 1799 Alaska became to all intents and purposes a private possession.

The events which led up to the transfer of Russian America and eastern Siberia to a private corporation are paralleled by the history of the Hudson Bay Company. In both instances charters were granted to lands about which little was known, and both these lands were in part of debatable sovereignty where aggressions of rival nations were to be expected. Probably both Charles II and Paul I were not unmindful of the fact that the acts of a private corporation could be disavowed should the political conditions in Europe lead to a protest on the part of a rival sovereignty too powerful to be ignored. On the other hand, actual possession by either of these corporations could be used as a valid claim of sovereignty should other conditions favor such a claim. In both instances the plan of monopolizing the fur trade of a vast country originated with men who knew by personal experience of the value of such a monopoly. The Hudson Bay Company owed its conception to the vision of two French fur traders, Groseilliers and Radisson, just as the formation of the Russian American Company was the result of the work of Shelikof and Golikof. In both instances the actual charters were obtained by court favorites, Count Rezanof at St. Petersburg and Prince Rupert at the court of St. James. Nor are the actual charters unlike in their provisions; for example, in the use of armed forces, exemption from taxation, and other features. It must be noted, however, that Charles II in 1670 granted a large part of his North American possessions in perpetuity with no regard for the future. Wiser counsel prevailed with Paul I, and his grant was only for 20 years. A search of the Russian archives may reveal what influenced the Tsar to this limitation—whether it was a deliberate act with a vision of the future or whether it had to do with industrial conditions and traditions prevailing in the Russian Empire. Probably the long-established system of leasehold grants in Russia compared with the freehold grants of England was the dominating factor in the decision. It is interesting to note that in recent years the United States has adopted the leasehold system and has applied it to a part of Alaska's resources, namely the coal, and that this is the first application of it on a large scale by the Federal Government.

Had the Russian American Company been given a fee simple to Alaska, it is probable that it would have entered upon its task of settlement and development on a permanent basis. The differences between the actions of the two American fur companies are very striking. The Hudson Bay Company built large posts, in some instances masonry forts, boat canals, and other permanent structures, but the Russian company except at Sitka and Kodiak had only a few stockaded posts. Though the Russian America posts were far easier of access, they were but indifferently supplied and but few definite transportation routes were established. On the other hand, the Hudson Bay posts stretching across the continent were reached by established routes of travel, and communication was kept up with England by ships making regular trips, first to Hudson Bay and Quebec, and later to the Pacific. The differences in the commercial genius of the two races undoubtedly had something to do with these contrasts, but the permanency of the occupation of one corporation as compared with that of the other was probably an equally strong factor. When the time came for a change, the Russian American Company surrendered its rights with nominally at least only a small payment for its actual equipment, but the Hudson Bay Company was only dispossessed of its sovereign rights by a payment of 15 million dollars and, moreover, retained absolute title to a tremendous tract of land.

It should be added that both monopolies performed valuable service to mankind by their settlements on a remote frontier and their exploration of unknown lands. In this, of course, the results achieved by the Hudson Bay Company far excelled those of its rival, partly because of the conditions mentioned above, partly because of its much longer history. When the Russian American Company was formed, the Hudson Bay Company had already established posts within the western system of ranges, and, had not this rival corporation intervened, it would in a few years have reached Bering Sea with its outposts, just as it reached the Pacific south of the Russian American possessions. As it was, the two companies first clashed in Southeastern Alaska and later became rivals on the Yukon River.

CHAPTER XII

The Russian American Company

THE ORGANIZATION of the Russian American Company under the direct patronage of the Tsar had been preceded by the amalgamation of all the important fur trading interests both of northeastern Siberia and of northwestern America. These were combined under the name "United American Company," with a capital of 724 shares worth 1,000 rubles each. This union was favorably regarded by the Tsar who directed that it should be patterned after the best practices of foreign European corporations.[1] At that time stock companies were a novelty in Russia. In fact, the Russian American Company is said to have been the first stock company chartered in the Tsar's dominion.[2] It is probably for this reason that there is some uncertainty as to the privileges and duties of the new company. The original charter appears to have been modified by royal edict from time to time, and it is probable that the authorities sought by this means to develop a workable charter. It remained to obtain a monopoly of the American fur trade and such other privileges as the Tsar was willing to grant. No doubt the United American Company was organized both to shut out competition so far as possible and also to prevent conflicting interests from opposing the granting of the monopoly now sought at St. Petersburg. There appears to have been but little difficulty in obtaining the monopoly, for it was granted the year following the organization of the United Company.

The ukase[3] signed by the Tsar on December 27, 1799, stated that ". . . having taken under our immediate protection a company organized for the above-named purpose of carrying on hunting and trading we allow it to assume the appellation of 'Russian American Company' operating under our highest protection." A further provision of the

[1] Pilder, Hans, "Die Russisch-Amerikanische Handels-Kompanie bis 1825," *Osteuropaische Forschunger*, Heft 3, Berlin und Leipzig, 1914, p. 18.

[2] *Ibid.*, p. 35.

[3] *Bering Sea Arbitration Case Presented on the Part of Her Brittanic Majesty to the Tribunal of Arbitration Presented to Both Houses of Parliament by Command of Her Majesty*, London, March, 1893, pp. 25-27.

preamble limits the grant to 20 years. The first clause asserts Russian sovereignty by right of discovery and occupation of that part of North America lying between the 55th parallel and Bering Straits, as well as over the Aleutian Islands. This is followed by a clause providing for the discovery and occupation "under prescribed rules" of new lands provided they are not occupied by or dependent upon other nations. The third clause will be quoted in full: "To use and profit by everything which has or shall be discovered in these localities on the surface and in the interior of the earth without competition from others." This gave monopolistic rights not only to the fur trade but also to mineral wealth. Privilege to establish settlements and to fortify them and to pursue free intercourse with these settlements by ships is given in the fourth clause, and the succeeding article permits commerce and trade with the people of other nations. A sixth article permits the company to employ in its business "free and unsuspected people having no illegal views or intentions." Provincial authorities are bidden to grant passports good for seven years to such free people who are sent out as settlers, hunters, and so forth. This article furthermore says that serfs and house servants will only be employed by the company with the consent of these landholders and that government taxes will be paid for all serfs thus employed. It appears from article seven that the timber of the Russian Empire was reserved, and exception is made to this company which is permitted to cut timber for repairs and "occasional construction of ships" without special permit. It is rather curious to find this germ of the present reservation policy presented in this ancient document. Article eight provides for sale to the company from government stocks in Siberia of quantities not exceeding 40 or 50 pounds of powder and 200 pounds of lead. The ninth article prohibits the seizure for debt of any individual stockholder's share of realty in the company. The interests of other individual traders or companies already in this region are provided for in article ten, by which they are allowed a certain length of time to close their business. In the 11th article the company is given judiciary powers in minor cases. By inference the major infractions of law are to be dealt with by the Siberian authorities. In this article, too, the company is allowed to maintain fortifications and to maintain its posts against foreign attack. A closing provision allows only partners of the company to be employed in the administration of their possessions.

As the new corporation was but a reorganization of the United American Company and as the privileges and duties of that company had already received royal sanction, they remained in force for the Russian American Company. The privileges of the company are fully set forth in various documents, but the obligations imposed on it are less clearly stated in these publications. It appears, however, that the company was obligated to assume the entire cost of administering the trans-Pacific colony, to establish agricultural colonies, to support churches and missions, and to maintain a small military force and magazines of supplies. Some of these obligations were probably imposed by ukases which were issued from time to time at a date later than the original charter. No taxes appear to have been imposed, but the company was subject to the imposts, chiefly on tea in its trade with China. It appears also that the natives of Alaska were obligated to pay to the company certain taxes in the form of furs. This provision has often been quoted as a deliberate attempt on the part of the Russian Government to enslave the Alaskan natives and place them in the servitude of the company. It is more probable that it was simply a transferring of the taxing power of the Government to the corporation. Previous to this time, Alaskan natives, like those of Siberia, were subject to a tax of furs. As the Russian American Company assumed all functions of government in the colony, it was only natural to transfer to it this power of taxation. It appears that, in addition to the 724 shares issued by the United American Company, the new corporation was authorized to issue 1,000 more shares and that foreigners were forbidden to invest in the enterprise. The management was in the hands of four directors elected annually by stockholders who had one vote for each 25 shares.

The Tsar encouraged the enterprise by purchasing 20 shares of stock in the new company, the profits of which he donated to charity, and members of the royal family and others of the court circle also became stockholders. Though this gave the company standing, it was by no means able to dispose of all its stock, and even 20 years later some unsold shares remained in the Treasury.[4]

[4] Pilder, *op. cit.*, p. 86.

Though the charter provided that an officer of the Imperial navy was to have the directorship of the American possessions of the company, yet there seems to have been no thought of supplanting Baranof who continued his energetic campaign for new fur hunting fields. The Englishman Shields had been sent in 1793 to explore the coast to the east and had reached Norfolk Sound. Here a wide field for sea otter was found, which was one of the chief reasons for the transfer a few years later of headquarters from Kodiak to Sitka. Three years earlier, Captain Becharof had skirted the west coast of the Alaska Peninsula and had found the portage route across its base by way of the lake which still bears his name.

In the meantime, Shelikof's plan for an agricultural colony was put into execution. Two vessels arrived at Kodiak in 1794 in which, by order of Catherine II, there were nearly 200 colonists, together with livestock and a supply of much-needed provisions. Though Shelikof, as has been previously pointed out, is usually credited with only desiring to impress the St. Petersburg authorities with his good intentions by this action, yet this seems hardly a completely rational interpretation of his motives. Shelikof knew from personal experience that agriculture and stock raising were possible at Three Saints Bay, and he had, moreover, broad vision. His instructions to Baranof bear witness to his vision, as is shown by the following quotation from a letter to the director dated Okhotsk, 1794, which has been translated by Bancroft:[5]

> And now it remains for us to hope that having selected on the mainland a suitable place you will lay out a settlement with some taste and with due regard for beauty of construction in order that when visits are made by foreign ships as can not fail to happen it may appear more like a town than a village and that the Russians may live in a neat and orderly way and not, as in Okhotsk, in squalor and misery caused by the absence of nearly everything necessary to civilization. Use taste as well as practical judgment in locating the settlement. Look to beauty as well as convenience of material and supplies. On the plans as well as in reality leave room for spacious squares and public assemblies. Make the streets not too long, but wide and let them radiate from the squares. If the site be wooded let trees enough stand to line the streets and to fill the gardens in order to beautify the place.

No doubt these plans, which were fantastic enough in view of the fact that Baranof's handful of exiles in the

[5] Bancroft, H. H., *The History of Alaska*, San Francisco, 1886, p. 353.

distant colony then faced starvation, were intended to impress the court at St. Petersburg; but yet there is good reason to believe that Shelikof's vision was broader than that of the men of his time or even of his successors in Alaska during the century which followed. Further evidence of Shelikof's sincerity is found in the project[6] of his widow to transfer her serfs from her Russian estate to the American colony. Natalia Shelikof had nothing to gain personally by the carrying out of this plan, and it is evidently simply an extension of her husband's project for agricultural colonies in the new possessions.

Another factor influenced Shelikof's agricultural projects, and that was the desire to provide food for his colony. He knew the difficulties of sending supplies from Russia, and his aim no doubt was to make Russian America self-supporting. Had Shelikof's successors been able to grasp the possibilities of local agriculture and a self-supporting community, there is serious question whether Russia would have relinquished her American possessions. These remained, however, throughout their history an outlying trading post of the Russian Empire which could only be provisioned at heavy expense.

Whatever may have been Shelikof's motives, the time was hardly ripe for agricultural colonists, and Baranof did not hesitate to divert the new supply of laborers to the more immediate needs of the company. Moreover, the new arrivals included a number of craftsmen whom the company very much needed. Therefore, many of the newcomers, a large part of whom were Siberian exiles or convicts, were distributed to the best interests of the company. Two years later 50 of them were established at Yakutat Bay where they eked out a miserable existence, almost starving to death the first winter. The region was but ill-adapted to agriculture, and there was but little game. A final end to this first colonizing project was made when the Yakutat settlement was destroyed by the natives (the Tlingits) in 1804. Had the group been placed on Cook Inlet, it would have become self-supporting and with proper management might have supplied some food to the colony.

The ship load of colonists which arrived in 1794 also included the Archimandrite and seven priests, the first missionaries to reach Alaska. These were not warmly welcomed by Baranof who apparently regarded them as so

---

[6] *Ibid.*, p. 382.

many more useless men to feed in his half-starved colony, and, moreover, he undoubtedly feared that they might intervene between him and the natives. On the other hand, the priests seem to have found little to endorse in the new colony and were loud in their complaints of the treatment they received and the conditions under which they lived. The first church was completed at Kodiak in 1796.

In spite of the adverse conditions, the priests undertook the work of proselytizing the natives and scattered out to various fields. This policy was evidently encouraged by Baranof who thus relieved himself from personal contact with men with whom he had little sympathy. Father Makar went to Unalaska in 1795 where he labored for several years. Father Juvenal visited Yakutat and then, returning to Kodiak, later went to a native settlement on the head of Iliamna Lake where he was killed by the natives. The spiritual welfare of the Kodiak natives was entrusted to Father Herman who opened a girls' school at Pavelovsk and continued his work at this locality for some 40 years. Iosaph, the Archimandrite, later returned to Okhotsk and was consecrated as bishop of Russian America; but on his return voyage the ship foundered, and he and several other priests were drowned.

Baranof's troubles with the priests were but the least of his difficulties. During the first year of his management provisions were scarce, several hunting parties were lost and vessels wrecked, and he himself suffered with rheumatism. In spite of all this, his efforts were never relaxed. In 1799 he went to Controller Bay where he not only lost some boats and their crews but also had a pitched battle with the natives. He continued his journey, however, and established a post on Baranof Island about six miles north of the present site of Sitka. About this time posts were also built on Iliamna Lake, on Nuchek, on Montague Island, and at the mouth of Kaknu River on the Kenai Peninsula.

Though Baranof collected many furs and paid dividends to his distant stockholders, yet for one reason or another he was in a constant turmoil. Naval officers employed by the company refused to obey his orders; foreign traders, especially American ships, invaded his field and offered serious rivalry to his enterprise; the natives were troublesome. His post on Iliamna Lake was soon destroyed; and in 1802 his fort on Baranof Island was taken by surprise, and most of the Russian garrison were killed. The few survivors from the massacre were rescued by an English vessel. Baranof returned to the scene of this tragedy and with the aid of three vessels and a large force captured the native fort on the present site of Sitka. Here was then started a settlement which for over a century was to be the capital of Alaska. Sitka is, therefore, the oldest white settlement, except for Kodiak, on the Pacific coast north of San Francisco. Besides the other difficulties, Baranof was constantly beset with the task of feeding his colony. Supplies were brought by ships from Okhotsk by the long overland route across Siberia. It was this condition that led to the use of the sea route from the Baltic as well as the negotiations with the Spanish colonies in California.

As was discussed in a previous chapter, the plan to use the sea route to the American colony appears to have been the project of Krusenstern, a captain of the Russian navy who sailed from the Baltic with two ships in 1803. With him went Rezanof whose interest in the Russian American colony had led him to accept residence in it as the Tsar's plenipotentiary. His first mission, however, was to establish relations with the Japanese, and in this he was unsuccessful. Meanwhile, one of the vessels, under command of Lisianski, reached Sitka in time to take part in the attack on the native fort. In the same year Rezanof, the new governor, arrived at Kodiak where he labored assiduously to improve the conditions of both the Russians and the natives. He established a school and at his own expense installed a small library, the first in Alaska. He even attempted a small museum which should illustrate the natural history of the colony.[7]

In 1805 Rezanof joined Baranof at the new settlement of Sitka which was threatened with starvation, only averted by the arrival of an American ship which, with its entire cargo, was purchased for use of the Russians. Even with this succor the colony spent a miserable winter, many dying from undernourishment and scurvy. By February there were eight deaths and 60 disabled by disease among the less than 200 Russians at Sitka. Something had to be done, and a voyage to San Francisco was decided upon. Though very hospitably received at San Francisco, Rezanof found the negotiations for supplies by no means easy. The non-intercourse law of the Spanish colony would probably

[7] Von Langsdorff, G. H., *Voyages and Travels in Various Parts of the World during the Years 1803-1807*, Carlisle, 1817, pp. 368-369.

have baffled a less experienced diplomat than Rezanof. He, however, secured not only the provisions but also the promise of the hand of the Spanish governor's daughter.

Rezanof returned to Sitka with his supplies and also with a broad plan for Russian expansions on the Pacific and commerce with the Spanish American colony. This plan and his love affair[8] required sanction of the Tsar. He therefore relinquished his overlordship of the American colony, probably all the more willingly because he found the details of administration and trade but little to his liking. In any event, he started for St. Petersburg with the draft of a treaty with Spain permitting intercolonial trade, but he died in Siberia. His broad vision of Russian dominance of the North Pacific died with him, and the Russian American colony continued as a private mercantile venture. Had Rezanof lived, the Russian flag would probably have still been flying on American soil, and a considerable part of the continent might have passed under the dominion of the Tsar.

From now on the colony was better supplied; partly from Russian sources, partly by Yankee clippers. Occasional vessels sailed from Kronstadt on the long, long voyage from the Baltic to Sitka. Many of the supplies, however, were still carried by the laborious pack horse route from Yakutsk to Okhotsk and thence by company vessel across the Pacific. In 1810 John Jacob Astor dispatched a vessel to Sitka with a letter offering to supply the Russian colony. Some supplies were received by Baranof from this source, but the trade relation presumably entered into was interrupted by the War of 1812, during which Astoria fell into the hands of the British.

In spite of his many requests to be relieved of his onerous duties, Baranof was continued as general manager until 1818 when he was relieved by Captain L. A. Hagemeister with Lieutenant S. I. Yanovski, Baranof's son-in-law, as deputy. Baranof, broken by years of exposure and heavy responsibilities, died in the following year at sea during his return voyage to Europe. His 20-odd years of service had established order in the remote colony. As the Spaniards refused to enter into trade relations, Baranof had in 1812 established a small colony on Bodega Bay in northern California known as Fort Ross, where some wheat was raised to supply Russian America. He had also placed a

[8] His first wife, the daughter of Shelikof, had died in 1802.—*Editor's note.*

post on one of the Hawaiian Islands, but did not live to see this project completed. Trade relations had been established with Canton, China, to which many furs were shipped direct from Sitka, in large part by American trading vessels.

Hagemeister took over a domain extending from Sitka to the Aleutian Islands. Posts were sparingly distributed through this vast domain, for at best the Russians clung to the edge of the continent, concerning the interior of which they knew almost nothing. Bering Sea had been explored, but, except for the post on the Pribilof Islands, its shores were not occupied by the Russians. The settlements then included five on the Aleutian Islands, four on Cook Inlet, one on Kodiak Island, two on Prince William Sound, and the capital at Sitka. Some 18 vessels had been built in the colony. Reforms were introduced into the administration by which the chief director became directly responsible to the crown for his administrative actions, and the fact that from now on naval officers were the governors of the colony improved the conditions of both natives and Russian employees.

An important feature of the new administration was the impetus it gave to the charting of coast lines and the beginning of inland explorations. The activities of naval officers stationed in the colony as well as the work of the several expeditions sent to these waters by the Russian Admiralty led to a rapid increase of accurate knowledge of the shore line. In 1820 the lower Kuskokwim was explored by Kolmakof, following an unsuccessful attempt in the previous year to ascend the Copper River. Other parties searched out the shores of Bering Sea and charted the coast line of the Alaska Peninsula.

In 1821 the charter of the company was renewed for 20 years by order of Tsar Nicholas. Captain M. I. Muravief succeeded Hagemeister as governor in 1820, but four years later relinquished the office to Lieutenant P. E. Chistiakof.

By this time Sitka had begun to assume the appearance of an important settlement. The town was overshadowed by the governor's house which was built on a rock, the summit of which stood some 80 feet above the rest of the settlement. This commodious building formed a citadel which was defended by 32 cannons. The rest of the settlement was surrounded with palisades flanked by towers at the angles. Muskets and swords enough for 1,000 men were kept in stock.[9] A small hospital was run by a surgeon with a student assistant. The work shops included a bell foundry and equipment to manufacture the iron work of vessels and other utensils. Some bells and agricultural implements were made at Sitka for the Spanish missions in California. There were about 300 Russians at Sitka, about 100 creoles, and about 400 natives. During the hunting season, however, more than three-quarters of them were employed elsewhere. Mail was received from Europe only once a year via vessel from Okhotsk, to which point it was carried by the long overland route across Siberia. The food was chiefly salmon of which 500,000 pounds were salted at Sitka each year. Potatoes and other vegetables were supplied from local gardens.

Up to 1818 employees of the company worked on shares but after that time were under wage. The *promishleniki* and creole hunters received 350 to 400 rubles annually, with rations, lodgings, light, and fuel. Those from Siberia served for seven years and were transferred to and from the colony free of charge. All grain was brought from California where fresh and salt beef, peas, beans, lye for tanning, and soap were obtained. In return, articles manufactured at Sitka, coffee, tea, sugar, woolen and cotton goods, and timber and furs were sent. Of these, only the goods manufactured at Sitka of iron and copper, lumber, and furs were produced in the colony.

The first man of distinction to govern the Russian American colony was Baron Ferdinand von Wrangell who succeeded Chistiakof in 1832. Wrangell had achieved distinction previous to this time for his exploration of the Arctic parts of Siberia. Under his initiative much exploration was accomplished, though he remained in the colony only four years. He has left a valuable record of conditions in the colony during the period of his governorship.[10]

In 1832 there were 652 Europeans in the colony, chiefly Russians. Of these, 406 were at Sitka. There were also in America about a thousand creoles. The native population of Kodiak and the Aleutian Islands who were regarded as subjects of the company numbered nearly 9,000. Sitka, the capital of the colony, called New Archangel by the Russians, is credited with a total population, including Europeans,

---

[9] Lutke, Frederick, *Voyage autour du monde, 1826-1829*, Paris, 1835, I, 104-105.

[10] Wrangell, Ferdinand, *Statistische und ethnographische Nachrichten über die Russischen Betsitzungen an der Nordwestküste von Amerika*, St. Petersburg, 1839.

creoles, and Aleuts, of 847, of whom 256 were women. Many of the clerks and mechanics were creoles, who had been educated for this service. All of the higher official positions at Sitka were filled by navy officers, including a dozen in all, a fact which gave the little capital some social distinction.

For administrative purposes Russian America was divided into five districts. Agents in charge of each district were stationed at Atka and Unalaska in the Aleutians, at St. Michael in Bering Sea, at Kodiak, and at Sitka. Small hospitals were maintained at several of these district headquarters and a larger one at Sitka. There were four churches and five chapels in the colony at this time and several schools for native children; there was also a school at Sitka for whites and creoles.

About 220 head of cattle were distributed among the islands and southwestern Alaska, together with some sheep, hogs, goats, chickens, and ducks. In spite of this livestock and the raising of potatoes and other vegetables, fish was still the principal diet of both Europeans and natives. The California settlement of Fort Ross had through poor management been able to contribute little in the way of food supply to the mother colony. The Russians then in North America knew nothing of agriculture, for they were sailors and hunters and could not take advantage of the products of the soil under any conditions. It is now known that the part of Alaska controlled by the Russians could have furnished at least the beef and potatoes needed by the few hundred Europeans. Another factor which led to the lack of interest in farming was the temporary character of the European residents. Most of those who came to the colony planned to return at the end of their seven year contracts. There were no settlements of permanent colonists except one or two on Cook Inlet, the descendants of ignorant peasants and convicts who had not the knowledge or ambition to take advantage of these opportunities. The educated men were naval officers who regarded this sojourn in the colony as a species of exile. There was no representative of an intelligent energetic pioneer stock such as settled the Atlantic seaboard of America. As a consequence, when Russia was ready to relinquish her overseas dominion, there were few who had any ties of affection to the colony.

The company did what it could to make their exiled employees more satisfied. Wrangell reports that the library founded by Rezanof had by 1833 grown to 1,700 volumes and that it included some foreign as well as Russian works. In addition there were about 400 Russian periodicals and newspapers, a collection of charts, atlases, and nautical and astronomical instruments. A magnetic observatory was built at Sitka in 1833.

While the Russian fur traders were gaining a foothold on the northwestern margin of the continent, their English rivals were steadily approaching the same goal from the east. The conquest of what is now Canada, confirmed in 1763 by the treaty of Paris, relieved the Hudson Bay Company of its competitors, the French traders. This was, however, succeeded by the even more serious rivalry of the Northwestern Fur Company whose agents were far more active than those of the older corporation. As has already been indicated, Alexander Mackenzie, the most daring of the Northwestern Company's agents, reached the Pacific near Queen Charlotte Sound in 1793 and thus became the first white man to cross the continent north of Mexico; four years earlier he had traced the great river which bears his name from Great Slave Lake to the Arctic Ocean. During the succeeding generation the English traders gradually occupied the region between Hudson Bay and the Pacific. Fort Vancouver, near the mouth of the Columbia River, was built in 1825. This act was clearly an invasion of the domain of another rival, for John Jacob Astor had established Astoria in 1811 as a post of the American Fur Company. Three years later, during the war between the United States and England, this post passed into the hands of the Northwestern Fur Company by purchase from the local partners in the enterprise. This deal was no doubt accelerated by the presence of an English man-of-war. Thus, the only strong American rival in the fur trade was disposed of.

Meanwhile the employees of the Hudson Bay and Northwestern companies had fought each other for control of the rich fur fields of the interior. This rivalry was by no means confined to ordinary competition in trade but included personal violence too. In 1821 this question was settled: the Canadian fur trade interests were consolidated by the amalgamation of the Northwestern Company with the Hudson Bay Company. As a result, one strong corporation practically controlled the rich fur fields stretching from the Atlantic to the Pacific, except insofar as the

Russians dominated the northwest coast. It was only natural that the next clash should be between the Hudson Bay Company and the Russian American Company.

Wrangell was succeeded as director of the company by Captain I. A. Kupreanof in 1836. Meanwhile, however, difficulties had already arisen with the Hudson Bay Company. Taking advantage of the clause in the treaties of 1824 and 1825, Russia had withdrawn the privilege of coastal trade from American and English citizens in 1834. Protests on the part of the British and American governments were unavailing. The Hudson Bay Company, loath to lose so valuable a field, had in 1834 attempted to establish a post at the mouth of the Stikine River. Wrangell, having received news of their coming, dispatched two armed vessels to prevent them. As a consequence, the English withdrew, and the Hudson Bay Company was loud in its protest. The Russians had, however, acted within their rights, and this post, which they called Fort Wrangell, remained in their possession. This not only prevented the English from trading on the coast, but also prevented access to the interior by the Stikine River where the Hudson Bay Company had planned to establish posts. Finding no relief through diplomatic channels, the Hudson Bay Company was forced to open negotiations with the Russian American Company and an agreement was reached in 1839. An instrument[11] was signed at Hamburg by Sir George Simpson, governor of the Hudson Bay Company, and Baron von Wrangell for the Russian American Company. By its terms the Hudson Bay Company leased for ten years a mainland strip of the Russian American colony extending from Cross Sound on the northwest to Dixon Entrance on the south at an annual rental of 2,000 land otter skins. The Hudson Bay Company was also to deliver each year at Sitka certain quantities of flour and other provisions at specified prices. A declaration of war between Russia and Great Britain was not to nullify the agreement, and in such contingency the Hudson Bay Company was permitted to withdraw its posts without monetary loss. The effect of this agreement was to give the Hudson Bay Company practically the control of the entire coast line and adjacent islands except the Alexander Archipelago from Cross Sound to the Columbia River. It also controlled the inland region stretch-

[11] Oliver, E. H. (ed.), *The Canadian Northwest, its early development and legislative records,* Publications of Canadian Archives, No. 9, Ottawa, 1915, II, 791.

ing eastward except insofar as this was in conflict with the interests of the United States, which had already protested against the English occupation of the Columbia River. This agreement between the two companies which was sanctioned by the Russian and English governments clearly recognized the suzerainty of the Tsar over the coastal mainland strip of Southeastern Alaska and was a strong argument in favor of our boundary contentions during the dispute with Canada.

The Hudson Bay Company now (1840) built a fort at the mouth of the Stikine River[12] and the same year another at the mouth of the Taku River south of the present site of Juneau; the former gave a route of communication with the posts in the interior, but the latter was soon abandoned. There were serious difficulties with the local natives who were turbulent, warlike people. This fact was well-known to the Russians who never subjugated them and were, therefore, probably quite willing to turn their difficulties over to the English.

An important event in the history of Sitka was the visit in 1842 of Sir George Simpson, governor of the Hudson Bay Company. A. K. Etolin, who was then the director of the Russian colony, received his distinguished guest with as much royal hospitality as the resources of the distant settlement permitted. Simpson has left a valuable record of the conditions in this little port.[13] He arrived on Easter Sunday and dined with the governor in the large room of Baranof castle, where about 70 were seated including all the Russian officials, sea captains, mates, and clerks. According to the testimony the holiday was celebrated by excessive drinking in which both sexes indulged. Simpson says:[14]

> In the service of the Russian American Company the officers are divided into two classes. The captain of the port, the secretary, three public and two private secretaries, two masters in the navy, the commercial agent, and the Lutheran clergyman form at present the first class and constantly dine by general invitation with the governor; while the civilian masters of vessels, the accountants, head engineers, and about twenty clerks and storekeepers form the second class and dine together in a club.
>
> The salaries of these officials independently of such pay as they may have according to their rank in the Imperial navy range

[12] Called Fort Stikine but generally known by the Russian name of Fort Wrangell.

[13] Simpson, Sir George, *Narrative of a Journey around the World during the Years 1841 and 1842*, 2 vols., London, 1847.

[14] *Ibid.*, II, 188.

between three thousand and twelve thousand rubles a year, the ruble being equal as nearly as possible to ten francs; while they are moreover provided with firewood and candles, with a room for each and a servant, and a kitchen between them. Generally speaking the officers are extravagant, those of five thousand rubles and upward spending nearly the whole and others getting into debt as a kind of mortgage on their future promotion.

The frugal mind of the experienced administrator notes that there are an unnecessary number of employees for the amount of work to be done. These total nearly 500, and with their families make about 1,200 souls in the establishment. The servants, however, appear to have been harder worked, for their hours of labor were from five until seven. At this time the workshops were well equipped, being so provided that all the machinery of small steamers was cast and manufactured.

Of the place as a whole, Simpson says:[15] "Of all the dirty and wretched places I have ever seen Sitka is preeminently the most wretched and dirty. The common houses are nothing but wooden hovels huddled together without order or design in nasty alleys." Whymper,[16] who visited Sitka 20 years later, records a more pleasing picture:

After passing the governor's house, which is perched on a rock and only reached by a steep flight of stairs, we found the bureau and workshops of the company and a number of better class houses of the employees. On the left of the street is shrubbery, the Club Gardens, with summer houses, card and supper rooms, and swings for the children, and a little farther the Greek church with its domes and spires of oriental style overshadowing a plain Lutheran structure within a few steps of it attracts our attention. Then came the clubhouse occupied by the married servants of the company—the schoolhouse from which scholars of promise were sent to St. Petersburg, and the hospital, a very neat and clean building. Beyond these were a few dozen cottages and shanties and then the woods with the one promenade of the place running through them.

The hospital finds favor, too, in Simpson's eyes, for of it he says: "In its wards and in short in all the requisite appointments the institution would do no disgrace to England." He also speaks of the Greek Russian priests and comments on the spirit of tolerance exhibited by the Russian government as evinced by the presence of the Lutheran clergyman. Thirteen vessels were counted in the harbor, the largest of 350 tons, of which two were steamers.

---

[15] *Ibid.*, p. 190.

[16] Whymper, Frederick, *Travel and Adventures in the Territory of Alaska*, New York, 1869, p. 98.

Simpson's reference to social life at Sitka is as follows: "New Archangel, notwithstanding its isolated position, is a very gay place—much of the time of its inhabitants is devoted to festivity; dinners and balls run a perpetual round and are managed in a style which in this part of the world may be deemed extravagant." Referring to a wedding he attended, he says, "The ladies were showily attired in clean muslin dresses with satin shoes, silk stockings, kid gloves, fans, and all other necessary or unnecessary appendages." Music was furnished by a good band, and the refreshments included champagne and liqueur. Of a farewell dinner with the governor, he says, "The glass, the plate, and the appointments in general were very costly; the viands were excellent; and Governor Etolin played the part of the host to perfection." The apparent aristocratic flavor to these descriptions is offset by another statement: "During this walk I took leave of several of my old friends, particularly of Katherine, the acknowledged belle of the place, who, though the tailor's daughter, has a host of suitors of all ranks."

While Sitka had some semblance of civilization, the outposts were of the most primitive character. Fort Constantine, located on Hinchinbrook Island, near the entrance of Prince William Sound, was built before the end of the 18th century. It was, therefore, one of the oldest posts in the colony, besides being of easy access. Yet some 40 years later when Belcher visited it, he describes it as follows:[17]

> This establishment of the Imperial Russian Fur Company consists of the official residence, eight Russians, fifty Aleuts, and other allies. The houses are included in a substantial wooden quadrangle furnished at its sea angles with two octagonal turrets capped in the old English style and pierced with loopholes and ports; the summits of the lines are armed with spikes of wood. It is calculated to sustain a tolerable siege under determined hands. The sleeping apartments, or "tween decks" as we should term them, are desperately filthy. The whole range is warmed by Dutch ovens and the sides being eighteen inches in thickness are well calculated to withstand the cold as well as to defy musketry. The native allies who live in huts outside are filthier than any Esquimaux.

Dr. Dall has left a valuable record of the life at the more isolated posts. Though his observations were made some 20 years later than those of Simpson, they will serve to illustrate this contrast.

---

[17] Belcher, Captain Sir Edward, *Narrative of a Voyage Round the World Performed in Her Majesty's Ship* Sulphur *during the Years 1836-1842*, London, 1843, I, 72-73.

He describes[18] the redoubt at St. Michael in 1865 as being composed of log buildings with plank roofs arranged in a square connected by palisades and flanked with bastions. The rooms were heated with a peculiar form of stove built of stone and smeared inside and out with mortar. After the stove had been thoroughly heated by wood fire, the coals were removed and the damper closed. These stoves, which were universally used in Russian America, once heated would hold the heat for many hours. Bath houses were to be found at even the most isolated posts, and no doubt they contributed greatly to the health of the Russian employees. Dall describes the commander of this redoubt, who also controlled the small posts of the adjacent region, as an old soldier

> . . . of great energy and iron will, with the Russian fondness for strong liquor and with ungovernable passions in certain directions. He has a soldier's contempt for making money by small ways, a certain code of honor of his own, is generous in his own way, and seldom does a mean thing when he is sober, but nevertheless is a good deal of a brute. He will gamble and drink in the most democratic way with his workmen and bears no malice for a black eye when received in a drunken brawl; but woe to the unfortunate who infringes discipline while he is sober, for he shall certainly receive his reward.

Dall quotes this petty tyrant as saying of his men: "You can expect nothing good of this rabble; they left Russia because they were not wanted there." Indeed, this company recruited its lower class of employees from among the criminal exiles of Siberia.

Dall records that the regular workman at St. Michael received 50 pounds of flour, a pound of tea, and three pounds of sugar a month, and that his pay was about 20 cents a day, though some received 30 cents. Apparently there was no meat in the ration, but large quantities of fish were consumed. Small offences were punished by imprisonment in guard houses or a thrashing administered by the commander in person. Some greater criminals were forced to run gauntlet, receive 100 or 200 blows with a stick, or be sent for trial to Sitka.

The commander of the sub-post at Nulato is pictured even less attractively by Dall. A Russian creole,[19] he was good humored, but was a mixture of stupidity and low cunning and could neither read nor write. Also,

---

[18] Dall, William H., *Alaska and its Resources*, Boston, 1870, pp. 10-13.

[19] *Ibid.*, pp. 44-46.

He was an insatiable drinker and ungovernable as a mad bull when drunk, though at other times quiet and unexcitable. . . . Notwithstanding his faults, most of which were hereditary, he brought up his children and treated his wife as well as his light allowed him to. He had a large proportion of generosity and hospitality in his character, was unusually free from any disposition to immorality, and was never known to sell any furs purchased by him and belonging to the Russian American Company to any of our party, as he easily might have done.

Nulato then consisted of an enclosure surrounded by buildings and stockades. On some of the buildings there were turrets pierced for cannon with an armament consisting of two old rusty six-pounders. The inhabitants of the place consisted of this trader in charge, his Indian wife and numerous children, one creole who could read and write and acted as clerk, two Russians, and a few half-breeds and Indians.

These descriptions of the Russian American colony give a picture of strong contrasts. The gaiety and luxury of the high officials of the colony are offset by the wretched hovels in which a large part of the population of Sitka lived. Kodiak at this time could boast of some good buildings, a church and a school for natives, but the other settlements were but frontier posts characterized by squalor and dirt, and in many instances commanded by illiterate Russians or creoles. A few Greek Catholic missions scattered among these posts were the only marks of civilization.

The contrast between the posts of the Hudson Bay Company and those of the Russian American Company is shown by Dall's description of Fort Yukon, which he visited the same year as he went to Nulato. Fort Yukon, located at the mouth of the Porcupine River, was the most isolated post of the English company. It is said that the commander, on shipping a cargo of furs to London, did not receive returns until seven years later. Dr. Dall[20] describes this remote outpost as follows:

The present buildings consist of a large house containing six rooms for the commander; a block of three houses of one room each for the workmen; a large storeroom; a kitchen; and four block houses or bastions pierced for musketry at the corners of the proposed stockade. . . . All the houses were strongly built, roofed with sheets of spruce bark and fastened down with long poles. The sides were plastered with white mortar made of shell marl, obtainable in the vicinity. Most of the windows were of parchment but those of the

[20] *Ibid.*, p. 103.

commander's house were of glass. The latter was provided with good plank floors and the doors and sashes were painted red with ochre. The yard was free from dirt and the houses with their red walls and white trimmings made a very favorable comparison with any of those in the Russian posts.

Dall states that the garrison consisted of the commander and six men, of whom five were Scotchmen, and two French Canadians; there was also a Church of England clergyman.

In spite of adverse conditions, the expansion of the Russian trade continued. A post had been built on St. Michael Island near the mouth of the Yukon in 1833 and about the same time at Kolmakof, on the Kuskokwim. A post was established at the mouth of the Unalakleet River in 1840 and at Nulato in 1841. By these new establishments, the Russians controlled the shores of Bering Sea and the Yukon and Kuskokwim rivers for 600 to 800 miles from tidewater. Attempts to establish posts on the Copper River were frustrated both because of the difficulties of the ascent of that turbulent stream and because of the hostilities of the natives. Though the Russians had by this time become skilled navigators and their vessels traversed the shore line without difficulty, yet their inland navigation ended where they encountered swift waters. They considered the Yukon unnavigable above the mouth of the Tanana, though steamers now ascend the river a thousand miles farther.

At the time that the Russians decided the upper Yukon was unnavigable, the Hudson Bay Company's post, Fort Good Hope, was already established on the Mackenzie, though it could only be reached by a canoe journey of a thousand miles or more, traversing many swift rivers. But the Russians had no such craft as the birch bark canoe of the Canadian voyageur. It was the Ojibway canoe that opened up the northwest of Canada, and it was its absence in Alaska that prevented the Russians from occupying the inland region. The small white birch of Alaska does not yield bark in sufficient size to make the large canoe of the voyageur. It is possible that the northern limit of the large birch tree may be regarded as one of the chief reasons why Alaska today is occupied by the Anglo-Saxons rather than by the Slavs. For had the Russians occupied the interior instead of securing only a foothold near tidewater, they might never have relinquished their valuable American possessions.

In the years from 1836 to 1839 the natives of Russian

America suffered severely under an epidemic. In spite of the efforts of the director, Kupreanof, the disease spread from the southeastern part of the colony, where it is said to have been introduced from British Columbia, through to Bering Sea and up the Yukon and Kuskokwim rivers. Thousands of natives died, though the Russians appear to have been largely exempt from the ravages. Wholesale vaccination of the natives was undertaken so far as the limited means permitted, but it seems that the disease ran its course rather than being checked by these efforts. In some settlements a third to a half of the native population was swept away by the scourge.

A renewal of the charter for 20 years was granted the company on March 5, 1841. This was on the same terms as the previous one, with some additional privileges as regards trade with China. A council of five officials of the company was established by this instrument with criminal jurisdiction in all but capital cases.[21] Not only was the furnishing of intoxicants to natives prohibited by the new instrument, but also their sale to Russians in the colony was forbidden. From all accounts, this drastic prohibition law seems to have had little or no effect in reducing drunkenness among the white employees of the company. Though the American fur trade was continued on a large scale, the profits were by no means as large as they had been under the old regime. Most of the higher naval officers sent to Sitka were men of ability, and the general conditions of natives and Russians were improved under their administration. Yet they were by no means experienced in business affairs, and the commercial side of the venture was not of the importance to them that it had been to the old trader Baranof. The company was hemmed in on the south by the English traders and did not have the men in its employ who could open up the rich fur fields of the interior.

During this period the chief directors of the colony were appointed from among the naval officers who had seen service in Russian America. Thus the chief directors, Captain Etolin (1840-45) and Captain S. V. Voevodski (1854-60), had both contributed to the increase of geographic knowledge of the colony which they governed.

The Russians by no means controlled the natives that were near their posts. Even at Sitka itself they maintained themselves only by their block houses and palisades which

[21] Bancroft, *op. cit.*, p. 569.

were armed with artillery. The Copper Indians drove out or massacred all the Russians who attempted to invade their domain. Wrangell was several times attacked by natives, the post at Yakataga was destroyed, and several battles were fought at other localities. In 1851, as will be discussed in the following chapter, the Koyukuk natives attacked the post at Nulato on the Yukon and killed practically all the natives as well as several whites. The attack appears to have been the result of intertribal warfare rather than being especially directed against the whites. It is noteworthy that the post at Nulato had been twice before this attack plundered and burned by the Indians, but during the absence of the Russians.

In spite of the supplies sent to the colonies either by vessels direct from Russia or by foreign vessels, many of the supplies were still sent by the expensive overland route to Okhotsk. As a consequence of this condition and the large pay roll of employees at Sitka and other places, the operating costs were high. The control of the company was not in the hands of shrewd business men such as those that dominated the Hudson Bay Company. The local employees, except for a few naval officers whose term of service was short, had no voice in the management of the company, which was controlled by men in St. Petersburg, but few of whom had firsthand knowledge of the conditions pertaining in the distant possessions.

A temporary boom was inaugurated at Sitka by the California gold discovery of 1848. Previous to this time the little foundry at Sitka had supplied some of the few implements needed by the Spanish ranchers of California. It is recorded that mission bells were cast at Sitka for the Roman Catholic missions of California. The first iron plows of the California ranchers were also made at Sitka, as were other simple tools. After the Mexican war, California became a possession of the United States and for a time looked to Sitka for some of its implements. With the influx of gold seekers there was a demand for all kinds of articles, and the warehouses at Sitka were emptied of previously unsalable goods that had accumulated for years.[22] This trade, however, was short-lived, for Sitka had no manufacturing plants and the routes across Nicaraugua and Panama gave the eastern merchants of the United States

[22] *Jahres Bericht der Russische Amerikanischen Companie für das Jahr 1848*, St. Petersburg, 1850, VIII, 712.

a quicker route to California than was available to the Russian company. Even the Cape Horn route was far shorter than that from Russia. Moreover, the influx of population, while it enabled the company to empty its warehouses of a lot of junk at good prices, also made it more difficult to obtain provisions from sources that now diverted their trade to the new market.

In spite of these difficulties, dividends were continued on the stock. It was evidently regarded as a good investment, for in 1850[23] it sold at about 270 rubles, though the annual dividend was then only about 15 rubles.

There were then in the employ of the company in America 697 officials. This number included many creoles, for the total Russian population of the colony was less than 500.

At this time an attempt was made to search for mineral wealth in the colony, a project no doubt inspired by the finding of gold in California. Of this unsuccessful attempt, more will be said hereafter. Significant too is the fact that from 1859 to 1864 I. V. Furuhelm, a mining engineer, served as chief director of the colony.

Plans for agricultural colonists in Russian America had long since been abandoned. The descendants of some of the early colonists still supported themselves on Cook Inlet and at other places to the southwest. A few cattle and sheep were raised, but the possibilities of the distant possession supplying its own grain were never recognized by the Russian officials. This is the more strange because even at that time grain was raised in parts of Siberia under conditions of soil and climate that were far less favorable than were those in the Cook Inlet region then occupied by the Russians. They did not, of course, have any knowledge of the fertile valleys of the interior.

American whalers, by the middle of the 19th century in spite of Russian prohibition, had made Bering Sea and the adjacent portions of the Arctic Ocean their own hunting ground. Here a lucrative industry developed, and the whalers did not hesitate to trespass on the domain of the company by engaging in the fur trade along the shores of Bering Sea. The Russians were unable to prevent this, and it remained for the Confederate privateer *Shenandoah* to place the first check on this industry by a raid in 1864. This vessel appeared without warning and destroyed upwards of 30 whalers without opposition, for there were no

[23] *Ibid.*, IX, 710-716.

Union war vessels in this sea. She subsequently continued her voyage across the Pacific and was the only vessel to carry the Confederate flag around the world. In 1851, the Russian American corporation attempted to take toll of the whaling industry by organizing a subsidiary company, but this enterprise met with only moderate success. Another venture was in cooperation with an American company to furnish ice and coal from Russian America to California, but this too met with failure.

On the Yukon River the Russians began to feel the competition of rival traders before the middle of the 19th century. Though Nulato, founded in 1841, was the highest Russian post on the river, the trading voyages were extended from there for some 200 miles to the mouth of the Tanana, and in time the Russians would undoubtedly have acquired the trade of the entire Yukon basin. But their more active rivals, the Hudson Bay traders, reached the great river by 1847 and built their post of Fort Yukon at the mouth of the Porcupine. From here their trading voyages were made down the river as far as the Tanana. So the two rival companies once more came into direct competition. Though the Hudson Bay Company was here trading with goods that were brought thousands of miles in canoes, yet they maintained a successful rivalry with the Russians who were separated from tidewater by less than a thousand miles of sluggish water navigation. In this field, as in all others where the two companies met, the English company again gained the advantage.

When the question of the renewal of the charter came up, the Russian Government insisted on certain administrative reforms which the company was loath to undertake. An immediate agreement was not possible, and negotiations were continued until the plan of transfer of the colony to the United States became a matter of negotiation. Meanwhile, the company continued its business under the direction of Prince Maksutof, who took charge of company affairs by order of the Tsar. Before we consider the transfer of Russian America to the United States, it will be desirable to review briefly the history of exploration up to this time.

CHAPTER XIII

Exploration During Russian Occupation

BY THE beginning of the 19th century the larger features of Russian America's coast line as far north as Cape Lisburne were fairly well known. This was chiefly due to the surveys of Cook and Vancouver, though the navigators of other nationalities made important contributions. With the recognition of Russian ascendency in the northwestern part of the continent the extending of these explorations was left to the Government of the Tsar. The St. Petersburg Government was, however, not ready to enter the field, and for some years the task fell to the Russian American Company. Baranof, its resident director, was anxious to learn about his extensive domain, but he had no means at hand for accurate surveys. However, his chief thought was to find new fields for the fur trade, and at no time during his long administration was there any evidence of a desire for a scientific exploration beyond that required by the immediate commercial needs of the company. Good harbors must be sought and located; fisheries had to be found; ship-building timber was needed; and, above all, there must be a constant endeavor to find natives to trade with and new fur fields to exploit. Incidental to this work a large amount of information was gathered regarding the details of the coast line, and some crude charting was done.

Baranof's successors were naval officers and among them were some, such as Wrangell and M. D. Tebenkof, who had high scientific standing. Under the inspiration and guidance of such men, scientific knowledge regarding Russian America was much extended. The vague statements and crude charts of the illiterate Russian fur hunters, upon which Baranof was chiefly forced to rely, were supplanted by the accurate observations and maps made by naval officers and trained navigators of the merchant marine. Another class of explorers was recruited from among the Russian half-bloods or creoles. These were youths who were trained in simple methods of navigation and survey at Sitka and a few even at St. Petersburg. Some notable explorations were accomplished by the creoles, who had the advantage over the Russians both in being thoroughly familiar with the conditions of travel in the country and in having a better understanding of the natives, with whom they had blood relationship. Among them was Alexander Kolmakof, who explored the lower Kuskokwim in 1829, and Andrei Glazunof, who discovered the Yukon River in 1834. In fact, it fell to the creoles to make the principal inland explorations, for with the exception of Zagoskin no Russian naval officer extended his surveys beyond tidewater.

Lieutenants Davidof and Khvostof were the first naval officers to enter the employ of the company. They served for nearly two years (1802-1803) in the colony, but their time was chiefly taken up with the navigation of supply ships and they accomplished little in the way of surveys. In 1804 Captain Lisianski, also a naval officer, reached Kodiak in command of the *Neva,* the first Russian vessel to reach the colony from Europe. Though he remained on the coast for nearly a year, he performed no very important geographic work. He was followed in 1810 by a visit to the colony of the Russian warship *Diana,* commanded by Captain Vassili M. Golofnin. Golofnin's voyage was one of inspection and investigation of the Russian American Company's posts, and eight years later he was sent out on a similar mission. His reports led to some much needed reforms, but aside from determining the position of some points along the seaboard, he accomplished no important geographic work.

The most important exploring voyage of this period was that of Captain Otto von Kotzebue in the brig *Rurik.* Kotzebue, an officer of the Russian navy, was a son of the German dramatist and was accompanied by L. A. Chamisso, the German poet-naturalist. His purpose was the general advancement of scientific knowledge, including the discovery of a northeast waterway, in the existence of which many learned men still obstinately believed. His vessel of 180 tons was built in Sweden, and the expedition was equipped with scientific instruments made in England. A special type of lifeboat was furnished by the English Admiralty, and the provisions included the then newly-discovered tinned meats, soups, milk, and vegetables. Among the members of the expedition were Choris the painter and Eschscholtz the surgeon and botanist whose names, together with that of Kotzebue himself as well as those of Chamisso and Shishmaref, the first lieutenant of the vessel, are fittingly preserved in the geographic nomenclature of Alaska. The expense of the undertaking was met by the chancellor, Count Romanzof, and it was guided by the instructions of the well-known navigator, Krusenstern. It was, in fact, the best-planned and best-equipped expedition which had been sent out from Russia.

Kotzebue sailed from Abo in 1815 and reached Kamchatka by way of Cape Horn the following year. His voyage was continued during the summer northeasterly to St. Lawrence Island, thence through Bering Straits and along the northern coast of Seward Peninsula to Kotzebue Sound. Returning, he visited the eastern end of St. Lawrence Island[1] and then sailed southward to the Pacific, visiting Unalaska. Kotzebue wintered in Hawaii and again went north in 1817, but did not notably extend his explorations. These explorations, of which the Alaskan portion included only a small part, were characterized by thoroughness and fully justified the elaborate preparations.

The demands of the fur trade soon led to other explorations of the littoral of Bering Sea. In 1818, Korsakof crossed from Cook Inlet to Iliamna Lake; thence to Bristol Bay; thence to the mouth of the Nushagak River, where he left Kolmakof to build a post; and thence traced the shore line northwestward to Kuskokwim Bay. The new post on the Nushagak River, called Alexandrovsk, afforded a favorable point of departure for explorations which were soon undertaken. The most important expedition was that of Vasilief, graded as a "lieutenant of the pilot corps" in the company service. In 1829, accompanied by the creole Lukeen as interpreter, he ascended the Nushagak, explored Tikchik Lake, and later reached the Holitna River by portage. This he followed to its junction with the Kuskokwim and descended that river to its mouth, returning to Alexandrovsk by tracing the shore line of Bering Sea. Vasilief was, therefore, the first Russian to reach the Kuskokwim River.

Vasilief's discovery of the Kuskokwim was made while Wrangell was governor of the colony. The latter was quick to realize the importance of the new field as a source for furs. He, therefore, in 1832 dispatched Alexander Kolmakof

[1] Kotzebue did not recognize this as a single island, but regarded it as a group, as had previous explorers.

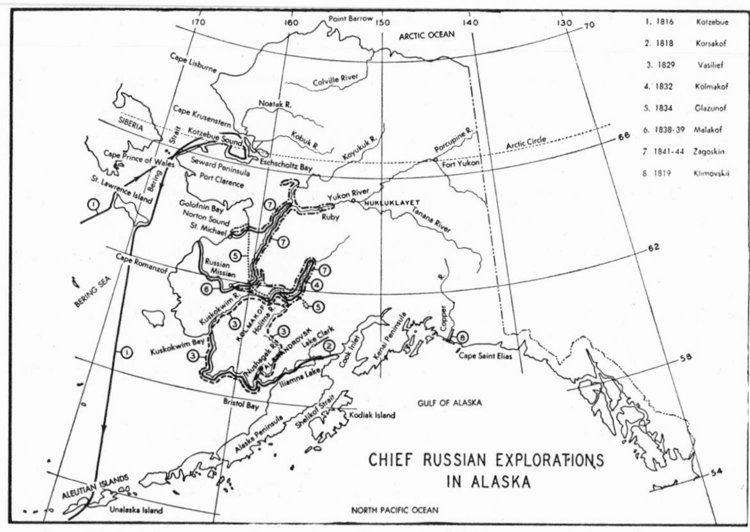

ROUTES OF RUSSIAN EXPLORERS IN ALASKA

to establish a post on the Kuskokwim. Kolmakof was a Russian creole and, though entirely illiterate, was both energetic and resourceful. He had made a good record as chief of the post, Alexandrovsk, at the mouth of the Nushagak. Accompanied by Lukeen, who had been a member of the previous expedition, Kolmakof reached the Kuskokwim by the route explored by Vasilief. He left Lukeen to build a post on the Kuskokwim about 100 miles below the Holitna. He also appears to have ascended the river as far as the mouth of the Takotna and was, therefore, the real explorer of the Kuskokwim above the Holitna. Kolmakof was, however, unable to use instruments, and therefore the results of his explorations were not very definite. His activities on the Kuskokwim included the appointment of chiefs of native settlements, the distribution of silver medals, and the baptism of several natives. He returned to his post during the winter of 1833 by the mouth of the Kuskokwim.

Lukeen remained several years on the Kuskokwim and explored some of its tributaries. He was a Spanish-Russian-American creole, born in the Fort Ross colony of California, and was Kolmakof's clerk. It is probable that he had knowledge of the use of the sextant and compass. From Lukeen's post, the Russians made frequent trips up the river as far as the mouth of the Takotna. It is reported that a son of Kolmakof in 1839 crossed the divide from the mouth of the Takotna to the Innoko basin. His object was to continue his journey to the Yukon, but hearing of the destruction of the Nulato post he turned back.

By 1829 the entire shore line from Cape Prince of Wales to Bristol Bay had been traced. In the charts of that date the course of the Kuskokwim is shown as far as the mouth of the Holitna River. The mouth of the Yukon, or Kwikpak,[2] is also indicated as a re-entrant in the coast line. There can be no doubt, therefore, that the Russians at that time knew of the existence of a great river lying west of the Kuskokwim, though no one had penetrated it to the head of its delta.

In 1833, Lieutenant Michael Tebenkof, later governor of the colony, built a post on St. Michael Island, 60 miles north of the mouth of the Yukon. This was named Michaelovski in his honor, but was afterwards changed to St. Michael. It gave a vantage point to explore the Yukon River, a plan which was almost at once put into execution. The leadership of the party of four was given to Andrei Glazunof. He was rated as quartermaster in company service, a creole educated at Sitka where he had learned the use of simple instruments. His knowledge of surveying was probably limited to taking compass bearings and the use of the sextant. He was, however, a keen observer and a man of energy and determination. Though the delta of the Yukon was known prior to Glazunof's exploration, no one had actually seen the river, and he can, therefore, well be called its discoverer. Glazunof had intended to reach the Yukon from the Pastol River, but his native guides feared the Eskimo of that part of the mainland; hence he decided on a more easterly course.[3] Accompanied by four men and several native guides, with two dog teams loaded with provisions and trading goods, Glazunof left St. Michael on December 30, 1833 (R.)[4] and traced the east coast of Norton Sound, then took a southeasterly course across a low divide to a river which he called the Anvik. It now seems certain that this was the Bonasila River, which

[2] The Eskimo name for the Yukon River.

[3] Wrangell, Ferdinand, *Statistische und ethnographische Nachrichten über die Russischen Besitzungen an der Nordwestküste von Amerika*, St. Petersburg, 1839, pp. 137-160.

[4] (R.) indicates the Russian method of computing dates, in accord with the old Julian calendar. One needs to add 12 days to get the equivalent date of the West, in accord with the Gregorian calendar.—*Editor's note.*

heads near the coast. He followed this river to the Yukon, where he arrived on January 24, 1834 (R.) in a half-starved condition. The natives of the Anvik settlement at first prepared for attack, but Glazunof soon established friendly relations with them. Later, having secured provisions, he continued his journey and followed down the Yukon to the mouth of Shageluk Slough; then, leaving the river, he took a southeasterly course and crossed by a low pass to the Kuskokwim River, which was reached February 19 (R.), near the present site of the settlement called Mountain Village. Continuing the journey upstream, Glazunof met Lukeen who guided the party to the newly constructed post of Kolmakof. Glazunof, though strongly urged against it by both Lukeen and the natives, resolved to attempt to reach Cook Inlet from this post.

He continued his journey up the Kuskokwim on February 25 and reached the mouth of a large easterly tributary which he called the "Tchalachuk" but which on modern maps is called the Stony River. A conspicuous mountain was sighted to the northeast which he called "Tanada" and which is one of the peaks in the unsurveyed headwaters of the Stony River. Here the native guides turned back, but the Russians boldly plunged into the unknown. For a week they plodded on, dragging their sleds along the icy surface of the river. Their slender stock of provisions finally gave out entirely, though eked out by both dog meat and dog harness, and they were finally forced to turn back. It appears that their most easterly point was probably about 50 miles from the Kuskokwim and not far from what are now called the Lime Hills. The return journey was made with great suffering until they secured provisions from the friendly natives of the Kuskokwim. So far as can be learned, Glazunof reached the Yukon by the same route he had come and then returned to St. Michael by the mouth of the river.[5] Glazunof lost his compass during his hard journey, a fact which detracts somewhat from the value of his notes.

The next recorded journey to the Yukon was made by Malakof, also a creole and probably a son of Vassili Malakof, Baranof's agent. Malakof, who was one of the most energetic of the company's agents, left St. Michael in February, 1838, and under native guidance reached the Yukon by way of the Unalakleet River portage. He ascended as far as

[5] His map suggests this, but the published narrative does not go into details.

the Koyukuk and hence was the discoverer of that river. During the following summer he came down the Yukon to its mouth by boat and was thus the first Russian to navigate the Yukon. It is reported that, having no mercury, he used syrup for an artificial horizon in determination of latitude. He returned the following year and established the post at Nulato. Here he left a trader by the name of Nordstrom, who remained until the following summer and then left by boat. Nordstrom became lost in the delta and was forced to winter with the natives. Meanwhile, the post was burned down. It was rebuilt by Vassili Derzhavin in 1841. Derzhavin, who had accompanied Glazunof to the Yukon, remained at Nulato in command of the post until he was killed ten years later in the Nulato massacre. From Nulato the Russian traders made occasional journeys up the Yukon as far as the mouth of the Tanana.

The explorations of the Yukon and Kuskokwim rivers chronicled above added much to the knowledge of inland Russian America. These were mostly made by creoles, who had been trained in simple methods of surveying and were energetic men who accomplished much. As yet, however, the work had not been well coordinated. The relative position of such posts as Kolmakof on the Kuskokwim, Nulato, and St. Michael was only approximately known. The agents located at these posts were known to be pushing their trade into each other's territories. Lukeen at Kolmakof was drawing the trade of the Cook Inlet natives. It was also known that there was a steady stream of furs from the Yukon to Kotzebue Sound, whence they were carried to the Tchuckchu Peninsula of eastern Siberia by the Eskimos, who there dealt with independent traders. The natives of the middle Yukon were being supplied with white man's stores by the return traffic over this same route. The discovery of the great Yukon and Kuskokwim rivers gave hopes to the Russian American Company of extending its trade into the inland region of North America. There was need, therefore, of a comprehensive survey of this new province with a more definite determination of geographic positions. By thus coordinating the explorations accomplished and extending them into the interior, the company hoped both to manage its own business more economically and to short-cut any possibility of rivalry. No doubt an additional motive was the fear of competition with the Hudson Bay Company. This rival company already occupied points on the Stikine and Mackenzie river valleys, and it was high time that the Russians should establish their claims to the region drained by the two great rivers recently discovered. In 1839, Wrangell, as was noted in the previous chapter, had negotiated the agreement with the Hudson Bay Company with reference to the English leasing of the coastal strip. This had brought him into intimate contact with the great rival fur company. It was, therefore, probably not a coincidence that Lieutenant L. A. Zagoskin of the Imperial Russian navy was dispatched to Sitka soon after Wrangell's return to St. Petersburg, and that about the same time an agent by the name of Frieman was sent to investigate the posts of the Hudson Bay Company. Frieman spoke English, and his purpose was to acquaint himself with the methods of the rival company and to learn of the geographic distribution of their posts. Zagoskin's mission was exploration and scientific survey. The reasons given for his journey were as follows:[6]

> The colonial administration did not possess sufficient data to determine the following important matters: How were the redoubts and settlements to be distributed to prevent their mutual interference in the trade with the natives? What routes should be chosen in this well-watered province to bring the posts into communication with the coast? By what regulations can the prevention of the fur trade direct with eastern Siberia be brought about?

Zagoskin's orders instructed him to explore the headwaters of the Kuskokwim and Yukon rivers, as well as the course of the Buckland River. He was also to trace the Togiak River and to investigate the establishing of a trading post on Kotzebue Sound. Although this comprehensive plan was impossible of execution, Zagoskin accomplished far more than any other inland Russian explorer. It can not be doubted that it was Wrangell's interest in science that led to Zagoskin's explorations being laid out on such a comprehensive plan. Zagoskin not only obtained valuable topographic data but he also collected insects, birds, and ethnologic and geologic specimens. Judging by the results, he was a keen observer and tireless worker. His positions were obtained by sextant. The longitudes, being determined by the aid of chronometer, as might be expected were not very close, but his latitudes were remarkably accurate.

---

[6] Erman, A. von, "Uber die Reise und Entdeckungen des Lieut. L. Sagoskins," *Archiv für Wissenschaftliche Kunde von Russland,* VI (1848), 499-552, 622-671; VII (1849), 429-466.

Zagoskin arrived in Sitka in April, 1841, and the following month went to St. Michael. His journey to the Yukon in the winter of 1842 was by the Unalakleet route. In March of the same year he ascended the frozen surface of the Koyukuk to the mouth of the Kateel and traced that river to its source, going as far as the Buckland-Koyukuk divide. Here he located the Indian trade route to Kotzebue Sound, which he describes as a well-beaten path. By this route, furs reached Siberia, thus causing a loss of trade to the company.

In the spring of 1843 Zagoskin ascended the Yukon by boat as far as the mouth of the Nowitna River, a southerly tributary. He, therefore, traced the Yukon for some 40 miles above the location of the present town of Ruby. His map depicts the Yukon and the adjacent hills with remarkable accuracy. It is, however, not easy to reconcile his description of rapids formed by large boulders on the Yukon at the point where he turned back with what is now known of the river. These rapids Zagoskin states were impossible to his heavy boat but were ascended by the natives with their lighter craft. There is swift water in the Yukon with some boulders about ten miles below the mouth of the Nowitna, caused by the Yukon cutting into the terrace carrying heavy boulders on the north side of the river. It is quite possible that at the time of Zagoskin's journey the Yukon at the mouth of the Nowitna may have been cutting the terrace on its northern bank and thus caused the rapids he refers to.

In any event, the Russians later found means of overcoming these rapids, for they are known to have ascended the Yukon as far as the old trading post of Nukluklayet, at the mouth of the Tozitna River, some 60 miles above the highest point of Zagoskin's journey. It is also most probable that some of these trading journeys took the Russians up the Yukon as far as the mouth of the Tanana River. This is shown by the fact that the mouth of the Tanana is represented on a Russian map of the date of 1861. Moreover, the lower Tanana natives are known to have had intercourse with the Russians as is shown by the large number of Russian words which the Indians have adopted into their language. As the Hudson Bay traders are known to have descended the Yukon as far as the mouth of the Tanana, it is there that the two great fur companies came into direct competition.

Deeming the ascent of the Yukon above the Nowitna impractical, Zagoskin returned to Nulato and later in the summer followed the Yukon to Ikogmut, the present site of Russian Mission. From this place an excursion was made into the Innoko valley[7] during the following winter, and later Zagoskin went to Kolmakof. A summer journey up the Kuskokwim as far as the mouth of the Takotna River completed Zagoskin's survey. From his highest point he had a good view of the inland front of the Alaska Range which he called the Chigmit Mountains. While Zagoskin, except for his journey up the Koyukuk, probably reached no place not previously visited by Russians, still he was the first scientific observer in the region. His map of the lower Yukon remained the only source of information up to the time of the Western Union Telegraph survey of 1865, and his map of the Kuskokwim was not superseded until 1898.

Nulato throughout the Russian occupation continued the highest trading post on the Yukon of the Russian American Company; however, as will be discussed later, the Hudson Bay Company had established two trading posts on the upper Yukon before the middle of the 19th century. From Nulato, the Russians made their trading journeys up the Yukon as far as the mouth of the Tanana and thus became familiar with this part of the river. Through the natives they knew of the presence of white men on the river above and, indeed, may have met Hudson Bay traders who descended the river. As more definite knowledge was important, Lukeen was dispatched up the river on a secret mission in 1863. He reached Fort Yukon, representing himself as a deserter;[8] but after obtaining the desired information about the rival post, he stole away in the night and returned to Nulato. He was, therefore, the first positively to establish the identity of the Yukon of the Hudson Bay traders and the Kwikpak of the Russians.

As has already been shown, the Russians had occupied Cook Inlet and Kenai Peninsula during the early history of the American colony and had extended their surveys westward to Iliamna Lake and eventually to Bristol Bay. They

[7] Though Zagoskin appears not to have explored the Innoko any great distance, yet his map depicts the course of that river with remarkable fidelity and also marks the course of the Dishna River and the lower reaches of the Iditarod. It is probable that he obtained this information from the explorations of the younger Kolmakof, made in 1839, as discussed above.

[8] Dall, William H., *Alaska and its Resources*, Boston, 1897, pp. 276-277.

appear, however, to have paid small heed to the great Susitna valley which opened out before them at the head of Cook Inlet. It is reported that they penetrated the headwaters of the Kuskokwim either from Cook Inlet or from Iliamna Lake in the early part of the 19th century, but this report is not verified; and if the upper Kuskokwim was visited at all, it was by some ignorant trader who left no record of his journey. The fur trade of the Susitna River was never exploited by the Russians except insofar as it reached their posts on Cook Inlet. In 1834 Malakof visited this river and is said to have extended the explorations ten years later. I have been unable to find any account of these journeys. It is certain, however, that by 1845 the Russians had a better knowledge of the headwater region of the Susitna than could have been obtained from the crude maps drawn by natives. A Russian map of that year indicates that a rough survey was made of the entire Susitna together with the Talkeetna River. The general course of the Matanuska River is also correctly delineated on this Russian map.

Of the examination of the Copper River during Russian days even less definite evidence is available. The Russians knew of this river early in the settlement of Alaska, for it furnished a means of communication with the inland natives who annually visited the coast. The Russians made several attempts during the early history of the colony to ascend the Copper River, apparently searching for copper; but they failed, partly because of the swift current of the stream and partly because of the hostility of the natives. The members of two of these early expeditions are said to have been killed by the natives.

The first successful attempt to ascend the Copper River was made in 1819 by Klimovskii.[9] Like so many of the Russian explorers, he was a creole and appears to have been quite illiterate. He ascended the river as far as the Chitina and possibly to the mouth of the Gulkana. His map indicates that he was able to approximate distances and directions, and he was, moreover, the first to describe the glaciers now called Childs and Miles, as well as Mount Wrangell, the volcano. He built a cabin on the left bank of the Copper above the mouth of the Chitina, and here for a time a trader was maintained by the company. How long is not known, but probably not many years, for in

[9] Wrangell, *op. cit.*, pp. 161-167.

1843 a party which attempted the ascent of the Copper turned back on account of the hostility of the natives.

Another disastrous attempt was made to penetrate the Copper River basin in 1847 by Serebrennikof, also a creole, with a party of 11 men. None of this party ever returned, for they were all killed by natives, and the only records of the journey are a part of Serebrennikof's notes made during the first part of his trip and surrendered by the natives. It is known that he ascended the Copper in boats and wintered near the mouth of the Chitina, probably at Taral. The following summer he continued the journey to the mouth of the Klutina and up that river, exploring the lake at its head, and thence returned to the Copper and started downstream. The subsequent movements of the Serebrennikof party are unknown except for a sole latitude observation which is reported to be 62° 48′ 45″.[10] If this be correct, he surely reached one of the passes leading from the upper Copper River to the Tanana. The reports of the natives are to the effect that he was killed during the winter while traveling with sleds. Therefore, his movements from June until at least the following December must be accounted for. There is some indirect evidence on this matter. In 1848 the natives reported to Hudson Bay traders at Fort Yukon that Russians had come to the Yukon by boat along a river flowing into it from the south and some distance above the post. This is described as a deep, sluggish stream that must have been Fortymile River, called Deep River on some of the earlier maps.[11] It is hardly possible that the natives would invent a story of this kind, and yet the only record of a Russian party that penetrated north of the Copper is the one led by Serebrennikof. The place of his last record was not more than a month's journey from the mouth of the Fortymile over long-established Indian routes of travel. It seems quite possible that he reached the Yukon. Against this interpretation is the fact that the Russians reached the upper Yukon "two or three years since"—and Serebrennikof's journey was made the same year as the record. This may have been carelessness of record or a misinterpretation of the statement of the natives. Had any other Russians reached the upper Yukon and returned to the coast, they could

---

[10] Allen, Henry T., *An Expedition to the Copper, Tanana, and Koyukuk Rivers in the Territory of Alaska, in the Year 1885*, Washington, D.C., 1887, p. 20.

[11] Murray, Alexander H., *Journal of the Yukon, 1847-48*, edited by L. J. Burpee, Publications of Canadian Archives, No. 4, Ottawa, 1910, p. 73.

not have failed to leave a record of such an important exploration.

The discovery of placer gold on the Stikine River in 1861 directed the Russian attention to this part of their colony. An expedition under Commander Bassarguine of the Russian navy was dispatched to investigate the Stikine River. A boat party from this expedition ascended the Stikine some 45 miles. As the river had long been known to the Hudson Bay traders, the results were of no great geographic importance, though they added to the more accurate mapping of the region. Worthy of note is the fact that the American geologist, William P. Blake, accompanied this expedition. He was thus the first geologist to examine any part of Alaska.

The inland Russian explorations chronicled above gave considerable knowledge of the lower courses of the Yukon, Kuskokwim, Susitna, and Copper rivers. They yielded much geographic information, yet were meagre considering the fact that the Russian occupation of Alaska's shore line continued for almost a century.

Far more important were the Russian surveys along the coast line. Though the English navigators, Cook and Vancouver, blocked out the larger coastal features of Russian America, yet it was the Russian naval officers and company employees who filled in most of the details. The field of their charting extended from Dixon Entrance to Point Barrow, from Cook Inlet to Attu, westernmost of the Aleutian Islands. The many officers and expeditions sharing this work can not here be reviewed. Special reference, however, must be made to Michael Tebenkof who, first as explorer and later as governor, did more than any one else to bring about a better knowledge of Alaska's coast. While governor, he compiled all the available cartographic information, assembling it in a series of charts of the entire coast line. These were first engraved at Sitka by the creole Tarentief and presumably printed for local use. Later these were gathered into an atlas published at St. Petersburg in 1852.[12] Tebenkof also published the first description of the hydrography of Russian America.

It has been indicated that with the recognition of Russian supremacy in the northwestern part of the continent other nations ceased the exploration of the shore line. How-

[12] An earlier atlas of Russian America was issued in 1828 by Gavrila Sarychef, a Russian naval officer, who accompanied the Billings expedition of 1791.

ever, the movement of English explorers and traders from the east did not cease. The previously mentioned exploration by Mackenzie of the river which bears his name in 1789 and his crossing of the continent four years later pointed out new fields for exploitation by the fur hunter. Early in the 19th century the Hudson Bay Company had established numerous posts in the Mackenzie River basin. Many explorations were made by the company men and by men sent out from England. Most of these did not touch Russian America. In 1826 Sir John Franklin descended the Mackenzie and traversed the Arctic to the westward as far as Return Reef on the North Arctic coast; and Captain F. W. Beechey, commanding *H.M.S. Blossom,* who had been dispatched to cooperate with Franklin, charted the south coast of Seward Peninsula to Cape Prince of Wales and added many details to the work of Kotzebue on Kotzebue Sound. A boat expedition under Beechey's mate Thomas Elson succeeded in reaching Point Barrow, northernmost cape of Alaska, which it was hoped Franklin could reach from the east. But as Franklin was blocked by the ice 200 miles east of Point Barrow, this part of the coast line represented a hiatus on the charts for ten years. In 1837, Peter Warren Dease and Thomas Simpson, of the Hudson Bay Company, descended the Mackenzie and followed the coast westward. Like Franklin they too were stopped by ice, but Simpson continued on foot and in native boats. He reached Point Barrow on August 4, 1837, thus completing the exploration of the entire coast line of the mainland of Alaska which had been begun by Bering about 100 years before.

Another impetus to Alaska exploration was given by the series of Franklin relief expeditions which were sent out by the British government between 1848 and 1853. While the primary purpose of these expeditions was to find and bring relief to Franklin, yet the commanders incidentally accomplished considerable exploration and charting. An added stimulus was the hope of finding a northwest passage which geographers were loath to give up. In 1849, Captain Thomas E. L. Moore in *H.M.S. Plover,* Captain Henry Kellet in *H.M.S. Herald,* and the yacht *Nancy Dawson* reached Kotzebue Sound. A boat expedition under Lieutenant Pullen was sent northward and, rounding Point Barrow, proceeded eastward to the Mackenzie River, which it ascended to a Hudson Bay post. A second expedition from these vessels explored the Buckland River. Other minor explorations were made by the crew of the *Plover* while she wintered in Kotzebue Sound. Thus Lieutenant Bedford Pim crossed the eastward end of Seward Peninsula to the Russian post at St. Michael; and Simpson, surgeon of the expedition, explored the Selawik River and made the first mention of the Kobuk River. The *Plover* spent the two following winters at Point Barrow, from which she continued to send out exploring parties.

In 1850, Commander Robert McClure in *H.M.S. Investigator* sailed eastward past Point Barrow and beyond the mouth of the Mackenzie until he was stopped by ice. His vessel was never brought through, but eventually his crew, by walking over the solid ice, was the first to make the northwest passage. The following year Captain Richard Collinson in *H.M.S. Enterprise* also passed Point Barrow and subsequently wintered on Walker Bay on the north coast of Alaska. In 1853, *H.M.S. Rattlesnake* under Commander Trollope wintered at Port Clarence on the south side of the Seward Peninsula, which some of the crew crossed during the winter.

Collinson left Lieutenant J. J. Barnard at St. Michael with orders to ascend the Yukon to learn whether the inland natives had any knowledge of the Franklin party. Barnard made his way to Nulato in the spring of 1851. A Russian was dispatched to request the Koyukuk natives to visit the post for a conference. As their chief had a score to settle with the Russian factor at the post for some real or fancied wrong, they killed the messenger and then set out for the post. They first attacked the native settlement, setting fire to their dwellings and killing those who broke out. They then attacked the Russians who apparently had no foreboding of trouble, for they slept peacefully during the killing of the natives in their village close at hand, undisturbed since the Indians had no firearms. After killing the Russian traders, the Koyukuks entered the room where Barnard was reading; a fierce fight ensued during which both Barnard and Derzhavin, the Russian factor, were killed, and the native interpreter was severely wounded. The other Russians took refuge in an adjacent blockhouse, opened fire with their guns, and finally beat off their assailants. The incident is but one of several illustrating the enmity between the Koyukuks on one hand and the Nulato natives and the Russians on the other. Though the attack has sometimes been credited to a lack of tact in dealing with the natives on the part of Barnard, it is more likely that the presence of the English officer at Nulato had no connection with the attack. The fact that the Koyukuks killed all the Nulato natives first before turning their attention to the whites indicates intertribal enmity. Had Barnard lived, he would probably have made the journey through to the Hudson Bay post of Fort Yukon and thus have forestalled some of the explorations made by the Western Union Telegraph surveys some years later. His immediate successor in this work was Robert Kennicott, who, as will be shown later, also died at Nulato.

The surveys of these Arctic expeditions were very carefully executed and are still the bases for most of the charts of the regions they cover. The accounts of the voyages are full and contain much valuable information, which up to very recent times was all that was available concerning Arctic Alaska.

In 1848, the American whaler *Superior*, commanded by Captain Roys, ventured through Bering Straits and was amply rewarded by a good catch. This example was followed by many others in succeeding years. The whaling industry along the Arctic coast of Alaska continued to be an important one for many years, though, as was indicated in the previous chapter, it received a serious setback during the Civil War because of the ravages committed by the Confederate privateer *Shenandoah*, which captured and destroyed a number of the vessels in the American whaling fleet. The experienced seamen who usually commanded these whalers added not a little to the geographic knowledge of the Arctic coastal region of Alaska.

The only other important American contribution during the period of Russian control was furnished by Lieutenant William Gibson, U.S.N., who, in command of the schooner *Fenimore Cooper* of the Rodgers' United States Northern Pacific Exploring Expedition, made surveys and explorations among the Aleutian Islands in 1855. Some of the other vessels of the same fleet passed through Bering Straits and into the Arctic Ocean.

In 1867, Captain Theodore Long, commanding an American whaler, sailed northward (he had no steam) into the Arctic Ocean and was able to approach within 15 miles of the large island lying north of Siberia, which he named

"Wrangell Land."[13] Long announced that a vessel could reach the Atlantic from Bering Straits along the north coast of Asia. This prophecy was fulfilled many years later.

In 1837, as has already been stated, the Hudson Bay Company had leased the coast strip of Southeastern Alaska and established a post at Wrangell, which they called Fort Stikine. The company traders soon became familiar with the lower Stikine. Meanwhile, the headwaters of the Stikine had been reached by McLeod, coming from the Mackenzie River. John Bell, another employee of the company, explored the Peel River, a westerly tributary of the lower Mackenzie, and in 1840 built Fort McPherson on its banks. This was separated by only a low divide from Bell River, flowing into the Porcupine River. By 1844, the Porcupine had been traced to its junction with the Yukon. The Pelly was explored by Robert Campbell in 1840 and 1842. He reached its headwaters from the Mackenzie by way of the Liard River. The systematic manner in which the Hudson Bay Company pursued its explorations is illustrated by the reasons given for Campbell's exploration. In 1839, Dease and Simpson had discovered the mouth of the Colville River, flowing into the Arctic Ocean. Supposing this river had its source somewhere west of the Mackenzie, the company instructed Campbell to traverse the Rocky Mountains and look for it. This fact also goes to show that at this time the Hudson Bay Company had no conception of the drainage system west of the Mackenzie. Campbell's tracing of the Pelly to its junction with the Lewes, where the two rivers combine to form the Yukon, was followed by the construction of a post at this locality. This was Fort Selkirk, built in 1848. In the previous year Alexander H. Murray had built Fort Yukon at the mouth of the Porcupine, thus giving the Hudson Bay Company two posts on the upper Yukon and effectually controlling the fur trade of a large inland province. Fort Yukon was built especially strong because Murray[14] well knew he was within the Russian domain and had reason to fear a Russian attack on this, the most isolated outpost of the great chain of Hudson Bay forts that stretched across the continent. Murray, as is shown by his journal, had a fairly accurate conception of the drainage features of the upper Yukon and also guessed that he was on the Kwikpak of the Russians. He

[13] "Das Neue Endeckte Polar Land," *Peterman's Mittheilungen*, XV (1869), 26-37.

[14] Murray, *op. cit.*

was not, however, aware of the fact that while he was completing his post Campbell was building another on the same river some 500 miles above him. It remained for Campbell to complete the exploration by tracing the Yukon River to the mouth of the Porcupine in 1850.

The Russians appear to have been well aware of the Hudson Bay post within their domain, for it is so marked on one of their maps in 1861. But with the exception of Lukeen's spying journey of 1863, already discussed, they made no attempt to investigate and did not protest. It is probable that they realized that with their clumsy boats they could not hope to reach the upper Yukon, and their business relations with the Hudson Bay Company were such that they did not care to raise the issue of trespass. On the other hand, the Hudson Bay traders were probably careful to avoid, as far as possible, direct contact with the Russians. They would not, however, have been true to their history if they had neglected the exploration of regions adjacent to their post. It is recorded that in 1863 Strachan Jones, then factor at Fort Yukon, descended the Yukon as far as Nukluklayet at the mouth of the Tozitna.[15]

The inland exploration of Russian America previous to 1865 was entirely due to the interests of the fur trade. Russian traders coming from the west and English traders pushing from the east had accomplished very important geographic results, but the data obtained at such labor and privation were not coordinated except insofar as it was possible by European cartographers. The next exploration to be recorded received its impulse from an entirely different source—the search for an overland telegraph route which should tie together Europe and America. This project was first advocated in 1857 by Percy Collins, but interest was then centered on an Atlantic cable. The failure of this cable determined the Western Union Telegraph Company to establish communication with Europe by a land line. Concessions were obtained from the Canadian and Russian governments, and in 1864 the explorations were placed in the hands of Colonel Charles S. Bulkley. The work of building a line of 6,000 miles, much of it through an almost uninhabited wilderness, was a stupendous undertaking. By keen foresight or good fortune the exploration of the Yukon

[15] Dall (*op. cit.*, p. 91), when exploring the Yukon in 1866 describes a meeting with Peter McLeod near the Tozitna River. McLeod described himself as a deserter from Fort Yukon. It is quite probable that he had been dispatched as a spy on the Russian post, as the latter had sent Lukeen to Fort Yukon three years earlier.

basin was placed under the direction of Robert Kennicott. Kennicott was a well-known naturalist who had spent some time at Fork Yukon, which he reached by the Mackenzie River route, and was, in fact, the first trained scientist to visit the Yukon River. In addition to having charge of the Yukon exploration, he was also director of the scientific corps. Kennicott enlisted the services of a number of young men who, though trained as scientists, agreed to do any work called for. Among these the most conspicuous was Dr. William H. Dall, then but 20 years old. Dr. Dall was destined to become during the next decade the leading authority on all matters relating to Alaska.

The first American party was landed at St. Michael in August, 1865. It had been planned to ascend the Yukon by steamer, but the boat provided proved worthless for this project. Therefore, Kennicott reorganized his parties to reach the Yukon by the Unalakleet River portage. After a preliminary trip across the portage, Kennicott returned, and his energies were now devoted to sledding parties by this route. He had planned to reach Fort Yukon by dog team during the winter, but this journey had to be deferred because of heavy administrative duties. Worn out by toil and exposure, Kennicott suddenly died on the banks of the Yukon near Nulato in May, 1866. He was alone, but the compass at his side gave mute evidence that the last effort of his life had been to extend his surveys. His name has been commemorated in that of Kennicott Glacier in the Copper River basin. By curious chance, the name of the first American naturalist to investigate Alaska, one who sacrificed his life to this work, is also perpetuated in that of the great copper mine lying near the glacier.

So well had Kennicott's work been planned and organized that, in spite of the great loss of his inspiration and leadership, the explorations were continued as he had laid them out. After his death Frank E. Ketchum and Michael Laberge, accompanied by the creole Lukeen, ascended the river by boat to Fort Yukon. It will be remembered that Lukeen had three years before visited Fort Yukon as a spy on the Hudson Bay Company. They returned to St. Michael, the next year made a winter trip to Fork Yukon, and during the summer traced the river as far as Fort Selkirk. They seem to have been the first to report the great lake on the upper Lewes River,which has been appropriately named Lake Laberge.

Meanwhile, Dr. William H. Dall had been appointed to succeed Kennicott in the scientific exploration of the Yukon and Norton Bay region. He reached Nulato by the portage route from St. Michael in November, 1866. Here he wintered, and the next June (1867), in company with Frederick Whymper, artist of the expedition, he reached Fort Yukon. The party returned to St. Michael in company with Ketchum and Laberge by way of the mouth of the river, being the first expedition to make this journey. At St. Michael, Dall learned of the success of the Atlantic cable and hence the abandonment of the entire project of exploration. He was, however, unwilling to relinquish his task of a scientific exploration of the Yukon and resolved to continue this work at his own expense. Bidding farewell to his companions who left for the States, he returned to Nulato and devoted another year to his investigations. Later Dr. Dall continued his Alaskan researches after the annexation by taking service under the Coast Survey.

It remains to refer to the other activities of the telegraph company explorers. A party under the leadership of Baron Otto von Bendeleben and including W. H. Ennis and D. B. Libby carried out an exploration of the southern part of the Seward Peninsula. So far as is known, this expedition was the first to traverse the portage route from the Fish River basin to Port Clarence. Here at Port Clarence several miles of telegraph line were actually constructed, the first in Alaska and all there was for over 30 years. Bendeleben reported the occurrence of placer gold in the region explored by him, and this seems to have been the first record of gold deposits occurring in that part of Alaska drained into Bering Sea. Libby returned in 1898 and was one of a party of prospectors to find the first valuable deposits in Seward Peninsula.

In 1865, J. T. Dyer and R. D. Cotter explored the region between the Koyukuk and Norton Bay. The Yukon delta was carefully surveyed in 1867 by Dyer and E. E. Smith, and in 1865 to 1866 Frederick L. Pope carried an exploration from the Fraser River to the Stikine. During the following year Michael Byrnes went from the Stikine River through to Atlin Lake which drains to the Yukon. Of the important explorations made by the telegraph company in Siberia, it is not necessary here to speak.

The Western Union Telegraph explorers in the course of three years practically completed the exploration and location of a route from northern British Columbia to Bering Straits. That their work was well done is shown by the fact that much of the route chosen by them has since been utilized for a telegraph line. However, the actual explorations were by no means the most important results achieved. Of the thousands of miles of explorations within Russian America there was relatively little that had not been previously visited by white men. The principal geographic results of this arduous toil were the knitting together and the coordination of the work of previous explorers. This was very largely done by Dall. No report of results was ever issued, for with the abandonment of the project the company, after expending about $3,000,000, lost interest, and it fell to Dr. Dall to gather up the loose ends and present them in systematic form. Above all, the Western Union Telegraph survey must be credited with the first systematic scientific exploration of Russian America, and this was due to the plans of Kennicott and their execution, so far as conditions permitted, by Dr. Dall. As a result, when Russian America was transferred to the United States, Dall was able to present an authoritative and comprehensive statement on the resources of this great land as well as an exposition of its natural history.

At the close of the Russian occupation of Alaska, all the larger features and many of the detailed features of its shore line were charted. The general course of the Yukon from its sources far south in British Columbia was fairly well known. None of its tributaries except the Porcupine and 100 miles of the lower Koyukuk and Innoko rivers had been explored. The Kuskokwim had been traced for a thousand miles from Bering Sea, but its headwaters lay in a large unexplored region. Of the Kuskokwim tributaries, only the Holitna had been traced to its source, but a few miles of the lower reaches of the Stony and other rivers had been explored. The Nushagak River and Iliamna Lake were fairly well known, but Lake Clark had not been visited by white men. A rough traverse had been made of the Susitna River, and the Copper River was known as far as the mouth of the Tazlina. Something was known through natives of the courses of the Alsek and Chilkat rivers, and the Stikine had long been in use as a route into the interior. Between the Yukon and the Arctic coast, the map of Russian America was practically a blank, though the mouths of the great Kobuk, Noatak, and Colville rivers had been discovered. In short, it can be said that when Russian America passed into the hands of the United States three-quarters of its area was still practically an unknown land.

CHAPTER XIV

Treaty of Annexation and Transfer

IT IS NOT difficult to find reasons for Russia's transfer of her American colony to the United States, though all the documents relating to this matter are not available at this writing. Russia, stretching across half of Europe and all of Asia, was presented with an enormous frontier to guard. The expansion of this frontier had led to more or less hostility from the Black Sea to the Amur and involved Russia in a series of wars. Serious domestic troubles followed the close of the Napoleonic wars, and then came wars with Turkey and Persia, a Polish insurrection, a war with Hungary, and difficulties with the Chinese along the Amur and with the Circassians in their Caucasian strongholds. The inadequate means of communication greatly hampered military operations in the remote regions in which the fighting took place, for at that time Russia was not knit together by the railways which now make her a unit.

These difficulties had culminated in the Crimean War, in which Russia was helpless even to guard her European possessions. In spite of her great population and resources, she was beaten by the allies who invaded her territory by an oversea expedition that Russia was powerless to beat off. This war also brought home the final proof that Russia was far from being a naval power, though this had been her ambition since the days of Peter the Great. On sea and land she had been worsted by English arms, and the English fur traders had forced themselves into the margins of her American colony.

During the Crimean War Russia's American colony was protected from English raids by the agreement made between the Hudson Bay and Russian American companies. This was, however, probably helped in a great measure by a suspicion that an attack on Russian America might be considered as opposed to the interests of the United States under the Monroe Doctrine. There can be no doubt that Russia feared the loss of her American colony to England. At that period England was the traditional foe of Russia. The two empires were opposed not only in Asia but also at the Dardanelles. Probably the principal motive for relinquishing what was to be called Alaska to the United States was to gain assurance that it would never become a part of the British Empire. Before the transfer some of the people of the west coast of British Columbia were advocating the purchase of at least the coastal strip of Russian America. It was not hard to foresee that in another war with England—which the close of the Crimean War seemed to make inevitable, for it settled none of the points at issue—Russia's rival might seize her North American colony. If a surrender of Russian America was to be made, it was best that it should be to the United States. Russia and the American Republic had preserved a close bond of friendship since the days of the Revolution. The two governments had never had a serious dispute, nor had they been rivals either in commerce or in zone of occupation. This friendship was the more closely knit because at various times they were both opposed to England. The Government of the Tsar could relinquish Russian America with all honor, for there could be no grounds for imputing any motives of fear.

That Russia's traditional attitude toward the United States was based on opposition to England is shown by the following statement credited to the Tsar Alexander II, with reference to his policy during the Civil War: "All this I did because of love for my own dear Russia rather than for love of the American Republic. I acted thus because I understood that Russia would have a more serious task to perform if the American Republic, with advanced industrial development, was broken up and Great Britain left in control of most branches of modern industrial development."[1] It will ever remain to the credit of farsighted Russian statesmanship that no chauvinistic argument about the hauling down of the Russian flag prevailed when it was recognized that a transfer of the distant possession would add to the safety of the empire. By this act one possible cause of future wars was avoided, and in any event a possession which could add nothing to the greatness of Russia and was a source of military weakness was got rid of.

It appears that the Tsar's Government made the first advances looking toward a transfer of Russian America

[1] A letter from Wharton Baker about the policy of Russia during the Civil War. New York *Sun*. January 2, 1902.

to the United States during the Polk administration. At that time the cry was "54-40 or fight." Had the United States made good this claim to territory, it would have carried our boundary to what is now the southern line of demarcation of Alaska. This would have effectually shut out the British Empire from the west coast. Russia was willing to relinquish her colony under these conditions, but nothing came of the proposal.

In 1859, negotiations were informally renewed for a treaty to bring about this transfer. This time the advances were made from the American side. Senator Givin of California, who appears to have taken up the project at the insistence of some of his constituents, had several interviews with the Russian minister at Washington. John Appleton, assistant secretary of the state, also took part in these negotiations. It was represented to the minister "that Russia was too far off to make the most of the possessions; and that as we are near we can derive more from them." Senator Givin hinted that we could pay as much as $5,000,000 for Russian America. Though the American negotiators stated that they were acting entirely unofficially, yet they claimed that their actions were sanctioned by President Buchanan. The results of the interviews were communicated to the Russian Premier, Prince Gortschakof, who in reply said that "the offer was not what might be expected; but that it merited mature reflection: that the Minister of Finance was about to inquire into the condition of these possessions, after which Russia would be in a condition to treat." He added his own opinion that the sum offered was not considered "an equitable equivalent." As will be shown, the emissary was dispatched to investigate the value of Russian America. With the change of administration and the outbreak of the Civil War, the negotiations were suspended.

Before discussing the renewal of the negotiations seven years later, let us pass in brief review the conditions of the Russian American Company and its possessions. Here will be found cogent reasons for a change of policy in the administration of the colony, and these had no connection with international politics.

Russian America had been a continuous source of trouble and scandal. The Tsar's Government had been powerless to prevent the perennial charges of maladministration in the affairs of the company. These were, no doubt, in part due to jealousy of the corporation which had been given monopolistic control of the American colony, yet in part they were well grounded. The charter of the Russian American Company seems to have been unique in the history of Russia, and the authorities were never quite masters of the situation. There was no representative of the crown in the colony, for even the navy officers there resident were, temporarily at least, in the employ of the company. There was no means of adequately enforcing the law, for the company had never been vested with plenary powers. Minor infractions were punished by the local director, but those charged with major offenses had to be transported to Siberia and then tried—a difficult and expensive undertaking. No adequate machinery of government for the colony had been developed, and St. Petersburg officials probably welcomed an opportunity to cut the Gordian knot by relinquishing the entire possession.

Though many reforms had been introduced into the administration of Russian America since the time of Baranof, yet there was still much to criticize. In 1859, an extension of the Russian American charter was asked for, but the authorities held the matter in abeyance until an investigation could be made of the alleged abuses of the natives. Paul Nikolaievich Golovin, an imperial chamberlain, was dispatched to Sitka to investigate. He was sent soon after the first definite negotiations for the transfer of Russian America to the United States had been entered upon. His mission was, therefore, twofold: (1) he was to investigate the alleged abuses existing under the corporate management of the colony and (2) he was to obtain data on the future value of the possession to Russia. It appears that Golovin's report was by no means entirely favorable to the methods of administration of the company. The renewal of the charter was refused, or at least deferred. No doubt the hope of selling the colony to the United States was an important motive in bringing about this refusal, for the Russian Government could not but know that the claims of the company might interfere with or entirely prevent such a transfer. Therefore, pending these negotiations, the colony was placed under direct imperial administration, and Prince Dmitri Maksutof was made the first imperial governor.

This left no one to plead for the retention of the colony. The naval officers and company officials who had served in the distant possession all regarded this service as a species of exile. Hardly a Russian of the educated classes called the colony his home or had any sentimental feeling about having it pass into foreign control. The Russian American Company, though still paying dividends, had long ceased to make the enormous profits that had resulted during Baranof's administration. Various efforts to develop the whale fishery or mining industry had been far from successful. Equally discouraging were the results of attempted commerce with California and Oregon in ice, coal, and fish. During the Crimean War the company had been at considerable loss in the destruction of ships and of a port in the Kurile Islands. Moreover, the natives, except for the Aleuts and those of Kodiak, had never been fully subjected. During the 80 years of Russian occupation, the relations between the Russians and the Indians were those of armed neutrality rather than of friendly trade. From Sitka to Nulato many of the posts were to all intents still held by force of arms. The entire colony contained only 600 Russians and 1,800 creoles. It is not necessary to go beyond the above-cited facts to find a reason for Russia's relinquishment of her American colony, though the international situation set forth above was the principal cause of this action.

Our own acceptance of the Territory is due chiefly to the broad view of William H. Seward. He recognized that the United States was destined to become a Pacific as well as an Atlantic power and that the acquisition of this northern territory would strengthen the nation in the western sea. It was a part of a broad plan, which included obtaining footholds at Samoa, at Panama, and in the West Indies, though Russian America alone was to be acquired during Seward's lifetime. Subsequent events have justified Seward's outlook, though over half a century elapsed before the entire plan was put into execution. The Civil War had brought Seward into numerous controversies with England, some of which were by no means adjusted. He, therefore, no doubt relished this diplomatic move, which meant the forestalling of the nation whose government had been by no means friendly during the long conflict. This was, however, only incidental to the broader considerations which determined his policy.

Both the Russians and our own people were profoundly interested in the projected overland telegraph line which should connect North America, Asia, and Europe. Both governments had given more or less support to the American company that had undertaken the enterprise. In this co-operation attention had been directed to Russian America, and it was probably the telegraph project as much as anything else which had attracted the attention of American statesmen to the little-known northwestern part of the continent.

The nation as a whole was not concerned with this distant land, though there was some clamor on the West Coast for fishing and trading rights in Russian America. I. S. McDonald, who in 1859 had attempted to secure the right to fish for cod on the Russian American coast, introduced a resolution into the legislature of the Territory of Washington in which he was serving as a member. In this the President was petitioned "to obtain such rights and privileges of the Government of Russia as will enable our fishing vessels to visit the ports and harbors of its possessions to the end that fuel, water, and provisions may be easily obtained, that our sick and disabled fishermen may obtain sanitary assistance, together with the privilege of curing fish and repairing vessels." This resolution was passed on January 13, 1866. Other forces were also at work to attract the attention of the West Coast to Russian America. Since the beginning of the 19th century, when Rezanof established trade relations between the Spanish and Russian colonies, there had been considerable commercial intercourse between California and Russian America. A contributing factor was the Fort Ross colony in California maintained by the Russian American Company, though not a commercial success until 1841 when it was sold to John A. Sutter.

The transfer of California to the United States removed many of the restrictions to trade and knit more closely the two isolated colonies. This was especially true during the period immediately following the '49 gold excitement. Until a route of travel was established across Central America, all supplies for California had to be transported by the long route around Cape Horn. Consequently, Sitka was the nearest settlement that could be drawn upon; and, as we have already seen, its warehouses were quickly emptied and its little machine shops strained to the utmost capacity to furnish the needed equipment. Sitka was, however, an isolated post, and it was not long before it was entirely drained of goods needed in California. Trade, however, continued in a small way, and vessels went south with cured fish and a little lumber and returned with such provisions as could be obtained.

California's rapidly growing and wealthy population soon made a demand for ice, and it was natural to turn to the northern colony to seek a supply. In 1851, California capitalists engaged in a project for bringing ice from Russian America. The first shipment of 250 tons is said to have been sold at $75. This business was organized under the name "American Russian Trading Company." The ice was shipped in part from Sitka, in part from Wood Island near Kodiak. At the latter place a number of buildings were erected for storing the ice. In all, about 20,000 tons were shipped to California, having a value of between $400,000 and $500,000. This was the first mineral product to be produced in Alaska. In spite of the high price received, the ice business seems soon to have languished. In 1855, the same California company received permission to mine coal at Port Graham on the Kenai Peninsula. Machinery brought around the Horn was installed, and operations began on a considerable scale; but the low grade of coal, which is lignite, was not adapted to steamer fuel, then offering the principal market for coal. As the coal proved unsuited for export, the mining industry soon languished also, as its only market was for local use.

These enterprises kept the Californians in close touch with the Russian colony. The rapid accumulation of wealth in the Gold State made it natural for its capitalists to look to the north for new ventures. It was the fur trade which next excited interest. In 1866, the California-Russian Fur Company was incorporated, of which John F. Miller was made president. Its purpose seems to have been to purchase the rights of the Russian American Company, or at least the leasehold owned by the Hudson Bay Company. Negotiations were opened through Senator Glynn with the Russian minister at Washington. He had, however, no authority in the premises. The negotiations were then transferred to St. Petersburg, where offers were made through the American minister, C. M. Clay. These negotiations came to nothing, but they did help to direct the attention of Seward to Russian America. They were probably one of the most important influences in bringing about the treaty of annexation.

Therefore, the Johnson administration had its attention directed to Russian America by the Territory of Washington, which requested fishing rights, and by Californians, who were asking for an interest in the fur trade.

The memorial of the legislature of Washington was communicated by Secretary Seward to Baron Stoeckl, the Russian ambassador, in February, 1866, with the suggestion that the countries come to some agreement with regard to the fisheries. This action led to a conference in which the transfer of all of Russian America was discussed. Stoeckl's visit to St. Petersburg at about this time led to his obtaining definite authority from his government for the sale of the American colony. He returned in March of the following year with power to act, and there remained only the question of the amount of the purchase price. Seward offered $5,000,000, the Russian Government demanded $10,000,000, and a compromise of $7,000,000 was finally agreed upon. To this amount $200,000 was added to compensate the Russian American Company whose rights were all extinguished by the treaty. The final assent of the Russian Government to the terms of the treaty reached Stoeckl by cable on March 29. He at once repaired to Seward's house and suggested that the treaty be signed the next day. "Let us do it tonight" was Seward's often-quoted reply. There was need of haste, not only because the Senate might soon adjourn, but also because England, and possibly other European powers, might find means to block the agreement. The treaty was signed at four o'clock in the morning on March 30 and was at once transmitted to the Senate.[2]

Fortunately for the treaty, the cooperation of Senator Sumner had been secured, and he was present at the signing of the treaty. Sumner was a bitter opponent of the Johnson administration, but in this affair he showed his ability to rise above partisan strife. As chairman of the Committee on Foreign Relations, his opposition would have been fatal to the confirmation of the treaty. He, too, must therefore share with Seward the credit of the Alaskan purchase. Probably because of Sumner's influence, there was comparatively little opposition to the treaty in the Senate, and it was ratified on May 28 by a vote of 38 to 3. The most interesting document bearing on the transaction is Sumner's

[2] The State Department was then housed in the building now occupied by the Washington Orphan Asylum, located at the corner of 14th and S Streets.

remarkable speech. In this, he not only summarized the physical features of the northern territory but also gave a remarkable forecast of its value to the nation. Half a century was to pass before the nation as a whole could be convinced of the accuracy of Sumner's prophecy. In closing his speech, he advocated that the name "Alaska,"[3] a corruption of the Aleut term for the mainland, meaning "great land," should be used to designate the new territory.

The publication of the treaty of acquisition aroused a storm of indignation in many quarters. This, no doubt, was largely owing to the unpopularity of the Johnson administration, which was shared by the entire cabinet. Seward himself was the special target of the anti-administration leaders who could not forgive him for remaining loyal to the President. The purchase of Alaska gave the opposition a new field of criticism, and now well-known designations of the new territory as "Seward's ice-box," "Seward's folly," and "Walrussia" found wide circulation in the partisan press. Congress adjourned without appropriating the money called for by the treaty. This action did not, however, deter Johnson and Seward from carrying out the plans of transfer; nor had the Russian Government, well-informed as to the conditions of American politics, any hesitancy about consummating the treaty. This document, moreover, provided that the payment should not be made until ten months after its ratification by both governments.

Meanwhile President Johnson made public the treaty in a proclamation dated June 20, 1867. Its terms were simple, including clauses describing the boundaries of ceded territory and providing for the retention by the Greek Catholic Church of its property located within Alaska. Another clause permitted the inhabitants to remain and become citizens of the United States; or, lacking such intent, to return to Russia within three years. Exception is made under this clause to the uncivilized tribes of Alaska, for they are not given citizenship. The other articles of the treaty simply provide for the method of transfer.

The West Coast merchants were not slow to seek an entrance to the new market. Even before the treaty was proclaimed, they petitioned the Government to permit the clearance of ships for Sitka and the free entrance of goods into Alaska, which was, of course, still in the hands of

[3] The natives of the Aleutian Islands called the adjacent Alaska Peninsula "Aliashka." This has been variously written Alakshak, Alayeska, Alaksa, or Alaxa.

the Russians. This courtesy was granted by the Russian authorities, and the collector of customs at San Francisco was directed to clear vessels for Sitka.

The first important administrative act with reference to the new possession was the dispatching of the revenue cutter *Lincoln* under the command of Captain W. A. Howard on a voyage of survey and investigation. On board the *Lincoln* was Dr. George Davidson of the Coast Survey, with a party of scientific assistants. This was the beginning of a long series of surveys and investigations made in Alaska by the Coast Survey, in connection with which Dr. Davidson was to render such distinguished service. T. A. Blake was attached to the expedition as geologist. It is significant that the first action on the part of the Government was to dispatch a scientific expedition to the new acquisition.

Alaska was still in Russian hands when Captain Howard and his colleagues made their official call on the Russian governor at Sitka on August 12. From Sitka the party set sail for Unalaska, and later visited Kodiak, Chilkat, and other places along the coast. Davidson supplemented the surveys and investigations made during the summer cruise by a large amount of material gained from the Russian officials. As a result, it was possible the next year, when the bitter opposition developed in Congress to the appropriation necessary to consummate the treaty, to present a carefully compiled summary of what was known about the geography and resources of Alaska.

Meanwhile the administration, nothing daunted by the failure of the House to grant the purchase fund, accelerated its plans for the transfer of the territory. It was typical of President Johnson's disregard of Congress that even before the ratification of the treaty by the Senate he should have appointed a commissioner to receive the transfer of the new territory. His choice for this important mission was General Lovell H. Rousseau. Captain Alexie Pestchurof of the Imperial Russian navy was appointed as Russian commissioner. The difficulty of then communicating with Sitka is shown by the fact that, though the commissioners sailed from New York for San Francisco on August 31, they did not reach Sitka until October 18. Though special facilities had been provided for this journey, it occupied over six weeks; now it is possible to reach Sitka from New York in less than two weeks by established transportation lines. A military escort had been provided for the Commission by dispatching General Jefferson C. Davis with three companies of troops[4] under date of September 6, 1867. General Davis was appointed commander of the military district of Alaska, and by virtue of this order became the first governor of the Territory. General Davis and his troops were dispatched on the steamer *John L. Stephens* and arrived at Sitka on October 10, eight days ahead of the Commission. Out of courtesy to the Russians, it had been ordered that no troops should be landed until the arrival of the Commission, so the poor soldiers had to content themselves with their cramped ship quarters, though anchored only a cable's length from the shore. General Davis and staff called on the Russian governor, Prince Maksutof, but otherwise the military members of the expedition remained on board ship. On Sunday during the long wait, Rev. J. O. Rainer, chaplain of the detachment, held services in the little Lutheran chapel. This was the first service held by an American clergyman in Alaska.

On the morning of October 18, the *Ossippee,* U.S.N., dropped anchor, with the Commission on board. There were also present at the same time the U.S. Navy vessels *Jamestown* and *Resaca.* Plans for the simple ceremony were quickly made. The American troops were landed under command of Captain C. O. Wood while the Russian guard was commanded by Captain Helruski. There were also under arms the soldiers and marines of the U.S. naval vessels. The commissioners, General Davis and staff, American naval officers, W. S. Dodge of the United States Customs Service, Prince Maksutof and his staff completed the official representation of the two governments. The wives of a number of the officials also attended the ceremony, including the Princess Maksutof, Mme. Gardsishof, wife of the Russian vice-governor, Mrs. Davis, Mrs. Weeks, Mrs. Wood, Mrs. McDougall, and Mrs. Dodge; and with them were a few American civilians. That there was some love of this isolated land by the Russian residents is shown by the fact that but few of the residents of Sitka witnessed the ceremony of lowering the Russian flag. At four o'clock on the afternoon of October 18, 1867, the Russian flag was lowered; and the boom of salutes of the American warships was replied to, gun for gun, by the Russian shore battery. As if in protest to the surrender of the Tsar's dominion in North America, the flag clung to the pole and could not

[4] C and H of the Second Artillery and F of the Ninth Infantry.

be lowered until a marine ascended, disentangled it, and dropped it on the bayonets of the Russian soldiers. After this interruption, Captain Pestchurof, turning to Commissioner Rousseau, said, "By the authority of His Majesty the Tsar of all Russia, I transfer to you, the agent of the United States, all the territory now possessed by His Majesty on the continent of America and in the adjacent islands, according to a treaty made between these two powers." General Rousseau replied, "I accept from you, as agent of His Majesty the Tsar of all the Russias, the territory which you have transferred to me as Commissioner on the part of the United States to receive the same." The American flag was then raised by the American commissioner's son, George L. Rousseau. Again the guns rang out a national salute, this time the Russian batteries leading and the American men-of-war replying. By this simple ceremony we became possessed of a territory embracing nearly 600,000 square miles which was destined within half a century to yield over half a billion dollars in wealth.

At about this same time, the Chilkat Indians hoisted at the settlement on Lynn Canal an American flag given them by the officers of the revenue cutter *Lincoln* which was cruising in those waters. There is evidence that a still earlier raising of the American flag took place. It is reported that Edward Lendecke, an American resident at Wrangell, on hearing of the treaty raised the flag before the official ceremony took place. One other flag-raising deserves to be noted. At the time of the annexation, Dr. William H. Dall was pursuing his lonely work of studying the geology and natural history of the Yukon region. The news of transfer reached him February 3, 1868, at Nulato, and he promptly raised the American flag, the first to float in Alaska north of Sitka.

The treaty had provided that the purchase price should be paid within ten months after the exchange of the ratification. These ten months were the momentous ones in the administration, for they included the adoption of the articles of impeachment of the President. The limiting date of payment fell during the impeachment trial, and Congress was, therefore, not ready to act in the matter. Seward had no difficulty in negotiating an extension of time of payment, for the Russian Government was, of course, entirely conversant with the political situation at Washington. The ending of the impeachment trial in May with the acquittal of the President left the way clear for the consummation of the treaty.

Seward was not loath to use every legitimate expedient to bring about the granting of the funds. During the 18 months that had elapsed since the treaty was signed, much had been published in regard to the newly-acquired territory, and indeed the American Government had acquired a great volume of information through its own agencies about the geography and resources of Alaska. The most important sources of information were the results of the investigation made by Dr. Dall and his associates of the Western Union Telegraph survey in the Yukon basin and northern Alaska and by Professor George Davidson of the Coast Survey of the Pacific littoral. The exact and disinterested information furnished by these scientists was an important element in convincing Congress of the value of the new territory. The fact that all those who were familiar with the region favored its annexation must have impressed the thinking man. There were, of course, many exaggerated statements made of the known resources of Alaska, but none of them was so absurd as those of the opponents of the treaty. Seward gained all the help he could toward the furthering of the project. Among others, he consulted the late Professor William Brewer of Yale. Professor Brewer gave as reasons for the acquisition of Alaska: (1) to prevent England from acquiring it; (2) to have a source of ice for California; (3) to secure the valuable fisheries which would be needed to feed our growing population; (4) to have a playground, as he expressed it, for the people of the West Coast. With the invention of the artificial ice machine, one of his reasons fell out; but he lived to see Alaskan fish distributed all over the continent, and Alaska visited annually by thousands of tourists.

The opposition to the treaty in the House of Representatives was based on three principal reasons. Of these, probably the most important was the antagonism to the President and his cabinet, especially Seward. There was also the long-standing constitutional dispute between the Senate and the House on the treaty-making power. The contention of the House was that any treaty that involved a grant of funds must be approved by it before it became law. The same argument had been used at the time of the Louisiana Purchase. It exasperated the House to be forced to make an appropriation called for by a treaty which, according to the Constitution, was the "supreme law of the land." Last, there were those in the House who were opposed to the acquisition of any new territory, and Alaska in particular. This latter group was the most violent in assailing Seward's policy and the most unguarded in its statements about the worthlessness of Russian America. Some attempt was also made to revive the old constitutional argument against the acquisition of foreign territory. This, however, had little weight with a nation which had in less than a century extended its boundaries across the continent solely on the basis of acquisition of foreign territory from foreign powers.

A part of the propaganda in favor of the treaty was based on the visit of the two Russian fleets, the Atlantic and the Pacific, to our posts during the Civil War. The rather absurd argument was used that the money paid Russia for Alaska should be considered solely as a recompense for her assistance during the hour of national peril. While there is no question that Russia had from the Revolution, because of her antagonism to England, shown a more friendly feeling toward the new republic, nevertheless the visits of the Russian fleets to Boston and San Francisco were inspired more in her own interests than in those of the United States. The Government of the Tsar, as shown by Professor Golder,[5] dispatched its war vessels to American ports in 1863 because war with England then seemed imminent, and friendly ports had to be sought. It was the safety of the few vessels which was the prime motive for this action, though it can not be denied that it had the important effect of indicating to England that war with the Union would mean war with Russia. Much, however, was made of this incident by administration supporters, and there is no doubt that the people as a whole felt a deep gratitude to Russia.

At about the close of the impeachment trial of President Johnson, a bill was reported to the House appropriating the money due Russia under the terms of the treaty. The debate was begun on June 30 and continued with great heat for some six weeks. Both the opponents and the advocates of the appropriation indulged in much foolish talk, though in this respect those in favor of the treaty had decidedly

[5] Golder, F. A., "The Russian Fleet and the Civil War," *American Historical Review*, XX (1915), 92 ff.

the best of the argument. Eliminating partisanship and demagoguery, we can reduce the arguments of the opposition to five. First was the constitutional one, which denied the power of the Senate and the Executive to commit the House to an appropriation of funds. Second was the worthlessness of Alaska. It was stated, and rightly so, that nothing was known of the presence of mineral wealth in Alaska, and that fur trade was languishing. While it could not be denied that there were extensive fisheries along Alaska's seaboard, it was argued that these could not be utilized because the climate was so wet that the fish could not be cured—this in spite of the fact that Russian America had been supplying California with fish for many years. Agriculture in this northern climate was held to be an idle dream. Carried away by their enthusiasm, the advocates of the treaty claimed that Alaska contained 300,000 square miles of agricultural land, a statement met with derision by their opponents. The danger of annexing a land which was non-contiguous was also dwelt upon. This was represented as a change of policy, fraught with untold possibilities of evil. The poverty of the nation was also set forth as a reason against the appropriation, and with telling effect. It was pointed out that there was an enormous war debt, that the cost of reconstruction governments was tremendous, and that all other government expenditures were increasing. The payment of $7,200,000 in gold meant an equivalent of $10,000,000 in the depreciated currency of that day. This argument was met by showing that the proposed grant of funds was but a bagatelle in the total expenditures of the nation. It was also argued that the cost of administration, estimated by the opponents at $3,000,000 annually, should deter us from entering this new field of colonization. This argument has long since proved invalid, for the National Government has never expended anything like this amount for administrative support. In fact, for many years the customs collector was the only civil official in the Territory, and he more than supported himself by his collections. The military posts, of course, involved expenditures, but this expense is hardly chargeable to civil administration.

The last important public act of Thaddeus Stevens' life was to support this bill and to defend the constitutionality of this act of the Johnson administration, which he had on other accounts so bitterly assailed. He died 16 days after the final vote on the law was taken. The strongest opposition to the treaty came from the inland states, a condition which was duplicated nearly half a century later when the government railroad for Alaska was opposed by the dwellers away from the seaboard. The final vote showed 80 Republicans and 33 Democrats in the affirmative, and 41 Democrats and two Republicans in the negative. No doubt there were some opposed to the policy who voted nevertheless for the appropriation, deeming it a matter of national honor. The new territory had been surrendered to us in good faith by Russia, and we could not honorably avoid the fulfillment of our financial obligation.

As the bill passed the House, it contained the following clauses: "[that it was] necessary that the consent of Congress shall be given to the said treaty before the same shall have full force and effect . . . that the consent of Congress is hereby given to the said treaty." The Senate, however, refused to give consent to this invasion of its prerogative, and the bill was promptly sent back with these clauses eliminated. It was finally accepted by the House in this modified form by a vote of 91 to 48, and became a law on July 25, 1868.

As is common in a matter involving such bitter controversy, charges of corruption were made after the granting of the funds. Definitely to prove or disprove corruption in regard to the acquisition of Alaska would require the examination of documents not available. It seems hardly likely, however, that corrupt means were used to bring about the appropriation of the money for payment to Russia. The amount involved was too small to tempt the Tsar's Government to become involved in our domestic politics, and there is no reason to suspect that it had so demeaned itself. The administration, even if it could stoop so low to carry through its policy, had no funds that could be used for such a purpose. Nor is it to be supposed that the commercial interests of the West Coast states that hoped to profit by engaging in the development of the new land were sufficiently sure of the profits to come that they would subscribe to a corruption fund. The mere fact that the strongest men in both parties and in both houses advocated the treaty and that the final vote was overwhelmingly in its favor argues against suspicion of their having been any corruption. In contrast, the opponents of the measure were either pure demagogues or those who were known to have a narrow point of view in national affairs. To offset the argument against the probability or even possibility of corrupt means having been used to bring about the final acceptance of the treaty, there are thus far only some vague charges of violent partisans. It can, therefore, be emphatically stated that no evidence has been produced of the gaining of any man's support by improper means.

Alaska became a possession of the United States at a time when partisan politics took their extremest form in the history of the country. Its acquisition was one of broad statesmanship, and for the time being leaders of all political faiths united with their opponents to the support of a national administration which many had previously united for the purpose of discrediting. It stands out as the one important accomplishment during the turbulent administration of President Johnson.

Public interest in Alaska subsided almost as quickly as it arose. The period immediately following the Civil War was one of rapid industrial development. Transcontinental railroads opened up vast regions to industry and commerce which had previously been inaccessible. There was no need of turning to this then-remote region to find fields for development and investment. Therefore, except for a few people on the Pacific seaboard who engaged in fur trading, Alaska attracted no population and was for a time almost forgotten by both the public and the Government. This was a period of neglect toward this northern Territory that continued almost unbroken for a generation. The first break was the excitement caused by the Klondike gold discovery, under the impulse of which thousands of people started for Alaska. Even this movement of population was insufficient to break completely the period of stagnation in Alaskan affairs, for it is only within the last decade that people have realized that the development of this northern country is a matter of national importance.

CHAPTER XV

The American Occupation

WHEN the commissioners arrived at Sitka to transfer Alaska to the United States, they found that some Americans had already preceded them. These enterprising real estate speculators had arrived on the first vessels that were cleared for Sitka, and upon landing had promptly staked lots throughout the little settlement, "including the governor's garden, the church, and the church property." All this was to the great bewilderment of the Russian officials who had never before witnessed a real estate boom. They, however, accepted the situation without protest, for they understood that Alaska already belonged to the United States. General Davis, the military governor, had received ample instructions from Washington as to his treatment of the Indians and Russians, but the orders were eloquently silent as to the policy to be adopted toward the newly-arrived American citizens. These, indeed, had no legal standing with reference to acquiring lands or entering into trade. Under date of October 26, 1867, the Secretary of the Interior ruled with reference

> . . . to attempts of American citizens to acquire preemption rights to lands at Sitka, the newly acquired Territory of Alaska, . . . such claims and settlements are not only without sanction of law, but are in direct violation of the provisions of the laws of Congress applicable to public domain secured to the United States by any treaty made with a foreign nation; and if deemed necessary and advisable, military force may be used to remove the intruders.

The administration had indeed recognized the necessity of providing a civil code for Alaska, for as early as July, 1867, President Johnson recommended to Congress "proper legislation for the occupation and government of the territory as a part of the dominion of the United States," and bills were introduced into the Senate to put this recommendation into effect. The law-makers were, however, then in no mood to heed the advice of the President. The only action taken was a year later, when the laws of the United States relating to customs, commerce, and navigation were extended to Alaska. At the same time control of the importation of breech-loading firearms and alcoholic beverages was placed in the hands of the President. A more remarkable statute passed at this time was the prohibition of the taking of all fur-bearing animals except under regulations prescribed by the Secretary of the Treasury. This last act, which except for the seals was never enforced, suggests that there were influences at work which hoped to obtain monopolistic control of the Alaskan fur trade. It was provided that any violation of these statutes should be tried in the federal district courts of Oregon, California, or Washington. These courts had, however, only very vague jurisdiction in Alaska in regard to other civil or criminal action. No other statutory law and—it was held by some—not even common law existed in Alaska. It is certainly true that, except for a few customs officials and the military, there was no means of enforcing law or maintaining order. It was held by the department that the Territory was "Indian country," and under this ambiguous authority the military governor was left to work out his own salvation, as well as that of several hundred Americans who had come north to try their fortunes in the new colony. Evidence of the conditions is found in an incident that happened at St. Michael in the summer of 1868. There arrived in port an American vessel whose captain had during the voyage abused his crew. Complaint was made to the Americans and in the absence of any federal official or legal machinery a court was formed, of which Dr. William H. Dall was made judge. The case was duly presented to a jury that found the captain guilty, and the court decreed that he should lose command of his ship which was then turned over to the mate. The significant fact is that there was no court in the world where the captain could find redress against these equitable but entirely illegal proceedings.

These political and commercial conditions, however, had by no means discouraged professional town site boomers. They staked lots, purchased and leased property of the Russians, and erected buildings. Among the newcomers were many of the best frontier type who desired to make permanent homes in the newly acquired territory and to take part in its industrial development. Trained as they had been under the frontier conditions of the West, they were slow to realize that, though under the American flag, they were living under a military despotism. True to the

American instinct of self-government, they organized a city under a self-granted charter. An election was soon held, at which about 100 votes are said to have been cast for nearly as many candidates. W. H. Wood was elected as mayor, and was accompanied into office by a full-fledged council, recorder, and surveyor. General Davis, recognizing that the sole legal means of enforcing law and order was by court martial and the bayonet, rather welcomed this farce of popular government, for it could not help relieving a difficult situation. For a brief time Sitka prospered; stores and buildings were erected; and in spite of the ruling of its being an "Indian country," the saloon was not lacking. At this time there was published the first Alaskan newspaper, the Sitka *Times,* issued in September, 1868. The editor, Barney O'Ragan, lacking a printing press and before the days of the typewriter, wrote his paper out by hand.

Though the records show that during the first two years some 70-odd vessels cleared for Sitka, there was no real commercial basis for a settlement of the size laid out. During the first year the Russian American Company gathered its employees at Sitka, preparatory to returning thence to their homes in Russia. As these numbered several hundred and they were all under pay, their expenditures, swelled by those of the U.S. troops, brought about an era of temporary prosperity. It is estimated that about $70,000 worth of business was done with the whites of Sitka during the first year. Upon the withdrawal of the Russians and the reduction of the garrison, business rapidly dwindled and the real estate boom collapsed. In fact, Sitka soon became of less commercial importance than during the Russian days when it was the supply point and industrial center of the fur company. Under the new conditions, its little foundry was closed and its shipyard was allowed to go to decay.

Though Sitka was the headquarters, Army posts were also established at Wrangell, at Kodiak, and on Cook Inlet. A fort was also built on Tongass Island at the entrance to Portland Canal, and at this lonely post troops were kept for some two years. Some soldiers were also sent to guard the fur seal rookeries on the Pribilof Islands. By 1871, the troops were all withdrawn except from Sitka and Wrangell. This occupation of Alaska by the Army served to maintain order to a certain extent, though the troops, being without means of transportation, could exercise authority only within the range of the gun at the fort. Moreover, the authority of the Army officers in civil affairs was never exactly defined. This matter will receive further consideration in the final chapter.

While Sitka attracted chiefly real estate speculators, other parts of the Territory were receiving a more permanent industrial advancement by the advent of the fur trader. Hardly was the ink dry on the treaty of annexation than the fur trader began to lay plans for an inroad into the new domain. In probably less than one per cent of the Territory was there any pretence of enforcing law and order. There was no means of enforcing the regulation in regard to the introduction of whiskey, and many among the newcomers had no scruples about using this beverage for trade with the natives. Small trading vessels visited the coast line from Dixon Entrance to St. Michael, and for a time the natives suffered far more than they did under the Russian regime. The law provided that the traders must be licensed, but this was a dead letter, for the few customs officials were powerless to enforce the statute. Near the Army posts some semblance of the suppression of this liquor traffic was maintained, but the military government was also hampered by lack of means of transportation.

In 1869, two white traders were murdered by the Kake Indians, apparently in retribution for the inadvertent killing of one of their tribe by a sentinel at Sitka. A detachment of troops was sent from Sitka and the Kake village destroyed. This unfortunate affair could probably have been avoided had the commanding officer understood the habits of mind and customs of the Indians. A recompense in blankets for the killing of the Indian at Sitka would have settled the matter. Other murders took place, and in but a few cases were the perpetrators punished. The military arrests recorded were largely those of natives for some minor infractions on visiting the posts and of white men who introduced whiskey among the Indians. There is no record that the criminal acts of other white men were punished. The conditions at Sitka illustrate the situation in regard to prohibition in Alaska. Though the bringing of whiskey into the Territory was prohibited, yet the official census of 1880 shows that out of a total white population of 215, 16 are recorded as being saloon-keepers.

Though the small trader was active in Alaska immediately

following the annexation, the most important industrial event was the organization of a powerful trading company. Among the first Americans to reach Sitka was an eastern businessman by the name of H. M. Hutchinson. Backed by ample capital, he quickly came to an agreement with Prince Maksutof for the purchase of the property of the Russian American Company. There was need of haste, for another group of California capitalists was already negotiating for the same prize and, indeed, is said to have had a verbal agreement with the Russian company with regard to the purchase. Be that as it may, Hutchinson's offer was accepted.[1] The purchase included the buildings, equipment, vessels, and other property of the company. In view of the fact that the Russian Government owned no property in its colony, and the treaty provided that all fortifications, buildings, and barracks should be transferred to the United States, it became a rather delicate situation as to who owned certain property. At Sitka, the Commission determined by personal investigation which structures were public; but elsewhere there was no such definite information. There may, therefore, be ground for the charge frequently made that the new corporation became the owner of certain structures in different parts of the Territory which rightfully belonged to the Government. It should be added, however, that these buildings had but little value except as fur trading posts and that the title to the land on which they stood remained vested in the Government.

The new corporation of Hutchinson, Kohl, & Company at once went actively to work to develop the fur trade. It took into its employ many of those who had served the Russian company. This gave it a decided advantage over its competitors who could be but indifferently informed as to conditions to be met with in this remote region. Headquarters were removed from Sitka to San Francisco, and the old Russian posts were taken over as rapidly as conditions permitted.

The fleet purchased of the Russian company included the steamers *Alexander, Constantine,* and *Fideliter,* together with the barks *Cyano* and *Menshikoff* and the sloop *Jabez Howe.* With these vessels, manned in part by Russians who had knowledge of the coast, the company soon estab-

[1] There is no published record of the purchase price. The extra $200,000 added by the treaty was understood to be for the Russian American Company. This probably nearly covered the value of its Alaskan holdings, and the money received from the American capitalists was in addition.

lished itself in the new possession. In 1868, Hutchinson, Kohl, & Company took over the Russian posts on the lower Yukon River. About this time the *Yukon,* the first steamer to be used on the Yukon River, was built. By 1868, the following trading posts had been established by the new company: Port Graham, Kenai, and Knik in the Cook Inlet region; Unalaska in the Aleutian Islands; and St. Michael. In 1869, the following were established on the Yukon: Kotlik, Andreafsky, Reunion, Mission, Anvik, Nulato, and Kokrines. In Southeastern Alaska, the fur trade was in the hands of the corporation which succeeded the Russian company.

Meanwhile, the Alaska Commercial Company was established in 1868, and in 1870 it secured the lease of the fur seal rookeries of Pribilof Islands. The two corporations were closely affiliated from the first, and in 1872 the Alaska Commercial Company purchased the property and interests of Hutchinson, Kohl, & Company. Official statements show that the Alaska Commercial Company issued 20,000 shares of stock having a par value of $100. From the same source, it is learned that no dividends were paid during the first three years of corporate existence and that the highest dividend up to 1876 was 15 per cent. This profit was not excessive, considering the risks of loss that those who took part in the new venture were subject to. The stockholders were apparently satisfied with the profits, for there was no change of ownership in the first decade, when the total number was 18, chiefly residents of California.

During the decade following annexation, the history of the Territory is practically that of the Alaska Commercial Company. Though this corporation, except in the Seal Islands, had no monopoly by law, the conditions of industry and transportation practically gave it such a monopoly. Some small traders continued to search out fields for commerce in their own vessels, but they could not rival a powerful corporation. It will be shown later that during this time the prospector began his search for precious metals and some beginnings were made to harvest the valuable fisheries, but these attempts as yet played only a small part in the industry of Alaska where the fur trade was all-supreme. Indeed, the value of the fur seal catch overshadowed that from all other industries. In the dozen years ending in 1880 Alaska had produced nearly $27,000,000 worth of furs and fish, but the value of fish production represented less than $3,000,000 of the total. Of this total fur product, only a small share went to the independent trader, most of it belonging to the Alaska Commercial Company.

The Alaska Commercial Company has been fiercely attacked both in governmental and in private publications. Charges of corruption of public officials both in Washington and in Alaska have been freely made. Above all, it has been laid at the door of the corporation that for many years it monopolized the industries of the Territory. It is not worth while to attempt here to consider the validity of these charges, as that would lead far afield from the purpose of this writing. The second charge, namely that the company practically controlled the fur trade and incidentally the transportation system of the Territory, no one will deny. This monopoly, aside from the seal fisheries granted by law, was, however, largely brought about by the physical conditions. Aside from the seal fisheries, the fur trade was not large enough to tempt more than one strong corporation to the field. This corporation had of necessity to supply its own system of transportation, and in this fact lay the key to the monopoly. Small traders could skirt the coast line in their own sailing vessels, but when it came to organizing fur trade on a large scale, steamers and supply stations were necessary; and by establishing and controlling these, the Alaska Commercial Company was able effectually to shut out any rivals. No grant of a monopoly of fur trade was, therefore, necessary to make the one company supreme. It needed only enterprise, business acumen, and capital to bring this about. Those who were loud in their denunciation of the company failed to find means to combat the enterprise shown in the development of the Territory.

The monopoly worked both for good and evil. There was good because it was better that a company should undertake the development of the fur trade on a permanent venture than that it should be controlled by a number of small independent traders who could be expected only to look after immediate profit. The company quickly recognized the evil in the use of alcohol in the fur trade, which the less responsible individual had less hesitancy in making use of. There can be no doubt that in general the natives received far better treatment at the hands of the Alaska Commercial Company agents than they did from the individual trader who did not look for a permanent field of trade. On the other hand, it is equally true that this monopoly discouraged individual initiative and deferred Alaska's industrial development. The company, while making good profits out of the fur trade, had no motive in encouraging other enterprises. No doubt difficulties were placed in the way of those who sought to enter the new field, probably both because it directly interfered with the operations of the company and because it was feared that the increase of population would lead to competition in the fur trade. The seas and rivers were open to all, but the vessels available for traveling over them were in the hands of the monopoly. It is not necessary to accept any of the charges against the company to believe this, for the conditions made a monopoly perfectly possible using only fair means, or at least those that were sanctioned by law and regulations. There can be no doubt that, directly or indirectly, this monopoly of the fur trade and its attendant features had much to do with the curtailing of Alaska's industrial advancement and with the discouraging of its settlement.

In 1880, 13 years after the annexation, the white population of Alaska was less than it had been during the Russian occupation. It would be unjust to lay the decrease of population entirely at the doors of the monopoly. A region where there was practically no civil or criminal law, where a man could neither purchase land nor transfer his estate by process of law, where no title to land could be acquired, offered small inducement to the colonist. Moreover, the first plan of colonization was proposed by the Alaska Commerical Company. This contemplated the bringing over and settling in Alaska some 500 Icelanders, and the company offered to pay the cost of transportation. Since it required legislative sanction on the part of Congress, nothing was done. Congress would take no action in Alaskan matters. The Government said in effect to the Alaska Commercial Company, "Take this great possession; do as you will with it; it's no concern of ours."

Under these conditions, the company can not be blamed for looking after its own financial interests rather than attempting to make available to the many the latent resources of the vast domain. It must, however, be credited both with having established the first system of transportation to the remote parts of the Territory and with doing its full share toward maintaining law and order.

CHAPTER XVI

American Exploration of Alaska

IT HAS been shown that in 1867 when Russia transferred her American possessions to the United States, though the coast line had been explored and in part charted, there was little known of the interior, except of the Yukon River and the lower courses of the Kuskokwim River. The exploration of these watercourses had hardly gone beyond a day's trip from the river banks. Seventy per cent of Alaska was then still practically unknown to white men.

For many years after the acquisition of Alaska the United States Government made no systematic effort to explore the interior. Such official explorations as were made were largely due to the initiative of some government employees, and often received but scant support, and in some cases even open opposition, from the authorities at Washington. It is, therefore, to the greatest credit of these early explorers that they carried out difficult projects with but little help and with no hope of any official recognition of their efforts. It should also be noted that much of the knowledge gained of the hinterland during the generations following the acquisition was due to the personal efforts of prospectors and fur traders and of the employees of periodicals.

The above statements apply to the explorations of the interior. Professor George Davidson's early exploration of the shore line, already referred to, was but the forerunner of a large amount of investigating and charting carried on by the Coast and Geodetic Survey. This work was not strictly exploration but more the searching out of the details of the shore line and the hydrography of the adjacent waters. Incidental to the charting, many scientific data relating to various subjects were collected by Coast Survey officers. The pioneers in this work were Professor Davidson and Dr. William H. Dall. Later, the work was extended by many naval officers who commanded Coast Survey vessels, notably the famous old *Patterson.* Up to 1898, the vessels were all commanded by officers of the Coast Survey. It is impractical to record here the many who have taken part in this coastal exploration. Suffice it to say that the charting of the shore line has been under way for over half a century and the results attained have been of inestimable value both to the navigator and to the scientist. The Revenue Cutter Service, now the Coast Guard, and a few vessels of the Navy have also aided in this charting of the coast line.

The first, and for many years the only, official expedition sent into the interior was led by Captain Charles Raymond, Corps of Engineers. In 1869, he ascended the Yukon to the mouth of the Porcupine. His mission was to determine whether or not the Hudson Bay post at Fort Yukon was within Alaskan territory. The question was decided in the affirmative, and the corporation was ordered to move its trading station to Canadian soil. The new site chosen, at Rampart House on the Porcupine River, proved 20 years later also to be in Alaska, and a second move was required.

In 1877, E. W. Nelson, the naturalist, was dispatched to St. Michael to establish a meteorological station at that place, under the auspices of the chief signal officer of the United States Army. The ostensible purpose was to obtain a series of accurate weather records, but the choice of a naturalist for this mission clearly indicates that other observations were also to be made. Nelson was the first government scientist, other than those of the Coast Survey, to go to Alaska; and his contributions to knowledge of Alaskan biology and ethnology are of great importance. His meteorological observations during four years of residence kept him closely tied to St. Michael, but he made some important explorations in the Bering Sea littoral and also made a voyage to Point Barrow in the revenue cutter *Corwin*. In December, 1878, Nelson, in company with Charles Peterson, a fur trader, carried an exploratory survey southward from St. Michael across the vast Yukon delta and on to the Kuskokwim River. They were the first white men to reach the Kuskokwim by this route, and Nelson's sketch map of the region still remains the only source of information on the geography of a part of this vast stretch.[1]

In 1879, John Muir and Rev. S. Hall Young, the veteran Alaskan missionary, visited what was afterwards called Muir Glacier and explored Glacier Bay. They were the first white men to examine the bay, though it had been seen in 1877 by Lieutenant C. S. A. Wood, U.S.A., while he was making some explorations in the Fairweather Mountains

---

[1] Nelson, Edward W., "A Sledge Journey in the Delta of the Yukon River." *Proceedings of Royal Geographic Society, N.S.*, IV (1882), 660-670.

in company with native hunters. Muir's published descriptions of Alaskan scenery drew much public notice and led in later years to the development of the favorite tourist route through Southeastern Alaska. Many years later Dr. Young recorded in a charming way his recollections of this voyage.[2]

The most notable contribution to the knowledge of Alaska's geography and resources was made by Ivan Petrof, a Russian Alaskan serving as an agent for the Tenth Census. He spent two years in traveling along the coast and on the lower Yukon and Kuskokwim, his familiarity with the native tribes and the Russian inhabitants enabling him to obtain much valuable data regarding regions not visited by him. His results and those of the several other experienced men who were employed in this work were compiled by Petrof in an admirable report and published by the Census Office. His general map of Alaska which accompanied the report, though largely based on the statements of natives and traders was remarkably accurate in delineating the general features of the geography. He seems to have been the first man to have a clear conception of the distribution of the mountain ranges in Alaska. In judging Petrof's geography, we must remember that outside of rough traverses of the Yukon and the lower Kuskokwim the interior of Alaska was known only through the reports of a few traders.

As will be shown later, George Holt, a prospector, following the route long known to the Indians crossed up the Chilkoot Pass in 1878; and between 1880 and 1882 many prospectors followed this route into the interior. Moreover, Aurel and Arthur Krause explored the Chilkoot Pass as well as the Chilkat basin in 1881, under the auspices of the Geographical Society of Bremen.[3]

This part of the interior was, therefore, well known to white men, though unsurveyed, when Lieutenant Frederick Schwatka, Cavalry, U.S.A., already experienced as an Arctic explorer, traversed it in 1883. Crossing the Chilkoot Pass (called by him Perrier Pass) with a small party, Schwatka built a raft at the headwaters of the Lewes and continued down the river in this unmanageable craft, running the various rapids,[4] to Fort Selkirk at the junction

[2] Young, S. Hall, *Alaska Days with John Muir*, New York, 1915.

[3] Krause, Aurel, *Die Thlinkit Indianer*, Jena, Germany, 1885.

[4] Schwatka portaged his outfit around Miles Canyon and White Horse Rapids. The raft was allowed to drift through and was caught below.

of the Pelly and Lewes. From this point on he was traversing a river which had been explored by the Western Union Telegraph agents and was already occupied by the fur traders. Schwatka continued his trip to Fort Yukon and thence to the sea. To Charles W. Homan, who accompanied

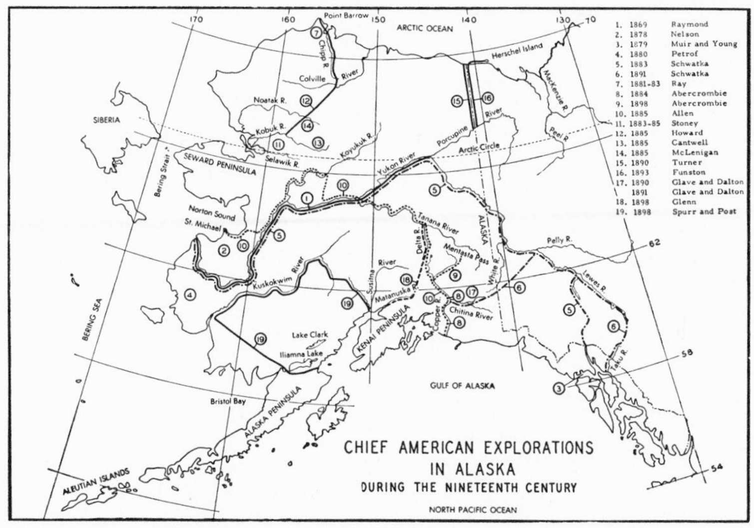

ROUTES OF AMERICAN EXPLORERS IN ALASKA

Schwatka as topographer and made sketch surveys throughout the entire journey, which were corrected by observations for latitude, belongs the credit of having made the first actual survey of the Yukon and Lewes rivers. Crude as it was, it has only in very recent years been superseded by better work. Schwatka's rather spectacular account of his trip down Alaska's great river, a journey which had been made by many others, did much to rouse public interest in this far away region, and during the following decade a number of exploring parties were sent out under various auspices.

Schwatka deserves great credit for having carried through his project in the face of decided opposition to it in Washington. The War Department[5] refused to sanction it. Fortunately, General Nelson A. Miles, then in command of the Department of the Columbia, took a broader view of the subject and directed Schwatka to go to Alaska "for

[5] Schwatka, Frederick A., *A Summer in Alaska*, St. Louis, 1894, p. 10.

the purpose of gathering all information that can be obtained that would be valuable and important, especially to the military branch of the Government."[6]

Schwatka's orders were eloquently silent about the trip to the Chilkoot and down the Yukon, probably because this journey would involve crossing Canadian territory. In view of the opposition to the project, it was necessary to keep the plan and departure secret. "Thus the little expedition, which gave the first complete survey of the third largest river of our country, stole away like a thief in the night and with far less money in its hands to conduct it through its long journey than was afterward appropriated by Congress to publish its report."[7]

During 1881 to 1883 a magnetic and meteorological station was maintained at Point Barrow by Lieutenant P. H. Ray, U.S.A. This was a part of an international plan for circumpolar observation. Ray explored the region inland 100 miles from his station.

Schwatka's results from his Yukon exploration led to the dispatching of Lieutenant W. R. Abercrombie in 1884 to explore the Copper River. Abercrombie failed in his mission, but ascended the river as far as the two great glaciers which discharge into it. These he named Miles[8] and Childs glaciers.

This work was taken up again in the following year by Lieutenant (later Major General) Henry T. Allen, Cavalry, U.S.A., who made one of the most remarkable journeys in the annals of Alaskan explorations. Allen, with four men, landed at the mouth of the Copper River in March, 1885, and made his way up that stream by boat for some 300 miles; then he crossed to the Tanana by way of the Suslota Pass and, securing another boat from the natives, continued his journey to the mouth of the Tanana. During this part of the journey the party were dependent entirely upon the country for food and were in a half-starved condition when they reached the Yukon about the end of June. With indefatigable energy Allen then, with one companion, crossed to the Koyukuk from near the mouth of the Melozi River and explored it almost from the Arctic Circle to its junction with the Yukon. Crossing by portage from the lower Yukon to Norton Sound, he made his way to St.

[6] Schwatka, Frederick, *Military Reconnaissance in Alaska*, Washington, D.C., 1885, p. 119.

[7] Schwatka. *A Summer in Alaska*, p. 11.

[8] The Geographic Dictionary says that this glacier was named by Allen in 1885.

Michael, whence he returned by steamer to the United States. No man through his own individual explorations has added more to a geographic knowledge of the interior of Alaska than has General Allen. Throughout his journey he made careful sketch surveys and noted all facts which came within his observation; and within one season he made maps of three of the larger rivers of the Territory, which until accurate surveys were inaugurated 12 years later were the basis of all maps. His reports are the work of a careful, painstaking observer who did his utmost to gain all the information possible.

After the return of the survivors of the ill-fated *Jeannette* expedition, which in 1879 had made St. Michael, near the mouth of the Yukon, its last port of call, a number of naval officers were sent to northeastern Siberia to recover the bodies and records of those who had lost their lives. By chance, one of them, Lieutenant George M. Stoney, became marooned on Kotzebue Sound for a couple of weeks in the summer of 1883; he utilized his time in exploring the delta of the Kobuk River,[9] which was then practically unknown. This trip roused Stoney's interest, and he induced the Navy Department to send him back the following year. He made the passage to Hotham Inlet by schooner, ascended the Kobuk River on a steam cutter for some 200 miles, and then by canoe up a tributary to its source. This season's work led to Stoney's being given command of a still more elaborate expedition in 1885. Stoney and his well-equipped party landed in Hotham Inlet in July. The equipment included a small river steamer. Winter quarters were established on the Kobuk, about 250 miles from its mouth, and the party spent the winter in extensive explorations. Stoney himself explored the headwaters of the Noatak and of the Alatna, the latter a tributary of the Koyukuk, and reached Chandler Lake, in which the Colville River has its source, as well as the head of the Selawik River, south of the Kobuk. Of Stoney's officers, Ensign Reed led a party from the winter camp to the Noatak River, and Assistant Engineer Zane reached the Yukon by way of the Pah and Koyukuk rivers; but the most noteworthy trip was that made to Point Barrow by Ensign W. L. Howard. Leaving the winter camp in April, with two white men and two natives he proceeded to the northeast across the Noatak to the valley of the Colville, followed this down in company with a party

[9] He called it the Putnam River.

of natives for some 20 miles, and then crossed to the headwaters of the Chipp River. Here he discarded the dog teams he had used up to this point for transporting his supplies, and descended the Chipp River to the coast in native skin boats, arriving at Point Barrow on July 15, the first white man to cross northern Alaska. The results of the expedition were a fairly accurate survey of the Kobuk valley and sketch maps of the Selawik, upper Colville, upper Noatak, and Alatna rivers. Stoney was the first to make instrumental surveys in the interior of Alaska. It is very unfortunate that his full report and maps were never published. The manuscript maps are still on file in the Navy Department, and the only record of this elaborate expedition is a brief statement of results prepared many years later.

In 1880, Captain C. E. Hooper of the U.S. Revenue-Marine Service penetrated the Arctic Ocean and explored a part of its shore line. This was the first of a series of many coastal explorations in the northern Bering Sea and the Arctic Ocean made by that service. Lieutenant J. C. Cantwell, during the summers of 1884 and 1885, made the expedition up the Kobuk. By use of steam launch and skin boats he succeeded in reaching Walker Lake, near the head of the Kobuk. His was the first party to reach the upper Kobuk; and, considering the conditions under which the trip was made, he prepared a very creditable map of the river. Charles H. Townsend, then of the U.S. Fish Commission, accompanied the party as naturalist in 1885. Another officer of the Revenue-Marine Service, S. B. McLenigan, in 1885 with one companion ascended the Noatak River some 300 miles in a native skin boat, carrying out his instructions in the face of many obstacles and maintaining a sketch survey throughout his journey.

Mount St. Elias (see picture, page 145), whose summit marks the boundary of Alaska, was long a subject of great popular interest, both because of its altitude, it being at one time considered the highest peak on the continent, and because it was the first point sighted by a white man on the mainland of Alaska. Bering, who discovered and named it, knew it only as a distant peak which loomed above the clouds, for he made no attempt to get near it. The mountain was also noted by Cook, Dixon, and Vancouver during their explorations of the coast line. In 1786, LaPerouse, while cruising along the coast saw Mount St. Elias; and Dagelet, his astronomer, calculated its altitude at 12,672 feet. Five years later Malaspina entered Yakutat Bay and surveyed Disenchantment Bay, its inland extension, which he hoped would prove to be a northeast passage. His determination of the altitude of the mountain at 17,851 feet came remarkably near the truth, considering the adverse conditions under which it was made. In 1837, Sir Edward Belcher visited Yakutat Bay in *H.M.S. Sulphur.* Tebenkof's atlas, published in 1852, gives the altitude of the mountain as 17,000 feet. In 1874, W. H. Dall and Marcus Baker, while cruising along the coast, made a rough determination of the altitude of Mount St. Elias and estimated it at 19,000 feet.

It was nearly a century and a half after Bering's discovery before any attempt was made to ascend the mountain or even to approach its base. In 1886, Frederick Schwatka, with Professor William Libbey and Lieutenant H. W. Seton-Karr, led an expedition supported by the New York *Times* to make the ascent of the mountain. So little was known of the conditions of travel that the party was foredoomed to disaster. Schwatka and Seton-Karr with a small party reached a point about 20 miles inland and obtained considerable geographical information which was of great use to the subsequent explorers. Two years later an altitude of 11,400 feet was attained by a party consisting of the Englishmen W. H. Topham, Edwin Topham, and George Broca, and an American, William Williams. A third attempt was made in 1890 by I. C. Russell and Mark B. Karr with six camp hands, under the joint auspices of the National Geographic Society and the United States Geological Survey, which, though unsuccessful, resulted in some important contributions to the geographic knowledge of the region. Russell and Karr would undoubtedly have reached the top had not a severe storm forced them to retreat after a four day wait in rude shelters in snow banks on the upper slopes of the mountain without fuel and almost without food. Russell, nothing daunted by this experience, in 1891 again essayed the ascent under the same auspices. During this attempt, he while alone succeeded in reaching a height of 14,500 feet, but he was again forced to return on account of severe storms. The results of Russell's two expeditions were a large number of data in regard to the glacial history of the region and a fairly accurate map of the slope of the mountain. Karr's determination of 18,100 feet at its height proved to be remarkably accurate if one takes into account the conditions with which he had to contend. The Coast Survey triangulation of the following year shows the elevation to be 18,024. The summit of Mount St. Elias was reached by the Italian, Prince Luigi, who followed the route which Russell had explored and very largely adopted the methods which Russell had recommended. Luigi, in 1897, landed at Yakutat Bay and, with a large and thoroughly equipped expedition, made his way across the 40 miles of snow and ice between the coast and the base of the mountain. In his ascent he practically followed Russell's route, reaching the summit on July 31, five weeks after leaving tidewater. Prince Luigi's expedition was carefully planned, and he showed himself a capable leader as well as an experienced mountaineer.

The location of the international boundary on the Yukon became a question of importance after the discovery of rich gold placers near it. The Canadians were first in the field. In 1888 the surveyor, William Ogilvie, and the geologist, George M. Dawson, made surveys of the route from the head of Lynn Canal in Southeastern Alaska to the mouth of the Lewes River. Ogilvie in the following year extended his surveys down the Yukon to the international boundary, and in 1890 continued his exploration to the head of the Porcupine, which had been surveyed in the previous year by J. D. McConnell of the Canadian Geological Survey.

Meanwhile, the United States Coast and Geodetic Survey had dispatched two parties to the boundary. One of these, under J. E. McGrath, established an astronomic station near the boundary on the Yukon, and the other, under J. H. Turner, made a similar station where the boundary crossed the Porcupine. In connection with this work, Turner with one companion made a trip with dog teams from the camp on the Porcupine to the Arctic Ocean in the winter of 1890, following as nearly as possible the 141st meridian. This was the second time that northern Alaska was crossed by white men, the first being three years before by Ensign Howard. The surveys of McGrath and Turner were limited to very small areas, but they were the first geodetic surveys in the interior of Alaska. Besides doing the work to which they had been especially detailed, they also kept meteorologic records and made corrections from their route traverses in the existing maps of the Yukon. Professor

I. C. Russell of the United States Geological Survey accompanied McGrath to the boundary from the mouth of the river, and thence came to the coast with a party of prospectors by way of Lewes River and Chilkoot Pass.

In 1893, Frederick Funston (afterwards Major General, U.S.A.) made his way into the Yukon via the Chilkoot Pass with a "roving commission" to collect plants for the Department of Agriculture. Following the well-traveled route to Fort Yukon, he made his way up the Porcupine River and wintered at Rampart House, the Hudson Bay Company Station. In March, 1894, Funston made a journey northward to Herschel Island with one Indian companion, following approximately the route to the Arctic Ocean which had been explored three years earlier by Turner. In 1904, A. G. Maddren and Wilfred Osgood made a summer trip into this same region under the auspices of the Smithsonian Institute. They ascended the Old Crow River, a northern tributary of the Porcupine, and explored the region near the international boundary.

In 1890, an expedition was sent out by *Frank Leslie's Weekly* for explorations in Alaska, which left the coast at Pyramid Harbor, ascended the Chilkat River, and after crossing the divide explored Lake Kusawa in Canada. There the party divided: A. B. Schanz and S. J. Wells descended to the Yukon, and E. J. Glave and Jack Dalton crossed the divide to Alsek waters and followed the Alsek River to the coast. In the following winter Wells crossed from the Yukon to the Tanana, and Schanz is said to have visited Lakes Clark and Iliamna. The exploration by Glave and Dalton of the Alsek was a daring piece of work, as its character at that time was entirely unknown. Its course through the St. Elias Range has not even yet been surveyed.

In 1891, Schwatka made his third trip to Alaska. In company with C. Willard Hayes of the U.S. Geological Survey and Frank Russell, a prospector, he ascended the Taku River, crossed the divide to Teslin Lake and, in folding canoes which had been transported across the pass by natives, went downstream to the Lewes River and continued to Fort Selkirk on the Yukon. Crossing overland to White River, near the point where it is intersected by the international boundary, they then continued up the White to its source; and though they were deserted by all of their Indian packers, the three white men went on through Skolai Pass and, after reaching navigable waters on the Nizina, built a boat and continued down to the Copper River, thus connecting with Allen's exploration. Dr. Hayes' report and map, based on a foot traverse, are remarkably complete and accurate, considering the exceedingly trying conditions under which the field observations were made and give much geologic and geographic information about a region which up to the time of its publication was practically unknown.

In that same year Glave (who later lost his life on the Congo) and Dalton made a second trip into the Alsek basin. This time they extended their journey to the White River basin. This exploit is of interest chiefly because it was the first time in the history of Alaska that horses were used on an extended journey.

Congress, in 1895, recognized the importance of an investigation of the mineral resources of Alaska, and by a small appropriation enabled the Geological Survey to send its first party to the north. George F. Becker, aided by C. W. Purington, made a preliminary investigation of the gold deposits, and Dr. W. H. Dall studied the coal deposits of the Pacific coastal belt. The following year J. E. Spurr, with H. B. Goodrich and F. C. Schrader, descended the Yukon and visited the more important placers of Alaska, and did some topographic as well as geologic mapping.

Of the thousands who entered the Yukon basin during the first years of the gold excitement only a small percentage had any conception of the difficulties with which they would be confronted, and still less had any previous training which fitted them for the work they had so rashly undertaken. Hundreds toiled over the Coast Range passes and made the mad dash to reach the El Dorado their fancies had painted; but discouraged at the outlook, continued down the Yukon to its mouth, having hardly been out of sight of its banks. The more venturesome prospector, however, found no risk too hazardous, no difficulty too great, and now there is hardly a stream which has not been panned by him, and hardly a forest which has not resounded to the blows of his axe. Evidences of his presence are to be found everywhere, from the almost tropical jungles of Southeastern Alaska to the barren grounds of the north which skirt the Arctic Ocean. While the prospectors have traveled far and wide in Alaska, they have as a class added little to the knowledge of its geography. As a rule they follow but two purposes: to find gold and to get through the country. The information obtained by them is seldom exact, even when available, for their conception of where they have been is often as vague as their ideas as to where they are going. Though their contribution to geographic knowledge is small, these pioneer prospectors at the expense of hard toil and suffering, if not of their lives, have blazed the way for the settler, miner, and surveyor.

The public interest aroused in Alaska by the finding of valuable placer mines in adjacent territory led to a demand for more definite information, and money was appropriated for investigation in Alaska under various bureaus of the Federal Government. The Coast and Geodetic Survey was enabled to expand its Alaskan survey which had been carried on ever since the purchase of the Territory. The Army established military posts to preserve order and to extend relief to the many ill-equipped and inexperienced argonauts. It later also built trails and telegraph lines which were to become of immeasurable advantage to Alaska, and made some surveys.

When in 1898 the Geological Survey began its systematic surveys and explorations in the interior of Alaska, the problems which confronted it were not easy. The public demanded the immediate publication of maps of unexplored or only partly explored regions. Such maps would have far greater value if they could be furnished while the excitement was at its height, so there was not opportunity for extensive areal mapping. The problem was to make surveys of the main routes of travel, which were chiefly confined to the larger rivers, and to include with these as wide areas as possible. The first season's work resulted in about 3,000 miles of instrumental traverses, with reconnaissance maps of an area of nearly 30,000 square miles, besides a more accurate survey of about 2,000 square miles. These traverses were largely confined to the more important rivers. The work had to be planned with a very incomplete knowledge of the geography, of the climate, and of other conditions of travel in the region, and all supplies and equipment had to be transported from Puget Sound ports. After landing in Alaska, the parties were entirely dependent on their own resources for transportation. The first year they made their way by following the waterways in canoes, which were carried on the backs of the men at the portages; but after some knowledge of the country had been gained, it was found that horses could be used to advantage for the transportation of supplies.

The general scheme of operations for the first year included exploration of the Kuskokwim, the Susitna, and the Copper rivers, as all three of these streams offered possible routes into the interior. The Copper River work was carried on by members of the Geological Survey under the auspices of the War Department, which organized two expeditions for the purpose, one under Captain (later Major General) Edwin F. Glenn and the other under Captain (Major retired) William R. Abercrombie.

Glenn, with a small detachment provided with pack horses, left the coast at Cook Inlet and made his way northward along the Matanuska, crossed the Copper River plateau, and descended the Delta River to the Tanana, whence he returned to the coast by the same route. Walter C. Mendenhall of the Geological Survey, who had been detailed to his party, made a route traverse throughout the journey in addition to doing his geologic work. At the Tanana, Lieutenant (later Colonel) J. C. Castner was detached from Glenn's party to continue the exploration to Circle on the Yukon. With two men he crossed the Tanana and attempted to make his way up the Volkmar River, but the lateness of the season made the plan impracticable. After losing both their horses, the three attempted to return to the Tanana on a raft. The raft was wrecked and everything lost, including their shoes. They reached the Tanana half dead with hunger and exposure where they were fortunate enough to find some friendly Indians. Some explorations were also carried on in the Susitna valley by Lieutenant H. G. Learnard and Sergeant William Yanert, also of Glenn's party.

The second Army expedition, under Captain Abercrombie, landed at Valdez on Prince William Sound. The heavy snowfall prevented an early start, but eventually the entire party, including horses, made its way inland by the Valdez Glacier route, which that year was used by hundreds of prospectors. After reaching the Copper, Captain Abercrombie left the party for a hurried trip to Mentasta Pass along the trail established by prospectors. Lieutenant P. G. Lowe, following a similar route, made his way to Fortymile and returned to the coast by way of the Lowe River and the White Pass Railroad. The rest of the party, under the leadership of F. C. Schrader of the Geological Survey, made surveys and investigations in the lower part of the Copper River basin.

The exploration of the Susitna was undertaken by George H. Eldridge and Robert Muldrow of the Geological Survey with five men. They made their way up the river from Cook Inlet, dragging their supplies in canoes against the swift current. At Jack River the boats were left; and with packs on their backs, the party pushed on to the Cantwell

UNITED STATES GEOLOGICAL SURVEY CAMP ON SNAG RIVER, 1898
Typical of exploring expeditions. Photo by A. H. Brooks.

River, confluent to the Tanana, but at this point were forced to turn back by the failure of provisions, and reached their boats in a half-starved condition. Rough surveys were made throughout the journey, and the approximate position and height of Mount McKinley were determined.

The longest exploration of 1898 was that made by Spurr and Post who ascended the Yentna, the left fork of the Susitna, portaged to Kuskokwim waters, descended the latter river to its mouth, and returned to Cook Inlet by a route which crossed the Alaska Peninsula.

The same year the two most important southern branches of the Yukon—the Tanana and White rivers—were surveyed. A party, led by W. J. Peters and with Alfred H. Brooks[10] as geologist, crossed the White Pass and went

[10] This, of course, is the author himself. He was making the first of his 24 trips to Alaska.—*Editor's Note.*

inland on the snow and ice to Marsh Lake where, after delaying until the ice broke up, they embarked in canoes for the White River, at which point the surveys began. The ascent of the river was made by dragging the canoes against the rushing current. Six weeks of this toilsome task in the glacial waters brought the party near the head of Snag River, a northern tributary of the White, whence the Tanana was reached by portage, after which the downstream trip to the Yukon was comparatively easy. Reconnaissance surveys of about 10,000 square miles were made by this party. The same year E. C. Barnard, following a similar route from the coast to the Yukon, made a survey of about 2,000 square miles in the Fortymile River basin.

In 1899, Peters and Brooks continued their explorations by a survey extending westward from Lynn Canal along the northern base of the St. Elias Range to the headwaters of the White and Tanana rivers and northward to the Yukon at Fortymile. The journey was made with horses, only five out of the original 15 reaching the Yukon.

In this year, too, the work of exploring the great waterways was extended north of the Yukon to the Koyukuk, which was mapped by Schrader and T. G. Gerdine. Leaving Fort Yukon in canoes, they ascended the Chandalar River, and after making a 16 mile portage reached Koyukuk waters and followed them to the Yukon. In the fall Schrader and Brooks met at St. Michael after the close of the work, decided to visit the newly-discovered placers at Nome, and made the investigation to be discussed in Chapters XXI and XXII.

The great demand for maps of important mining districts forced the Geological Survey in 1900 to postpone further explorations. One party, under the leadership of Schrader, Gerdine, and Spencer, mapped a large area in the Copper River basin, both geologically and topographically; another, under Barnard, Brooks, Peters, and Mendenhall did similar work in Seward Peninsula.

In 1901, the work in northern Alaska was resumed, and a network of surveys completed connecting the Yukon, Koyukuk, and Kobuk rivers, the Arctic Ocean, and Kotzebue Sound. Schrader and Peters made a trip which included a journey the entire length of Alaska from its southernmost limit to Point Barrow. Starting in winter, they traveled to the Koyukuk with dog teams, thence ascended one of the north forks of that stream with canoes, crossed to a branch of the Colville, and followed it to its mouth. They then skirted the coast westward to Point Barrow and finally southward to Cape Lisburne, where they were so fortunate as to find a steamer. In the course of their journey they traversed the Endicott Mountains and brought back the first authentic information in regard to this great range. Theirs was the most notable exploration that has been made by the Geological Survey. In the same year Mendenhall and D. L. Reaburn also made surveys and explorations in this northern region. They reached the mouth of Dall River on the Yukon in June, ascended that stream in canoes, and then by an 18 mile portage reached Koyukuk waters. They descended the Koyukuk to the mouth of the Alatna River, which they ascended for about 100 miles, and then made a second portage which brought them to the Kobuk River, which they followed to its mouth. This expedition is of particular interest in that it made the first instrumental survey from the Yukon to tidewater. The topographic survey was begun at Fort Yukon and carried through to Kotzebue Sound. During the same season, Brooks was engaged in geologic studies in Southeastern Alaska, and Gerdine, A. J. Collier, and D. C. Witherspoon did areal mapping in Seward Peninsula.

The work for 1902 was planned to include an exploration of the largest unexplored area in southern Alaska and the running of a traverse to the Yukon which should connect the previous surveys of the Susitna, Kuskokwim, and Tanana rivers. To this end a party led by Brooks and Reaburn, with L. M. Prindle as assistant, extended a survey northwest from Cook Inlet through the Alaska Range and, bending northeast, passed close to the base of Mount McKinley and on to the Cantwell River, whence they took a northwesterly route across the Tanana to Rampart on the Yukon. During the same season, the areal mapping of the Copper River basin was extended by parties led by Schrader, Gerdine, Mendenhall, and Witherspoon, while Collier studied the geology of the Yukon and Peters made a detailed topographic survey near Juneau.

It was largely through the surveys of Gerdine and Prindle that the vast region between the Yukon and the Tanana became known. To Witherspoon, J. W. Bagley, and F. H. Moffit we owe our knowledge of the southern slope of the Alaska Range between the Copper and the Susitna rivers. While many topographic engineers have engaged in mapping, the important services of D. C. Witherspoon deserve special mention. Starting in 1899 as assistant to Gerdine, he began his independent work in the upper basins of the Copper and Tanana rivers in 1902. From that date until 1918, he spent every summer in Alaska mapping. The area of his surveys during 20 years of faithful service is greater than that of any other man.

To Moffit we owe our first knowledge of the geology of the Kenai Peninsula and of the northeastern part of Seward Peninsula, but the Copper River basin has been his special field. Collier's Alaskan investigations (1900 to 1902) were chiefly in Seward Peninsula. Henry M. Eakin and A. G. Maddren have, during ten years of service, done important work in the exploration of Alaska and in the deciphering of its geology. Southeastern Alaska has been investigated by A. C. Spencer, F. E. and C. W. Wright, Adolph Knopf, P. S. Smith, E. M. Kindle, R. M. Overbeck, Theodore Chapin, and J. B. Mertie. To George C. Martin we owe most of our knowledge of the coal and oil resources of Alaska. Prince William Sound has been the field of research for U. S. Grant and B. L. Johnson, who also with Martin have studied the Kenai Peninsula. The Alaska Peninsula was investigated by W. W. Atwood, H. M. Eakin, T. W. Stanton, and Martin. The Iliamna region was mapped by Martin and Witherspoon. S. R. Capps has given special attention to the Alaska Range, but has also done important work elsewhere. The surveys in the Kuskokwim region have been made by R. H. Sargent, P. S. Smith, C. E. Giffin, G. L. Harrington, and J. B. Mertie. Smith's most important service has been in Seward Peninsula and in the Kobuk and Noatak regions.

Many geologists have taken part in the explorations and study of Alaskan glaciers. Among the earlier workers are F. E. Wright, Harvey Fielding Reid, and G. H. Gilbert. The most complete studies are those of R. S. Tarr and Lawrence Martin.

These earlier explorations of the Geological Survey have been set forth in some detail as being examples of pioneer work. In the course of the many years of surveys and explorations, many others have been made of no less importance, but they are too numerous to be here recorded.

Of the 150 or more parties which the Geological Survey has sent to Alaska, hardly a single one has failed to execute the work allotted to it. This is largely due to the special fitness, by nature as well as by experience and training, for the undertaking of those who were entrusted with the leadership of the expeditions. The parties have usually been made up of a few carefully chosen men, and the physical work and discomforts, as well as the hardships, have been shared by leaders and men alike. In connection with the topographic surveys, geologic investigations have gone hand in hand, in some instances somewhat detailed studies having been undertaken, in others the work being purely of a preliminary character.

Subsequent to the work done in collaboration with members of the Geological Survey in 1898, the Army continued to send out expeditions. In the following year some more or less detailed surveys were carried on in connection with constructing the military trail across the Chugach Mountains from Valdez. These operations as well as some minor explorations were carried on under the direction of Captain Abercrombie. Oscar Rohn, a civilian employee of Abercrombie's party, with one companion made a daring journey in which he crossed the Wrangell Mountains to Tanana waters and then returned to Copper River, making a sketch map as well as geologic observations.

Another party, provided with horses and a large river steamer, was sent to Cook Inlet under the command of Captain Glenn. The most notable contribution of this expedition to geographic knowledge of Alaska was Lieutenant Joseph S. Herron's exploration in the upper Kuskokwim basin. Following the general route previously traversed by Spurr and Post, Herron crossed the Alaska Range and entered the unexplored great lowland which lies to the northwest. Here considerable time was lost in a search for natives to act as guides, during which the early frosts killed the grass and the pack horses had to be abandoned. At length, with the aid of Indian guides, Herron's party reached the Yukon in the early winter. C. E. Griffith, a topographer of Glenn's command, led a small party from Knik Arm, Cook Inlet, to Eagle City on the Yukon. His route led partly through the region previously explored by Glenn and Mendenhall and partly over the well-traveled trail which leads from Valdez to Eagle City. George W. Van Schoonhoven, also of Glenn's party, attempted with a full equipment of horses to reach the Tanana from Cook Inlet. He first followed the route surveyed by Eldridge and Muldrow in the previous year, but turned back at the

Cantwell, reporting the route impassable. In this, he was mistaken, for Brooks and Reaburn in 1902 crossed the Cantwell where he turned back, and then continued through to the Tanana without serious difficulty.

Later the Signal Corps of the Army began the construction of telegraph lines, and as a result has connected by wire the most important points, both inland and on the coast. Reconnaissance surveys have to a certain extent been carried on, subservient and preliminary to the construction of the telegraph lines.

In 1894-95 the United States and Canadian governments made joint preliminary surveys of a part of the then-disputed *lisiere* of Southeastern Alaska. After the international boundary convention of 1903, more accurate surveys were made of the area lying on the two sides of the newly-established frontier. After a decade of continuous field work, maps were made of the entire boundary line from Portland Canal on the south, northwesterly to the summit of Mount St. Elias, and thence northward to the polar sea, along the 141st meridian.

In the Coast and St. Elias ranges of Southeastern Alaska, these precise surveys were carried out under almost insuperable difficulties. Supplies were taken up the torrential glacial streams to the head of navigation and thence sledded far inland across glaciers and carried by men up perilous declivities. The engineers themselves in ascending innumerable ice-clad peaks with their heavy instruments performed feats of mountaineering that but few have equalled in North America. The ascents worthy of permanent record in the annals of mountaineering are so numerous that they can not be recounted here. Among these, may be mentioned that of A. C. Baldwin, head of an American party which surveyed the ice- and snow-covered mountains north of Mount St. Elias and the slopes of Mount Logan in 1913. This party reached the northern base of St. Elias after a 60 mile sled journey and ascended the mountain from the north up to an elevation of 16,000 feet. Frederick Lambert, head of a Canadian party, made the first ascent of Mount Natazhat (13,440 ft.) in 1912.

The boundary in the Yukon basin traverses no high ranges, but here the surveys were beset by the difficulties of transport. Long journeys had to be made far from the established route of travel along the Yukon. This involved the development of a transport system, by sledding in the winter and by boat and pack train in the summer. Finally the survey and demarcation of the international boundary were carried through to the Arctic Ocean. The work north of the Porcupine was done by Thomas Riggs, Jr., afterward governor of Alaska. On July 18, 1912, Riggs with his Canadian colleague, J. D. Craig, set the northernmost boundary post on the shores of the Arctic Ocean. In addition to marking the boundary through thousands of miles of the trackless wilderness, this great survey has yielded a large fund of geographic information.

Ernest Leffingwell, between 1906 and 1914, devoted five years to the exploration of the Arctic littoral of Alaska, and in the Canning River region extended his surveys 50 miles inland. Working without scientific aid and in part alone, except for some Eskimo companions, Leffingwell did a remarkable piece of geographic and geologic work. He not only carried on his work unaided but also at his own expense.

The American explorations which have been chronicled above were chiefly devoted to geology and geography, and the other sciences received only collateral attention. In addition to these, a large amount of biologic investigation has been done. It would lead too far afield to chronicle all these here. Dall and Kennicott were the pioneers in this field, followed by E. W. Nelson who, as already shown, explored the Yukon and Kuskokwim deltas. Among these earlier biological workers should also be mentioned H. W. Turner, weather observer and naturalist, who was at St. Michael from 1874 to 1877 and later made biological investigations in the Aleutian Islands. Henry W. Elliot was the pioneer of the many naturalists who have studied the seal rookeries of the Pribilof Islands. In more recent years systematic investigation of the distribution of animal life of Alaska has been made by the Biological Survey. This includes the work of Wilfred W. Osgood along the Yukon River, on Cook Inlet, in the Iliamna Lake region, and on the Alaska Peninsula. The studies of Edward A. Prible, also of the Biological Survey, of the fauna of the Mackenzie River basin have thrown much light on the natural history of Alaska. Charles Sheldon, naturalist and big game hunter, has also made many long journeys in Alaska. His most important exploration was in 1907-08 when, in company with Harry Karstens who afterwards climbed Mount Mc-

Kinley, he devoted a year to a biological survey of the region lying at the northern base of Mount McKinley.

No part of Alaska has excited greater interest among explorers than the region adjacent to Mount McKinley (see picture, page 293). This mountain stands 20,300 feet above sea level and is, therefore, the highest in North America. Its snow summit is clearly visible both from tidewater and from the Yukon basin, and it was long known to the whites before its stupendous altitude was recognized. Vancouver made one of the earliest references to it when he was searching out the shore lines of Cook Inlet in 1794. Though the mountain was well known to the Russians under the name "Bulshaia Gora," meaning great mountain, since the early part of the 19th century, they did not mark it on their maps. Long before this, countless generations of Indians had viewed it, those of the Pacific watershed calling it "Traleika" and those who saw only its inland slope calling it "Denali." The early prospectors knew of Mount McKinley, Harper and others having seen it from the Tanana River as early as 1878. In 1889 Frank Densmore journeyed from the lower Tanana to the upper waters of the Kuskokwim and for days was in plain view of the mountain. It was probably his account of the mountain that led the Yukon pioneers to call it "Densmore's Peak." Years rolled by, and still no one had brought back a sufficiently definite description of this mountain to interest the cartographers and geographers.

In 1896, W. A. Dickey, a Princeton graduate and later a prominent mining man of Alaska, made a prospecting trip up the Susitna River. For days as he dragged his boat against the swift current of the river, he was in sight of the mountain. Though having no instruments, Dickey made a careful estimate of its height and finally became convinced that it was over 20,000 feet. This remarkable estimate of height was confirmed by Robert Muldrow who in 1898 accompanied the Eldridge expedition, already described. Upon his return, Dickey published the first definite description of this, the highest peak on the continent, which he named Mount McKinley. In 1899, Captain Herron, during his exploration of the upper Kuskokwim, had the same fine view of the mountain as that of the prospector, Densmore, ten years before. By then, several expeditions had roughly blocked out a vast unexplored area in the center of which lay Mount McKinley. It remained, therefore, to traverse this area and reach the slope of the mountain. This was done by Brooks and Reaburn in the summer of 1902. It was no part of this survey to attempt the ascent of the mountain, but the geologic investigation called for a visit to its slopes, and to this party belongs the credit of being the first to reach the base of the mountain and to climb to snow line.

As a result of this expedition, which determined the

TWO VIEWS OF MOUNT McKINLEY

The highest mountain in North America raises its huge bulk almost directly from the plain below to a towering 20,300 feet above sea level. Photos by F. H. Moffit (lower) and S. R. Capps (upper).

position of Mount McKinley, explored a route to its base, and confirmed its stupendous height, an interest was developed among mountaineers and explorers in this little known part of Alaska.

The first attempt to scale the mountain was made by James Wickersham, then judge of the district court and later delegate from the Territory. He had previously mountaineered in the Cascades, and his several years of judicial duties in Alaska, involving long journeys in both winter and summer, gave him a fund of experience for overcoming the physical obstacles of this undertaking. In the early summer of 1903, Wickersham, leaving his court at Fairbanks, reached the base of the mountain by an overland journey. The party was ill-equipped for the ascent, and after reaching an altitude estimated at 10,000 feet was forced to turn back.

[Since this first unsuccessful attempt, there have been many later ones, some of them successful; but the initial ascent of Mount McKinley is obscured by controversy. For this, Dr. Frederick A. Cook is primarily responsible. After two unsuccessful attempts that resulted in important contributions to geographic knowledge through explorations that encircled the base of the mountain in 1903, he put forth his claim to having reached the summit in 1906. This claim has been completely rejected by later climbers who have presented conclusive evidence to prove that his story is false and that it is physically impossible for any human being to make the ascent by the route he said he followed in the eight days that he said he spent in climbing after leaving the other members of the expedition.

[In 1910, the famous "Sourdough Party" from Fairbanks set out to climb the mountain in order to disprove Cook's story and to plant a flagpole on the top so that the stars and stripes might be seen by telescope from Fairbanks, 175 miles off. Two of them, Pete Anderson and Billy Taylor, reached the summit of the north peak. A third, Charley McGonagall, stopped just short of the goal, having finished his stint of carrying the flagpole and leaving the completion of the job to the other two men. The fourth, Tom Lloyd, leader of the group, got no higher than about 11,000 feet; but, returning ahead of the other three, made some sensational claims about having reached the summit himself. These were widely publicized and, when the truth was learned, caused some skepticism to be directed at the whole enterprise. It is now, however, accepted that Anderson and Taylor actually did scale the north peak and that McGonagall, though he did not go to the summit himself, discovered the pass that made the ascent possible. The north peak, however, is not really the summit of the mountain since its altitude is some 300 feet less than that of the south peak. This fact the Sourdoughs neither knew nor cared about since a flag on the south peak would not have been visible from Fairbanks: they accomplished their purpose by ascending the north peak; had they wanted to, they could certainly have climbed the south peak too.

[In 1912, the south peak was the scene of one of the most heart-breaking defeats in the history of mountain climbing. For all practical purposes it was conquered by Belmore Browne, H. C. Parker, and Merl La Voy at that time. The two former had been with Cook for part of the time in 1906 and all three had made an unsuccessful attempt on Mount McKinley in 1910, when they were obliged to turn back after reaching 10,300 feet. When they were within a few minutes' easy climb from the top, they were suddenly struck by a terrific blizzard that forced them to retreat in order to save their lives. They had overcome all the difficulties of the ascent and had really conquered the mountain, but they did not quite reach the peak and so technically can not be credited with being the first to achieve that goal. That honor went the following year to Hudson Stuck, Harry Karstens, Robert Tatum, and Walter Harper who reached the top of the south peak and thus, on June 17, 1913, stood at the summit of the North American continent.][11]

[11] Dr. Brooks, quite obviously, never completed this chapter, his manuscript breaking off abruptly with the account of the Wickersham attempt to scale Mount McKinley. I have taken the liberty of adding the last three paragraphs to his text in order to give a sense of completeness to the chapter by briefly relating the most important incidents in the story of the conquest of Mount McKinley that follow that first unsuccessful attempt.—*Editor's note.*

CHAPTER XVII

Notes on the Beginnings of the Alaskan Mining Industry

EVEN under the Russian regime some attempts were made to develop the mineral resources of Alaska. These were chiefly directed to finding a coal supply which was needed for the several steamers used in Alaskan trade. The demand for coal in California led the Russian American Company even to hope for an export trade. With the waning of the fur trade and with the California gold excitement, a search for this precious metal was also undertaken by the directors of the company. They even tried to mine gold in California on company account, using employees of the company. These, however, soon found that the local rules made it possible for them to mine on their own account, and they promptly went to work for themselves.

In 1849, Peter Doroshin, a graduate of the Imperial Mining School at St. Petersburg, was sent to the colony to investigate its mineral resources. He devoted some four years to the task, during which time he traveled extensively and visited many of the localities where lignitic coal had been found along the Pacific seaboard of Alaska. He did not, however, see any of the high grade coals. On his recommendation[1] a coal mine was opened at Port Graham, Cook Inlet, equipped with machinery sent from Boston. Though some experienced miners were imported from Germany, most of the laborers were ignorant of mining, and the cost of operations was inordinate. At one time there were 131 men working at the mine with a daily output of only 30 to 35 tons. A shipment of coal sent to San Francisco was sold for less than the cost of mining. This ended the plans for an export trade in coal. As a matter of fact, these coals are of an inferior grade and were then less accessible than the coals of Vancouver Island which were then being developed to supply the Pacific coast trade. Though this venture proved a financial loss, yet the mine

[1] Golder, F. A., "Mining in Alaska before 1867," *Washington Historical Quarterly*, VII, (1916), 233-238.

continued to supply coal for the local use of the company.

Doroshin's investigations had been in part directed to the finding of gold. He visited the California gold fields and directed systematic prospecting for placer gold in the Kenai Peninsula. In his general choice of locality he showed a broad knowledge of Alaska's geology. At the time of his survey the coastal strip, including the then-unknown Juneau gold belt, was under lease to the Hudson Bay Company and not available for possible mining sites. The inland region was practically unknown and for the most part inaccessible. The Alaska Peninsula and other parts of the Pacific littoral were not favorable to the occurrence of placer gold. Under these conditions, the Kenai Peninsula was possibly the most favorable place to search for gold placers. He probably chose the west side of the peninsula because this was better known than the eastern part and was readily accessible from the settlements on the shores of Cook Inlet. Making his way inland, he crossed the belt of coal-bearing rocks which he knew was not gold-bearing, and gave his attention to the western margin of the more highly altered rocks forming the backbone of the Kenai Peninsula, and now known to be locally mineralized.

Though Doroshin eventually reached the mountains near the center of the Kenai Peninsula, his first prospecting appears to have been done on the bars of the Kenai River, near Cook Inlet. It is quite possible that colors of gold had been previously found in this vicinity by someone from the neighboring Russian settlement and that Doroshin was guided in his search by such information. Realizing that the fine colors of gold he found in the bars were not of local origin, Doroshin followed the Kenai valley into the mountains. Here, on a tributary now known as Russian River, he did considerable digging. Though he sluiced out several ounces of gold, the first mined in Alaska, he found no placers which could be profitably exploited. Doroshin desired to continue his search; but the company, discouraged with the meagre results of two years of investigations, did not permit it. This ended the only attempt at Russian gold mining in Alaska.

The Russian American Company was not, however, unmindful of the possibility of finding mineral wealth. According to Professor Golder, a contract was drawn in 1863 with Ivan Furuhelm, who came to Russian America to investigate the possibility of a mining industry. By this instrument the rights of all minerals in the colony were conveyed to Furuhelm under a lease for seven years, he to pay a royalty and at the end of the term all mine equipment, as well as improvements, to revert to the company. Probably fortunately for the lessor, who could not have developed profitable mines within seven years, the transfer of the Territory prevented this remarkable instrument from ever going into effect.

Meanwhile, other influences were at work which were destined to lead to the discovery of gold in Alaska. The discovery of gold in California in 1848 had brought to the West Coast a large number of men of adventurous disposition who were looking for new fields of activity. Under the influence of the California mining laws, both statutory and developed by local usage, the American prospector was developed. In this new field, except for a few old Spanish grants, all lands belonged to the public domain. Everyone was at liberty to seek his fortune with shovel and pick, and this condition developed the vocation of the prospector. The vast mineral wealth of the great cordillera of Western America was then practically unknown, but the opportunity lay before the prospector and he was destined during the next generation to search out the most inaccessible parts of the region stretching from Mexico to Bering Sea. Moreover, the number of prospectors was much augmented by the Civil War, which developed a spirit of adventure among the young men in both the Northern and Southern armies.

The route of the prospector to Alaska lay through Western Canada, and it was in British Columbia that the first of the series of important placer gold discoveries was made which were to yield untold millions. The first of these discoveries was made on the Stikine River in 1861. This river had then long been known as it furnished the route of travel between the coast and the interior Hudson Bay posts. The gold placers were found on the bars of the Stikine, probably by Hudson Bay Company employees. In any event, it is certain that A. Choquette, a French-Canadian voyageur, who came to the coast as an employee of the Hudson Bay Company, was one of the first to engage in mining, and it is probable that he was the discoverer. He wore the typical dress of the voyageur and from his buckskin shirt was nicknamed "Buck," and the locality of his mining operations was known as "Buck's Bar." Near here he lived with his Indian family for many years, during the course of which he maintained a small trading post. Other placer discoveries were also made on the bars of the river, but these seem to have all been on the Canadian side of the boundary. During low water these bars were exposed and furnished placers on which $3 to $10 could be made daily with the aid of a "rocker." This rocker was a simple device with which the California miners were familiar for extracting gold from the gravels. The Stikine River discoveries attracted probably 100 or more American and Canadian miners. They received no welcome either from the Russian authorities or from the Hudson Bay Company employees.

In 1871, the Cassiar district in northern British Columbia was discovered by Henry Thiebert, a French-Canadian, and Harry McCulloch from St. Paul, who came into the country from the east by way of the Liard River. Hearing of the presence of white men on the Stikine, they returned to the coast by that route; and going to Victoria they rapidly disseminated the news of the gold discovery. This news started the first stampede northward, and within the next two years several thousand miners came to Wrangell en route for the new camp. Steamers were put into use on the Stikine, including the *Flying Dutchman.* By 1875, the Cassiar district had a mining population of over 1,000, and the value of the gold production was over $800,000. But both population and production soon fell off. Its importance to Alaskan mining was the influx of prospectors, some of whom scattered out along the coast of Southeastern Alaska. Some of them in about 1874 found placer gold on the Unuk River at or near the international boundary, but it proved to be of no commercial importance. Others made their way up the coast and found placer gold on Shuck River, a southerly tributary of Windham Bay, about 70 miles south of Juneau. The exact date of this find or the name[2] of the discoverer is not recorded. Placer gold was probably first found on a tributary of Shuck River about 1875. During the following two years, some 30 or 40 men visited the scene of the discovery. Some placer mining was done, but the very large estimates[3] of production are probably wide of the mark. It is more than probable that a few thousand dollars worth of gold was the value of the entire output of this district. Had it been larger, the new camp

[2] Mix Sylva is reported to be the name of the discoverer, but this has not been verified.

[3] Reported to be as high as $40,000.

would have attracted much more interest among the Cassiar miners who wintered at Wrangell to the number of 200 or 300. Whatever the amount of gold mined, this was the first to be produced in Alaska, except for the few ounces recovered by the prospecting of the Russian mining engineer, Doroshin.

Meanwhile, auriferous quartz veins had been found near Sitka, and some abortive attempts had been made to mine them. It is reported that a soldier named Doyle stationed at Sitka, in 1871 found some gold-bearing quartz in a stream tributary to Silver Bay, but little heed was given to the discovery. In the same year another gold-bearing ledge was found on Indian River about one mile from Sitka. Claims were located by W. Dunlap, M. Batten, and S. Melletish, and a little work was done on them. In the following year Michael Haley, an experienced lode miner from California, came to Sitka as a soldier, and it was he that undertook the first systematic lode development. Haley worked on a number of properties, but the most systematic developments were made on the Stewart Mine, located about 15 miles south of Sitka. This was developed on a ledge discovered in 1872. Here Haley was the first to recover gold from an Alaskan quartz mine. He did so by crushing the rich ore with the aid of pestle and mortar. In 1877, the Stewart Mine was taken over by a Portland, Oregon firm called the Alaska Gold and Silver Mining Company, capitalized at $300,000, the first corporation organized for precious metal mining in Alaska. A five stamp mill was erected, the first in Alaska, but the venture did not prove a financial success. The Sitka gold discoveries would undoubtedly have attracted more attention had they not been almost coincident with the finding of the placers of the Cassiar district in British Columbia in 1871. It has been the history of Alaskan mining that the prospector was ever ready to desert a lode district for a reported discovery of placer gold. Be it remembered also that up to 1884 no one could obtain title to a mineral claim in Alaska. Mining claims were held only by squatters' titles and common consent. There was, therefore, small incentive to exploit mineral deposits except rich placers from which immediate returns could be made.

Though the Sitka lodes for many years were destined to play a small part in Alaska's mining history, yet they served mainly, along with the Cassiar placer discovery, to draw a mining population to the Territory. Indeed, at this time there were few in Alaska except the fur trader and the miner. A census taken at Sitka in 1880 gave a return of 444 citizens. of whom 82 are classed as miners. That other vocations were not entirely neglected is shown by the fact that this small population included 18 saloon keepers.

In 1879, John Muir and S. Hall Young, on the journey already referred to in the previous chapter, threaded the mainland coast southward from Glacier Bay, in an Indian canoe. During their remarkable journey of exploration, they visited Windham Bay where there were then a few prospectors working on the Shuck River placers. Muir expressed the opinion that an extension of the gold belt would be found north of Taku Inlet, and this prophecy seems to have inspired the miners to prospect in what is now the Juneau district.

The plan for a search of the mainland coast for gold originated at Sitka and apparently in the minds of N. A. Fuller, a merchant, and George E. Pilz, a German assayer. The latter had come to Sitka to erect the stamp mill already referred to. He claimed to have received specimens of gold ore brought to him by the Indians from near the present site of Juneau. Be that as it may, the two prospectors, Richard T. Harris and Joseph Juneau, who were grubstaked for a search of the mainland coast north of Windham Bay, appear to have had no very definite plans as to the locality to be chosen for prospecting. Harris had been a clerk in a store at Wrangell, and later both he and Juneau had worked in the Stewart Mine near Sitka. Juneau was a Frenchman and a nephew of the founder of Milwaukee. Though it was generally believed that these men were grubstaked by Fuller, this belief is not borne out by Harris' own statement, which is as follows:

In the year 1880, Richard T. Harris and Joseph Juneau entered into an agreement with George E. Pilz of Sitka, and the Hall Brothers of San Francisco, to prospect the mainland of Alaska for gold and silver lode and placer mines. The agreement provided that Harris and Juneau as compensation for such service reserved the right to locate all gold placers they should find and Pilz and Hall Brothers in their turn should receive the first location on every quartz vein discovered by Harris and Juneau, but the latter should have the right to stake the extension of such quartz vein. In addition to the mining claims Harris was to receive $3.00 and Juneau $2.00 for every day spent in prospecting.

It is evident from the character of this agreement that the backers of this enterprise were seeking lode mines rather than placers.

Harris and Juneau, with three Indians, left Sitka on July 19, 1880, in a dugout canoe. They first prospected on Windham Bay, where they found some placer mining. Then they visited Sumdum and Snettisham bays, and skirted the north shore as far as Berners Bay. Returning, they landed at Salmon Creek, north of the present site of Juneau, where a few colors of gold were found. Then they made a camp at the mouth of Gold Creek on August 17, where Juneau is now located. On Gold Creek they found good prospects of alluvial gold, and also some quartz float carrying gold and galena. Returning to Sitka for more supplies, they again reached Gold Creek on September 20. This they then ascended to Snow Slide Gulch, and then climbed the summit which separates this stream from Quartz Gulch flowing north. Here they stood on what was subsequently developed as the Alaska-Juneau Mine. Through this divide they climbed down into Silver Bow basin, which lies at the head of Gold Creek. Here they found rich placers and auriferous veins, and they located many claims.

The two white men now organized the Harris Mining district and adopted a code of laws. They also staked a town site and named it Harrisburg. On their return to Sitka in November of the same year, the specimens and reports they brought back created the wildest excitement. Every available craft was soon put into commission to transport gold seekers to the scene of the new discovery. The first to arrive was a group of 30 who reached Gold Creek on December 6. They were soon followed by others. By the summer of 1881 there were upwards of 100 miners in the new camp. The name Harrisburg was changed in 1881 to Rockwell in honor of a naval officer who assisted the miners. A few months later it was changed to Juneau, after one of the discoverers, the name Harris being retained to designate the mining district.

The most important event in Alaska's mining history was the development of the Treadwell group of mines. They have produced gold to the value of over $60,000,000. These lodes occur on the eastern slope of Douglas Island opposite Juneau and close to tidewater. This slope was heavily timbered and covered with moss; and, except for the occurrence of alluvial gold in the talus, derived from the lode, there was probably little or no evidence of the great gold deposit subsequently developed. As in all new gold camps, claims were often staked irrespective of any actual discoveries. It is probable that the locator of the "Paris lode," the first of the Treadwell group to be staked, had little to guide him but the surface colors of gold and some mineralized quartz. The Paris lode covered approximately the present site of the great "Glory Hole," which marks the place of the earliest mining on the Treadwell group.

It is not recorded who actually staked the Paris lode, but the first record of ownership shows that it belonged to Joseph Pierre Erussard, generally known as French Pete, who was a trader from Sitka. As he was not a prospector or miner, it is probable that he acquired title by grubstake, or possibly by barter. The name suggests that it was originally staked for French Pete.

Among the early arrivals at Juneau was John Treadwell, a California contractor and mining engineer. He came north to examine a property located in the Silver Bow basin, but did not find it up to his expectations. About the same time French Pete arrived at Juneau on a steamer with a stock of trading goods, but without money enough to pay the heavy lighterage charges. Apparently his only asset was the Paris lode which he sold to Treadwell to raise money for lighterage. The official records show that the claim was sold for $5, but the actual transaction involved a payment of $400 or $500 which was probably paid in lighterage service. This has often been cited as an example of a man selling a rich claim at a nominal price. As a matter of fact, the claim was not worth more to the owner who had neither the experience nor the capital to develop a large body of low-grade ore. It was the genius of John Treadwell which made the Paris lode valuable. No one but an experienced engineer with farsightedness could have realized that an ore body which carried less than $10 a ton could be profitably exploited in as remote a region as Juneau was at that time. Therefore, Treadwell, though not the original owner of the property that bears his name, was the real pioneer who developed it into a mine. With French Pete, on the other hand, it was a pure gamble. It is quite possible that he never even saw the claim which he sold for all it was worth at that stage of development. Treadwell, the engineer, must share equally with Harris and Juneau, the prospectors, the honor for the pioneer work in the Juneau district, for it was his genius that led to the camp's being developed into a lode district.

In 1882, Treadwell built the first mill in the Juneau district on Douglas Island. This contained five stamps and was provided with ore taken from a shoot about 20 feet wide along the foot wall of the Paris lode. This ore body milled gold to the value of $8 to $10 a ton. Developments soon showed that the major part of the ore body was of so low a grade that it could be profitably exploited only on a large scale. In 1885, a 120 stamp mill was erected, followed three years later by the installation of 240 more stamps. Meanwhile, the ore body had been traced to the north and south, and the increase was therefore justified. More were gradually introduced until at the present time the four mines of the Treadwell group include some 900 stamps.

After Treadwell had acquired title to the lode properties, a dispute arose with miners who were engaged in washing the rich talus material derived from the lode. By law Treadwell was entitled to the gold placers on his property as well as the lode. The miners thought otherwise. A miners' meeting was called at Juneau, and its decision was that Treadwell was to have only the lode gold. It was eminently a case decided on equity and not on law, but with this decision Treadwell was forced to be content, and probably many thousands of dollars worth of gold were washed from the Treadwell property which by law belonged to the owner of the lode.

The early workings at the Treadwell Mine were in the great pit known as the Glory Hole whose sides enclosed some 13 acres. Now the workings reach depths of over 2,000 feet, and the mining operations are carried on far under the Gastineau Channel which separates Douglas Island from the mainland. Power was first secured by a combination of water power and a steam plant burning coal. Later oil was substituted for coal, and now much of the power is derived from large hydro-electric installations. The operations of the four mines, the Treadwell, Mexican, 700-foot, and Ready Bullion, have been on such a large scale that economies have been introduced which have made it possible to work lower grade ore than anywhere else in the world, said to be as low as only $3 a ton in recent years. There is no waste handled from the mine,

THE TREADWELL MINE
This enormously rich gold deposit has yielded millions of dollars in low-grade ore: left, the famous "Glory Hole," photo by A. H. Brooks; right, a crusher plant, photo by Sidney Paige.

all the rock and ore hoisted being put through the mill. The combination of conditions for economic mining existing at Juneau are hardly paralleled in any other mining camp in the world. These are cheap ocean freight rates, which reduce the cost of both labor and supplies; water power and abundant timber; and favorable climatic conditions. In the early history of the Treadwell, the ore body was undercut, and hence no hoisting was required. Though this condition no longer exists on Douglas Island, where the ore bodies are mined below sea level, yet it holds for the mines located on the mainland. Here the strong relief makes an enormous tonnage of ore available above the level of the working tunnels. All these conditions make for cheap exploitation and have made possible the profitable development of low-grade ores of the Juneau type. In the aggregate, there has been very little high-grade ore mined at Juneau. The small plants for mining the rich shoots occasionally found have never been very profitable, but on the other hand enormous production has been made and is being made from the low-grade ore bodies. This work has required the highest technical skill as well as enormous capital investments.

While Treadwell was developing the mine on Douglas Island, many prospectors were engaged in sluicing the gravels of Silver Bow basin, drained by Gold Creek. Here the richest deposits were the hillside placers whose gold was derived direct from the weathering of the mineralized lode whose outcrop skirts the southern margin of the basin. This development, though very lucrative for a time, soon had to give way to exploitations on a larger scale. The placers, though rich, were soon exhausted since they were not very extensive. Meanwhile, the lodes in the mainland belt were also receiving attention. In 1882, W. I. Webster built a five stamp mill near the present site of the Ebner Mine, a locality which could then be reached only by a difficult horse trail. This was the first mill built on the mainland in the Juneau district. During the next ten years, a dozen small mills were built in the Gold Creek and Sheep Creek basins, but none was a financial success, for the ores were not rich enough to permit of profitable exploitation except on a large scale. It is only since the large developments of the Alaska-Gastineau and Alaska-Juneau of the past few years that the mainland lode production has been large. Besides the Treadwell Mine, the most successful venture in the first 20 years of mining at Juneau was the development of the low-grade placers of the Silver Bow basin. As has already been stated, the richest parts of this placer were mined by small operators in the early history of the camp. In 1889, a group of claims was united and developed by the American Gold Mining Company, and the property later passed into the hands of the Nowell Mining Company. During ten years of mining, nearly half a million dollars worth of gold was recovered.

Mines had been developed and a number of mills built in the Juneau district several years before there was any legal ownership of mining claims. Mining property was held by squatters' rights and transferred to other ownership by common consent. These conditions speak well for the standards of citizenship and public spirit maintained in this little isolated community whose affairs were administered with the almost entire absence of a civil and criminal code. The miners made their own laws and enforced them themselves. While important questions were settled by the miners' meetings, lesser affairs were taken care of by an elected commission of three, one of whom acted as justice of the peace. A jail was maintained, but fine and banishment were the more common punishments meted out for minor offences. The selling of firearms and whiskey to Indians was punished by banishment, and thus the miners solved a problem which had vexed the military authorities for many years.

In 1881, there was some trouble with the Indians who killed several white men. The murderers were captured and promptly hanged, this being the first capital punishment inflicted in Alaska. Since there was some fear of the Indians, four militia companies were organized and armed with rifles loaned by the Government.

With the enactment of the civil code for Alaska in 1884, conditions changed completely. Appointed United States commissioners took the place of the elected officials of the miners. Disputes were no longer arbitrated by the miners' meetings, but were tried in a regular court of law. This providing a legal machinery for the settlement of property disputes in regard to mining claims was not an unmixed blessing. For a quarter of a century the development of the Juneau district was hampered by legal disputes. The new law, though it legalized the acquisition of mineral claims, and was therefore an important advance, yet brought with it the long train of rules and court decisions which have so hampered the mining industry. Nowhere has there been a better example of the inadequacy of the American mining code than in the history of the Juneau district.

The early history of Juneau is evidence that the pioneers were essentially law-abiding citizens. In spite of the absence of legal authority, order was maintained and the community submitted to the laws. The only serious exceptions were the anti-Chinese riots of 1886. These were part of the general movement extending throughout the western states in which the white miners by force prevented the employment of Mongolian labor. In 1886, a house in which Chinese were living was blown up at Juneau, and in August about 100 Chinese miners were taken by a mob from the Treadwell Mine and placed on two small sailing vessels which were ordered to leave. The single United States marshall stationed at Juneau claimed, and no doubt rightly so, that he was powerless to prevent this outrage, for it appears that the majority of the community was in sympathy with the mob. A. P. Swineford, the energetic governor, attempted to have the Chinese, who had reached Wrangell, brought back by the naval authorities. The little *Pinta* was the only naval vessel on the coast, and her commander stated that his force was not large enough to cope with the situation. The expelled Chinese were not brought back, and from that day to this no Mongolian labor has ever been employed in Alaskan mines, though many find work at the fish canneries during the summer months.

The many prospectors who came to Juneau in its early history soon searched out the northern and southern extension of the gold belt. This, as has already been shown, had been recognized as far south as Windham Bay long before the discovery of Juneau, and some evidence of it to the north as far as Berners Bay is reported to have been found as early as 1886. The first stamp mill was erected at Berners Bay in 1890, and during the next decade four others were built.

After the discovery of the Juneau district the most important event in the mining history of the Pacific coast of Alaska was the development of the beach placers at various localities. These gold deposits are formed by concentration through the beating of the surf on sands and gravels whose gold contents are not high enough to warrant exploitation, at least by the crude methods then in vogue. Their method of formation determines that their location is at such localities as are swept by the full force of the ocean waves, a fact which of necessity makes them difficult of access. It appears that the first discovery of beach gold was made near Yakutat in 1880 by a party led by James Hollingwood. As the story goes, two of the white men in the party were killed by natives, and Hollingwood fled. There is no definite record of this murder, and it is probable that the narrative has been embellished to give it a more dramatic setting. It appears that the first actual mining of beach gold was in 1887 on the outer margin of Khantaak Island, which lies near the entrance of Yakutat Bay. These placers proved neither very rich nor extensive. About the same time, beach gold was found on the outer strand line of Lituya Bay. These deposits proved rich enough to afford good profits to the individual miners working with shovel and rocker. The discovery attracted much attention, and upwards of 100 men started for the scene. Though the Lituya Bay deposits were not extensive, yet they afforded a living to more than a score of miners during the next decade. About 1898, gold was found in the very inaccessible Yakataga beach, and this has been exploited in a small way ever since. Since the early 90's, there has been some beach mining on the southwestern part of Kodiak Island and on Popof Island, adjacent to Unga. There was also a little

MINERAL RESOURCES

Alaska's wealth in minerals is not confined to its gold but also includes such things as coal beds (upper left, photo by A. H. Brooks), magnetite as seen in the black portion in upper right (photo by F. H. Moffit), copper as shown by the huge nugget in lower left (photo by J. B. Mertie), and marble being quarried at Tokeen (lower right, photo by A. H. Brooks).

mining of placer gold on the eastern side of Cook Inlet as early as 1889. None of the beach placers of Alaska's Pacific seaboard has yielded any large quantities of gold. They have, however, for many years furnished a living to a score or two of men. During 30-odd years of mining, gold to the value of over $500,000 has been won from this type of deposit.

For many years lode mining was confined entirely to

the Juneau district. The only exception was the discovery of an auriferous lode on Unga Island in southwestern Alaska by George C. King in 1884. On this, a five stamp mill was erected in the following year, and a 40 stamp mill built in 1891.

The influx of prospectors following the Juneau and Lituya discoveries led to much search of the seaboard region for placer gold. In 1888, gold was found on Resurrection Creek in the Kenai Peninsula, and a little mining was done; but the discovery excited little interest. Six years later, the richer placers of Bear and Palmer creeks were found. These discoveries on Kenai Peninsula were a continuation of the initial work done by the Russians earlier. They attracted a large number of miners, and by 1896 the excitement had drawn several thousand people to the Kenai Peninsula and the adjacent region. This was soon overshadowed by the Klondike excitement, however, and most of the miners were soon drawn away. Still, placer mining in the Kenai Peninsula continued, reaching a maximum output in 1899 when the value of the gold production was $150,000. Though auriferous lodes were found in this field as early as 1896, no developments were made for nearly ten years. Auriferous lode mining began in the Willow Creek district in 1908 and near Valdez on Prince William Sound in 1910.

The Alaskan mining industry had its beginnings on the Pacific seaboard of the Territory, where mineral resources were developed on a large scale before the more remote parts of the Territory became known. The most important events in the history of the gold mining industry of this part of the Territory have been sketched above. Copper mining, too, had its beginnings in Southeastern Alaska as early as 1880, and by 1901 the Pacific slope of the Territory had developed an important copper mining industry. Here, too, began the mining of the coals of the Territory, first during the Russian days and later under American auspices. Marble quarrying began in Southeastern Alaska in 1902 and gypsum mining a little later.

Meanwhile, however, enterprising prospectors penetrated the great inland region of Alaska and adjacent parts of Canada and eventually found the gold of the Klondike which was destined to draw the attention of the entire civilized world to this northern region.

CHAPTER XVIII

Notes on the First Prospectors on The Yukon

IT IS reported that the Hudson Bay traders found fine colors of gold on some of the tributaries of the Yukon near Fort Selkirk before the middle of the 19th century. Even if this report be true, nothing of importance to the mining industry developed, for no attempt was made to follow up the discovery by prospecting and the information was kept secret and attracted no miners.

The first authentic report of the finding of gold was the discovery by Robert McDonald, a Church of England missionary, at Fort Yukon. In the course of a journey to the north of the Yukon, probably made in 1863, McDonald found gold in the alluvium of a stream that has never been identified. Long after, some prospectors, believing that they had reached the scene of this discovery, named a stream Preacher Creek in honor of the clergyman who was the first to report placer gold on the Yukon. It is quite possible that McDonald's discovery was on one of the creeks of the Birch Creek district, where 30 years later profitable mining was begun. But wherever he may have found the gold, certainly the tradition that the deposit would yield "gold by the spoonful" was a gross exaggeration. Such a find would have broken even the iron bonds of the Hudson Bay Company's discipline, and its servants at Fort Yukon, whose annual wage did not exceed $200, would have deserted to become gold miners.

Among the great horde of gold seekers that came to California in the middle of the 19th century, there were many adventurous spirits who found the search for mineral wealth to their liking and hence made it their permanent vocation. Thus developed the American prospector, a type of pioneer destined to have a profound influence on the exploration and settlement of the western half of the continent. From the earliest settlement of America, the fur hunter had been the pioneer, and he must be credited with much of the searching out of new land. But the progress of settlement slowly crowded the fur hunter into new fields, and as a consequence he was always far beyond the frontier established by the pioneer colonists. The fur hunter, be he trader or trapper, is by his vocation opposed to the settler and the consequent opening up of a new land to commerce and industry, for this results in depriving him of a livelihood. Not so the prospector, who in his quest for gold invaded the field of the trapper. The success of the prospector depended on rendering accessible the mineral fields, and he therefore welcomed the settler and the attendant improvement of commercial conditions. Therefore, the prospector, and not the fur hunter, was the pioneer who smoothed the way for the settler; and it was largely due to his efforts that the cordilleran regions of the United States and Canada as well as Alaska were opened up.

W. P. Blake, the American geologist who accompanied the Russian expedition up the Stikine River in 1863, was the first to have a broad conception of the geology of the cordilleran region with reference to the distribution of the mineral deposits. On the basis of his observations and studies, he ventured the opinion that the cordilleran gold-bearing zone extended through Western Canada and into what was then Russian America. Half a century of prospecting and mining has verified his bold prophecy.

The overflow of prospectors from the California gold fields led to the discovery of the placers of the Fraser River in 1859, of the Stikine basin in 1861, and of the Caribou district in 1865. The route to the latter was by way of Fort Wrangell and, consequently, through the then newly-acquired Territory of Alaska. As was shown in the previous chapter the influx of prospectors led to the finding of gold in Southeastern Alaska; it inevitably followed that some adventurous spirits among them would in time overcome the opposition of the coast Indians and find their way to the Yukon basin from which they were separated by only one range of mountains, and that broken by numerous low passes. Meanwhile, however, a few prospectors had found their way into the Yukon basin by the long-established Hudson Bay Company's route from the Mackenzie River.

Among the small group of prospectors who reached the Yukon in the early 70's, two stand out prominently—Arthur Harper and Napoleon Leroy (always known as "Jack") McQuesten. Both were men of strong character with vision far beyond that of most of their vocation, and both devoted the best part of their lives to furthering the development of the Yukon basin. The financial success of these pioneers was but very moderate considering their opportunities, but they will ever be remembered for the important part they played in opening up the Yukon to the prospector and miner.

Harper was an Ulsterman, having been born in the County of Antrim in 1835. He came to New York as a boy and when 20 years old went to California. By the 60's he had become a prospector and had found his way to British Columbia. Like Blake, the geologist, Harper seems to have had a conception of the broader orographic features of the western cordillera, for according to Ogilvie[1] his study of Arrowsmith's map of Northwestern America led him to the conclusion that an extension of the mineralized zone would be found in the Yukon basin. Ogilvie[2] has traced Harper's journey to the Yukon in detail, and his account need not here be repeated. Suffice it to state that Harper, with three companions, left Munson Creek near the head of Peace River in September, 1872, and went to Fort Yukon by way of the Liard, Mackenzie, Peel, and Porcupine rivers. Harper's party arrived on the Yukon on July 15, 1873. It included Frederick Hart,[3] from Antrim County, Ireland; George Finch, from Kingston, Ontario; and Andrew Kansellar,[4] a German. This journey of over 1,500 miles, which occupied nearly a year, was in part through an entirely unexplored region and the rest through territory where the only white men were Hudson Bay traders; and the party lived almost entirely on fish and game. It was an achievement far beyond many a well-advertised and well-provisioned exploring expedition.

While Harper was planning his search for new gold fields, Jack McQuesten had conceived a similar undertaking. McQuesten was born in Litchfield, New Hampshire, in 1836. He was drawn to the West by the California gold rush and later went to British Columbia. At the time of the Fraser River excitement he was working at the Gamble Mills, near the present site of Vancouver.[5] McQuesten mined and prospected in the Fraser River region until 1863, when he joined the rush to the Finlay River placers.

[1] Ogilvie, William, *Early Days on the Yukon*, Ottawa, 1913, pp. 87-91.

[2] *Ibid.*

[3] He died at Dawson in 1908.

[4] In some accounts this name is given as A. Gensler.

[5] Letter from L. N. McQuesten to Albert McKay, dated July 1, 1905.

During the next ten years he was chiefly engaged in trapping and in the fur trade; part of this time he was in the employ of the Hudson Bay Company. In 1871, he heard of the purchase of Alaska by the United States and resolved to go to the Yukon basin. This plan was put into effect in 1872 when McQuesten, with two companions, went up the Liard, intending to cross to Frances Lake and reach the Yukon by way of the Pelly. They wintered at the mouth of Nelson River, where a Hudson Bay post is located. McDougal, the agent, evidently dissuaded McQuesten and his companions from choosing the difficult Frances Lake and Pelly River route and persuaded them to take in preference the well-established one by way of the lower Mackenzie and Porcupine rivers.

That spring, as indicated above, Harper and his companions arrived on their journey to the Yukon. Harper's route from Peace River clearly shows that he too had intended to reach the Yukon by way of the Pelly, a plan no doubt based on Arrowsmith's which shows it to be the shortest route to the Yukon. After meeting McQuesten, the Harper party decided to follow the Hudson Bay Company route. Before beginning his long journey down the Mackenzie, McQuesten made a hurried trip to Fort Resolution, on Great Slave Lake, and then followed Harper down the Mackenzie. He crossed by the Rat River portage to the Porcupine and arrived at Fort Yukon, in company with Alfred Mayo and George Nicholson, in August, or about a month after the Harper party.

These first prospectors on the Yukon found the pioneer fur traders already in possession. The latter had, however, done little more than take over Fort Yukon, from which the Hudson Bay Company had been expelled, and the Russian posts on the lower river. The tributaries of the Yukon were then no better known than in the days of the Russian occupation. In the whole length of the Yukon there were probably not half a dozen white men. The posts were supplied by a small steamer which ascended the river as far as Fort Yukon every summer, bringing in supplies and returning with furs. This trade was in the hands of the Alaska Commercial Company. The agents of the company gave the prospectors a warm welcome and supplied them so far as their meagre stores would permit. McQuesten has recorded that Moses Mercier, the trader at Fort Yukon, let him have 50 pounds of flour, the first he had had for two years. Later, when these prospectors were driven to St. Michael by lack of supplies on the Yukon, they were again warmly welcomed and furnished with such supplies as were available.

The charge is frequently made that the Alaska Commercial Company attempted to exclude the prospector from the Territory, whose fur trade it practically monopolized. But such experiences as the above do not justify these charges, and an unbiased examination of the available records has revealed no evidence to substantiate them. There is no doubt that the company charged full measure for the service it rendered the early Yukon placer camps, yet it still remains to be proved that these charges were very exorbitant considering the uncertainties of the business caused by the roving character of the population and the risks of loss by sea and river transportation or by fire. Later, when large fleets of ocean and river boats carried supplies to the Yukon and the relatively large fixed population gave assurance of a certain market, all commercial companies maintained high prices with profits entirely out of proportion to the risks involved. This was in part due to the abundance of gold as compared with other commodities, in part to the get-rich-quick atmosphere which permeated all classes of men. It also came about because of the lack of foresight on the part of the leading businessmen, who could not see anything but immediate profits, and the lack of good management, causing great losses which had to be borne by the communities.

Harper had the mental attitude of the typical prospector. At Fort Yukon he found among the Indians some native copper which had come from the White River, and he at once recognized a field for prospecting. But without considering that copper on the White River, because of its remoteness from transportation facilities, was absolutely worthless, he and his companions started on a 500 mile journey into an unknown region to find the source of this native copper; if he had found it and could have transported it to New York, he would have had to sell at a tremendous financial loss. Harper and his companions slowly made their way up the Yukon against the swift current, prospecting as they went. On the lower reaches of Fortymile River, they found some fine gold in the bars, but they were dissuaded from going up by the Indians who told of an impassable canyon beyond. Continuing to the White River, they ascended that stream until the low water and swift current prevented further progress with a boat. Harper's description[6] of the country indicates that he reached the middle flat of the White and probably wintered near the mouth of what is now called the Snag River. Here the party prospected. Their winter supplies consisted of only 300 pounds of flour, and they subsisted chiefly on moose, which were then very abundant in the White River valley. They made a fruitless search for the source of the native copper which the Indians had long mined for their own use. It was not until 17 years later that the source of the placer copper was found by Schwatka and Hayes, and the locality proved to be some 50 miles above where Harper made his search. Later, promising lode deposits were found, but to this day, half a century after Harper's search, the region has proved too inaccessible to permit of mining development.

Meanwhile, McQuesten and his companions had gone down the Yukon to the mouth of Beaver Creek, where they built a winter camp and prospected in the vicinity. The choice of locality was quite likely determined by the story of McDonald's find of gold some ten years before on an easterly tributary of the Yukon. McQuesten found some fine gold in the bars of Beaver Creek but nothing that would pay for mining at that time. Like Harper, McQuesten was dependent on moose meat for subsistence.

Both Harper and McQuesten now realized that prospecting was impossible in this remote region without a local supply base, so they and their companions all went to St. Michael, the distributing point for the Yukon, during the summer of 1875. McQuesten, Hart, and Mayo there entered the service of the Alaska Commercial Company. Harper, in company with George Finch and John McKniff, secured supplies, came back up the river to the mouth of the Tanana, and spent the summer prospecting in the vicinity. Harper at this time probably ascended the Tanana at least as far as what is now known as Harper's bend where he then or later built a cabin. This in 1878 was the scene of the murder of Mrs. Bean, the wife of the first trader to establish himself on the Tanana.

Harper found no gold on the Tanana and rejoined McQuesten, who had established the post called Fort Reliance six miles below the present site of Dawson. Later, Harper

[6] Ogilvie, William, *The Klondike Official Guide*, Toronto, 1898, p. 48.

again made a long prospecting trip, including the head of Fortymile and thence across the divide to Sixtymile and down that stream to the Yukon. On Sixtymile he found his first encouraging prospects and determined to go to work on them. The gold was so fine that quicksilver was necessary to recover it, and nothing could be done until this was secured. Meanwhile, Harper joined McQuesten in the fur trade. With him, however, this was only a means of obtaining a livelihood while continuing his search for gold. During the next decade Harper continued to make prospecting trips when his business affairs permitted, but there is little record of these journeys. It is known that he made several journeys into the Tanana valley, in the course of one of which he traversed the upper reaches of Fortymile valley. It also appears that he visited the Stewart River, in the lower parts of which he had found a few colors of gold on his first journey up the Yukon in 1873. But of only one trip is there any definite information. In 1878, Harper and Mayo ascended the Tanana,[7] a distance estimated at 250 miles, and brought back some black sand and gold dust, the result of prospecting the river bars. The first 40 miles of this journey were made on the little steamer *Yukon*.[8]

Though so far as is known Harper himself never located a claim which proved to carry workable gold deposits, yet he was in fact the discoverer of gold in the Yukon. By his arduous journeys distributed through a decade he gained a general familiarity with the distribution of auriferous gravels in the central Yukon basin. He was the first to find gold on the bars of the lower reaches of Stewart and Fortymile rivers, on the upper part of Sixtymile, and in the Tanana valley, probably near the present site of Fairbanks. In addition to determining the general distribution of gold, Harper acquired during his prospecting a conception of the broad features of relief and drainage of the central Yukon basin, then practically unmapped and known only through the vague reports of the Indians. As Harper was the first to appreciate the latent mineral wealth of the Yukon, so he was also the first to make this wealth known through his letters to his friends in the Cassiar and other placer camps of British Columbia. It was in

[7] Letter of E. W. Nelson, April 13, 1909. Cf. Brooks, Alfred H., "Mt. McKinley Region," *United States Geological Survey Professional Paper 70*, Washington, D.C., 1911, p. 25.

[8] Mayo, A. H., Statement in Fairbanks *Times*, December 16, 1912.

large measure these letters, as well as McQuesten's, that publicized these new fields to other prospectors. Harper was, therefore, the discoverer of gold on the Yukon and the pioneer prospector whose efforts directly led to the discovery of Fortymile, the Klondike, and Fairbanks. These, in turn, led to the finding of gold at many other Yukon camps, and also at Nome.

Though all honor is due Harper, the pioneer prospector, his friend and long business associate, Jack McQuesten, played an equally important part in bringing about the industrial development of the Yukon. It appears that after his first venture in prospecting on Beaver Creek in 1873 he himself gave little attention to the search for gold. Instead, he devoted himself particularly to the fur trade and made many journeys down the Yukon to St. Michael, carrying down furs and bringing back supplies, while Harper, as we have seen, was making his difficult journeys in search of gold. This division of effort was part of the plan formulated when McQuesten, Harper, and Mayo formed a partnership,[9] the task of looking after the trading interests falling especially to McQuesten. Once satisfied that the Yukon was gold-bearing, the men realized that their most important problem was to establish a reliable source of supplies. Both McQuesten and Harper were without capital, so until they could find gold deposits that could be profitably mined they were forced to turn to the fur trade as the only source of livelihood in the region.

McQuesten in 1874, as has already been stated, built a post on the east bank of the Yukon six miles below the present site of Dawson which he called Reliance. This was the headquarters for the upper Yukon trade during the next six years. Here McQuesten traded with the Indians and, so far as he was able, supplied the needs of the few prospectors in the region. In course of time he formed his partnership with Harper and Mayo and did most of the fur trading of the Yukon above Nulato. This venture appears to have been given financial support by the Alaska Commercial Company, though the traders had more or less independence and followed their own policies. All three of the partners married Indian wives, and thus it became impractical for them to follow the roving vocation of prospecting, for the fur trade was the only sure source

[9] Letter of McQuesten dated July 1, 1905.

of income and without it they could not support their families and educate their children. McQuesten and Harper, however, never lost sight of the mission which had first brought them to the Yukon. They looked upon the fur trade as only a temporary source of income until the gold mines could be developed. It was impossible to carry on systematic prospecting without an assured source of provisions and miner's supplies, and to this object they devoted themselves, doing only such prospecting as circumstances permitted, Harper doing most of the searching.

As a consequence of the hard labors of these two pioneers, the paths of the prospectors who came later were much smoothed: there was at least the beginning of a steamboat service on the Yukon; Fort Reliance, though inadequately supplied, offered an outfitting point and a headquarters for prospectors; McQuesten and Harper had available a large amount of information about the conditions of travel and prospecting. In other words, these two men had by their unaided efforts opened up the great Yukon valley to the prospector. At that time neither the American nor the Canadian government had made any surveys or investigations of the Yukon basin above the mouth of Porcupine River, nor had they made any efforts to establish trails or in other ways to open up the country to settlement. This pioneer work, now considered a governmental task, was almost entirely the work of Harper and McQuesten. Also, the letters they sent to their old prospecting companions in the Caribou and Fraser River districts concerning the Yukon discoveries performed an important service, for these were without doubt one of the important influences in starting the stream of prospectors northward.

It was characteristic of the two pioneers that they made no attempt to reap a quick profit out of the prospectors who came to the Yukon during the decade that preceded the Klondike discovery. Though prices of provisions were very high, the profits, because of the uncertainties of the trade, losses by sea and land, and bad credit, were by no means commensurate to the risks. This policy was, of course, in part to be credited to the financial backing of the Alaska Commercial Company; but the influence that brought it about was that of their representatives, Harper and McQuesten.

Probably the greatest service rendered, and this was

due especially to McQuesten, was the credit extended to the miners. McQuesten never turned a miner from his post because of lack of funds. Year after year men were supported who had not made good at their prospecting ventures. McQuesten made these credits to a large extent at his own personal sacrifice. In not a few cases the prospectors imposed on his generosity and developed into little more than dead beats; these were the very ones who complained that monopolistic greed was closing the Yukon to the prospector. Loud were their complaints that the Alaska Commercial Company was strangling the Yukon, though they had been living for years on the bounty of Jack McQuesten, its agent. Another typical feature of McQuesten's policy was the distribution of supplies, which were often exceedingly scant in the early days of mining. All provisions were divided equally among all who were in the country, no matter what their financial standing. If the supplies were so scant as to threaten starvation, a certain number of men would leave in the fall for the outer world by way of St. Michael or Chilkoot Pass. According to the stories of the old-time prospectors, shortage of provisions was the normal condition. One spoke of an especially hard winter when his allotment of provisions consisted of three bags of flour and a new method of snaring rabbits.

All this goes to show that McQuesten and Harper were guided in their actions by a broad vision of the latent wealth of the Yukon gold fields; that they were willing to wait for the future to obtain their share of the wealth which their pioneer work was destined to let others reap. Broken by his long years of toil, Harper died the year after the discovery of the Klondike with but little return for his sacrifice. McQuesten, though he lived to see the great developments which he had prophesied, died in 1909, a poor man.

While Harper and McQuesten were establishing themselves on the Yukon, great changes had been wrought in Southeastern Alaska by the influx of prospectors at Fort Wrangell bound for the Cassiar and later by the discovery of the gold deposits at Juneau. Among this restless population there were some who desired to reach the Yukon, and no doubt the information disseminated by the letters of McQuesten and Harper had reached some of them. It was generally known that streams flowing into the Yukon lay beyond the rugged range whose precipitous slopes lay close to Juneau. Some information about the transmontane region had been obtained by the Western Union Telegraph explorers in 1866-67. One of these, Michael Byrnes,[10] a Cassiar miner, had in 1867 reached a lake in the upper drainage basin of the Yukon which he called Taku Lake and which appears to have been Lake Atlin. It has been generally believed that Byrnes reached the interior by the Stikine valley, but it is equally probable that he arrived by the Taku River whose lower reaches had been explored by the Hudson Bay traders. Be that as it may, it is certain that the Taku River and the low passes which connect it with the Stikine valley near Telegraph Creek were explored by the Western Union Telegraph parties. Byrnes, whose explorations were interrupted by the sudden closing of the Western Union surveys, must be credited with being the first white man to reach that part of the Yukon basin lying nearest the coast region of Southeastern Alaska. The information he obtained was embodied in the official maps of Alaska;[11] and, no doubt, among the prospectors who first reached Southeastern Alaska there were some who knew him and had obtained first-hand information from him by word of mouth.

More important, however, was the geographic knowledge obtained by the coast natives who in their trading expeditions had penetrated far into the interior by way of the Chilkat River basin, Chilkoot Pass, and the Taku River. The Chilkat natives well knew that the shortest route from the coast was from the head of Lynn Canal and over Chilkoot Pass to the headwaters of the Lewes River. Anxious to maintain their trading monopoly with the interior Indians, they jealously guarded the route to the Yukon by way of this pass. These Indians were very independent and warlike, and the individual prospectors ran serious risks in attempting to traverse their domain.

The first to make this attempt was one George Holt, about whose history little is known. Holt was killed by an Indian at Knik near Cook Inlet in 1885, and the story of his journey over the Chilkoot was never definitely known. Holt's statements of his accomplishments and discoveries were so exaggerated as to leave doubts as to where he had

[10] Dall, William H., *Alaska and its Resources*, Boston, 1870, p. 507.

[11] "Alaska and Adjoining Territory," *United States Coast Survey*, Washington, D.C., 1869.

actually been. It is known, however, that in the summer of 1875[12] Holt with one white man crossed Chilkoot Pass, followed the chain lakes to the headwaters of the Lewes River, and traced this as far as Marsh Lake; from here he made an overland journey through a low pass to a river he called the Hootalinqua, believing it was the same river which had been visited by Byrnes in 1867. His identification, however, was wrong, and the native name of the stream he visited is Teslin; it is about 70 miles north of the real native Hootalinqua discovered by Byrnes. This error of identification was perpetuated by the prospectors who followed Holt.[13] Holt returned to the coast by way of Chilkoot Pass in the same summer. He claimed that he was forced to leave the country because of threats made by the Indians at the place he turned back. It is more probable that lack of provisions had forced him to return and that the Indian threats were those of the coast natives whom he had avoided by chance or design on his way inland. He claimed to have found good prospects at the farthest point of his journey; and if this be so, it was probably the float gold which occurs on the bars of the Hootalinqua. Holt was at Sitka in the winter of 1875-76, and his story found sufficient credence with the post commander to lead to the formulation of a plan to send an officer with Holt to the Yukon the following spring. The withdrawal of troops prevented the execution of this plan. Holt appears to have realized that the Chilkats would not allow him to retrace his steps over the Chilkoot without military support, and so far as is known he never again visited the Yukon basin. His later fantastic embellishments of his rather remarkable journey were probably made in the hope of getting support for another expedition. One other story with reference to Holt deserves mention. He is said to have sent out the first gold to come from the Yukon. This was dispatched from St. Michael in 1880 and contained two small nuggets said to have been procured from a Tanana Indian. This was probably some gold which Harper had found, for there is no evidence that Holt was on the Yukon at that time, though he may have been at St. Michael in the employment of the Alaska Commercial Company where the gold passed through his hands.

---

[12] Quinan, W. R., "Discoverer of the Yukon Gold Fields," *The Overland Monthly*, 1897, pp. 340-42.

[13] Hayes, C. W., "An Expedition to the Yukon District," *National Geographic Magazine*, IV (1892), 133.

The stories of Holt, the letters of Harper and McQuesten to Cassiar miners, and above all the spirit of enterprise which pervaded the pioneers of that period led to definite plans for prospecting the upper Yukon basin. These culminated in 1878 when a small party of miners, among whom George E. Pilz, an assayer from Sitka,[14] appears to have been the guiding spirit, attempted to reach the interior by the Chilkoot Pass route. The hostility of the Chilkat Indians led to the abandonment of this undertaking. The project was revived again two years later when a group of prospectors at Sitka applied to Captain L. A. Beardslee, U.S.N., commanding the *Jamestown* for protection against the natives. Pilz seems to have been one of the principal instigators of the second expedition, though he did not accompany the party, as is shown by the official list. The following document[15] shows the organization of this party:

We, the undersigned miners, do hereby pledge ourselves to accept and be guided by Edmund Bean as our captain or leader of the consolidated parties of prospectors now in Sitka and proposing to search for gold in the interior of Alaska Territory, going by water up Chatham Straits and landing at the Indian village of Chilkat. We hereby pledge ourselves to behave orderly, accept and obey the lawful commands of our leader, and otherwise acquit ourselves as becomes orderly, sober, and reasonable men. We also agree that no spirituous liquor shall be carried by any of us into the Indian country for the purpose of trade or barter with the natives. We furthermore do agree and pledge ourselves that if Captain Beardslee, Commander of the U.S.S. *Jamestown,* will furnish us with such escort as in his judgment is proper, to Chilkat we will be guided by him or his officer or representative with us and afterward by our mining leader, Edmund Bean.

(Signed)

Edmund Bean
Robt. A. Duggan
Geo. G. Langtry
Thos. Lineham
Dankert E. Peterson
James Fallon
Patrick McClinchey
William Zoble
M. A. Hayes
Antone Marks
Dennis Barrett
Thos. Kiernan
Geo. Harkrader
J. Newton Masson
Fred. Cushman
Preston Nonteman
James McCluskey
John Lemon
S. B. Mathews[16]

[14] Letter of George E. Pilz dated March 11, 1907.

[15] Beardslee, Captain L. A., "Reports Relative to Affairs in Alaska and the Operations of the U.S.S. *Jamestown,*" *Senate Document No. 71, 47th Congress, First Session,* Washington, D.C., 1882, p. 61.

[16] R. Steele joined the party later.

In response to this request Captain Beardslee directed Lieutenant E. P. McClellan to accompany the miners in the ship's launch. The McClellan party included three officers, 13 men, and Marcus Baker of the Coast Survey as scientific observer; they bore the following message to the Indians:

U.S.S. Jamestown
Off Sitka, May 20, 1880

To the Chiefs of the Chilkats,
Klotz-Kutch and Elqueslik:

Chiefs:

You have sent to me, through the Skeenga-Stockeen and Stikeech Indians, in whom you and I place confidence, an invitation to the white men to come and prospect in your country, and have promised to be their friends. The men who now come are those I have invited in your name. I feel sure from what I know of the bravery and honesty of the Chilkats that you will keep these promises.

Therefore I send them, and the Great Father in Washington will be greatly pleased to hear that they have gone and more pleased to hear next fall that you all have remained friends.

The officer who delivers this letter acts as my representative.

(Signed) L. A. BEARDSLEE,
Commander U.S. Navy and Senior Representative
of the Government

This message seems to have had a great influence with the Indians, for they agreed not only to let the miners pass through their country but also to furnish packers to carry the supplies over the Chilkoot summit. Later in the summer Captain Beardslee visited the Chilkats in person and discussed with the native chiefs the whole matter of the relations of the whites and Indians. With him was Major Gouverneur Morris, collector of customs, who for the sake of impressing the natives on this ceremonious occasion donned his old Civil War uniform. Captain Beardslee, by his tact and diplomacy, effectually broke the Indian opposition to the coming of the white man. The short route from tidewater to the upper Yukon now lay open to the prospector.

The Bean party arrived at Lake Bennett on June 17 and began whipsawing lumber and building boats. On July 4 the entire party started downstream, but apparently divided soon after. Details of the journey are lacking, but it is known that 15 of the prospectors continued the journey to the mouth of the Hootalinqua. Three of the party ran the Miles Canyon[17] and thus were the first to attempt this dangerous passage. Later, they ascended the Hootalinqua, which had been reached by Holt five years before. It is not known how far they went up the river, but they did not reach Lake Teslin, about 100 miles from the mouth. This party appears to have been closely followed over the Chilkoot Pass by James Wyn (Slim Jim) and John McKenzie.[18] It is not known where these last two miners went after crossing the Chilkoot, but it is probable that they too were bound for the Hootalinqua, where Holt reported that he had found placer gold.

So far as is known, all these prospectors returned to the coast in the fall (1880) by way of Chilkoot Pass. They had verified Holt's story of finding gold on the Hootalinqua bars. Above all, they had found a route into the interior which was feasible to experienced prospectors and this news, spread among the prospectors of Juneau and Sitka, was to bear fruit during the next few years.

In the following year two members of the original Bean party, George G. Langtry and Patrick McClinchey, with two other prospectors, crossed the Chilkoot and followed the Lewes River to the mouth of the Big Salmon River and then ascended that stream. A little gold[19] was mined by them on the bars of the Big Salmon, the first won from the upper Yukon. This party returned to the coast in September of 1881.

Juneau was then the headquarters for prospectors, and the bringing out of fine gold from the Yukon naturally caused considerable local excitement. As a result, probably more than a score of miners started for the upper Yukon in the spring of 1882. These prospected the Lewes River, and two parties ascended the Pelly River as far as Hoola Canyon. About a dozen of these miners reached Jack McQuesten's post, Fort Reliance, in September, 1882, and were the first to arrive by the Chilkoot Pass route. Among these were Thomas Boswell, Joseph Ladue, Howard Franklin, Frank Densmore, and others who were destined to take an important part in the development of the Yukon. These men wintered at Fort Reliance and in the following year prospected on Sixtymile and Fortymile. Though they

---

[17] "The Upper Yukon: Notes on a gold prospecting trip," New York *Herald*, December 21, 1881, p. 8.

[18] Dawson, George M., "Report on an Exploration in the Yukon District," *Geological Survey of Canada, Annual Report, 1887, Part B,* 1888, p. 180B.

[19] Reported to be several hundred dollars in value, but this is probably greatly exaggerated. See *Life in Alaska*, the letters of Mrs. Eugene S. Willard, Philadelphia, 1884, p. 135.

found encouraging prospects, all but two, Joe Ladue and George Powers, were forced to leave in the fall on account of shortage of food and to make the long upstream journey to Chilkoot Pass. That same year (1883) a party of four[20] (Richard Poplin, Charles McCoskey, George Marks, and Benjamin Beach) reached the Yukon from Juneau and prospected the Stewart River with good results. On returning to Fort Reliance in the fall, they found it deserted, for McQuesten's steamer had broken down before reaching the post. In need of food, they therefore made their way to the mouth of the Tanana and there wintered.

In the following spring Poplin and McCoskey returned to the Stewart where they convinced themselves of the presence of gold in commercial quantities, but lack of supplies compelled them to return to Juneau. Boswell and Franklin, who had been to the Yukon in 1882, returned by way of the Chilkoot in 1884 with Henry Madison; the three prospected along the Lewes and made the discovery of "Cassiar Bar"[21] where they began systematic mining. Later they were joined by Michael E. Hess.[22] These four produced the first considerable amount of gold mined on the Yukon, the total recovery probably being one or two thousand dollars. Since the bars are accessible only at low water, they went down the river in the fall and wintered with McQuesten at Fort Reliance. Boswell had learned of the Stewart River discoveries from Poplin and, with John Fraser, sledded to the Stewart in the spring of 1885 where they successfully mined all summer. It is said that some of the bars yielded as high as $100 a day. Here they were joined later[23] by Poplin, Peter Wyburg, F. Moffit, and Joseph Machiel. Mining was very successful and in August Boswell came to Fort Reliance for provisions. McQuesten had wintered in San Francisco but came back in the summer with 30 tons of miner's supplies, the first to be brought to the Yukon. He brought these supplies up the Stewart on his steamer. The Stewart River miners had resolved to keep their discovery secret. The news, however, leaked out, and during 1885 and 1886 probably 75 miners worked on the Stewart River bars, recovering gold to the value of about $75,000.

---

[20] Letter of McQuesten dated July 1, 1905.

[21] Everette, Willis E., "The Upper Yukon River," Extract from Report, *Mining and Scientific Press*, LIV (1887), 251. Cf. Dawson *Daily News*, August 17, 1914.

[22] Hess, Michael E., "Gold Diggings," Letter in Sterling (Illinois) *Gazette*, March 27, 1896.

[23] Letter of McQuesten dated July 1, 1905.

Up to 1886 all the mining of the Yukon was on the Canadian side of the boundary. Many prospectors, however, had been searching for gold in the Alaskan Yukon. The best organized expedition was that of Edward L. Schiefflin.[24] Schiefflin was the discoverer of the Tombstone camp in Arizona where he had made considerable money.[25] In 1882 he organized a party to prospect on the Yukon. It is quite possible that Schiefflin may have known or even grubstaked one of the Bean party of 1880. If so, the fact of the occurrence of gold on the Hootalinqua may have been accepted by Schiefflin as proof of his theory that a well-defined gold belt stretched parallel to the Pacific seaboard from Cape Horn to Bering Sea.[26] This wild theory and his restless spirit of adventure were doubtless the controlling influences of his venture. Schiefflin himself had no plans to reach the Hootalinqua but intended finding his gold belt nearer Bering Sea. He probably knew of Harper's discovery of gold on the Tanana. There is evidence, however, that Schiefflin had at least an understanding with, and possibly gave financial aid to, some of the prospectors who crossed the Chilkoot in 1882,[27] and that his own venture into the lower Yukon valley was part of a broader plan to prospect the entire Yukon.

In the summer of 1882 Schiefflin chartered a schooner at San Francisco and, placing a small steamer on board, sailed to St. Michael.[28] His party of five included his brother Albert, Henry de Wolfe, and Professor Jacobson of the Royal Berlin Museum. Their small steamer, the *New Racket*, slowly made its way up the Yukon to some place near and above the mouth of the Tanana where they wintered. The stream tributary to the Yukon from the west about 20 miles above the mouth of the Tanana, now called Schiefflin Creek, is supposed to be the scene of the prospecting of this party. Schiefflin found some placer

[24] He was born in western Pennsylvania in 1848 and died in the mountains of Oregon, where he was prospecting alone, on May 14, 1897.

[25] Blake, W. P., "Tombstone and its Miners, a report on the past and present conditions of mines of Tombstone, Cochise County, Arizona, to the Development Company of America," *Mining Engineering*, New York, 1902, pp. 14-15.

[26] It is most probable that Schiefflin had talked with W. P. Blake, the first geologist, as has already been shown, to appreciate the broader features of the geology of the northern cordillera.

[27] Willard, *op. cit.*, pp. 230-31.

[28] It is said that this steamer had been equipped with pumps to lift water for sluicing the auriferous alluvium from river bars. This indicates that Schiefflin knew of the gold in river bars and that his quest was for placers. (See Dawson *Daily News*, August 17, 1914.) This boat was actually used for this purpose on the bars of Stewart River in 1886. (See Haskell, William B., *Two Years in the Klondike and Alaskan Gold Fields*, Hartford, Conn., 1898, p. 51.)

gold, but nothing that would justify the continuation of the venture.[29] There is a story that one of the men came to Sitka by way of the Chilkoot Pass during the winter of 1882-83. If such a remarkable journey had been made, it would undoubtedly have been definitely recorded. It seems probable, however, that one of the party did make his way up the river and come out over the pass in the fall of 1883 with some of the many prospectors who made the journey that year. Meanwhile, Schiefflin sold his boat to the then newly-organized firm of McQuesten, Harper & Mayo and returned to California. The expedition was without tangible results, but it did help to dissipate some of the ignorance about Alaska and at least established the fact that auriferous mineralization occurred in this new field. Above all, it was the first invasion of mining men with capital into the Yukon basin.

The first prospecting trip into the Kuskokwim basin was made by George Marks and Benjamin Beach in 1883. Six years later, Frank Densmore with several companions also went into the Kuskokwim valley. The exact route of these parties is unknown, but they probably crossed from one of the southern tributaries of the lower Tanana to the headwaters of the Kuskokwim. In 1884, Joseph Ladue and George Powers prospected the White River country, and this region was again visited by Howard Franklin, Mike Hess, and Henry Madison. During their journey, Hess and Madison crossed the divide to the upper Tanana and thus were the first to visit this part of Alaska.[30] Franklin and Madison spent the early summer of 1886 in prospecting on the McQuesten, a tributary of the upper Stewart; but, discouraged at the outlook, they returned to the Yukon in August. Franklin then went up the Fortymile, where on September 7 he found coarse gold in the river bars about 25 miles from the mouth and a little later on Franklin Creek, a tributary of the main river.[31]

This discovery was the turning point in the history of Yukon mining. Up to that time no coarse gold and no very rich placers had been found, nothing, in fact, that justified the presence of the 100 or more miners who were

---

[29] See Patterson, W. D., "Alaska," *Mining and Scientific Press*, XLVI (1883), 68-69; "Alaska Mines," *Ibid.*, XLIX (1884), 64; letter of Schiefflin; *Reply of the Alaska Commercial Company to the Charges of Gov. Alfred P. Swineford of Alaska*, San Francisco, 1887, pp. 68-69.

[30] Ogilvie, *Early Days on the Yukon*, p. 111.

[31] Letter of McQuesten dated July 1, 1906. See also Dawson *Daily News*, August 17, 1914. By some the discovery of the Fortymile placers is credited to Michael O'Brien.

MINING METHODS OF EARLY DAYS, I

Upper: Hopper on a dump box; center: Steam points in operation; lower: Self-dumping hoist and tram. All photos by Sidney Paige.

MINING METHODS OF EARLY DAYS, II

Upper: China pump, photo by Sidney Paige; center: Pipe and wheel, photo by F. H. Moffit; lower: Arrastra, photo by F. H. Moffit.

then in the country. Harper's faith in the country was at last vindicated. Moreover, Franklin's discovery was on the Alaskan side of the international boundary. Above all, these gold deposits were at such shallow depths that a quick return for the labor expended was assured.

No attempt was made to keep the discovery secret, and in a short time Stewart River was deserted and the entire population of the Yukon was engaged in mining on Fortymile. Harper was quick to realize the importance of the find and moved his trading post from the mouth of the Stewart to the mouth of the Fortymile, where a settlement quickly sprang up. It soon became only too evident that unless word could be got to McQuesten, who had gone to San Francisco, to increase the normal shipment of supplies, there would not be enough food the following summer for the expected influx of miners. It was, however, too late to send out a message by steamer, for the river was frozen. A meeting was held and volunteers called for to make the long journey over the Chilkoot Pass. No one had at that time attempted a winter journey to the coast. A man named Thomas Williams[32] offered to make the trip, and with one companion, "Indian Bob," started off. Williams had been a river captain[33] and appears to have had little experience in winter travel. His inexperience made for unnecessary difficulties, but his perseverance and pluck were admirable. In a nearly starved condition the two men finally reached Chilkoot Pass in January, 1887, where they were snowed in for several days. Williams became too weak to travel. The Indian finally left him in a snow hut and managed to reach J. J. Healy's trading post at the head of Dyea Inlet. Here he was cared for and soon returned with white men. They succeeded in bringing Williams to the post, but he died in a few hours. Williams' package of mail and bags of nuggets, which were later dug out of the snow by William Stewart of Juneau, gave concrete evidence of the gold discovery and proclaimed to the world the important news.[34] Thanks to Williams' heroic sacrifice, the needed provisions were sent to the Yukon, and mining could be continued. The development of the Fortymile district established the Yukon as a mining camp, and during the succeeding decade probably 100 or

[32] Notes from Frank Brandham, who went to the Yukon in 1887.

[33] It is reported that he had been on the Mackenzie River.

[34] Williams' diary is said to have been found but has since disappeared.

more prospectors crossed the Chilkoot to reach the new diggings.

In 1893, two Russian half-breeds, Poitka and Sonoiska,[35] grubstaked by McQuesten, discovered gold in the Birch Creek district. Birch Creek soon became the center of gold mining in the Yukon, and Circle City, with a population of 500 in 1895, the supply point and the largest settlement on the Yukon. Birch Creek continued to be the most important camp until the development of the Klondike in 1896 and 1897. Meanwhile, there was some mining in the Rampart district where John Mynook, a Russian half-breed, had found gold in 1893. The presence of placer gold in this region had been established by Schiefflin and by Hess[36] who spent the summer of 1888 in a lonesome search for gold in this part of the Yukon. O. C. Miller, who mined on a tributary of Hess Creek in 1893, was the first to produce any gold in the Rampart district.

Natives are said to have shown Harper some small nuggets of gold in 1878 which came from the Koyukuk. John Bremner, a trader and prospector who was killed by two Koyukuk natives in 1888[37] seems to have been the first to search for gold in this basin. His murder was promptly punished by a party of miners who caught and hanged the two Indians. But there appears to have been but little mining in the Koyukuk until 1893, when Tramway Bar was discovered.[38] It was not, however, until 1899 that any considerable gold production was made in the Koyukuk.

In the decade following the Fortymile discovery the value of Alaskan Yukon gold production rose from $30,000 in 1887 to $800,000 in 1896. The summer mining population in the same decade rose from less than 200 to over 1,000 men. More than half of these wintered on the Yukon. By 1894 two rival companies had established steamship service and trading posts on the Yukon. The region was still without government, but order was maintained and primitive justice enforced by miners' meetings.[39] All min-

[35] Goodrich, Harold B., "History and Conditions of Yukon Gold District to 1897," *United States Geological Survey, 18th Annual Report, Part III*, Washington, D.C., p. 118. See also McQuesten's letter of July 1, 1906.

[36] He died at Fortymile in 1892.

[37] Notes from Captain A. Fredericks, then at Nulato.

[38] Notes from N. V. Hendrick who went up the Koyukuk with a steamer in 1893, built a ditch, and mined considerable gold.

[39] Notes furnished by Frank A. Reynolds, U.S. commissioner at Circle, taken as transcripts from old record books of the district.

ing during this epoch was of the simplest character. The gold-bearing alluvium was shoveled into sluice boxes made of hand-sawed lumber. Shafts and drifts were made in the frozen ground by thawing with hot rocks or wood fires, but little mining was done in the winter.

In winter the miners were idle, except for the work of hauling supplies, and congregated in Circle City. This town had its "opera house" where in 1895 George Snow, the pioneer actor of the Yukon, gave performances with his troupe which included several women. By this time there were quite a number of women at Circle who had made the difficult journey through the Coast Range pass. "Dutch" Kate Wilson was in 1888 the first white woman to cross Chilkoot Pass.[40] The winter hauling was done chiefly with dogs, but Bill McFee had brought two horses in over Chilkoot Pass in 1888, the first to reach the Yukon. Except for the sawmill of Ladue and Harper at Fortymile and another at Circle, all the sawing of lumber was laboriously done by hand. Little heed was given to the spiritual needs of the miners. Bishop Bompas had a mission at Fortymile, but other missions were chiefly devoted to work among the natives. There was a Roman Catholic mission at Stewart River in 1886. There was no representative of the United States Government from one end of the Yukon to the other, except a collector of internal revenue at Circle City. This official, David Ross, vainly attempted to prevent the bringing of whiskey into the Yukon, which was then illegal. The law, however, did not prevent the saloons from doing a thriving business. Those were the happy days at Circle to which the old pioneers frequently refer. Jack McQuesten was by virtue of inherent openheartedness, integrity, and keen intelligence the leader of the community. No one with a hard-luck story was ever turned away from his counter because of lack of money. He had trust in the integrity of the pioneer and seldom was the trust abused. Above all, he had such faith in the country that he was ready to stake his all on its future development. The community was thoroughly democratic and entirely American. The close contact between its members welded them together and Americanization went on unconsciously. Nowhere was the typical American, with his self-confidence, energy, perseverance, and democratic ideals, more definitely developed than in these little com-

[40] Notes from William McFee of Fairbanks.

munities along the Yukon, made up of the most diverse nationals. Irish, Swedes, Russians, Turks, English, Scotch, Germans, and Italians here became as true Americans as were those pioneers from New England, Montana, and the West Coast.

While these advances were going on in the Yukon, even more important developments were being made in the coast region, as was pointed out in the preceding chapter. The success of the Treadwell Mine plus the discoveries at Yakutat, Lituya Bay, Yakataga, the Kenai Peninsula, and elsewhere raised the annual value of the gold production along the coast from $20,000 in 1880 to about $2,000,000 in 1896; to this must be added for the latter year about $800,000 from the Yukon districts. Meanwhile, as we shall see later, there had also been an important development of the fisheries. Hence, since the beginning of mining in 1880, the white population of the Territory had risen from a few hundred to about 8,000, of whom probably 1,000 were on the Yukon. Much charting had been done along the coast, and many exploring expeditions had penetrated the interior. Steamboat service had been established along the coast and on the Yukon River. Therefore, when the Klondike discovery in 1896 attracted thousands of gold seekers, their paths had been somewhat smoothed by the toil and sacrifice of the pioneers who had gone before. But there were still large areas of the interior practically unknown, many rivers that had never been traversed by white men, and many mountain passes that remained to be discovered. Hence large fields for geographic and mineral discovery still lay open to the new hordes of gold seekers.

CHAPTER XIX

The Klondike Gold

ALASKA'S real development dates from the discovery in 1896 of the marvellously rich placers of the Klondike district, placers which were destined to yield gold to the value of over $150,000,000. The Klondike district lies in the Canadian Yukon, but a short distance from the Alaskan frontier. To reach this El Dorado, it was necessary for men to traverse a part of Alaska, and thus the Territory became better known. Moreover, many of the horde of gold seekers attracted by the Klondike turned their attention to Alaska. This fact led eventually to the discovery of many new placer districts, as well as of auriferous lodes and of copper, coal, and other mineral deposits. Had it not been for the lure of the Klondike gold, Alaska's mineral wealth would, no doubt, have lain dormant for many years. The great influx of population and the establishment of lines of transportation, including steamboat service, building of trails, later of wagon roads, and eventually of railroads, were brought about by the Klondike gold. Therefore, while these deposits belonged to Canada, Alaska benefited directly by their exploitation.

When the gold excitement carried tens of thousands of people northward into a region almost unknown, without trails or roads, along a dangerous and almost uncharted coast line lacking all guides to navigation, across unsurveyed passes and down unmapped rivers, into a territory having only a mere skeleton of government and almost without laws, then and not until then did the Government and people of the United States begin to realize the criminal folly of their attitude of neglect toward Alaska. Army posts were now established, laws enacted, U.S. commissioners and marshalls appointed, the Coast Survey given funds to begin the enormous task of charting the coast line in additional detail, and other steps taken to make amends for the long neglect of the rich territory. The United States Geological Survey was authorized to begin the important work of exploring and studying the mineral resources of Alaska which has continued to the present day. Later came the systematic investigation of the fisheries, agricultural lands, and forests. It is evident, therefore, that Alaska's modern history begins with the Klondike discovery.

The Klondike River flows into the Yukon from the northeast about 120 miles above the international boundary, and not more than six miles above McQuesten's old post of Fort Reliance. Klondike is a corruption of "Tron-diuck," the Indian name of the stream.[1] As early as 1887 a miner had prospected along the bank of the Klondike for some 40 miles above its mouth. He reasoned erroneously that the gold came from the head of the river, and therefore passed unheeded the mouth of Bonanza, where a decade later enormously rich placers were to be mined. The Klondike River had since the days of the Hudson Bay traders been known as a good hunting ground for moose and caribou, and it is possible for this reason that they called it "Deer River." In any event, it was generally known to the early Yukon prospectors as "moose pasture" and no one regarded it as a favorable field for gold.

The Indians had a fish camp at the mouth of the Klondike, and its valley was a favorite hunting ground of theirs. Here for several years came George W. Carmack with his Indian family and relatives to catch salmon, which at certain seasons of the year ascended the Klondike River in great shoals. Carmack had come to Alaska during the early days of the Juneau excitement and had spent his time chiefly in trading, but had also done some prospecting. His wife was a Tagish Indian from the upper Yukon country, and among her people he had a cabin which was something of a trading post; this was located near the present site of Carmack. Through his Indian relatives and through long residence, he had become a man of considerable influence among the Tagish tribe. He had also spent some time among the Chilkats on tidewater at the head of Dyea Inlet.[2] Prospecting with him had been only a side issue, for mostly he engaged in hunting or fishing or occasionally in cutting timber for the town of Fortymile. In

[1] According to Ogilvie, the termination "diuck" means "small water" or "small stream." "Tron" is Indian for "hammer." The Klondike was a famous salmon stream. Fish traps were placed by the Indians at the mouth and barriers made by driving across the channel stakes which were hammered in. Therefore, "Tron-diuck" means "small hammer water or stream." See Ogilvie, William, *Early Days on the Yukon*, Ottawa, 1913, pp. 115-118.

[2] Carmack had taken some small contracts from miners to transport supplies across Chilkoot Pass.

the summer of 1896 Carmack was as usual at the Indian fishing camp at the mouth of the Klondike.

Meanwhile, unknown to Carmack, gold had been found and some mining done in the Klondike basin by Robert Henderson,[3] a Nova Scotian who had followed the sea for many years but had turned prospector and long searched for gold in Colorado. He arrived in the Yukon in 1894 by way of the Chilkoot Pass with a view to trying his luck in the Fortymile or Birch Creek districts. On his way down the river he stopped at the then newly-established post of Ogilvie, and here he found Joe Ladue, an old-timer on the Yukon. Ladue, like Harper and McQuesten, had implicit faith in the country and was especially impressed with the potential wealth of the district immediately tributary to his post. He persuaded Henderson to prospect in the Canadian Yukon, then practically deserted by the prospectors who had gone to Fortymile and the then newly-discovered Birch Creek district 200 miles below. Henderson was sufficiently impressed with Ladue's statement to decide on trying his luck in this region. After securing some supplies he, with one companion, ascended Indian River, which drains the southern part of the Klondike district. Quartz Creek, a northern tributary, was ascended, and the two went as far as the divide, where they could look down into the Klondike basin, but they were forced to return to the Yukon for supplies. Henderson was enough impressed with the outlook to devote the next year to prospecting in the Indian River basin; but his success was only moderate.

In the spring of 1896 Henderson won about $600 from the gravels of Quartz Creek, the first gold to be mined in the Klondike basin. Not satisfied with this, he crossed the Klondike divide and found good prospects on a stream which he called Gold Bottom but which was afterwards called Hunker Creek. Here with four others he started mining in the early summer of 1896. When provisions ran low, he returned to the Yukon, this time deciding to reach the scene of his discovery by way of the Klondike River.

During the two years that Henderson was at work, Joe Ladue was assiduously spreading the news of the finding of a new placer district. As a consequence, quite a few prospectors visited the region; but Henderson's finds were

[3] The statements about the discovery of the Klondike are taken chiefly from Ogilvie, *op. cit.*, pp. 115-136.

too small to draw many from the producing creeks on the Alaskan side of the boundary. Nor was the interest in Henderson's discoveries general enough to reach Carmack at his fishing camp at the mouth of the Klondike. Therefore, he was quite surprised when in July Henderson appeared with a boatload of supplies bound up the river. In accordance with the custom of the country, Henderson invited Carmack to visit his mine and stake a claim. Carmack, who was loyal to his Indian companions and insisted on their sharing in any new venture, did not please Henderson, who probably had not been on the Yukon long enough to overcome a prejudice against the natives. To this attitude Carmack took exception, and the two men seem to have parted with some mutual distrust.

Some weeks later Carmack with two Indians, Skookum Jim and Tagish Charley, decided to pay a visit to the scene of the Henderson discovery. Their route led them along Bonanza Creek, where they found some colors of gold. After a 25 mile tramp they reached Henderson's camp, but they were not very cordially received on account of the presence of the Indians. Carmack was, moreover, not greatly impressed with the importance of Henderson's find and decided not to stake a claim.

On their return, the party ran out of provisions, and on August 15 Jim undertook to find a moose. He shot one on what was then called Rabbit Creek, and while awaiting the arrival of his companions found some coarse gold in the gravel of that stream. Since the moose meat gave them ample provisions, the three men spent two days in prospecting, and on August 17 Carmack staked Discovery Claim on Rabbit Creek, which he named Bonanza Creek; the two Indians took One Above and One Below. Meanwhile, others had been looking for the scene of Henderson's mining, and within three days of Carmack's staking a number of other claims were located on Bonanza Creek by prospectors who had no knowledge of the previous discovery. It was, therefore, the improvidence of Carmack and his two Indians which led them not to take provisions enough for their journey to Henderson's camp, and hence the killing of the moose, which led them to be the discoverers of Bonanza Creek. Had it not been for this fact, Edward Monahan and Greg Stewart would have been the discoverers, for they staked claims on Bonanza on August 19.

PIT ON EL DORADO CLAIM, KLONDIKE REGION
Photo by Sidney Paige.

Carmack proceeded to Fortymile a few days later with a raft of saw logs, taking with him about $12 worth of gold which he had discovered while prospecting. He appears to have been not very communicative about his discovery.

In any event the old miners gave little credence to his report, for he was not regarded as an experienced prospector. Many prospectors, however, probably to the number of about 50, did visit the Klondike, drawn hither because of Henderson's reports and especially because of Ladue's enthusiastic accounts of the region. Since all the prospectors coming down the river passed Ladue's post, most of them were induced to visit the Klondike. As a consequence, the early stakers were mostly recent arrivals. By September a general movement had started from Fortymile, and 100 or more men had poled up the river to the Klondike where they were joined in October by about 20 who came from Circle by steamer.[4] By the end of November about 500 claims had been staked in the district, though there had been but little mining.[5]

Henderson had continued work, and Carmack had opened up his claims and done a little sluicing with good results, finding one $25 nugget. Two other nuggets had also been found, each worth over $200. While many had found good prospects, the extraordinary richness of the placers was not recognized until November 3, when coarse gold was found near the surface of the ground on Claim No. 21 Above Discovery on Bonanza Creek. Here the gravels yielded an average of $3.35 to the pan, equal to nearly $500 to the cubic yard. It is probable that the gold contents of the richest gravel previously found on the Yukon were less than $10 to the cubic yard. From this discovery dates the real Klondike excitement. But in spite of these rich finds, the total recovery of gold from the Klondike in 1896 probably did not exceed a few thousand dollars.

Meanwhile, Henderson, the discoverer of the district, fared but ill. Long before the news had reached his isolated camp on Gold Bottom Creek, Bonanza and its tributaries had been staked. Even his own creek was named Hunker after the man who had first recorded a claim on the stream, for Henderson had delayed taking this step. He was forced to content himself with the one claim which he had developed and which was not among the rich ones of the district.

Henderson was later rightfully recognized by the Canadi-

[4] Dunham, Samuel C., "The Alaska Gold Fields and the Opportunities They Offer for Capital and Labor," *Bulletin of the Department of Labor, No. 16*, Washington, D.C., 1898, pp. 316-330.

[5] *Report of the Commissioner of the Northwest Mounted Police Force for 1896*, Ottawa, 1897, p. 234.

an Government as the discoverer of the Klondike, but beyond this recognition he received little reward for his hard pioneer work of two years. On the other hand, it is equally certain that the discoveries of the Carmack party were far more important than those of Henderson. Carmack, however, must share with the two Indians credit for the discovery of the richest creek in the district. Credit is also due to the faith of the old-timer Joe Ladue, whose counsel led Henderson and many others to turn their attention to the Klondike. It was the optimism of Ladue, like that of Harper and McQuesten in earlier days, which led to the opening up of the great gold fields of the Yukon valley.

Early in September, 1896, Ladue had moved his sawmill and trading post to the mouth of the Klondike River. There he located a town site and erected the first building. The site was later surveyed by William Ogilvie, then Dominion land surveyor stationed at Fortymile. At Ogilvie's suggestion, the new town was named Dawson City after the distinguished Canadian geologist who had made the first report on the geology and mineral resources of the Canadian Yukon in 1887. Ogilvie himself had contributed greatly to the knowledge of the country by making the first survey of the routes from tidewater at Lynn Canal over the Chilkoot and White passes to the international boundary below Fortymile. It was characteristic of Ogilvie's modesty that he should have named the town Dawson after his colleague in the pioneer work rather than after himself as the miners would have been glad to do, for he was both well-known and well-liked among the pioneers. It fell to him to settle many disputes on the rich claims of the Klondike, whose boundaries he established by surveys. Ogilvie inspired such implicit confidence in his integrity that his decisions, though they involved property worth millions of dollars, were never called in question. He afterwards performed distinguished service as Governor of Yukon Territory. Though he saw many making fortunes, he remained true to his ideals, never took advantage of his official position to make money, and died after performing invaluable services to the Northland, a poor man.

At the time of the Klondike gold discovery, there were about 1,700 white men in the Yukon basin, of whom at least 1,000 were on the Alaskan side of the boundary. In the winter of 1896-97 this population was increased by 500. Of this total probably 1,500 were in the Klondike district where the town of Dawson was beginning to take form with a population of about 100. The increase in population was chiefly drawn from Juneau and other Alaskan settlements, for as yet no gold had been shipped out and the outside world had received only scant information about the new discovery. By the spring of 1897 quite a few gold seekers had come to Alaska; they made their way over the Coast Range passes and reached the Klondike by the time the ice had broken on the Yukon.

Mining had been carried on during the winter months as best it could be by the crude methods then in use. All of the deposits to the depth of mining were frozen solid and could not be excavated except by thawing. This was done by wood fires and hot rocks, a very slow and laborious process. It was not until 1898 that Clarence Berry devised a method of thawing by the use of steam. In spite of the difficulties, much frozen gravel was mined during the winter of 1897-98, and when the summer thaw came the material was shoveled into sluice boxes. It was not until then that the fortunate miners could definitely realize what riches they had. In some instances the product of winter mining would yield as high as $20,000 or $30,000 in gold from a few days' sluicing. Fortunes were literally realized overnight, and the intense excitement caused by the occasional panning out of rich pockets of gold during the winter in the cabins was increased almost to the breaking point. Many a miner who had struggled for years to make a bare living now came to realize that he was rich beyond all dreams.

Meanwhile, the outside world did not realize that this northern region had proved to be one of the richest gold camps in the world. Rumors were plentiful, but they were given little credence; and it was not until gold began to be shipped out during the summer of 1897 that the world became convinced of the existence of a new El Dorado. The return trips of the first steamers from the mouth of the Yukon in the summer of 1897 began to bring in the gold which had been recovered from mining on the Klondike. Of these the first to arrive was the *Excelsior,* which steamed into San Francisco on July 16 with nearly $400,000 worth of Klondike gold. Two days later the *Portland* arrived at Seattle with about $700,000 in Klondike gold. This gold was definite evidence of the richness of the new field, and within a few weeks the name Klondike was known all over the civilized world. My own first news of the discovery came to me in the Ural Mountains of Russia in scarcely a month after the arrival of the gold ships at the Pacific ports.

At once a tide of emigration started northward, the first to go being those who had had previous experience in the Northland. These could make their preparations quickly, for experience had taught them and they knew also the best routes of approach. Before the winter set in, some 2,000 more had reached the Klondike, swelling the population to nearly 5,000, and the winter frost and consequent closing of the river found several thousand more stranded on the way. Some travel continued both in and out of the Yukon all winter long, but the real rush started in the spring of 1898.

Because of the failure of some of the up-river steamers to arrive and the unexpected increase of population, there was some shortage of provisions at Dawson during the winter of 1897-98. This fact was impressed on the newcomers, and the less experienced ones disposed of their stock of supplies and turned back to the coast. The trading companies also urged that as many men as could should go down the Yukon to lower river stations where supplies were abundant. As a consequence, there was much alarm from fear of starvation, especially among the inexperienced. Very exaggerated reports of the shortage of provisions reached the States in the fall of 1897; these were largely due to those who had fled from Dawson before the close of navigation.

The United States Government had at this time no official representative at Dawson,[6] or indeed on the entire Yukon. Its only source of reliable information was two Army officers who reached Fort Yukon in September. They were hundreds of miles from Dawson, and their reports were based on second-hand information and chiefly on the statements of those who had fled from Dawson at the first rumor of a shortage of provisions. Consequently, when by a resolution of December 9, the Senate called upon the Secretary of War for information regarding the lack of food in the Yukon, he replied that the information at hand indicated that if provisions were not sent in there

[6] A United States consul was later appointed, stationed at Dawson.

would be starvation by March. A week later an appropriation of $200,000 was made for the purchase of food; also, the use of reindeer or other means of transportation into the interior was authorized. This was a generous act, passed by Congress in the honest belief that action was necessary in order to save human lives. But it was done without knowledge of the true facts or the means of obtaining them.

Meanwhile the Canadian Government had the situation well in hand. Its force of most efficient Northwest Mounted Police on the Yukon aggregated nearly 100 men, commanded by experienced officers well qualified to meet any conditions which might arise on this remote frontier. Inquiry at Ottawa would have established the fact that there was no serious shortage of food.[7] Experienced Army officers at Fort Yukon were out of reach of mail and could not be consulted, or better counsel would have prevailed. The Canadian Government would, moreover, have given the necessary information to select the most feasible methods and routes to take supplies into the interior and thus have prevented the United States Government from taking a leading part in an *opera bouffe* performance. Also, while the discussion on food shortage was progressing and weird plans were being formulated for reaching the "starving miners," scores of men were coming out over the winter trail from Dawson, and thousands of gold seekers were carrying their supplies across the Coast Range passes and sledding them down the frozen river. Anyone short of supplies at Dawson would have taken his sled and made his way to the coast.

All these facts were ignored by the authorities, who relied on the advice of self-styled Alaskan experts whose sole knowledge of the Territory had been gained from the deck of an ocean steamer. This was a direct result of the governmental attitude toward Alaska for a generation and showed how little attempt had been made to gain knowledge of this important possession.

The plan for a relief expedition was ill-advised, though the result of a generous impulse to help those in distress. Its execution was little short of ridiculous. To those who had experience in the North, it seemed that if supplies were

[7] *Annual Report of the Department of the Interior for the Year 1898*, Ottawa, 1899, pp. 317-320.

to be sent in they must be transported over the White or the Chilkoot Pass and down the river with horses and dogs, a method then being used by thousands of gold seekers. But this method, it appears, was not deemed sufficiently spectacular by those in control. Reindeer must be used. A party was at once sent to Norway that, with commendable energy, though at enormous expense, collected 500 reindeer and landed them in New York on a chartered vessel on February 27, 1898. At a cost of $10,000, a special train took these government pets across the continent, and another specially chartered vessel transported them to Haines Mission near Skagway. By this time interest in the enterprise had begun to wane. The first startling discovery was that no supplies were needed. A second damper on the enthusiasm was the fact that the reindeer was utterly unfitted for use in the region to be traversed. The reindeer is an admirable means of transport in the tundra region of Alaska, where occurs the lichen used as food. The upper Yukon is, however, timbered, and there is no "reindeer moss" except at high altitudes, which it was impossible for the expedition to traverse. Therefore, the whole plan proved impossible of execution and was formulated on an utter ignorance of the country and of the habits of the reindeer. The promoters of this foolish enterprise attempted to justify their expenditures of nearly $200,000 by recommending that the reindeer be used by the parties then being organized by the Geological Survey and the Army. After a careful investigation the offer was declined. By June all but 160 of the original 540 reindeer had died. A part of this remnant finally reached the Yukon with their Lapland drivers. It had been a useless expenditure of public funds which were so badly needed in other fields for Alaskan development. The story of this famous fiasco has, however, served to enliven many a lonely Alaskan campfire.

A side issue of the same project was the employment of "snow locomotives." This was a private project, the purpose of which was to haul supplies over the Chilkoot Pass with a species of traction engine. This too recommended itself to the Washington authorities, and a contract was solemnly entered into for the delivery of supplies to Dawson at $500 a ton. This did no harm, for the machines never left the beach at Dyea. The possibilities of the snow locomotives crossing Chilkoot Pass were about equal to their ability to climb the Washington monument.

The Paris papers took the keenest interest in these projects, but finally abandoned faith in the reindeer and snow locomotives to the balloon transportation advocated by a French aeronaut. Pictures of balloons carrying huge cargoes of freight over barren wastes then began to appear in Paris papers instead of the Santa Claus teams that were supposed to depict the carrying of supplies into the Yukon. The English papers took the matter more seriously and gravely discussed international laws bearing upon the question of permitting the reindeer which were under the military authorities to traverse British soil. American papers had a temporary flurry of interest in the reindeer, but the blowing up of the *Maine* and the serious situation regarding Cuba and Spain soon drew attention away from this episode.

One of the unfortunate after effects of the ridiculous reindeer relief expedition is that in the minds of many it brought proof that Alaska was not adapted for a reindeer industry. Few could realize the vast extent of the Territory and therefore grasp the fact that the great barren grounds bordering Bering Sea and the Arctic Ocean and the moss-covered uplands of the inland region were the natural habitat of the reindeer while the upper Yukon basin was not. Actually the reindeer, as will be indicated later, has become an important element in the civilization of the Alaskan Eskimo; and, as suggested in an earlier chapter, it also will in the years to come probably furnish an important source of meat both for local consumption and for export.

Meanwhile, the whole civilized world had become excited by the Klondike gold. The general movement toward the Klondike, begun during the summer of 1897, reached its culmination the following spring. Of the two main routes of approach the quicker but more arduous, for it required the crossing of a sharp summit, was that by the Coast Range passes, chiefly the Chilkoot, and down the river to Dawson. Probably upwards of 60,000 people started for the Klondike during the years 1897 and 1898. The larger part of them came from the United States, but there were of course many Canadians, and nearly every civilized nation of the world was represented among the gold seekers. Many elaborately organized expeditions started from London, and all the British colonies had large representation. Even the most conservative Paris paper, *Le Temps,* dispatched a special corespondent to the Klondike. As a prelude, *Le Temps* issued a special Klondike supplement with a map showing the route to the gold field, accompanied by some remarkable illustrations which represented French artists' conceptions of life in the Northland.

The West Coast ports were the gathering points of the gold seekers, and of these Seattle was the most important. Vancouver was the outfitting point of the Canadian and English expeditions. San Francisco had so long been the center of Alaskan trade, being the headquarters of the Alaska Commercial Company, that it too was thronged with Klondikers during the winter and spring of 1898. Parties were also organized at Atlantic ports with the purpose of reaching their goal by the perilous voyage through the Straits of Magellan and thence northward. This bizarre plan was formulated partly through a spirit of adventure and partly through the old tradition of the gold seekers of '48, so many of whom reached their goal by way of Cape Horn. The mental attitude of a large portion of the gold seekers was that of having entered upon the great adventure, and often the more perilous and difficult the plan, the more it appealed to them. Therefore, instead of adopting the rational plan of choosing the direct route by rail to Seattle or Vancouver and thence by steamer to the Yukon or to the head of Lynn Canal near Chilkoot Pass, these people preferred some difficult or indirect route.

Any man with sufficient capital—say $500 or $1,000—for outfit and transportation charges could reach the head of Lynn Canal from any place in the United States in two weeks. If of stout heart and strong physique, he could sled and carry his equipment across the Chilkoot to water transportation on the inland slope in not over two months more. The building of a boat or raft and the passage down the river would not take over one month more. Therefore, the Klondike could be reached in not more than three and a half months. Yet probably most of the Klondikers occupied at least six months in reaching their goal, and many chose routes to the interior which required a year of arduous travel, and not a few spent two years on the trail. All this wasted time was largely due to the entire lack of experience of most of the Klondikers.

Men coming directly from the farms, workshops, and counting houses could not have the knowledge of frontier conditions which would enable them to economize their strength and time. As a consequence, they made blunders in choice of routes and, above all, hampered their progress and wasted their energies by foolish equipment. The merchants in the outfitting ports were as ignorant as the gold seekers themselves. Stores were filled with folding stoves and collapsible frying pans, with cumbersome and perfectly useless sheepskin-lined clothing, with patent sleds and boats, and with innumerable remarkable mechanisms for the recovery of gold. The man who was found greasing his rubber boots at Chilkoot Pass so as to make them waterproof and pliable was but one example of the type of tenderfoot that swarmed northward by the thousands. It was men like these who suffered needlessly, and many died from exposure, scurvy, and accidents which were caused solely by their own ignorance. It is the stories of such tenderfeet that now have become traditional which have so magnified the dangers and hardships of the Klondike trail.

Much of this suffering and death would have been avoided had it not been for the stepmother-attitude of the American people. When the Klondike was discovered, a generation had passed since we had acquired the Territory. Yet its rivers and passes were unsurveyed, its coast line uncharted, and almost no effort had been made to evaluate its resources. Except for the Pacific seaboard, "No law of God or man ran north of fifty-three." In contrast to this is the attitude of the Canadian Government. When the Klondike rush came, exploratory surveys and preliminary investigation of mineral wealth of the Canadian Yukon had been completed. The Northwest Mounted Police had established a government and maintained order. This fine body of frontier police were not only ready to take action against the criminal but also prepared to succor those that were ill and in distress. A Klondiker crossing the Chilkoot passed from a condition of chaos—from the standpoint of government—on the Alaskan side to a well-organized district on the Canadian side, where the criminal had no chance and where those in distress could always find help.

In the late winter and early summer of 1898 Skagway, then the largest town in Alaska, was absolutely dominated by a picturesque rascal with a long criminal record who went under the name of "Soapy Smith." He and his gang of well-organized thugs swindled and robbed at will without hindrance from the United States officials then in the district. At the impending outbreak of the Spanish-American War, this scoundrel actually had the impudence to offer to the President the services of an Alaskan regiment, for which he had selected himself as commanding officer. At the time he made this offer, he had a criminal record which entitled him to a life sentence in jail. Soapy Smith finally met a well-merited death by being shot by an engineer, Frank H. Reid, a member of a posse of outraged citizens whom the apathy of the officials forced to take the law into their own hands. Unfortunately, Reid himself was killed by Smith and thus was sacrificed as a victim to our misgovernment of Alaska.

While this was happening, a few miles away across the border law and order were absolutely maintained. The fact that among the many Canadian officials who were sent to the Klondike there were those who could not resist the temptation to enrich themselves at the expense of the miners does not detract from the excellence of the general policy adopted by Canada towards her frontier possessions. And there was no monopoly of official grafters on the Canadian side of the boundary. Viewed from the standpoint of percentage of total officials, we probably had the advantage; but our grafters had not the opportunities that were afforded by the Klondike mines.

It is estimated that on January 1, 1898, there were some 6,000 persons in the Canadian Yukon, of whom 5,000 were in Dawson and the Klondike district. There were also over 1,000 white men in the Alaskan Yukon, chiefly stranded gold seekers who had not been able to reach their goal. The latter were augmented during the winter by several hundred men who left Dawson over the winter ice for fear of famine and reached the better provisioned posts on the Alaskan Yukon. The official Canadian records show that about 28,000 gold seekers came into the Yukon by way of the Chilkoot and White passes during the winter of 1897-98. Probably about 5,000 or 6,000 started for Dawson by way of St. Michael and the lower Yukon, but of these something like two-thirds for one reason or another did not reach their goal. These estimates indicate that of the total of about 60,000 who started for the Klondike only some 34,000 arrived there. At the same time that the people were streaming into the Yukon, there was also an outward current of those who were discouraged and disgusted. These discouraged Klondikers probably aggregated some 8,000, of whom at least 6,000 must have gone out by way of St. Michael. Some of the others went back by the long upstream journey to the Chilkoot; others sought their fortunes in adjacent parts of the Alaskan Yukon. At the close of navigation about 30,000 men were left in the Yukon region, of whom some 13,000 were in the Klondike district. By official count the population of Dawson was 4,206.

This record by no means includes all the movements of population induced by the Klondike gold. It is probable that some 40,000 people landed at the several ports in Southeastern Alaska. At Wrangell, which was the point of departure for the Stikine route, some 5,000 landed. Over 35,000 went to Skagway and Dyea. Of these, hundreds, probably a couple of thousand, turned back at their first view of the difficulties that confronted them. Others found it to their advantage to stay on the coast, and the greater part of them built up the town of Skagway. The route over the Valdez Glacier attracted some 3,000 adventurous spirits, and probably 1,000 landed at or near the head of Cook Inlet. Even the far-away Kobuk region attracted some 500, and several hundred more essayed the difficult Alsek and Copper River routes. A great number, probably aggregating some 2,000, attempted to reach the Klondike by the so-called all-Canadian routes, either directly overland from Edmonton or by way of the Mackenzie River. Casting up these figures, one reaches a total of some 54,000. But of all that left their homes a certain percentage either found occupation before they sailed from the West Coast ports or became discouraged and turned back. It is probably safe to place the westward and northward movement of population started by the Klondike gold discovery at something like 60,000. It will also be conservative to assume that every Klondiker had at least two dependents or financial backers. Therefore, there would be nearly 200,000 who had a more or less direct financial interest in the gold rush.

The educational value of the movement to the Klondike has been more than a minor factor in the building of the nation. Our great northwest territory became known to the nation; and while the exaggerated statements about the hardships and perils as well as the harshness of the climate at first broadcast many untruths, yet at least Americans learned that there was such a place as Alaska. Moreover, thousands reached the West Coast who except for the lure of gold would never have seen the Pacific. A better knowledge of our great West and its people was thus broadcast. These were the broadening influences that affected to greater or less extent the whole people. In addition, there was the influence of half a hundred thousand who actually reached the shores of Alaska and, in some cases, even its great interior. The large part of them had come from a sheltered life and thus by actual contact came to know frontier life, that life which has been such a strong influence in moulding American character by developing initiative and self-reliance. Many a man from the farm, desk, or workshop came to know for the first time what it meant to be thrown entirely on his own resources. Life on the Klondike trail was a great winnowing process. A man stood on his own feet. If he had the basal character, he won; if not, he became a derelict. A small percentage failed through lack of moral stamina, for there was ample opportunity to go to the dogs in the northern gold camps. On the other hand, many a man who had not developed beyond mediocrity in his own community, tightly bound by tradition and custom, found in Alaska his opportunity and rose to his true level. This last of our frontiers, therefore, has played a part in developing breadth of view and character among our people.

CHAPTER XX

The Klondike Trail

THE KLONDIKE of 1898 embraced all classes of men and nearly all nationalities. In the matter of education, social standing, and experience they differed greatly; but one trait was common to all—the possession of more initiative and determination than the average man. It was this characteristic that differentiated them from the masses. This trait led the preacher to leave his pulpit, the plumber his tools, the teacher his pupils, and the farmer his plow. It was the restless spirit in each community that felt the call and, often staking everything on the venture, made his way northward. In two days on the Klondike trail, I became acquainted with a British mining expert from South Africa, a Swedish engineer, an old California hunter, a steamfitter from New York, a farmer's boy from Vermont, and a young Irish lord. This was typical of the trail, except that the majority were Americans.[1]

What records there are indicate that about 75 per cent of the newcomers were Americans. All were welcome under the Canadian laws and given an opportunity to take part in the new venture.

The average man who started for the Klondike had but one thought, and that was to find gold. Of the country he was going to he knew nothing, and his principal concept was a land covered with ice and snow that lay in the polar region. If he had been told that winters in the Klondike were more healthful than those in New England, that the summer temperature frequently ran about 70°, he would have laughed his informant to scorn, for he was bent on adventures in the Arctic amidst icebergs and polar bears. And as he was going to a wild country, there must be wild Indians, so arming himself against savages was but following the first instinct of self-preservation.

[1] A census of Dawson in 1899 showed a total population of 4,445. Of this number 3,205 were Americans, 645 Canadians, 325 from Great Britain; the rest included Arabs, Austrians, Belgians, Chinese, Danes, Dutch, Finlanders, French, Germans, Greeks, Indians, Italians, Japanese, Norwegians, Russians, Spaniards, and Swedes. Therefore, a total of 20 nations were represented in the small isolated town. Cf. *Report of the Commissioner of the Northwest Mounted Police Force for 1899*, Ottawa, 1900, p. 54.

A man of this type—and his knowledge represented the average—quickly fell a prey to the first merchant who "specialized in Klondike outfits." The limit on equipment purchased was then usually determined by length of purse. In general, the poorer men were in better condition for the trail than the wealthier ones, for their movements were not so hampered by elaborate outfits.

Having bought his outfit in some West Coast city, the tenderfoot took his next step in proclaiming to the world that he was a Klondiker: he donned the full regalia. The favorite costume was a corduroy or canvas suit, high-laced boots, and a felt hat with a remarkably wide brim and leather hat band, in cowboy style. On account of local police regulations, he was not permitted to strap on his pistol, which the average Klondiker regarded as an essential now that—as he believed—he was close to the frontier.

One of the first necessities was to obtain passage to Alaska. This task was much simplified for many by their finding in the Pacific towns, and even on the East Coast, Alaskan transportation companies, often with very long names and luxurious offices. An affable agent explained that these companies were backed by solid capital and owned a large palatial fleet, only in part then available since most of the vessels were under construction or on their way around the Horn. Assurance was given of the immediate sailing of one of the "smaller vessels" of the company, but passage must be booked at once, for there were many applicants. This last statement of the agent would often prove to be nearest the truth.

The purchase of a ticket usually included the signing of a contract by which the passenger relinquished all rights as a citizen and a man. When after long, weary waiting the vessel finally proved to be an old Puget Sound freighter or an ancient whaler that had been taken out of the boneyard at San Francisco, the average Klondiker found it was too late to back out; but, in fact, he was usually in such a rush to go north that he paid little heed to the character of the craft in which he embarked. Once started, he was likely to find that the vessel had twice the number of passengers she should carry and, besides full holds, was also carrying a high deck load. But this was all part of the game, and the Klondiker, though he might grumble much at the poor food which was characteristic of this type of vessel, adjusted himself as best he could.

If the voyage was made in the spring or summer, it would usually prove a delightful one. As the steamer threaded its way for a thousand miles among the islands and fiords, the lowland dweller could not help being awed by the rugged magnificence of the scene spread before him. To many a one came an undying love of the Northland, and never again would these be reconciled to living in a more subdued and civilized environment. A voyage of a week would bring the vessel to the head of Lynn Canal, where the passengers and their freight would be dumped without ceremony on the beach. Landing would be at Dyea or Skagway, some five miles apart, according to the choice of the traveler. The vessel then returned for another rich cargo.

Many a Klondiker when landed on the shores of Lynn Canal found himself for the first time in his life thrown on his own resources. He was but an atom among the great mass of gold seekers, each of whom was struggling to get forward. There was no unity of action on the trail, each one being for himself. One who fell by the wayside might be passed by hundreds and no helping hand be extended. The mob of gold seekers were newcomers who had not yet learned the first principle of frontier life—unity of action and mutual help. Therefore, the newly landed Klondiker must pitch his own tent, alone transport his cargo of supplies, and learn to cook his meals. Nor could he learn much from watching the crowd, for most were as green as he. The sprinkling of old frontiersmen was so small as to be lost amid the crowd of tenderfeet, or *cheechakos* as they were called in Alaska.[2]

Two routes led across the Coast Range from the head of Lynn Canal to navigable waters on the Lewes River,[3] routes which converged at Lake Bennett. The shorter left the coast at Dyea and ascended the steep coast wall of Chilkoot Pass (3,100 ft.) about 20 miles from tidewater, descended to Crater Lake on the inland front, and then reached Lake Bennett at a distance of 30 miles from the sea. A rough horse and sled trail led from tidewater to the base of a steep 500-foot climb to the summit. From

[2] *Cheechako* is an Alaskan coast Indian word for newcomer. It has become corrupted to designate a greenhorn or tenderfoot. In contrast to this, the experienced prospector who could make raised bread and not depend on baking powder was called a *sourdough*.

[3] The name Yukon River is by definition confined to the stream formed by the junction of the Lewes and Pelly rivers. Of these, the Lewes River heads near the Chilkoot Pass and may be considered the source of the Yukon.

FROM DYEA TO DAWSON

Many Klondikers started at Dyea (upper photo, by W. C. Mendenhall, 1898), crossed the pass through the mountains, and in going down the Yukon braved such hazards as Miles Canyon (center left, photo by A. H. Brooks) and Five Finger Rapids (center right, photo by J. B. Mertie) before reaching Dawson (lower photo, by W. C. Mendenhall).

here on it was not possible to use either sleds or pack horses, and all supplies had to be carried on the backs of men. From the summit, the descent of about 1,000 feet to Lake Bennett was by easy grade except for the first declivity down to Crater Lake. The longer route over White Pass (2,800 ft.) left the coast at Skagway. There the grade to the base of the last ascent was gentle, but the route led first through a heavily timbered valley for some ten miles and then through a steep-walled canyon whose declivities gave but perilous footing. The base of the ascent to the pass is about 18 miles from tidewater. From here the ascent of about 800 feet is steep, but it was feasible for both sleds and horses. From the summit of White Pass a gentle descent for some 20 miles led to Bennett, 40 miles from the coast.

By spring of 1898 transportation on both routes had been much improved. A wagon road had been built from Skagway to the base of the White Pass. At the Chilkoot an aerial tram had been constructed for carrying freight up the last steep ascent. Those who had the money to pay for transportation over these established lines were confronted with no serious obstacles to their journey into the interior. By hired transport, however, the cost of freight supplies to Bennett was from 20 to 50 cents a pound, and there were relatively few who could afford this luxury.

For many months thousands toiled along the rough trails, dragging their heavily-loaded sleds. It was a heart-rending task, especially in the late spring when the snow became soft and the coast end of the trail became muddy. Three to four hundred pounds were all that two men could drag on a loaded sled, and so, with the average outfit weighing seven or more tons, frequent relays were necessary. When the base of the Chilkoot was reached, the real test of physical endurance came. Here each man made up his pack of 50 to 100 pounds and carried it up the steep 500-foot declivity, then returned for another load. It is no wonder that many failed in this final test, sometimes from lack of physical strength, but more often through lack of mental and moral stamina. Many breakdowns were due to improper food, caused by sheer ignorance of cooking.

The physical wrecks of the Chilkoot were almost all due to such causes and not to the cold, as is often stated. In fact, the climate with its bracing cold was admirable. If a man lacked the physical constitution for the work, or as was more often the case if he did not know how properly to prepare his food and care for himself, he would go under. Many died from the strain, and others turned back as physical wrecks. But these failures were only a very small percentage of the total. No doubt the percentage of death to the total number was much smaller than in any equal body of men who were leading sedentary lives. There were no serious epidemics. Some typhoid developed in coast towns. There was one epidemic of spinal meningitis at Dyea in the spring of 1898, with a total death toll of about 20. Because of infection in the water there was an epidemic of typhoid at Dawson in the summer of 1898, but it was checked by the enforcement of sanitary regulations by the officials. The total deaths from typhoid at Dawson during this year were 84, and from all sources 137.[4] This, in a town of 4,000 with an additional transient population of 15,000 to 20,000, is an index of the healthful character of the climate.

The danger to the average individual on the White and Chilkoot passes was almost nil. A few fell into swift glacial streams and were drowned. A very few wandered from the trail and, weakened by hard work, died of exposure. One exception must be made: During the height of the travel on April 3, 1898, a great snowslide took place near Chilkoot Pass which buried 142, of whom 43 perished. Including these, the deaths by accident and exposure on the Chilkoot and White pass trails were less than a third of one per cent. The addition to this total of those who died by disease will still leave the deaths at less than one per cent.

It has been shown that Skagway was for a few months controlled by criminals. These were, however, of the card sharp and swindler type, and few had the courage to become robbers. There was some thieving and robbing of caches on the trail, but this amounted to but little in the aggregate. In a few instances vigilance committees were formed and thieves punished by lashing in public. There were also a few cases of shooting and murders, but these were very exceptional. The old typical bad man of the West never gained a foothold in the North. Public opinion was against him, and flight after a crime was impossible. Moreover, if he ventured on Canadian soil, the Mounted Police made short work of him. No one went armed on the Klondike trail, for a weapon was but a useless burden. The criminal element in the North was never of the picturesque border-ruffian type. So far as it existed, its center was the saloon

[4] *Report of the Commissioner of the Northwest Mounted Police Force for 1898* (Part III, Yukon Territory), Ottawa, 1899, pp. 22-23.

and dance hall. Even the loose woman who infested the gold camps had acquired through facing the hardships of the trail some elemental good qualities unknown to her class as represented in the centers of civilization.

Those who took part in the Klondike rush of 1898, while they could not attain success unless inured to hardship and strenuous toil, faced no great dangers. The climate was far better than the gold seeker found who reached California in 1849 across the deserts of the West or through the swamps of Central America. Nor did he run danger of physical violence from Indian or white outlaws, as did his prototype of half a century before. Hardships he had, but the actual physical dangers of his trail, if he were intelligent and experienced, amounted to but little. There were dangers of glacial streams and snowslides on the coast side of the passes, but the records show that these were not so great as those met in threading the thoroughfares of some of our great cities.

The down-river trip was, of course, not without danger, especially to these argonauts who had little if any knowledge of guiding boats in swift waters. Much has been written about the dangers of running the famous Miles Canyon and the White Horse Rapids. These forbidding looking waters were indeed a serious barrier, and many a Klondiker who had toiled for months to reach this point lost a part or all of his freight at these places. The loss of life, however, was insignificant. In 1898, 7,080 boats went down the Yukon carrying about 28,000 passengers, and of these 23 were drowned in all, five at White Horse.[5] This is a most astounding record to anyone who has seen the hundreds of makeshift crafts, mostly greatly overloaded and manned by inexperienced crews. Even assuming the police record to be incomplete, the number drowned would still be only a small fraction of one per cent of the total number who went down the Yukon.

The great horde of gold seekers were essentially law-abiding. Though the coastal towns of Alaska were for a time infested by a criminal element, it never became a serious menace to a community, except for those few months at Skagway. Relatively few professional criminals ever reached the Yukon. They were discouraged by the Mounted Police, and above all the sentiment of the community was against them. Saloons, gambling and dance

[5] *Ibid.*, p. 56.

houses, and houses of ill fame were found in all the northern mining camps; but the rougher criminal element found it an unattractive field. The cordon of police, as well as the difficulties of travel, made it almost impossible for the thief, the robber, and the murderer to make his escape. Not half a dozen murders were committed during all this wild stampede, and thefts were exceedingly rare. While the police records show nearly 650 arrests in Yukon Territory during 1898, most of these were cases of drunkenness, disorderliness, or vagrancy. According to the record these include charges of "letting out bush fire, non-payment of wages, wounding a dog, fishing on Sunday, damage to raft," and other minor infractions;[6] this indicates a strictness in the enforcement of laws and regulations hardly to be expected on a remote frontier. Of the total arrests, less than 150 were for more serious crimes, and of these over half were concerned with the inmates of the houses of ill fame.

Even though, as has been shown, the perils of the Klondike trail have been greatly exaggerated, we should not detract from the credit due those who, by facing the unknown dangers and hardships of the North, opened up a new empire. These were stimulated by the same spirit of adventure and search for the new which three centuries before had brought to America the first colonists, whose descendants pushed their way through the passes of the Appalachians and eventually across the continent to the Pacific. The Klondiker had a lesser task and fewer hardships and perils, yet all credit for his will to do and to suffer should be given him.

While the Klondike trail thus lacked the picturesqueness and romance loaned to the early days of the West by the outlaw, yet it had a flavor all its own. The horde of gold seekers toiling up the steep slopes of the Chilkoot created their own atmosphere of romance and adventure. Here was a line of men, each with his heavy burden, winding its way to the summit in close marching order. This line for months was never broken, night or day. At the summit, each toiler threw down his pack and added it to the confusing aggregate of freight which covered the narrow crest line close at hand. Half-buried in the snow was a tent over which waved the British flag, and here the customs house duties must be paid. The guard of Mounted

[6] *Ibid.*, pp. 119-139.

Police in their red jackets added color to the scene, and above towered snowy peaks on every hand. Once at the summit, the Klondiker's heart-breaking toil was over and he could sled his supplies down to Bennett with little labor. At Bennett the number who crossed the Chilkoot was reenforced by those who had crossed the White Pass, and here quite a tent settlement grew up, a year later to become of still greater importance when connected with the coast at Skagway by a narrow-gauge railroad.

The shores of Bennett were forested and here many of the Klondikers built their boats to use when the ice went out in June. Some extended their sled journey 100 miles or more beyond. Every means of conveyance was tried on the Klondike trail. Dogs and horses were the most common, but sleds drawn by oxen, burros, goats, and sheep were also seen. The mass of gold seekers, however, used hand sleds. A flat, narrow sled with a steering pole in front was the favorite. The use of animals involved the hauling of feed, which constituted an additional burden. It is sad to relate that many used their animals barbarously. Much of the White Pass trail was lined with dead horses. Many a man would drive his stock until it could go no more. Now and then a thrifty one who ran out of feed would push his horses or oxen to the limit and then, before the poor animals died of hunger or exhaustion, would slaughter them and hang out a sign on his tent, "Meals $2.50." The price of a cup of coffee and two crullers was 50 cents. Nearly everything, however, sold at $1 a pound, whether bacon or wire nails. Horse feed, when it could be bought, sold usually at $500 a ton. A bunk in a tent without blankets cost $1 a night. All drinks were $1, but cigars were only 50 cents.

Next to crossing the pass, the building of the boat was the most serious task. Could a man afford it, he could buy lumber from several small mills on the trail at the rate of $500 a thousand board feet with, as one man expressed it, no rebate for knotholes. More often, the Klondiker whipsawed his own lumber, a wearisome task. With this green lumber and even greener builders, boats of most remarkable design were constructed. After the boat had been built, oars were hewn out of green spruce; and in these crazy crafts the Klondikers started on the 500 mile downstream journey to Dawson. Many were the accidents, for much of the run was broken by boulders and reefs, by no means easy to navigate by a skillful boatman. Though many outfits were lost, the loss of life, as already shown, was exceedingly small. The crafts were of every size and description. They varied from huge scows, carrying many tons of freight and horses, to one-man cranky skiffs, graceful canoes, and clumsy rafts. Some small steamers were also built at Bennett which made the run to Dawson successfully, passing through Miles Canyon and White Horse, Five Fingers, and Rink rapids.

On the whole the down-river journey was one continuous source of joy for those who had toiled over the passes. Usually no attempt was made to row with the clumsy oars, and the craft drifted along guided by a long stern sweep. It was a lazy life and many succumbed to it, losing all interest in seeking gold. The nearer they approached their goal, the less interest they had in prospecting. Thousands of them reached Dawson and, finding the goal which it had taken months of toil to reach not what their fancies had painted, continued their easy journey down the river, after spending a few days, or even only a few hours, tramping the streets of the town. Indeed, scores of boats manned by would-be Klondikers passed Dawson after only a few minutes' halt on the river banks. In the fall of 1898 there were many small boats at St. Michael which had been laboriously built on the upper lakes and whose crews had traced the whole course of the river without even attempting to prospect.

These slackers were of course, the exception, for almost all who reached Dawson at least made an attempt to prospect. Most of them after a hasty but laborious visit to the gold-bearing creeks found that all the creeks within reach of Dawson had been staked from mouth to source. There was no chance for anyone arriving during the summer of 1898 to find an unstaked claim. Those who wished could easily obtain work at the mines at wages of $15 a day and board. An experienced placer miner could also obtain leases, or "lays" as they were called, under which he worked the ground, taking 50 per cent to 80 per cent of the gold recovered, the balance going to the owner. Still larger were the opportunities to open up "wildcat" ground. Many an owner was glad to have someone open up his claim on a percentage basis. The *cheechako* was a fair mark for those who did not want to work themselves. Many an inexperienced man spent months of hard toil on a claim which the experienced man knew was worthless. On the other hand, some profited by their very ignorance. Thus one man, not knowing that placer gold was found only in the deposits of watercourses, cheerfully went to work high on the valley slope of Bonanza Creek. His efforts to find placer gold in such a place were jeered at by the experienced miners. By chance, however, he found a former river deposit which because of the elevation of the land now stood 100 feet or more above the present valley bottom. This was the famous "White Channel" of the Klondike whose gravels have yielded millions of dollars worth of gold.

It was the chance discoveries like this which encouraged the average Klondiker to believe that the discovery of gold was pure luck. It was only later that the more intelligent prospectors realized that the distribution of gold followed definite laws and that, though these were obscure and not well-known, it was wise not to ignore them. This northern region, where the cost of living was very high and the physical obstacles to mining and travel were very great, was no place for the hit-or-miss type of prospector. In the long run, it was only he who made use of geology by at least observing the simple facts relating to the occurrence of gold placers and making intelligent deductions who succeeded.

Another type among those who arrived in Dawson was those who had more or less money for investment. Among these were many whose ignorance of mining and often of all business matters made them an easy mark for those who had worthless claims to dispose of. But by far the larger number were shrewd businessmen, quick to see a financial opening. Often such men realized at once that their ignorance of mining prevented their entrance into this field, and they seized on other opportunities that opened. The temperament of the community was democratic, and a man's vocation in no way affected his social standing. Thus preachers went to work with pick and shovel, jewelers became pot hunters, stockbrokers opened shops, and lawyers started restaurants. Three bright young sisters who had had good business training, finding no work as stenographers, opened a hand laundry which proved a great business success. While much the larger number who arrived in Dawson were enterprising enough to find more gainful occupations, there were a considerable percentage who idly walked the streets and spent their money in the saloons, dance halls, and gambling houses.

Thanks to the Northwest Mounted Police, there was no lawlessness, no rowdyism. A man was safer at Dawson or on the creeks than in many of our large cities. Men kept in their unlocked cabins huge quantities of gold, and unarmed, transported it to the banks at Dawson. While outwardly the town had all the picturesqueness of a mining camp, with its crowded saloons and gambling tables and gaily-dressed women of the underworld, vices were only of the obvious sort and were conspicuous only because there was no attempt to hide them, as is done in the centers of civilization. Except for occasional fines, the police made no attempt to interfere with the women of the underworld, of whom there were hundreds. If, however, a robbery or assault occurred in a house of ill fame, it was promptly raided by the police and closed. Public gambling was a conspicuous feature of the social life. It was, however, carried on under definite rules, and the police made short shrift of the dishonest gambler. In fact, there was far more dishonesty among certain small promoters, who lay in wait for the guileless *cheechako* and sold him worthless mining claims or stocks. Many of the keepers of gambling houses and saloons were men of the sturdy type of frontier honesty. Their word could be relied upon, and they were respected by the better class in the community. Rascals of the Soapy Smith type, who so long dominated Skagway, were not tolerated in Dawson.

The one serious blot on the life in the Northland was the large number of women of the underworld. For a number of years during the earlier part of the Klondike and Nome excitement such women were encountered everywhere. Since they always had plenty of money, the best accomodations on the steamers and in the hotels were reserved for them. In the early days of Dawson and other gold camps, women of this type were more numerous than the respectable ones. This condition made it very trying for the better class of women to travel, though in the settlements there were always enough of them to form a society of their own. In justice to the women of the underworld who went North, or who became such women after their arrival, it should be said that they included a large number who by sharing the hardships of the frontier had developed certain stalwart qualities unknown to their class in civilized communities.

During the summer of 1898 Dawson was in a continuous state of overflowing population. The town as then built was for a population of about 4,000 people, yet during the height of travel there were probably 10,000 to 15,000 people there. In the flat next to the river there were many large buildings and back on the hill slopes were innumerable small cabins. In addition, tents were pitched, crowded into every available plot of ground. Lodgings were almost impossible to find. Bunks and cots were frequently used for two, sometimes for three, shifts of sleepers. With almost continuous daylight, little distinction was made between day and night. All saloons and many stores were kept open throughout the 24 hours. A business engagement for two o'clock might mean in the morning or in the afternoon.

While many idle men tramped the streets, there was always work for those who sought it. Wages were $1 an hour. This was not high considering that meals cost $1.50 to $3, and a cot or bunk for 12 hours cost $2. A man and team cost $75 to $100 a day. Drinks which cost $1 during the winter fell to 50 cents during the summer. Before the first upper river boat arrived, whiskey was scarce and sold for $100 a gallon. The first cargo of whiskey to arrive from St. Michael was sold wholesale for $80,000. In June a weekly newspaper, *The Klondike Nugget,* sold for 50 cents a copy. Land on the main streets sold at from $500 to $1,000 a front foot.

The Canadian policy was to furnish a good government and aid the miners by building trails and roads, the cost of which was levied on the community. Every miner had to have a license for which he paid an annual fee of $10. Rather heavy charges were made for all official records and papers. A tax of 10 per cent was made on all gold mined,[7] except that each operator was allowed $2,500 worth of gold without tax. There was much evasion of this tax by smuggling gold out of the country, though the penalty for such action was the confiscation of the gold. This tax also had a tendency to keep gold in the country, though it passed currently in exchange below its true value. Gold scales were familiar sights in every shop, saloon, and hotel. Hardly any money circulated, barter being in unre-

[7] This tax was later reduced to 2½ per cent.

fined gold "dust" and nuggets. Though the Canadian Government collected in 1898 upwards of $1,000,000 in taxes from the Klondike, it was all spent on policing, road-building, and other civic items.

While, as has been shown, the great mass of gold seekers chose the shortest route to the Klondike by one of the Coast Range passes, yet many other routes were also chosen. Among these, the one from the mouth of the Yukon was of most importance, for it was by this route that the bulk of heavy supplies reached Dawson. This route involved an ocean voyage of 3,000 miles across the North Pacific, through the Aleutian Islands, and thence across Bering Sea to St. Michael. The shallow delta of the Yukon afforded no port for ocean vessels, so landing was made 50 miles to the north at St. Michael Island, which had but an indifferent harbor. Here transfer was made to river steamers and, after an ocean voyage of 90 miles not unattended by dangers, the Yukon was entered by one of the many narrow channels which thread its delta. Once the Yukon had been reached, the journey to Dawson involved only the tedious stemming of its current for 1,800 miles to Dawson. A journey by this route would under fair conditions occupy about six weeks or two months. This lower Yukon route to Dawson attracted many gold seekers, primarily those who had enough money to make it unnecessary for them to essay the dangers and hardships of the Chilkoot Pass.

While the project as outlined above seemed simple enough, yet in fact there were not enough boats on the river to transport the passengers and supplies. It was a field that attracted many newly-born transportation companies.

The usual procedure was to secure by charter or purchase any sea-going vessel, usually an old freighter; load it with passengers, freight, and materials for a river steamer; and set sail for St. Michael. Each passenger, in addition to paying $300 to $500 for transportation, would sign an agreement by which he was to perform any work necessary for the success of the enterprise. As a consequence, he might find himself a stevedore, ship's roustabout, stoker, or wood carrier. He would help run the ship to St. Michael, build the river steamer, and chop and carry wood on his way up the river. The contract always provided that the destination was to be Dawson, time and conditions per-

DIFFICULTIES OF THE KLONDIKE TRAIL

Upper: Unloading horses from steamer "Protection" at Valdez in 1898, photo by F. C. Schrader; lower: Abandoned steamers at St. Michael in 1904, mute evidence of blasted hopes, photo by A. H. Brooks.

mitting. Since much time was lost in these enterprises which were handled by men inexperienced in the country, only a very few expeditions of this type ever reached Dawson. Hence, many a Klondiker found himself after three or four months of hard labor, a privilege for which he had paid several hundred dollars, dumped out in the fall of the year on the banks of the Yukon, 500 to 1,000 miles from Dawson.

Another type was the cooperative companies. In these the stockholders contributed the funds to buy the outfit and their services to perform the labor. These usually landed at St. Michael with a knocked-down river boat which all assisted in putting together. All questions were decided at stockholders' meetings, and the officers and crews of the steamer when it was ready were elected by ballot. Probably no class of enterprise met with more dismal failure than these cooperative transportation and mining companies. Probably 40 or 50 of them started for Dawson from St. Michael during the summer of 1898. The lower river was lined with these little tubs desperately struggling against the current on one hand and a shortage of fuel on the other. Failing to get up the Yukon, a large number started up the Koyukuk. Here they wintered; and many in the spring, abandoning their steamers, made their way back to the Yukon in small boats and on rafts. It used to be said that in the summer of 1899 every Indian on the Koyukuk owned a steamer.

While these new ventures in transportation up the Yukon were mostly dismal failures, yet many passengers were taken to Dawson from St. Michael in 1899 by the two strong companies which had for some years been operating large steamers on the Yukon. These were carried in comparative comfort and faced none of the dangers or hardships of the other Klondikers.

Among the routes which found great favor in 1898 was that by the Stikine River to Telegraph Creek, thence by trail to Teslin Lake and down the Hootalinqua which drained into the Lewes. Probably nearly 5,000 people landed at the old Russian post of Fort Wrangell in the winter and summer of 1898. About half of these reached Telegraph Creek, and possibly 200 or 300 eventually reached Dawson. In the summer of 1898 a project was launched for building a railroad into the interior by this route, and this was one of the principal reasons that it attracted so many.

A corporation sold tickets to hundreds of people for transportation by this route. It is said to have delivered one passenger to his destination: this distinguished individual made his trip down the Hootalinqua in a dugout canoe paddled by two Indians.

Another favorite route was by way of the Valdez Glacier to the Klutina, a tributary of the Copper River, and thence up the Copper across two divides to the Yukon. A few score even essayed the swift waters of the Copper itself as a route into the interior.

Several hundred landed at the head of Disenchantment Bay, a branch of Yakutat Bay. Thence they sledded 20 miles over the Hubbard Glacier to the Alsek River and then started up that swift stream. Much of the Alsek valley is steep-walled, and several glaciers discharge into its swift waters. Here there is no timber except willow. Many died on this route of scurvy and exposure; quite a few were drowned or lost on the glacier. Probably not over a score were able to ascend the river through the mountainous part of its valley to the open country beyond. Here they found themselves, after a year of incredible toil and exposure, not five days' walk from the coast at Lynn Canal. Those who still had the Klondike fever made their way to Skagway and thence by one of the well-beaten trails to Dawson. They had lost a year in this venture.

From Pyramid Harbor, 30 miles from Skagway, an easy route into the interior had been discovered by Jack Dalton in 1890. This was especially suited for stock, and in 1897 and 1898 hundreds of animals were taken to the Yukon by this route. It also attracted a few prospecting parties who were provided with horses.

It has been shown that probably 50,000 gold seekers actually reached Alaska and the Klondike in 1898. Of these, many made a good living, a few grew fabulously rich, but the majority were financially losers by the venture. In 1898 the Klondike produced gold to the value of about $10,000,000, while the total value of Alaska's mineral wealth was $12,000,000. Had this wealth been equally divided among the gold seekers, each man's share would have been $250. This amount would have represented his reward for months of toil and hardship. As a matter of fact, it would not have paid for his expenditures for equipment. It is evident, therefore, that as a financial venture the world was a loser by the Klondike gold rush.

MAIN STREETS IN FRONTIER TOWNS, ABOUT 1901

Upper: Fort Wrangell, photo by A. H. Brooks; center: Nome, photo by W. C. Mendenhall; lower: Skagway, photo by A. H. Brooks.

Yet measured by the building of character and physical strength, the world was better off. Who can measure the good done by the broadening influence of the frontier life, by the development of self-reliance and strengthening of character, by the facing of hardships and dangers? Measured by standards of good citizenship, the influence of the Klondike rush was not a loss but a great gain.

CHAPTER XXI

The Nome Gold Discovery

THE TOWN of Nome stretches along the beach of the southern shore of the Seward Peninsula, which forms the westernmost promontory of the mainland of Alaska. Only 60 miles of water separate Cape Prince of Wales, westernmost point of the peninsula, from the Siberian coast, and in clear weather the opposing mainland can be seen from both shores. A Russian vessel, blown out of her course, landed on Seward Peninsula as early as 1732, and during the succeeding century its shores were traversed by many explorers; but the interior remained practically unknown to white men until 1865, when a Western Union Telegraph expedition made its way from Golofnin Bay on the east by way of the Niukluk and Kruzgamepa rivers to Port Clarence on the west. In the following year some 15 miles of telegraph line were constructed along the western part of this route, the first built in Alaska. This was done under the direction of W. H. Ennis and D. B. Libby, as we have seen in a previous chapter. The latter returned to Alaska many years later as a prospector. He claims to have found colors of gold on the Niukluk River in 1865; and if this is true, it was the first gold found in the Seward Peninsula.

The peninsula continued to be regarded as a barren waste for many years after the building of the telegraph line. Whalers had a rendezvous at Port Clarence, where they anchored in the early summer while waiting for the ice cap to break on the Arctic Ocean. Occasionally a trader came from the nearest permanent posts, Unalakeet and St. Michael, and bartered with the natives, but otherwise conditions were as primitive as during the Russian occupation.

In 1879 a small schooner visited the shores of Norton Sound. It was found that some of the natives had a heavy, silver-colored mineral which they were using as slugs in their muzzle-loading guns or as cores in the moulding of bullets. One of the crew, W. T. Hofner, who had been a student at the Freiburg School of Mines in Germany, recognized this mineral as galena. He secured a large sample

VIEWS OF NOME BEACH

Upper: Storm beating against Front Street, photo by J. B. Mertie: center: Landing at Nome in 1899, photo by A. H. Brooks; lower: West part of Nome beach during the gold rush, photo by F. C. Schrader.

of the material, and on his return to San Francisco interested John C. Green in a project to search for the deposit. Green organized a small company, and in 1881 he and several others were landed at Golofnin Bay. Guided by the natives, they found a deposit of galena ore, which they called the Omalik, in the Fish River basin. There was started the first lode-mining enterprise in Alaska, except for the little done at Sitka. Work was continued for a number of years, but for one reason and another the venture was not successful.

Among the employees of this company was a sailor by the name of John Dexter who finally left the service, married an Eskimo woman, and established a small trading station at Cheenik on Golofnin Bay. Until the Klondike excitement there were no white prospectors in the region, but Dexter managed to interest the natives in the search for gold, he himself being incapacitated for prospecting by rheumatism. He secured gold pans and taught the natives their use. It is not definitely known who found the first gold, nor where and when the first discovery was made. One story credits the discovery to Tom Guarick, an Eskimo, who is said to have found gold on Ophir Creek in 1897. According to another story, a Norwegian grubstaked by Dexter by the name of Johansen found gold and did some sluicing at the mouth of the Casadepaga River in 1894. Whoever it may have been that did the mining, it is certain that for several years previous to 1896 a little placer gold passed through Dexter's hands and also that no rich discoveries had then been made.

The Klondike gold excitement drew some prospectors to Golofnin Bay. Among these was a party under the leadership of Daniel B. Libby who, as already indicated, had 30-odd years before supervised the building of the telegraph line at Port Clarence. With him were L. S. Melsing, A. P. Mordaunt, and H. L. Blake. These men, probably guided by previous discoveries, found gold on what they called Melsing Creek, a tributary of the Niukluk River, in March, 1898. A little later the rich deposits of the near-by Ophir Creek were found. Mining began in the spring of 1898, and gold to the value of $75,000 was recovered that year. The return tide of unsuccessful searchers for gold in the Kotzebue Sound region brought other prospectors into the country, so by midsummer there were several hundred miners in the region tributary to Golofnin

Bay. But interest in the new district hardly extended beyond its borders. The discovery was reported at St. Michael in 1898, but there was a general apathy toward the news there, only 100 miles away. Among the thousands of discouraged and disgusted Klondikers who passed through St. Michael that summer, it was impossible to awaken any enthusiasm for new gold fields. They had only two thoughts: one to board a south-bound steamer, the other to forget their unsuccessful quest for gold in the Northland.

Among those who were attracted to new gold discovery on Ophir Creek was Jafet Lindeberg, a native of Norway who was destined to play a most important part in the development of gold mining on the Seward Peninsula. Lindeberg arrived in St. Michael during the summer of 1898 under contract to take charge of the purchase of reindeer for the United States Government at Plover Bay, Siberia.[1] As it proved that the hostility of the natives made the plan unpractical, Lindeberg was relieved of his contract by Dr. Sheldon Jackson, the government agent. He then made his way to Ophir Creek on the Seward Peninsula to try his fortunes in the new gold field. Here he met with Jon Brynteson and Eric O. Lindblom, both naturalized Americans of Swedish birth. Brynteson was an experienced iron miner from Michigan who had come to Golofnin Bay at the suggestion of the Swedish missionary at Cheenik. The plan was to develop some lignitic coal on Norton Sound for use of the miners. This plan fell through, and Brynteson turned to prospecting. Lindblom was by vocation a tailor and was living at San Francisco when the Klondike rush started. Bound for Kotzebue Sound, he shipped on the whaler *Alaska,* which he deserted at Port Clarence. A friendly Eskimo took him to Golofnin Bay in his big skin boat, and thence Lindblom made his way to Ophir Creek.

These three men, whom chance had brought together, formed in August, 1898, a prospecting partnership and, making their way to Golofnin Bay, secured an open boat in which they skirted the southern shore of Seward Peninsula, prospecting as they went. Arriving at the present site of Nome, they made their way up the Snake River and prospected the tributaries, everywhere finding some gold.

---

[1] Lindeberg's own statement. See *United States Geological Survey Bulletin, No. 328,* Washington, D.C., 1908, pp. 16-18.

The stream they named Anvil Creek was found to be the most promising and here on September 22, 1898, they located the "Discovery Claim."

It appears that the Lindeberg party was more or less guided to its goal by the finding of colors of gold near the present site of Nome by a group of prospectors who had been blown ashore during the previous July. This party was headed for the Sinuk River, where it was rumored that gold had been found. It included N. C. Hultberg, H. L. Blake, J. L. Haggalin, and Brynteson. The men halted at Snake River only until the storm blew over, and none except Brynteson was sufficiently impressed with the importance of the field to continue a search in that vicinity.

At any rate, it is certain that the Lindeberg party was the real discoverer of the valuable placers at Nome and the first to stake claims. These men fashioned some crude rockers and during the short remaining open season recovered some $1,800 worth of coarse gold from the gravels of Anvil Creek, the first to be mined in the Nome district.

This incident shows what chance will do. At the time of the discovery there were thousands of men in Alaska and several score in the peninsula who had spent years of their lives in prospecting. Yet this discovery was made by three men who had at most spent not over three months at prospecting and only one of whom was an experienced miner. Though pure luck had made these men the discoverers, yet Lindeberg, their leader, was a man of exceptional natural ability, and it was therefore not chance that subsequently made him the leading mining man of the community which later sprang up at Nome.

Joined by other men from Golofnin Bay and Ophir Creek, the Nome mining district was organized on October 18, and the claims duly recorded. About 40 men filed on some 7,000 acres of prospective placer ground.

When the district was formed, the season of navigation had practically closed, and communication was cut off from St. Michael, the nearest regular port of call of ocean steamers during the summer. However, rumors of the rich discovery gradually reached other parts of Alaska, and during the fall of 1898-99 many men arrived from St. Michael and even from the Yukon. During the winter the news reached Dawson and thence was carried to the outside world. There were thousands of disappointed gold seekers in the Klondike and along the Yukon, and many of these started for the new camp. The world at large was far from being convinced of the authenticity of these reports, for it had developed considerable skepticism of the wild tales emanating from the Northland during the Klondike excitement. Late in June, 1899, several vessels reached Nome, then called Anvil City, from Puget Sound, of which the steamer *Garonne* was the first. These found a population of around 400 living in tents and in a few driftwood cabins. Mining began on June 20, and the steamers returning to Seattle brought the confirmatory news of placer gold in the new camp. It was not until then that the rumors were taken seriously and that any real excitement about Nome arose. As a result, several steamers sailing for St. Michael touched at Nome to discharge passengers and freight. These newcomers, together with those from the Yukon, swelled the population by the fall of 1899 to nearly 3,000. By this time a veritable frenzy seized the people of the Yukon, and near-by settlements were almost depopulated as a result of the rush to Nome.

Meanwhile, in the early summer there was anything but a contented community at Nome. The newcomers had found the whole country covered with location notices and very little mining being done. The professional claim-stakers had followed their usual practice of blanketing the creeks with location notices under powers of attorney, thus holding many claims without mining or prospecting in the hope of taking advantage of any discoveries made through the labor of others. In the early part of July probably not over 500 men were engaged in mining, while upwards of 1,000 were idle with no hope of employment as miners nor opportunity to prospect on unstaked ground. At that time, mining was limited to Anvil Creek and a few adjacent streams. The idle men believed that many of the locations were illegal, as they undoubtedly were under a strict interpretation of the law which requires a gold discovery on each claim before it is staked. Obviously, a man who had staked 20 to 50 claims in a few days could not have determined whether they were gold-bearing. It was also charged that many claims had been located by aliens and therefore were not legal pre-emptions. Under these conditions, it is not to be wondered at that an era of "claim-jumping" began, during which practically every property of any prospective value was re-staked. It was not uncommon to find a claim corner marked by half a dozen or more stakes, each one of which represented a different claimant.

The nearest United States commissioner was at St. Michael, and there was therefore practically no means of enforcing civil law. In fact, there were no representatives of the Government at Nome except an officer and a small detachment of soldiers that had been sent over from the Army post at St. Michael in the spring. On the commandant of this handful of soldiers, Lieutenant Spaulding, rested the responsibility of maintaining law and order among a thousand discouraged and angry men, a task made all the more difficult because he was without any actual legal authority. He deserves great credit for meeting the situation as far as lay in his power by patrolling property to which there were rival claimants and attempting to settle the constantly arising disputes. Discontent was rife, and matters went from bad to worse.

On July 10 a so-called "miners' meeting" was called for the purpose of discussing the situation, and a resolution was there presented[2] setting forth the grievances of those who believed that the claim locations had not been made in accordance with United States statutes. While it must be admitted that the unlimited staking was undoubtedly illegal, yet this meeting was mainly attended by those who, for one reason or another, had not succeeded in getting hold of placer claims. Had these discontented men spent less time in protesting and airing their grievances and more time in prospecting, they would have been better off, for subsequent operations have shown that there remained much valuable placer ground that had not been pre-empted. The organizers of this meeting had formulated a definite plan. Resolutions were to be introduced declaring all existing locations void. News of the passage of these resolutions was to be signalled by a bonfire at Nome to men stationed on Anvil Mountain eight miles away. When this signal was received, the rich claims on Anvil Creek and adjacent creeks were to be re-staked. In other words, this meeting, ostensibly called for the good of the whole community, was actually to be used for the benefit of a small inner ring.

The conspirators had, however, not counted on the action of Lieutenant Spaulding who, sensing that the meeting

[2] Dunham, S. C., "The Yukon and Nome Gold Region," *Annual Report of the Commissioner of Labor*, Washington, D.C., 1900, pp. 849-50.

was called to make trouble, attended it in person. On the introduction of the resolution, he promptly made a motion for adjournment, and carried it by ordering a sergeant and a few soldiers to clear the hall with fixed bayonets.[3] This action, entirely illegal, was an application of good common sense and without doubt prevented further complications in the community. It must be classed as one of those extra-legal actions which have so often saved the situation in Alaska.

The tension grew day by day, and physical conflicts between rival claim owners became not infrequent. To rectify matters, the military promulgated the following order on July 13:

> To put an end to apparent misunderstandings, the following statement is published:
>
> All disputed titles, whether to mining claims or to town lots, shall at once be brought before the civil authorities for settlement. So long as the civil authorities can handle such matters, the military authorities will take no action. In case it becomes necessary for the military authorities to act, the claim or lot will be held in its condition at the time, neither party being allowed to do any work to change the condition of the same.
>
> While there exists no objection to the holding of orderly meetings for the discussion of ordinary business affairs, in any meeting held for the purpose of acting in district affairs no person is entitled to participate except claim holders. Any attempt so to participate by other persons is illegal, and the proper steps will be taken to prevent it.
>
> Decisions and orders of the civil courts will be supported by the entire power and authority of the United States troops.
>
> No persons will be allowed to carry firearms, revolvers, or pistols. Anyone violating this order will have said firearms confiscated.

This order, though undoubtedly intended to relieve the situation, was far from having this effect. The ownership of practically every placer claim which had been exploited was rightfully or wrongfully disputed, and had this order been strictly enforced mining at Nome would have ceased. Such an eventuality would have worked great hardship on many bona fide property owners who depended on the summer yield of their mines for capital to make more extensive development in the following season. To meet this condition, a modification of the order was made on July 27 as follows:

[3] Morrow, William W., "The Spoilers," *California Law Review*, IV (January, 1916), 99.

The instructions contained in the order of July 13, 1899, posted at Anvil City [Nome], will be amended so as to permit original locators at work on their claims to continue their work in the event that anyone jumps the claim. The matter can afterwards be settled by the civil authorities.

The situation was suddenly relieved in an unexpected manner. It was accidentally discovered that the beach sands were rich in gold. It appears that the beach placers were found almost simultaneously by a soldier of the barracks and John Hummel, an old Idaho prospector who was too sick to leave the coast. Within a few days the mutterings of the discontent were almost silenced because it was found that good wages could be made with rockers on the beach. All the idle men went to work as fast as they could obtain implements. As it gradually became known that the beach sands for several miles were gold-bearing and could be made to yield from $20 to $100 a day to the man, another frenzy seized the people of Nome. A large part of the population went to work with shovels and rockers. During the height of the excitement, it is estimated that there were 2,000 men engaged in beach mining. The yield of the beach placers is estimated at more than $1,000,000, and this was practically all taken out with hand rockers in less than two months.

The beach placers by public consent, and as it subsequently proved by law, were open to all comers. Anyone with a shovel and rocker could be almost assured of good wages in beach mining. The gold recovered was widely distributed and freely spent. Many a man worked on the beach only long enough during the day to win the gold which he spent in gambling halls at night. Should he be cleaned out, he would mine gold enough the next morning to pay for his breakfast. During the gold mining, stores were drained of their stocks of shovels, and lumber for making rockers was at a premium. The beach gold is very fine, about 60 particles or colors having a value of one cent. It was, therefore, necessary to recover it by amalgamation with mercury. The usual practice is to have a copper plate coated with mercury in the bottom of the rocker, and over this the gold particles passed and were caught. When copper plates were not available, the bottom of the rocker was sometimes lined with silver dollars coated with mercury. The gold-bearing layer was only a few feet below the surface, the overburden being sand. Unlike the creek gravel, this material was not frozen and could easily be shoveled. Men usually worked in pairs, one working the rocker and the other digging the auriferous sand.

There was one legal complication relative to beach mining which threatened to be serious but which ended rather ludicrously. Previous to the discovery of the beach gold, many so-called "tundra claims" had been staked which stretched inland from the ocean. A group of these, including the richest beach deposits, had been segregated and had passed into the control of one company. When beach mining began, this company claimed that it owned the beach and warned off all trespassers unless they paid a royalty of 50 cents a day for the privilege of mining along the water front. Most of the miners, however, contended that a 60-foot strip from high water was public property and paid no heed to the warning against trespassing. The company thereupon appealed to the commandant of the troops, and he warned off all beach miners. The order was not obeyed, and he finally arrested about 300 men. At this time the situation reached the point of absurdity. Since there was no civil magistrate at hand before whom these men could be tried, no building in which they could be confined, nor any funds from which they could be supported while awaiting trial, the perplexed officer was forced to discharge all his prisoners—who all promptly returned to their rockers on the beach. Later decisions of the Land Office have not upheld the claims of this company to the gold on the beach, for a strip of the beach 60 feet wide is reserved for public use and has remained open for mining to all comers.

In the summer of 1899 I was engaged in exploration of the upper Tanana. When I arrived at Eagle on the upper Yukon, I found the place alive with excitement about Nome. Realizing the importance of securing authentic information about the new camp, I resolved to return to Seattle by way of Nome instead of choosing the shorter route to the coast by way of the White Pass and the then newly-constructed railroad to Skagway. I boarded the first down-river boat with difficulty, for it was already crowded with passengers from Dawson. It had received the culls from the Klondike who would not venture until the future of the new El Dorado was assured. The majority of my fellow-passengers were those who form the parasites in a new gold camp—men and women who will not venture until the flow of gold is assured. Gamblers, thieves, thugs, and women of the lower world crowded the steamer to its capacity. My sleep under a table in the dining room was broken by the noise of a gambling game going on over my head. After a week of discomfort I reached St. Michael and here fell in with F. C. Schrader, also of the Geological Survey, who had explored the Koyukuk River during the summer and was now bent on a similar mission to my own. Had I known of this plan, I would have been saved a long journey. We united forces and set sail for Nome on a flat-bottomed harbor boat, the famous *Sadie*. For 24 hours our crowded vessel was tossed on the turbulent waters of Bering Sea before we were landed at Nome on October 1, to find the ground already covered with snow.

Nome and its environment in the bleak weather of the fall was not attractive. A forbidding line of breakers separated the beach from the waves of Bering Sea. Through these breakers all landings had to be made from the vessels, which were compelled by the shoal waters to anchor about

MINING AT NOME

Upper left: Early dredge on Nome beach, photo by Sidney Paige; upper right: Sluicing on beach west of Nome, photo by A. J. Collier; lower left: Old beach near Cape Nome, photo by A. H. Brooks; lower right: Mining old beach 40 feet above sea level, photo by A. J. Collier.

two miles from the shore. The beach rises gradually to a sharply-cut scarp 100 yards from the breakers, and in this occurs the gold which made Nome so prosperous that year. From the scarp stretches the more covered plain or tundra for several miles back to the base of rolling hills. Along the seaward margin of the tundra stretched the town, consisting of driftwood cabins, tents, and a few

MINING IN NOME AREA

Upper left: Sluicing at No. 1 Dexter; upper right: Rocking on Boulder Creek; lower left: Recovering the gold of Topkok beach; lower right: Panning on Boulder Creek. All photos by A. H. Brooks.

frame and galvanized iron buildings which sheltered nearly 3,000 people. Except for a few main stores and warehouses, all the large buildings were saloons, dance halls, or gambling houses. In these, trade was brisk during 24 hours of the day, for as a result of the beach mining all had gold.

During the first three weeks in October, Schrader and I made such excursions into the adjacent region as conditions permitted, carrying our equipment and supplies on our backs. Though our observations were limited, one important conclusion was arrived at: that the region adjacent to Nome had been elevated and that certain low, seaward-facing escarpments marking the margins of terraces were most likely to be ancient sea beaches. The logical deduction from this analysis was that ancient sea beaches should be found in the tundra plain and that these would most likely be gold-bearing. This interpretation of the recent geologic history proved to be correct, and therefore the discovery of the ancient beach placers was precast on purely geologic evidence several years before their discovery was made. Strangely enough, though the facts and deductions were presented in a widely distributed publication[4] which was in the hands of thousands of the gold seekers of 1900, so far as I know not a single one paid any heed to the search for ancient beaches. In fact, the data were still further elaborated after a more detailed investigation the following year and again failed to excite any interest among these would-be prospectors.[5] The first ancient beach mining was in 1904, and it was then with some disgust that many experienced prospectors discovered that attention had been directed to this type of deposits and their probable loci some four years before. As one old prospector expressed it, "We thought the khaki-pants men did not know anything, and then found that the location of the gold beach placers was printed in a book." This piece of work was indeed a triumph for the practical application of geology, though the problem was a very simple one. It had, however, a permanent effect, for from that time on every experienced Alaskan prospector pays close heed to the results of the geologist.

During this same summer a few enterprising men struck out to seek new fields. Some went eastward and found gold on a number of southward-flowing streams, including Bonanza and Solomon rivers, but were unable to prove its presence in commercial quantities. Others went westward and named and staked Cripple and Penny rivers. Gold was also found during this season in the gravel of some streams near Cape York, and the York mining district was organized.

The yield of the beach placers gave the settlement great prosperity. Prices were high, as there was a scarcity of everything except gold. Before the last out-going steamer

---

[4] Schrader, F. C. and Brooks, Alfred H., "Preliminary Report on the Cape Nome Gold Region, Alaska," *Special Publication the United States Geological Survey*, Washington, D.C., 1900.

[5] Brooks, Alfred H. and others, "A Reconnaissance of the Cape Nome and Adjacent Gold Fields of Seward Peninsula, Alaska, in 1900," *Ibid.*, 1901.

departed, lumber cost from $150 to $250 a thousand and coal from $50 to $100 a ton. Fresh meat, mostly reindeer brought from Siberia, commanded $1 a pound; eggs were $3 to $4 a dozen. The cost of meals varied from $1 to $2.50. Beer, whiskey, and other drinks were sold at $1 a glass. A few small watermelons which had reached Nome sold at from $5 to $7 each. A supply of fresh vegetables and meat was expected to arrive on the *Laurada,* but she was wrecked on the Pribilof Islands in October. Small cabins, on lots staked on the tundra in back of the town with nothing but squatters' title, found a ready market at $600 to $700; corner lots on the main street, also with uncertain titles, sold for as high as $10,000. The Nome *News,* the first newspaper, began publication on October 9 and sold at 50 cents a copy. It was owned and edited by Major J. F. A. Strong, already a veteran newspaperman in the North who afterwards became governor of the Territory. A few days later the first copy of the Nome *Weekly Gold Digger* was issued. Wages were $10 a day but at times rose to $2 an hour. The abundance was reflected in the thriving business carried on day and night by a score of saloons and gambling rooms.

In 1899 there was only one judge for the entire Territory. The influx of gold seekers into the interior led this judge, C. S. Johnson, to make the long circuit down the Yukon River, holding court at various places. He arrived at Nome in the late summer and held court in a large leaky tent, attired in a slicker and high rubber boots. Judge Johnson made the important decision, in which he was subsequently upheld by a higher court, that the staking of a claim by an alien could not be contested by an individual and that the question of citizenship would only arise when patent was requested from the United States Government. This practically settled the question of whether claims being staked by aliens could be opened to relocation. Judge Johnson appointed a U.S. Commissioner and suggested that a provisional city government be organized by common consent. The term of court was very brief, for the judge was needed in other parts of his enormous district. He wisely refused to accede to the many requests for placing claims in the hands of receivers.

On October 16, a spirited election was held and a full complement of city officials balloted for. There were no strictures on the suffrage: men and women, citizens and aliens—all voted. The so-called "miners' ticket" carried the election. This government was maintained for a year but, having no legal authority, could not assess taxes and in consequence was in financial difficulties before the year was out. Order was, however, maintained by this government until the great influx of people in the summer of 1900 when the task proved too great.

The greatest need in the fall of 1899 was for a hospital, for the surface waters of the tundra, universally used in the town, had become infected with typhoid germs and there was an epidemic of the disease. It is estimated that there were as many as 200 cases at one time; and since there was only one small Army hospital, it was impossible to give the patients proper care, and hence the mortality was large.

Though the town of Nome was "wide open" in the fall of 1899 and its population of the most mixed variety, the sentiment of the community could not abide lawlessness, for the population embraced but few of the criminal class. Some gold robberies and some shooting affrays were the sum total of violence. One instance is worthy of record. Among the riff-raff which the camp had attracted were a dozen well-known criminals who, had they been left for the winter, would have made trouble. At the request of the city authorities, Captain D. H. Jarvis, who commanded the revenue cutter *Bear,* arrested them and transported them, without legal authority, to Seattle, where he turned them loose. This extra-legal procedure would undoubtedly have led to an award for damages had the victims brought a case in court. But the criminal record of this bunch of rascals was such that courts and court officers were the things they shunned; they were, therefore, only too glad to fade away into obscurity upon being released.

The results of this first season of mining were as follows: Up to January 10, 1900, about 4,500 claims were recorded in the Nome district; but probably not more than 50 claims were developed and not more than 100 were prospected. These 50 claims probably yielded over $1,500,000 in gold. The beach mining operations described above were more of a dramatic incident in the history of the region than anything of permanent commercial significance, for the richest part of the Nome beach was worked out the first year. The only other district on Seward Peninsula in which any mining was done in 1899 was on Ophir Creek, where gold variously estimated at $50,000 to $100,000 was taken out. Surface prospects were also found in the Solomon River region and near Cape York. A result of far greater importance than the actual mining was that some knowledge of the character of the deposits and the condition of operations had been gained. Although this information availed little to the more inexperienced men who were to invade the peninsula during the following year, yet it was of great practical benefit to those who did the actual mining in 1900.

CHAPTER XXII

The Gold Seeker at Nome

THE RETURN of the steamers in the fall of 1899, bringing probably 1,000 people from Nome, started the excitement which was to culminate in the following spring. It was not until the summer's output of gold of about $3,000,000 was brought from Nome that the outside world realized the importance of this new placer field. During the following winter, interest in Nome grew rapidly, and it was evident that a rush comparable to that of the Klondike two years before would begin with the breaking of the ice.

Professional promoters and stock jobbers were not backward in taking advantage of this excitement, and there was the usual crop of flamboyant prospectuses. Scores of companies were incorporated to mine gold at Nome, and much stock was sold. Though not a few of these ventures were intended to be legitimate enterprises, practically all of them were doomed to failure because of the complete ignorance on the part of most of the promoters of the character of the deposits, suitable methods of mining, and general commercial conditions. Beach mining enterprises were the favorite because of the supposed richness of the placers and especially because no capital was required to purchase claims. The almost incredible record of the first year's beach mining appealed to the popular mind, and its interest was maintained through the newspapers and through the circulars of the mining and transportation companies, which published the most preposterous statements. The "Golden Sands of Nome" became the popular slogan.

Not a few so-called mining experts asserted that the gold in the beach was inexhaustible because the supply was constantly being renewed by the waves from the ocean bottom. As a matter of fact, the beach placers were formed by the action of the waves in concentrating the gold contained in the gravels of the tundra. The movement of the gold was, therefore, from the shore outward, and the heaviest concentration was just below the surface line.

It was easy to maintain that, if a man with a rocker could make $20 a day on the beach, a plant which could handle 20 times as much would yield untold wealth. There was a flood of gold-saving devices, varying from a patent gold pan hung on a pivot and turned by a crank to complex aggregates of wheels, pumps, sieves, and belts, which required a 100 horsepower engine for their operation. The "Golden Sands of Nome" slogan inspired thousands to engage passage for this El Dorado months in advance of the sailings. Reaching Nome was far easier than going to the Klondike, for the gold seeker could be landed at his destination from an ocean steamer. Here there was no winnowing of the persevering and enterprising from the shiftless and indolent as occurred at Chilkoot Pass, the gateway to the Klondike. In consequence, the crowd of men who reached Nome were less well fitted for frontier life than those who went to Dawson.

As during the Klondike rush, a swarm of new transportation companies were organized, and every type of vessel started for Bering Sea. Fortunately, in the early summer good weather prevails on the North Pacific and Bering Sea; therefore, most of the great fleet, though many of the boats were unseaworthy, arrived at their destination. The foolhardy nature of some of these voyages is illustrated by the fate of the *Liza Anderson*. This vessel was a small, ancient Puget Sound side-wheeler excursion boat which had long been out of commission. Salvaged from the boneyard, she took on over 200 passengers and put to sea. Heavy weather soon showed that the old craft was entirely unseaworthy, and every wave threatened to put an end to the vessel. The terrorized and infuriated passengers decided to hang the captain who had imperilled their lives by putting out to sea in such an old tub. But better counsel prevailed, chiefly because he was the only seaman aboard. The *Liza Anderson* finally did reach Dutch Harbor in the Aleutian Islands, and there her bones still lie. Another example is that of a small schooner manned by amateur sailors who constituted a cooperative society. The captain obtained good observations every day and confidently plotted his course on the chart. After crossing the North Pacific, this night school graduate in navigation discovered that he was in error some 800 miles on his longitude and had reached the western instead of the eastern end of the Aleutian chain.

In 1900 the ice on Bering Sea broke unusually early, and on May 23 the old steam whaler *Jeannie* dropped anchor at Nome, the forerunner of a large fleet to follow. By July 1, upwards of 50 vessels had discharged passengers and freight on the Nome beach. The census of 1900, taken in June, showed 12,488 at Nome. It is estimated that by midsummer over 18,000 people had landed on Seward Peninsula, this in addition to some 2,000 who had wintered at Nome.

During the height of the rush there was a solid row of tents stretching along five miles of the beach, and the water front was piled high with freight of all kinds. The newcomers found little to encourage them. Those that had wintered in the peninsula had industriously extended their claim stakes so that a man could travel for days and hardly be out of sight of a location notice. To add to the discouragement and confusion, smallpox was introduced from one of the vessels; and had it not been for the prompt action of Captain D. H. Jarvis of the Revenue Cutter Service, it would have become a serious epidemic. The inexperienced men who landed at Nome, not finding the El Dorado their fancies had painted, were loud in their denunciation of the region. Many in the course of a few days' tramping of the beach became self-styled experts on placer mining and strenuously announced that the auriferous gravels of the peninsula had practically been exhausted. Their pessimism was only exceeded by their ignorance, for the region which they condemned was in the following two decades destined to produce nearly $80,000,000 worth of gold.

During the month of July every conceivable kind of gold-saving appliance was installed on the shore, but few except those of simplest design paid even running expenses. Nevertheless, there can be no question that a strong company controlling a considerable strip of the beach could by the use of mechanical excavation have profitably extracted what gold had been left in the sands. But under the conditions of public ownership of the beach, if values were found in any given locality, men swarmed in with rockers and quickly worked out that spot. This made it impossible to extract the beach gold at a profit by other than light equipments readily movable from one rich spot to another.

Probably the most ill-conceived enterprises were those planned to dredge gold under the sea. Though the upper layer of these underwater sands contains a little fine gold, the difficulties of excavation are such as to make it improbable that it can be profitably mined. The severe storms and lack of shelter prevent the use of dredges, except possibly during one month of the year. Many of these dredging schemes were based on the theory that the auriferous sands were swept in from the sea. The fallacy of this conclusion has already been pointed out, but it was held by some who were entirely ignorant of the origin of the beach gold and who refused to be instructed. On August 9, a severe southwesterly storm practically demolished the more elaborate appliances for gold-saving and strewed the beach for miles with debris. This ended beach mining for that year except where the simplest apparatus was in use.

Among the thousands who rushed to Nome there were many who were entirely unfitted to cope with the physical conditions inherent in the subpolar region. Though there were no physical obstacles to reaching Nome such as tested the endurance of the Klondikers, for anyone with $200 could reach Nome from anywhere in the States by rail and steamer in two or three weeks, still the climatic and other physical conditions in the Seward Peninsula were far more severe than those in the Yukon valley. Except in the eastern part of the peninsula, there is no timber; therefore, the only material for cabins was the driftwood logs along the beach. This source of timber was very rapidly depleted, and after the first few years of mining was practically gone. A man opening up a claim had as a rule to obtain Puget Sound timber for his sluice boxes. The same conditions affected fuel supply. When the driftwood was gone, coal and petroleum had to be brought from the States. The stunted willow along the watercourses afforded fuel for cooking, but in only exceptional places was it ample enough for winter fuel.

There is practically no game on the Seward Peninsula except ptarmigan and migratory birds, such as ducks and geese. The caribou had practically disappeared before the coming of the white man. The region is not adapted to the growing of even hardy vegetables, except that in favored localities a few small gardens could be maintained. As a consequence, the prospector could rely on no food from the country except fish. Even fur-bearing animals are far less numerous on the Seward Peninsula than in the "upper country," as the miners call the Klondike and the Alaskan Yukon. Therefore, there was little chance of supplementing the gains from mining by winter trapping. Though the summers at Nome are exceedingly pleasant, the fall is bleak and wet and the winter characterized by severe winds from which there is no shelter. Where all the necessities and many of the luxuries of life can be obtained, as in Nome itself, living conditions are very comfortable, the most serious drawback being the entire isolation from the time of the closing of the ice in November until its break in late June. At a few other communities along the southern shore of the peninsula, too, the winter life is not unbearable.

In the Yukon the prospector may go into the hills, build a comfortable cabin, be certain of fresh meat by killing moose or caribou; he can also clear a bit of land and raise his own potatoes or other vegetables. If he has a horse, he will find summer pasture and by clearing more land can raise his own oats. A line of traps will give him occupation during the long winter, as well as some revenue. He can thus lead a comfortable frontier life, and will need only a few hundred dollars worth of supplies from the outside world. As a consequence, there are hundreds, if not thousands, of miners living a life of independence in their isolated cabins in the Yukon and Kuskokwim basins and in other inland regions. All this is unknown on the Seward Peninsula, where the prospector must spend the winter at Nome or one of the smaller settlements. He must gain by mining enough money to purchase his lumber, his fuel, and practically all his food. Under these conditions many individual miners lose heart, and as a consequence mining operations are chiefly carried on by the large corporations with hired labor. A large percentage of the employees are in Alaska for the summer months only and do not feel themselves permanently identified with the Territory.

Such conditions as these were faced by the horde of inexperienced gold seekers that reached Nome during the summer of 1900. Most of them, totally unfitted for the life of this forbidding region, quickly became discouraged, and the return steamers were packed with such discouraged gold seekers. It is probable that of the 18,000 that landed not more than 5,000 remained for the winter. The temper of the community was for claim staking and claim jumping and not for prospecting. My journey through the southern half of the peninsula in 1900 indicated that not more than 300 or 400 of the thousands of gold seekers had the perseverance actually to do any prospecting in that region which was more than a day's walk from the beach. It was not until the country was rid of the *cheechakos* that the vast gold resources of the peninsula became known.

In 1899 the complaint at Nome had been, as we have seen, that, there being no civil court, important enterprises were retarded because of the impossibility of having disputes about ownership of mining property settled by law. During the winter this complaint had been brought to the attention of Congress, and a statute was passed forming a new judicial district which included the Seward Peninsula. The newly-appointed judge, Alfred H. Noyes of Minnesota, with the court officials arrived in Nome on July 19. Alexander McKenzie, an intimate friend of the judge, who accompanied the party as an unofficial member, was destined to wield for a brief period more power than any federal official in the North.

There were rival claimants to every mining property which had been located in the Nome district. Among the many claims of disputed ownership there were a few of special importance, because these were already known to be very rich in gold. These included a group owned by Lindeberg and his associates, who had incorporated under the name of Pioneer Mining Company, and another purchased from the original locators by Charles D. Lane for the Wild Goose Company. The jumpers of these very rich claims had united in placing their interests in the hands of a firm of Nome attorneys. With these attorneys McKenzie is reported to have come to an agreement, and so the legal firm at once filed complaints in the court on behalf of its clients. The action of the court is presented by Judge William Morrow of the Circuit Court of Appeals as follows:[1]

---

[1] Morrow, William W., "The Spoilers," *California Law Review*, IV (January, 1916), pp. 103-104. An interesting account of the legal complications at Nome in 1900, by a lawyer who played an important part in them, is also contained in Lanier McKee's *The Land of Nome*, New York, 1902.

The Judge immediately appointed McKenzie as receiver in all the cases embracing all the original claims of the two companies on Anvil Creek. The order was made without notice and directed McKenzie to take immediate possession of the property, which he did. It was further ordered that the persons then in possession of the claims should deliver to the receiver their immediate possession, control, and management, and the order expressly enjoined the defendants from in any manner interfering with the mining or working of the claims by the receiver, or with control and management. The amount of the bond required by the judge of the receiver was five thousand dollars in each case.

Judge Morrow in his scholarly presentation then goes on to show the illegality of this action. He presents evidence that McKenzie had entered into a secret agreement with the attorneys for the plaintiffs, by which he was to receive a certain percentage interest of the profits. He continues by saying that "McKenzie was therefore not a disinterested person in these cases, but his relation to the litigation was such that he was absolutely unfitted for the office of receiver; and this the court must have known, if not directly, certainly from all the surrounding circumstances."

The situation was then as follows: McKenzie, a personal friend of the judge, was in possession of all the richest mines in the district, worth, as subsequently proved, millions of dollars. He was not only in possession, but was mining gold to the value of hundreds of thousands of dollars. No representatives of the original owners of the mines were permitted on the properties, and there was no check on the amount of gold being taken out of the ground. Judge Noyes refused the petition of the original claim owners for leave to appeal to the Circuit Court of Appeals.

Such a situation would have baffled men of less determination than the group which opposed McKenzie. To their credit be it stated that, though the court had failed them, they made no attempt to take the law into their own hands. No doubt the greatest credit for circumventing this bold conspiracy belongs to Lane, leader of the original group of claim owners. An old California miner and frontiersman and man of affairs, Lane never lost his courage. Since there was no legal redress except through the Circuit Court of Appeals, 4,000 miles away, the petitioners sent to San Francisco and laid their case before this court. Their application was granted by Judge Morrow; and McKenzie, the receiver, was ordered to restore the claims.

Returning to Nome, the lawyers for the defendants filed the necessary papers in local court and made demand on McKenzie for restitution of the properties. By this time McKenzie realized that he controlled the court at Nome and, confident that his strong political backing in the States would protect him, refused to obey the order of the court. Judge Noyes, dominated by McKenzie, was afraid to take action and refused to compel the receiver to vacate the mines.

Nothing was left but a second appeal to the Circuit Court. Time was precious, for it was now the middle of September and in six weeks the ice would close in and communication with the outside world would be interrupted for eight months, except by a 1,500 mile journey by dog team. Again the attorneys went southward, and this time the Circuit Court directed two United States marshals to proceed to Nome, enforce the previous order of the court, arrest McKenzie, and bring him to San Francisco.

Meanwhile McKenzie had become worried and decided at least to make sure of the gold which he had already won from the claims and which he was illegally holding. He therefore, accompanied by an armed body of his friends, started for the bank, in the vault of which the gold was locked. His opponents, however, had been prepared for this action and also arrived at the bank, well-armed. Each of these two groups of armed men demanded access to the vault. The young teller acted promptly by closing the vault door and, turning the combination lock, announced that no one should enter. Meanwhile, a hurry-up call to the barracks near by brought a file of soldiers with fixed bayonets. The bank was quickly cleared and bloodshed narrowly averted.

Two deputy marshals, armed with the writs from the Circuit Court, arrived in October and immediately arrested McKenzie. McKenzie refused to deliver the key to the safe deposit box containing the gold of which he had despoiled the claims. The marshals then, under protection of the military, broke open the box and seized the gold, found to be of $200,000 in value. McKenzie was tried in San Francisco and sentenced to a year in jail. Judge Noyes, generally believed to be more of a tool of the McKenzie ring than a conspirator, was sentenced to pay a fine of $1,000. He was removed from office by the President, but served until the summer of 1901. Two other conspirators, the district attorney Wood and an agent of the Department of Justice named Frost, received jail sentences of four and 12 months respectively.

In concurring with the court opinion on this case Judge Rowe[2] says:

> I am of the opinion that the evidence and record show beyond any reasonable doubt that the circumstances under which and the purpose for which each of those persons committed the contempt alleged and so found were far graver than is indicated in the opinion of the court, and that the punishment awarded by the court is wholly inadequate to the gravity of the offenses. I think that the records in evidence show very clearly that the contempt of Judge Noyes and Frost were committed in pursuance of a corrupt conspiracy with Alexander McKenzie and with others not before the court and therefore not necessary to be named; by which the property involved in the suits mentioned in the opinion among other properties were to be unlawfully taken under the forms of law from the possession of those engaged in mining them, and the properties thereof appropriated by the conspirators. For these shocking offenses it is apparent that no punishment that can lawfully be imposed in a contempt proceedings is adequate. But a reasonable punishment may here be imposed and I am of the opinion that in the case of the respondent Alfred H. Noyes a sentence of imprisonment in the county jail for eighteen months should be imposed.

This, however, was a minority opinion, and Judge Noyes escaped a jail sentence. His punishment, though, was destined to be still greater at the bar of public opinion. He continued in office until midsummer of 1901, but no one trusted him even when his decisions were just. Embarking on the steamer and while still anchored off the coast, he continued to issue court orders, locally known as "deep-sea injunctions," some of which conflicted with each other. Despised by the entire community, he left without a friend. By his actions he had not only thrown the question of ownership of property into unutterable confusion, but he had shaken the faith of the people in the honesty of the courts.

Fortunately, confidence was restored by his successor, Judge James Wickersham, and gradually the chaotic conditions left by Noyes were brought into order so that the harvesting of the rich gold deposits could be taken up systematically. The only redeeming feature of this disgraceful episode of the Alaskan courts is that it gave Rex Beach the plot for his dramatic novel, *The Spoilers*.[3]

---

[2] Harrison, E. S., *Nome and Seward Peninsula*, Seattle, 1905, pp. 68-69.

[3] Beach has also published an exposé of the affair under the title "The Looting of Alaska," *Appleton's Book-Lovers Magazine*, VII (January to May, 1906).

While the fight was going on for possession of the rich claims, mining operations had virtually stopped, except on the beach which was open to all. Men who made promising discoveries dared not open them up for fear the court would throw their claims into the hands of a receiver and they would find their gold taken by others. As a consequence, the mining of creek placers was almost at a standstill, except on the rich claims near Nome, and most of these were not operated by their owners.

The phenomenally rich beach placers at Topkok, at the mouth of Daniels Creek 40 miles east of Nome, were discovered in March of 1900. The deposit was practically mined out in six weeks, before the arrival of most of the gold seekers. It yielded over $600,000 worth of gold, most of which was contained in a narrow strip of beach less than 600 feet long. The gold contents of this beach placer probably averaged $150 to the cubic yard, and it is indeed the richest placer of its kind ever discovered. During the mining, three men are reported to have recovered gold to the value of $10,000 in three days. In July, the owners of the claims adjacent to the beach induced the military authorities to stop the beach mining, but by this time the strip had been practically mined out.

But little gold was recovered from Nome beach in 1900, although thousands of men directed their energies to the task. In the early summer, the beach was crowded for ten miles with *cheechakos* bound to their erroneous slogan, "The Golden Sands of Nome." With the small recovery, interest gradually dropped off, and all mining finally ended in August when the entire beach was swept by the waves of the furious storm already mentioned. It carried away all the wonderful gold-mining devices, besides many supplies and tents. Beach mining on the shores of Bering Sea thus ended forever as an important industry, though to this day many a man ekes out his grubstake by rocking out a few dollars worth of gold from the Nome beach.

Thanks to the enterprise of Charles Lane a narrow-gauge railroad and telephone line were built in the summer of 1900 from Nome to Anvil Creek. This made the richest claims readily accessible. One of the most important discoveries of the year was the finding of high gravels containing gold on the divide between Anvil and Dexter. This, like the finding of the elevated beaches, had been forecast by Schrader and me on the basis of the geologic examinations made the year before. On the whole, considering the unfortunate legal complications and the burden of such a large horde of inexperienced men, the result of the summer's work was not bad. Gold was mined to the value of $4,750,000. Some of the bolder spirits among the miners had sought for new fields, and as a result gold had been found in the Bluestone district near Port Clarence, in the Solomon River region east of Nome, and in the Kougarok lying in the very heart of the peninsula. Placer gold had also been found in the extreme northeastern part of the peninsula near Kotzebue Sound. In 1899 a mining district had been organized at York near Cape Prince of Wales, but the returns of gold from the mining of 1900 showed nothing of promise; however, in the summer of 1900 I found some stream tin in the York district and this was the beginning of a tin mining industry which, though not large, is the most important on the continent. All this showed that auriferous mineralization was widespread and augured well for the future.

During the height of the excitement there was a good deal of lawlessness at Nome, and life and property were none too secure. A number of robberies occurred on the city streets. During my many years of Alaskan journeys, beginning with the Klondike rush and including visits to every important mining camp, I found Nome in 1900 the only spot in which I had the slightest apprehension of being robbed. At Nome, since I carried a large sum of money, I went armed, as did many others. The reasons for this lawlessness were two: (1) Nome had attracted many of the criminal class who found no difficulty in reaching it, and (2) those federal agencies which were above suspicion were engaged in other work than the handling of the rougher criminals. However, as the crowd melted away in the fall, conditions improved and lawlessness gradually ceased.

The systematic and large mining enterprises begun at Nome in 1901 have been continued to the present day and have been gradually extended over the entire peninsula. The first attempt at improving mining methods was the installing of large pumping plants to elevate water to a high level for purposes of hydraulicking; the plan was economically unsound and was soon abandoned. It is surprising that experienced miners should not have seen the fallacy of such projects: it is evident that the pumping of water, simply to use its force of gravity when running down, is uneconomical. Especially with the high cost of fuel at Nome, such projects were doomed to failure. In 1901 the more rational project of bringing in water by long ditch-lines was started. The credit for the conception and construction of the first long ditch, that to the Kigluaik Mountains, belongs to W. L. Leland and W. M. Davidson, who were among the earliest to obtain a broad grasp of the mining problem. The success of the so-called Miocene Ditch led to a great many ill-advised enterprises at ditch construction. It soon became only too evident that the small precipitation in the Seward Peninsula (15 to 22 inches) and the topography made the region unsuitable for hydraulic mining and that water was scarce even for the necessary sluicing of the gold gravel. But before this discovery, many hundreds of thousands of dollars had been wasted on ditch construction.

Among the early enterprises were some small gold dredges. Some of these were successful as early as 1903, but the real beginning of this form of mining was a large dredge installed by Leland on the Solomon River in 1904. Since then dredging has greatly increased; in 1914, 22 of these great excavators were operated and recovered gold to the value of $2,400,000. Since that year, however, mining on Seward Peninsula has been on the decline for reasons partly local, partly world-wide.

As has already been shown, the Geological Survey predicted the finding of ancient and elevated gold-bearing beach lines. The first of these, the so-called "second beach line," was discovered in the winter of 1904-05, and this was followed the next year by the discovery of the "third beach line." The latter was near the base of the hills and hence near the source of the gold; it included, in fact, some of the richest gravels that have been mined on the Seward Peninsula. This last discovery revitalized mining, and during the succeeding four years some $6,000,000 were recovered from this source.

Though for some years placer mining has been on the decline in the Seward Peninsula, there are still large deposits of gold-bearing gravels which are untouched. They await the attention of those who are willing to invest large amounts of capital and to employ experienced engineers who can devise means of exploiting placers of lower gold content than those that have previously been mined.

CHAPTER XXIII

Early Alaska Transportation

THE PERIOD of evolution from man-carried burdens to railroad transport, from raft and dugout to steamboat, is coextensive with the advance of man from savagery to civilization, a period to be measured by many thousands of years. In Alaska, however, the most primitive modes of transport are often found side by side with the most highly developed: the prospector leaving a railroad coach and shouldering his heavy pack becomes a beast of burden, as was the man of the stone age; the tourist may photograph from comfortable steamers the little bark canoe of the Yukon native; a modern ocean steamer anchored at Nome will be visited by the primitive skin boats of the Eskimo.

Less than two decades ago no Alaskan valleys had echoed to the whistle of the locomotive, and a score of its navigable rivers had never felt the rhythmic chug of the steamer. Now there are over 700 miles of railroad in the Territory, and some form of steamboat service is found on nearly all Alaskan rivers. Of the tens of thousands who essayed the heart-breaking task of dragging and carrying their supplies through the passages in the mountainous coastal barrier, there were probably few who could realize that within a few years it would be possible to reach the Yukon by rail in not as many days as they took months for the journey.

Transport is the very essence of frontier life. Progress of industry and settlement are absolutely controlled by the means of transport. The pioneer whose mission is to obtain furs or to harvest rich deposits of placer gold can by hard labor carry out his projects through means of transport of his own development. If, however, other resources are to be utilized, such as the fertility of the soil, beds of coal, deposits of copper and gold veins, and if permanent settlements are to be made and homes to be built, steamboats, railroads, and wagon roads must be provided.

While much the larger part of Alaska is still almost as inaccessible as it was in its earliest history, yet the railroads, the automobile roads already built, and the well-established steamer service have revolutionized the transport system. This fact, and this alone, has made possible the beginnings of a systematic industrial development of the Northland. The relative efficiency and approximate cost of the most important means of transport in Alaska are shown in the following table:

Relative Efficiency of Alaskan Means of Transport

Type	Weight carried	Miles traveled in 24 hours	Approx. cost per ton mile	Notes
Back packing	50 lbs. per man	12	$25.00	Wages $7.50 per day.
Pack horse	200 lbs. per horse	12	12.00	Based on actual chgs.
Dog sled	100 lbs. per dog	15	2.50	Based on actual chgs.
Wagon road	500 lbs. per horse	20	.60	Two-horse team at $20 per day.
Railroad[1]	700 tons per train	300	.08	Frontier railroad.
Canoe or poling boat	1000 lbs. per boat	20	1.50	Two men, wages at $7.50 per day.
River stmrs.	500 tons	250	.05	Average of river steamer freight.

Though the cost figures given in this table are only an approximation, yet they give a measure of the difficulties with which the pioneer who provides his own transport has to contend and show why large industrial advancement is only possible when modern means of transport are available. Historical evidence of this truth is also found in the evolution of Alaskan settlement and industry. Until the Klondike gold was discovered in the 1890's, the only settlements in Alaska of any importance were at tidewater. The great interior contained only a few roving prospectors, and a dozen trading posts on the Yukon and Kuskokwim rivers were the only permanent settlements. The extraordinarily rich gold deposits of the Klondike and later those of Fairbanks, Nome, and other camps made possible certain industrial advancements, but these constituted no permanent prosperity. It is only the construction of railroads and wagon roads which has led to the development of the resources of inland regions other than the rich placers.

When we took over Alaska from Russia, commerce, as has been previously pointed out, was confined to that of the fur trader along the coast and the lower courses of the Yukon and Kuskokwim rivers. The coastal settlements

---

[1] Cf. "Railroad Routes in Alaska," *Report of Alaska Railroad Commission, 62nd Congress, 3rd session, H. R. Doc. 1346,* 1913, pp. 114-130.

were served by a few smaller steamers, and extraneous commerce was by sailing vessels chiefly operating between Sitka and Petropavlovsk on the east shore of Kamchatka. Once a year a ship arrived direct from Kronstadt on the Baltic. The few overland journeys of the Russians were by dog teams, and traffic on the rivers was by skin boats or scows.

The steamers carrying the Commission and the troops to Alaska in 1867 were among the first ocean steamers to be seen in these waters.[2] At this time the steamer, *John L. Stephens,* also made her first voyage from San Francisco to Sitka. This inaugurated a monthly service which was the only communication with Alaska for 20 years, when a semi-monthly service was begun.[3] These vessels ran from San Francisco to Sitka and Wrangell, with occasional stops at other settlements in Southeastern Alaska. After 1871 when the Cassiar gold discovery of British Columbia was made, a field which was reached by the Stikine River route, the Wrangell call became the most important, for this city was then the industrial center of Alaska. It could also be reached by a small vessel operated by the Hudson Bay Company which gave an intermittent service between Victoria and Wrangell.

For over 20 years the traveler who wished to go beyond Sitka had to rely on the occasional vessels of the Revenue Cutter Service or the fur companies, or on the small craft of the fisherman and the small trader, for there was no regular communication with other Alaskan ports. There was no mail service outside of Southeastern Alaska until 1891 when a contract was made to carry mail to Unalaska during the summer months.[4] It fell to the Alaska Commercial Company, which took over the fur trade of the Russian American Company and obtained the first lease on the Seal Islands, to establish communication with Alaskan ports other than those of Southeastern Alaska. The company posts on Cook Inlet, Kodiak, Unalaska, and St. Michael were reached by vessels running to San Francisco. At first small steam schooners were used, later vessels of

---

[2] The Russians had only small coastal vessels driven by steam, their trans-Pacific traffic being all by sailing vessels.

[3] Andrews, C. L., "Marine Disasters of the Alaska Route," *Washington Historical Quarterly,* VII (1916), 24.

[4] In 1878, the entire expenditure for the Alaskan mail service was $18,000, which provided monthly service to Sitka and Wrangell. By 1898, only seven post offices had been established in the Territory. In 1920, there was a total of 159 post offices of all classes.

1,000 tons or more. Early in the 70's a more or less regular communication was established with the principal ports, later developing into a regular carrier service. By 1879 the steamer *St. Paul* was making a seasonal call at St. Michael, and the famous little steamer *Dora* was supplying the ports on the Aleutian and Pribilof islands. Later the steamers running to Kodiak and St. Michael became public carriers, and the same was true of the river steamers on the Yukon.

The *Dora* is perhaps the most famous of Alaska's vessels, and has a record of 40 years of service. At different times she has served as a poacher of seal on the high seas, as a transport for furs and supplies, as a passenger boat, and finally as a fish boat. Originally built as a brig, she was later given steam power and for years plowed the dangerous waters of Bering Sea. From 1891 to 1900, the *Dora* plied between Sitka and the ports to the westward as far as Unalaska. In 1900, she carried the local traffic from St. Michael to Nome and other settlements along the southern coast of Bering Sea. Later, for many years, she was the mail boat between Seward and Alaska Peninsula ports. The *Dora,* in spite of her great age, was always a staunch sea craft and weathered many a fierce gale that carried her hither and yon, for she had little steam power. She has perhaps the record for carrying more passengers with more discomfort than any vessel which ever reached Alaskan waters. (See picture page 418.)

Though the reaching of Alaskan ports in the early history of the Territory presented many vexations, delays, and difficulties, these were the least of the transportation obstacles met with by the pioneer. Once landed with his outfit, he had to make further progress entirely on his own efforts. It was then a question of packing his supplies on his back, building his own boat, or, where conditions favored, making use of dog teams.

Countless generations of Alaskan natives have used the dog for transport, and he is to Alaska what the yak is to India or the llama to Peru. The climatic and topographic features of the Pacific seaboard are not favorable to sledding: the winter snows do not last long enough; and the heavy timbers and steep slopes also make the use of dog teams impractical. But the gently rolling upland region of the interior with its broad flat valleys and lack of thick timber furnished admirable sleigh routes, especially over the smooth surfaces of the many watercourses. The long cold winters also favored sled transportation, the season extending from November to May. The snowfall seldom exceeds three feet, but it remains continuous all winter, a fact which also favored the use of sleds.

Hand sleds have been used as well as dog sleds, and many a gold seeker dragged his heavy sled for hundreds of miles. From 150 to 200 pounds is all a man can pull over an average trail. But in sledding over river or lake ice he can take advantage of fair winds by employing improvised sails of the type used on the upper Yukon during the Klondike rush. The dog sled is, however, the typical mode of transport in inland Alaska as well as for the tundra region of the Bering Sea and Arctic Ocean. Originally there were two rather sharply differentiated types of sled dogs in Alaska, the malemute or Eskimo dog and the "husky" or dog introduced from the Mackenzie valley, probably by the Hudson Bay traders.

The malemute, originally the sled dog of the Bering Sea and Arctic coastal region, is now widely distributed in the interior. The same family of dogs is found along the entire Arctic coast of Canada and in Greenland and has provided the power for most of the sleds of the Arctic explorers. Their short, stocky build, their strong shoulders, their pointed ears and noses, and their gracefully arched tails are familiar to all through the illustrations in narratives of polar adventure. A good-sized malemute will weigh 75 or 80 pounds. The malemute varies in color from almost snow white to black, gray, and mottled.

The husky has longer legs and body than the malemute, is loosely built, and has a dense though shorter coat of fur. His resemblance to a timber wolf is very strong, and he appears to be a much more powerful animal than the malemute. He is more vicious too, but he is nevertheless perhaps the favorite sled dog, especially in the heavy freighting of the interior.

The Yukon Indians also had a dog on the first coming of the white man. It resembled the malemute but was smaller and not so powerful. These dogs, generally called "Siwash," are probably the degenerate offspring of the coastal malemute; and generations of underfeeding and abuse have produced an inferior breed. It is probable that the Athabascans, the true Indians of the interior, got their first knowledge of sled dogs from the Eskimo.

The pure breeds of both malemute and husky are rapidly disappearing along the well-traveled routes by the inbreeding of native with imported stock. Many drivers prefer these cross-breed dogs, the offspring of native dogs and collies, setters, pointers, spaniels, Newfoundlands, and St. Bernards. The pure-bred imported dogs, while more intelligent and tractable than the native animals, have not their endurance and resistance. One of the great faults is the tenderness of their feet on a rough trail. Some of the half-breeds, however, combine the endurance of their native blood with the intelligence and gentleness of their imported ancestors, and these make the most valuable draft animals. A common practice is to use an outside dog as the intelligent leader of a team of more hardy native dogs. The leader, controlled by the commands of the driver, guides the dogs that follow.

Dried salmon is the standard dog food throughout Alaska. It is surprising how much work a dog can perform on a pound and a half of salmon a day. Large dogs engaged in continuous travel should, however, receive from two and a half to three pounds of food a day. They show the greatest endurance when fed a diet of fish and a cereal, such as rice or oatmeal, and bacon or lard at a ratio of one to one and a half; and the best practice is to cook all the food, which, of course, is necessary for the cereal. Dogs are fed only at night, no morning or noon meal being provided. Most of the Indian dogs, and indeed many of those owned by whites, in summer are much undernourished. This makes them most arrant thieves, and every cache of provisions must be carefully barricaded against dogs. Even well-fed sled dogs are not to be trusted and will devour or destroy footwear and even their own harness. The native dogs require no housing in the coldest winter weather and after being fed will curl up and sleep in the snow, even though a blizzard be howling. Their shaggy skins are proof against the mosquito, ever present in summer, but these insects sometimes torture them by stings about the eyes and nose.

There is no standard size for an Alaskan dog team. A prospector may drag a sled loaded with his 200 or 300 pounds of supplies with the aid of a single dog, or a driver may have a team of nine dogs or more. A driving team, however, usually includes not less than five or not more than nine dogs. Much larger teams are sometimes used

THE ALASKAN DOG TEAM

Dogs are widely used for hauling sleds over the snow on cross country trips (left), but they are sometimes also used in a less orthodox fashion such as (right) pulling a wheeled vehicle over the railroad tracks on the Seward Peninsula. Photos by J. B. Mertie.

for heavy freight. There is a known instance of dogs being used for hauling the heavy steel shaft of a gold dredge from Knik, at the head of Cook Inlet, to the Iditarod district, a distance of nearly 500 miles; the route led over a mountain pass in the heart of the Alaska Range and, though the journey was performed under great difficulties, the trip was completed successfully.

Sled dogs are hitched both tandem and in pairs, with an extra leader. For tandem driving, traces are used, and the rig is not unlike that for horses. In pair driving, the traces of each dog are merely hitched to a single tow line. If the dogs are staggered along the tow line, the team can adjust itself to any width of trail. The fan-shaped rig of Greenland, by which each dog is attached to the sled by a separate tow line and the team spreads out radially, is not adapted to narrow trails and is unknown in Alaska. Each dog is fitted with a padded leather collar from which his traces reach back and are attached to the tow line.

Distance of a day's trail for a dog team and weight pulled vary so much, depending on condition of trail, on gradient of course, and on weight and endurance of dogs, that it is difficult to generalize. Where a new trail is being broken and where there are steep gradients, 50 pounds to the dog is an ample load. Indeed, in some cross-country journeys, this load may have to be reduced to 30 or 40 pounds. On the other hand, over a smooth, hard, level trail, strong dogs have been known to drag as much as 300 pounds. It is probably safe to say that a good dog on hard, level trails should haul 100 pounds—that is, about 25 per cent more than his own weight. This load he will not take over 15 or 20 miles a day. Reduce this weight to 50 pounds, and the dog should make 25 miles a day. The famous dog races at Nome have shown that a dog team hauling only the empty sled can average nearly 90 miles a day for five days.[5] The winter mail contracts call, on the average, for a speed of 22 miles a day; but the carriers frequently exceed this, runs of over 40 miles a day having been recorded. The mail carriers haul from 50 to 75 pounds of weight per dog.

Many long journeys have been made over well-beaten trails by good "dog mushers" where a day's average travel was 25 miles. This, however, is hard work for the driver as well as the dogs. The driver seldom rides on the sled, except on down grades, but runs behind, guiding and steadying it by the handle bars. Where a new trail has to be broken through new snow, a man on snowshoes goes in advance of the team.

The dog sleds are eight to 12 feet long and about 20 to 24 inches wide. They are strong, built of hickory or oak, and made not too rigid. A certain looseness and pliability allow the runners to follow the tracks. Small sleds weigh about 75 pounds, large ones nearly 200. For freighting, flat sleds are used, sometimes with a "gee pole" for guiding at the front where the driver helps haul the load, sometimes with the gee pole at the rear. Travel sleds are made with a basket superstructure and two handles at the rear. These are used by the driver to guide the sled, and when opportunity offers he steps on the rear of the sled for short rides.

Dogs are also used in summer to a limited extent as pack animals by both Eskimo and Indian, and occasionally a lone prospector will be found to make a similar use of them. A dog will pack 20 or 30, even 40, pounds. Unless thoroughly broken, these dogs are difficult to control, and one of their favorite tricks is to lie down in water, pack and all.

Back packing is the most primitive and laborious mode of transport and is resorted to only when all other means fail. As an actual means of forwarding supplies, it is used only between navigable waters, namely on portages.

[5] A speed of nine miles an hour for four hours has been recorded in some of the dog races.

A portage is chosen, so far as circumstances permit, so as to afford firm footing and easy grades. The Chilkoot Pass is the most famous portage in the world, for thousands of tons of supplies have been carried across it. It lies some 20 miles from and 3,100 feet above tidewater; and, as has been indicated earlier, the approach to it, though easy enough at first, becomes steep and difficult. To the place called the "Scales" sledding was feasible; but from here on a steep climb to the summit had to be made, and transport was on the backs of men. This portage provided the test that winnowed out the strong from the weak, the stout-hearted from the failures. The average man found, at least at the start, that 50 pounds was a heavy load up the steep ascent; many learned later to carry 100 pounds, though such a burden was a serious strain on the heart and some whose determination was greater than their strength succumbed under it. Over an ordinary portage with hard trail and no grade, most physically strong men will carry 100 pounds; and experienced packers will take 150 or even 200 pounds on a cross-country trip, through the hills and mountains. But relatively few will carry more than 50 pounds, and that amount not over 15 miles a day.

In the Pacific seaboard region of Alaska the best grasslands are along the shores of Cook Inlet, on the Alaska Peninsula, and on Kodiak Island. But these areas are by no means all the grazing lands, and grass is sufficiently abundant elsewhere to make the use of horses feasible for summer journeys. There is much good pasturage in the Susitna valley, especially on its western margin in the Yentna River basin. The Copper River has less grazing land in its basin, but it suffices for the traveler. Summer pastures sufficient for pack train are widely distributed in the great inland region beyond the Pacific ranges and northward as far as the Arctic Mountains which divide the Yukon waters from those flowing northward into the Arctic Ocean. Some splendid grasslands are found in this region, for example along the Tanana and its tributaries. In other places again, such as north of the Yukon, the grass is scant, but patches sufficient for a pack train can usually be found at distances not exceeding a day's march. Horses have been used by the Geological Survey as far north as the Arctic divide, and the International Boundary Commission took a pack train all the way to the Arctic Ocean along the 141st meridian, north of the Porcupine

River. As Bering Sea is approached, nutritious grass becomes scanter and is confined chiefly to the highlands, the extensive lowlands being chiefly covered with moss and marsh grass. In this region only careful planning and search for pasture will permit the use of pack horses. Much the same is true of Seward Peninsula, though the Geological Survey expeditions have traversed its entire area with pack trains. There is some grassland even in the Arctic Slope Region of Alaska, but not in sufficient abundance to make long pack train trips feasible. It is probably safe to estimate that there are in Alaska some 300,000 square miles in which the grass is sufficiently abundant to permit the use of a pack train.

Horses were brought to the Yukon as early as 1885, but they were relatively little used until the Klondike rush. The first long pack train trip in Alaska was that made in 1891 by E. J. Glave and Jack Dalton when they went from the coast into the Lake Kluane region, previously discussed in Chapter XVI. The Army explorations of 1898 were made in part with pack horses, and in 1899 the Geological Survey first used horses. That summer W. J. Peters and I made the journey from Haines in Southeastern Alaska to Eagle on the Yukon, a distance of nearly 600 miles, that has already been referred to (Chapter XVI). In 1902, I made what is perhaps the longest pack horse journey ever accomplished in Alaska, from Cook Inlet, round the base of Mount McKinley, and on to the Yukon at Rampart. In 105 days the pack train traveled some 800 miles with the personnel going entirely on foot. At the start the horses were each loaded with 250 pound sacks; but, as provisions were consumed at the rate of about 21 pounds a day, the packs gradually became lighter. On the other hand, some of the least strong of the horses were so weakened by the arduous trail and by the insect pest that they had to be shot before the journey was half over; at the end of the trip only nine of the original 20 animals remained.

During such journeys the animals find their food in the native grasses which are very nourishing. There is in Alaska, however, no natural curing of grasses such as takes place in the arid states of the West. When frost comes, about the middle of September, the horse feed is practically ruined. Therefore, the use of pack horses in Alaska is pretty much limited to the season from June 1 to the middle of September. By feeding grain one can considerably extend the season, but as a horse will eat up his own load in 10 or 15 days such use is impractical for long journeys.

Horse sleds, like pack animals, only came into general use after the Klondike discovery. Their efficient use is limited to roads which must be at least passable after the winter snow comes. In the early days there was much horse sledding over the ice of the Yukon and other rivers. But even this implies the breaking of a trail, and the use of horse sleds is now limited to established winter roads. Before good sled roads were available, many so-called "double enders" were in use. These are small sleds, not unlike the freight sleds pulled by dogs, that are drawn by a single horse or by two driven tandem.

Before trails passable for sleds were established, a mode of transport called "raw hiding" was sometimes resorted to. In this, freight was securely lashed into bales which were encased in raw hides to which the traces of horses were attached. Such bales could be dragged over any trail, and even over bare ground, on which the horse could find footing, for it was of no importance which side of the load was on top. It was, of course, on account of the friction, a very inefficient use of horse power and little, if any, improvement over the back load. Now, where roads have been built or other good sledding conditions are found, winter horse freighting is by the familiar double- or bob-sled, known in all the northern states.

During the early years of the introduction of reindeer into Alaska much was said about their use for transport. It was pointed out that the advantages of the reindeer over the dog were that he found his own food and could be used as pack animal in the summer and sled puller in the winter. The enormous use of reindeer transport in Siberia appeared fully to justify these contentions, yet after 30 years of reindeer breeding in Alaska their use in transport is almost negligible. In Siberia a sled load of 270 to 300 pounds is easily hauled for long distances by the reindeer. But these are the large Tungus animals which average at least a third larger than the Alaskan reindeer, are used as saddle animals, and will carry a rider even through deep, soft snow; as pack animals they will carry from 100 to 200 pounds. It is difficult to understand why a similar use in Alaska has met with such indifferent success. In the earlier days of the reindeer experiments Laplanders were chiefly used for training both the reindeer themselves and the Eskimos in their use. This was undoubtdly, as can now be seen, a mistake. The Laplander had both the ignorance and the lack of adaptability to a new environment inherent to his semi-civilized state. He was dealing with a Siberian animal much wilder than the more highly domesticated one of his own land. The small "pulka" or Lapland sled, fashioned out of half a log and rounded at the bottom, while making a good passenger vehicle, was not adapted to hauling freight; and the freight sled with runners was new to him. Moreover, in Lapland the reindeer was chiefly used to carry men and light loads, and there was no use of the animal to transport heavy freight for long distances, such as had been done in Siberia for many generations. As a means of domesticating the Alaskan reindeer and of training the natives in their use, the Laplander was almost a complete failure.

Reindeer transport had, however, a more thorough test by some of the mail contractors. These men with a keen idea to business fully realized that if the reindeer could be substituted for dogs there would be a material profit in the change. The reindeer subsists on food of his own finding, and it costs $75 to $100 a year to feed a dog. After a period of careful test by men who had the initiative of the frontiersman, the experiment of substituting reindeer for dogs as mail carriers was on all but a very few routes entirely abandoned.

There are some evident reasons why the reindeer could not be substituted for the dog. Most of the established dog team routes are along the large waterways, and in the great inland regions of Alaska the lichen or reindeer moss grows only on the highlands above timber line. Obviously the sled reindeer could not be driven to the highlands to obtain its pasture. Local climatic conditions were also an obstacle. A thaw followed by a freeze might cover the pastures with ice and make the lichens unavailable to the reindeer. In contrast to this, the general use of dog teams made the furnishing of dried salmon for dog feed a well-established industry along the watercourses. The reindeer will eat little except its regular food of lichens, but the dog is omnivorous in its appetite. It should be added, however, that the great tundra areas of Bering

Sea and of northern Alaska are the natural home of the reindeer. The barren ground region has as yet but little population save for the native whose mode of life has long been adapted to the use of dogs. Hence the substitution of the reindeer can only be brought about very gradually; the change of a people from a nomadic to a pastoral life must be a work of generations.

The following description by Jarvis illustrates the use of reindeer as sled animals:[6]

> All hands must be ready at the same time when starting a deer train, for, just as soon as the animals of the head team start, they are all off with a jump, and for a short time keep up a very high rate of speed. If one is not quick in jumping and holding on to his sled, he is likely either to lose his team or be dragged along in the snow. They soon come down to a moderate gait, however, and finally drop into a walk when tired. They are harnessed with a well-fitting collar of two flat pieces of wood, from which a trace goes back on each side to the ends of a breast or single tree that fits under the body. From the center of this a single trace runs back to the sled either between or to one side of the hind legs. In the wake of the legs this trace is protected with soft fur, or the skin will soon be worn through with the constant chafing. Generally there is a single line made fast to the left side of a halter and with this the animal is to be guided and held in check; but this line must be kept slack and on only when the deer is to be guided or stopped. By pulling hard on this line, the weight of the sled comes on the head and the animal is soon brought to a standstill, though often this is only accomplished after he has gone in a circle several times and you and the sleds are in a general mix-up. No whip is used and none should be, for the deer are very timid and easily frightened and once gotten in that state are hard to quiet and control. A little tugging on the lines will generally start them off even when they balk. The sleds in use are very low and wide with very broad runners.

During the past decade much advance has been made in the training of sled deer by the Eskimo, mainly because of the supervision and encouragement of W. T. Lopp and his assistants of the Alaska Reindeer Service. The use of sled deer is gradually becoming a part of the industrial life of the Eskimo, and the more intelligent herders are showing an increasing facility in handling them. The superintendents of the Alaska Native School and the Reindeer Service are making much use of reindeer in their winter journeys of inspection. The journeys of one winter using reindeer aggregated 1,300 miles, and the average normal day's travel was 28 miles. It is also worthy of note

[6] Jarvis, D. H., *The Cruise of the U.S. Revenue Cutter* Bear *and the Overland Relief Expedition,* Washington, D.C., 1899, p. 47.

that native reindeer races have established a record of ten miles in 27 minutes, 20 seconds and that the pulling capacity of a single deer is 1,600 pounds for a distance of 250 yards. A sled reindeer should make 25 miles a day for a journey of 100 miles or so, hauling the driver and 50 or 75 pounds, perhaps 300 pounds in all. The reindeer tire easily in soft snow and must then be frequently rested.

The argument for the use of reindeer is presented by Carl O. Lind of the Alaska Reindeer Service:[7]

> Our trip, which demanded 45 days for its accomplishment, was successfully done before Christmas. In all we traveled about 1,000 miles under adverse conditions, and four out of seven deer made the return trip with us, hauling 100 to 200 pounds. If dogs had been used they could not have hauled their own provisions for the time, and much less anything for the drivers. The deer hauled the whole load of the driver, their own provisions being picked up by themselves whenever we stopped. No shelter was needed. When the most furious wind sweeps its path, the deer simply faces it with an open mouth and with an expression of satisfaction and joy. . . . It goes uphill and downhill alike. Trail or no trail, it will haul its 200 pounds or more day after day; yes, week after week.

The argument against the use of reindeer has been presented by the late Archdeacon Stuck:[8]

> There is not a dog less in Alaska because of the reindeer. . . . Speaking broadly, the reindeer is a stupid, unwieldy, intractable brute, not comparing a moment with the dog in intelligence or adaptability. . . . The rein with which he is driven is a rope tied around one of his horns. He has no cognizance of "gee" and "haw," nor of any other vocal direction, but must be yanked hither and thither with the rope by main force; while to stop him in his mad career once he is started it is often necessary to throw him with the rope.

Some use of Alaskan reindeer as pack animals has been made, but this mode of employment is not yet well developed. The large Siberian reindeer will carry 100 to 150 pounds, but the smaller animal of Alaska will on the average probably not carry over 50 pounds. The burden is carried in cloth hampers hung over the animals and made secure by a lashing going over the back and around the animal's belly. Unless thoroughly broken, the pack-bearing animal must be led. There appears to be no question that the pack reindeer will find a use in the tundra regions where there is not enough grass to support horses. Its employment

---

[7] Jackson, Sheldon, *14th Annual Report on the Introduction of Domestic Reindeer into Alaska*, Washington, D.C., 1906, pp. 104-105.

[8] Stuck, Hudson, *Ten Thousand Miles with a Dog Sled*, New York, 1914, p. 402, p. 407.

on long journeys has not been tested. Difficulties of herding when the deer are in pasture present themselves, and as yet but few reindeer have been broken to the pack.

The evidence in hand shows that the Eskimo reindeer has clearly demonstrated the fact of the utility of the sled reindeer to his mode of life. For his purpose the deer is no doubt more suitable than the dog, for his life is spent in the tundra region, where reindeer pastures are usually abundant. On the other hand, experience up to the present has shown that the needs of winter transport for the whites can better be served by the dog and the horse than by the reindeer. As has already been suggested, the value of the reindeer to both native and white as a source of meat and hides has been fully demonstrated.

It is roughly estimated that about 480,000 square miles of Alaska's area are, by virtue of the physical condition, suited for winter dog transport. Of this area, about 220,000 square miles, or less than half, have the physical condition that makes the use of reindeer practical. This gives a rough measure of the relative value of the two draft animals; yet, as has been shown, there are other factors which must be given consideration in making this comparison.

Water transportation has been the saviour of the province. Without Alaska's enormous coast line, aggregating over 20,000 miles, and her extensive river systems that give access, though in part only with great difficulties, to the most remote parts of the Territory, industrial advancement would have been impossible. The Alaskan Yukon and Kuskokwim basins include upwards of 5,000 miles of waters navigable for river steamers. It is these great arteries of commerce that have served chiefly in the past to open up the interior to settlement.

Long before any steamers had navigated these rivers, these waters had been much used for transportation in various ways. The inland natives of Alaska were, it is true, a land folk who made relatively little use of the rivers. Their only boat was a small bark canoe, too frail and light to be used for transport. Downstream journeys were made by crude rafts and occasionally by a hastily improvised skin boat made by the stretching of the hide of a moose or caribou over an ill-constructed framework. They had, however, no means of transportation upstream, except the frail canoes which could be pushed against only a slight current. As has already been shown, the

Russians were indifferent boatmen, and their clumsy river craft were but ill-adapted to upstream navigation. The first good river boats in Alaska were those introduced by the Hudson Bay voyageurs whose boats included both the double pointed bateaux, using both oars and poles as water power, and the bark canoes.

There were, as has been previously pointed out, no trees on the Yukon large enough for dugouts and, because of the small size of the white or canoe birch trees, no possibility for making practical large bark canoes. Therefore, the Yukon pioneers were forced to provide boats built of whipsawed lumber. This common type was a flat-bottomed boat, sharply pointed at the bow and with a rather narrow stern, of the general type of a dory, and some 18 to 24 feet long. Later the Yukon poling boat was devised. This was a long, narrow, tapering craft, admirably adapted to upstream journeys, against swift current and in shallow water. The poling boat was 20 to 30 feet long, and at

NATIVE TRANSPORTATION METHODS ON WATER

Upper left: Eskimo "tracking," photo by A. H. Brooks; upper right: Eskimo in kayak, photo by A. H. Brooks; lower left: Indians in birch bark canoe, photo by W. C. Mendenhall; lower right: Indian propelling canoe with hand push poles, photo by A. G. Maddren.

midship its bottom measured from 12 to 20 inches, with tapering sides, giving it two and a half to three feet of beam at the gunwale. Though tapering rapidly at both ends, it is usually built with snub nose at both bow and stern. The Yukon poling boat was no doubt an adaptation of similar types of craft long used on the western rivers. Up to the time of the use of steamers, the Ohio River keel-boats, said to have been first used in 1793, with their expert polers were the only crafts which would go up-stream. These Ohio River boats were 50 feet long, but only 12 to 15 feet wide, and were propelled by 10 polemen. Their form and mode of use were identical with the Mississippi craft.

It is surprising with what facility good polemen can push a loaded boat of this type up swift streams and with barely enough depth of water to float the craft. With fair conditions two good men could take a ton of supplies up-stream at the rate of 10 to 20 miles a day, and with a lighter load 30 miles a day were not uncommon. In the early days of Yukon mining it was not infrequent for a party of men to make the journey from Fortymile to Lake Lindeman, the head of boat navigation, a distance of nearly 600 miles, in a month, an average speed of nearly 20 miles a day. This included the time spent in making the difficult portage around White Horse Rapids and Miles Canyon, and also the easy navigation of Laberge and other lakes of the upper Lewes River.

In these upstream journeys propulsion by poling was varied by "tracking." This consisted in dragging the boat by lines of men walking on the shore. By attaching two lines to the boat, the men can readily steer it from the shore; and if good footing can be obtained, they can drag half a ton or more of supplies upstream at the rate of ten miles or more a day. Where the stream is shallow and the current swift, much wading is usually necessary to ease the boat over the bars. Where there are steep-cut banks and the water is too deep to pole, the boat must be pulled by the bushes and trees along the banks. This method of proplusion, formerly called "bushwhacking" on the Ohio River, is slow and tedious; and a whole day may be consumed to advance a few miles. It is not uncommon to use dogs as draft animals in taking boats up streams.

It was the Canadian explorers like William Ogilvie who first introduced the Peterborough canoes on the Yukon,

TRANSPORTATION ON STREAMS

Early trail blazers found Alaska's streams both a help and a hindrance. Pack trains had to swim them (upper left); men had to cross them on rafts (upper right) and to portage from one to another (lower left). But the Peterborough canoe (lower right) made them good highways. Photos on right by A. H. Brooks, on left by J. B. Mertie.

and later this craft was much used by the Northwest Mounted Police. Just as the poling boat has been the craft of the prospector, so the canoe has been the craft of the explorer. In general modeled after the Ojibway bark canoe, the Peterborough is an admirable swift water boat, carries a large cargo, and is so light that it can be portaged a long distance. This model is built in sizes varying from 17 to 24 feet in length with a beam of 40 to 52 inches. The favorite canoe of the explorer is about 19 feet long and 46 inches wide. Such a boat built of cedar will, when dry, weigh about 120 pounds and in an emergency can be packed by a single man across a portage. It will safely carry a cargo of half a ton besides a crew of two or three men. With a fair wind it makes a fairly good sailing craft. When it is equipped with six foot paddles, ten foot poles, and good tracking lines, there are no inland waters navigable to any other craft on which a Peterborough canoe can not be used. I have used a Peterborough provided with a small coaming and with canvas air-tight compartments in fairly heavy weather on Bering Sea. In river navigation, punctures by snags or rocks of thin cedar planking are not uncommon, but these are quickly and permanently repaired by strips carried for the purpose. The Geological Survey in the course of its explorations and investigations in Alaska has used these canoes on about 15,000 miles of the watercourses of Alaska. During the Klondike rush, when every type of craft was used, folding canoes and boats were not uncommon. Though easier to portage than Peterboroughs, they are useless for upstream work, being too flimsy to buck a current. They have found use in explorations, because they can be packed on a horse and transported overland and they are a necessity for cruising rivers too deep to ford, the banks of which are untimbered.

The introduction of the light portable gas engine has greatly modified Alaskan water travel. Many prospectors avoid the labor of poling and tracking by its use. In shallow rivers air propellors have been successfully used. Nearly every Yukon Indian now has some sort of gas boat to visit his fish wheels and to travel from place to place.

Coastal navigation has also been completely revolutionized during the past two decades by the gas engines. Previous to 1900, the prospector and the fisherman traveled chiefly in crafts propelled by sail and oars, but now the use of power boats is almost universal. The favorite craft is the Columbia River fishing boat, 20 to 30 feet long, of the lifeboat type, and admirable for heavy weather. These, formerly propelled solely by sail and oars, are now equipped with economical heavyweight gas engines.

The Western Union Telegraph exploring expeditions had for part of their project the steam navigation of the Yukon River. Two flat-bottomed boats about 60 feet long, the *Wilder* and the *Lizzie Horner*, were shipped to St. Michael in 1866, but neither succeeded in entering the mouth of the Yukon. Navigation of the Yukon continued by small boat until the newly organized Alaska Commercial Company brought in its first small steamer, the *Yukon*. This boat was 50 feet long with 12-foot beams, was equipped with two engines, and drew when loaded 18 inches of water; it was built by John W. Gates of San Francisco. On July 4, 1869, with Captain Benjamin Hall as master and John R. Forbes as engineer, the *Yukon* left St. Michael and 27

TRANSPORTATION BY BOAT

Upper: "S.S. Scotia" taking on wood on Taku Arm, photo by Sidney Paige; center: The "Dora," photo by D. F. Higgins; lower: The "Sarah" loaded with Fairbanks stampeders, photo by L. M. Prindle.

days later arrived at Fort Yukon, having completed the first steam navigation of the lower 1,000 miles of the Yukon River. Within the next ten years three other small steamers were brought to the Yukon and navigated the river up as far as Fort Selkirk,[9] 1,700 miles from Bering Sea. These boats were chiefly used in the fur trade, but they also supplied the few prospectors then in the region.

With the influx of miners after the discovery of gold in the Fortymile district, a larger vessel was demanded. In 1889, the Alaska Commercial Company built the *Arctic*,[10] 140 feet in length with a 28-foot beam. By this time the annual freight taken up the Yukon was largely the trading goods and provisions to supply the Alaska Commercial Company posts. Freight charges to the upper river were $50 a ton, passenger rates $150. The freight rates were very reasonable, and the passenger rates affected but few of the miners, who arrived mostly by the Chilkoot Pass route. In 1892, the North American Trading and Transportation Company entered the Yukon as a rival in fur trade and transportation. Their first boat, the *Portner B. Ware,* of about the same size as the *Arctic,* ascended the Yukon for some 200 miles in September, but was frozen in before it reached the mining camps. The organization of this company was due to the energy of J. J. Healy, a pioneer Alaska fur trader. He long maintained a trading post at Dyea, the gateway of Chilkoot Pass, and from information obtained from the miners became convinced of the industrial importance of the Yukon. As the managing head of a great commercial company, he was a commanding figure on the Yukon during the Klondike days, but he died a pauper in 1910.

With the Klondike rush came an enormous expansion of Yukon River traffic. In 1898 and 1899 between 75 and 100 steam-driven vessels were plowing the muddy waters of the great river and its tributaries. In 1900, five transportation companies were operating 33 river boats on the Alaskan Yukon, and a dozen steamboats were navigating the Canadian waters above. There is no record of the traffic during the height of the Klondike travel; but in 1901, when it had greatly subsided, 35 boats carried 25,000 tons of freight up the Yukon, and the passenger traffic

[9] The first trip above Fort Yukon, made in 1875, ascended the Yukon as far as the site of Fort Reliance, about six miles below Dawson.

[10] The *Arctic* brought the first cargo of provisions to the then newly-discovered Klondike in the fall of 1896, but soon after was caught in the ice and wrecked.

upstream and downstream aggregated 2,500 persons. This was at a time when the building of the White Pass & Yukon Railroad had, by establishing a through freight and passenger service from Skagway, greatly reduced the traffic on the lower river. The tariffs were in 1901 $85 a ton for freight and $125 a passenger, from St. Michael to Dawson.

During this period large packets were built for the Yukon service[11] comparable to those used on the Mississippi. Their masters and pilots were recruited from the Mississippi and Columbia rivermen, the former having the prestige of having operated large boats, the latter being more experienced in handling steamers in swift water. The larger steamers had lengths of 222 feet, beams of 42 feet, depths of six feet, and horsepower of 1,000. For many years they were all wood burners, for the several attempts to use the local lignitic coal were unsuccessful.[12] In 1906, many of the boats were changed to oil burners, the petroleum being brought from California. These large packets proved to be uneconomical, and there has been a gradual change to smaller boats of from 400 to 600 tons which could be efficiently used on the small tributaries of the Yukon. With the decrease of gold mining, steamer traffic has already decreased. In 1919, only nine steamers were operated in the Alaskan Yukon, carrying a total of less than 10,000 tons of freight.

In general, the Yukon is open to navigation from June until October. The ice-free season, however, varies in different parts of the basin. Above Dawson, the river is usually clear of ice soon after the middle of May, and steamers can be operated well into October. Navigation on the lower Yukon is possible from the last week in May until the end of September. The ice, however, often does not go out of the Yukon delta until July, and the river there may be frozen again by the middle of September. One reason for the high freight rate on the Yukon is that the expensive equipment and, to a certain extent, the personnel too are idle for eight to nine months in the year. All the profits must be made during the short season of navigation.

Nothing emphasizes the slow growth of means of transportation in Alaska more than the history of its road con-

[11] Gross tonnage, 800 to 1,211.

[12] During the Klondike days wood for steamers was sold at $15 and $25 a cord, but the more normal price is $4 to $8.

EARLY ROADS, I

These roads were frequently rather crude affairs as is shown by the wagon road (left) up Gold Creek and that to the Jualin Mine in the Berners Bay district (right). Photos by C. W. Wright.

struction. The Russians during nearly a century of occupation built less than five miles of wagon road in their American possessions. During the next 30 years, up to the time of the Klondike gold discovery, we added barely another five miles to the total length of wagon road. At the 50th anniversary of the annexation of Alaska, there were only 980 miles[13] of wagon road in the Territory, an area of nearly 600,000 square miles and a population then of nearly 70,000. At this time, the Government had spent a total of $3,970,000 on road and trail construction in Alaska, of which $1,700,000 had been collected by direct local taxes. Alaska had in turn produced minerals, fish, and fur up to a total value of $800,000,000. It is questionable whether any other one country in the world has shown such a notable industrial advancement with such a scant outlay of public funds for transportation facilities.[14]

A little construction and some improvement of roads at Sitka were done by the military authorities between 1867 and 1877, but beyond this bit there was no building of roads until after the discovery of the Juneau gold. In 1882, a horse trail was built by the miners for two miles up Gold Creek, and later this was changed to a wagon road which, by 1888, had been extended into the Silver Bow basin. The building of this road in part through a steep-walled valley was an expensive undertaking and all of it was paid for by local mining industry. In 1898, a law was passed authorizing the construction and maintenance of toll roads and bridges in Alaska,[15] a privilege

[13] In addition, there were 620 miles of winter sled road and 290 miles of improved trail.

[14] Government railroad construction at this time was beginning to rectify matters.

[15] The law provided that the toll rates must be approved by the Secretary of the Interior.

EARLY ROADS, II

Backpacking man and dogs (left, photographer unknown) hike along Fairbanks-Valdez trail; they will probably cross an old-fashioned bridge like that shown on the right (photo by F. H. Moffit).

of which, however, few availed themselves. The Chilkat Indians had long regarded the Chilkoot Pass trail as a toll road owned by them, a monopoly which the pioneer miners soon disregarded and claimed the right of carrying their own burdens over it without charge. When the Klondike rush started, a wagon road was constructed from tidewater at Dyea for eight miles to the entrance of the canyon, and during the height of the travel it carried on a brisk business.

In the spring of 1898 George A. Bracket completed 15 miles of wagon road from Skagway to the base of the final steep 1,000 foot climb leading to the summit of the White Pass. This road traversed the heavily timbered flat of Skagway River for some five miles, and beyond led along the precipitous slopes of a rocky defile. At that time the Bracket road was the longest and most difficult piece of highway construction that had been attempted in Alaska. Remnants of this pioneer road are still visible from the White Pass & Yukon Railroad where they can be seen clinging to the sides of precipitous cliffs. Bracket's troubles, however, did not end with the building of the road, for he found it difficult to collect the toll of $20 a ton to which he was legally entitled. Many Klondikers could see no reason for paying toll on a route through which they had had a sled trail before the building of the road. Some of the toll collectors were roughly handled. But the controversy over toll was short-lived, for by May of 1898 the railroad surveyors had arrived and the railroad company bought the wagon road,[16] both for the prevention of competition in the haulage of freight and for hauling use in construction.

Jack Dalton, in 1898, built a horse trail from Pyramid

[16] The price paid for the wagon road was $40,000.

Harbor on Lynn Canal to the top of the pass at the head of Klehini River. This opened up a route into the interior well suited for horses and cattle which Dalton had explored. No trail work was necessary beyond the pass where the country was open. Dalton himself drove in several herd of beef cattle and horses, reaching the Yukon either at Five Finger Rapids or at Fort Selkirk at the mouth of the Pelly. The Dalton trail was the best pack horse route into the interior, but it was not much used even before the completion of the railroad and the venture was not a financial success.

In addition to the above, a few toll bridges have been built at various places in Alaska. On the whole, however, the toll road and bridge act of 1898 was entirely ineffective in opening up Alaska.

In 1904, Congress made a second attempt to provide roads for Alaska without appropriating any funds. This effort compelled the United States commissioners to appoint a road overseer in each district, who was to receive the magnificent wage of $4 a day, the average wage at that time being $6 to $10 a day. Recognizing that the poor overseers would be at a financial loss for every day of employment, the law specified that they were to be paid for only ten days in the year. In this time these philanthropists were not only to construct roads but also to notify every man in their district that they must give two days' work to road building each year, or in lieu thereof to pay a head tax of $8. This law was evidently framed on the ancient statutes of many of the Eastern states, by which road building was made the duty of every citizen and a knowledge of road engineering was recognized to be inborn in every American. For generations this ancient fallacy hampered the development of good roads, and it was done away with only after the inauguration of modern highway construction.

No fault can be found with the principle of the Alaska Road Act of 1904, of throwing the burden of road construction on the Territory. But this should have been done by a proper system of local taxes, and the funds collected spent by qualified engineers. In Canadian territory, this was recognized from the start, and the royalty collected on the Klondike paid for the excellent system of highways in the Yukon Territory. The Alaskan law was almost futile in providing means of communication, though a few local sled roads and trails were improved, most of which were badly located and poorly constructed.

The extensive federal exploration of Alaska inaugurated in 1898, chiefly by the Geological Survey and, for the first few years, by the Army, included many long journeys. Many of these exploring expeditions used horses and, incidental to their advance, many miles of rough trail were established. These were subsequently followed by others and, in lieu of better trails, became established as routes of travel. A few are still in use, and we still hear of the "Gem Trail" and the "Survey" and "Army" trails. Far more important than these trails to betterment of means of communication were the maps and reports which resulted from the work of these expeditions. All had as part of their mission the location of possible routes for wagon roads and railroads. The actual areal mapping fell chiefly to the Geological Survey which, before the epoch of road and railroad construction that began some five years later was inaugurated, had made contoured reconnaissance maps of nearly all the routes which were subsequently chosen or considered for wagon roads or railroads. This work admirably furnishes conclusive proof of the value of topographic maps. The cost of the areal topographic surveys of Alaska has been far less than it would have been had it been necessary to carry out explorations for every road and railroad project. These maps gave information on the best general route, and it was only necessary for the engineer to make his location survey.

Many of the reports of this exploring expedition made more or less definite recommendations for road and trail construction. For example, in 1903, incidental to the discussion of the future of placer mining,[17] I recommended that a million dollars be spent in building wagon roads to the inland placer camps. The recommendation included a road from Valdez to Eagle or Fairbanks as a main highway and many other local roads. The opinion was then expressed that several of the Yukon gold camps had probably already spent more money in the transport of supplies than the cost of wagon roads. This was probably an exaggeration, but that such a generous project for wagon roads was sound is proved by the fact that most of those

[17] Brooks, Alfred H., "Placer Mining in Alaska," *United States Geological Survey Bulletin, No. 225*, Washington, D.C., 1904, pp. 56-57.

it included have, during the 20 years that have since elapsed, been completed or are under construction.[18]

Though the trails established by these early exploring expeditions were of use to the prospector, they were little more than cuts through the timber, with here and there some small bridges. The only actual trail construction by such an expedition was that built under the direction of Major W. R. Abercrombie from Valdez inland. Abercrombie, commanding the Copper River expedition of the U.S. Army, landed at Valdez in the spring of 1898. His parties, as already noted in Chapter XVI, subsequently made their way inland over the difficult and dangerous Valdez Glacier route and also explored other passes through the coastal mountain barrier. Abercrombie recommended that a military trail be built inland from Valdez by a route which would avoid the glacier. This was authorized in 1899, and during the summer Abercrombie constructed a horse trail to the summit of Thompson Pass, thus surmounting the most serious obstacle to inland travel. During the following five years a crude pack trail was built through to Eagle on the Yukon, under appropriations granted by the War Department. Good service was rendered the pioneers by this trail, but its construction is chiefly significant in being a forerunner of the splendid work done by the Army in road construction in Alaska.

Since the law of 1904 was found futile in opening up Alaska, a new statute was enacted in 1906. This provided for an Alaska Road Commission of three Army officers, one to be detailed from the Corps of Engineers. This board was authorized to construct and maintain military and post roads, bridges, and trails from funds collected by the existing license taxes outside of incorporated towns. Thirty per cent of these taxes was reserved for maintenance of schools for whites and 25 per cent for care of the insane; the remainder was to be used for road construction and to this was added a direct appropriation of $150,000. This law marked the real beginning of road construction in Alaska, and its beneficial effects have been felt throughout the Territory ever since its enactment.

The original act left but little to be desired. Its immediate and continued success, however, was almost entirely due

[18] It is worthy of note that C. W. Purington, then of the Geological Survey, was the first to present definite estimates of the cost of road construction in Alaska and to substantiate by actual figures their need to the placer mining industry. See his "Roads and Road Building in Alaska," *Ibid., No. 263*, 1905, pp. 217-228.

to the fact that Brigadier General (then Major) Wilds P. Richardson, a man of exceptional executive ability, was chosen to be president of the board and continued in this office until 1917 when he was recalled for military duty. At the time of his detail, General Richardson had had eight years of almost continuous service in the Territory, during which time he had pioneered on the Yukon, built trails, and established Army posts. These duties had given him a broad knowledge of Alaska and her people, and his duties in road location and construction soon made him the leading authority on the subject of Alaskan transportation. His duties and responsibilities were arduous, for not only had he to carry on road building under very adverse physical conditions but also he had to meet constant criticisms from local residents who could not realize that an annual grant of only a few hundred thousand dollars could not begin to meet the needs for wagon roads.

Richardson was quick to grasp that the crux of the transportation problem was to establish a trunk line of communication between open waters on the Pacific and the inland region. He, therefore, almost at once established a sled road between Valdez on the coast and Fairbanks, the largest settlement in the interior, a distance of 370 miles. Year by year this route was improved, and it passed by successive stages from dog trail to sled road to wagon road and finally to a fair automobile road. For years this was a main artery of mail routes and passenger trail into the interior, and it has only recently been superseded by the completion of the government railroad. Richardson's vision extended even further, for he conceived the bold project of an extension of this road through to Nome, thus giving an overland route to this remote community. This larger project he unfortunately could not carry out because of lack of funds. In addition to the main highway, now known appropriately as the Richardson Road, many local roads and trails were also built.

Richardson's many years of service devoted to the interests of Alaska are one of the outstanding features of federal administration of Territorial affairs. After his return to military duty, his work was most efficiently continued by the officers of the Engineer Corps to whom the task was assigned. By 1920, the Commission had built 4,890 miles of road and trail, of which 1,031 miles were wagon road. There had been expended in construction and maintenance a total of $5,498,000, of which $3,370,000 were from direct appropriations and the rest from local taxes. Meanwhile, some roads and trails had been built by the Forest Service and by the Territorial Road Commission.[19] Thus great progress has been made, but the industrial needs of the Territory demand at least an equal mileage of roads and trails to that already constructed.

One of the most important acts of Congress for the benefit of Alaska was the authorizing in 1900 of military cable connection with Alaskan ports, the establishment of land telegraph lines, and wireless stations. The original act was passed largely through the personal efforts of Major General A. W. Greely, then chief signal officer. Thanks to Greely's efforts, cable communication with Juneau and other Alaskan ports was established by 1903, and by that time land lines had been extended over much of the inland region.[20] Later all important Alaskan towns were given some form of electrical communication, cable, telegraph, telephone, or wireless.

The first aids to navigation in Alaskan waters were 14 buoys placed in Peril Strait in 1906.[21] The hundreds of vessels which traversed Alaskan waters during the Klondike excitement, carrying thousands of passengers and millions of dollars worth of freight, were transported through these dangerous waters with hardly a single aid to navigation. The losses of ships in Alaskan waters have been appalling. These were in part, of course, due to the natural physical conditions; but they are chargeable also to the lack of sufficient aids to navigation and the lack of adequate charts, a problem which the Coast Survey, with its very limited facilities,[22] has tried hard to meet. Alaska's vast shore line still has only one life-saving station, which was established at Nome in 1905. The Revenue Cutter Service, now the Coast Guard, has, however, from the beginning of its cruises in northern waters rendered much aid to wrecked vessels and has been the means of saving many lives.

---

[19] It is estimated that the cost of wagon road construction in Alaska at the prices of 1920 will be from $5,000 to $6,000 a mile.

[20] It should be remembered that the Western Union Telegraph Company built and operated some 15 miles of telegraph line in Seward Peninsula as early as 1867. The construction of long distance private telephone lines was begun at Nome in 1900, but telephones had by then been in use for a number of years at Juneau. Nearly all Alaskan towns of over 400 population have a telephone system.

[21] The Russians had one lighthouse in Alaska. This was a light placed in the cupola of the "Baranof Castle" at Sitka. It was maintained by the Army for a few years after the annexation and then abandoned because of lack of funds.

[22] In 1920, about ten per cent of Alaskan waters had been charted in the detail needed for navigation.

CHAPTER XXIV

Fisheries

ALASKA'S broad expanse to the sea, broken shore line, and innumerable waterways have given the physical conditions favorable to the development of her great fishing industry, the most important of the Territory. Her salmon fisheries have a world-wide renown, but it is not generally known that Alaskan waters have furnished cod to the West Coast market for upwards of a half century and that her halibut banks have long supplied the Atlantic market. While the salmon catch has no doubt reached its maximum and Alaska's halibut banks are threatened with depletion, her great resources in cod, herring, and other fishes are almost untouched.

The total value of Alaska's fishery products is now upwards of half a billion dollars, and the value of the annual catch runs to tens of millions of dollars. Much of this represents the value of the canned salmon, but the output of other fish products is on the increase and will in time make up for a reduced output of salmon, which no doubt will come, and in fact must come, if the salmon fisheries are not to be entirely depleted.

Long before the coming of the white man the Alaskan natives had devised means of catching fish, especially salmon, in large numbers. Indeed fish have always been the principal food of Alaskan Indians and Eskimos. It has been estimated that under primitive conditions the Alaskan natives caught on the average about 500 pounds of fish annually for every man, woman, and child in the Territory. This would make the weight of the annual catch about 15 or 16 million pounds. Much the larger part of this catch was salmon, but it also included cod, halibut, herring, tomcod, and some fresh water fish.

Fish was also the principal article of food of the whites during the Russian occupation and, except for some potatoes, was practically the only food that the colony yielded, all other provisions being imported. In 1827, some 500,000 pounds of salmon were salted at Sitka for local use of the colony, and an even larger product came from other localities such as Cook Inlet and Kodiak Island. The employees of the Russian American Company received a ration consisting chiefly of fish, the consumption being about 50 pounds per month per person. In addition, the Russians exported some salted salmon to California and the Hawaiian Islands, but this did not become an important industry. As has already been shown, the Russians were not by training or tradition a seafaring people and it was only force of circumstances that drove them to navigate the Pacific and to draw on the sea for food. To these landsmen, the Pacific Ocean was simply an obstacle to be overcome in reaching the valuable furs beyond the sea. Though the Russians in their chase for the sea otter and the fur seal achieved some dexterity in coastal navigation, they preferred to travel and find their livelihood on land, and they utterly failed to develop a fishing population and to reap the rich harvest of fisheries which their American colony offered them.

The Russians even ignored the cod fisheries on their own shores of Siberia until they were developed by American fishermen from across the Pacific. Captain Matthew Turner seems to have been the pioneer fisherman in these waters. In 1857, he crossed the Pacific in the brig *Temandra,* 120 tons, with the purpose of trading on the Amur River. Much to his surprise he found cod fish in the Gulf of Tartary, and during the next few years he made several voyages to these banks for cod. His discovery attracted a number of other fishing vessels. In 1863, Captain Turner also discovered cod banks near the Shumagin Islands off the southwest coast of Alaska. In his little schooner *Porpoise,* 45 tons, he brought back 30 tons of cod, the first to be caught on the Alaskan coast by American fishermen. His example was followed by others, and the Alaskan cod fishing industry became important enough by 1867 to be one of the principal arguments used in favor of the annexation of Russian America.

Long before the arrival of the cod fisherman the American whaler, as has been pointed out earlier, had reached the Alaskan shores. It seems desirable here, though some repetition will be unavoidable, to review briefly the history of the whaling industry in Alaska. The pursuit of whales, which for centuries had been conducted on the Atlantic and adjacent seas, was extended to the Pacific at about the close of the 18th century, and there it greatly expanded.

By 1839, there were 555 American whalers, the majority of them engaged in Pacific sperm whale fishing. The whale fisheries of the Pacific-Alaskan coast were first visited in about 1835, and the hunt was soon extended into Bering Sea. In 1848, Captain Roys, commanding the American ship *Superior,* ventured through Bering Straits into the Arctic and made an enormous catch. As a consequence, a great stimulus was given to the industry: by 1852, 278 American vessels were engaged in whaling along Alaska's coast line, and in 1855, 154 American whalers traversed the straits. Meanwhile, the Russians had organized their own whaling company to take part in this industry that had developed along her shores; but there were neither men nor material for the purpose, and the enterprise was a failure. In 1864, as we have seen, the American whaling fleet was ravaged by the Confederate privateer, the *Shenandoah,* which destroyed 34 vessels. Stories of this "fire ship" are still current among the Eskimos of Bering Sea. At that time the whalers were without steam power and hence fell an easy prey to the cruiser.

With the introduction of petroleum for illuminating purposes and the depletion of the whale fisheries, the industry rapidly declined. In 1902, only eight vessels were employed in Alaska, and now this industry has almost entirely disappeared. All that is left of it is shore whaling with small steamers from stations located at several places. Fertilizer is the chief product of these shore stations.

The salting of salmon for local use and in a small way for export continued after the purchase of Alaska. It was not, however, until 1878 that the foundations of the great salmon industry of today were laid with the building of two small canneries, one near Sitka and one at Klawak on the west coast of Prince of Wales Island. From these small beginnings the gigantic present industry was developed. In 1920, 27,482 persons were employed in Alaskan fisheries, using 788 vessels and 5,950 smaller boats; the total capital investment was $70,986,221, and the gross value of the product was $41,492,124. Most of this was devoted to the salmon canneries which put up 4,429,463 cases with a value of $35,602,800, and which had a capital investment of $62,550,727.

The salmon, the great fish food of the world, is widely distributed along the shores of the North Pacific and Bering Sea. Salmon occur as far south as California and north to the Arctic, and are abundant on the Siberian coast and the northern islands belonging to Japan. The salmon fisheries of Oregon, Washington, British Columbia, and Alaska have been exploited on a very extensive scale. Salmon canning has also been developed in a small way by Japan on the Siberian coast.

The salmon industry has certain peculiarities imposed on it by the habits of the fish. Salmon have their home in the sea, but they spawn in fresh water. With the act of spawning the life cycle of the Pacific salmon is completed, and the adult fish dies. The young salmon, hatched in fresh water, make for the sea after a period of three to 12 months, where they mature and return to fresh water to spawn and die. As yet the records are not complete enough to determine accurately the span of years between the migration of the young fish to the sea and their return to the fresh water breeding ground. It is known, however, that this period varies with different species, probably from two to seven years. It was formerly supposed that the young salmon on reaching the sea wandered far out into the ocean and, with a remarkable instinct, always returned to the same stream in which they had been hatched. It is now believed that during the period of maturing in salt water the salmon remains for the most part near the scene of birth and close to the margin of the submerged continental shelf. When the breeding year arrives, the salmon then make their way to the nearest fresh water stream. There are instances on record to show that salmon have wandered far from the scene of their hatching, sometimes a thousand miles or more. Little is known of the cause of the long migrations, but the search for food is probably a factor.

Salmon appear to be peculiarly sensitive to the detection of small percentages of fresh water in the sea. When the breeding season and year arrive, the salmon's reaction to fresh water appears to draw it toward the source of that fresh water. It is possible that the time of arrival of the breeding salmon on the coast and in the streams may be determined by flood conditions brought about by the melting of winter snows, seasonal rainfall, or maximum discharge from melting glaciers. The relation of the salmon run to seasonal changes is not a direct one, and the determination of the elements in the problem must be based on intensive studies not yet made of each district. It

ALASKA'S SALMON

Upper left: Humpback salmon on riffles of stream, photo by F. H. Moffit; upper right: Salmon jumping falls, photographer unknown; lower left: Native fish wheel on the Tanana, photo by J. B. Mertie; lower right: Tidal fish trap of 1898 on Cook Inlet, photo by W. C. Mendenhall

appears probable, however, that for various causes there is a freshening of the sea water near the shore which attracts the salmon and eventually leads the fish to the near-by streams emptying into the ocean. Since the salmon while maturing remain in the ocean near the mouths of the streams where hatched, they are most likely to ascend the same watercourses when the spawning period arrives. It has been proved, through marking the young planted in certain streams or artificial hatcheries, that a part, and probably a large part, of the spawning salmon return to the fresh water streams of their nativity; but, on the other hand, marked salmon have been caught a thousand miles from the scene of their hatching.

There is a rather indefinite cycle in the run of the various salmon species. While the absolute cycles have not yet been determined, it is now well known that in certain years the number of salmon in the streams and along the adjacent shore line is far larger than in others. Though the reasons for the fluctuation in different years are but imperfectly understood, it is quite possible that they were originally established by some natural cause which killed off most of either the spawn or the young salmon in a particular year. As a consequence there would be a dearth of salmon at the end of the cycle when the matured fish were due to return to spawn. The cycle when once established would continue indefinitely because of the scarcity of breeding fish and hence of spawn.

There are in Alaskan waters five species of salmon[1] whose habits differ somewhat. The time of arrival in the spring varies with each species and also according to latitude and locality. It is probable that the time of the salmon run for each locality is determined by the spring run-off caused by melting snows or by rains. The five species of salmon all belong to the genus called by the naturalists *Oncorhynchus.* The scientific names of the different species are the common names given by the Russians who were the first to become familiar with the salmon.

The king or chinook salmon *(Oncorhynchus tschawytscha),* the largest of the five species, has an average weight of 22 pounds with individuals ranging up to 70 and even 100 pounds. Alaskan king salmon average somewhat larger than those found farther south. King salmon range as far as any of the genus, occurring as far south as Monterey Bay in California and north to the Yukon and probably in the rivers emptying into the Arctic Ocean. They are also found on the Siberian and Japanese coast. The king salmon is the first of the genus to search for the spawning ground. Their run on the Alaskan coast is principally in May and June. King salmon are found along the continental shelf in Southeastern Alaska during all months of the year and are the only variety extensively caught outside of the spawning season. Deep sea salmon fishing for the king is carried on by trolling from small launches and dories, chiefly off the west coast of Prince of Wales Island. Many of the Alaskan king salmon have a white or pale pink flesh. Because of the unfortunate prejudice of the public in favor of red salmon, the king is less valuable for canning than some of the other fish. This prejudice is entirely without foundation, for the color of the flesh has nothing

[1] Cobb, John N., "Pacific Salmon Fisheries," *United States Fish Commission Report,* Washington, D.C., 1920.

to do with the nutritive value of the fish or with its taste. Because of the size of the fish, the delicacy of its flavor, and its being caught throughout the year, the king salmon is much used for shipment in frozen form.

The red salmon, sockeye or blueback *(Oncorhynchus nerka)*, is the most important species from the standpoint of consumption. Its average weight is about six and a half pounds. Commercial fisheries of red salmon are found as far south as the Columbia River, but the species ranges down to the Sacramento River in California. Red salmon occur along the entire Alaskan coast line as far as Bering Sea and probably also in the Arctic rivers. The species is especially abundant in the Bristol Bay region of Bering Sea, which furnishes the greatest red salmon catch in the world. It also ranges along the Siberian coast and the northern Japanese islands. The red salmon run of Bering Sea and the Alaska Peninsula begins in June and extends into August, but it is somewhat later in Southeastern Alaska. The deep red color of the flesh of this salmon has, in view of the prejudice of the public, made it the species most sought for by the canneries. Its canned product commands a higher price than any other species. About 40 per cent of Alaska's catch is red salmon, and half of this comes from Bristol Bay.

The silver or coho salmon *(Oncorhynchus kisutch)* averages about six pounds in weight, with an occasional fish running up to 30 pounds. This species is found as far south as California and north to the Yukon River, and also along the Asiatic coast. The coho runs in Bristol Bay during July, and in Southeastern Alaska during August and September. Coho are valuable for canning, for the flesh is reddish in color but paler than the red salmon.

The humpback or pink salmon *(Oncorhynchus gorbuscha)* ranges as far south as California and north to the Yukon and the rivers emptying into the Arctic Ocean, and is also found on the Siberian coast. During the breeding season the males of this species are much distorted: the back has a decided upward arch, from which it derives its name of humpback. This salmon is most abundant in the waters of Southeastern Alaska where it runs from June to September. Here large numbers of humpback are canned. About half of the salmon catch of the Territory is humpback, and 80 per cent of this catch comes from the waters of southern Alaska. The flesh of the humpback is soft and pink in color.

The chum salmon *(Oncorhynchus keta)* ranges from California to Arctic Alaska but is especially abundant from Puget Sound to Southeastern Alaska. It averages about eight pounds in weight, but individuals weigh as much as 16 pounds. During the breeding season the jaws of the male chum become greatly distorted, and from this feature the fish received the unfortunate local name of "dog salmon." Partly from this name and partly because the flesh is white and less oily than that of other species, the canned product commands a lower price than the other species. Indeed, for many years the Alaskan chum was not canned but was utilized only as a salt fish with a market largely in Japan. Later, when Japan developed her own salmon fisheries, especially after the annexation of the southern part of the island of Sakhalin, this market was lost to Americans. Now the canning of chums is increasing, the catch being about ten per cent of the total salmon and most of these being taken in the waters of Southeastern Alaska. Though canned chum are sold at a lower price than are other salmon, the industry has the advantage over the canning of other salmon because of the longer season. Chum begin to run in Southeastern Alaska during June and continue into September.

The Alaskan natives have always caught salmon only after they entered the fresh water streams, and indeed those of the interior often only after the fish had traveled hundreds or even a thousand miles or more upstream. They employed a crude form of trap and some seines, but mostly dip nets or fish spears. The Russians caught salmon much as did the natives, but they also used more elaborate barriers *(zapors)* on the streams. They paid no heed whatever to the necessity of conserving the fisheries.

During the past 20 years small fish wheels have been introduced among the Yukon Indians. These are turned by the current and, as they require no physical effort on the part of the fisherman, have won great popularity. They are now used almost to the exclusion of other types of gear. The disadvantage of them is that success depends on the salmon run being close to the bank where the wheel is moored. In times of flood water during the salmon run —an unusual occurrence—the fish may travel upstream some distance from the bank, thus missing the wheel; and this will result in a shortage of salmon and possibly suffering among the natives.

There have been several seasons since the introduction of fish wheels when such a shortage has occurred, and each time the smallness of the salmon catch has been charged to some activity of the white man. One year it was claimed that the introduction of petroleum-burning steamers on the Yukon had polluted the waters and killed the salmon; another, 1919, that the location of a cannery on the Yukon delta had kept the salmon out of the river. The first contention is too absurd to need reply. The second one will be seen to lack merit when it is remembered that the Yukon delta presents a 100-mile front to the sea with innumerable channels. The supplying of a small cannery with salmon from one of these channels could in no way deplete the Yukon. Such fishing has been carried on throughout the delta of the Copper River for upwards of 30 years. The fallacy of these contentions is best shown by the fact that, in the years succeeding the introduction of oil-burning steamers and the cannery at the mouth of the Yukon, the salmon were as abundant as ever.

Nevertheless, the regulation of fisheries at the mouths of the large rivers demands earnest attention. The assurance of an ample salmon supply to the natives and whites of the interior must be safeguarded. On the other hand, if there are salmon fisheries which the world can draw upon for food without depleting the salmon stock or cutting off the supply of local residents, it will be the part of wisdom to allow these to be developed. While the interests of the cannery man are of small import as compared with the residents of the Territory, popular clamor based on ignorance of the facts should not shut out commercial fisheries so far as they accord with fish conservation.

During the early development of the cannery industry, no restraints were placed on fishing; and had not wiser counsel prevailed, salmon fishing in Alaska would now be a thing of the past. In justice to the cannery men, it should be noted that they were the first to advocate the conservation of the fish and to take steps toward rectifying some of the evils: A salmon hatchery was constructed by a combination of packing companies in 1891, long before the Government took similar action; this hatchery, at Karluk, was operated in 1896 by the Alaska Packers Association which also began to regulate the fishing. It is to be regretted that under the fierce competitive conditions of the last ten years there have been only too many engaged in salmon canning whose sole purpose was immediate profit and who paid no heed to the conservation of the fish, thus giving little assurance of a permanent industry. Such men are ready to circumvent fishery regulations, the enforcement of which on account of the geographical extent of the industry, the physical conditions, and the insufficiency of inspectors and proper boats is exceedingly difficult.

There are three principal methods of catching salmon: by seines, by gill nets, and by traps. Some salmon are also caught by dip nets and some by trolling. Each method finds its principal use in different parts of Alaska. In Southeastern Alaska and on Prince William Sound, the deep channels close to shore especially favor the use of the trap sometimes called the pound net. A trap consists essentially of a long net hung on piles, which stretches out from the shore usually several thousand feet. This turns the salmon into a compartment built of nets, where they are caught. A trap costs many thousands of dollars but once installed is cheap to operate, and the fish remain alive in it until needed.

The small fisherman usually makes his catch with a seine or gill net. One type of seine is dragged up on the beach by man or steam power. This calls for a shelving beach and formerly was used more than it is at present when restrictions have been placed on fishing near salmon streams. However, it still finds extensive use along the Alaska Peninsula and on Kodiak Island. The purse seine is one dropped from a fish boat, dragged around a school of fish, and then hoisted aboard. This can be used in deep water and far from shore and has its greatest employment in the Bristol Bay region of Bering Sea. The gill net is supported either by poles, when it is stationary, or by floats. It is used most widely on the tidal flats such as those of the Stikine and Copper rivers. The catching of salmon by dip nets, formerly extensively practiced by the natives, is almost a thing of the past. Dip nets are, however, used to supply the cannery located at the canyon of the Copper River.

The fishermen who supply the salmon canneries as a rule work by contract, receiving so much a fish for their catch. If the fishing gear is furnished by the cannery, which is the usual practice, the price is lower than when the fisher-

SALMON CANNING

Upper: Hauling in a trap, photo by S. R. Capps; center: Inside the cannery, photographer unknown; lower: Typical cannery of Southeastern Alaska, photographer unknown.

men supply themselves. Most canneries own their own fish traps, in which case the trap tenders are paid by the day. A few of the salmon trap owners may, however, be entirely independent of the cannery; and if one of these has a good location, he often gets a much larger return on his investment than does the cannery man.

So far as physical conditions permit, salmon canneries are located as near the fishing grounds as possible. A proper cannery site demands a place for a wharf accessible to ocean vessels and also shelter for the fishing fleet. An abundance of running water is needed for the cleansing of fish and equipment, and water power is very desirable. These conditions are not always met with at fishing grounds, and transportation of fish to the cannery must be provided. Fish are brought to canneries sometimes as far as 100 miles or more. Since a salmon must be canned within 48 hours after being taken from the water, the distance to the cannery is an important item. If the fish spoils before being canned, the loss falls on the cannery, for the fisherman is paid at his nets. The salmon are delivered by the fisherman to scows anchored or brought to a convenient point at the fishing ground. Here he receives a receipt for the number of fish he brings. The scow is then towed to the cannery, and the fish are delivered to the cutting room by means of a mechanical conveyor on which the salmon are thrown with a two-pronged fork.

In the early days of the industry the preparation of the fish and placing them in cans was done by hand. Gradually machines were devised, and in a modern cannery the hand cleaning and filling of cans has all been done away with. The last machine to be introduced was the "iron chink." It dresses the fish, removing head, tail, and fins; opens it; and thoroughly cleans it—thus taking the place of from 15 to 20 workers. After this process the fish is cut by mechanical means and then thrust into a can already provided with salt by another ingenious mechanism, and the filled cans are then passed slowly through a steam bath on a mechanical conveyor, a process which partly cooks the fish and expels most of the air. The can then goes through another machine which places the top on the can and crimps it, for in a modern cannery no solder is used. The covered cans are then run into a huge oven where they are cooked for from 90 to 120 minutes. The canning process thus finished, the cans are submitted to inspection by experts. Lacquering and labeling of cans is also done by machinery. A modern salmon cannery is thoroughly sanitary: large amounts of running water are used in cleaning the fish, everything is kept scrupulously clean, and after closing time in the evening all parts of the cannery are washed down with steam and hot water.

A variation of the above-described method is introduced by having part of the work done by hand. Some canneries, too, still solder on the tops, a process that is also done by machinery. One complete set of machinery which starts with the uncleaned fish and ends with the cooking oven is called a "line." Small canneries may have only a single line, large ones as many as five. A single line is operated by from 20 to 30 men and in theory should turn out 20,000 to 25,000 cases of salmon, each case containing 48 one pound cans. In practice, however, many of the single line canneries do not pack more than 5,000 or 10,000 cases. The run of the salmon and the favorable or unfavorable weather conditions control the pack of the cannery, no matter what its capacity. A steady and regular run of fish is favorable to the small cannery. Irregular runs, with very heavy maxima, can be taken care of by a cannery of large capacity but will swamp a small cannery.

In general, the quality of Alaskan canned salmon has stood the test of actual use through all parts of the world. The percentage that has been found unfit for food is so small as to be negligible. With but very few exceptions, the whole tendency of cannery men has been to establish a reputation by taking scrupulous care to manufacture only a strictly hygienic product. A visit to almost any cannery will convince the most sceptical that Alaskan canned salmon is one of the safest of manufactured foods. This has been due largely to the high standards set by the cannery men themselves. The provision made for federal inspection of canneries is so small that only a very occasional visit can be paid to the many different plants.

The habits of the salmon limit the season of fishing for canneries to from one to three months each year. Therefore, the great salmon canning industry, in which some $70,000,000 are invested, must get its entire returns in only a few months. For at least nine months of the year the huge plants, with thousands of vessels and fish boats, are idle. A large percentage of the canneries is in regions of very meagre local population, a fact which necessitates the importation each year of many thousands of employees who must be transported north and south for the brief fishing season.

During this brief active season the canneries are veritable hives of industry. The buildings are crowded with workmen, usually of many races. A great stream of fish boats, large and small, moves back and forth, scows of fish arriving and empty ones departing. Many canneries are equipped with radio to communicate with their tugs which bring in the scows, and it is constantly buzzing. The season of fishing over, the canneries are as deserted as a tomb. In place of hundreds of employees is found only a single watchman. Radios are out of commission; fish boats, scows, and barges are hauled up on the ways and the freight ships have left for southern ports.

The labor question has always been a serious one to the cannery man. Formerly nearly all the cannery crews—that is, those employed in the actual fish preservation—were Chinese; but now, with the relative decrease of Chinese labor, many races and nationalities are employed. Japanese have in part supplanted the Chinese, but one also finds Philippines and Mexicans and a few whites. Fishermen are chiefly whites, but many natives are employed when they are available.

As a consequence of the control exercised by the physical conditions, the canning of salmon has in large measure been built up quite independently of all other local industries. Many of the companies transport the larger part of their supplies and most of their labor north in the spring, and return with the labor and the canned product in the fall, utilizing only their own vessels. The employees earn their money in Alaska and spend it in the states where they make their homes. Cannery supplies are also from the States, and hence Alaskan merchants are deprived of any profit. In this type of operation the Territory reaps no benefit. Its population is not employed by the canneries, its commercial interests are not advanced by the industry.

On the other hand, the canneries are as a rule only too glad to utilize all local sources of labor, and they import their employees only because of the scant local population. Since employment is not for exceeding one-third of the year, obviously the fisherman and other cannery laborers must find means of supports for the other two-thirds. The most obvious source of labor is the natives, who can spend the rest of the year in hunting or fishing. The canneries welcome this condition and employ as many natives as possible, for it is to their commercial advantage to do so. Out of a total of about 30,000 employed in the fisheries, some 5,000 are natives and therefore local residents. This figure does not include all the resident labor, for many of the fishermen now are whites who make their homes in Alaska throughout the year. This class of men is increasing, as fishermen are finding some employment during the winter months in catching salmon for the refrigerating plants that are operated for most of the year.

There is also a class of canneries to which the criticism suggested above does not apply. These are located in regions served by public carriers and have no freight or passenger vessels of their own. Where accessible to such towns as Ketchikan or Cordova, they purchase their supplies in part from local dealers and their cannery employees are drawn to a certain extent from the local settlements.

But in general it is true that salmon canning has developed as a special industry which is in no way coordinated with or dependent on others of the Territory. The interests of the employees, from superintendent to workman, are in no way identified with the Territory. To these Alaska is simply a place of lucrative employment for a short time each year, but they make their homes and raise their families outside of the Territory. As a consequence, a certain antagonism has grown up between the residents and the cannery men. The former claim that the latter are reaping a rich harvest from local resources and are doing nothing in return. The latter reply by pointing to the large taxes[2] which are paid by them to federal and territorial governments and claim that they receive but little direct benefit from these, since neither expends any considerable part of the taxes on fisheries for the benefit of the fishing industry. There is clearly a tendency on the part of the Territory to increase the tax on the salmon industry; and since but the smaller part of those connected with the fishing interests are residents of Alaska, the industry has little voice in the territorial government.

The usual charge made by Alaskans against the cannery men is that they have made huge fortunes by despoiling

[2] In 1920, the salmon canneries paid a total of $301,096.43 in taxes in addition to an estimated four millions for income taxes.

the salmon fisheries. Both parts of this charge have a basis of truth when applied to individuals and corporations, but neither is strictly true when applied to the industry as a whole. To consider first the question of inordinate profits:

It has been pointed out that the quantity of salmon in any given region varies enormously from year to year. One year the shores and streams will be alive with salmon, and fishermen and canneries will be fairly swamped with fish. In another year there may not be enough salmon to justify the operation of canneries throughout the season. This fluctuation in numbers has a certain rhythmic swing for each species and district; and when more facts are accumulated, it will probably be possible to forecast whether a given year will be a fat or a lean season. As it is now, the cannery man, though he may hazard a guess, can not be sure whether he should make preparations for a large or small run. Be it noted also that the fluctuation is by districts and species; hence a shortage in one locality may be offset by a large catch in another. Therefore, the canneries in a region of small catch may not find any increase in price to counterbalance the small product.

The expense for operating a cannery is almost the same for a small catch as for a large one. Most of the actual canning is done at a contract price of so much a can. The contractor, very often a Chinaman, hires and feeds his own employees. His contract always allows so much a can, but there is a minimum number of cans specified for which he must be paid regardless of whether the supply of fish permits this or not. This contract usually provides for an assurance of about 20,000 cases on each line of cannery machinery operated. Should the catch not equal this amount, the cannery man loses the difference. Moreover, most of his other expenses are the same, whether he makes a full pack or not. His mechanics, crews of vessels, and other employees are most often paid by the season, with in certain cases a bonus on the number of fish caught. He must provide the tins, boxes, and other equipment for a full pack and must meet the cost of holding this investment over another year if it be not utilized. If he operates his own freight carriers, this expense goes on irrespective of the size of the catch. It will be evident that during a season of small run the canneries will be operated at a loss. It is as if a manufacturing plant had to be operated at full capacity, no matter whether it received raw material or not.

On the other hand, given a good run of salmon, the profits are in many instances very large. There are cases of a cannery paying a considerable part of its installation costs in a single season when the run happened to be large. The fact of the enormous expansion of the industry shows that on the whole it has been very profitable. This was especially true of the first two years of the European war when salmon commanded a high price because of its desirability as food for army supplies. Later the Government restricted profits by fixing the price of salmon, but even this was high enough to assure a good profit. On the whole the salmon canning industry, at least as it has been carried on, involves large risks, with possibilities of both large losses and large profits. This is a feature which appeals to the type of speculator on the frontier. Among the risks, in addition to the size of the salmon run, are those by fire and marine accidents. Insurance rates against fire and marine disasters are exorbitant. Some of the larger companies carry their own insurance. A large part of the marine losses along the Alaskan coast are cannery vessels, and underwriters have made their rates accordingly. Taking it by and large, and in spite of the small fortunes made by lucky individuals, the Alaskan salmon industry has probably not paid inordinate profits in view of the risks incurred. Its expansion has been more because of the possibilities of speculative profits than because of the certainty of large returns.

The question of inordinate profits under our present conception of government is left to the individual. In the long run such matters adjust themselves by free competition and individual effort. On the other hand, the matter of the exhaustion of salmon reserves is naturally one of first importance. It affects Alaska directly but also the people of the United States as a whole. The Alaskan salmon fisheries are now supplying the world with 250,000,000 pounds of very nutritious food annually.[3]

This figure indicates what an important item of food the Alaskan salmon is. It is evident that no private interests or profit-making should interfere with the perpetua-

[3] For the three year period 1918-1920, the figures of the Bureau of Fisheries show 340,162,232 pounds, 233,517,675 pounds, and 220,844,740 pounds respectively. These figures include canned, mild-cured, pickled, frozen, fresh, dry-salted, and dried and smoked salmon.—*Editor's note.*

tion of the salmon run. The spawn from one pair of salmon will furnish 2,500 young fish. In theory, therefore, 80,000 salmon should be enough to stock the waters to furnish an annual catch of the hundred millions which is the maximum catch of any one year thus far. However, an unknown but only a small part of the spawn actually develop into mature salmon since many of the eggs do not hatch because they are not fertilized, the physical conditions are unfavorable, or the eggs are eaten by trout or other enemies. Again, the young salmon, or fry, have many enemies such as eagles and other birds, trout and other fish. It is even true that salmon are mutually destructive and that one species maturing earlier will feed on another. It will probably be safe to assume that not over five per cent of the spawn carried to the breeding grounds actually hatches out and matures into adult salmon. Assuming this estimate to be correct, the number of breeding males and females sufficient to maintain an annual catch of 100,000,000 adult fish must approximate nearly 2,000,000. In the dearth of actual facts, even this figure may be far too low.

Whatever the number of breeding fish needed to perpetuate the stock, all in excess of this number which are allowed to escape are lost as a source of food to the world. The problem, therefore, is to permit and even to encourage the catching of all the salmon in excess of the number required to maintain supply. Be it noted also that the number of young salmon that can be bred in any particular stream or lake is determined by the food supply. For this reason even an unfished stream will never exceed a certain quantity of salmon.

Two lines of action have been taken to prevent exhaustion of salmon fisheries. The first is to enforce certain regulations which have for their purpose the assurance that a certain percentage of fish will escape the nets and traps and reach the breeding ground. These regulations, without going into details about them, apply to forms of fishing gear used and to the place and time of use. Fishing may be restricted to certain parts of the season, may be prohibited in selected areas altogether for a given period of years, or may be limited so that there is a 36 hour period in each week when no fishing is allowed. Unfortunately, the main purpose of these regulations has been obscured because they were combined to a certain extent with taxes, which have nothing to do with the conservation of fish. It is also true that the Fish Commission has never had adequate funds to enforce these regulations.

The second method is to establish artificial hatcheries where a certain number of fry are annually freed. These hatcheries are now liberating about 100,000,000 young salmon. It is well established that these hatcheries have done much in certain localities to maintain the supply of salmon or even to restock the fisheries which have been depleted, but of the six hatcheries half are operated by the Federal Government and half by cannery companies which by law receive certain rebates from their taxes in accordance with the number of fry they release. In justice to the cannery companies, so often accused of ruthlessly destroying the salmon fisheries, it should be recorded that one of these—the Alaska Packers Association—established a hatchery long before the Government took the matter up. A simple solution of the problem of maintaining the salmon fisheries would seem to be to establish enough hatcheries to assure an abundance of fry. Assuming that this would take 20 times as many salmon as are now being released, it would cost at pre-war prices about $400,000. The federal and territorial taxes now paid by canneries would be sufficient to cover this cost.

Probably no one will concede that it is practical to supplant the natural hatching of salmon, and every one will admit that some means must be devised to check overfishing. The present law and regulations thereunder do not seem to be adequate, and certainly the machinery thus far provided for their enforcement is entirely inadequate. New canneries are constantly being established and closer fishing undertaken. Fish traps are increasing in number. In spite of the valiant efforts of the Bureau of Fisheries, the salmon fisheries are only too evidently being depleted.

An undoubtedly effective solution to the problem would be to limit the number of canneries and above all the number of traps. If the law provided for leasing fishing sites, especially trap sites, for a period of perhaps 25 years, with a just royalty and provision for renewal, the question would be settled. It would then be to the interest of the lessee to assure a good supply of salmon during his period of occupancy. He would not only see that his own fishing was in the interests of conservation but also be an active agent in helping the suppression of illegal fishing. This would be in strong contrast to the present conditions, where there is cut-throat competition between those engaged in the industry. A good many know that the present methods will assuredly lead to a decline of the industry and spend their efforts in securing a large immediate return. Such a policy would give a permanency to the industry and an identification of the fishing interests with those of the Territory.

On the other hand, the granting of monopolistic rights to any part of the fishing ground would be adverse to the small operator and the newcomer. Such rights would undoubtedly fall to those having large capital, and the small fisherman would disappear. Here we find the same clash between the interests of conservation of raw material, best brought about by a monopoly, and the advantages of free competition, with its lower prices and equal opportunities for all. With the present public attitude it is not likely that this method of conservation will be tried out.

Though much the greater part of the salmon catch is canned, there are various other means of preserving the fish for shipment to market. Mild curing consists in slightly salting the salmon, which has been cleaned and cut into two pieces and then shipped in cold storage. Most of the mild-cured salmon goes to North European countries, where it is smoked before reaching the consumer. The pickling of salmon is the oldest of all Alaskan industries, but it is no longer an important one. At one time much dried and salted salmon was shipped to Japan from Alaska. After the Japanese took the fisheries of Sakhalin from Russia, they got salt salmon from their own coast, and the industry ceased. The native method of curing salmon is by smoking, especially in the interior where the semiarid climate favors this process. The Yukon Indian, however, uses no salt and but very little smoke, the process being largely one of sun-curing. The white man's process of smoking is preceded by pickling. Smoked salmon is very delicious, but the Alaskan product finds only a home market. The real salmon eater accustomed to the fine fresh fish prefers the smoked to the canned product.

The freezing of Alaskan salmon and their shipment to the Atlantic seaboard and to Europe is a growing industry. It has the advantage of a much longer fishing season. The large king salmon is the best for freezing, and in certain localities this can be caught by trolling for much of the year. The king salmon banks are for the most part on the outward exposed coast line of the islands of Southeastern Alaska. Fishing in these waters is not practical during the winter storms; therefore, the cold storage plants can not be operated for salmon for more than seven or eight months of the year. Since these same plants can, however, be operated for icing halibut, there is really no closed season. This is in strong contrast to the canneries, which are closed during much of the greater part of the year. Therefore, the icing plants are of great value to the Territory in encouraging a permanent population and hence the local industries. Now, upwards of 2,000,000 pounds of frozen salmon are shipped from Alaska, put up at eight different plants.

The utilization of the offal and other waste material in the manufacture of oil, fish meal, and fertilizer is as yet but little developed. In most of the canneries this valuable by-product is dumped into the sea. It appears that the cost of a plant for utilizing the by-product is so large that only at very large canneries or closely-grouped individual canneries can such equipment be economically used. No doubt the time will come when canners will be obliged to utilize all parts of the fish, an eventuality that will work a hardship on the small cannery man in isolated localities. It would appear, however, that in the many places where canneries are closely spaced and where sheltered waterways give easy communication, all the waste products could now be economically utilized. Possibly a fertilizer industry might be developed by some form of bounty or relief from taxation for a given period of years.

The halibut *(Hippoglossus hippoglossus)*, largest of the Alaskan food fishes, is found up to 300 and 400 pounds in weight. It is essentially a deep water fish, being found on the fishing banks at depths of from 10 to 50 fathoms. Halibut are found at these depths both in the bays and fiords of the broken shore line of the Pacific seaboard and on submerged banks farther out to sea. Virgin halibut banks are characterized by their very great abundance of fish. Their numbers seem almost unlimited, and they afford splendid opportunities for the fisherman. This very opportunity, however, encourages over-fishing and rapid depletion. Though halibut fishing was not begun in a large way on the Pacific until about 1890, already the center of the industry which started on the coast of Oregon and Washington has moved northward to Southeastern Alaska.

In a generation there has been a very striking depletion of the Pacific halibut banks, and the industry has only been maintained by the finding of new fisheries.

Halibut banks are widely distributed along the Alaskan coast line. The fishing of these so far has been chiefly along the coast of Southeastern Alaska and along the Alaska Peninsula. There are believed to be important halibut banks along the Aleutian Islands which have thus far been but little investigated. Though there are still many halibut banks containing an abundance of fish, the industry is relatively declining. Formerly it was second only to the salmon industry. It appears that without drastic action the Alaskan halibut banks will be fished out, as to a large extent those of the Atlantic seaboard have been. If this valuable food fish is to be preserved, means of protection will soon have to be taken. Many of the halibut banks lie outside of the three league limit and are, therefore, not under our control; hence, protective measures can only be by international agreement. The reason for rapid exhaustion of halibut fisheries is that the most valuable fish is the small or so-called "chicken halibut" which is the fish demanded by the public. These relatively small fish are under the breeding age; their destruction means the destruction of the species. It must be left to the experts to decide what manner of protection to the young fish should be attempted by international agreement. The national importance of this matter is shown by the fact that nearly 90 per cent of the halibut consumed in the eastern market comes from the Pacific, chiefly from the Alaskan banks. If the halibut is to be counted on as a future source of food, it must be protected by drastic international agreements and regulations.

Though halibut schooners began to visit the Alaskan waters as early as 1895, the first systematic development of these fisheries began in 1899 when an icing plant was established at Petersburg in Southeastern Alaska. The fishing grounds, first located in the sheltered waterways of Southeastern Alaska, are now on the more exposed banks to the westward.

Halibut fishing has been extended during the last 20 years by the general introduction of gasoline marine engines among fish boats, a fact which has made the fisherman more independent, for he can carry his catch to ports of his own choosing in a fairly expeditious manner. The typical boat of the present is a staunch seagoing craft from 40 to 60 feet long, capable of making from five to eight knots an hour under gasoline power. Much larger vessels are also employed. From such boats a small fleet of dories is sent out at the fishing banks. Each dory, manned by two men, throws out its trawl, 1,000 to 2,000 feet long; to this smaller lines are attached at intervals of 15 feet, baited with herring, and the whole system is anchored to the bottom. When the trawl is hoisted, the halibut are killed at the surface of the water with a club. The fish are cleaned and may be packed in ice from a near-by glacier or salted on board or, if a plant be accessible, may be delivered for freezing. Much the larger part are packed in ice and shipped from the nearest port of call of regular steamers. Halibut fishing can be carried on throughout the year except for brief periods governed by local weather conditions. Upwards of 150 vessels and over 1,000 men are employed in the Alaskan halibut fisheries.

Cod, as has been shown, was the first fish to attract American fishermen to Alaskan waters, and that as early as 1865. The Pacific cod is of the same species as the Atlantic variety *(Gadus macrocephalus)*, though the naturalists have recognized certain minute differences between the two. The Alaskan cod ranges in weight from six to 40 pounds or more. Cod occur along the entire Pacific coast of Alaska, but all the important fisheries are on banks located from Kodiak southwestward along the Alaska Peninsula and northward in the deeper waters of Bering Sea. The largest fisheries are those of the offshore banks, whose total areas are roughly estimated at 30,000 square miles[4] with depths ranging from 20 to 70 fathoms. The inshore banks are closer to shore and include the bays and more or less sheltered waterways of parts of the Alaska Peninsula and Bering Sea. These include an area of at least 10,000 or 15,000 square miles. In addition, there are unexplored cod banks along the Aleutian Islands. All these form the largest cod fish banks in the world, and their exploitation has as yet been but begun. There is more or less annual migration of cod, the general movement being inshore during the summer months.

The early fishing for cod was by vessels which sailed from Pacific ports, usually San Francisco; a vessel, having

[4] Cobb, John N., "Pacific Cod Fisheries," *Bureau of Fisheries, Document No. 830*, Washington, D.C., 1916.

caught and salted the fish on board, would then return with its cargo. This great loss of time for the entire fishing crew, because of the long north and south voyages, led in 1876 to the establishment of a permanent fishing station at Pirate Cove on Popof Island. This was followed by others, and now much of the cod fishing is carried on from these shore stations. Auxiliary power boats have now displaced the sailing craft of the past in the cod fisheries. Cod fishing is now carried on in part with small boats, the catch of which is prepared at the shore stations, and in part with large vessels, the fish being salted on board. The fishing method is by hook and line and is not unlike that used for halibut.

Some 15,000,000 pounds of cod are annually caught in Alaskan waters, and this is but a fraction of what it could be were there a larger market for the fish. It has been found impossible to compete with the Atlantic cod fisheries in most of the export trade.

Herring are probably the most abundant and widely distributed of Alaskan food fishes. The Pacific herring *(Clupea pallasii)* is very similar to the Atlantic herring, which since earliest times has been an imoprtant source of food for the nations of North Europe. As found in Alaska, the herring averages about a foot in length and a little under a pound in weight. The herring, essentially a deep water fish, reaches the shallower littoral zone of the ocean during the spawning season.

Herring are found along the entire Pacific seaboard of Alaska and in the Bering Sea, and they range at least as far north as Bering Straits. The best herring are those of the northern part of the Gulf of Alaska and Bering Sea. Those in the waters of Southeastern Alaska are small but suitable for canning. The general movement of herring is toward shallow water during the spawning season, but their migrations are rather irregular at a given locality. An abundant run of herring in one year may be followed by an almost total dearth of fish in the succeeding one, followed by still greater abundance of fish in the third year. In the cold waters of Bering Sea the large shoreward migration of herring is short, in some places only of a fortnight's duration, much shorter than in the Pacific. The spawning season of the herring is during June on Bering Sea, between April and June in the Pacific.

The exploitation of the Alaskan herring industry is

but in its infancy. As yet the Alaskan smoked herring has not been able to compete with the imported fish from Scotland and the Scandinavian Peninsula to any great extent. The European herring are sold at a cheaper price and are better prepared than the Alaskan fish. It is unfortunate that the only considerable use of Alaskan herring has been in the manufacture of fertilizer. Though this industry is as yet of small extent, it should be discouraged, for a valuable food product should not be thus used. It should be noted, however, that an increase in the demand for Alaskan herring as a food fish would undoubtedly check their use for the less valuable fertilizer. In the end, therefore, this waste of food will correct itself, though meanwhile some fisheries might be depleted. These are, however, so enormous that it is inconceivable that any demand for fish fertilizer would suffice to lead to an exhaustion of the herring fisheries. Another phase of this question is that the exhaustion of any part of the herring banks might affect the salmon industry. It is known that the herring is one of the principal foods of the salmon, and it has been charged that over-fishing for use of a fertilizing plant of certain herring banks in Southeastern Alaska is one of the causes for a decreased run of salmon. This charge is not founded on definite facts, and it can not be given much weight; yet it deserves consideration in the problem of the conservation of the salmon.

There are many other food fishes of Alaska which have been but little utilized. The Dolly Varden *(Salvelinus malma)* and steelhead *(Salmo gairdneri)* trout are widely distributed and very abundant in Alaskan streams. They weigh from eight to 15 pounds, with individuals running up to 30 pounds. They are an excellent food and are valued for shipment fresh, frozen, pickled, and canned. The so-called Atka mackerel *(Pleurogrammus monopterygius), a* most excellent fish, are found in enormous numbers in the Aleutian Islands. They have long been used by the Aleuts but are hardly known outside of Alaska, though a few small export shipments have been made. This fish resembles somewhat the Atlantic mackerel, though of an entirely different species. Those that have attempted to introduce them into the West Coast market have been confronted with the pure food law which prevented their sale under the name of Atka mackerel. Designated as a variety of mackerel, they could be more easily introduced than under some name entirely unknown to the public. The Dungeness crab *(Cancer magister)* is exceedingly abundant in Southeastern and central Alaskan waters. There are a few crab canneries in this district, but the industry is as yet small. The clam resources of Alaska are enormous, and a clam-canning industry has been started. The innumerable other food fish of the Alaskan waters need not be listed, for, though locally used, they give no promise of being the basis of an important industry.

It has been shown that the marine fisheries of Alaska are capable of being developed on a large scale and will in time come to be an even more important source of food. At present, only the salmon fisheries, which have certainly been exploited up to the limit of safety and probably beyond it, are of world-wide importance. The Alaskan halibut fisheries are large, but for the reasons given above they are seriously threatened with exhaustion. The herring, cod, and other food fishes will be had in enormous quantities when a market develops. Take it all in all, Alaskan fisheries are most important to the nation, for they can with proper protection be made to furnish an enormous supply of food to our growing population.[5]

---

[5] A number of Dr. Brooks' lacunae in this chapter have been filled by providing the required statistical information as presented in the *Annual Report of the Governor of Alaska,* Washington, D.C., 1921. I am also indebted for several bits of similar information to the Juneau office of the United States Fish and Wildlife Service.—*Editor's note.*

CHAPTER XXV

Agriculture

NO STATEMENTS about Alaska have been received with greater incredulity than that the Territory promises potential agricultural resources. Even among those long resident in Alaska, there are not a few who sneer at the attempts at agricultural development and hold that, except for the raising of potatoes of an inferior quality and a few hardy vegetables, the Territory can not produce any food crops. There are several reasons for this attitude, but the principal one is that the size and geographic extent of Alaska baffle the mental concepts of the average man. It is hard to visualize a territory whose dimensions, east and west, north and south, are as large as those of the United States. It is as if one were attempting mentally to coordinate the rich lands of Texas with the arid and cold regions of Montana. Thus they who have dwelt amidst the sombre fiords of Southeastern Alaska, with its precipitous slopes reaching upward to the zone of glaciers and perpetual snow, can see no field for the farmer. Again, the placer miner from the tundras of Nome, where at best the vegetation is but scant, rightly scorns the thought of agriculture. To grasp the agricultural possibilities of Alaska, one must traverse the fertile valleys of the Yukon and its tributaries and, above all, visit the prosperous farmers of Fairbanks. One must see the fields of oats, rye, barley, and even wheat of the Tanana valley. The developments yet made are but small, for the farms can not develop beyond the local demands for agricultural products. Though the day will come when the increasing population of the States must draw on the farming lands of Alaska for foodstuffs, yet in the immediate future the Alaskan farmer can only hope to find a market among the local population that has been attracted by other resources.

The most persistent opponents of agricultural development in Alaska are those who desire to maintain in the public mind a picture of the Northland as a field of adventure and physical endurance. Prosperous farmers and happy families are a discordant element in the mental picture of facing the terrible dangers and hardships which have been dwelt upon by so many writers. A true picture of the inland region with its grass and flowers would rob these authors of their heroics and make their writings unsaleable. Besides, many are sincere in striving to preserve the picturesqueness of the old frontier life, which is fast disappearing from the larger communities.

Even among some of the earlier American explorers, however, there was some concept of the agricultural possibilities of Alaska. Notable among these was Dr. William H. Dall who over a half century ago recognized that the climatic and soil conditions of the Yukon valley were no bar to farming. Indeed, even the Russians established some agricultural colonies on Cook Inlet for their superannuated employees, and these have been maintained to the present day. The Russians, however, had little knowledge of the interior where are the best farming lands. They did raise some potatoes in the coast region, but no attempt was made to introduce seed adapted to the climate and soil and their success was but moderate.

Most of our knowledge of Alaska's agriculture is due to the labor of Dr. C. C. Georgeson of the Department of Agriculture. For a quarter of a century he has carried on a scientific investigation of the agriculture of Alaska. Dr. Georgeson came to the Territory during the Klondike gold rush, a period when the psychology of the residents was inimical to all enterprises except the exploitation of rich placer mines. By his broad vision he was able to foresee the future and to forecast the development of farming which has since taken place. For many years he received little help or encouragement from the local residents, and even some of the governors of the Territory refused to accept his conclusions. Gradually the growing population led to the establishment of gardens, and later land was cleared for forage crops. Dr. Georgeson's prophecy that wheat could be commercially raised in Alaska was long doubted by many who conceded the possibilities of maturing the hardier grains and vegetables. The plant breeding of Dr. Georgeson, however, finally developed a variety of wheat which has now for a number of years been successfully raised by the Tanana farmers. Indeed, during the war the local wheat was ground in a feed mill and the flour locally used, and since then a small mill has been built that promises to supply the community with flour.

Before suitable wheat was developed, varieties of oats, barley, rye, and potatoes were bred, adapted to the climatic conditions by Dr. Georgeson and his assistants. Experiments with alfalfa, clover, and other forage crops are now being made to develop suitable varieties. Nor has horticulture been neglected, the Sitka station being chiefly devoted to this phase of agriculture. The breeding of cattle and sheep for Alaskan lands is also under way, and recently some yaks have been introduced. Besides the Sitka station, agricultural experiment farms are maintained at Kodiak, devoted to cattle and sheep; at Matanuska on the government railroad; at Fairbanks; and at Rampart on the Yukon. The last is very inaccessible to the inland population and is chiefly given over to plant breeding.

It is only an occasional tourist who visits the experiment stations and farming region of Alaska. Yet there is quite a percentage of these Alaskan travelers who, after visiting a few glaciers and Indian settlements on the coast, will probably declaim their ignorance of Alaska by asserting that the country is entirely barren. More exasperating, however, are the statements of those residents in the Territory who, from sheer ignorance or prejudice, make similar statements. One is reminded of the writings of two centuries ago, when the fertile lands of Ontario were described in similar terms.

In Chapter IV of this book Alaska was divided into five vegetation zones, as follows: (1) the forest lands of Southeastern Alaska, (2) the grasslands of the southwest, (3) the woodland of the interior, (4) the tundras, and (5) the Alpine zone. Of these, the last two can be eliminated from consideration here, as they have no agricultural value. But arable and stock-raising lands are to be found within the other three regions.

The densely forested lands of Southeastern Alaska are chiefly valuable for their timber for lumber, and especially for pulpwood. Climatic conditions are unfavorable to the raising of grain, even were the cost of clearing these lands for extensive farming not prohibitive. These lands, however, are adapted for vegetables and fruits, and in favored localities some market gardening is carried on, notably at Haines on Lynn Canal, famous for its strawberries. Near the larger settlements there are some dairy farms.

In the occasional open glades, and where land has been cleared, grass grows luxuriantly. With the growth of population the development of scattered farms in the bottom lands, which are not of large extent, will increase. On the whole, not much farming can be expected in the coastal forest zone. The total area of possible farming lands here is said to be approximately 11,000 acres. Most of this, however, will not be utilized for many years, and much of it will probably always be more valuable for timber than for agriculture.

The grasslands of southwestern Alaska, including Kodiak Island, the Kenai Peninsula, and the Alaska Peninsula, contain in the aggregate much arable land. In the absence of timber, the land can be brought under cultivation at no great cost. During the growing season the climate is rather cold and wet and not so well-suited to farming as the inland region. There are in this province enormous areas of grasslands suitable to the raising of cattle and sheep. This fact was known to the Russians, who raised some cattle at Kodiak. Cattle can graze for eight months of the year, and indeed sometimes during the entire winter. The establishment of a cattle raising industry for export in this region will no doubt come. Its limits will be set not by the amount of pasturage but by the extent of arable lands suitable to the growing of forage for winter feeding. Data on the quantity of arable lands are lacking. The present most serious drawbacks to the beginnings of a cattle raising industry are the lack of ocean transport and the presence of the large brown bear. The bear are now protected by law but must be exterminated before cattle and sheep raising is encouraged. No surveys have been made of the grasslands which grade upward into moss-covered uplands of the tundra type and are suitable only for reindeer pasture. In view of the growing demand for beef and mutton, it can be confidently predicted that these cattle and sheep ranges will be utilized. There is, however, at present no definite information about the extent of these pastures, but it is probably safe to estimate them at not less than 3,000,000 acres. The most favorable localities for experimentation are some of the small islands adjacent to the Alaska Peninsula and the northern part of Kodiak Island.

The interior woodland province is *par excellence* the farming region of Alaska. The farming lands of this province lie in the main valley of the Yukon as far down as the timber extends and the valleys of the southern tributaries, notably that of the Tanana. It also includes the upper basin of the Kuskokwim and the lower reaches of the Susitna and Matanuska valleys. Broadly speaking, three types of plant formations are found in this province. There are swampy areas in the valley bottoms in which the chief trees are stunted black spruce and willows, and these mark lands which are not very fertile or promising. There are also in the valley bottoms well-drained areas in which are found the large white spruce, cottonwood (poplar), and birch; and these are well adapted to farming. On the slopes similar trees are found, but here grass is more abundant and the birch and cottonwood are the prevailing trees. These form the best of the agricultural lands. Such lands grade upward into less fertile lands where the stunted spruces dominate. This land too, when burnt off, can be cultivated. Just at timber line, the growth of native grasses is especially abundant. These grasslands too must be counted as arable, but they will probably be chiefly valuable for grazing. At still higher altitude, the grass becomes scant and eventually the zone of moss and reindeer pastures is reached. The lands thus far cultivated in the Yukon are the dry lands of the valley bottoms and the richer lands of the lower slopes.

There is considerable variation in soil, and this is, of course, an important factor in the matter of agriculture. The best soil thus far cultivated is a fine loam which occurs in a broad belt along the northern slope of the Tanana valley. Here in its virgin condition it is covered by a thick growth of birch and cottonwood. The origin of this loam is not definitely known. In the Fairbanks district it has been formed from a silt deposit which varies in thickness from a few feet on the higher slopes to 100 feet or more farther down. Similar soil occurs on the lower reaches of the Matanuska valley, apparently derived from a similar silt. The silt of these soils is probably a wind-blown deposit or, in other words, a loess. In contrast to these loess soils on the north slope of the Tanana valley, sandy soils occur on the south slopes. These are very previous and, in this region of only 15 inches of precipitation, have thus far been found too dry for agriculture. Similar dry sandy soils occur on the south side of the lower Matanuska valley and in the region extending through to the town of Anchorage. No doubt, such lands will eventually find their use, but with the abundance of better lands near at hand they have thus far been avoided by the homesteaders.

These contrasts of soil conditions have been set forth to show that local conditions determine the distribution of agricultural lands. The classification of Alaskan lands must, therefore, first take account of the climatic provinces which determine the length of growing season and rainfall, and then of the local soil conditions. It should be noted, however, that the average amount of rainfall varies greatly from place to place. It will, therefore, be necessary to make a more exhaustive study of soils and rainfall than has yet been made to determine what part of the inland woodland area can be rightfully classed as farming land.

There are certainly thousands of acres in the Tanana valley in which the loam soil is found and this is probably all farming land. Similar soils are believed to occur in the region lying between the lower Tanana River and the Kuskokwim valley, but their extent is not known. Good lands are also found on the benches of the Yukon valley as far down as the Catholic mission of Holy Cross where successful farming has long been carried on. It is probably safe to estimate the arable lands of the Yukon and upper Kuskokwim basin to aggregate some 5,000,000 acres.

To the tyro in Alaskan matters, one soil condition often appears to preclude all hope of farming. That is that in most places the virgin soil remains frozen throughout the year at depths varying from 18 to 24 inches below the surface. Under virgin conditions only the upper foot and a half or two feet thaw out during the summer. This perpetual ground frost is a peculiarity of much of the subpolar area of the world. At Fairbanks the ground frost has been found to depths of 300 feet. This ground frost is a survival of a colder climate of the glacial period. It has been preserved into a warmer climatic period by the non-conductive mat of moss and other vegetation. Its presence has not prevented the luxuriant growth of grass and trees of a fair size. Indeed, I have seen a fair crop of oats in a field where frost occurred two feet below the surface. Good crops, however, can not be raised with a frozen subsoil. With the stripping of the surface mat of vegetation and the cultivation of the soil, the ground frost disappears; that is, the seasonal frost does not reach down to the depth of the permanent frost. The permanent ground frost of some of the virgin lands is, therefore, no detriment to agricultural development. There appears to be no permanent ground frost in the lower Susitna valley where the better agricultural lands are found.

In addition to the farming lands of the lower Matanuska valley already referred to and of the adjacent parts of the Susitna valley, there are others on the west side of the Susitna River. Some of the best lands of this region occur in the basin of the Yentna River. There are also tremendous areas of bench lands on both sides of the Susitna basin, some of which are covered by good soil, and the rest have some agricultural value. Agricultural lands are found too around the upper part of Cook Inlet. The farming lands of the Susitna-Matanuska region which are immediately adjacent to the Alaska railroad are estimated to include 291,000 acres. The area on the west side of the Susitna valley and the estimated area of the agricultural lands of the Cook Inlet region will total probably an additional million acres.

The Copper River basin is as a whole uninviting to the farmer. Except near and in the high mountains the rainfall is scant. Along the base of the mountains the growing season is short. Much of the Copper River basin is occupied by a high plateau, swampy and covered with only stunted timber. The soil is wet and the growing season is short. Such conditions prevail over much of the region lying between the Chugach Mountains on the south and the Alaska Range on the north. This plateau is, however, traversed by some sharply cut valleys, along the lower slopes and narrow bottoms of which some arable land is found. In these valleys some successful farming has been done, and the raising of vegetables at other localities is also possible. Grass is scarce on the plateau. It is worthy of note, however, that where the plateau has been burnt over grass grows luxuriantly in many places, and the second growth of spruce is much more rapid than before burning. It is worthy of careful consideration whether this land might not well be systematically burnt off, with the plan of inducing grass to grow. It is also possible that a method of reforestation might be found which would utilize these lands that now have no value.

To sum up, the agricultural lands of Alaska are chiefly in the interior and the best developed are in the Tanana valley. It is probable that the Territory includes some

ALASKAN AGRICULTURE, I
Garden (upper) and dairy farm (lower) near Fairbanks; photos from Brooks collection, photographers unknown.

100,000 square miles[1] of potential agricultural lands. In addition, there are tracts of grazing lands whose area can not now be estimated.

The Alaskan farmer has already accomplished much, and much more still can be accomplished. In Southeastern Alaska there are a few dairies and many market and home gardens. Vegetables and fruits are the only farm products raised on any considerable scale which have had any markets. In the Yukon and Susitna basins, there is an increasing number of homesteaders, most of whom support them-

[1] This is Dr. Georgeson's estimate. None of the factual information concerning farming and pasture lands presented in this chapter was given in Dr. Brooks' manuscript. I have filled the lacunae as best I could after finding that many estimates have been made and that most of them vary greatly from each other. The assistance rendered by the University of Alaska Department of Agriculture and the University Extension Service in tracing down the necessary information is hereby acknowledged.—*Editor's note.*

selves in part by other industries such as mining, roadhouse-keeping, trapping, and fur raising. Besides many kinds of vegetables, including potatoes, beets, cauliflower, lettuce, asparagus, peas, beans, and celery, the farmers have raised large quantities of oats, rye, and barley and some buckwheat and wheat.

Thus far the only farm product which might be raised for export is beet sugar. The sugar beet can be matured and contains some 17 per cent of saccharine, which is higher than the average for other regions. A sugar beet industry would have an advantage in that the beets could be frozen in the fall and thawed when needed, which would do away with the necessity of manufacturing the sugar during only a few months of the year. On the other hand, the raising of sugar beets requires much hand labor and could not be carried on with the present scant population.

ALASKAN AGRICULTURE, II

Upper: Harvesting potatoes near Hot Springs, photo by L. M. Prindle; lower: Grain field near Fairbanks, photographer unknown.

There is at present not sufficient acreage of cultivated land in any one district to start such an industry. In the Fairbanks district and adjacent parts of the Tanana valley, and in the Matanuska valley are found the best possibilities and the largest number of acres under cultivation. The best hope for a sugar beet industry will be through some scheme of colonization by which a sufficient amount of land can be brought under cultivation and a supply of labor assured. There will be many difficulties in carrying out such a project, and it probably must be done under governmental auspices. Before it is entered upon, more exhaustive studies than any yet made should be undertaken to determine the areas best adapted to the raising of beets as well as of the yield that can be counted upon.

It has been shown that grasslands are widely distributed in the Territory and that those in the southwest of Alaska probably offer a field for stock raising. It appears likely that these may yet be drawn upon for a supply of meat for our growing population. There is also much grassland in the interior, notably in the Yukon and Kuskokwim basins. In this province, however, the season of pasturage is only about three months long. It is not probable that beef could be raised for export with eight or nine months of feeding necessary. There are, however, some areas like that of the upper White River basin where there are some winter pasturages. Whether these are extensive enough for cattle raising on a large scale remains to be seen. For the present it must be held that stock raising in the interior will be limited by the local market for the product, but there seems to be no reason why the inland region should not supply its own beef.

CHAPTER XXVI

Schools and Missions

THE DEVOTED and heroic work of Alaskan missionaries well deserves complete record, but it can only be outlined here. For long over a century men of many creeds have conscientiously labored to uplift the Alaskan native. Even though viewing their work in retrospect makes it clear that many earnest efforts have been misdirected and that by no means all who have entered upon this difficult task have been fitted for its problems, yet no one can doubt the high ideals which have been the motives of the movement as a whole. The few exceptions in a large group of missionaries serve but to emphasize the high character of the many men and women who have engaged in this noble work.

During the Russian days some schools, supported by company funds, were provided for the whites and creoles, but the education of the natives was entirely in the hands of missionaries of the Russian church. As in all other matters, there was a shameful neglect of education in Alaska for nearly 20 years after the annexation. Finally, as will be shown, a small appropriation was made for schools. For many years that part of the annual grant devoted to education was allocated to the various missions, but later wiser counsel prevailed and a system of government native schools was established. Meanwhile, schools for the whites were organized in the more accessible and larger communities. When Alaska became a territory, the education of the whites was turned over to the local officers; and since this, a good school system has been established. The schools of the large towns are comparable in standards to those in the States, and many of even the smallest settlements have very creditable schools. These are entirely supported by taxes levied in Alaska; the cost of native schools, as in the States, is carried by the Federal Government.

A detailed account of the present white schools of the Territory will not be necessary, for these maintain the same standards as those in the States. The Territory has provided fairly liberally for its schools, and most of even

SCHOOL AND MISSION BUILDINGS
Typical are the early school building at Mosquito Point (left, photo by J. B. Mertie) and the Episcopal Mission at Tanana (right, photo by F. H. Moffit).

the smaller communities have educational facilities. The law makes the establishment of schools for whites obligatory where a community contains five or more children of school age. These are managed by local committees, but are under the supervision of a territorial commissioner of education. They are provided for by territorial taxes and grants. The incorporated towns have their own school systems, supported by local taxes. Alaskan teachers are much better paid, even allowing for the difference in the cost of living, than are those of the older Eastern states. In 1920, there were 67 schools in the Territory, including eight four-year high schools, with a total enrollment of 3,482 pupils and 165 teachers. Eleven communities maintained night schools, with an enrollment of 408, for the teaching of foreign-born residents. Most Alaskan children are sent to the States for higher education, for until recently there was no school of collegiate grade in the Territory. In 1917, the legislature provided funds for the construction of an agricultural and mining school near Fairbanks. A building was constructed, but the territorial College of Agriculture and Mining was not opened until 1922. The Territory has a board of education of which the governor is *ex officio* president, but the territorial commissioner of education is the administrative head of the schools.

The Russian Period

It is commonly assumed that Russia's administration of Alaska was directed entirely to the commercial exploitation of her colony and that no thought was given by the Imperial Government to the welfare of its distant subjects. Such opinions are far from being justified. In no field is it more evident that Russia had something more than a commercial interest in her American colony than in her support of its schools and missions. Primitive though these may have been when judged by modern standards, they compared favorably with similar institutions in the mother country.

Peter the Great, whose broad plans of Russian expansion and empire-building led, as we have seen, to the discovery of Russian America, was also the founder of the first system of schools for his domain. His projects were advanced and expanded by his successors, notably by Catherine II, during whose reign the first American settlements were made. In 1782, Catherine appointed a commission to make recommendations for a plan of elementary education in Russia; and under her successor, in 1802, the first minister of education was appointed. Popular education was, therefore, receiving earnest attention by the Imperial Government when the first charter was granted to the Russian American Company. No doubt for this reason that charter included a clause for the support of schools as well as missions in the new colony.

The educational projects formulated at St. Petersburg received but scant support from the first governor, hard-headed old Baranof, who could see no merit in anything that did not contribute to his immediate profits. Among his successors, however, were men of high character who gave strong support to the schools and missions, regarded by Baranof with nothing but aversion. It is certainly remarkable that before the close of the Russian administration four district schools had been founded at Sitka for the education of the 600 Russians and probably not over 2,000 creoles who constituted the entire civilized population of the Russian American colony. At this time too some 16 missions administered to the spiritual needs of the colony, and their work was largely among the natives. Those who are inclined to sneer at Russia's administration of her American colony should realize that Russia did far more for the education and christianizing of her American subjects than we did for the first 20 years after annexation.

As has already been shown, Shelikof, who established the first Russian colony in America, attempted some teaching and christianizing of the native children. As the principal instigator of the organization of the Russian American Company, although he did not live to see his plan completed, Shelikof was sympathetic with the plan of teaching and converting the natives, if for no other reason than because a civilized subject would be far more valuable to the company than a savage.

More disinterested work for the civilization of the natives was started in Russian America with the arrival at Kodiak of the first missionaries on September 24, 1794. At the will of the Holy Synod a little band of monks, led by the Archimandrite Iosaph, set out from Moscow in January and made the long journey across Siberia and the Pacific, the first of their church to go beyond the seas. These simple men did not lack religious enthusiasm, but they were little fitted for the task which confronted them. Coming from the peasant class, with but little education, and having lived for most of their lives in monasteries, they had had no experience to help them grapple with the frontier or to deal with a rough trader like Baranof. The monks with their purely religious training and experience could not deal with those whose lives had been directed to more practical ends. Baranof regarded them as useless supernumeraries who could give him no help in his difficult task of providing food for his colonies and dividends for his stockholders. Both the lack of warmth in their reception and their religious zeal to baptize the heathen natives led the monks soon to scatter out to the native settlements. In their own estimation, these early missionaries performed marvels, for their leader within a year was able to report: "The Lord be praised! We have baptized 7,000 Americans and performed 2,000 marriage services."[1] There is no record, however, to show what moral influence the monks had on this horde of new converts.

Father Herman, the most prominent of this group, rendered the most lasting and devoted services. Of his life Professor Golder has given us a delightful picture. He was destined for 40 years to render devoted service to the Kodiak natives. Father Herman came to Alaska from the Valaam Monastery on Lake Ladoga, not far from the Finnish-Russian boundary. His training, simple tastes, and religious fervor gave him a preference for a life far from the abode of man. This and his constant troubles with the fur traders led him to found a retreat on what is now

[1] Golder, F. A., *Father Herman, Alaska's Saint,* Pullman, Washington, 1915.

called Spruce Island, a few miles from the town of Kodiak; there he established his mission of New Valaam. Here he built a chapel and a home and school for native orphans which was continued for many years after his death in 1837. Father Herman, though a recluse, never hesitated to visit Kodiak and other settlements where he felt his influence would do good.

Meanwhile, the Archimandrite Iosaph had returned to Russia to be consecrated bishop of the American colony. He and a band of devoted followers were lost in 1799 on the return voyage with the foundering of the *Phoenix,* the first vessel built in Alaska. Of the original group of monks, Father Makar labored among the natives of the Aleutian Islands and, according to the ecclesiastical records, won the entire population to Christianity. Father Juvenal visited Yakutat and in 1796 opened a school at Three Saints Bay, the site of Shelikof's first colony. His pupils were, however, soon transferred to Kodiak, where a native school had been opened by Father Herman. Juvenal himself visited the western shores of the Kenai Peninsula, and eventually crossed Cook Inlet and made his way to Iliamna Lake, where he was killed by the natives, the first martyr to the Christian faith in Alaska.

It will not be possible here to trace the work of the many Russian priests who performed noble service in Alaska. That all of those who came, however, were not true to the spirit of their faith is suggested by a regulation of the company forming a part of the charter of 1821, which provided that "priests must live virtuous lives, and must be supported and aided by the company officials." This may have been a slander on the priests introduced by Baranof's influence, for almost throughout his term he was constantly at war with them. And yet, in spite of the conflict, he gave freely of his own means toward the construction of churches at both Kodiak and Sitka. Whatever may have been the morals of the priests as a whole, they are known to have included some mischief-makers who could not resist the temptation to mix with temporal affairs. But the fact that Baranof's successors had little trouble with the priests is an indication that he was much at fault in the quarrel. No doubt, however, the priests, who included many well-educated men, found it easier to deal with the naval officers who succeeded Baranof in the government of the colony than with the ignorant and almost illiterate trader. The small class of meddlesome ecclesiastics who had made much trouble in Baranof's time, chiefly by their secret and sometimes false reports to the Holy Synod, practically wholly disappeared under his successors.

Though it is not practical here to trace the history of the Russian church in Alaska and of its large clergy, most of whom did much to uplift the natives, still no account of Alaskan missionaries would be complete without some reference to Father Veniaminof, the eminent priest, scholar, and scientist.

Ivan Veniaminof, a graduate of the Irkutsk seminary, came to Russian America as a young priest in 1824. His first mission was at Unalaska where his earnestness and pleasing personality quickly won him the respect and admiration of the Aleuts. He soon mastered the Aleut language, of which he wrote a grammar. For nine years he labored among these people and not only made a large number of converts but also did much to improve their physical conditions. Veniaminof's vision, however, extended far beyond his priestly duties; and he was the first of the group of missionaries, albeit but a small one, to study the land and its people. His publications on the Aleut language and ethnology are still the standard works of reference on the subjects to which they pertain. Moreover, he made many notes on the natural history of the islands, with observations on volcanoes and detailed records on meteorology. His were also the earliest scientific records on the seal herds of the Pribilof Islands, and his the best estimates of the native population of Russian America. Veniaminof was without doubt the most prominent intellect that developed in Russian America; Governor Wrangell, who was of equal intellectual standing, had become prominent as a scientist and explorer before he came to America.

It was on Wrangell's recommendation that Veniaminof was transferred to Sitka in 1834, and there for two years he labored among the natives and familiarized himself with their language. In 1839, he was recalled to Russia for consultation on church affairs, and there he presented a plan for reorganization of the colonial missions. In the following year he became bishop of Russian America and Kamchatka, under the name of Innocence. Realizing that his field required men of special training, he in 1841 established an ecclesiastical school at Sitka which four years later was raised to the rank of seminary. He hoped by this means to train the priests not only in the language of the people they were destined to serve but also in their customs and traditions. Such a project might well have been considered by the later founders of Alaskan missions belonging to other creeds. Measured by some of its graduates, this school must have set itself fairly high standards of education. It was supported by the Holy Synod, and it is recorded that in 1857 it had a grant of 7,000 rubles.

Veniaminof seems to have been free also from sectarian prejudices, for it was during his regime as bishop that a Lutheran chapel and minister were established at Sitka. This was for the benefit of the Protestants in the colony, mostly Finlanders and a few Swedes. The project had the strong support of Etolin, an Alaskan creole, himself a Protestant, and soon to become governor, who later gave an organ to the Lutheran chapel which was built. It is said that Roman Catholic priests, too, were invited to the colony to administer to those of their own faith among the employees of the company. These actions on the part of the bishop showed a spirit of religious tolerance which has by no means always been shown by all his successors in Alaskan missionary work.

Bishop Veniaminof is described as "a very formidable athletic man" standing six feet three and "quite herculean and clever." One of his disciples says, "When he preached the word of God all people listened and listened without moving. Nobody thought of fishing or hunting while he spoke, and nobody felt hungry as long as he was speaking, not even little children." Simpson, the English explorer, a more disinterested witness, says of the bishop:

> His appearance to which I have already alluded impresses a stranger with something of awe, while on further intercourse the gentleness which characterizes every word and deed insensibly moulds reverence and love; and at the same time his talents and attainments are such as to be worthy of his exalted station. With all this the bishop is sufficiently a man of the world to disdain anything like cant. His conversation, on the contrary, teems with amusement and instruction; and his company is much prized by all who have the honor of his acquaintance.

In 1858, the seat of the bishopric was removed to Yakutsk, and the colony lost its most distinguished man. Veniaminof continued to rise in the hierarchy and before his death reached the highest place in the church, becoming Metropolitan of Moscow. But with the transfer of the bishopric, Sitka also lost the seminary, which moved to Yakutsk. And after Veniaminof's departure there seems also to have been a general decline of church activities in the colony. Many of the reports of the Russian authorities are very critical of the work of the missionaries, in some cases even impugning their morals. Among them there were, however, many earnest, conscientious men who devotedly gave themselves to their tasks. Still, it is true that some who took part in this work were ignorant and performed their religious tasks in but a perfunctory way. This is especially true of the deacons, many of whom were creoles with but little education and at best unfitted for their tasks. Many of the outlying chapels were visited only once a year; and even where such visits were made by good men, they could have little influence in raising the standards of living and morals of their flocks.

In spite of all this the Russian church remained up to a few years ago the strongest single sect in Alaska. Under the treaty of annexation it maintained its Alaskan property and permission to continue its missionary work. The earnestness of the Holy Synod to continue in this field is shown by the fact that until the revolution of 1917 a large annual grant was made to the Alaskan Russian church, which was part of the bishopric of the United States. In 1890, the Russian church reported its communicants in Alaska at over 10,000, all natives or creoles, and the value of its property at over $300,000. In the same year the Protestant and Catholic churches had less than 2,000 communicants and property worth only $25,000. Such figures indicate that nearly a quarter of a century after the annexation in 1867 the Russian church was the only one that had made any marked progress in christianizing the natives. Some of the missionaries of other creeds, who arrived in Alaska at least half a century after the Russian church was well established and counted among its communicants at least half of the natives who had any close contact with the whites, by no means showed proper consideration for this field of authority of the older church. Among the first efforts of some of the early Protestant church work in Alaska were attempts to convert not natives from paganism to Christianity but communicants of the Russian church to Protestantism.

Something has been said of the educational work of the Russian church among the natives. Native schools were maintained at Sitka, Kodiak, Unalaska, and a few other places; but many of the Russian missions made no attempt at even the most elementary teaching, and it should be noted that the education of the natives was by no means regarded as the most important function of the church.

Aside from the church seminary at Sitka, the other schools of the colony were chiefly devoted to the education of the children of Russian officials and the training of servants of the company, principally drawn from the creoles. The first school for Russians and creoles was opened at Sitka in 1805, but it did not amount to much until about 1820 when it passed under the control of naval officers. This school was maintained by the company under the terms of the charter. The first real progress in the school occurred when Etolin was placed at its head in 1833. Himself a creole and first educated at Sitka, later to be sent to Russia, Etolin was probably the most remarkable of the native-born colonists, and by sheer ability he rose to be governor of the colony as well as an officer in the Russian navy. This colonial school became still more important when the theological seminary was removed to Yakutsk in 1858, for it then became the highest institution of learning in the colony. Its curriculum included navigation, bookkeeping and some other commercial courses, English, and theology. Its training was for company servants and also, as it appears, for lay brothers for church service. In 1862, it received an annual grant of 24,000 rubles from the company and 3,750 rubles from the Holy Synod in Russia to support religious teaching. In 1862, its pupils numbered 27, a good showing considering that the colony contained only a few thousand civilized people, including Russians and creoles. A girls' and a boys' school were also maintained at Sitka to take care of the orphans of company employees and to give elementary instruction to the children of the lower classes. In the meantime, under Veniaminof's leadership, the teaching of reading and writing to native children was undertaken at a number of the missions.

This brief review shows that the provision made for education in Russian America was by no means contemptible. The standards of education and schools appear to have been higher than the average of the Russian Empire of today. Certainly these efforts were far superior to any made by us in the 20 years following the annexation. We allowed the Russian schools at Sitka entirely to disappear and made no provision for the education of the many intelligent creoles of Alaska, who so far as any action on our part was concerned might lapse into barbarism. We were equally at fault in making no provision for the natives, neither schools nor missions being provided.

When later missions and schools were established, much criticism was leveled at the shortcomings of the Russian church and of its priests. It was pointed out that no English was taught, that no industrial schools were established, that many of the priests were satisfied with the formal observation of the church services and paid little heed to the improvement of the physical and moral conditions of their flocks. Above all, attention was directed to the lack of knowledge among many of the Russian priests of modern sanitation and physical welfare. There was, no doubt, much truth in these criticisms. On the other hand, however, it should be noted that it was the Russian church and priesthood that prevented the Alaskan natives from practically reverting to barbarism. It was the graduates of the Sitka school who during this period of total neglect maintained such standards of education and morals as were maintained at all. While a good many of the church servants were more or less illiterate half-breeds—mostly, however, lay brothers—the missions included enough educated men of high ideals to maintain some standards of education and the torch of Christianity. Alaska also contained a few educated Russians, mostly native-born, who threw their lot with the new American colony, never dreaming that the great American republic would both repudiate its treaty obligations by not looking after its new citizens and utterly neglect its new possessions. We owe a debt of gratitude to this little band of Russian priests who stood by their missions when Alaska became absolute chaos so far as government schools or missions were concerned.

Aside from their deep knowledge of the Alaskan natives, the Russian priesthood had an advantage in that their ritual and wonderful coloring of robes and church fittings made a greater appeal to the simple and immature native minds than did the simpler settings and services of the Protestant sects. Perhaps this fact will account for the predominance of Russian Catholics among the Alaskan natives. It is evidence of the narrowness of some of the Protestant missionaries who went to Alaska that they failed to recognize the great good that had been accomplished by the Russian church, whose priesthood was far better qualified to deal with the natives than they were themselves. Direct invasions of the Russian parishes, as at Sitka, Kodiak, and Unalaska, were by no means uncommon. Such action brought confusion to the minds of the simple natives, who could not understand why a new form of Christianity foreign to them, their parents, and often their grandparents should be forced upon them. This was done at a time when much the larger portion of the Alaskan natives were entirely unconverted to Christianity. It was easier and far more comfortable to establish missions in the larger settlements and undertake the conversion of Russian Catholics to Protestantism than to strike out into the wilderness as the true pioneers of the church had done. Such action is, however, not calculated to win the support of intelligent people.

Missionary Work after 1867

As has been previously indicated, the Hudson Bay Company traders invaded the Russian American territory in the upper Yukon before the middle of the 19th century. A decade later came the missionaries of the Church of England. Of these the first was the Rev. W. W. Kirby, later archdeacon, who arrived at Fort Yukon in 1861 and devoted about a week to preaching to the Indians. In 1862 Archdeacon McDonald arrived on a similar mission. It appears that at this time no regular mission was established at Fork Yukon, probably for the reason that the church was well aware that the Hudson Bay Company was trespassing on Russian territory and might at any time be summarily expelled. The Church of England, however, by no means neglected this field, and its missionaries at various times visited the tribes along the Yukon as far down as the mouth of the Tanana and as far up as the boundary and beyond. For a time a mission was maintained at La Pierre house on the Porcupine, known to be well within Canadian territory, and from here missionaries made not infrequent journeys to the Yukon. The veteran missionary, Bishop Bompas, was at Fort Yukon in 1869 when the Hudson Bay Company was forced to abandon the post by order of Captain Raymond, who raised the American flag and thus finally ejected the British corporation. Bishop

Bompas, however, finding that the American churches exhibited no anxiety to take possession of this mission field, was not willing to abandon it. Most of his missions were in the Canadian Yukon; but in 1888, through the Rev. T. H. Carnahan, he established St. James Mission at the mouth of the Tozitna River, 18 miles below the Tanana, near a trading post known as Fort Adams. This was maintained until 1891, when it was turned over to the Rev. J. L. Prevost of the Methodist Episcopal church.

Meanwhile, the natives of the coastal region were utterly neglected by both the Government and American churches, and their interests were looked after only by the Russian church with its limited resources. The powerful Russian company, which in spite of its shortcomings had maintained some measure of discipline among the nátives and above all refrained from introducing alcohol among them, was succeeded by a horde of small traders who sailed hither and yon among the native settlements and whose chief stock in trade was whiskey. Under these conditions it was inevitable that the natives be debauched wherever they were within reach of this malicious influence. For this debauching of the natives by the freebooting traders, the American people are responsible. No one was interested enough in the faraway colony to give it a civil government.

Though the importation of whiskey was somewhat checked by the customs officials, the natives were soon taught to distill their own alcohol from molasses, the importation of which was strictly legal. There can be no question that during the first 15 years of American rule the natives retrograded and, had these conditions continued, would eventually have reverted in part to barbarism. It is not pleasant to record that our treatment of the Alaskan natives during this period was worse than that of the Russian American Company. The Army officers stationed at Wrangell, Sitka, and other places did what little they could under the law and with the facilities given them to suppress the abuses. Appeals were also made to American churches, but these for many years appear to have received scant attention. Meantime, various earnest missionary societies were advocating doing something for the Alaskan natives.

It remained, however, for Clah, a British Columbia Indian, known to the whites as Philip McKay, to start the missionary work among the natives of Alaska. Clah, who had been educated at the Methodist mission of Fort Simpson, arrived at Wrangell in the summer of 1876 with seven Indian companions to cut wood for the Army post. This group of Indians had learned to respect the Sabbath and on Sunday met for worship under the leadership of Clah. Captain S. P. Jocelyn, commander of the post, encouraged them by providing a meeting place. This came to the attention of the Rev. Thomas Crosby, head of the Fort Simpson mission, and he visited Wrangell in the fall of 1876 and held a meeting with the Indians at which some 36 subscribed to a church fund which was afterwards turned over to the Presbyterians. Through Jocelyn's influence, Clah was induced to stay at Wrangell and open an Indian school and mission under American auspices. The zeal of the Wrangell natives to attend this school is evidence of the neglect that had been shown them.

After Clah, the Methodist Indian, the Presbyterians were the first to take up the Alaskan work, though similar plans were at that time also being matured by Father Segher of the Roman Catholic church. Credit for this work belongs to the Oregon Presbytery. As early as 1869, the Rev. A. L. Lindsey of Porland had become interested in the Alaskan missionary field, chiefly because of a conference he had held with William H. Seward after his northern journey. Dr. Lindsey continued for a number of years to gather information about Alaska and to interest the Presbyterian church in this field, but he had no success until 1877 when he secured the assignment of J. C. Mallory to this work. The opening of the mission at Wrangell is recorded in the official report of the missionary board as follows:

> In May at Dr. Lindsey's expense Mr. Mallory was furnished with the necessary funds to enter the field at once, explore the ground, and take charge of a small school already opened at Wrangell. [This is the Indian school noted above.] He visited Sitka, Fort Wrangell, and the intervening regions and very industriously prosecuted the work. He assumed responsibility for the school and employed Philip McKay [Clah], a native convert, to assist. The work was progressing encouragingly when Mr. Mallory, having accepted a government appointment in Arizona, was forced to leave the ground. Mrs. A. R. McFarland, a member of the First Presbyterian church at Portland, a woman of large and successful experience on the frontier, was secured to fill the vacancy; and she carried on the work without serious interruption. On the eve of Mrs. McFarland's departure Dr. Sheldon Jackson, having arrived at Portland on a visit and being desirous of seeing the region beyond, acted as an escort, going up and returning by the same mail steamer.

For some time after, the Wrangell mission was entirely supported by the Presbyterian Church of Portland and, indeed, chiefly by its pastor, Dr. Lindsey. Hence it was due entirely to Dr. Lindsey's initiative that the first Protestant mission was established in Alaska, and the credit for the work at the Wrangell mission is due to Mrs. McFarland and to the Rev. S. Hall Young who joined her in the following year, having been sent to Alaska by the Presbyterian Home Missionary Board. At the same time, 1878, the Rev. John Brady, later to become governor of Alaska, was dispatched to Sitka, where he maintained a Presbyterian mission for about six months when he resigned. It is probable that Brady, recognizing that he was operating in competition with the Russian church which had been established at Sitka for 75 years and of which most of the natives were at least nominally members, found his task distasteful. Dr. Young, however, continued his work at Wrangell and in other parts of the Territory for many years and, indeed, became the dean of Alaskan missionaries.

Mrs. McFarland soon discovered that Wrangell, like the rest of Alaska, was practically beyond the pale of the law, for the military forces were withdrawn in 1877. She therefore called a meeting of the Indians in February, 1878, being supported in this act by the revenue collector, J. C. Dennis, the only government representative in the district, who was attempting to maintain order but was without legal authority. The following resolutions were passed and signed by many of the Indians present:

I. We concur in the action of Mr. J. C. Dennis, deputy collector of U.S. customs, appointing Toya-at, Matthew, and Sam to search all canoes and stop the traffic of liquor among the Indians.

II. We who profess to be Christians promise with God's help to strive as much as possible to live at peace with each other, to have no fighting or quarreling, no tale-bearing among us. These things are sinful and should not exist among Christians.

III. For any troubles that arise among the brethren between husbands and wives, or if any man leaves his wife, their brethren Toya-at, Moses, Matthew, Aaron, and Lot shall have authority to settle the troubles and to decide what punishment shall be imposed and, if fines are imposed, how much the fines shall be.

IV. The authority of these brethren is binding upon all, and no person is to interfere with them, as they are appointed by Mr. Dennis and Mrs. McFarland.

V. To the above we subscribe our names.

It is not to be supposed that this covenant stopped all the Indian troubles at Wrangell, but it did have much good effect. Moreover, it bears testimony to the intelligence of the Indians who saw the need of such action. With the withdrawal of the troops, all semblance of governmental authority ceased; the Indians had long since lost much of the restraint of tribal government and customs. When the Washington government scuttled ship, it fell to a woman missionary and a deputy collector to do what they could to establish order.

Dr. Young's arrival in Wrangell left Mrs. McFarland free to devote herself entirely to her cherished project of founding a home for Indian girls. Two years later the work of the mission was extended by the establishment of a school at what was afterwards named Haines on Lynn Canal. The credit for this project belongs to Mrs. McFarland and Dr. Young, but its execution was due to an Indian woman, the wife of a white trader named Dickson. Dickson opened a trading post and his wife a school for the people of her own race. This work was carried on almost unaided for a year, when the Rev. E. S. Willard and wife arrived at Haines to open a mission. This new mission was, however, not given adequate support or any definite means of communication with the outside world. Therefore, the devoted missionary and his wife suffered entirely unnecessary hardships.

Meanwhile Dr. Young, who was of an adventurous disposition, made many long canoe journeys among the fiords and islands of Southeastern Alaska. In the course of these he made, in company with John Muir, the important exploration of Glacier Bay referred to in Chapter XVI. Dr. Young thus attained an intimate knowledge of the physical features of his work and, above all, learned to know the natives, their language and customs. This knowledge, gained at great hardship, was of inestimable service in the extension of the Presbyterian missionary work which followed during the next few years.

Credit for the pioneer Protestant missionary work among the natives of Southeastern Alaska unquestionably belongs, then, to Mrs. McFarland and Dr. Young. It should be noted, however, that while their names, along with that of Willard, must stand first on the roll of honor, Dr. Sheldon Jackson, too, rendered most important service to the cause. His work will be discussed in the following section of this chapter.

Though the Presbyterians were the first to organize their work in the missionary field, other churches, too, had at almost the same time been awakened to the spiritual needs of the Alaskan natives. The first Catholic missionary to visit Alaska was Father Emile Petitot, well known for his important contribution on the geography and ethnology of the Mackenzie basin, who in 1870 reached the Yukon River by the Hudson Bay route down the Porcupine River. But recognizing that the Church of England had already occupied the upper Yukon, he made no efforts to establish a mission.

Archbishop Segher was the pioneer Catholic missionary in Alaska. He appears to have long been interested in the Alaskan field and made his first journey along the coast as far west as Kodiak in 1878. His careful study of this region led him to decide that the Pacific littoral of the Territory was already well occupied by the Russian church, and he had no desire to spend his energies in converting the communicants of the Russian church to Roman Catholicism. He, however, established a chapel at Wrangell, then the largest white settlement in Alaska. Bishop Segher's reconnaissance in this field had but served to enhance his enthusiasm, and he well knew that there were many natives far beyond the reach of the long-established Russian church. Hence, he made another journey to Alaska, during which he reached the mouth of the Yukon and made the difficult journey up-river to the Indian settlement of Nulato. Here he found an entirely unoccupied field lying between the Church of England missions on the upper river and the Russian missions of the lower river.

His long-cherished plan for a mission at Nulato was finally carried out in 1886. In July of that year the bishop, accompanied by Father Pascal Tosi and Father Aloysius Ribot, crossed the Chilkoot Pass and made a difficult and dangerous journey down the river in boats of their own construction. Finding a settlement of miners at the mouth of the Stewart River, the bishop left his two priests at that place and continued downstream to Nukluklayet, his only attendant being a man named Fuller. The season was too late for them to continue the voyage by boat so that, waiting until the ice came, the travelers made their way by sleds. Fuller, who had during this journey developed symptoms of insanity, on November 28, 1886, shot the bishop, killing him instantly. The locality of the murder is near the mouth of the Koyukuk, and the tragic event is commemorated in the name of a small prominence called

"Bishop Rock." The companions of the bishop reached the lower river the following summer and began that missionary work in this field which has continued to the present day.

Meanwhile, northwestern Alaska had also been visited by a representative of the Catholic church. In 1883, the Rev. P. F. Healy, S. J., visited Unalaska, St. Paul in the Pribilof Islands, St. Michael on Bering Sea, and as far north as Point Hope on the Arctic Ocean. This appears to have been the first missionary penetration of the Bering Sea littoral, but it was not immediately followed by the establishment of stations. As in other parts of Alaska, the Catholic fathers refused to undertake the proselytizing of natives who were already under the influence of the Russian church, as were those of Bering Sea.

In 1879 the Rev. S. E. Howry and the Rev. A. E. Baer of the Society of Mennonites visited Kodiak and Cook Inlet in the interests of missionary work. Like Bishop Segher, they decided that this field was well occupied by the Russian church, and they abandoned their project. The Moravian church was one of the first to invade this northern field. In 1884, two of its clergy, J. A. H. Hartman and W. H. Weinland, made a long journey into the lower Kuskokwim and Bristol Bay region, including a difficult overland trip from Goodnews Bay to Nushagak. Finding this area entirely unoccupied, Weinland, with the Rev. J. H. Killbuck, returned in the following year and formed the mission of Bethel on the lower Kuskokwim and thus began a task which has been successfully continued to the present time by the Moravian church. Killbuck, who was a full-blooded Delaware Indian, continued his splendid work among the natives of Alaska until his death in 1922. His was a life of unselfish devotion.

Though the Church of England had, as already shown, even during the Russian regime carried on missionary work on the upper Yukon, the American Episcopal church neglected Alaska until 1885, when one of its members, the Rev. Octavius Parker, became a government school teacher at St. Michael. The following year he was joined by the Rev. John Chapman, and an Episcopal mission, the first in Alaska, was established at Anvik on the lower Yukon. Here for over 35 years Mr. and Mrs. Chapman successfully carried on their devoted work among the Indians. Mr.

Chapman, both by seniority and service rendered, earned the title of dean of Alaskan missionaries.

In the years to follow, many other Episcopal missions were founded in Alaska, notably the one at Point Hope by Dr. J. B. Driggs in 1890. The first great impetus given to the Episcopal missions was with the coming of the bishop. The Right Reverend Peter Trimble Rowe was made bishop of Alaska in 1895; and during the next 20 years, he was destined to become intimately acquainted with even the most remote parts of the Territory. An indefatigable traveler, Bishop Rowe was ever on his journeys, with dog team in winter, with canoe or boat in summer. He not only came to know the natives of his vast diocese but also became the friend and adviser of the whites as well. Modest, with a tolerance toward all creeds, and possessed of a sympathetic understanding of the frontiersman achieved by few if any other churchmen, Bishop Rowe came to be respected and loved by all who knew him.

Metlakatla in Southeastern Alaska is undoubtedly the most successful of missions that has ever been organized on the northwest coast. William Duncan, its founder and for nearly half a century its leader, who was born in Yorkshire, England, in 1828, was sent to Port Simpson in British Columbia as a lay missionary in 1857 by the Church Missionary Society. After a few years' work at Port Simpson, Duncan moved his converts to Metlakatla, a near-by island, and there the settlement prospered for a number of years. Duncan's principle was that it was not sufficient to make converts of the Indians; he felt that they must also be made self-supporting under the new industrial conditions imposed by the invasion of their hunting and fishing grounds by the white men. He, therefore, gradually transformed his mission into a self-supporting colony. His religious services were devised by himself and adapted to the simple ideas of the natives. Father Duncan, as he was always called, ruled his mission with an iron hand and was intolerant of outside interference, but he was beloved by all his converts.

When the bishop of the diocese attempted to dictate the form of his religious services and teachings, Duncan refused to obey and was peremptorily relieved of his charge. The agents of the American Church Missionary Society then took possession. The Metlakatlans, however, would have none of them and insisted that Duncan was their minister and teacher. For a time the hitherto peaceful settlement was set by the ears by this ecclesiastical interference, and several riots threatened. Duncan then took the bold step of transferring his colony across the near-by frontier into Alaska. A conference with the Washington authorities gave him assurance of protection; and, in 1887, 823 out of a total of 948 Indians at Metlakatla followed Duncan to the land of promise. A bay on the north side of Annette Island had been chosen for the new colony and was called New Metlakatla. This move showed the devotion of the natives to Duncan, for thereby they abandoned to the bishop all their buildings, the fruit of many years of labor.

The new colony flourished almost from the start. A saw mill was installed, a salmon cannery built, and many substantial buildings erected. Annette Island was set aside for the use of Duncan's Indians by Congressional act in 1891. The federal authorities left Duncan to his own devices, and there was no meddlesome bishop to contend with. The natives learned carpentry, seamanship, boat building, and other trades; and like the Pilgrim fathers they could worship God in the manner of their own choosing. In the decade which followed some of the Metlakatlans migrated to other parts of Alaska and engaged in various industries, chiefly lumbering and fishing. Though the influence of the colony was thus extended, Metlakatla itself lost in population, and by 1910 it numbered only 465. In 1898, Duncan reported that his colony received $11,000 in subscriptions from outside friends; and with this and his own means he founded the Metlakatla Industrial Company, which after seven years had a paid-up capital of $54,000, of which $3,000 belonged to the natives. The company owned a saw mill, cannery, and general store. Duncan's own share of the stock in the company was $40,000, and this was the basis of the fortune that he left to the community on his death. Duncan also states that between 1888 and 1894 he received allotments totalling $12,700 from the federal educational funds for Alaska.

As the Indians became civilized and industrially independent, they began to chafe under Duncan's paternal rule. These natives belonged to Tsimshian stock; previous to their civilization they were closely identified in customs with their kindred, the Haidas, and they are among the most intelligent Indians of the northwest coast. Duncan's principle was to keep them far apart from the whites, and to bring this about he refused to give any instruction beyond the lowest grades. As a consequence, the Metlakatlans found themselves at an industrial disadvantage with the other natives, who were better educated. Though practically all the natives loved and respected Duncan, dissatisfaction grew at some of his policies. Finally the natives petitioned for a government school, which Duncan refused to permit. In 1912 a memorable conference was held by Walter Fisher, then Secretary of the Interior, at Metlakatla at which the natives in a dignified manner set forth their grievances. One and all of the speakers, who were chiefly old men and original founders of the colony, acknowledged their deep gratitude to Duncan; but the upshot was that a government school was founded and Father Duncan's reign practically ceased, though he continued to reside in the village and to lead in the church work. The government school was crowded with pupils, and the natives themselves contributed toward its support. So great was the desire to learn that the teacher was compelled to start a night school for adults. Gradually changes were instituted in the form of government, and a democracy was substituted for the old autocratic rule.

These facts are here set forth because it has been charged that the displacing of Duncan as teacher was the result of Washington bureaucracy. The change was brought about by the natives themselves, who were fully competent to judge of their own needs. Duncan died in 1918 and left his entire estate, which aggregated over $100,000 and had been amassed at Metlakatla, on trust, the income to be used by the community.

Duncan clearly demonstrated what could be accomplished by a proper system with the more intelligent natives of Southeastern Alaska. Though he instilled religious principles in his flock, and his children are among the most pious of Alaskan natives, yet he realized that the great problem was to make his people industrially independent, for without such independence they could not do their part in the body politic. Duncan's good business training as a youth and his native shrewdness led him to recognize and to utilize for his people the available commercial opportunities. His success as a missionary and teacher was due to several reasons outside of his personality which, as in all such work, is of first importance: he worked to elevate the entire community; he achieved industrial independence for his colony by sound business management; he avoided pauperizing the natives by making them find their own means of support; and in his religious and secular education he adapted his teaching to the simple minds of his people. His success, however, was only possible because he was dealing with exceptionally intelligent natives and because the region in which he labored had such resources as fish and timber which could profitably be developed without a great amount of capital.

Duncan's plan of uplifting the entire community rather than, as has been done at many missions, educating the brightest children, often to make them unfitted for the environment to which they must return, could well be copied. The native boarding school, at one time very popular, is by no means an unmixed evil; for it has often happened that the graduates who have lost their native arts and crafts have found no means of subsistence. Mr. Chapman's 30-odd years of service at Anvik was on Duncan's principle of seeking to advance a community rather than selected individuals; but he labored under the handicap of having less intelligent natives than had Duncan and the fact that there were no good industrial opportunities like those of Southeastern Alaska. W. T. Lopp has founded a number of similar industrial communities in Southeastern Alaska as part of his work of educating the Alaskan natives.

The Work of Sheldon Jackson

The civil government organized by the residents of Sitka in 1868 attempted to provide a school for the community. A building was purchased and, with the assistance of the Army officers, a school was maintained for several years, but it seems to have been discontinued when the military forces were withdrawn in 1877. The project was revived in 1879 through the efforts of Capt. L. A. Beardslee, the naval commandant who succeeded the Army officer in the government of the Territory. At that time there were 108 Russian and creole children at Sitka, and the teacher of the school, Alonzo E. Austin, performed valuable service in teaching English to these young Americans who were being entirely neglected by the Washington Government. This school was but a makeshift and its work in strong contrast to the educational facilities offered at Sitka previous to the annexation.

At this time the only attention the Government had given to education in Alaska was by compelling the Alaska Commercial Company by terms of its lease of the seal rookeries to maintain a school for natives on the Pribilof Islands. This was for a long time the only school north of Sitka except such as were maintained by the Russian church. For a time the company, entirely on its own initiative, also maintained a native school at Unalaska. The Pribilof school, which was under the direct supervision of the resident government agent, was for a long time the best in Alaska. By terms of its lease the company also provided medical attention for the Pribilof Islands. Thus the only help given Alaskan natives outside of a few missions was that furnished by a private corporation.

The first civil code for Alaska, enacted in May, 1884, had provision for the education of Alaskan children, carrying an appropriation of $25,000. This clause was to be put into effect by the Secretary of the Interior. In the following March he authorized the commissioner of education to take action. Dr. Sheldon Jackson was then appointed United States special agent for education in Alaska.

Dr. Jackson's connection with the founding of the Wrangell mission has already been noted, but it was only that of a casual traveler. At this time his designated field of activity was in Arizona and New Mexico and his journey to Alaska but a vacation. Though his observations extended but little beyond those obtained from the deck of a steamer, his interest had been aroused, and his indomitable energy and enthusiasm led him to assume the voluntary task of arousing enthusiasm and gaining financial support for evangelistic work in this new field. The task, once assumed, became the principal work of his life.

His first venture into Alaska by no means won the approval of the Presbyterian Home Missionary Board, which by a tactful resolution suggested that his assigned field of activity was sufficient to absorb all his energies. Jackson, however, wielded a tremendous influence in the Presbyterian church both because of his strong personality and because he was then editor of a widely circulated journal, *The Rocky Mountain Presbyterian.* In its columns he valiantly espoused the cause of the Alaskan missions and supplemented this effort by many public addresses. In spite of the opposition of the church authorities he continued making summer tours in Alaska and, without official warrant, assumed responsibility for the support of missions. His position was much strengthened by the publication in 1880 of a book on Alaska, the first to be issued since Dall's famous work of a decade before. As Jackson's knowledge of the Territory at this time had been gained by only three casual visits, the book was chiefly a compilation. On the whole it was a fairly creditable piece of work, though full of errors that could have been avoided by a more careful study of Dall's work. By virtue of this book and his innumerable addresses, Jackson became, at least in church circles, the authority on Alaska, a position entirely unwarranted by his knowledge of the Territory. The records, however, show that the money raised for the Alaskan Presbyterian missions was almost entirely the result of his personal efforts. It is also true that, though his Alaskan journeys were only hasty ones, his visits to the then-isolated missions were a powerful influence in encouraging the men and women to continue their difficult labors. What coordination of work there was was largely due to his efforts.

By virtue of his important services in thus arousing public interest in the Alaskan natives and in securing money for the Presbyterian missions, he attempted for a long time to have his self-appointed office of supervisor of Alaskan Presbyterian missions recognized by the Board, but without success. Finally in 1885, he was placed in charge of the Sitka mission and church, but without any control of the other missions, and here he spent about six months, a period which covered the only personal experience he had in Alaskan missions. With characteristic independence Jackson promptly transferred the center of Presbyterian missions from Wrangell to Sitka and thus dominated the situation. He threw himself into the work of building up the Sitka station, which now became the famous "Sheldon Jackson Institution."

Jackson was so widely known by his addresses and publications on Alaska and had himself been so active in securing a civil government for the Territory that it was perhaps logical that he should now be charged with the organizing of a school system. It was held by the federal authorities that the appropriation would not justify a salary of more than $1,200, which, measured by purchasing power, is as high as any salary since paid for the same position.

Since this was not considered a sufficient recompense, the Presbyterian Board agreed to pay an equal sum. It is rather remarkable that the Presbyterian church did not see fit to recognize the important service that Jackson had performed for its Alaskan missions until his appointment as federal agent of schools. Too, the action of appointing as federal agent of education a man who at the same time became the agent of a church certainly deserves criticism, for it can not be considered other than illegal. So far as Dr. Jackson is concerned, however, it should be recorded that, though he may be charged with being somewhat overliberal in his allotments of government funds to the Presbyterian missions of which he had charge, he made every effort to induce other churches to enter his field. Indeed, had it not been for Jackson's personal appeals, it is probable that the other churches would have long delayed the taking up of Alaskan missionary work. Several of the new missions could not have been started except for the liberal grants made by Jackson from government funds.

Jackson's task was no easy one, for with only a small grant of funds he was charged with the duty of establishing schools over an area of nearly 600,000 square miles, for a population of over 30,000 people, in a region almost entirely inaccessible to regular means of transportation. For a number of years he did not attempt to start schools except along the established routes of travel bordering the Pacific seaboard. His policies were shaped so as to obtain all the help from outside agencies possible, and this of course meant the church missions. White children were few, and their needs were in a measure provided for by establishing schools at the principal settlements in Southeastern Alaska. Between 1887 and 1892 the total appropriation available was $205,000, of which $112,200 were allotted to the missions, $61,500 to the Presbyterian missions. The large allotment to the latter was due to the fact that the Sheldon Jackson Institute at Sitka was built up as an industrial school which in theory was to serve the whole Territory, though in actual practice the pupils were nearly all from near-by localities.

Jackson's original commission provided that he should reside at Sitka, the capital; but this was not to his liking, and he soon had his headquarters transferred to Washington and made only summer journeys to Alaska. From this vantage point his personal appeals to Congress gave him an increase of appropriations—these in 1889 reached $50,000, to be reduced again in 1892 to $30,000. Unfortunately, while his energetic personality won for him many friends, it also made him bitter opponents, and there was a constant row on about Alaskan educational affairs. His enemies included some of the best people in the Territory; they were, however, powerless to oppose him at a distance. Residence in Washington gave him opportunity to exercise much influence in Alaskan affairs, including federal appointments, and this fact did not increase his popularity in Alaska. One of the sources of strong criticism and even stronger commendation was Jackson's management of the government reindeer herd, a subject that needs to be discussed in some detail.

The plan for the introduction of reindeer into Alaska originated with the Revenue Cutter Service. Beginning in 1879 revenue cutters had annually visited the Alaskan shores of Bering Sea and the Arctic Ocean, and thus their officers came to have an intimate knowledge of the physical conditions of this province and of its Eskimo inhabitants. Their cruises also extended to the Siberian coast, where domesticated reindeer had long been in use among the natives. The experienced mariners of the service could not help being impressed by the identity of the topography, vegetation, and climate of the lands on the two opposing shores, which at Cape Prince of Wales are separated by only 56 miles. They also observed that, while the Alaskan Eskimo depended entirely on fish and game for food and clothing, some of the Siberians had advanced beyond the hunting stage and become a pastoral people because of their reindeer herds. The presence of the wild reindeer or barren ground caribou on the Alaskan side of Bering Sea and the Arctic Ocean gave definite proof that the environment here was favorable to the domesticated animal.

The first recommendation for the introduction of domesticated reindeer into Alaska was by the naturalist, Dr. Charles H. Townsend, who accompanied the *Corwin* Arctic expedition in 1885, during the course of which he made a long journey up the Kobuk River, already referred to in Chapter XVI. Townsend added the following observations[2] to his description of the caribou or wild reindeer:

[2] *Report of the Revenue Marine Steamer* Corwin *in the Arctic Ocean in the Year 1885*, Washington, D.C., 1887, p. 88.

Notwithstanding the fact that large herds of reindeer are kept in a state of domestication by the Chuckchees at East Cape and other well-known places on the Asiatic side of Bering Straits, with whom the natives of the Alaska side communicate regularly, there appears to be no domestication of the species whatever in Alaska nor indeed in any part of North America. In time, when the general use of firearms by the natives of upper Alaska shall have reduced the number of this wary animal, the introduction of the tamer variety, which is a substantial support to the people just across the Straits, among our own thriftless, alcohol-bewitched Eskimos would be a philanthropic movement, contributing more toward their amelioration than any system of schools or kindred charities. . . . Something tending to render a wild people pastoral or agricultural ought to be the first step toward their advancement.

This suggestion of Dr. Townsend met with the hearty endorsement of Captain M. A. Healy commanding the *Corwin* who, however, had no means or authority to put it into effect. Five years later Dr. Jackson made his first journey to Arctic Alaska, with Captain Healy on the *Corwin*. Healy, who had a deep personal interest in the welfare of the Eskimo, impressed upon Jackson the desirability of introducing reindeer among the natives. Dr. Jackson, with his remarkable mental alertness, was quite willing to accept Healy's opinions, especially as he himself was entirely ignorant of the Eskimos and their environment. Upon his return to Washington in the fall of 1890, he recommended an appropriation from Congress to carry out Healy's plan, but he met with failure. Jackson, however, with his usual energy, made a public appeal for funds and gathered by subscription some $2,400 and authority for Captain Healy to transport the reindeer from Siberia to Alaska. During the summer of 1891 Jackson with the aid of Healy purchased 16 reindeer in Siberia and landed them on Unalaska Island. The project, like so many other of Jackson's, though admirably conceived, lacked practical sense in the execution. Instead of transporting the animals to the Seward Peninsula, the nearest part of Alaska and the one best suited to their habits, he had them carried 1,000 miles to the Aleutian Islands, which were not especially favorable to reindeer life. Here they were put ashore and, with no care taken of them, all died. Therefore, the money subscribed was all wasted.

Another and entirely independent plan for the introduction of reindeer should also be recorded. In the summer of 1890, W. T. Lopp and H. R. Thornton established the Congregational mission at Cape Prince of Wales. Through the natives they learned of the Siberian reindeer. Some of the Cape Prince of Wales natives owned interests in Siberian herds and were, of course, familiar with the reindeer industry. Lopp and Thornton were led to formulate a plan for introducing reindeer into Alaska by cooperating with the natives, transporting them across Bering Sea in the large native skin boats. Their means for carrying out this project were very small; and when Jackson arrived the next summer with ample funds and the use of a vessel, their own plan was abandoned. Lopp, however, continued his interest in the reindeer industry and was destined before many years to become the highest authority on the subject. He secured some deer for the missions, and his herd was the most successful of any in Alaska; he was also the first to carry out the plan of training natives to become reindeer herders and owners. Later he was placed at the head of the Reindeer Service and eventually headed all the educational work for the natives. He was without question the man to whom the eventual success of the reindeer enterprise is due, and it was not until he took hold of it that practical results were obtained.

Dr. Jackson, undaunted by the failure of his first reindeer venture, continued to importune Congress for funds, but he secured no money until 1894 when $6,000 were granted. Meanwhile, he had imported, with the aid of the Revenue Cutter Service and private subscription, some 295 animals. These were placed on the Seward Peninsula and, with the 1,000 animals later brought in entirely at government expense, were the stock from which the present herd, numbering some 200,000, are descended. During the next decade grants from the Government aggregated some $222,000. As the original cost of the reindeer and their transportation did not exceed $20,000 in all, it is evident that much money was spent on their care. This is especially striking in view of the fact that the reindeer feeds himself and that the natural increase will be ample reward for the herdsman. These large expenditures led to much criticism of the reindeer project which culminated in an investigation of the whole matter by a trustworthy and disinterested government official in 1905. As a consequence of his report the policy of introducing reindeer into Alaska was subjected to entirely unjust criticism, for the faults were not in the project itself but in its execution; Congress reduced the annual grant from $25,000 in 1905 to $9,000 in 1907.

The reindeer herd had by 1905 increased to 10,235 deer, but only 38 per cent had during a decade been transferred to the natives for whose use they had been imported, the Government still retaining title to only 30 per cent. It was part of Dr. Jackson's plan to give a part of the herds to missions that, in turn, were to turn them over to the natives in such numbers and on such terms as they saw fit. The profit of the balance was to accrue to the support of the missions. This plan was not only unauthorized by law but in part unconstitutional, for it made a direct gift to a church institution. The fact that Dr. Jackson, though no doubt actuated by the best of motives, was willing to carry out his plans by ignoring the supreme law of the land proved him to be unfitted for the task he had in hand.

Jackson also presented a large number of reindeer to Laplanders and other Scandinavians without any authority in law. These included a few Lapps brought over as reindeer herders during the early years of the project; there were also a number who arrived as by-products of the famous Klondike relief expedition already described, which had been largely fostered by Jackson. This importation, besides the 500 animals, included 100-odd herders, men, women, and children. Jackson seems to have seized the opportunity to further one of his favorite projects, the colonizing of northern Alaska by Lapps. Most of the imported Lapps either became discouraged and returned home or deserted at the time of the gold excitement. Those that remained, after having all their expenses paid by the Government, also received as gifts a considerable number of reindeer. These gifts were completely illegal, and it is hard to believe that the government officials would have continued the practice. Moreover, even if legal, the whole plan of Lapp colonization was utterly without merit. Why any intelligent person should want to transplant in the lands belonging to the Eskimo a people who at best were only a stage or two beyond them in civilization it is impossible to understand. If the plan had succeeded, we should have had to support the Eskimo population in addition to having taken up the civilization of the Lapps.

Though, as has been shown, the plan for the introduction of the reindeer into Alaska was due to others, the credit for gaining the necessary financial support belongs entirely to Dr. Jackson. Had he shown an equal amount of energy in the execution of the plan, the Reindeer Service would have been in far better condition. There need be no further evidence sought of the adaptability of the reindeer to Alaskan conditions than the survival of the project after 15 years of gross mismanagement.

Up to the influx of population between 1898 and 1900, there were comparatively few white children in the Territory, and the educational needs of these had been taken care of, so far as practical by the funds available, by establishing schools in the larger settlements. In 1900, the law provided that the schools in the incorporated towns should be under the supervision of the local communities. This left to the Bureau of Education only the administration of the schools in the smaller settlements. In 1905, the white schools were placed under the supervision of the Territory, and their support came entirely from local taxes.

This influx of population following the Klondike discovery drew further attention to Alaska and led to the establishment of many churches and chapels for the whites. The rather full statistics about missions and churches available for 1903, as shown in the following table, are of interest in indicating the status of religious work at about the close of the Jackson regime, and they are in one sense a testimony of the church activities which he had aroused:

MISSIONS AND CHURCHES IN ALASKA, 1903

Church	Number of Missions and Churches	Personnel: clergymen and lay teachers, physicians, nurses	First Mission	
			Place	Date
Russian	16	50	Kodiak	1794
Presbyterian	16	39	Wrangell	1877
Catholic	10	34	Wrangell	1878
Moravian	4	13	Bethel	1885
Episcopalian	14	33	Anvik	*1886
Methodist	6	9	Unalaska	1886
Baptist	2	8	Kodiak	1886
Friends	3	8	Kotzebue Sound	1887
Evangelical	3	16	Yakutat	†1887
Independent	1	2	Metlakatla	1887
Congregational	4	5	Cape Prince of Wales	1890
Lutheran (Norwegian)	1	3	Teller	1898
Total	82	220		

* The Church of England maintained missions in the Alaskan part of the upper Yukon from 1837 to 1891.

† There was a Swedish Lutheran mission at Sitka from 1842 to 1867.

During the 20 years of his service Jackson had accomplished much, even though the results were hardly commensurate with his expenditure of a million dollars of public funds. About 2,000 native children were enrolled in 40 widely scattered schools, having an average attendance of nearly 1,000. Dr. Jackson's untiring efforts were also an important contributing cause to the expansion of the Alaskan missionary work of the various churches. By his many addresses he not only awakened interest in the Alaskan field but also, in many instances by direct or indirect grants of public money, gave important financial support to the missions. The direct subsidizing of the missions, under the plan of making them contract schools for the education of natives, had by 1895 been found to be illegal and was discontinued. Indirect support was, however, continued by appointing as school teachers the missionaries themselves who thus drew their salaries from the Government.

The revelations published in 1906 of the condition of Alaskan school and reindeer affairs practically ended Dr. Jackson's control, though he continued in the service until his death a few years later. In spite of his many errors of both omission and commission, principally caused by an almost entire lack of administrative ability, Dr. Jackson performed a most important service to the people of the Territory, especially the natives. It was his task to gain support for the schools and missions, and it was very unfortunate that this should not have been made his work rather than the disbursement of funds and the administration of business affairs, for which, as the records only too plainly show, he was by temperament entirely unfitted. He gave over a quarter of a century of unremitting hard toil toward his self-chosen task, and he literally wore himself out in the public service.

Jackson's public addresses on Alaska numbered thousands, and his editorship for many years of a widely circulated sectarian paper whose columns he freely used to advance his plans made him widely known throughout the country. As the paid agent of the Presbyterian church he had, of course, its powerful support; and other churches to which he had allotted government funds also gave him strong moral support. For many years Jackson was the only federal official who spent his summers in Alaska and his winters in Washington, and it was only natural that he should come to be regarded in official circles as the final authority on Alaskan affairs.

Jackson by his personal efforts secured from Congress a total of $1,112,000 for the schools and for the Reindeer Service. This he spent on his various projects, often with apparently little concern for fiscal regulations or even law. In addition to this, and especially in the earlier years of his connection with Alaskan affairs, he raised large sums of money by private subscription for missions. Because of all these things Jackson for many years exercised a most powerful influence on Alaskan affairs, including not only schools and missions but also matters concerning the civil government of the Territory. There can be little doubt that many federal office holders in Alaska owed their appointments, or their removals, largely to Jackson's influence.

Dr. Jackson's great service to Alaska was in awakening the conscience of the American people to their long neglect of the distant colony. Without his untiring efforts civil government would doubtless have been longer delayed. Alaskans, both white and native, owe a great debt of gratitude to this man, for it was through him that knowledge of the Territory became widely disseminated.

To deny Jackson's services to the people of Alaska would be to belie the facts set forth above. On the other hand, a Jackson myth has been growing up in missionary circles which is equally far from the truth. Many honestly believe that he was a pioneer missionary in the Territory, though the facts show that, except for a few months spent at Sitka, he never did any missionary work in Alaska during his 30 years of service. He has also been represented as having undergone great hardships and as having made many perilous journeys; but this is also untrue, for nearly all his trips were made on steamers and the discomforts were no more than those that have been met by thousands of travelers in Alaska. Above all, Dr. Jackson has been credited with a profound knowledge of Alaska. This is a great exaggeration, for at best his knowledge was very superficial. In fact, it was his ignorance of the physical conditions in the Northland and of its people which led him to make many egregious blunders of administration. To prove this statement, it is necessary only to compare Jackson's own writings with the publications of others of the same date. Perhaps it was inevitable that a man so active in so many fields should not be able to go very deeply into any one subject and therefore be essentially superficial in his writings. Another factor coupled with this was Jackson's fondness for sensational statements, no doubt in part developed as necessary to the propaganda to which he devoted most of his life. Jackson also had a weakness for being the central figure in every situation and was given to taking credit to himself for the work of others.

But in spite of his many faults Jackson accomplished much for Alaska, and it must be said of him that he never spared himself but rather wore himself out physically in carrying out his difficult self-imposed task. For all of this he deserves full measure of credit. His was, however, a different field from that of such pioneer missionaries and teachers as Archdeacon McDonald, Bishop Segher, Mrs. McFarland, Dr. Young, Bishop Rowe, Dr. Chapman, Mr. Duncan, and Mr. Lopp, who sacrificed all and devoted their lives to the betterment of the natives of Alaska.

The Achievement of the Missionaries and Teachers

Missionaries in Alaska, like their brethren in other fields, have had their full share of criticism. One of the well-worn arguments against all this missionary work consists in claiming that the native is better off under his own code of moral conduct, developed by a natural evolution to meet the conditions of his environment, than under a superimposed one which ignores this evolution. Assuming that the native code of morals be adequate, yet the fact remains that it breaks down upon contact with a superior race, and the native without the priests is morally adrift. Moreover, the moral code of the native, though it may have enabled him to establish a crude social system, is certainly inferior to that of Christianity. Therefore any forward step, be it ever so small, is toward ultimate civilization. Even the greatest critics of missionary efforts have never developed a substitute for its methods and ideals. Without the heroic efforts of the missionary, the moral and physical conditions of the Alaskan native would be not only at a low ebb compared with those of the white man but even at a lower standard than they were before the coming of the superior race. While the native never had a better friend than the true Alaskan pioneer, in his wake there follows a certain number of the lowest class of white man who regards the Indian and the Eskimo as proper subjects for his nefarious operations. From these debauchees the native finds his only protection in the missionary and his teachings. If, as is sometimes charged, the results of many years of time and money devoted to missions are not very evident, it can be replied that the lifting of savages to civilization is not the work of a day nor even of a generation. It is the universal experience that the second generation of christianized Indians are far more amenable to moral training than the first, even though the teaching of the parents may be without visible results.

One fact must ever stand to the credit of the Alaskan missionaries: during the great excitement attending the discovery of the various gold fields they, as a class, stood steadfastly to their ideals by remaining with their people. This was a true test of their ideal to serve, for it must have been a tremendous temptation to take advantage of their opportunities to make the money they sadly needed for their dependents and old age. The few exceptions who could not resist the lure of gold and deserted their flocks but serve to prove the high ideals of the vast majority.

Among the many who have engaged in this noble work there were some who were unfitted for their task. The life of the Alaskan missionary requires a certain adaptability to environment which was not possessed by all whose conscience called them to this field. Not all had intelligence or education enough to grasp the psychology of the primitive races. They lacked the breadth of view to adapt their teaching to the conditions and concepts of their flocks. Some through sheer ignorance and stupidity attempted to uproot and destroy all of the native customs and traditions. To such a class belongs that one who in reprehensible ignorance of the meaning of the totem poles directed his natives to burn them, supposing them to be idols; this is very much as if a civilized community were directed to destroy all its memorials and tombstones. Equally in such a class is that missionary who reported with self unction that he had induced his converts to break away from the old and very sanitary custom of cremating the dead; in his poor little narrow mind he supposed that he had thus saved the souls of the departed and was too ignorant to realize that in his backward step he was simply helping to imperil the lives of the living.

Most of the missionaries in Alaska have been both intelligent and well-educated. Among them, however, are enough half-educated and stupid ones to make it plain that all those who send out missionaries have not yet learned that religious fervor is not the only requisite to successful missionary effort. No doubt the best results in training men and women for this field of service would be obtained if a special school could be maintained. Here the general education obtained elsewhere should be supplemented by special instruction in the ethnology of the natives, including such things as their traditions and social systems. The curriculum should also include instruction that would help to teach the natives in utilizing their local resources like carpentry, canning, agriculture, and weaving. It should also include instruction in hygiene, sanitation, and nursing. The graduates of such schools would enter their work equipped to help their people and not learn these things at the expense of their flocks.

In the early years of missionary work it was by no means fully recognized that the great problem was to educate the native to support himself under the new conditions imposed by the advent of the white man. There can be no doubt that it would be better to leave the native as he was than to educate him out of his environment. Children were taken to mission schools and taught white standards of living. After growing up under such conditions, they returned to their native life, often entirely unfitted for their environment. They had acquired tastes in food, clothing, and living conditions without any means of gratifying them. In such instances their book lore was of no practical value to them, and they had lost the native arts of fishing, hunting, and trapping without which they could not gain a livelihood. In too many cases the result of the education, especially of the girls, was disastrous to their morals. There were, indeed, a number of attempts on the part of the missionaries to give an industrial education; but these were by no means always successful, partly because of lack of funds and partly because those charged with the work were themselves ignorant of what they were supposed to teach and often without practical knowledge of what form of training was best adapted to their environment. There are records of selected native children being sent to the States and being taught such trades as saddlery and millinery which were, of course, of no value to them in their home settlements.

Another evil practice among some missionaries was that of making gifts of food and clothing to Indians who were fully able to provide for themselves. Such a practice simply encourages indolence and develops pauperism. The native should be taught to take care of himself under the conditions imposed by his environment. Father Duncan, than whom no one has understood the Indians better, said:

> A missionary should be a man who will look at the Indian as a whole, take him body and soul, and try to lift him up. My endeavor has been to try to make him self-supporting. . . . They are not in a position at present to cope with the white man. First bring them up to manhood: Teach them how to maintain themselves and then send them out in the world. . . . The system of making presents of food and clothing to individuals and uncivilized Indians can not be too strongly condemned; its tendency is to sap self-reliance—foster indolence, pauperism, and discontent.

The late Archdeacon Hudson Stuck, who long lived among the Alaskan Indians, also recognized the evils of educating the native out of his environment. In speaking[3] of a mission-trained boy who did not know how to handle a dog sled, he says:

> This incident gave further point to a danger that accompanies mission work among natives wherever it is carried on. Here was a youth of 20, mission-bred for ten years, well-grown, well-appearing, polite-spoken, and with a fair English education and a good deal of general education, who had been used for a long time as Eskimo interpreter. But he had never made a sled or a pair of snowshoes or a canoe in his life and was unpracticed in the wilderness arts by which he must make a living unless he were to depend upon mission employment. . . . It is not unnatural that to a school teacher school-learning should assume an unreal and disproportionate importance; it is not unnatural that ladies of gentle rearing should fail for a time to see that the essential part of an Indian's education is training to make an Indian living.

In 1907, Dr. Harlan Updegraf, an experienced educator, took charge of Alaskan schools and the Reindeer Service. With him was associated W. T. Lopp, whose 17 years of experience as a teacher in northwestern Alaska gave him a most intimate knowledge of the natives and who was the

[3] *A Winter Circuit of our Alaska Coast*, New York, 1920, pp. 36-37.

best authority on the reindeer. Under this efficient leadership the Alaskan service was soon well organized, including local district superintendents and a system of inspection of schools. The confidence of Congress was won, and the appropriation for the native schools was doubled. Unfortunately, the prejudice against the Reindeer Service, caused by its long history of mismanagement, could not be overcome and for many years only a pittance was granted for this work.

Since 1910 Mr. Lopp has been in charge of the Alaskan work of the Bureau of Education. When he entered this duty, he had had 20 years of service in Alaska that fitted him most admirably for his difficult task. His splendid record is due to his intimate knowledge of the Territory and, above all, to his sympathetic understanding of the Alaskan native and his needs. So quietly has Mr. Lopp carried on his work that but very few realize his wonderful service and self-sacrificing devotion to his task. Under his management the educational facilities have been greatly expanded and a medical service for the natives has been organized, including a number of widely scattered hospitals. The Reindeer Service has also been improved, so far as the slender means would permit, and above all its original purpose of getting the animals into the hands of the natives has been carried out. In 1920, there were 67 native schools in Alaska with 133 teachers and an average attendance of about 2,000 pupils. Six native hospitals and 22 medical officers were also maintained in Alaska. Following the general plan of Father Duncan, Lopp has established a number of self-supporting industrial communities among the more intelligent of the Alaskan natives. At Metlakatla and elsewhere he has organized a system of self-government for the community, a system which is most admirably adapted to bring the natives to an understanding of the principles of our government and fits them for rapid absorption into the body politic. Interest in the reindeer industry has been stimulated by the holding of annual winter reindeer fairs at convenient centers. These fit well into the customs and traditions, for they are but a revival of the trading marts which annually took place in the past. In this praise of the Alaskan work of the Bureau of Education, one must not overlook the fact that many of the missions have developed on the same lines: industrial education has been introduced, medical and hospital work has been greatly expanded, and principles of self-government have been inculcated. In some cases this last has been accomplished by a revival of some of the principles of local community or tribal government, which with the introduction of the white man's laws and customs had fallen into disuse.

It is safe to conclude that the proper methods for civilizing the Alaskan natives have now been developed, and there is every evidence of success to come with future generations. This is true in spite of the fact that among the more primitive and less intelligent natives the progress is so slow that the teachers must frequently become discouraged. In some cases it will take a number of generations to bring the natives to civilization. A contrast to this is the success achieved among the more intelligent, where a single generation of teaching has brought the people to a status of self-respect and self-support by which they have already achieved the goal of good citizenship. Governor Thomas Riggs, whose many years of service in Alaska both as engineer and governor have given him a comprehension of the natives, says:[4]

> There is no doubt in my mind but that the natives of Alaska can be so developed in education and in industry as to become a great factor in the economic life of the Territory. In Southeastern Alaska is found the greatest progress. There are many natives of full or mixed blood who have assumed the responsibilities of citizenship and who are able to compete on equal terms with their white neighbors. Among them are found clergymen, teachers, merchants, and navigators. They own their own homes and fishing vessels, and some are comparatively wealthy. In certain towns such as Metlakatla, Klawock, and Hydaberg the land they occupy is set aside by proclamation for their sole use, but they can in no way be classed as reservation Indians. They are free to come and go as they wish; they are not supported by the Government; and the land is simply held for their exclusive occupancy. . . . The Eskimos who inhabit the Yukon delta, Seward Peninsula, and the Arctic coast are being developed along other lines, principally in reindeer herding. The native of the Yukon drainage does not adapt himself so readily to changed conditions of life: he is not so intelligent nor so adaptable as the Thlinkit or the Eskimo; his problem is indeed a difficult one.[5]

[4] *Annual Report of the Governor of Alaska*, Washington, D.C., 1920, p. 59.

[5] The statistical data concerning Alaskan schools presented in this chapter are from the *Annual Report of the Governor of Alaska*, Washington, D.C., 1921. Dr. Brooks had left blank spaces to be filled out with the information that has been thus provided.—*Editor's note.*

CHAPTER XXVII

Government of Alaska

ALASKA WAS the first of the non-contiguous lands acquired by the United States. The history of its government—or perhaps better, lack of government—clearly illustrated how unfitted the American people were to cope with the problems of colonial administration. This history is chiefly one of a succession of errors, of omissions and commissions, which must ever be painful for Americans to recall. It is a fact, though hardly to be credited, that, during the first 17 years that followed the raising of the American flag at Sitka, Alaska literally had no government. During this first epoch, the few that took any interest in Alaska's welfare bent their energies to securing some form of civil administration. This finally attained, there followed another 11 years when the growing population of this northern territory fought for the principle of representative government. A delegate to Congress was finally granted in 1906, an act which so strengthened the hands of those carrying on the struggle that six years later a local territorial government was granted. It was, therefore, nearly half a century before the American principle of self-government was applied to this, our oldest colony. Meanwhile, more or less autonomous local governments had been conceded to the newer possessions of Hawaii, the Philippines, and Porto Rico. No doubt the long struggle of Alaskans for the recognition of their rights educated the nation, and the newer colonies were able to reap the benefit.

As was indicated in Chapter XV the first attempt to govern Alaska was on the basis of a military despotism. But even this form of administration was not carried to its logical conclusion. The authority of the commanding officer was very circumscribed. Though he had ample authority to deal with the native population, his control of the whites was based on the assumption that certain ancient statutes ran to Alaska on the theory that it was an "Indian country." This classification of Alaska as Indian country was an executive opinion, and the contention was not supported in the courts when the matter was brought to issue. Some situations arose during Alaska's early history which would be ridiculous if they were not such painful evidence of our neglect of the Territory.

Among the few statutes passed after the annexation was one prohibiting the introduction of alcohol into Alaska and its sale or barter with the Indians. Under this act a man was arrested in 1874 at Wrangell by the military and sent by the first steamer to Oregon for trial. There he was promptly discharged by order of the court because the law provided that "no person apprehended by military force, as aforesaid, shall be detained longer than five days after his arrest and before removal." Though it was shown that the prisoner had been dispatched by the quickest means of transportation, yet he was actually in custody over 90 days. Hence he was discharged on a writ of *habeas corpus,* though undoubtedly guilty. But even this did not end the difficulties of the Army officers. The prisoner, a gambler by the name of Hugh Waters, now brought suit for damages against Major J. B. Campbell, by whose order he had been arrested, and after a jury trial was awarded $3,500. This was the reward of the officer who had conscientiously tried to enforce law in the Territory. No wonder that William Gouverneur Morris, the special Treasury agent, writes:

> Let an officer arrest a blackleg for selling ardent spirits and be sued in civil damages by the card sharp, the jury who will try the case against him will be informed by Judge Deady that "he is the peer of any man in his court seeking justice, and his profession as a gambler does not prevent him from standing on the same plane as any citizen who has been subject to illegal arrest." This is all very fine, but if I find it necessary ever in Alaska to take any responsibility for the preservation of life and property, or for the prevention of murder, rapine, or bloodshed, or a wholesale Indian massacre, I am hereafter going to give Judge Deady's court a wide berth.

The judge who discharged Waters also stated in his opinion that "it is a mistake to suppose that the Territory of Alaska is under military rule any more than any other part of the country, except as to the introduction of spirituous liquors." This action left the Territory without any semblance of government, for no other administrative machinery was provided; and the law became entirely inoperative since it was a physical impossibility for the military to deliver prisoners within five days to civil authorities located over 1,000 miles away.

Whiskey selling, therefore, went on merrily, for the commandants of the post would not punish infractions of the law, except by committing the offenders to the guardhouse. It is to the credit of the Army officers stationed in the lonely posts that they did not hesitate to assume authority and commit the more flagrant offenders to the guardhouse. The rights of these corrupters of the Indians proved a matter of grave concern to the lawmakers, for in 1876 a Senate resolution called on the President for a full report of the military arrests in Alaska. This report was duly furnished, but it was promptly forgotten by those who had demanded it before it was printed.

It appears that the only criminal law which was operative in Alaska was certain federal statutes intended primarily for vessels on the high seas. In 1879, one John Williams assaulted one E. R. Roy with a pistol and wounded him. The crime was not denied, but it seemed that there was no federal statute covering assault with a deadly weapon. Therefore, Williams was discharged by the court, which announced in its decision: "It appears that there is no punishment provided for an assault with a dangerous weapon committed within the exclusive jurisdiction of the United States if committed *on land,* even if such assault should involve, as it may and did in this case, an attempt to commit murder." The judge adds at the close, "By this ruling the defendant will escape punishment for what appears to have been an atrocious crime, but the court can not inflict punishment where the law does not so provide."

Thus it was announced, 13 years after the annexation, that there were no statutes under which criminal offences could be punished in Alaska. The Alaskan Indians were far better off than the whites. They had their own tribal codes and, moreover, were governed under the treaty as being "uncivilized tribes." This condition not only was criminally unjust to the Americans who had gone to the colony, but also was a direct violation of our treaty with Russia. One clause in this instrument assured to the Russians remaining in the Territory that they "shall be admitted to the enjoyment of all rights, advantages, and immunities of citizens of the United States, and shall be maintained in the free enjoyment of their liberty, property, and religion."

Though the law prohibited the importation of alcoholic beverages, there was apparently no prohibition against the operation of stills, for a deputy collector at Wrangell was warned in 1878 that the Treasury Department "has no jurisdiction over the crime of distilling spirits without paying a tax therefor"; and, with reference to the destruction of stills, "my own opinion is that a customs officer should be very careful how he assumes any such responsibility." It stands to the credit of the few scattered revenue collectors that they did not hesitate to suppress, so far as lay within their power, the distilleries whose product had such a baneful effect on the natives and endangered the lives of the whites. The difficulties under which the customs officials operated are illustrated by the following extracts from their reports:

M. P. Berry writes from Sitka in 1877:

> There is no necessity for using vigilance to prevent the landing of liquor; the Indians make all they want; and in town here I have been informed that there are two discharged soldiers and eight different Russians running stills.

From Wrangell, J. C. Dennis writes in February, 1878:

> Is it policy for me to let white men and Indians understand that I have no legal right to interfere with the liquor traffic? No, sir, that would be the worst thing that ever happened. Should I stop raiding on whiskey makers, in 24 hours the town and Indian village would be flooded, and hell would be to pay. . . . The fines that I have imposed I propose to turn over to the mission school at this place to be used for church purposes, unless the Department should disapprove my actions and order them refunded. In such event I should be compelled to resign my position, for no man can execute the customs laws faithfully without assuming certain authority not conferred by the statutes. The policy of the Government toward Alaska has been a disgrace.

He writes again on March 18:

> The want of law here is daily more keenly felt. I am annoyed continually by Indians and whites who come to me to settle disputes. What can I do? In many instances the charges are so aggravating that I must act to prevent bloodshed.

A few months later he resigns his office of deputy collector, writing in part as follows:

I take this step on account of the manner in which the Department is running the Territory. I have acted in the capacity of arbitrator-adjudicator until forbearance has ceased to be a virtue. . . . Again the prospect for Congress to extend law and order over this country looks gloomy, and in the absence of law at this post no compensation that the Government could offer me would be any inducement for me to act in the capacity of deputy collector another year.

Though the federal courts did provide for punishment in case of actual murder, it appears that almost any other crime could be committed without infraction of law. The presence of troops in Southeastern Alaska had, in spite of the conditions just outlined, a very restraining effect on both the whites and the natives; and the commanding officers, assisted by the collectors of customs—the only representatives of government—labored valiantly through such means as lay within their power to maintain order. Ninety per cent of the Territory was, however, absolutely without any governmental control. The fact that some measure of order was maintained by common consent rather than by governmental authority speaks well for the character of most of the white pioneers of Alaska.

Even that small measure of protection afforded by the troops was lost in 1877 when they were withdrawn from all Alaskan posts. The Nez Percé war had made an urgent demand for every soldier of the small United States Army. With no thought given to the possible effect in Alaska and with no attempt made to replace them with other authority, the soldiers were withdrawn.

Since the first Russian settlement the natives of Southeastern Alaska had been turbulent, and with the withdrawal of the soldiers they became restless. Urgent appeals for protection were sent to Washington by the customs officials, but without avail. In the winter of 1879, matters came to a crisis at Sitka. The whites, of whom there were but a handful, armed themselves and stood ready to face several thousand natives. Fortunately, there was among the natives some discord which prevented an immediate outbreak. Meanwhile, the monthly mail steamer carried the news southward. The appeal for help reached Captain Holmes A'Court commanding *H. M. S. Osprey,* anchored at Victoria. Captain A'Court at once set sail, and soon the Americans at Sitka were under the protection of the guns of a British man-of-war. This incident finally awakened the Government to the fact of its disgraceful attitude toward Alaska, and after seven weeks of guard duty the English vessel[1] was relieved by the *Alaska* of the American Navy. On June 12 the U.S.S. *Jamestown* arrived and remained at the Alaskan station for several years. From this time on until civil government was established in Alaska, the Territory was, nominally at least, under the jurisdiction of the Navy Department. This arrangement had the advantage that a vessel could better visit the isolated settlements and enforce order than could the land forces.

The naval officer who now assumed the guardianship of the Territory found himself in the same dilemma as had his predecessor of the Army. Of his position, he writes:[2]

> The arrival of the *Jamestown* was welcomed by all as furnishing the solution to the various problems. I as her commanding officer, being provided with sufficient power to control dangerous characters, to suppress illicit distilling and traffic, and to protect those who needed protection, and with orders so broad in their scope that I could be able to pursue any course I might think best to adopt, fell naturally into the position of head to this otherwise headless community. Both whites and Indians manifested a disposition to rely upon the Government for every thing and to look upon me as a representative of their government sent in answer to their appeal to supply all of the deficiencies incident to the entire absence of any other governing power or code of laws. . . . The problem presented to me was how to govern a mixed community of whites and Indians with no code of laws but the Revised Statutes of the United States, the United States Naval Regulations, and the Treaty with Russia. . . . Should the Indians refuse to recognize my authority, the means at my disposal were not sufficient to enforce obedience; and if the whites refused, there was no method which I could adopt to coerce them which would not render me personally liable to civil proceeding.

The first branch of the Government to be represented in Alaska was the Revenue Cutter Service. For a long time this service was hampered in its patrol duty of Alaska for lack of suitable vessels and equipment. When in 1877 the troops were withdrawn, the *Wolcott,* was ordered to this northern post. Her commander, Captain James M. Seldon, borrowed three 12 pounders from private owners for the use of his vessel and secured powder and ball through the courtesy of the Army post at Port Townsend.

---

[1] Meanwhile the Revenue Cutter *Oliver Wolcott* had arrived, but neither her armament nor the size of her crew was sufficient to cope with the situation; hence the *Osprey* remained on guard duty until the arrival of the *Alaska*.

[2] Beardslee, Captain L. A., "Reports Relative to Affairs in Alaska and the Operations of the U.S.S. *Jamestown*," *Senate Document No. 71, 47th Congress, First Session*, Washington, D.C., pp. 16-17.

To such extremes was this energetic officer driven to obtain means to carry out his instructions. Moreover, the vessel was unsuited for cruises on the open waters of the Pacific and could operate only along the sheltered waterways. This is simply cited as another example of neglect on the part of the Washington departments.

The principle duties of the cutters were to visit the Pribilof Islands and look after the Government's interests in the seal fisheries, but gradually it fell to them also to patrol all the more remote seaboard of the Territory. For many years there was no federal agency north of the Pribilof Islands, and the commanders of the cutters undertook so far as lay in their power during the summer cruise to enforce law and order. Notable in this work was Captain M. A. Healy who, as commander of the *Corwin,* was the terror of every evil-doer and the friend of everyone in distress north of the Aleutian Islands. It is said that every native both loved and feared him, and the threat that Captain Healy would call him to account kept many a renegade Eskimo from breaking out.

With the development of mining in the 1870's and 1880's and the increased exploitation of the fisheries, attention was finally attracted to the shameful neglect of Alaska. It could no longer be charged that Alaska was only the abode of a few fur hunters and needed no government. The increased population drew attention to the utterly chaotic condition of government, including both criminal and civil law. In 1879 Morris in an official report[3] says that

> . . . there is no law by which a man can acquire title to any land whatever, either within settlements or away from home. The sole exceptions were the Russian titles to certain lots at Sitka, and a few other places provided for under the treaty. . . . Anyone who settles upon land in Alaska intending to hold the same by occupation until necessary pre-emption laws can be passed . . . [is] liable any moment to be ejected therefrom neck and heels by armed forces of the United States; and yet we are told the country is still unsettled. . . . A man can not sell a piece of property in Alaska and give a deed for it which will be legal . . . and for the same reason a man can not mortgage a piece of land. . . . Likewise, a man dying in Alaska is unable to dispose of his property by will. . . . There are no laws regarding the estates of deceased, no probate judges, and no one having any authority to administer upon any estate. . . . A man may be murdered, his will forged, and his estate scattered

[3] Morris, William Gouverneur, *Report on the Customs District, Public Service, and Resources of Alaska Territory,* Washington, D.C., 1879, pp. 118-121.

to the four corners of the earth, and there is no power in a court of chancery to redress it. Alaska is the paradise of the dishonest debtor, for there is no law of any kind throughout the land for the collection of debts.

The first bill providing for a civil government in Alaska, together with a court and the necessary officials, was reported to the House in 1880. Four years elapsed before any action was taken. Finally by act of Congress on May 17, 1884, the so-called "Organic Act" was passed. Thus it was 17 years before "the Constitution followed the flag" to this northern colony.

The Organic Act, though far from perfect, did bring some measure of order out of chaos. After its passage a man could settle in Alaska, knowing that he would not be deprived of the constitutional rights of an American citizen. A criminal code was enacted and the judicial machinery for its enforcement was provided. One of the most important features of the new laws was the extension of the United States mining laws to the Territory. Alaskans had, however, to wait 14 years longer for the right to take up homesteads. Provision was made for four United States commissioners, located at Wrangell, Juneau, Sitka, and Unalaska; but so far as resident officials were concerned it left the great inland region and all of northern Alaska "no man's land." Instead of enacting a code of criminal and civil laws suitable to the Territory, Congress took the easier course of extending the laws of Oregon to Alaska, with the rather vague proviso that "so far as the same may be applicable and not in conflict with the provisions of this act or the laws of the United States." Nevertheless, though this act left very much to be desired, the northern colony reacted almost at once to improved conditions. Prospectors began seeking mineral wealth in the remote corners of the Territory, and the garnering of the rich fisheries began on an extensive scale.

John H. Kinkead was appointed the first governor under the authority of the Organic Act. He arrived in Sitka in September, and on the 15th the officer commanding the U.S.S. *Pinta* formally relinquished his shadowy authority over Alaska to the civil authorities. This act, which was carried out with all due pomp and ceremony, can be said to mark the beginning of the government of Alaska, for the various makeshifts at control and execution of laws should not be dignified by the term government.

As has already been shown (Chapters XVII and XVIII) the movement of the prospectors into the Yukon basin had begun some years earlier, and by the time the Organic Act was passed the entire length of the great river had been traversed by these indefatigable pioneers. During the succeeding decade small communities sprang up in the placer districts of the interior. These were remote from any governmental control, for the only representative of the Government in all inland Alaska was a revenue collector whose duties were to prevent the importation or manufacture of intoxicants, prohibited by the new law. The miners were thrown on their own resources to maintain order. Fortunately, the institution known as the "Miners' Code" was recognized in the statutes relating to acquisition of mineral lands in the following clause: "The miners of each mining district may make regulations not in conflict with the laws of the United States or with the laws of the state or territory in which the district is situated governing the location, manner of recording, and amount of work necessary to hold possession of a mining claim." Under the authority the Alaskan miners made their own regulations regarding mining claims and, in the absence of any federal official, enforced their own decrees.

From this beginning it was but a natural evolution to enact laws and rules regarding other affairs of these isolated communities. Under these conditions there developed democracies of the purest type, resembling in a manner the government in some of the cantons of Switzerland and the earliest colonial settlements of New England. The miners met and by majority vote enacted a mining civil and criminal code. If any member of the community believed that a wrong had been done him, he called a miners' meeting, and the case was settled by majority vote. Similar action was taken in criminal cases. As imprisonment was impractical, there were only three punishments: hanging, banishment, and fines. In the code established at Circle City in 1893, murder was punished by hanging, assault and stealing by banishment, and minor infractions by fines. And lest it be thought that these pioneers had no thought of the refinements of life, it should be noted that the use of profane and obscene language was punishable by a fine; such a regulation is

EARLY BUILDINGS AT CIRCLE CITY

Upper: U.S. Customs House, 1896, photo by J. E. Spurr; center: Jail, 1904, photo by A. H. Brooks; lower: Fire engine house, photo by A. J. Collier.

more suggestive of puritanical New England than of the average man's conception of pioneer life on the Yukon.

In these communities the recorder was the only permanent official. He was elected by the miners, who also determined the fees he was to receive. The old record book at Circle City presents a picture of the life of the community. There are many pages of record devoted to a murder trial. It is worthy of note that the trial took place the day after the shooting, and the acquittal of the defendant on the plea of self-defense was clearly established by the testimony of witnesses transcribed in full. All who attended the meeting signed the verdict of "not guilty" which was spread on the record. There can be no doubt that justice was rendered—and without expense to the community and with a promptness that could well be emulated in our courts. This record also shows the banishment of a few thieves or other undesirable members of the community. In summer, these criminals were given a boat—in winter, a sled—and enough provisions to carry them to the next post, and were warned never to return.

Many civil suits are recorded involving disputes over claims or cabins, and these cases when acted on were settled for all time. This old record also reflects other phases in the life of these pioneers. There were no clergymen or justices of the peace; marriage took place by the simple signing of a certificate by the man and woman with two witnesses, all duly spread on the record. The pathetic attempt to give these a legal standing is shown by the fact that the marriages were certified to by the official signature of the "deputy collector of internal revenue," the only federal official in 400,000 square miles of inland Alaska.

These communities were above the average in their intellectual interests. In 1893, a library was established by the miners at Circle City, which then had about 300 inhabitants. Several hundred books were purchased by popular subscription. The well-thumbed copies of such classics as the writings of Herbert Spencer, Victor Hugo, George Eliot, and Shakespeare give evidence of the intellectual tastes of these miners.

The town of Circle City was but one example of a number of self-governing mining settlements that sprang up in different parts of the Territory. Miners' meetings continued as an important element in the government of the Territory up to the time of the inrush of population during the Klondike excitement. The large numbers who arrived at that time, plus the fact that they had little unity of purpose or ideals and for the most part no training in frontier conditions, made the miners' meetings an impractical method of control. The custom gradually fell into disuse, though, as has already been shown, it was revived in 1899 at Nome in a somewhat modified form and is still occasionally appealed to in the more remote settlements. It has, however, played an important part in maintaining order and in protecting life and property during the middle period of Alaska's history, and it deserves critical study by a trained historian.

While the Yukon miners were establishing well-regulated communities, the seaboard region under direct Federal Government was far from being well administered. The Governor, who had little authority and no means of enforcing it, was marooned at Sitka on an island and out of touch with most of the Territory. He could appoint notaries and was at the head of a "militia" which did not exist. His only important function was drawing the attention of Congress to the needs of Alaska by his annual reports.

The United States commissioners had much greater authority, but they were scattered out over a wide territory and at best could accomplish but little. The most important phase of the new law was the providing of a judge and court officials. So much publicity has been given to the proved corruption of the court at Nome in 1900, described in Chapter XXII, that it is only fair to record that nearly all judges in Alaska have maintained a high standard of honesty and justice. Unfortunately, the same is not true of all the minor officials who have been sent to Alaska. While there were many who were entirely upright and conscientious, there were also those who took advantage of their positions to plunder the people. A premium was put on trouble-makers by providing that certain officials were to be paid by fees, so that the more trouble that was stirred up in the community, the greater was the income of those who were supposed to be working in the cause of law and order.

The difficulties of patrolling the coast made whiskey-smuggling easy; and the revenue collectors, except at such time as a cutter was present, could do little in the way of apprehending the smugglers. For a time opium smuggling was carried on. Vessels sailing north would secure opium in a British Columbia port, carry it to Alaska, and bring it back to the States marked as some staple commodity in the ship's manifest. This practice, of course, involved the connivance of the master of the vessel; but since the profits were large, it was not impossible to find a captain who would run the risk.

Though the Organic Act of 1884 was at least a recognition of the fact that Alaskans were entitled to some form of government, yet it was at best only a makeshift. After a test of four years Governor A. P. Swineford writes:[4]

> Aside from the partial administration of justice by the United States district court and the four United States commissioners acting principally as justices of the peace, the government of Alaska is little, if any, better than a burlesque, both in form and substance. There is no legislature, and there are practically no local laws applicable to the wants and urgent necessities of a territory so isolated, and aside from the preparation of an annual report . . . there is no duty enjoined upon the governor the performance of which is possible, no power he can exercise, no authority he can assert. . . . Authority to require performance of duty, in the absence of any power to compel it, amounts to nothing.

The shortcomings of Alaska's machinery of government did not stand out clearly until the Klondike excitement. Probably 50,000 people went north at this time, including some of the worst criminals. On the Canadian side of the boundary the situation was kept well in hand by the Northwest Mounted Police, who had not only ample force but also full authority to maintain law and order. How well this superb body of men acquitted itself is long since a matter of historical record. In Alaska, on the other hand, no means were provided for meeting the new conditions. That the result was not complete chaos is due rather to the general high character of the gold seekers than to any action on the part of the Government. For a time, as has been previously pointed out, lawlessness was rampant at Skagway and other smaller communities, but before long the better element asserted itself and by extra-legal action maintained a semblance of law and order.

One of the corrupting influences among the minor officials was the whiskey trade. Alaska was in theory dry territory, but every hamlet was crowded with saloons, every one of

---

[4] Swineford, A. P., *Report of the Governor of Alaska, fiscal year 1888*, Washington, D.C., 1889, pp. 45-46.

which was of course a law-breaker. The sentiment of the community was against prohibition, and those who attempted to enforce the law received neither help nor sympathy. By a curious conflict of law or regulation, one branch of government issued federal licenses for the sale of intoxicants and another was charged with the duty of preventing it. The prohibition law was an absolute farce, and fortunately a high license law was substituted in 1900. This met the desires of the community and was generally enforced. Seventeen years later the same communities were destined to vote overwhelmingly for prohibition.

In 1895, the first grant of funds was made to investigate the mineral wealth of Alaska. An appropriation of $5,000 to investigate the gold and coal resources of the Territory by the United States Geological Survey was made; this work, described in a previous chapter, has been continued to the present day. During the Klondike epoch, effort was made to meet the changed conditions by additional legislation. In 1897, a surveyor general, *ex officio* secretary of the Territory, was provided as well as additional commissioners. A year later, another statute was enacted which provided among other things for rights of way for railroads and toll roads. It also permitted the purchase of not exceeding 80 acres of land for business purposes and allowed the sale of government timber for use within the Territory. This was the first recognition of the rights of any Alaskan settler to land which he occupied and improved, except for mining claims. Nearly a whole generation had passed since the annexation before this elementary step for the encouragement of the colonist was made. In 1898 also, a steamboat inspection district was established in Alaska, a work inaugurated by Captain Whitney who set up headquarters at Sitka and began that series of extensive travels over Alaskan waters that he has continued to the present day. At about the same time, the experimental work of the Department of Agriculture was begun by Dr. C. C. Georgeson which has been continued by him ever since.

The discovery of the rich placers at Nome again centered public attention on Alaska. Hence, in 1899 Congress provided a criminal code and in the following year the first complete civil code for Alaska. Again, however, the labor-saving device of enacting practically the code of Oregon was adopted rather than providing statutes which were adapted to Alaskan conditions.

The new law provided additional United States commissioners, making it now possible to give all the settled parts of the Territory a resident federal official. These officials were appointed by the federal judges of each of the districts into which Alaska was divided. Each judge sub-divided his district into as many precincts as the distribution of population demanded; and since the size and number of precincts could be varied at any time, it was possible to adjust the system to the more or less shifting population. Each of these commissioners is justice of the peace, recorder, probate judge, commissioner of deeds, road supervisor, and coroner. It was in these officials that the government of Alaska was practically vested, for they were responsible to the Department of Justice and not to the Governor of the Territory. The latter is in effect an official of the Interior Department and at this time, isolated at Sitka away from the main routes of travel, was less in touch with his domain than if he had resided in the city of Washington.

The new law also provided for an elaborate system of taxation. Nearly every business was taxed for a license, varying, for example, from a taxidermist shop at $10 to a brewery at $500. There was no tax on placer mining, but quartz mills paid an annual tax of $3 a stamp. Railways were taxed $100 a mile, and vessels and river steamers paid $1 a net ton.

After 1900, there were many statutes enacted which were intended to meet the many needs of the Territory. These need not be considered in detail here. Suffice it to say that gradually Alaska was provided with a complete set of laws, though some of the legislation was ill-advised.

The extensive system of taxation provided by the law of 1900 and the various pieces of experimental legislation that followed intensified the desire of Alaskans for representation in Congress. The opinion was well-nigh universal that Alaska should be represented in Washington by a delegate elected by the people. The census of 1900 had shown a white population of over 30,000, and this and the industrial advances made it impossible longer to say that the Territory was the abode of only a few fur hunters. In 1906, Congress authorized the election by the people of Alaska of a delegate from the Territory. The immediate result was the presence in the halls of Congress of a man who represented the people of Alaska; before this time, Congressional committee rooms had swarmed with self-appointed delegates, a few of whom were honestly striving for the good of the Territory as a whole but most of whom were using the self-styled designation of representative as a cloak to further some personal scheme.

Alaskans were by no means satisfied with the gain of a delegate and hence continued their efforts for complete territorial government. There were some residents who honestly believed that the sparseness of population, more or less of a roving character, made it inadvisable to enact a territorial form of government. And a strong opposition also developed among certain large corporate interests which feared that they would be overtaxed by a local legislature. Nevertheless, home rule was practically the only issue at every election of delegates, and in each case the affirmative vote was overwhelming; therefore, it could not be denied that the majority of Alaskans favored a territorial form of government. But it was some time before Washington could be convinced of the wisdom of the proposed action. Some projects for a commission form of government, similar to that of the Philippines, were launched, but these found small favor either among Alaskans or in Congress. Opposition in Congress to home rule was partly through ignorance of Alaska, both its resources and population, and partly through fear on the part of some that a territorial form of government would eventually lead to statehood. On the part of conservatives it was considered that a grave menace to our institutions would result from the admission of a non-contiguous state. The very ignorance of Alaska in Washington was, however, one of the strongest reasons for allowing this distant possession to manage its own affairs.

In 1912, the territorial form of government was granted, though the act included many restrictions on the powers of legislation. It was felt that the Alaskans could not be trusted to legislate on the excise laws, for it had been charged that the Territory was controlled by the saloon element; yet four years later by a popular referendum the Territory voted overwhelmingly for prohibitiion. An appeal had then to be made to Congress to put this wish into effect through the vote of the people. The home rule bill as it passed the Senate provided for only one legislative body. Overwhelmed by the tradition of a bicameral legislature, the House changed the bill and provided for a senate and a lower house. No one seemed to realize the inconsistency of the plan of having two bodies of men elected in the same way by the same people to perform the same duty. It is an evidence both of how much Americans are bound by tradition and of how our fetish of government is restriction and safeguard rather than fixing responsibility.

The enactment of the territorial legislative law brings the history of Alaskan government to its present status. Home rule has, of course, by no means solved all the problems of government. But these are not unlike those of the other commonwealths of the Union. The Federal Government, as the principal landholder of the Territory, still dominates its destinies; and wise legislation at Washington still remains the most important factor in the opening up of this vast territory.

Index

Addendum

On pages 294 and 295, an account by Burton L. Fryxell, editor of the first edition, tells of attempts, successful and unsuccessful, to climb Mt. McKinley between 1903 and 1913. The following covers the same period in Alfred Brooks' own words. It is composed of sentences and phrases excerpted from the twenty two page publication MOUNTAIN EXPLORATIONS IN ALASKA (Alpina Americana No. 3, Amer. Alpine Club, Philadelphia) published in 1914. Although his punctuation has necessarily been altered to permit condensation, Dr. Brooks' own exact choice of language has been faithfully retained.

About the time that Wickersham left the mountain to return to his judicial duties at Fairbanks, the second party to essay the summit landed at Tyonek, under the leadership of Dr. Frederick A. Cook. This party included Robert Dunn, who had had considerable Alaska experience. The route of approach to the mountain and the method of travel accorded with plans proposed by Mr. Reaburn and the writer,[11] except in the one important particular of starting a month later, which foredoomed the attempt to failure. Two attempts were made to climb the mountain; on the second an altitude about 11,000 feet was attained. The party returned to the coast by a remarkable journey through the heart of the Alaska range, a feat never before attempted. Three years later, in 1906, Doctor Cook again essayed the ascent of Mount McKinley. His party, including Professor Herschel Parker, Belmore Browne, R. W. Porter, topographer, and Fred Printz, veteran packer, spent most of the summer south of Mount McKinley in exploring the region tributary to the Susitna. They tried without success to cross the range at the head of the Yentna. The attempt to reach the summit from the south was equally futile, but the journey added much to the geographic knowledge of the region.[12]

In 1910 a party was organized at Fairbanks to attempt the summit. It included Thomas Bloyd, William Taylor, Pete Anderson, and Charles McGonogill, all Alaska prospectors and provided only with such equipment as their winter-bound town of Fairbanks could afford. These men were familiar with the region about the

---

[11] See: Brooks, A. H. and Reaburn, D. L., "Plans for Climbing Mount McKinley," NATIONAL GEOGRAPHIC MAG., Vol. 14, 1903.

north base of the mountain and inured by long experience to the difficulties and hardships of Alaska winter travel. A base camp was established on the Muldrow Glacier on March 25th, and from this supplies were advanced by the joint efforts of the entire party. Finally, on April 3rd Taylor, Anderson, and McGonogill made the final dash to the top (of the north peak, 850′ lower than the south). McGonogill turned back about 500 feet below but the other two not only scaled the north summit, but carried with them and planted on top a fourteen foot pole. Dr. Hudson Stuck after describing this ascent says, "This is the true narrative of a most extraordinary feat, unique—the writer has no hesitation in claiming—in all the annals of mountaineering."[12]

Professor Herschel Parker and Mr. Belmore Browne, nothing daunted by their hard previous experiences, organized a third expedition, in 1912. This time they sledded their supplies up the Susitna, crossed the Alaska range and reached the northeast base of the mountain on April 19th, then up the route established by the Fairbanks party two years before. The highest camp was made at an altitude of about 16,600 feet on the northeast ridge of the mountain. From here the party pushed their way on June 29th in the teeth of a howling blizzard to within a few hundred feet of the top (of the south peak). This altitude was only gained at the imminent risk of their lives, and its attaining must ever stand as one of the heroic episodes in the annals of Alaska mountaineering.

Another attempt was made July first, but again the party was overwhelmed by storm; lack of food necessitated abandonment of further efforts.

The highest peak of Mt. McKinley had not yet been conquered. This was accomplished by Dr. Hudson Stuck, Archdeacon of the Yukon, and Mr. Harry Karstens, a prospector of Fairbanks. Both men had seen much experience in Alaskan winter and summer travel. After a long sledge journey, base camp was established at 4,000 feet. Thence the route led to the Muldrow Glacier, the one discovered by the Fairbanks party in 1910. With dog teams, supplies were moved to 11,500 feet where the serious difficulties of climbing began. (Following the route of preceding parties) the highest camp was made in the Grand Basin early in June between supplies were carried to this altitude. On June 7th, 1913, the ascent to the south summit was made on a bright clear day. The top of the continent was thus mastered.

the two summits at about 17,000 feet, and two to three weeks

---

[12] Dr. Brooks completely ignores Cook's false claim to have returned and climbed McKinley with Ed Burrill in eight days later in 1906; and he similarly ignores Lloyd's false claim that all four of the Sourdough party climbed both peaks of McKinley in 1910. But what both parties did do he presents correctly, the first historian of whom this can be said.

Corrections and Clarifications for First Edition

In the early parts of this book, a number of altitudes of mountains and passes are mentioned. Some of there were in Dr. Brooks' manuscript, and some were inserted later. There appear to be only two that differ seriously from currently accepted figures: those of Mt. Crillon and Mt. Illiamna. However, for purposes of comparison, altitudes from three different sources are given below:

Altitudes

Mountain	Blazing Alaska's Trails	Brooks Alpina Americana, 1914	Dictionary of American Place Names, 1967
Blackburn	16,200	16,140	16,390
Broad Pass	2,400		2,300
Crillon	15,900	12,727	12,700
Dall	9,000		8,756
Fairweather	15,292	15,399	15,300
Foraker	17,000		17,400
Hubbard	16,000	14,950	14,950
Illiamna	10,617	12,066	10,016
Isanotski	8,032		8,025
La Perouse	10,740	10,756	10,728
Logan	19,500		Canadian
McKinley	20,300		20,320
Natazhat	13,440		13,435
Pogromni	6,500		6,568
Redoubt	11,270	10,198	10,197
Russell	11,350	11,600	11,670
Seattle	10,000	10,175	10,070
Shishaldin	9,387		9,372
Spurr	11,500	11,069	11,100
St. Elias	18,024		18,008

In addition, the following errors have been noticed:

Page 124, Line 7: Date should be 1771 (See page 152). On both pages "Coppermine" River is preferable to "Copper Mine."

Page 161, top of page: correct name is Jean Francois Galoupe de La Perouse; middle paragraph: Dagelet, not Malaspina, was the first to measure Mt. St. Elias. (See page 279.) Also, Malaspina got it almost exactly correct; not more than 2000 feet in error. It should also be pointed out that Malaspina, although an Italian, took possession for the Spanish Crown; bottom of page: Verendrye, not Verandrye.

Page 162, line 12: Northwest Fur Company, not Northwestern Fur Company.

Page 213, five places: Northwest, not Northwestern.

Page 223, bottom of page: 1865, not 1864, since this raid took place in June, 1865, after the Civil War. This mistake is repeated on page 240 and on page 430.

Pages 243, 258, 259, and 265: In the text, Brooks refers to Dr. Dall. The degree was not conferred until after the events described.

Page 243, bottom of page: In Brooks' tribute to Kennicott, he mentions the copper mine, but could not know that the name would become a household word as the company grew into a world wide organization. Curiously, the name became Kennecott.

Page 279, second paragraph: Mark B. Kerr, not Karr; also Russell and Kerr, not Russell and Karr. The confusion is with Seton-Karr mentioned slightly above. Also George Broke or H. G. Broke, not Broca.

Page 288, third paragraph: Harry, (not Harvey) Fielding Reid.

Page 290, end of paragraph four: Frederick Lambart, not Lambert.

Page 291, third paragraph: Henry W. Elliott, not Elliot.

Page 474, Line 10, second paragraph: Fort, not Fork Yukon.

BLAZING ALASKA'S TRAILS is unique. It is the work of a man long dead, and in it there has not been the opportunity to view history in the light of later happenings and interpretations. Therefore, it is not surprising that many people have noted shortcomings. Some of these have been obvious to the editors, among which are the following: Chapter 1, Relief and Drainage, is perhaps a poor one to start with since, to many people, the subject holds little interest. The chapters on agriculture, fishing, transportation and fisheries likewise have been singled out as out-of-date and of little present value. However, everything in this book is of some interest to someone, and more harm than good would be done by eliminating chapters.

A more serious charge deals with the omissions. The history of the era described by Brooks is intimately associated with the history of mining. Therefore the lack of inclusion of such subjects as the discovery of copper at Kennicott or gold at Fairbanks or any other placer district besides Nome, seriously detracts from its value as a history. Again, however, if chapters on these subjects were written and included, it would no longer be Brooks' book and a unique contribution to Alaskana would cease to be. Perhaps that task can be left to other men and other times.

Memorial of Alfred H. Brooks

In 1926, Doctor Brooks' old friend and colleague, Phillip S. Smith, wrote a memorial which was published in volume 37 of the BULLETIN OF THE GEOLOGICAL SOCIETY OF AMERICA. This tribute, by a man who himself left his mark on Alaska, is published in full below. The Geological Society of America has given its permission to do this.

Memorial of Alfred Hulse Brooks
By Phillip S. Smith[1]

Introduction

"Alaskan Scientist, Explorer, Historian." These few descriptive words, carved on an enduring granite shaft in one of Washington's most beautiful cemeteries, mark the last resting place of the body of Alfred Hulse Brooks. His useful life, which came suddenly to an end November 22, 1924, left a profound imprint on the science of geology, not only through his own direct personal contributions, but through his ability to develop other geologists and to administer and coordinate their work and interpret their results.

From his ancestry of old pioneer stock he inherited sound American principles, deep patriotism, and strong incentive to productive endeavor. His father, Major T. B. Brooks, an eminent mining engineer and geologist, whose work on certain iron-ore deposits of upper Michigan marked a prominent milestone in American geology, gave to his son a lasting trend toward love and appreciation of nature. To his father's influence also must be attributed the sound patriotism that led him to anticipate his country's need and answer her call when the great war loomed and broke. To the happy, congenial home of his boyhood with his father and his three sisters may be traced many of the qualities that endeared him most to his friends and associates.

---

[1] Manuscript received by the Secretary of the Society, January 2, 1926.

Early Years

He spent his early years under diverse conditions, and the training he received followed no systematic plan. Born at Ann Arbor, Michigan, July 18, 1871, he went with his family to Germany when he was only six months old, and he remained there until he had reached the age of five years, when the family returned to America and made their home in Newburgh, New York. On his return to America the child was, of course, so completely a "foreigner" that he was more or less the butt of his companions; yet his life at Newburgh was very happy. A beautiful house and grounds, with animals and equipment that were a source of constant joy to the children, congenial friends and neighbors, a family circle in which adults and children participated on more or less equal footing—all helped to make the Newburgh period a series of red-letter days in his memory. In 1883 his mother died, and for several years a sister only a few years his senior became the mistress of the house—a fact that probably intensified the close mutual reliance of the members of the family on one another and made each a partaker in the family responsibilities rather than a mere onlooker. At Newburgh he received his elementary education in schools and from private tutors, but by far the most potent influence he felt in those days was that of his father, who fascinated his boy with tales of his own experience, encouraged in him a spirit of inquiry, and taught him how to find answers to his own questions from books and from his own observations.

Major Brooks, the father, had a strong desire to acquire land, wherever he happened to be and whatever might be the quality of the land. This trait brought him into close though informal association in business with Prof. Raphael Pumpelly, who had done geologic and prospecting work in northern Michigan on lands having possible value for their content of iron. The close friendship between the elder Brooks and Pumpelly, which began in 1866, also led the two to undertake about 1888 the development of the Roseland Plantation, a tract of about 5,500 acres, near Bainbridge, Georgia, under the name of the South Georgia Live Stock and Planting Company. This plantation was the winter home of the Brooks and Pumpelly families for many years. Its operation gave a multitude of incentives to outdoor life, in which all members of both families participated, thus strengthening family ties. Rides through the pine woods about Roseland, the charm of the care-free life, the close companionship of friends—all left in his mind an ineffaceable memory of pleasure, duty, and happy growth.

First Work on Geological Survey

His first professional work of the kind to which he later devoted his life was begun in 1888, when he served as field assistant in a topographic party of the United States Geological Survey, in charge of H. L. Smyth, that was mapping certain areas in southern Vermont. Apparently Brooks was used in running traverses and in performing such similar jobs as usually fall to the lot of the younger, less experienced members of a survey party. In the next year (1889) he was out again with a topographic party of the Survey under Fred J. Knight, this time in the vicinity of Marquette, Michigan. Here he employed many of the methods he had learned from his father, and he must have felt special satisfaction in realizing that in this work he was retracing some of his father's footsteps. He does not appear, however, to have been keenly interested in the geology of the district. In fact, we know from his own lips that for a long time he was most strongly attracted toward a career as a topographer, and he was disposed to resent the fact that some of his assignments tended to divert him from topography to geology.

At the conclusion of his work in Michigan, late in the fall of 1889, he went with his family to Germany and remained there throughout 1890 and the early part of 1891. During this period he traveled some and he studied a good deal in the Polytechnik at Stuttgart and Munich. This trip to Germany, however, was not made directly for educational or similar purposes; it was determined upon because of the desire of his stepmother, his father having married again in 1886, to return to her native country. This life abroad undoubtedly stimulated the investigative spirit of the young student and broadened the foundation for much of his maturer work.

While the Brooks family was still abroad, Professor Pumpelly developed, with Major Brooks, a plan to have the United States Geological Survey, under the direction of Prof. C. R. Van Hise, investigate certain potential iron-ore lands in northern Michigan—a job for which some financial assistance had been obtained from the forerunner of the Chicago, Milwaukee and St. Paul Railroad, which owned large tracts of land in that region. On the acceptance of this plan by the Geological Survey, young Brooks was invited to return to the United States and take part in the field-work with F. W. McNair, J. R. Finlay, Samuel Sanford, and others. He gladly accepted the opportunity, and in June, 1891, was at work on the job. It was hard work, but in it he learned many of the geologist's methods in a more or less frontier country, remote from settlements or even trails, where back-packing was the only practicable means of transporting supplies and equipment, and where in consequence only the bare necessities of existence and work could be taken along. All this was valuable experience on which to build his subsequent work in Alaska.

Student at Harvard

At the end of his field-work in Michigan, in December, 1891, he decided to go to Harvard, and after submitting a statement of his training and experience he was admitted to the scientific school of that university. Here he, like most other scientific students of that period, soon fell under the spell of Prof. N. S. Shaler, who marshaled great assemblages of natural objects and phenomena into organized hosts, enthralling in magnitude of conception and touching all phases of every-day life as it responded to conditions in nature. Under this magnetic personality and stimulating environment, Brooks delved more and more deeply into geology and became acquainted with many students of that science who continued in later years to be his associates. R. E. Dodge, M. A. Read, J. E. Spurr, and C. W. Purington are among those to whom he constantly refers in his letters of that period as participating in his studies and in his relaxations. Throughout his college course Brooks knew definitely what he wanted and went after it with unremitting enthusiasm. Unfortunately, his physique could not stand the strain of his unceasing work, and in March, 1893, he was compelled to consult a doctor, who found his condition so serious that he was ordered to stop work and was soon afterward sent to his home at Roseland, Georgia, to recuperate. Either the trouble was discovered opportunely, in its early stages, or the healthful conditions at Roseland and his good general physical resistance prevailed, for he built himself up rather rapidly and within a month or so was more or less actively at work around the plantation. When he had sufficiently regained his strength, he and A. F. Foerste began a geologic study of the Tertiary formations of parts of Georgia adjacent to Bainbridge and made a section along the Apalachicola River. Later in that same year he worked up some of his notes and petrographic sections of the rocks of Orange County, New York, the county in which his home at Newburgh was situated.

In the fall of 1893 his health was so completely restored that he was able to return to Harvard and continue his studies. Apparently his academic status did not concern him deeply, though he

some of his American colleagues and gained a lasting appreciation of the work of such men as A. C. Lawson and R. A. Daly. The interest then awakened in him in some of the problems of Russia and Siberia was revived when his Alaskan studies led him to turn to the consideration of these countries because of their proximity to Alaska.

At the close of the Geologic Congress, in September, 1897, Brooks decided not to return to the United States, but, after further travel, to go to Paris and study at the Sorbonne. Here he studied principally petrography and geology, working in La Croix's laboratory and attending lectures by Fouqué, Bertrand, and De Launay.

Beginning of Alaskan Career

He had spent only a few months in his studies in Paris when he received a cable from the Geological Survey, offering him a chance to return and serve as a member of one of the parties that would be sent to Alaska in the spring of 1898. This was an opportunity that he had long wanted. His close association with Doctor Hayes, who had made a notable exploratory trip to Alaska in 1891, had long before fired him with an interest in that Territory, and he had several times applied for assignment to work in Alaska if the Survey ever had the opportunity to undertake investigations there. Furthermore, he welcomed the chance to utilize his geologic knowledge in directing the intelligent development of a new region on sound scientific principles. It was, therefore, with great joy that he accepted this assignment and within a day had closed his academic work and was on his way back to Washington. For the next few weeks there was a lively scurry to make the necessary preparations, because he reached Washington only in March and the expedition left Seattle April 5, 1898.

This was the beginning of Brooks's Alaskan career—a career to which he unceasingly devoted his best efforts for a quarter of a century, and in which he established a reputation not only in his chosen profession, but as an empire-builder, that made him more revered and better known than any other man connected with the development of this great Territory.

The party to which Brooks was attached as geologist was in charge of W. J. Peters, and its plan was to survey the lower part of White River and as much of Tanana River as time would permit. This trip contemplated the survey of an area that had been seen only in part by white men, and even for the part seen there were not maps sufficiently definite to be of material assistance in a new exploration. The party ascended White River—a turbulent glacier-fed stream, which, according to all available information, including that of the natives, could not be ascended in boats—and its tributary, Snag River, for a distance of about 150 miles, a portage of 5 miles, and a journey down the Tanana of more than 600 miles. The party achieved all the main objects of the trip, studied all phases of the physiography and geology of the region, and suggested many interpretations that have stood the test of later, more detailed investigation. Brooks's own realization of the incompleteness of some of the records covering this area are well stated in his report on this trip, for he says: "Only those who are familiar from personal experience with the present conditions of exploring such a region can understand why scientific observation must be more or less fragmentary. The explorer must, of necessity, spend a large part of his energies and time in overcoming the physical obstacles to his progress, and geologic investigation, except of the most hasty kind, can be made only at such times as conditions of traveling permit. These facts the reader should bear in mind when he feels like criticising the author for leaving so many important questions unsettled." This warning might well be repeated to any one who fails to rank Brooks's work among the outstanding examples of a contribution to the geology of a frontier region.

Pyramid Harbor–Eagle Trip

The next year (1899) Brooks made another reconnaissance trip, this time from Pyramid Harbor (a boom town, now deserted, southwest of Skagway), by way of Klehini River and the headwaters of the Alsek, to Lake Kluane, across the upper White River basin to the basin of the Tanana; thence down the Nebesna to a point where the party crossed the Tanana, and thence along the divide north of the Tanana to Forty-mile River and Eagle, on the Yukon. In addition to Brooks, this party consisted of W. J. Peters, topographer in charge, and four assistants and camp hands. The equipment and supplies were carried by a pack train of 15 horses. Some measure of the mere physical stress of the trip may be gained from the facts that the party moved camp more than 600 miles in 66 days; that in going that distance they had to chop 40 miles of trail—an exercise in which all of its members participated; that 8 of their 15 horses became exhausted and had to be shot before completing the trip; that they had to build their own boat to get across the Tanana, and that their route compelled them to cross many glacial streams, in trips so hazardous that their success seemed almost impossible. In spite of these physical difficulties Brooks obtained a wealth of data regarding the region and especially regarding its mineral deposits. His report on the district states that his aim was to give such facts and conclusions as would be of practical value rather than to attempt a technical treatment of the large amount of material collected. To this aim he adhered closely, and his conclusions, especially those relating to the mineral deposits, are clear-cut and definite, even though at the same time he set forth many uncertainties. Although supplemented and modified in detail by the more complete data gained by later work, the fundamental conclusions he reached have proved well founded and remarkably accurate.

First Survey of Nome Region

After completing the long field trip from Pyramid Harbor to Eagle, the party started to go home by way of the Yukon to Saint Michael, where they expected to take an ocean steamer to Seattle. On arriving at Saint Michael, however, they met a Geological Survey party consisting of T. G. Gerdine and D. C. Witherspoon, topographers, and F. C. Schrader, geologist, who had recently completed surveys in the Koyukuk-Chandalar regions. They also encountered a rush of gold-seekers bound for Nome, a hundred miles distant across Norton Sound. The desirability of obtaining information regarding this new gold camp decided Brooks, Schrader, and Witherspoon to make a hurried examination of Nome. It was then October and work had been stopped on nearly all the placer diggings because the creeks were frozen. Most of the equipment of the Survey party had been worn out on the trips already made and had been discarded, so that the new work was done mainly from Nome as a base, by back packing sleeping bags, provisions, and instruments into the adjacent mountains and gulches on circuits of several days each. In spite of these difficulties, the main geologic features of the country were correctly determined, and a topographic sketch map was prepared by Witherspoon, showing the region within a radius of ten miles of Nome.

The unsanitary conditions at some of the camps caused Brooks to become infected with typhoid fever. On reaching Seattle he was miserable, and he became so much worse that on his arrival in Washington he was in a dangerous condition and was put to bed, where for weeks he was critically ill. His good physical condition and the unremitting care of his friend and associate, T. W. Vaughan, finally pulled him through and he went ahead preparing his reports. In spite of his illness, a report that made 50 printed pages, covering the work around Nome, with maps and illustrations, was completed and transmitted to the Secretary of the Interior by the Director of the Survey on February 1, 1900, less than three months after the party returned to the States. Even at that, the Director felt called on to apologize for the delay in sending the report and mentioned Brooks's illness as the explanation.

This preliminary report on the Nome region was characteristically full of valuable yet guarded interpretations, which, however, were not so hedged about by qualifications that they were meaningless. Rather they were sufficiently marked by warning signals that commanded attention, and then the author's interpretations were thoroughly and definitely given. The report thus resembled a well-made harbor chart that first called attention to the dangers of the coast and the entrance and then outlined the safest route through the obstructions.

Typical warnings and advice from this report are:

> "In the coming spring (1900) it is expected that there will be a very large influx of population into Nome and adjacent regions. . . . It is evident, therefore, that the region, compared with other parts of Alaska, will be densely populated, and it is not likely that the high rate of wages paid last year will be maintained. . . . It must be remembered, however, that the beach placers, like all others, are not inexhaustible, and that they do not by any means extend along the whole coast. . . . It would be very wise for all inexperienced newcomers to save money for their return passage. . . . There will be good opportunities at Nome for experienced miners. . . . We believe that the Nome region has a great future."

Survey of the Nome Region

After completing the preliminary report on the Nome region Brooks turned at once to the preparation of the report on his Pyramid Harbor-Eagle trip and completed it before leaving for the next field expedition, in June. The widespread interest in the Nome region and the great influx of prospectors led the Geological Survey to send into the Nome region and the western part of Seward Peninsula a geologic party in charge of Brooks, with G. B. Richardson and A. J. Collier as assistants and five camp hands, and a topographic party in charge of E. C. Barnard, while another party, in charge of W. J. Peters, topographer, and W. C. Mendenhall, geologist, with four assistants and camp hands, went into the eastern part of the peninsula. The party in charge of Brooks brought back geologic information regarding a tract of more than 6,000 square miles, and although he disclaimed the idea that the report on the work done was more than a hasty summary of a preliminary reconnaissance of the gold field, the conclusions expressed were remarkably broad and sound. Characteristically, in writing this report, Brooks stressed the need of making it of immediate and practical value to the miner and prospector and the intelligent reader not specially versed in geology, rather than indulging in abstruse or speculative theories of interest principally to specialists in geology. As a result, the report was of wide use and became a notable force in directing intelligent prospecting and development. Unfortunately, some of the suggestions and predictions made were not followed for several years. For instance, in 1900 the probability that ancient gold-bearing sea beaches would be found was predicted in the following terms:

> "As these coastal plain deposits were laid down on the margin of the ocean, we should expect old sea beaches to be found in these gravels. If such beaches are found, they are likely to prove as rich as the present beach at Nome. It would, therefore, be well for prospectors to examine carefully the seaward escarpments which mark the limits of the terraces. These bluffs are quite likely to mark an old sea beach. In such types of deposits we should expect their extension to be more or less parallel to the present coastline."

In spite of this definite suggestion, made in 1900 and published in 1901, it was the winter of 1904-05 before the rich ancient buried beaches were actually discovered and their exploitation begun.

Southeastern Alaska Work

By the time the office work of the report on the Nome region was completed another field season had come around, and late in June, 1901, Brooks started for southeastern Alaska to investigate mining developments in that region. In this project he was associated, both in the field and in the office, with C. C. Brayton. Most of the field studies were carried on in the Ketchikan district, where in the course of two months the party traveled about 1,200 miles, mostly in a small gasoline launch, visited more than 150 claims and mines, and made reconnaissances of about 2,000 square miles. In order to realize the difficulties under which the work was done, it should be remembered that it rained more or less on 45 of the 60 days spent in the region. At the conclusion of the work in the Ketchikan region, late in September and early in October, the party worked on the general geologic features and relations of the region to the north and visited the mining developments near Juneau.

Southeastern Alaska is an intensely difficult region for geologic work. It embraces sedimentary rocks ranging in age from early Paleozoic to Tertiary, igneous rocks of various composition and modes of formation, complex structure produced during different periods by mountain-building forces and profound intrusive activity, and economic products of greater variety than are found in any other Alaskan mining district. The intricate problems connected with these different phases of geology are still not completely solved, but the start toward their solution then made by Brooks has been of inestimable service to later workers in this field and has long been a valuable guide to the prospector and miner. The results of this field-work were rapidly put in shape for publication and within a year the report was published and in use.

Trip to Mount McKinley Region

In 1902 Brooks again went to Alaska, this time in charge of a party whose task was to obtain all possible information regarding the geology, topography, geography, and mineral resources of the vast unexplored tract along the western and northern slopes of the Alaska Range. In this work he was assisted by L. M. Prindle, assistant geologist; D. L. Reaburn, topographer, and four camp hands. The party traveled with a pack train of 20 horses, only 11 of which survived to arrive at Rampart, where the expedition closed its field-work. In 105 days the party moved about 800 miles and obtained geologic information regarding an area of at least 10,000 square miles. This may reasonably be regarded as Brooks's greatest piece of exploratory work. The party left Seattle May 15, 1902, and put ashore at Tyonek, on the western shore of Cook Inlet, on May 27. From Tyonek they worked northward to Beluga River; thence along the slopes of Mount Susitna to Skwentna River, a swollen, rushing torrent that swept horses and men off their feet whenever they attempted to cross. Finally, swimming the Skwentna, they went through a region of heavy timber and brush, where continuous trail chopping was necessary; then up the Kichatna until they discovered a pass that they called Rainy Pass, which led into a valley tributary to the Kuskokwim, and thence northeastward along the front of the mountains. This last part of the route was far better for travel, except for the crossing of the roaring, glacier-fed streams, which was always exciting, though not pleasant, as occasionally a horse would be swept off its feet and rolled over; but, fortunately, none were lost.

When near Mount McKinley, Brooks made a side trip to the ridges within nine miles of the summit of this stupendous mountain, which had never before been approached by white men. While he realized that the plan of the exploration on which he was engaged precluded any attempt to scale the mountain, he could not but feel regret that there was neither time nor means for reaching a higher altitude. Still eastward the party pushed its way across the Nenana, the last of the large streams flowing northward from the mountains, and later met a white man and some natives, the first human beings they had seen in nearly three months. On September 1 they crossed Tanana River, headed for Rampart, on the Yukon, which they reached on September 15, in spite of the assurance of the Indians whom they met on the Tanana that it was impossible to take horses through to the Yukon. In his account of this trip Brooks writes: "To the natives [on the Tanana] the arrival of white men from the mountains seemed little short of miraculous." When we consider the lack of information then available about this country and the difficulties of travel, we can only indorse the Indians' conclusion that the advent of this little band of hardy white explorers was indeed "miraculous."

February 23, 1903, marked a most important date in Brooks's life, for on that day he married Mabel Baker, of Washington. This marriage was the beginning of an ideal home life—one that was unusually happy and congenial. Mrs. Brooks is a highly cultured woman of keen intellect, who shared actively her husband's personal and scientific interests and at all times had a sympathetic understanding of the man and the scientist. She collaborated with him in putting many of his manuscripts into final form, and in fact will complete some of his unfinished work. At their home their friends could always count on finding genial hospitality, friendly comradeship, and stimulating association. Later, two children were born, Mary (1905) and Benton (1909), in whom Brooks renewed many of the joyous memories of his own very happy childhood.

Placed in Charge of Survey's Alaska Work

The early investigations of Alaska had been administered mainly by a committee of Survey geologists and topographers. This form of administration proved cumbersome and failed to place direct responsibility for coordinated planning and execution. Finally, in 1902, the Director placed the supervision of the geologic work in Alaska under Brooks, and that of the topographic work under R. U. Goode. In spite of the harmonious cooperation of Brooks and Goode, this plan did not work out so well as might have been desired, because in Alaska the two kinds of work are necessarily tied so closely together in actual operation that usually a party consists of both geologists and topographers, and the proper coordination of their work requires one directing head. As a consequence, on the death of Mr. Goode, in June, 1903, Doctor Hayes recommended to the Director that a new unit be established to handle all Alaskan affairs for the Survey; that this unit be placed in the Geologic Branch and made coordinate with the existing divisions of geology, chemistry and physics, and mineral resources, and that Brooks be placed in charge of it. This plan was approved both by the Director and by the Secretary of the Interior, and early in July, 1903, the new unit began its work and Brooks began his career as the recognized administrative officer in charge of one of the Survey's major activities, though for a long time before this he had taken a large part in the councils of the office and in the preparation of its plans.

Although throughout most of the following 20 years his principal duties in the Survey were administrative, he never ceased gathering at first hand information relating to Alaska. It is true that after 1903 he made no long full-season trips, such as he had made from 1898 to 1902, yet he spent several months of every year in the field visiting all the parties wherever possible and making independent trips to mining camps and other areas concerning which supplementary information was desired. In all, he made 24 trips to Alaska. As a consequence, he never ceased to be a fieldman, and his point of view in all his administrative work was never that of a desk autocrat, but always that of an investigator working sympathetically with his men, who were constantly confronted with unusual conditions. His greatest strength in administrative work was his willingness to place responsibility on his assistants, holding them accountable for their results, but not attempting to interfere with the details of their plans and methods.

Although there were some heart burnings when Brooks was placed in charge of the Alaskan work, the splendid spirit in which he conducted his organization built up such a spirit of loyalty, regard, and admiration among his assistants that the Alaskan unit became conspicuous for its *esprit de corps,* even in an organization like the Survey, which has long been remarkable for that spirit.

Geology and Geography of Alaska and Other Publications

Brooks not only did not abandon his field work, but he actually increased his productive investigation and study during his period of administrative responsibility. This fact is shown not only by publications based on his own observations, but by publications in which he interpreted or correlated the work of others. One of the most noteworthy examples of his excellence in summarizing the work of others as well as interpolating his own views was the report entitled "The Geography and Geology of Alaska," published by the Geological Survey as a professional paper. This volume was started as a short magazine article, but as data were accumulated it gradually outgrew these provisional bounds, so that when first submitted for publication by the Survey in 1903 it was equivalent to 200 printed pages. The results of new explorations, however, kept pouring in, and in order to make the volume complete additional subjects required treatment. The manuscript was therefore withdrawn for supplementary data and was not resubmitted until late in 1904. It was finally printed and distributed in 1906. The vast amount of information first brought together in a book of more than 300 pages at once stamped the author as the authority on Alaska and gave him an international reputation. Although this volume was necessarily in large part compiled from the work of others, Brooks's own familiarity with a considerable part of the territory justified him in reaching and expressing many personal conclusions, some of which were even at variance with those expressed in the reports from which his information was taken. So thoroughly was his work done that even today, twenty years after its publication, there is no more complete and accurate book on the general geology and geography of this territory, although, of course, many of its details could be amplified or modified in the light of the more complete data now available.

Every year from 1904 to 1916 and from 1919 to 1923 he prepared a statement on the whole Alaskan mineral industry. This statement took the form of an estimate, issued immediately at the end of the year, and a more complete analysis prepared after the data from most of the producers had been collected and digested. He was also alert to anticipate the public need for data on special topics, working these up in the midst of his numerous other duties. Good examples are his timely reports on Alaska coal —its distribution, its possible markets, and its utilization—a topic which he early sensed had great importance in the development of the Territory and the problems relating to it. The first of his reports on this subject was printed in 1905, and subsequent contributions were made public in 1910, 1911, and 1913.

Other subjects that he considered in a broad way were the "Geologic features of Alaskan metalliferous lodes," published in 1911; "The future of gold placer mining in Alaska," published in 1915; "Antimony deposits of Alaska," published in 1916; and "The future of Alaska mining," published in 1920. It was not only in the reports bearing his name, however, that those who were intimately associated with Brooks recognized his authorship. Among the many reports turned in to him for publication some were so incomplete and otherwise unsatisfactory that they could not be utilized in the form in which they were submitted by their authors. Many of these papers were worked over by Brooks during his scanty spare time; suggestions and constructive criticisms were made, and if the author was not available, or if Brooks felt that the author could not satisfactorily remedy the defects, he himself did the work, even though it might require weeks of writing the text or of drawing the necessary illustrations.

To resume the more or less chronological story of Brooks's life: In the field season of 1911 he was attached to the party of the Secretary of the Interior, Walter L. Fisher, during its visit to Alaska. Brooks's wealth of information regarding the Territory was a source of much assistance to the Secretary in helping him to get a broad view in the short time at his disposal. This association was the beginning of a personal friendship and a mutual appreciation that undoubtedly contributed to the selection of Brooks as a member of the Alaska Railroad Commission when it was established in 1912.

While Brooks was with the Secretary on this trip, Doctor Hayes, the Chief Geologist of the Survey, resigned to accept employment in one of the large oil companies operating in Mexico. After thorough consideration of all the geologists who might effectively fill the position thus vacated by Doctor Hayes, the Director offered it to Brooks. Brooks, however, though deeply appreciative of the recognition that actuated the offer, requested that he be allowed to continue his Alaskan work. The public notice sent out by the Survey regarding this matter contains the following statement:

> "While regretting Mr. Brooks's choice, both Secretary Fisher and Director George Otis Smith, of the Survey, have approved the same, and Mr. Brooks will continue in charge of the Alaskan geologic work. Mr. Brooks states that he has reached the decision after careful consideration of the matter, and while he fully recognizes the honor conferred by the offer of the higher office, he believes that his field of greatest usefulness lies in the continuation of administration of the Geological Survey work in Alaska, work which he believes has in reality hardly begun."

Applied Geology

Brooks took occasion, on his retirement from the presidency of the Geological Society of Washington, in December, 1911, to deliver a notable address on "Applied geology," as he styled the trend of geology toward the solution of practical problems. In this address he discussed subjects that had always been very close to his heart, and his championship of them in this paper was only the written expression of the championship that he, following his father's example, had displayed throughout his own scientific work and throughout his direction of the work of others. The concluding paragraph of this address may well be quoted as summing up what may be regarded as his fundamental geologic creed, and it emphatically proves his estimation of pure science:

"As I see it, there lies no danger in the present trend toward applied geology, provided our applied geology rests on a broad basis of scientific research. If the spring of pure science is cut off, the stream of applied geology must soon run dry. There is no field of pure geology which will not yield results applicable to questions of material welfare. On the other hand, any given investigation in applied geology may lead to problems of paleontology, petrography, geophysics, or other branches of pure science. In view of the pressing demand for results, we are justified in giving precedence to those fields of investigation which promise the earliest returns of material value. There is, however, grave danger that, carried away by the present furor for practical results, we may lose sight of our scientific ideals. Applied geology can only maintain its present high position of usefulness by continuing the researches which advance the knowledge of basic principles. Future progress in applied geology depends on progress in pure geology."

Alaska Railroad Commission

The controversies regarding the acquisition of certain mineral claims in Alaska and the general interest that had been stirred up by the supporters and antagonists of "conservation," whatever that much-abused term means, had brought Alaska more clearly into public sight and had indicated that something should be done by the Government for the development of the Territory. Among the various suggestions made, some of which had been carried far enough to be outlined in bills presented to Congress, was one to study the location of possible railroad routes in the Territory. Already, in 1906, Brooks, with his usual perspicacity in discerning key problems, had discussed the possible railroad routes. This clearness of vision, as well a his acknowledged unique and comprehensive knowledge of Alaska and its resources that were pertinent to any railroad enterprise, caused him to be selected as one of the commissioners when, on August 24, 1912, Congress passed an act creating a commission of four to "conduct an examination into the transportation question in the Territory of Alaska . . . to make report of the facts to Congress, . . . with their conclusions and recommendations in respect to the best and most available routes for railroads in Alaska, which will develop the country and the resources thereof for the people of the United States." . . .

The Alaska Railroad Commission, consisting of Major J. J. Morrow, Corps of Engineers, U. S. Army, chairman; Alfred H. Brooks, vice-chairman; L. M. Cox, civil engineer, U. S. Navy; and C. M. Ingersoll, consulting engineer, of New York City, convened as soon as possible, after their appointment, at Seattle and sailed for Alaska September 10. They examined personally as many of the routes as the season and other conditions would permit, and returned to Seattle by November 17. The Commission returned to Washington by way of Ottawa, studying several Canadian railroads, so as to obtain additional pertinent data. All the information obtained was compiled and incorporated in a report, prepared in Washington between December 2, 1912, and February 6, 1913, which was transmitted by President Taft to Congress with his favorable indorsement of the recommendations made.

The Commission recommended the construction of a railroad from Chitina, on the Copper River, to Fairbanks, though it also indicated the desirability of another line that should make available the mineral resources of the lower Susitna and Matanuska valleys and afford possible extension into the Kuskokwim region.

The report was, of course, the expression of the views of the Commission as a body, but it is obvious that the ability of the Commission to amass such a comprehensive array of data in the short time available must have been due to their guidance by Brooks's familiarity with sources of information and with the means of accomplishing desired aims expeditiously. The railroad that was ultimately built by the Government does not follow the principal route proposed by the Commission; it follows the route from Seward to Fairbanks that was discussed by the Commission. This change in the route was regarded by Brooks as a mistake. It was not, in his judgment, in accord with the facts nor with the best mode of developing the Territory.

Daily and Malte-Brun Medals

Recognition of the high value of the scientific contributions made by Brooks was brought to a focus by his service on this Railroad Commission and by the appearance in 1911 of his monograph on the Mount McKinley Region, a report that was started to describe his trip in 1902, but that was later amplified to embrace a larger area and to include the results of the work of a great number of explorers and others. This recognition was in part expressed in April, 1913, when the American Geographical Society presented him its Charles P. Daly gold medal "in recognition of the excellence and importance of his work in exploration and mapping Alaska." Brooks deeply appreciated this honor, but, with his customary modesty, he wrote in his letter of acceptance:

> "I must therefore regard this award as made not so much for personal merit, but rather as a recognition of the value of the geological work of my colleagues and myself in exploring Alaska. . . . I am sure that this will inspire us to continue our efforts to increase the geologic knowledge of Alaska."

In May, 1913, the Société de Geographie of Paris unanimously awarded the Conrad Malte-Brun gold medal to Brooks, expressing "its appreciation of and admiration for the great scientific service rendered by our laureate," and characterizing his work in the Alaskan service as follows: "He has directed it ever since with a zeal equaled only by his ability, and has given to his numerous collaborators an example of untiring energy."

Another honor that came to Brooks in 1913 was his designation as one of the delegates to the Twelfth International Geologic Congress. After having spent part of the field season of 1913 in Alaska, he returned to attend the meetings of the Congress at Toronto in August, and then joined the excursions through the Canadian Cordillera, visiting many of the mining camps in British Columbia.

Preparation for Military Service

The outbreak of the European War in 1914 turned the attention of every one to that catastrophe. Brooks, with his customary clearness of vision and his resourcefulness in drawing conclusions from his observations, early became imbued with the idea that this country should realize its need for preparedness. The recognition of a problem was to him the incentive for constructive suggestions for its solution. In this case his suggestion took the form of a memorandum to the Director that was transmitted to the War Department in May, 1915. It suggested the establishment of a roster in the War Department of the engineers and others in the Government service whose special qualifications might be of value to the military establishment in time of war, especially if these engineers could be given some preliminary training in military methods. The obvious merits of this suggestion and its practicability must have appealed at once to those in the War Department into whose hands the memorandum came, for in acknowledging its receipt, in a letter dated June 5, 1915, General Macomb stated that the plan had been carefully studied, and that they saw great possibilities in it. In fact, he stated that he believed "the idea is going to have a much wider application than Mr. Brooks indicated." In looking back at the National Defense Act of June 3, 1916, we may well believe that the creation of the Reserve Corps for all kinds of line duty, and also for various staffs and departments, may possibly have been what General Macomb meant by "wider application."

Preparedness, however, was not only a thing for others. To Brooks it meant personal action, so when a citizens' training camp was established at Fort Oglethorpe, Georgia, he applied for admission to it and was accepted. He was also probably instrumental in getting other geologists in the Survey—Sidney Paige, H. G. Ferguson, and J. F. Hunter—to join this training camp. While this training camp lasted, during May, 1916, he threw himself with whole-souled interest into the task of learning the new duties of a private soldier. His letters relating to his new experiences bubble over with enthusiasm. They contain such expressions as: "Tell everybody not to miss it [the training camp] on any account. . . . It is great to have some one else have all the responsibility. In fact, this has been one of the finest things I ever did."

After his experience at training camp and his usual trip to Alaska during the field season, Brooks came back with an even deeper sense of his responsibility to his country as its relation to Europe became increasingly more involved, and on December 5, 1916, the Director of the Survey transmitted to the Chief of Engineers, with his approval, Brooks's application for a commission in the Engineer Officers' Reserve Corps. Many delays in acting favorably on this application ensued, but on April 23, 1917, a commission was issued to him as Captain in the Engineer Officers' Reserve Corps. Brooks reported to the training camp near Washington on May 17 and his service in the Survey was discontinued soon afterward. Until late in July his whole time was devoted to training at the camps near Washington. Finally, he was commissioned as major and later orders came for him to go abroad. On August 15 he embarked from New York on the *Andania* and reported to the Chief Engineer of the American Expeditionary Force in France early in September.

Chief Geologist, American Expeditionary Force

The fact that geologists might be of service to the American forces in France seems to have been realized first by General S. A. Cheney and Colonel Ernest Graves, who needed geologic advice in handling problems relating principally to water supply and military mining. On their recommendation that geologists should be attached to the headquarters staff, the Chief of Engineers selected Brooks and permitted him to name his assistant. Brooks chose Captain Edwin C. Eckel, an engineer of long experience, who had been with him at training camp and with whom he had formerly been associated in the Survey. Apparently the possible military service of geologists was not well understood or appreciated in the Army, for after a month or so Captain Eckel was assigned to other duties, and only after an earnest appeal by Colonel G. A. Youngberg, the head of the Division of Front Line Engineering, was the geologic section continued. The personnel attached to the geologic section under Brooks as chief geologist underwent many changes from time to time. Captain (later Major) M. F. La Croix was soon assigned to Eckel's place. In April, 1918, Lieut. T. M. Smithers was assigned to the section for temporary duty, and in July a plan for adding several geologists to the force was approved. Under this plan Lieut. R. S. Knappen, Lieut. H. F. Crooks, Lieut. Wallace Lee, and Lieut. Kirk Bryan, who were already in the service in positions that did not utilize their geologic knowledge, were added to the section and ordered to report as soon as they could be spared from their other duties. Request was also made on Washington for eight additional geologic officers, but the signing of the Armistice interrupted this plan, and only one of these officers arrived in France.

The geologic section of the American Expeditionary Force was charged with the duty of collecting and presenting information relating to the physical conditions of the terrain as they affected the construction of field-works, the source and quality of water, the distribution and occurrence of road metal, and such other subjects as were related to the application of geology to military matters. Most of the data had to be compiled from existing publications, as there was little time or opportunity to collect original information. In all, some forty-eight formal reports and thirty-one maps were prepared by the geologic section, besides numerous memoranda and much informal advice. In terms of area the eight geologic engineering maps relating to field fortifications covered more than 7,800 square kilometers, and those relating to water supplies covered nearly 15,000 square kilometers. These figures show what a surprisingly large amount of work was done by the geologic section, for it should be remembered that during all the time the section was in existence, except the two months just preceding the Armistice, the personnel on the average included only two geologists and one clerk.

Although we may suppose that for some time the headquarters

staff hardly knew what kind of a *lusus naturæ* a geologist was, Brooks, through his personality, his quick comprehension of problems, and the practicality of the reports he prepared, demonstrated the usefulness of geology to military operations. He was promoted October 3, 1918, to the rank of Lieutenant Colonel, and when he left the service General Pershing in a personal letter to him said: "Your work was of a constructive character in a field new to military service, and the results of your efforts were becoming manifest to all."

After the Armistice, Brooks spent some time in closing up the work he had in hand and attending to all the details required in terminating his service in the Army. On February 6, 1919, he was directed to proceed to Paris for duty with the American Commission to Negotiate Peace, an assignment that lasted until April 19. Brooks's principal duty with the Commission appears to have been the preparation of an analysis of the iron, steel, and associated industries of Lorraine, the Sarre District, Luxemburg, and Belgium. In this task he was assisted by Lieut. H. F. Crooks, who compiled the data on which many of the statistical tables are based, and Major La Croix, who was especially conversant with conditions in Belgium and parts of Luxemburg. As already noted, both of these officers had at one time been attached to the geologic section of the A. E. F. The value of the service rendered the Commission was specifically recognized by General Pershing in a personal letter to Brooks, in which he said: "You have been specially commended by members of the Peace Commission for the excellence of your work in investigating and reporting upon the iron, steel, and related industries of Central Europe."

Soon after completing his work with the Peace Commission, Brooks received orders to return to the United States. He arrived on April 28, 1919, and on May 3 was honorably discharged from the service and was at once reinstated in his old post in the Geological Survey. The net results of his military service may be summarized as follows: He reached the rank of Lieutenant Colonel, won the right to wear three gold war service chevrons, and for the first time "sold" geology to the military establishment through the sheer force of having delivered useful service.

Resumption of Duties in the Geological Survey

Back in the Survey, he at once picked up the broken threads of his Alaskan work and threw himself into the double task of arranging for the coming field season and of writing up some of the accumulated results of his application of geology to military uses.

In August he accompanied John Hallowell, assistant to the Secretary of the Interior, to Alaska to study some of the many general problems relating to the development of the Territory, as well as to get information regarding the progress made in his own special fields of study. This trip was marked everywhere by ovations to Brooks. His return after two years' absence was greeted by all Alaskans as the home-coming of a much-loved and honored son.

In the spring of 1920 the certainty that Alaskan matters required more thoughtful consideration than had ever been given to them led John Barton Payne, Secretary of the Interior, to appoint a committee of representatives of the Interior, Post Office, and Agricultural Departments to advise him "as to what immediate steps can be taken to better conditions in Alaska—what industries can be developed and resources exploited to give employment to a resident population which, in turn, will give a home market for Alaskan products." Brooks was the representative of the Interior Department on this committee and its chairman. The committee brought in a report full of terse, practical suggestions and recommendations, many of which have been adopted.

With the completion of the Alaskan Committee's report, Brooks made a flying trip to Colgate University, New York, where he received the honorary degree of D. Sc. in recognition of his lifetime service to science, and especially of his contributions to the knowledge of geology and geography of Alaska. In July, 1920, the Secretaries of the Interior and the Navy visited Alaska, and Brooks accompanied them on part of their trip, and then made hurried examinations of the condition of the mineral industry in some of the adjoining regions, returning to Washington in October.

In the midst of his regular duties, Brooks found time to take an active part in the proceeedings of many of the scientific societies in Washington, and in 1921 was honored by election to the presidency of the Washington Academy of Science. His address on "The scientist in the Federal service," delivered on his retirement from that office, was a luminous statement of the vagaries of the Government service, a clear exposition of the limitations and opportunities of that work, but above all was a graphic picture of that army of men who express their recognition of public duty and self-sacrifice by action rather than words. The lessons taught by this keen, analytical dissection of the scientist in the Government service is equally applicable to research work in general, and the pitiless exposure of sham and the sympathetic understanding of real investigative work apply alike to the labors of many scientists, both within and without the service.

One of the recognitions of Brooks's service and of the organization he had built up was the definite establishment on April 1, 1922, of the Alaskan unit of the Survey as an independent branch, coordinate in rank with the other field branches. In the official announcement of this action, the Director wrote:

"This change is hardly more than a change in name, as the Alaskan work has long been only nominally under the administration of the Geologic Branch. . . . It has long been apparent that, in both theory and fact, the Division of Alaskan Mineral Resources is the Geological Survey of Alaska, but no less evident is the economy effected and the efficiency attained by continuing it as an integral part of the much larger organization carrying on similar work throughout the United States. . . . Mr. Brooks's official title as chief of the branch will be Chief Alaskan Geologist, which he has been in fact so long."

Trip to Alaska and Japan with Department of Commerce Party

The Department of Commerce, which is charged, among other things, with duties relating to many Alaskan industries and trade in general, decided to study several of the problems relating to an area in the North Pacific. Accordingly, C. A. Houston, the Assistant Secretary of that Department, with several specialists from both his own and other Government departments, planned to visit in 1922 some thirty points in Alaska and the adjacent islands, and then to go to Japan. This trip offered so unusual an opportunity to have Brooks visit many out-of-the-way places in Alaska that the Director of the Survey desired to have him attached to this party. On the other hand, the great benefit that would be gained by having a man so conversant with Alaska as Brooks available to discuss matters with Secretary Houston made Brooks's addition to the party highly acceptable to the Department of Commerce. The party left Seattle in June, 1922, on the coast guard cutter *Mojave* and visited much of the coastal portion of southern and western Alaska and adjacent islands, as well as parts of the coast of Siberia and Japan. While in Japan, Brooks suffered a slight stroke, which somewhat paralyzed his leg and side and necessitated his leaving the party and returning at once to Washington. When he reached Washington, although he was under a doctor's care, he had recovered sufficiently to attend to his official duties in the Survey. In fact, his realization of his condition and of what he wanted to accomplish made him force himself to work when, for his health's sake, he should have rested at home. He was a true soldier, however, and his sense of obligation to the office, to

Alaska, and to science did not permit any relaxation or faltering in giving at all times his full measure of service.

Trip to Australia with Second Pan-Pacific Scientific Congress

The Pan-Pacific Scientific Congress, which had been formed to discuss problems relating to countries contiguous to the Pacific, was to hold its second meeting in Australia in 1923. Many of the problems to be discussed necessarily related to matters concerning which Alaska could either contribute data or might benefit by the reports from other countries. Brooks was therefore named as one of the delegates to this convention from the United States. The other geologists in this delegation were N. M. Fenneman, H. E. Gregory, and T. W. Vaughan. In addition to attending the formal meetings, the delegates traveled extensively through Australia and adjacent regions. Brooks prepared and read several papers at the Congress and took part in excursions to Melbourne, Sydney, Adelaide, and Tasmania, visiting many of the mining districts in areas adjacent to his route of travel. He returned from this trip benefited not only in health, but mentally stimulated by the companionship of his associates and by the examples he saw of new applications of science to constructive empire-building.

Closing Days

On the completion of his office work, during the winter and spring of 1923-24, he again went to Alaska and visited several of the Survey parties in the field. As he was no longer able physically to undertake strenuous exertion, however, he had to content himself with visiting the more accessible camps. In spite of his physical infirmity, he was as much interested as ever in Alaska and gladly drew on his wealth of information to aid his associates or the prospectors and miners in the solution of their problems. He returned to Washington early in October, 1924, and with his characteristic vigor plunged at once into his accumulated office duties. When his associates entered his room, after office hours, on November 21, they found that, without any premonitory warning, he had collapsed at his desk. Almost at once he became unconscious, and in less than twelve hours he had passed away. He had just completed an article on "The future of Alaska," which he was to deliver at the Brooklyn Institute of Arts and Sciences the next day, and had lantern slides packed and everything in readiness to go to Brooklyn in the morning. It was a trip to which he had looked forward with much pleasure, especially as he was to be accompanied by his wife. Doubtless, the strain of completing the article, which he felt contained things that "must" be said about Alaska, was the last burden that proved too much for his already overtaxed body. It was, however, the way in which he would have liked to make the supreme sacrifice.

An attempt has here been made to trace in more or less chronological sequence the larger events in Brooks's life. The composite story told by these events is a story of extensive travel and experience, enormous productivity, and innumerable personal contributions to science and to the work of his associates. Some measure of his productivity is afforded by the bibliographic list of his writings that is appended to this sketch. That list, however, tells only part of the story, because every publication that was prepared under his administration of the Alaskan work bears the imprint of his criticism and constructive comment. During the period that he served in the Alaskan work the Geological Survey published over 380 reports and over 420 maps, covering more than 235,000 square miles of exploratory or reconnaissance topographic mapping and 220,000 square miles of geologic mapping, each equivalent to nearly 40 per cent of the entire area of Alaska—a monumental achievement whose energizing force came in large measure from Brooks.

The foregoing facts, however, give only a clue to the personal qualities and charm of the man. He was of medium height, stockily built, of ruddy complexion, his hair and beard sandy until somewhat bleached and thinned by advancing years. He enjoyed walking, and, in addition to his tramps while engaged in fieldwork, during the last 15 years, made a practice while in Washington of walking daily from his home to his office, a distance of more than three miles, regardless of the weather. Other than this he took part in practically no other form of athletic exercise, though for some years he was interested in fencing, belonged to a fencing club, and engaged in bouts as time and opportunity permitted. He was not deft with his hands, and therefore found no pleasure in manual tasks that serve many men as an antidote to mental work. He lacked to a surprising degree the gaming instinct. Cards, games of chance, or competitive contests not only failed to interest him, but bored him nearly to distraction. He did enjoy the theater and found in it occasional relaxation. His greatest joy, however, was in conversation, no matter with whom or on what subjects, provided the talk was informative and the participants presented interesting, authoritative, or novel views. He would sit up until late in the night, in his home or in the field, talking with friends and associates. Those who have traveled with him on a long ocean voyage all bear witness that he was the center of an animated group, discussing problems and always having something to say that was well worth hearing. Probably his love of conversation was due to the fact that he was always alert to learn, and that he found this a sure method of accumulating knowledge. He was an omnivorous reader and loved to collect books. As a young man in college, his greatest single item of expense was for the purchase of books, and he was always loath to throw away even a circular that he had received.

Brooks's method of writing was in many ways unique. He dictated very little, but instead wrote voluminously in a large, rather illegible hand. The activity of his thoughts usually far outstripped that of his pen, so that many of his sentences and even some of his words were incomplete. The remarkable feature of his work, however, was that he did not go over these drafts in detail, changing a word here and there, transferring sections or amplifying ideas, but instead he practically disregarded the first draft and wrote another, almost as if it were brand new and original. The mere task of having reduced his thoughts to written words seemed to clarify his expression and to perfect the arrangement of his later drafts. In this way he would frequently rewrite an article three or four times, leaving the correction of minor details, such as spelling and punctuation, mainly to his secretary. This practice kept him from becoming wedded to an expression simply because he had once written it in a certain way, and undoubtedly improved his style, making it terse and pointed, so that the reader was never in doubt as to his meaning.

Conclusion

Perhaps the most outstanding quality of Brooks was his intellectual honesty—honesty of purpose, honesty in the methods he practiced, and honesty in the support of the conclusions he reached. This quality is all the more remarkable because in exploratory work, whether that term applies to broad explorations in a new country or in a new realm of thought, there is neither time nor opportunity for the same minute scrutiny of details as there is in a restricted investigation in more thoroughly cultivated fields. In fact, the successful explorer must paint with broad strokes and bold outlines. Brooks did this, always leaving the picture clear and distinct, but at the same time, because he realized the necessary imperfections in his data, he pointed out those features that should be accepted only tentatively and that might require supplementary touching up or actual redrawing.

Whether his intellectual honesty expressed itself through his humor, or *vice versa,* is as inconsequential as the age-long question of which was first, the hen or the egg. Certain it is that his appreciation of the humor of a situation or the ludicrousness of a proposition gave him a poise that made him an excellent counselor, who was never swept off his balance by sophistry or self-deception. It was his humor or his intellectual honesty that prevented his spelling science with capital letters and worshiping at the shrine of a pure science, undefiled by application to human needs and served by acolytes who speak in language unintelligible except to the elect. It was his humor that made him an agreeable companion and conversationalist or an opponent to be feared. His was a kind humor, however, that was not employed to hurt or antagonize unjustifiably the object toward which it was directed, and it was never used to be "smart" or "clever."

He had a disciplined and well-stocked mind that was by no means of "meteoric" or "inspired" quality. All that he got was won through hard work and unremitting application. This naturally prevented him from making glittering generalities and snapshot judgments himself, and made him distrust the soundness of the work of others who indulged in these practices. He required of himself hard work in the field, hard work in the study, and hard work in expressing carefully and accurately his conclusions, in order that he might measure up to his standards of intellectual honesty. He naturally measured others by similar standards, though he never was a driving taskmaster to his subordinates. It was, perhaps, the hard work by which he reached his conclusions that prevented his readily changing his opinions when formed. This characteristic sometimes resulted in his continuing to place values on the work of some of his associates that were not always in accord with the opinion of others equally competent to judge critically.

In a tribute paid to the memory of this great scientist, Doctor George Otis Smith has said:

> "The one word best describing Alfred Brooks is loyal. He was loyal to those he loved, his family, and his friends. He was loyal to his science and to the organization of which he was a member for nearly 30 years. He was loyal to his chosen field of activity and to his country. This unswerving allegiance, the outstanding trait of the man, translated itself into abiding friendships, devoted service, and effective patriotism."

We do not differ with Doctor Smith as to the facts or as to the accuracy of the term "loyal" to describe Brooks. We would go further, however, and suggest that loyalty was another manifestation of the intellectual honesty of the man, who, seeing clearly his relation to himself, to his family, to his associates, and to his country, accepted the responsibility that this knowledge implied and met it to the limit of his ability.

With all the honors and regard that came to Brooks from learned societies, from those highest in administering the affairs of the nation, from his associates, from every Alaskan, Brooks's intellectual honesty prevented him from ever becoming self-important. He never strove to get into the limelight and never pushed himself or his ideas forward. When his opinions were asked he was always glad to express them frankly, but he never expressed them in a way that could be called oracular. Of the many charming illustrations that might be given of the innate modesty of the man, the following statement, taken from his letter acknowledging the congratulations of his associates on the completion of 25 years of service on the Survey, is perhaps the most appropriate one with which to close this sketch of Brooks of Alaska:

> "Were the day clear I could see Mount McKinley from the window. As I picture in my mind its stupendous height, I compare it to our science. Many have assailed its flanks; some have proclaimed untruths about it; some have climbed by great effort well up the slopes; a very few, the best by natural selection, have reached the summit and there attained the broad vision denied those at lower altitudes. As for me, I am satisfied to have been able to traverse the great lowland to the base and to climb the foothills."

Bibliography

Preliminary petrographic notes on some metamorphic rocks from eastern Alabama. Alabama Geological Survey, Bulletin number 5, 1896, pages 177-197.

Description of the Buckhannon quadrangle, West Virginia. (Alfred H. Brooks and J. A. Taff.) United States Geological Survey, Geologic Atlas, 1896, Buckhannon folio number 34, 4 pages, maps.

The crystalline and metamorphic rocks of northwest Georgia. (Alfred H. Brooks and C. W. Hayes.) Abstract in Journal of Geology, volume 5, 1897, pags 321-322. Science, new series, volume 5, 1897, page 97.

Age of the white limestone of Sussex County, New Jersey. (Alfred H. Brooks and J. E. Wolff.) Abstract in Bulletin of the Geological Society of America, volume 8, 1897, page 397. Journal of Geology, volume 5, 1897, page 322. Science, new series, volume 5, 1897, page 96.

The age of the Franklin white limestone of Sussex County, New Jersey. (Alfred H. Brooks and J. E. Wolff.) United States Geological Survey, Eighteenth Annual Report, part 2, 1898, pages 425-458, map.

Notes on the geology of the Tanana and White River basins, Alaska. Abstract in Science, new series, volume 9, 1899, page 622.

A reconnaissance in the Tanana and White River basins, Alaska, in 1898. United States Geological Survey, Twentieth Annual Report, part 7, 1900, pages 425-494, maps.

A reconnaissance from Pyramid Harbor to Eagle City, Alaska, including a description of the copper deposits of the upper White and Tanana rivers. United States Geological Survey, Twenty-first Annual Report, part 2, 1900, pages 331-391, maps.

A reconnaissance from Pyramid Harbor to Fortymile River, Alaska. Abstract in Science, new series, volume 11, 1900, pages 825-826.

Preliminary report on the Cape Nome gold region, Alaska. (Alfred H. Brooks and F. C. Schrader.) United States Geological Survey, special paper *a*, 1900, 56 pages, maps. Abstract in Mines and Minerals, volume 20, 1920, pages 534-537.

Ice cliffs on White River, Yukon Territory. (Alfred H. Brooks and C. W. Hayes.) National Geographic Magazine, volume 11, 1900, pages 199-201.

A reconnaissance of the Cape Nome and Norton Bay regions, Alaska, in 1900: Reconnaissances in the Cape Nome and adjacent gold fields of Seward Peninsula, Alaska, in 1900. (Alfred H. Brooks, assisted by G. B. Richardson and A. J. Collier.) United States Geological Survey, special paper *b*, 1901, pages 1-185, maps.

An occurrence of stream tin in the York region, Alaska. United States Geological Survey, Mineral Resources of the United States, 1900 (1901), pages 267-271.

Glacial phenomena of the Seward Peninsula, Alaska. (Alfred H. Brooks and A. J. Collier.) Abstract in Science, new series, volume 13, 1901, pages 188-189.

A new occurrence of cassiterite in Alaska. Science, new series, volume 13, 1901, page 593.

The placer gold fields of the Nome region, Alaska. Mining and Metallurgy, volume 24, 1901, pages 249-252.

Some notes on the Nome gold region of Alaska. (Alfred H. Brooks and F. C. Schrader.) American Institute of Mining Engineers, Transactions, volume 30, 1901, pages 326-337, map.

Navigation of Tanana River, Alaska. Engineering and Mining Journal, volume 73, 1902, page 355.

Copper deposits of the White, Tanana, and Copper River regions, Alaska. Engineering and Mining Journal, volume 74, 1902, pages 13-14.

The coal resources of Alaska. United States Geological Survey, Twenty-second Annual Report, part 3, 1902, pages 515-571, map.

Preliminary report on the Ketchikan mining district, Alaska, with an introductory sketch of the geology of southeastern Alaska. United States Geological Survey, Professional Paper 1, 1902, 120 pages, maps.

Geological reconnaisance in southeastern Alaska. Bulletin of the Geological Society of America, volume 13, 1902, pages 253-266, map.

Northwestern America and northeastern Asia; a criticism. Science, new series, volume 15, 1902, pages 909-910.

A reconnaissance in the Mount McKinley region, Alaska. Abstract in Science, new series, volume 16, 1902, pages 985-986.

Proposed surveys in Alaska in 1902. Reprint from National Geographic Magazine, volume 13, number 4, 1902, pages 133-136, map.

An exploration to Mount McKinley, America's highest mountain. Journal of Geography of Chicago, volume 2, number 9, 1903, pages 441-469. Smithsonian Annual Report, 1903, pages 407-422, 9 plates.

Plan for climbing Mount McKinley. (Alfred H. Brooks and D. S. Raeburn.) National Geographic Magazine, volume 14, number 1, 1903, pages 30-35, map.

Placer gold mining in Alaska in 1902. United States Geological Survey, Bulletin 213, 1903, pages 41-48.

Stream tin in Alaska. United States Geological Survey, Bulletin 213, 1903, pages 92-93.

Placer mining in Alaska in 1903. United States Geological Survey, Bulletin 225, 1904, pages 43-59.

The mining industry in Alaska. Engineering and Mining Journal, January 14, 1904.

The geography of Alaska. Reprint from National Geographic Magazine, volume 15, number 5, 1904, pages 213-220.

Description of topographic model of Alaska. Geological Society of Washington, 151st meeting, Science, new series, volume 19, 1904, pages 544-546.

Administrative reports on investigations of mineral resources of Alaska. United States Geological Survey, Bulletin 259, 1905, pages 13-17; Bulletin 284, 1906, pages 1-3; Bulletin 314, 1907, pages 11-18; Bulletin 345, 1908, pages 5-17; Bulletin 379, 1909, pages 5-20; Bulletin 442, 1910, pages 5-19; Bulletin 480, 1911, pages 5-14; Bulletin 520, 1912, pages 7-16; Bulletin 542, 1913, pages 7-17; Bulletin 592, 1914, pages 7-17; Bulletin 622, 1915, pages 7-14; Bulletin 642, 1916, pages 7-15; Bulletin 662, 1917, pages 3-10; Bulletin 692, 1919, pages 3-10; Bulletin 712, 1920, pages 3-10; Bulletin 714 (and G. C. Martin), 1921, pages 97-103; Bulletin 722, 1922, pages 69-74; Bulletin 739, 1923, pages 45-50; Bulletin 755 (and G. C. Martin), 1924, pages 51-56; Bulletin 773, 1925, pages 63-69.

Placer mining in Alaska in 1904. United States Geological Survey, Bulletin 259, 1905, pages 18-31.

The geography of Alaska, with an outline of the geomorphology. Eighth International Geographic Congress, report, 1905, pages 204-230, map.

The investigation of Alaska's mineral wealth. American Institute of Mining Engineers, Transactions, volume 35, 1905, pages 376-396.

The Alaskan Range; a new field for the mountaineer. American Geographical Society, Bulletin, volume XXXVII, number 8, 1905, pages 468-480.

Geologic reconnaissance map of Alaska. Bulletin of the Geological Society of America, volume 17, 1905, pages 695-700.

The outlook for coal mining in Alaska. American Institute of Mining Engineers, Bi-monthly Bulletin, number 4, 1905, pages 683-702, map; Transactions, volume 36, 1906, pages 489-507, map.

Railway routes. United States Geological Survey, Bulletin 284, 1906, pages 10-17, 8 plates.

The geologic survey of Alaska. Popular Science Monthly, volume 68, 1906, pages 42-54.

The mineral resources of Alaska. American Mining Congress, 8th Annual Session, Proceedings, 1906, pages 194-214.

Recent publications on Alaska and Yukon Territory. Economic Geology, volume 1, 1906, pages 340-359.

Gold and silver, Alaska. United States Geological Survey, Mineral Resources of the United States, 1905, pages 127-134; 1906, pages 134-146 (1906-7).

Railway routes in Alaska. National Geographic Magazine, volume 18, number 3, 1907, pages 164-191.

The mining industry in Alaska in 1905 and succeeding years. United States Geological Survey, Bulletin 284, 1906, pages 4-9; Bulletin 314, 1907, pages 19-39; Bulletin 345, 1908, pages 30-53; Bulletin 379, 1909, pages 21-62; Bulletin 442, 1910, pages 20-46; Bulletin 480, 1911, pages 21-42; Bulletin 520, 1912, pages 17-44; Bulletin 542, 1913, pages 18-51; Bulletin 592, 1914, pages 45-74; Bulletin 622, 1915, pages 15-68; Bulletin 642, 1916, pages 16-71; Bulletin 662, 1917, pages 11-62; Bulletin 692, 1919, pages 11-42; Bulletin 712, 1920, pages 11-52; Bulletin 714 (and G. C. Martin), 1921, pages 59-95; Bulletin 722, 1922, pages 6-67; Bulletin 739, 1923, pages 1-44; Bulletin 755 (and S. R. Capps), 1924, pages 3-49.

The geography and geology of Alaska; a summary of existing knowledge. United States Geological Survey, Professional Paper 45, 1906, 327 pages, maps. Abstract in Science, new series, volume 25, 1907, pages 946-947.

The Kougarok region, Alaska. United States Geological Survey, Bulletin 314, 1907, pages 164-181.

The Circle precinct, Alaska. United States Geological Survey, Bulletin 314, 1907, pages 187-204.

The Paleozoic section of the Upper Yukon. (Alfred H. Brooks and E. M. Kindle.) Abstract in Science, new series, volume 25, 1907, pages 181-182.

The distribution of mineral resources in Alaska. United States Geological Survey, Bulletin 345, 1908, pages 18-29, map.

Paleozoic and associated rocks of the Upper Yukon, Alaska. (Alfred H. Brooks and E. M. Kindle.) Bulletin of the Geological Society of America, volume 19, 1908, pages 255-314, map.

Gold, silver, copper, lead, and zinc, Alaska. United States Geological Survey, Mineral Resources of the United States, 1907, pages 139-150; 1908, pages 277-285; 1909, pages 223-232; 1910, pages 307-320; 1911, part 1, pages 406-420; 1912, part 2, pages 523-535 (1908-13).

Sketch of geology of Mount McKinley region. In "To the top of the continent," by Frederick A. Cook, 1908, New York, pages 237-259.

The gold placers of parts of Seward Peninsula, Alaska, including the Nome, Council, Kougarok, Port Clarence, and Goodhope precincts. (Alfred H. Brooks, A. J. Collier, F. L. Hess, and Philip S. Smith.) United States Geological Survey, Bulletin 328, 1908, 343 pages.

The Alaska of today. American Review of Reviews, volume 40, 1909, pages 49-62.

Mineral resources of Alaska. United States Geological Survey, Bulletin 394, 1909, pages 172-207. National Conservation Committee Report (60th Congress, second session, Senate Document 676), number 3, 1909, pages 572-603.

Alaska and its mineral resources. American Mining Congress, 11th Annual Session, Papers and Proceedings, 1909, pages 258-268.

Mining and mineral wealth of Alaska. Alaska-Yukon-Pacific Exposition, Seattle, Washington, 1909. Department of the Interior, Alaskan Exhibit, Washington, D. C., 1909, 46 pages.

Alaska coal and its utilization. United States Geological Survey, Bulletin 442, 1910, pages 47-100, map.

The Mount McKinley region, Alaska, with description of the igneous rocks and of the Bonnifield and Kantishna districts, by L. M. Prindle. United States Geological Survey, Professional Paper 70, 1911, 234 pages, map.

Geologic features of Alaskan metalliferous lodes. United States Geological Survey, Bulletin 480, 1911, pages 43-93, maps.

Report on progress of public lands in Alaska during 1910. United States Geological Survey, Bulletin 480, 1911, pages 15-20.

The future of Alaska coal. American Mining Congress, 14th Annual Session, Report of Proceedings, 1911, pages 291-298.

Geography in the devopment of the Alaska coal deposits. Association of American Geographers, Annals, volume 1, 1911, pages 85-94.

Applied geology. Journal of the Washington Academy of Sciences, volume 2, 1912, pages 19-48. Smithsonian Institution, Annual Report for 1912 (1913), pages 329-352.

Railway routes from the Pacific seaboard to Fairbanks, Alaska. United States Geological Survey, Bulletin 520, 1912, pages 45-88, maps.

Gold deposits near Valdez, Alaska. United States Geological Survey, Bulletin 520, 1912, pages 108-130, map.

A description of methods of placer mining. United States Geological Survey, Water-Supply Paper 314, 1913, pages 269-303.

The coal resources of Alaska. (Alfred H. Brooks and G. C. Martin.) International Geological Congress, XII, Canada, The Coal Resources of the World, I, lxiv-lxv, 2, 1913, pages 541-552, map.

The Chisana placer district, Alaska. United States Geological Survey, Bulletin 592, 1914, pages 305-320, maps.

Mineral deposits of Alaska. United States Geological Survey, Bulletin 592, 1914, pages 18-44, 1 plate.

The development of Alaska by Government railroads. Reprint from Quarterly Journal of Economics, volume XXVIII, May, 1914, pages 586-596.

Antarctic exploration. Mining Magazine, volume X, number 4, April, 1914.

Gold, silver, and copper in Alaska. United States Geological Survey, Mineral Resources of the United States, 1913, part 1, pages 213-225; 1914, part 1, pages 125-137; 1915, part 1, pages 175-186 (1914-6).

Mountain exploration in Alaska. American Alpine Club, Alpina Americana, number 3, 1914, 22 pages, maps.

The future of gold placer mining in Alaska. United States Geological Survey, Bulletin 622, 1915, pages 69-79.

The geography of Alaska in its relation to man. Abstract in Annals of the Association of American Geographers, volume 6, 1916, page 123.

The petroleum fields of Alaska. American Institute of Mining Engineers, Bulletin number 98, 1915, pages 199-207, maps. Transactions, volume 51, 1916, pages 611-619, maps.

Preliminary report on the Tolovana district, Alaska. United States Geological Survey, Bulletin 642, 1916, pages 201-209, map.

Antimony deposits of Alaska. United States Geological Survey, Bulletin 649, 1916, 67 pages, maps. Abstract in Journal of the Washington Academy of Sciences, volume 6, 1916, pages 567-568.

Gold, silver, copper, and lead in Alaska. United States Geological Survey, Mineral Resources of the United States, 1916, part 1, pages 171-183; 1919, part 1, pages 227-233; 1920, part 1, pages 441-446; 1921, part 1, pages 599-602; 1922 (and S. R. Capps), pages 637-642 (1917-25).

The physiographic provinces of Alaska. Abstract in Journal of the Washington Academy of Sciences, volume 6, 1916, pages 252-253; Association of American Geographers, Annals, volume 6, 1917, page 123.

Memorial of Charles Willard Hayes. Bulletin of the Geological Society of America, volume 28, 1917, pages 81-123.

Underground water and its relation to field-works. United States Army, American Expeditionary Force, Engineering Field Notes, Number 27, June, 1916.

Military mining. United States Army, American Expeditionary Force, 1918, Occasional papers (No. 62), the Engineering School.

Water supply of Commercy quadrangle, with map; scale, 1:80,000. United States Army, American Expeditionary Force, 1918.

Water supply of Metz southwest quadrangle, with map; scale, 1:50,000. United States Army, American Expeditionary Force, 1918.

Water supply of Metz southeast quadrangle, with map; scale, 1:50,000. United States Army, American Expeditionary Force, 1918.

Water supply of Metz northwest quadrangle, with map; scale, 1:50,000. United States Army, American Expeditionary Force, 1918.

Water supply of Metz northeast quadrangle, with map; scale, 1:50,000. United States Army, American Expeditionary Force, 1918.

Water supply of Verdun northeast quadrangle, with map; scale, 1:50,000. United States Army, American Expeditionary Force, 1918.

Water supply of Verdun northwest quadrangle, with map; scale, 1:50,000. United States Army, American Expeditionary Force, 1918.

Water supply of Mézières southwest quadrangle, with map; scale, 1:50,000. United States Army, American Expeditionary Force, 1918.

Water supply of Lunéville northeast quadrangle, with map; scale, 1:50,000. United States Army, American Expeditionary Force, 1918.

Water supply of Sarrebourg southwest quadrangle, with map; scale, 1:50,000. United States Army, American Expeditionary Force, 1918.

Water supply of and geological notes on the Rhine Valley. United States Army, American Expeditionary Force, 1918.

The Lorraine iron field and the war. Engineering and Mining Journal, volume 109, 1920, pages 1065-1069.

Alaska's mineral supplies. United States Geological Survey, Bulletin 666, 1919, 14 pages.

Application of geology to war. Abstract in Journal of the Washington Academy of Sciences, volume 10, 1920, pages 331-333.

Military mining in France. Engineering and Mining Journal, volume 109, number 10, 1920.

The iron and associated industries of Lorraine, the Sarre district, Luxemburg, and Belgium. (Alfred H. Brooks and Morris F. La Croix.) United States Geological Survey, Bulletin 703, 1920, 131 pages, 2 plates.

The use of geology on the western front. United States Geological Survey, Professional Paper 128, 1921, pages 85-124, plates.

The geological survey of Alaska. Pan-Pacific Scientific Conference, First, Proceedings, Special Publication number 7, part 3, 1921, pages 683-688, 1 figure.

Note on the Tertiary geology of Alaska. Pan-Pacific Scientific Conference, First, Proceedings, Special Publication number 7, part 3, 1921, pages 797-800.

A petroleum seepage near Anchorage, Alaska. United States Geological Survey, Bulletin 739, 1922, pages 133-135.

The scientist in the Federal service. Journal of the Washington Academy of Sciences, volume 12, number 4, 1922, pages 73-115.

Notes on topographic surveys in Alaska. Bulletin of the American Geographical Society, volume 36, number 11, 1924.

Alaska's mineral resources and production, 1923. United States Geological Survey, Bulletin 773, 1925, pages 3-52.

The value of Alaska. The Geographical Review, volume XV, number 1, 1925, pages 25-50.

The future of Alaska. Annals of the Association of American Geographers, volume XV, number 4, 1925, pages 163-178.

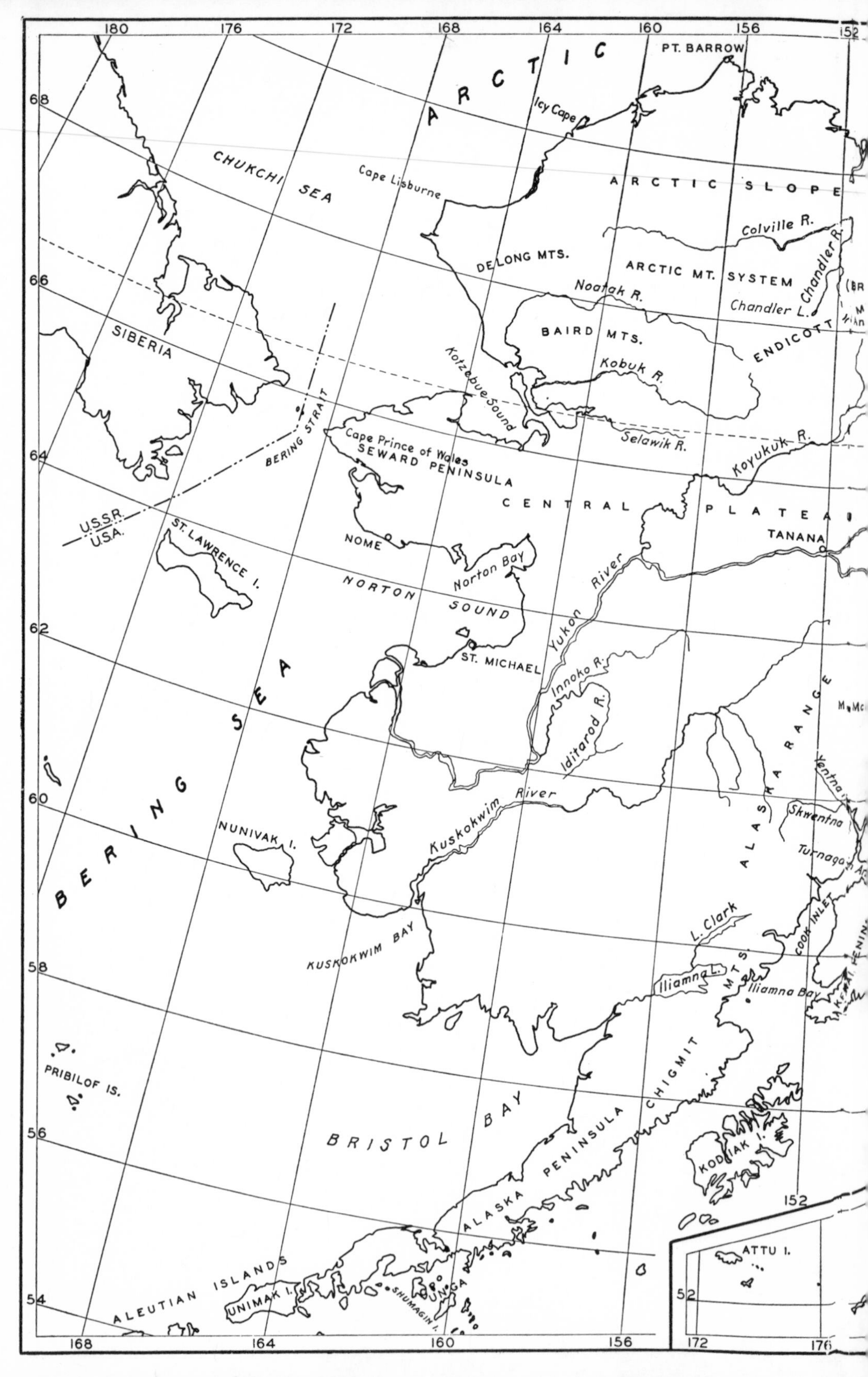

180
176
172
168
164
160
156
152
ARCTIC
PT. BARROW
Icy Cape
CHUKCHI SEA
Cape Lisburne
ARCTIC SLOPE
Colville R.
DELONG MTS.
ARCTIC MT. SYSTEM
Chandler R.
Noatak R.
Chandler L.
BAIRD MTS.
ENDICOTT
SIBERIA
Kotzebue Sound
Kobuk R.
BERING STRAIT
Cape Prince of Wales
SEWARD PENINSULA
Selawik R.
Koyukuk R.
U.S.S.R.
U.S.A.
ST. LAWRENCE I.
CENTRAL PLATEAU
TANANA
NOME
Norton Bay
NORTON SOUND
Yukon River
ST. MICHAEL
Innoko R.
BERING SEA
Iditarod R.
ALASKA RANGE
Yentna
Skwentna
Kuskokwim River
NUNIVAK I.
Turnagain Arm
COOK INLET
L. Clark
KUSKOKWIM BAY
Iliamna L.
Iliamna Bay
MTS.
CHIGMIT
PRIBILOF IS.
BRISTOL BAY
ALASKA PENINSULA
KODIAK I.
ALEUTIAN ISLANDS
UNIMAK I.
SHUMAGIN I.
UNGA
ATTU I.
68
66
64
62
60
58
56
54
52
172
176